Guidebook to
The Freedom of Information
and Privacy Acts

Guidebook to The Freedom of Information and Privacy Acts

compiled and edited
by Robert F. Bouchard
and Justin D. Franklin

Clark Boardman Company, Ltd.
New York, New York
1980

Fourth printing, October 1981

Library of Congress Cataloging in Publication Data

Bouchard, Robert F.
   Guidebook to the Freedom of information and Privacy acts.
   Includes text of the acts.
   Bibliography: p.
   Includes index.
   1. Government information—United States. 2. Public records—Law and
legislation—United States. 3. Records—Law and legislation—United
States. 4. Privacy, Right of—United States. I. Franklin, Justin D., joint
author. II. United States. Laws, statutes, etc. Freedom of information act.
1980. III. United States. Laws, statutes, etc. Privacy act of 1974. 1980.
IV. Title.
KF5753.B68   342'.73'0853   79-27406
ISBN 0-87632-310-7

Preface

The United States government has for decades gathered information about every facet of American life, including personal information about individuals. Until recently all but a very small portion of this information was unavailable to the general public and to the very individuals whom the information concerned. An increasing public awareness of the existence of this information gathering by the government, which in many instances was not only damaging but erroneous, led to the enactment of the Freedom of Information and Privacy Acts. Further indignation by the public has resulted in recent amendments to these Acts which facilitate obtaining more information by individuals. Presently, the government may still censor certain types of information, and in some instances the information obtained has been so censored as to be useless. This will probably change as well, as public consciousness demands that all governmental information be made available in uncensored form to the persons concerned. However, it is not the purpose of this book to examine the philosophy behind the Acts, government policies, or public reaction.

Guidebook to the Freedom of Information and Privacy Acts is a compilation of materials from various sources, and is intended as a practical guide to the federal Freedom of Information and Privacy Acts. Its purpose is to explain the Acts and tell how to obtain information under them.

The general purpose of FOIA is to strengthen the public's right to know, while the Privacy Act is intended to give the individual better control over the gathering, dissemination, and accuracy of agency information about himself or herself. FOIA gives any person a right of access to everything in agency records except for the nine statutory exemptions. The Privacy Act gives individuals a right of access to certain records that contain information about themselves. An individual may utilize either FOIA or the Privacy Act, or both, to seek access to information in agency records, and is entitled to the cumulative total of access rights under the two Acts. The two Acts are different in scope, and provide different procedures as to fees, time limits, judicial review, and other matters. They also have different sources of guidance: The Justice Department provides guidance to agencies on FOIA, while the Office of Management and Budget provides guidance on the Privacy Act, though with legal assistance from Justice.

Chapters One and Two of this book contain the full texts of the Acts followed by a section-by-section analysis with interpretative court decisions.

Chapter Three is a practical guide to the use of FOIA and the Privacy Act, complete with sample letters and forms. Chapter Four discusses business data requests and the present legal status of suits to bar the government from revealing submitted information. The recent Supreme Court decision in *Chrysler v. Brown,* which involved this problem, is included in full with an analysis. Footnotes, except for the *Chrysler* decision, are at the end of each chapter.

The addresses of selected federal government agencies which may be contacted for various information are included in the Bibliography. Because of the obvious relevance of the individual state statutes covering privacy and freedom of information, the full text of each state's statute is included in Appendix C. A general index completes the volume.

Robert F. Bouchard

Justin D. Franklin

Contents

CHAPTER 1
The Freedom of Information Act   **1**

The Act, 5 U.S.C. §552   1

An Overview   8

What is the Freedom of Information Act?   8

What Background Factors Help to Explain
FOIA's Enactment, Impact, and Limitations?   9

   Historical Factors   9

   Legal Factors   9

   Psychosocial Factors   10

What is the Statutory Structure of FOIA?   11

What Do the Nine FOIA Exemptions Cover?   11

   Exemption 1   12

   Exemption 2   12

   Exemption 3   13

   Exemption 4   13

   Exemption 5   14

   Exemption 6   14

   Exemption 7   15

   Exemption 8   19

   Exemption 9   19

What Procedures Must a Requester Follow?   19

What Procedures Must the Agency Follow?   20

What Will Happen if the Matter Goes to Court?   21

How Does FOIA Interrelate with the Privacy Act?   21

How Does FOIA Affect Business Information?   22

What References and Services Can Provide
Further Help on FOIA Problems?   25

CHAPTER 2
The Privacy Act   **27**

The Act, 5 U.S.C. § 552a   27
An Overview   39
Introduction   40
Computers and Privacy   41
The Privacy Act: A General Assessment   44
  Legislative History   45
  Recognition of Individual Interests   45
    Collection   46
    Maintenance of Files   46
    Disclosure of Records   47
  Restrictions on Federal Agencies   49
    Collection of New Data   49
    Maintenance of Files   50
    Disclosure and Dissemination   52
  Civil Remedies   52
The Privacy Act and the Social Need for Reform   54
  The Law Enforcement Exemptions   55
  Privacy and the Public's Right to Know   57
    The FOIA Exemptions   58
    The Agencies as Guardians of Privacy   61
    Interaction between the FOIA and the Privacy Act   63
Conclusion   67

CHAPTER 3
Government Data Requests   89

How to Use FOIA and the Privacy Act   89

Recommendation   89

Introduction   89

Which Act to Use   91

The Freedom of Information Act   91

Legislative Background   91

How to Request Government Documents   93

Information Available under the Freedom of
Information Act   93

Locating Records   94

Making a Request   94

Fees   95

Sample Request Letter   96

Requirements for Agency Responses   96

Reasons Why Access May Be Denied   97

Exemption (b) (1): Classified Documents Concerning National
Defense and Foreign Policy   97

Exemption (b) (2): Internal Personnel Rules and Practices   98

Exemption (b) (3): Information Exempt under Other Laws   98

Exemption (b) (4): Confidential Business Information   99

Exemption (b) (5): Internal Communications   100

Exemption (b) (6): Protection of Privacy   100

Exemption (b) (7): Investigatory Files   101

Exemption (b) (8): Information Concerning Financial
Institutions   101

Exemption (b) (9): Information Concerning Wells   101

Appeal Procedure   102

Sample Appeal Letter   102

Taking Your Case to Court   103

The Privacy Act   104

Legislative Background   104

How to Request Personal Records   105

Information Available under the Privacy Act   105

Locating Records   106

Making a Request   107

Fees   108

Sample Request Letter   108

Requirements for Agency Responses   109

Disclosure of Records   109

Reasons Why Access May Be Denied   110

General Exemptions   110

Exemption (j) (1): Files Maintained by the CIA   111

Exemption (j) (2): Files Maintained by Federal
Criminal Law Enforcement Agencies   111

Specific Exemptions   112

Exemption (k) (1): Classified Documents Concerning
National Defense and Foreign Policy   112

Exemption (k) (2): Investigatory Material Compiled for Law
Enforcement Purposes   112

Exemption (k) (3): Secret Service Intelligence Files   113

Exemption (k) (4): Files Used Solely for Statistical Purposes   113

Exemption (k) (5): Investigatory Material Used
in Making Decisions Concerning Employment, Military Service,
Federal Contracts, and Security Clearances   114

Exemption (k) (6): Testing or Examination Material Used Solely
for Employment Purposes   114

Exemption (k) (7): Evaluation Material Used
in Making Decisions Regarding Promotions in the Armed
Services   114

Appeal Procedure for Denial of Access   115

Sample Letter for Appealing Denial of Access   115

Amending Your Records   116

Sample Letter for Request to Amend Records   117

Appeal Procedure for Agency Refusal to Amend Records   117

Sample Letter for Appealing Agency's Refusal to Amend
Records   118

Taking Your Case to Court   119

Other Rights Provided under the Privacy Act   120

CHAPTER 4
Business Data Requests   123

How to Use FOIA and Reverse-FOIA Action   123

Summary of Findings and Recommendations   123

Substantial Competitive Harm Test   124

Processing FOIA Requests   124

Notice to the Submitter   124

Identification of Confidential Information by the Submitter   125

Determination of Confidentiality by Agencies at the Time of
Submission   125

Substantive Disclosure Rules   125

Agency Proceedings   125

Reverse FOIA Cases   126

Paperwork   127

Introduction: What's at Stake   127

Nature of Fourth Exemption Information   128

Corporate Concerns   129

Why Business Data is Requested   131

Purpose of this Report   133

Business Data Requirements of Government   135

Recommendation   136

Brief History of the Fourth Exemption of the Freedom of Information
Act   137

Understanding the Fourth Exemption   137

Trade Secrets   137

Early Approaches to Confidential Business Information   138

Competitive Harm Test   141

Beyond the Competitive Harm Test   143

Agency Procedures for Processing Requests   145

Introduction   145

Notice to the Submitter   147

Identification of Confidential Information by the Submitter   151

Determination of Confidentiality by Agencies at the Time of
Submission   155

Practical Difficulties   155

Agency Regulation   156

What if an FOIA Request is Made for Documents Undergoing
Presubmission Review?   158

Recommendation   159

FDA's Substantive Disclosure Rules   160

Problems with FDA's Rules   162

Rules of Other Agencies   163

Limitations on Substantive Disclosure Rules   165

Recommendations   166

Agency Proceedings   166

Agency Decision Procedures   167

Legal Problems with Existing Procedures   168

Other Comments   170

Recommendation   171

A Note on Time Limits   172

Reverse-Freedom of Information Cases   173

Introduction   173

Jurisdiction   175

Basis for Relief   175

Administrative Procedure Act   175

Freedom of Information Act   176

Trade Secrets Act   176

Scope of Review   178

Arguments for De Novo Review   178

Arguments against De Novo Review   179

Recommendation   181

Other Procedural Matters   182

Exhaustion of Administrative Remedies   182

Venue   183

Recommendation   184

Restrictions on the Scope of Relief in Reverse-FOIA Cases   184

Time   184

Other Disclosure Statutes   185

Release of Business Data by Third Parties   186

Recommendation   186

Bibliography

Selected Law Review Articles and Notes   207
Addresses of Selected Government Agencies   210

Appendices

A. Chrysler v. Brown

[1]   Opinion of the Court   223

[2]   Analysis   248

B. Two Government Memoranda to All Agencies and Legal Departments re: Chrysler v. Brown

[1]   Memorandum from Ass't Attorney General Barbara Babcock to All Agency General Counsels on "Reverse" Freedom of Information Act Cases. Issued June 21, 1979   251

[2]   Memorandum from Robert L. Saloschin, Director, Office of Information Law and Policy, To All Federal Departments and Agencies on Chrysler v. Brown. Issued June 19, 1979   258

C. State-by-State Freedom of Information Statutes   265

Index to State Statutes   435

General Index   437

CHAPTER 1

The Freedom of Information Act

The Act, 5 U.S.C. § 552

(a) Each agency shall make available to the public information as follows:

(1) Each agency shall separately state and currently publish in the Federal Register for the guidance of the public:

(A) descriptions of its central and field organization and the established places at which the employees (and in the case of a uniformed service, the members) from whom, and the methods whereby, the public may obtain information, make submittals or requests, or obtain decisions;

(B) statements of the general course and method by which its functions are channeled and determined, including the nature and requirements of all formal and informal procedures available;

(C) rules of procedure, descriptions of forms available or the places at which forms may be obtained, and instructions as to the scope and contents of all papers, reports, or examinations;

(D) substantive rules of general applicability adopted as authorized by law, and statements of general policy or interpretations of general applicability formulated and adopted by the agency; and

(E) each amendment, revision, or repeal of the foregoing.

Except to the extent that a person has actual and timely notice of the terms thereof, a person may not in any manner be required to resort to, or be adversely affected by, a matter required to be published in the Federal Register and not so published. For the purpose of this paragraph, matter reasonably available to the class of persons affected thereby is deemed published in the Federal Register when incorporated by reference therein with the approval of the Director of the Federal Register.

(2) Each agency, in accordance with published rules, shall make available for public inspection and copying:

(A) final opinions, including concurring and dissenting opinions, as well as orders, made in the adjudication of cases;

(B) those statements of policy and interpretations which have been adopted by the agency and are not published in the Federal Register; and

(C) administrative staff manuals and instructions to staff that affect a member of the public;

unless the materials are promptly published and copies offered for sale. To the extent required to prevent a clearly unwarranted invasion of personal privacy, an agency may delete identifying details when it makes available or publishes an opinion, statement of policy, interpretation, or staff manual or instruction. However, in each case, the justification for the deletion shall be explained fully in writing. Each agency shall also maintain and make available for public inspection and copying current indexes providing identifying information for the public as to any matter issued, adopted, or promulgated after July 4, 1967, and required by this paragraph to be made available or published. Each agency shall promptly publish, quarterly or more frequently, and distribute (by sale or otherwise) copies of each index or supplements thereto unless it determines by order published in the Federal Register that the publication would be unnecessary and impracticable, in which case the agency shall nonetheless provide copies of such index on request at a cost not to exceed the direct cost of duplication. A final order, opinion, statement of policy, interpretation, or staff manual or instruction that affects a member of the public may be relied on, used, or cited as precedent by an agency against a party other than an agency only if:

(i) it has been indexed and either made available or published as provided by this paragraph; or
(ii) the party has actual and timely notice of the terms thereof.

(3) Except with respect to the records made available under paragraphs (1) and (2) of this subsection, each agency, upon any request for records which (A) reasonably describes such records and (B) is made in accordance with published rules stating the time, place, fees (if any), and procedures to be followed, shall make the records promptly available to any person.

(4) (A) In order to carry out the provisions of this section, each agency shall promulgate regulations, pursuant to notice and receipt of public comment, specifying a uniform schedule of fees applicable to all constituent units of such agency. Such fees shall be limited to reasonable standard charges for document search and duplication and provide for recovery of only the direct costs of such search and duplication. Documents shall be furnished without charge or at a reduced charge where the agency determines that waiver or reduction of the fee is in the public interest because furnishing the information can be considered as primarily benefiting the general public.

(B) On complaint, the district court of the United States in the district in which the complainant resides, or has his principal place of business, or in which the agency records are situated, or in the District of Columbia, has jurisdiction to enjoin the agency from withholding agency records and to order the production of any agency records improperly withheld from the complainant. In such a case the court shall determine the matter de novo, and may examine the contents of such agency records in camera to determine whether such records or any part thereof shall be withheld under any of the exemptions set forth in subsection (b) of this section, and the burden is on the agency to sustain its action.

(C) Notwithstanding any other provision of law, the defendant shall serve an answer or otherwise plead to any complaint made under this subsection within thirty days after service upon the defendant of the pleading in which such complaint is made, unless court otherwise directs for good cause shown.

(D) Except as to cases the court considers of greater importance, proceedings before the district court, as authorized by this subsection, and appeals therefrom, take precedence on the docket over all cases and shall be assigned for hearing and trial or for argument at the earliest practicable date and expedited in every way.

(E) The court may assess against the United States reasonable attorney fees and other litigation costs reasonably incurred in any case under this section in which the complainant has substantially prevailed.

(F) Whenever the court orders the production of any agency records improperly withheld from the complainant and assesses against the United States reasonable attorney fees and other litigation costs, and the court additionally issues a written finding that the circumstances surrounding the withholding raise questions whether agency personnel acted arbitrarily or capriciously with respect to the withholding, the Special Counsel shall promptly initiate a proceeding to determine whether disciplinary action is warranted against the officer or employee who was primarily responsible for the withholding. The Special Counsel, after investigation and consideration of the evidence submitted, shall submit its findings and recommendations to the administrative authority of the agency concerned and shall send copies of the findings and recommendations to the officer or employee or his representative. The administrative authority shall take the corrective action that the Special Counsel recommends.

(G) In the event of noncompliance with the order of the court, the district court may punish for contempt the responsible employee, and in the case of a uniformed service, the responsible member.

(5) Each agency having more than one member shall maintain and make available for public inspection a record of the final votes of each member in every agency proceeding.

(6) (A) Each agency, upon any request for records made under paragraph (1), (2), or (3) of this subsection, shall:

> (i) determine within ten days (excepting Saturdays, Sundays, and legal holidays) after receipt of any such request whether to comply with such request and shall immediately notify the person making such request of such determination and the reasons therefor, and of the right of such person to appeal to the head of the agency any adverse determination; and
>
> (ii) make a determination with respect to any appeal within twenty days (excepting Saturdays, Sundays, and legal holidays) after the receipt of such appeal. If on appeal the denial of the request for records is in whole or in part upheld, the agency shall notify the person making such request of the provisions for judicial review of that determination under paragraph (4) of this subsection.

(B) In unusual circumstances as specified in this subparagraph, the time limits prescribed in either clause (i) or clause (ii) of subparagraph (A) may be extended by written notice to the person making such request setting forth the reasons for such extension and the date on which a determination is expected to be dispatched. No such notice shall specify a date that would result in an extension for more than ten working days. As used in this subparagraph, "unusual circumstances" means, but only to the extent reasonably necessary to the proper processing of the particular request:

(i) the need to search for and collect the requested records from field facilities or other establishments that are separate from the office processing the request;

(ii) the need to search for, collect, and appropriately examine a voluminous amount of separate and distinct records which are demanded in a single request; or

(iii) the need for consultation, which shall be conducted with all practicable speed, with another agency having a substantial interest in the determination of the request or among two or more components of the agency having substantial subject-matter interest therein.

(C) Any person making a request to any agency for records under paragraph (1), (2), or (3) of this subsection shall be deemed to have exhausted his administrative remedies with respect to such request if the agency fails to comply with the applicable time limit provisions of this paragraph. If the Government can show exceptional circumstances exist and that the agency is exercising due diligence in responding to the request, the court may retain jurisdiction and allow the agency additional time to complete its review of the records. Upon any determination by an agency to comply with a request for records, the records shall be made promptly available to such person making such request. Any notification of denial of any request for records under this subsection shall set forth the names and titles or positions of each person responsible for the denial of such request.

(b) This section does not apply to matters that are:

(1) (A) specifically authorized under criteria established by an Executive order to be kept secret in the interest of national defense or foreign policy and (B) are in fact properly classified pursuant to such Executive order;

(2) related solely to the internal personnel rules and practices of an agency;

(3) specifically exempted from disclosure by statute (other than section 552b of this title), provided that such statute (A) requires that the matters be withheld from the public in such a manner as to leave no discretion on the issue, or (B) establishes particular types of matters to be withheld;

(4) trade secrets and commercial or financial information obtained from a person and privileged or confidential;

(5) inter-agency or intra-agency memorandums or letters which would not be available by law to a party other than an agency in litigation with the agency;

(6) personnel and medical files and similar files the disclosure of which would constitute a clearly unwarranted invasion of personal privacy;

(7) investigatory records compiled for law enforcement purposes, but only to the extent that the production of such records would (A) interfere with enforcement proceedings, (B) deprive a person of a right to a fair trial or an impartial adjudication, (C) constitute an unwarranted invasion of personal privacy, (D) disclose the identity of a confidential source and, in the case of a record compiled by a criminal law enforcement authority in the course of a criminal investigation, or by an agency conducting a lawful national security intelligence investigation, confidential information furnished only by the confidential source, (E) disclose investigative techniques and procedures, or (F) endanger the life or physical safety of law enforcement personnel;

(8) contained in or related to examination, operating, or condition reports prepared by, on behalf of, or for the use of an agency responsible for the regulation or supervision of financial institutions; or

(9) geological and geophysical information and data, including maps concerning wells.

Any reasonably segregable portion of a record shall be provided to any person requesting such record after deletion of the portions which are exempt under this subsection.

(c) This section does not authorize withholding of information or limit the availability of records to the public, except as specifically stated in this section. This section is not authority to withhold information from Congress.

(d) On or before March 1 of each calendar year, each agency shall submit a report covering the preceding calendar year to the Speaker of the House of Representatives and President of the Senate for referral to the appropriate committees of the Congress. The report shall include:

(1) the number of determinations made by such agency not to comply with requests for records made to such agency under subsection (a) and the reasons for each such determination;

(2) the number of appeals made by persons under subsection (a)(6), the result of such appeals, and the reason for the action upon each appeal that results in a denial of information;

(3) the names and titles or positions of each person responsible for the denial of records requested under this section, and the number of instances of participation for each;

(4) the results of each proceeding conducted pursuant to subsection (a)(4)(F), including a report of the disciplinary action taken against the officer or employee who was primarily responsible for improperly withholding records or an explanation of why disciplinary action was not taken;

(5) a copy of every rule made by such agency regarding this section;

(6) a copy of the fee schedule and the total amount of fees collected by the agency for making records available under this section; and

(7) such other information as indicates efforts to administer fully this section.

The Attorney General shall submit an annual report on or before March of each calendar year which shall include for the prior calendar year a listing of the number of cases arising under this section, the exemption involved in each case, the disposition of such case, and the cost, fees, and penalties assessed under subsections (a)(4)(E),(F), and (G). Such report shall also include a description of the efforts undertaken by the Department of Justice to encourage agency compliance with this section.

(e) For purposes of this section, the term "agency" as defined in section 551(1) of this title includes any executive department, military department, Government corporation, Government controlled corporation, or other establishment in the executive branch of the Government (including the Executive Office of the President), or any independent regulatory agency.

An Overview

This overview answers those questions most critical to a working knowledge and understanding of the Freedom of Information Act:

What is the Freedom of Information Act?   *page 8*

What background factors (historical, legal, and psychosocial) help to explain FOIA's enactment, impact, and limitations?   *page 9*

What is the statutory structure of FOIA?   *page 10*

What do the nine FOIA exemptions cover?   *page 11*

What procedures must a requester follow?   *page 19*

What procedures must an agency follow?   *page 20*

What will happen if the matter goes to court?   *page 21*

How does FOIA interrelate with the Privacy Act?   *page 21*

How does FOIA affect business information?   *page 22*

What references and services can provide further help on FOIA problems?
    page 25

What is the Freedom of Information Act?

The Freedom of Information Act ("FOIA"), 5 U.S.C.§552, is the chief federal law on openness in government. FOIA is an open records law, but it has served as a model for two recent federal open meetings laws, the Sunshine Act and the amended Federal Advisory Committee Act.

Originally passed in 1966, effective in 1967, and amended in 1974 and 1976, FOIA provides that "any person" has a right, enforceable in court, to access to all "agency records" — generally, any record in the possession of a federal agency — except to the extent the records or parts of them may be covered by one of FOIA's nine exemptions. FOIA thus applies to almost the entire range of federal activities and has resulted in a much more open government. As might be expected, FOIA also generates numerous disputes and uncertainties.

What Background Factors Help to Explain FOIA's Enactment, Impact, and Limitations?

Historical Factors

A ten-year campaign in Congress, in which representatives of the news media played a leading role, culminated in FOIA's enactment in 1966 as a revision of the Public Information Section of the Administrative Procedure Act. Complaints during the 1972 Moorhead hearing about bureaucratic foot-dragging in administering FOIA, largely voiced by public interest groups such as those of Ralph Nader, coupled with widespread concern during the 1973-74 Watergate period over excessive government secrecy, resulted in the 1974 FOIA Amendments. In addition, historical factors may help illuminate some of the policies that underlie particular exemptions.

Legal Factors

Both information itself and records, which are repositories of information, may be treated as forms of property, i.e., as capable of being owned and transferred. See 5 U.S.C. § 301, in which federal records are treated as a form of federal property. However, because of the peculiar nature of information, together with the importance of the ability to control access to it in determining the allocation of power among individuals, public and private organizations, and nations, concepts of property law are but one of several legal factors that help place FOIA in proper perspective. The other factors, which may directly or indirectly affect FOIA's impact or which are noted for comparative purposes, include:

(a) the constitutional principle of separation of powers including the privileges of the three branches;

(b) the rules of pre-trial discovery and evidence in litigation;

(c) other federal laws on access to federally held information, such as the two open-meeting laws mentioned above, the Privacy Act, and the large number of statutes referenced by FOIA Exemption 3, discussed below, most of which affect but a single program or agency;

(d) federal laws on private access to non-federal records, principally records of federally aided schools pertaining to identifiable students and records of credit reporting firms pertaining to identifiable consumers; also, insofar as access is effected by making or obtaining a copy, federal copyright laws may be noted here;

(e) federal laws which authorize or require federal entities to obtain information or records from non-federal sources, material which then may be subject to federal access laws; and

(f) open-records and open-meetings laws of state and local governments and of other nations.

Psychosocial Factors

These factors, which may operate on requesters, on agencies holding information, are often difficult to identify or measure. They nevertheless may be important in generating or in resolving struggles over access. Factors *favoring* openness include:

(a) the traditions of discourse, the free exchange of information, and competition of opinions among scientists, scholars, and participants in democratically run organizations;

(b) the effort to assuage feelings of distrust and alienation experienced by increasingly educated and unrestrained populations toward increasingly bureaucratic, remote, impersonal or powerful institutions, especially government;

(c) specific needs or desires for information about competitors, adversaries, or others who present risks or opportunities;

(d) a desire to publicize one's self, one's views, or one's agency, form, or group, or to counteract suspicions;

(e) curiosity or anxiety.

Factors *limiting* openness include:

(a) individual privacy values;

(b) an employee's identification with his job and his employing organization;

(c) traditions of autonomy or esprit de corps in a business, agency, or other group;

(d) fears among those within or dependent upon an agency that its openness in some areas may involve costly burdens, disturbing precedents, failures of function, or other risks;

(e) the traditional cautiousness of most lawyers and some managers about disclosing potentially damaging information about those they represent;

(f) inertia in not seeking or providing information, or a sense of satiation induced by information glut.

What is the Statutory Structure of FOIA?

FOIA has five subsections. Subsection (a) provides for three types of access to agency records, depending on their general nature and presumed public importance: by publishing them in the Federal Register (§(a)(1)), by placing them in an agency reading room with an index (§(a)(2), which covers three types of records likely to have precedential value), or by making them available upon a request made in accordance with agency rules (§(a)(3), which covers the vast majority of agency records). Subsection (a) also provides for fees, judicial review of agency denials of access, attorneys fees, disciplinary action, and contempt (§(a)(4)), access to votes of agency members (§(a)(5)), and time limits for agency responses to requests for records (§(a)(6)).

Subsection (b) contains the nine exemptions, discussed below.

Subsection (c) provides that FOIA is not authority to withhold information from Congress.

Subsection (d) requires each agency to make an annual report to Congress on its denials and requires the Justice Department to report on litigation and on its efforts to encourage agency compliance with FOIA.

Subsection (e) is a redefinition of the term "agency" so as to subject the records of nearly all executive branch entities to FOIA. (Other legislation may in rare instances subject other entities, such as the Copyright Office, to FOIA.)

What Do the Nine FOIA Exemptions Cover?

Note: FOIA exemptions are discretionary exceptions from the Act's compulsory disclosure requirements, and any prohibitions against disclosure must be found elsewhere. There is a fair amount of uncertainty in the interpretation of most of the exemptions and their application to particular records and circumstances, and there is a constant flow of court decisions dealing with these questions. Accordingly, the following discussion must be read as only a summary that is subject to possible qualifications and modifications.

Exemption 1: This covers national security information, i.e., information requiring protection in the interest of defense or foreign relations, which has been properly classified under the standards and procedures of an Executive Order for protecting such information. The current order is No. 12065, which provides for "Top Secret," "Secret," and "Confidential" classifications. This order replaced Order No. 11652 as of December 1, 1978. In *E.P.A.* v. *Mink,* 410 U.S. 73 (1973), the Supreme Court held that the mere fact of classification of a record precluded any further judicial inquiry whether it was covered by this exemption. Exemption 1 was amended in 1974 to overturn this ruling. Exemption 1 as amended is discussed in the Attorney General's "Blue Book" on the 1974 FOIA Amendments. . . . Recent interpretations of the amended exemption appear in *Halperin* v. *Dept. of State,* 565 F.2d 699 (D.C. Cir. 1977); *Weissman* v. *CIA,* 565 F.2d 692 (D.C. Cir. 1977); *Phillippi* v. *CIA,* 546 F.2d 1009 (D.C. Cir. 1976), *Ernest Bell* v. *U.S.A.,* 563 F.2d 484 (1st Cir. 1977); and *Ray* v. *Turner,* 587 F.2d 1187 (D.C. Cir. 1978).

Exemption 2: This covers internal agency matters which are more or less trivial in the sense that there is not substantial and legitimate public interest in their disclosure; also, probably, internal agency instructions to investigators, inspectors, and auditors, but only to the extent that such instructions constitute confidential investigatory techniques and procedures the disclosure of which would seriously hamper the detection of violaters. The leading case is the Supreme Court's decision in *Dept. of Air Force* v. *Rose,* 425 U.S. 352 (1976), which held this exemption applies to trivia of the type just indicated, and expressly left open whether it also applies to instructions of the type just indicated.

In 1978 there were court of appeals decisions in two circuits which generally appear to answer the latter question in the affirmative. *Caplan* v. *Bureau of Alcohol, Tobacco & Firearms,* 587 F.2d 544 (2d Cir. 1978); *Ginsburg, Feldman & Bress* v. *Federal Energy Administration,* 591 F.2d 717 (D.C. Cir. 1978) (affirming by a 4 to 4 vote without opinion the decision of District Judge Flannery in No. 76-27, D.D.C. 1976). Doubts were raised, however, by the decision in *Jordan* v. *U.S. Department of Justice,* 591 F.2d 753 (D.C. Cir. 1978) decided by the same court and on the same day as the affirmance in the *Ginsburg* case. The *Jordan* decision involved access to prosecutional guidelines rather than sensitive investigatory techniques and procedures, but the rationale used to reject a claim of exemption under (b)(2) would on its face apply also to the latter type of material.

In 1979, in a District Court decision by Judge Oberdorfer in the same circuit as had decided the *Ginsburg* and *Jordan* cases, the *Jordan* decision was discussed, distinguished as to the type of records sought, and treated as not representing the views of a majority of the Court of Appeals for the D.C. Circuit on whether Exemption 2 protects sensitive investigatory techniques. *Sturgeon* v. *U.S. Department of Treasury,* — F.Supp. — (No. 77-1964 D.D.C. 1979) (suit for access to portions of Secret Service manuals). Nevertheless, the protectability of sensitive investigatory law enforcement techniques and instructions, remains somewhat clouded, at least as to its statutory basis, at this writing.

Exemption 3: This is a cross-reference to various other federal withholding statutes, and protects under FOIA material which another statute protects, provided that the other statute either (a) prohibits disclosure, or (b) confers discretion to withhold or release and either (i) provides criteria to guide such discretion or (ii) specifies the type of material to which discretion applies. Congress tightened this exemption somewhat in 1976, to overturn the Supreme Court's decision in *FAA* v. *Robertson,* 422 U.S. 255 (1975), which had held that a broad discretionary withholding provision in the Federal Aviation Act was referenced by Exemption 3. It has been said that there are roughly 100 provisions in federal legislation which are referenced by Exemption 3, but most of them, like the Internal Revenue Code provision protecting income tax returns, apply to the records of only one agency.

Exemption 4: This covers trade secrets and other confidential business information furnished to an agency from outside the government. Few problems arise over trade secrets in the strict sense; most of the disputes are over whether other business information is truly confidential. The leading court decision interpreting what is confidential business information under Exemption 4 is "National Parks I" (*National Parks and Conservation Ass'n* v. *Morton,* 498 F.2d 765 (D.C. Cir. 1974)). This decision indicates that claims of confidentiality by a business in submitting information, or promises of confidentiality by an agency in asking for it, are pertinent and significant but not wholly dispositive in determining whether Exemption 4 applies. *National Parks I* provides two alternate tests: First, where the agency needs the information, must rely on purely voluntary cooperation to obtain it, and will not be able to obtain it in the absence of some assurance of confidentiality; second, where release of the information would be likely to cause substantial competitive injury to the business that furnished it. The second test comes into play more often than the first as a basis for withholding business information.

The rule of redaction (the duty to release reasonably segregable non-exempt portions of a requested document) applies in this area as under other FOIA exemptions. The passage of time usually tends to erode the applicability of Exemption 4 to particular material; thus, a document that is likely to disclose the future plans of a business firm may lose its confidential character after the plans become known or have obviously become obsolete. There is some authority that Exemption 4 does not apply to information from a non-profit entity, even though the same type of information from a business corporation would be protected and even though the release would cause financial injury to the entity. The scope of this interpretation is uncertain and its soundness is subject to question.

As to discretionary release of information within Exemption 4 and the means available to the affected business to prevent such release, see below.

Exemption 5: This covers internal communications within the executive branch of the government to the extent they are "deliberative," or are covered by the attorney-client or attorney work product privileges. Important cases on Exemption 5 include, e.g., *Mink* v. *EPA,* 410 U.S. 73 (1973); *NLRB* v. *Sears,* 421 U.S. 132 (1975); *Montrose Chemical Corp.* v. *Train,* 491 F.2d 63 (D.C. Cir. 1974); *Wu* v. *National Endowment for Humanities,* 460 F.2d 1030 (5th Cir. 1972); *Vaughn* v. *Rosen* ("Vaughn II"), 523 F.2d 1136 (D.C. Cir. 1975); and *Mead Data Central* v. *Air Force,* 575 F.2d 932 (D.C. Cir. 1978). Almost all the cases deal with the "deliberative" privilege, the purpose of which is to preserve free and candid internal dialogue leading to executive branch decision making. The exemption thus protects advice, recommendations, proposals, and the like, but does not protect essentially factual matter, or even opinions on questions of fact, except as such material may be inextricably intertwined with deliberative matter or with a deliberative process. An Exemption 5 document must be pre-decisional, and the document may lose its character as such if an agency "adopts" the document, i.e., authoritatively indicates that the document is the agency's explanation of its decision or statement of its policy.

On May 5, 1977 Attorney General Bell sent a letter to all federal agencies which was largely designed to discourage the use of Exemption 5 where release of the document would not involve a sufficient prospect of actual harm to legitimate public or private interests to justify defense of a possible suit.

Exemption 6: This covers information about individuals, disclosure of which would be a "clearly unwarranted invasion of personal privacy." To be covered, information must be (a) about an identifiable individual, (b) an invasion of the individual's privacy if disclosed to others, and (c) "clearly unwarranted" to disclose. According to the Attorney General's Blue Book on the 1974 FOIA Amendments, release of information about an individual may invade his privacy if it is information which he "could reasonably assert an option to withhold from the public at large because of its intimacy or its possible adverse effects upon himself or his family." Medical files and personnel files are very likely to contain much Exemption 6 material, but so may other records. Exemption 6 does not apply if the injury to the individual is counterbalanced by a public interest favoring release. In performing this balancing, there is some question whether the public interest to be weighed is that in a release to the particular requester or that in a release to the entire public. The clear weight of authority, however, is that it is sometimes permissible to weigh the private injury and the public benefits of a release to the particular requester. Thus, home addresses may not be exempt from release to state income tax authorities or scholarly researchers for specified beneficial purposes, but would be exempt from release for unspecified or random uses such as commercial solicitation.

Any Exemption 6 material must be disclosed, so far as that exemption is concerned, if the identity of the individual can be adequately protected by deleting matter that might identify him, and of course Exemption 6 cannot be used to deny an individual access to information about himself. The Supreme Court's decision in the *Rose* case, cited above under Exemption 2, also deals with Exemption 6 and cites many of the other important Exemption 6 decisions.

Exemption 7: This exemption, which was amended in 1974, exempts "investigatory records" which are compiled for "law enforcement purposes" to the extent that one of six types of harm specified in clauses (A)-(F) are present. An investigation is for "law enforcement purposes" if it is violation-oriented or if it is a personnel background security investigation. General agency audits, reviews, or "investigations" of the manner in which the agency accomplishes its mission are not "law enforcement" investigations. *Rural Housing Alliance* v. *Department of Agriculture,* 498 F.2d 73 (D.C. Cir. 1974). The exemption applies to civil as well as to criminal law enforcement investigations, *Williams* v. *IRS,* 479 F.2d 317 (3d Cir. 1973), *cert. denied,* 414 U.S. 1024 (1974), and *Chamberlain* v. *Alexander,* 419 F.Supp. 235 (S.D. Ala. 1976). A comprehensive discussion of this exemption and each of its six clauses is found in the Attorney General's Blue Book on the 1974 FOIA Amendments. The principal features of the six clauses are discussed below:

Exemption 7(A):Interference with Enforcement Proceedings. Many of the

FOIA requests and resulting FOIA litigation involving Exemption 7(A) stem from efforts by persons who have civil or criminal disputes with government agencies to use the FOIA to aid them in these disputes. Under subsection (a)(3) of the FOIA "any person" may request reasonably described records and thereafter may bring suit, and thus, one's status as the subject of a government investigation or as a party opposing the government in court does not preclude use of the FOIA. Ordinarily, litigants or subjects of a government investigation or case do not have any greater or lesser rights under the FOIA than other persons. However, where the FOIA requester-plaintiff is involved in a law enforcement matter to which his FOIA request pertains, a number of decisions have dealt with the scope and application of the 7(A) Exemption, and perhaps more important, with the burden of proof which the government agency involved has to meet to establish the requisite 7(A) "interference."

In the leading case on Exemption 7(A), *NLRB* v. *Robbins Tire & Rubber Co.,* 437 U.S. 214 (1978), the Supreme Court rejected the position that a 7(A) "interference" must always be established on a document-by-document basis, and held that determinations as to the proper application of Exemption 7(A) to the records in dispute could be made generically, based on the type of record involved. More particularly, the Supreme Court found that the NLRB proved "interference" with its pending unfair labor practice enforcement proceeding by showing that all the records withheld were witness statements obtained for use in the enforcement proceeding. The primary basis for the Court's decision was its acceptance of the NLRB's claim that release would create a great potential for witness intimidation.

The *Robbins Tire* interpretation of Exemption 7(A) is in accord with numerous lower court decisions. These decisions generally support the view that the 1974 amendments to Exemption 7 did not change the original Congressional intent that the FOIA should not be used to provide an actual or potential defendant with earlier or greater access to open investigatory files pertaining to his case. See *United States* v. *Murdock,* 548 F.2d 599 (5th Cir. 1977); *Title Guarantee* v. *NLRB,* 534 F.2d 484 (2d Cir. 1976), *cert. denied,* 97 S. Ct. 98 (1976); *Climax Molybdenum Co.* v. *NLRB,* 539 F.2d 63 (10th Cir. 1976); *Roger J. Au and Son, Inc.* v. *NLRB,* 538 F.2d 80 (3d Cir. 1976); *New England Medical Center Hospital* v. *NLRB,* 548 F.2d 377 (1st Cir. 1976). See also, *Bryant* v. *Internal Revenue Service,* 76-2 U.S.T.C., par 9613, 28 A.F.T.R. 2d 76-5643 (D. Maine 1976).

A major problem confronting the courts and government agencies has been the impact of *Robbins Tire* and other court decisions on the government's burden of proof for establishing the 7(A) Exemption in instances where there are hundreds or thousands of records involved in the FOIA suit. If a detailed *Vaughn*-type index (*Vaughn* v. *Rosen,* 484 F.2d 820 (D.C. Cir. 1973) is required, there can be a resulting serious practical impediment to the government's enforcement proceeding, arising out of the process of preparing such an index, and also from making the index available to the plaintiff. Indeed, because information in the index could itself disclose the parameters of the government's case, including gaps in what its investigators know, some courts have permitted the *in camera* filing of *Vaughn* affidavits and/or indices. See *Kanter* v. *Internal Revenue Service,* 433 F.Supp. 812, 823-824 (N.D. Ill. 1977); *Tarnopol* v. *F.B.I.,* 77-2 U.S.T.C., par 9666 (D.D.C. 1977); *Steinberg* v. *Internal Revenue Service,* Civil. No. 77-2202 (S.D. Fla., decided January 25, 1979).

Even if a *Vaughn*-type index can be filed *in camera,* experience with FOIA cases involving large numbers of documents related to an open civil or criminal law enforcement proceeding has shown that a practical interference can result from the diversion of limited agency resources from the law enforcement proceeding to the preparation of detailed *Vaughn*-type affidavits and indices for the FOIA case. For this reason, in certain recent cases decided after the *Robbins Tire* decision, courts have rejected the plaintiff's motion for detailed document-by-document *Vaughn* indices and found instead that the government could meet its burden by submitting "generic" type affidavits which group the documents into categories and specify the type of harm which would flow from releasing documents in a given category. See *Anheuser-Busch, Inc.* v. *Internal Revenue Service,* Civil No. 78-1326 (D.D.C. November 27, 1978), on appeal to C.A. D.C., No. 78-2300; *Lyle* v. *Internal Revenue Service,* 78-2 U.S.T.C., par. 9740 (N.D. Ga. September 26, 1978); *Simons* v. *Semrick,* Civil No. H-77-1487 (S.D. Tex. August 18, 1978); *Stephenson* v. *Internal Revenue Service,* Civil No. C-78-1071A (N.D. Ga. November 15, 1978); *Steinberg* v. *Internal Revenue Service,* Civil No. 77-2202 (S.D. Fla. January 26, 1979).

On the other hand, *Bristol-Meyers Co.* v. *F.T.C.,* Civil No. 77-1275 (D.C. Cir. August 22, 1978) can be read as requiring a government agency, even after *Robbins Tire,* to engage in a document-by-document *Vaughn*-type proof exercise to support a 7(A) Exemption claim for investigatory records related to an open enforcement proceeding, at least in some situations, including certain ones where the records sought are not available in discovery. In this regard, see *Britt* v. *Internal Revenue Service,* 78-2 U.S.T.C., par. 9841 (D.D.C. 1978), where Exemption 7(A) was held not to apply *per se* to a document that had been denied the plantiff in discovery proceedings in a pending Tax Court case. And *cf. Ray* v. *Turner,* 587 F.2d 1187, 1203-1214 (D.C. Cir. 1978) (concurring opinion). It would appear that agencies may not be able to avoid FOIA disclosures in conjunction with agency adjudicatory proceedings by the simple expedient of adopting nonstatutory discovery rules barring all prehearing disclosure of investigatory records. The fact that documents sought through FOIA are not available in discovery in related agency adjudicatory or judicial proceedings may strongly suggest, but may not always automatically mean, that the Exemption 7(A) applies.

Finally, despite some uncertainty, the better view supports the availability of the 7(A) Exemption for investigatory records in a file that has been technically closed but which may be pertinent to another and still active proceeding. *New England Medical Center Hospital* v. *NLRB,* 548 F.2d 377, 385 (1st Cir. 1976); *AMF Head Division of AMF* v. *NLRB,* 564 F.2d 374 (10th Cir. 1977).

Exemption 7(B): Depriving a Person of a Fair Trial or an Impartial Adjudication. This exemption, which is aimed at prejudicial publicity, is rarely asserted.

Exemption 7(C): Unwarranted Invasion of Personal Privacy. To a great extent, the law concerning Exemption 6, which prohibits disclosures of any records that would result in a "clearly unwarranted invasion of personal privacy," is applicable here, although the omission of the word "clearly" where the records are investigatory means that the burden of proof to justify withholding is lower under 7(C). See *Deering Milliken* v. *Irving,* 548 F.2d 1131, 1136 (4th Cir. 1977). And *cf., Dept. of Air Force* v. *Rose,* 425 U.S. 352, 378-379. fn. 16 (1976).

It has repeatedly been held that Exemption 7(C) should be construed to protect the identity of certain individuals who provide information to law enforcement agencies during the course of an investigation. In such situations 7(C) may duplicate the first part of Exemption 7(D), discussed below. The privacy interest being protected in such instances is not necessarily confined to the protection of any personal details about himself which the individual may have furnished, but rather is related to his interest in being free from the harassment or opprobrium which may flow from public knowledge that he provided information about another to a government law enforcement agency. See *Maroscia* v. *Levi,* 569 F.2d 1000 (7th Cir. 1977); *Shaver* v. *Bell,* 433 F.Supp. 438 (N.D. Ga. 1977); *Forrester* v. *U.S. Dept. of Labor,* 433 F. Supp. 987 (S.D. N.Y. 1977); *Lobosco* v. *Internal Revenue Service,* 41 A.F.T.R. 2d 596 (E.D. N.Y. 1977); *Luzaich* v. *United States,* 435 F.Supp. 31 (D. Minn. 1977), *aff'd* 564 F.2d 101 (8th Cir. 1977).

Exemption 7(D): Confidential Source and Information. The first part of this exemption protects, in records of any law enforcement investigation, the identity of a confidential source, but not the information furnished. The second part protects, in addition to the source's identity, any confidential information he or she furnished to criminal law enforcement authorities in the course of a criminal investigation or a lawful national security intelligence investigation. This exemption should not be confined to those instances where either an express promise of confidentiality is given to the individual, or where there is a specific reference on the document itself to maintaining the confidentiality of the informant's identity, but should also apply if the source provided information in circumstances from which an assurance of confidentiality may be reasonably inferred. See *Nix* v. *United States,* 572 F.2d 998 (4th Cir. 1978); *Evans* v. *Dept. of Transportation of United States,* 446 F.2d 821, 823-824 (5th Cir. 1971), *cert. denied,* 405 U.S. 918 (1972); *Bast* v. *Internal Revenue Service,* 42 A.F.T.R. 2d 5078 (D.D.C. 1978). An area of some controversy has been whether the protection of a source's identity under 7(D) can apply to a source which is another law enforcement organization, including foreign sources such as Scotland Yard. One court has held such identities to be protectible, *Church of Scientology of California* v. *U.S. Dept. of Justice,* 410 F.Supp. 1297 (C.D. Cal. 1976), and the rationale underlying the exemption — to enable federal law enforcement agencies to obtain information that would not be forthcoming in the absence of confidentiality — applies to other law enforcement organizations as well as to individuals.

Exemption 7(E): Investigative Techniques. Under 7(E) investigatory records reflecting special techniques or procedures of investigation not otherwise generally known to the public may be withheld. This exemption is rarely used. See *Ott* v. *Levi,* 419 F.Supp. 750, 752 (E.D. Mo. 1976), where a 7(E) claim was upheld as to certain F.B.I. laboratory reports which disclosed techniques used in arson investigations.

Exemption 7(F): Safety of Law Enforcement Personnel. This exemption protects matter which would endanger such personnel, particularly undercover agents.

Exemptions 8 and 9: These exemptions, which are rarely used or interpreted, respectively cover records relating to the examination of banks and other financial institutions by agencies that supervise them and the records containing oil well information.

What Procedures Must a Requester Follow?

Each agency has issued FOIA regulations (published in the Federal Register and the Code of Federal Regulations) telling the public how to address letters to the agency requesting access to the agency's records, what fees for searching and copying may be charged, how to appeal an initial denial to a higher level in the agency, and the like. These procedures may sometimes be waived for reasons of public interest, simplicity, or speed; for example, some offices may furnish some types of records in response to telephone requests. Agencies do not ordinarily insist that requesters comply in every respect with the pertinent agency regulations in order to obtain access to agency records.

A request must "reasonably describe" the records to which access is desired, in order to enable the agency to determine what it is for which a search will be made. The mere fact that a request may seek thousands of documents and entail a burdensome search does not invalidate the request. Where substantial search and copying fees may be involved, an agency may provide in its regulations for payment of an advance deposit.

The requester does not have to explain why he wants access to the records, but to do so is often helpful for several reasons: it may sometimes result in a faster or less expensive search; it may sometimes result in a discretionary grant of access to material that is exempt from compulsory disclosure; it may help demonstrate a public interest in release which could counterbalance an individual privacy interest under Exemption 6, or which could lead to a waiver or reduction of the search or copying fees chargeable under the agency's regulations. For similar reasons, a requester may be well advised to include his telephone number in his request along with an offer to discuss the request with the agency should the agency so desire.

What Procedures Must the Agency Follow?

The agency must mail the requester a determination to grant or deny access within ten working days after the request is received at the proper agency office. Ordinarily, a grant of access gives the requester the opportunity to inspect the records, to obtain copies, or both. A reason (an exemption) must be given for any denial, and the requester must be informed of his rights to appeal to a higher official in the agency, and to judicial review in the event the appeal is not totally successful. Appeals must be acted on within twenty working days. Time extensions up to another ten days are possible in defined special circumstances, and the requester can sue if the time limits are violated, treating delay as denial. If, however, an agency responding to such a suit can demonstrate that it is exercising "due diligence" in processing the matter and that the delay results from "exceptional circumstances," the court can grant the agency more time. Where an agency has made such a showing, a general agency rule of "first come, first served" has been upheld. *Open America* v. *Watergate Special Prosecution Force,* 547 F.2d 605 (D.C. Cir. 1976). *Contra, Hamlin* v. *Kelley,* 433 F.Supp. 180 (N.D. Ill. 1977).

What Will Happen If the Matter Goes to Court?

The case will get expedited consideration compared to most other civil litigation. The agency has the burden of proving that the withheld records, or the deleted parts of them, are exempt. The most common form of proof is by affidavit, which may have to be very detailed, describing each withheld document and explaining the application to each of the exemptions claimed. See *Vaughn* v. *Rosen,* 484 F.2d 820 (D.C. Cir. 1973). The court also has express authority to inspect the withheld material *"in camera"* (in chambers without plantiff's participation), but such inspections are far from automatic. The court will decide the case de novo, may award the plaintiff attorney's fees, and may, if it finds the withholding may have been "arbitrary and capricious," order the Special Counsel of the Merit Systems Protection Board to investigate and, if sufficient cause is found, to require appropriate disciplinary sanctions for the responsible agency officials, a power very rarely used. About 700 FOIA cases have been decided with opinion, some by the Supreme Court, and several court cases are pending.

How Does FOIA Interrelate with the Privacy Act?

The Privacy Act, 5 U.S.C. §552a, governs the manner in which the Federal Government collects and uses certain information about individuals, and it grants individuals a right to access, subject to certain exceptions, to records pertaining to themselves. An individual may utilize either the Privacy Act or FOIA or both to seek access to information about himself in agency records, and is entitled to the cumulative total of access rights under the two Acts. Some agencies have created single units to process requests under both Acts. But the two Acts differ considerably in purpose, scope, procedures, and effects.

The general purpose of FOIA is to strengthen the public's right to know, while the Privacy Act is intended to give the individual better control over the gathering, dissemination, and accuracy of agency information about himself. FOIA gives any person a right of access to everything in agency records except for the nine exemptions. The Privacy Act gives individuals a right of access to certain records that contain information about themselves, and it restricts disclosures which agencies can make of these records to other persons and agencies without the subject individual's consent. But the restriction against disclosing records about the individual to others is subject to various exceptions, listed in subsection (b) of the Privacy Act. FOIA constitutes one of the exceptions to this restriction, and thus FOIA is an important limitation on the individual's protection under the Privacy Act from access by other persons to records about himself.

The two Acts also are different in scope: all agency records are under FOIA, but only records in a "system of records" are subject to the Privacy Act. A "system" is defined as a group of records from which information is retrieved by the individual's name, social security number, or other individual identifier. Also, the concepts of "records" under the two Acts are different: under FOIA a record is any repository of information, while under the Privacy Act a record is defined, in effect, as an item of information about an individual that has been recorded.

The two Acts provide different procedures as to fees, time limits, judicial review, and other matters. They also provide different sources of guidance: the Justice Department provides guidance to agencies on FOIA, while the Office of Management and Budget provides guidance on the Privacy Act, though with legal assistance from Justice.

Whether information about an individual is protectible from requests by other persons depends chiefly on Exemption 6 of FOIA, discussed above. If the information is under FOIA Exemption 6 and is also in a Privacy Act "system," the Privacy Act eliminates the agency's option to make a discretionary FOIA release unless the intended release is expressly authorized by other provisions of the Privacy Act, 5 U.S.C. §552a(b).

How Does FOIA Affect Business Information?

The legal principles determining what business information an agency *may* withhold are generally fairly clear, although these principles may sometimes be difficult to apply with assurance to particular information. Because of the 1979 decision by the Supreme Court in *Chrysler Corp. v. Brown, Secretary of Defense,* 60 L Ed2d 208, discussed below, the legal principles that determine what business information an agency *must* withhold have become somewhat more clear, although the application of those principles remains subject to various doubts.

FOIA Exemption 4 is the basic guide to the kinds of information contained in agency records and received from and pertaining to identifiable business firms that may legally be withheld in response to an FOIA request. As discussed earlier, Exemption 4 generally applies when release of the information would involve a substantial risk of competitive injury to the business which directly or indirectly furnished it. In addition, Exemption 3 may authorize (or require) withholding of specialized types of business information, typically in certain lines of business of particular concern to a single agency which administers a statute referenced by Exemption 3. Also, Exemptions 8 and 9 obviously authorize withholding of certain business information, respectively of financial institutions and oil producers. Finally, 18 U.S.C. § 1905, a general criminal statute prohibiting release of business information unless "authorized by law," has often been asserted — both by an agency denying an FOIA request and by a business firm which had furnished information in bringing a "reverse FOIA" suit to enjoin an agency from releasing it under FOIA — as a prohibition against release, either on the theory that it is an Exemption 3 statute or that it is an independent prohibition against release. Under the *Chrysler* decision, § 1905 is now clearly an independent prohibition against releases not authorized by law, but its scope remains somewhat unclear.

The Supreme Court's decision in *Chrysler* held that Exemption 4, like other FOIA exemptions, permits but does not require agencies to withhold business information covered by that exemption, but that 18 U.S.C. § 1905 does require agencies to withhold business information if such information is both exempt under FOIA and also within the scope of 18 U.S.C. § 1905, unless release of such information is "authorized by law" within the meaning of § 1905. The Court did not rule on the scope or coverage of Exemption 4, nor on the scope or coverage of 18 U.S.C. § 1905, except as to the meaning of the phrase "authorized by law" in the latter statute. As to this phrase, the Court held that, contrary to the decision of the third circuit court of appeals, neither 5 U.S.C. § 301 nor the applicable Labor Department regulations provided legal authority within the meaning of 18 U.S.C. § 1905 for a release. Such authority can only flow from a statute conferring it, a properly adopted regulation based upon such a statute, or (a point not considered by the Court) the Constitution. In a footnote at the end of its opinion, the Court stated that it was remanding to the lower courts the issue whether the information from *Chrysler* was exempt under FOIA, and that it was not deciding the "relative ambits of Exemption 4 and § 1905," but strongly suggested that § 1905 is not significantly broader than Exemption 4, and left considerable doubt whether it is much narrower, at least where the release of the information is "not authorized by law" within its meaning. The Court also made clear that reverse FOIA suits, while not authorized by FOIA or 18 U.S.C. § 1905, are authorized under Section 10 of the Administrative Procedure Act, 5 U.S.C. §§ 702, 701-706.

Business information may enter agency records through regulatory, procurement, or almost any other kind of government activity. It is not possible to describe all the kinds of information from business concerns found in agency records that may (and often must) be withheld by the agency, but important general categories that are likely to contain largely protectible information include, e.g., trade secrets in the strict sense of a valuable secret formula, process, or the like; technical designs or data of value to the company or to its competitors; internal cost information for current or recent periods; information on financial condition, the release of which might injure the company; resumes of key company personnel and data on how they are utilized; and information on customers, sources of supply, or business plans that are valuable to the company and not known to competitors.

The more damaging the release of the information would be to the company, the greater the likelihood that the agency will be able to withhold it, will in fact do so, and will be enjoinable if it should decide to release. The principal limitations on this statement are situations (a) where the agency feels it lacks, and the company does not supply, enough support for an agency determination that the information is exempt and for the agency to meet its burden in defending a FOIA suit of proving the exemption applies, and (b) where the agency believes that release of the information is authorized by law and should be made. Sometimes a company seeking to persuade an agency to protect purportedly confidential business information will have to educate the agency with respect to the competitive harm that would result from disclosure.

Some agencies provide procedures whereby a company can obtain a determination in advance of submittal as to whether or not the agency considers the information withholdable under Exemption 4. The alternative, of course, is for the agency to obtain the information if it can, and await a FOIA request before considering the applicability of Exemption 4. From the government's point of view, the principal advantage of predetermination is to facilitate the voluntary submission of business information to an agency by providing some advance assurance to the company that its confidences will be kept. The apparent attractions of predetermination procedures must be weighed against the time and effort they require in reviewing material which, if in fact it should ever be requested under FOIA, may have to be reviewed again to see if the potential for injury is still present when measured against the effects of time, the arguments of the requester, and possible new caselaw. Regardless of any predetermination procedures, agencies practically without exception will notify a company so that it can protect its interests if there is a real possibility of the agency releasing over the company's objections company-submitted information that is even arguably protectible.

What References and Services Can Provide Further Help on FOIA Problems?

1. *Attorney General's Memorandum on the 1974 Amendments to the Freedom of Information Act,* February 1975 (the A.G.'s "Blue Book" on the '74 FOIA Amendments), for sale by the Superintendent of Documents, U.S. Government Printing Office, Washington, D.C. 20402, 90 cents.

2. The Joint Congressional *Source Book* on the 1974 FOIA Amendments, March 1975, containing legislative history and other materials including item 1 above, for sale by the Superintendent of Documents, Stock No. 052-070-02805-0, $4.80.

3. *Attorney General's Memorandum on the Public Information Section of the Administrative Procedure Act,* June 1967 (the A.G.'s "Blue Book" on the original FOIA, now partly obsolete due to amendments and caselaw), for sale by the Superintendent of Documents, 25 cents.

4. The Senate *Source Book* on the original FOIA, 1974, Senate Document 93-82, containing legislative history and other materials including item 3 above, for sale by the Superintendent of Documents, $2.85.

5. *Freedom of Information Case List.* As of this writing, the March 1979 Edition of the Case List is expected to be available during April, to replace the August 1978 Edition. The Case List is an alphabetical list of court decisions on the Freedom of Information Act, 5 U.S.C. §552, including cases with opinions not yet reported, with notations as to the exemptions or other issues involved in each case, and with a topical index and other aids to users. It is issued approximately twice a year by the Office of Information Law and Policy, Department of Justice, and is reprinted in the Access Reports Reference File and, as to some editions, in the Congressional Record. It is also available for purchase from the Government Printing Office.

6. *Access Reports,* a biweekly newsletter on Freedom of Information and Privacy, published by Plus Publications, Inc. of Washington, D.C.

7. *Federal Information Disclosure: Procedures, Forms, and the Law,* James T. O'Reilly, Shepard's Inc. and McGraw-Hill, August 1977. This treatise is a useful reference work.

8. *Litigation Under the Amended Federal Freedom of Information Act,* edited

by Christine M. Marwick. Fourth edition, Aug. 1978, Project on National Security & Civil Liberties of the ACLU Foundation.

9. Chapter 3A, the Freedom of Information Act, in Kenneth Culp Davis' *Administrative Law of the Seventies,* supplementing his Administrative Law Treatise, June 1976, Lawyers Co-operative Publishing Co.

10. Chapter 5, "The Freedom of Information Act and Related Legislation," in Vol. 1 of Kenneth Culp Davis' *Administrative Law Treatise,* 2d ed. (1978), published by K.C. Davis, University of San Diego, Ca. 92110.

The foregoing is not a complete list of useful material on FOIA, its administration, and related matters. Valuable articles, too numerous to cite here, appeared from time to time in the National Law Journal, the Public Administration Review, the Administrative Law Review, and various other law reviews, including those of Harvard, Columbia, and Michigan. Other sources include the FOIA regulations of the agencies which are published in the Code of Federal Regulations, the annual FOIA reports to Congress of the Justice Department and other agencies training materials of the Office of Personnel Management, and the reports of various federal study commissions.

CHAPTER 2

The Privacy Act

The Act, 5 U.S.C. §552a

(a) Definitions. For purposes of this section:

(1) the term "agency" means agency as defined in section 552(e) of this title;

(2) the term "individual" means a citizen of the United States or an alien lawfully admitted for permanent residence;

(3) the term "maintain" includes maintain, collect, use, or disseminate;

(4) the term "record" means any item, collection, or grouping of information about an individual that is maintained by an agency, including, but not limited to, his education, financial transactions, medical history, and criminal or employment history and that contains his name, or the identifying number, symbol, or other identifying particular assigned to the individual, such as a finger or voice print or a photograph;

(5) the term "system of records" means a group of any records under the control of any agency from which information is retrieved by the name of the individual or by some identifying number, symbol, or other identifying particular assigned to the individual;

(6) the term "statistical record" means a record in a system of records maintained for statistical research or reporting purposes only and not used in whole or in part in making any determination about an identifiable individual, except as provided by section 8 of title 13; and

(7) the term "routine use" means, with respect to the disclosure of a record, the use of such record for a purpose which is compatible with the purpose for which it was collected.

(b) Conditions of Disclosure. No agency shall disclose any record which is contained in a system of records by any means of communication to any person, or to another agency, except pursuant to a written request by, or with the prior written consent of, the individual to whom the record pertains, unless disclosure of the record would be:

(1) to those officers and employees of the agency which maintains the record who have a need for the record in the performance of their duties;

(2) required under section 552 of this title;

(3) for a routine use as defined in subsection (a)(7) of this section and described under subsection (e)(4)(D) of this section;

(4) to the Bureau of the Census for purposes of planning or carrying out a census or survey or related activity pursuant to the provisions of title 13;

(5) to a recipient who has provided the agency with advance adequate written assurance that the record will be used solely as a statistical research or reporting record, and the record is to be transferred in a form that is not individually identifiable;

(6) to the National Archives of the United States as a record which has sufficient historical or other value to warrant its continued preservation by the United States Government, or for evaluation by the Administrator of General Services or his designee to determine whether the record has such value;

(7) to another agency or to an instrumentality of any governmental jurisdiction within or under the control of the United States for a civil or criminal law enforcement activity if the activity is authorized by law, and if the head of the agency or instrumentality has made a written request to the agency which maintains the record specifying the particular portion desired and the law enforcement activity for which the record is sought;

(8) to a person pursuant to a showing of compelling circumstances affecting the health or safety of an individual if upon such disclosure notification is transmitted to the last known address of such individual;

(9) to either House of Congress, or, to the extent of matter within its jurisdiction, any committee or subcommittee thereof, any joint committee of Congress or subcommittee of any such joint committee;

(10) to the Comptroller General, or any of his authorized representatives,

in the course of the performance of the duties of the General Accounting Office; or

(11) pursuant to the order of a court of competent jurisdiction.

(c) Accounting of Certain Disclosures. Each agency, with respect to each system of records under its control, shall:
(1) except for disclosures made under subsections (b)(1) or (b)(2) of this section, keep an accurate accounting of—

(A) the date, nature, and purpose of each disclosure of a record to any person or to another agency made under subsection (b) of this section; and

(B) the name and address of the person or agency to whom the disclosure is made;

(2) retain the accounting made under paragraph (1) of this subsection for at least five years or the life of the record, whichever is longer, after the disclosure for which the accounting is made;

(3) except for disclosures made under subsection (b)(7) of this section, make the accounting made under paragraph (1) of this subsection available to the individual named in the record at his request; and

(4) inform any person or other agency about any correction or notation of dispute made by the agency in accordance with subsection (d) of this section of any record that has been disclosed to the person or agency if an accounting of the disclosure was made.

(d) Access to Records. Each agency that maintains a system of records shall:

(1) upon request by any individual to gain access to his record or to any information pertaining to him which is contained in the system, permit him and upon his request, a person of his own choosing to accompany him, to review the record and have a copy made of all or any portion thereof in a form comprehensible to him, except that the agency may require the individual to furnish a written statement authorizing discussion of that individual's record in the accompanying person's presence;

(2) permit the individual to request amendment of a record pertaining to him and:

(A) not later than ten days (excluding Saturdays, Sundays, and legal public holidays) after the date of receipt of such request, acknowledge in writing such receipt; and

(B) promptly, either—

(i) make any correction of any portion thereof which the individual believes is not accurate, relevant, timely, or complete; or

(ii) inform the individual of its refusal to amend the record in accordance with his request, the reason for the refusal, the procedures established by the agency for the individual to request a review of that refusal by the head of the agency or an officer designated by the head of the agency, and the name and business address of that official;

(3) permit the individual who disagrees with the refusal of the agency to amend his record to request a review of such refusal, and not later than thirty days (excluding Saturdays, Sundays, and legal public holidays) from the date on which the individual requests such review, complete such review and make a final determination unless, for good cause shown, the head of the agency extends such 30-day period; and if, after his review, the reviewing official also refuses to amend the record in accordance with the request, permit the individual to file with the agency a concise statement setting forth the reasons for his disagreement with the refusal of the agency, and notify the individual of the provisions for judicial review of the reviewing official's determination under subsection (g)(1)(A) of this section;

(4) in any disclosure, containing information about which the individual has filed a statement of disagreement, occurring after the filing of the statement under paragraph (3) of this subsection, clearly note any portion of the record which is disputed and provide copies of the statement and, if the agency deems it appropriate, copies of a concise statement of the reasons of the agency for not making the amendments requested, to persons or other agencies to whom the disputed record has been disclosed; and

(5) nothing in this section shall allow an individual access to any information compiled in reasonable anticipation of a civil action or proceeding.

(e) Agency Requirements. Each agency that maintains a system of records shall:

(1) maintain in its records only such information about an individual as is relevant and necessary to accomplish a purpose of the agency required to be accomplished by statute or by executive order of the President;

(2) collect information to the greatest extent practicable directly from the subject individual when the information may result in adverse determinations about an individual's rights, benefits, and privileges under Federal programs;

(3) inform each individual whom it asks to supply information, on the form which it uses to collect the information or on a separate form that can be retained by the individual:

(A) the authority (whether granted by statute, or by executive order of the President) which authorizes the solicitation of the information and whether disclosure of such information is mandatory or voluntary;

(B) the principal purpose or purposes for which the information is intended to be used;

(C) the routine uses which may be made of the information, as published pursuant to paragraph (4)(D) of this subsection; and

(D) the effects on him, if any, of not providing all or any part of the requested information;

(4) subject to the provisions of paragraph (11) of this subsection, publish in the Federal Register at least annually a notice of the existence and character of the system of records, which notice shall include:

(A) the name and location of the system;

(B) the categories of individuals on whom records are maintained in the system;

(C) the categories of records maintained in the system;

(D) each routine use of the records contained in the system, including the categories of users and the purpose of such use;

(E) the policies and practices of the agency regarding storage, retrievability, access controls, retention, and disposal of the records;

(F) the title and business address of the agency official who is responsible for the system of records;

(G) the agency procedures whereby an individual can be notified at his request if the system of records contains a record pertaining to him;

(H) the agency procedures whereby an individual can be notified at his request how he can gain access to any record pertaining to him contained in the system of records, and how he can contest its content; and

(I) the categories of sources of records in the system;

(5) maintain all records which are used by the agency in making any determination about any individual with such accuracy, relevance, timeliness, and completeness as is reasonably necessary to assure fairness to the individual in the determination;

(6) prior to disseminating any record about an individual to any person other than an agency, unless the dissemination is made pursuant to subsection (b)(2) of this section, make reasonable efforts to assure that such records are accurate, complete, timely, and relevant for agency purposes;

(7) maintain no record describing how any individual exercises rights guaranteed by the First Amendment unless expressly authorized by statute or by the individual about whom the record is maintained or unless pertinent to and within the scope of an authorized law enforcement activity;

(8) make reasonable efforts to serve notice on an individual when any record on such individual is made available to any person under compulsory legal process when such process becomes a matter of public record;

(9) establish rules of conduct for persons involved in the design, development, operation, or maintenance of any system of records, or in maintaining any record, and instruct each such person with respect to such rules and the requirements of this section, including any other rules and procedures adopted pursuant to this section and the penalties for noncompliance;

(10) establish appropriate administrative, technical, and physical safeguards to insure the security and confidentiality of records and to protect against any anticipated threats or hazards to their security or integrity which could result in substantial harm, embarrassment, inconvenience, or unfairness to any individual on whom information is maintained; and

(11) at least thirty days prior to publication of information under paragraph (4)(D) of this subsection, publish in the Federal Register notice of any new use

or intended use of the information in the system, and provide an opportunity for interested persons to submit written data, views, or arguments to the agency.

(f) Agency rules. In order to carry out the provisions of this section, each agency that maintains a system of records shall promulgate rules, in accordance with the requirements (including general notice) of section 553 of this title, which shall—

(1) establish procedures whereby an individual can be notified in response to his request if any system of records named by the individual contains a record pertaining to him;

(2) define reasonable times, places, and requirements for identifying an individual who requests his record or information pertaining to him before the agency shall make the record or information available to the individual;

(3) establish procedures for the disclosure to an individual upon his request of his record or information pertaining to him, including special procedure, if deemed necessary, for the disclosure to an individual of medical records, including psychological records, pertaining to him;

(4) establish procedures for reviewing a request from an individual concerning the amendment of any record or information pertaining to the individual, for making a determination on the request, for an appeal within the agency of an initial adverse agency determination, and for whatever additional means may be necessary for each individual to be able to exercise fully his rights under this section; and

(5) establish fees to be charged, if any, to any individual for making copies of his record, excluding the cost of any search for and review of the record.

The Office of the Federal Register shall annually compile and publish the rules promulgated under this subsection and agency notices published under subsection (e)(4) of this section in a form available to the public at low cost.

(g)(1) Civil Remedies. Whenever any agency

(A) makes a determination under subsection (d)(3) of this section not to amend an individual's record in accordance with his request, or fails to make such review in conformity with that subsection;

(B) refuses to comply with an individual request under subsection (d)(1) of this section;

(C) fails to maintain any record concerning any individual with such accuracy, relevance, timeliness, and completeness as is necessary to assure fairness in any determination relating to the qualifications, character, rights, or opportunities of, or benefits to the individual that may be made on the basis of such record, and consequently a determination is made which is adverse to the individual; or

(D) fails to comply with any other provision of this section, or any rule promulgated thereunder, in such a way as to have an adverse effect on an individual,

the individual may bring a civil action against the agency, and the district courts of the United States shall have jurisdiction in the matters under the provisions of this subsection.

(2)(A) In any suit brought under the provisions of subsection (g)(1)(A) of this section, the court may order the agency to amend the individual's record in accordance with his request or in such other way as the court may direct. In such a case the court shall determine the matter de novo.

(B) The court may assess against the United States reasonable attorney fees and other litigation costs reasonably incurred in any case under this paragraph in which the complainant has substantially prevailed.

(3)(A) In any suit brought under the provisions of subsection (g)(1)(B) of this section, the court may enjoin the agency from withholding the records and order the production to the complainant of any agency records improperly withheld from him. In such a case the court shall determine the matter de novo, and may examine the contents of any agency records in camera to determine whether the records or any portion thereof may be withheld under any of the exemptions set forth in subsection (k) of this section, and the burden is on the agency to sustain its action.

(B) The court may assess against the United States reasonable attorney fees and other litigation costs reasonably incurred in any case under this paragraph in which the complainant has substantially prevailed.

(4) In any suit brought under the provisions of subsection (g)(1)(C) or (D) of this section in which the court determines that the agency acted in a

manner which was intentional or willful, the United States shall be liable to the individual in an amount equal to the sum of:

(A) actual damages sustained by the individual as a result of the refusal or failure, but in no case shall a person entitled to recovery receive less than the sum of $1,000; and

(B) the costs of the action together with reasonable attorney fees as determined by the court.

(5) An action to enforce any liability created under this section may be brought in the district court of the United States in the district in which the complainant resides, or has his principal place of business, or in which the agency records are situated, or in the District of Columbia, without regard to the amount in controversy, within two years from the date on which the cause of action arises, except that where an agency has materially and willfully misrepresented any information required under this section to be disclosed to an individual and the information so misrepresented is material to establishment of the liability of the agency to the individual under this section, the action may be brought at any time within two years after discovery by the individual of the misrepresentation. Nothing in this section shall be construed to authorize any civil action by reason of any injury sustained as the result of a disclosure of a record prior to September 27, 1975.

(h) Rights of Legal Guardians. For the purposes of this section, the parent of any minor, or the legal guardian of any individual who has been declared to be incompetent due to physical or mental incapacity or age by a court of competent jurisdiction, may act on behalf of the individual.

(i)(1) Criminal Penalties. Any officer or employee of an agency, who by virtue of his employment of official position, has possession of, or access to, agency records which contain individually identifiable information the disclosure of which is prohibited by this section or by rules or regulations established thereunder, and who knowing that disclosure of the specific material is so prohibited, willfully discloses the material in any manner to any person or agency not entitled to receive it, shall be guilty of a misdemeanor and fined not more than $5,000.

(2) Any officer or employee of any agency who willfully maintains a system of records without meeting the notice requirements of subsection (e)(4) of this section shall be guilty of a misdemeanor and fined not more than $5,000.

(3) Any person who knowingly and willfully requests or obtains any record concerning an individual from an agency under false pretenses shall be guilty of a misdemeanor and fined not more than $5,000.

(j) General Exemptions. The head of any agency may promulgate rules, in accordance with the requirements (including general notice) of sections 553(b)(1), (2), and (3), (c), and (e) of this title, to exempt any system of records within the agency from any part of this section except subsections (b), (c)(1) and (2), (e)(4)(A) through (F), (e)(6), (7), (9), (10), and (11), and (i) if the system of records is:

(1) maintained by the Central Intelligence Agency; or

(2) maintained by an agency or component thereof which performs as its principal function any activity pertaining to the enforcement of criminal laws, including police efforts to prevent, control, or reduce crime or to apprehend criminals, and the activities of prosecutors, courts, correctional, probation, pardon, or parole authorities, and which consists of (A) information compiled for the purpose of identifying individual criminal offenders and alleged offenders and consisting only of identifying data and notations of arrests, the nature and disposition of criminal charges, sentencing, confinement, release, and parole and probation status; (B) information compiled for the purpose of a criminal investigation, including reports of informants and investigators, and associated with an identifiable individual; or (C) reports identifiable to an individual compiled at any stage of the process of enforcement of the criminal laws from arrest or indictment through release from supervision.

At the time rules are adopted under this subsection, the agency shall include in the statement required under section 553(c) of this title, the reasons why the system of records is to be exempted from a provision of this section.

(k) Specific Exemptions. The head of any agency may promulgate rules, in accordance with the requirements (including general notice) of sections 553(b)(1), (2), and (3), (c), and (e) of this title, to exempt any system of records within the agency from subsections (c)(3), (d), (e)(1), (e)(4)(G), (H), and (I) and (f) of this section if the system of records is:

(1) subject to the provisions of section 552(b)(1) of this title;

(2) investigatory material compiled for law enforcement purposes, other than material within the scope of subsection (j)(2) of this section: *Provided, however,* that if any individual is denied any right, privilege, or benefit that

he would otherwise be entitled by Federal law, or for which he would otherwise be eligible, as a result of the maintenance of such material, such material shall be provided to such individual, except to the extent that the disclosure of such material would reveal the identity of a source who furnished information to the Government under an express promise that the identity of the source would be held in confidence, or, prior to the effective date of this section, under an implied promise that the identity of the source would be held in confidence;

(3) maintained in connection with providing protective services to the President of the United States or other individuals pursuant to section 3056 of title 18;

(4) required by statute to be maintained and used solely as statistical records;

(5) investigatory material compiled solely for the purpose of determining suitability, eligibility, or qualifications for Federal civilian employment, military service, Federal contracts, or access to classified information, but only to the extent that the disclosure of such material would reveal the identity of a source who furnished information to the Government under an express promise that the identity of the source would be held in confidence, or, prior to the effective date of this section, under an implied promise that the identity of the source would be held in confidence;

(6) testing or examination material used solely to determine individual qualifications for appointment or promotion in the Federal service the disclosure of which would compromise the objectivity or fairness of the testing or examination process; or

(7) evaluation material used to determine potential for promotion in the armed services, but only to the extent that the disclosure of such material would reveal the identity of a source who furnished information to the Government under an express promise that the identity of the source would be held in confidence, or, prior to the effective date of this section, under an implied promise that the identity of the source would be held in confidence.

At the time rules are adopted under this subsection, the agency shall include in the statement required under section 553(c) of this title, the reasons why the system of records is to be exempted from a provision of this section.

(l)(1) Archival Records. Each agency record which is accepted by the Administrator of General Services for storage, processing, and servicing in accordance with section 3103 of title 44 shall, for the purposes of this section, be considered to be maintained by the agency which deposited the record and shall be subject to the provisions of this section. The Administrator of General Services shall not disclose the record except to the agency which maintains the record, or under rules established by that agency which are not inconsistent with the provisions of this section.

(2) Each agency record pertaining to an identifiable individual which was transferred to the National Archives of the United States as a record which has sufficient historical or other value to warrant its continued preservation by the United States Government, prior to the effective date of this section, shall, for the purposes of this section, be considered to be maintained by the National Archives and shall not be subject to the provisions of this section, except that a statement generally describing such records (modeled after the requirements relating to records subject to subsections (e)(4)(A) through (G) of this section) shall be published in the Federal Register.

(3) Each agency record pertaining to an identifiable individual which is transferred to the National Archives of the United States as a record which has sufficient historical or other value to warrant its continued preservation by the United States Government, on or after the effective date of this section, shall, for the purposes of this section, be considered to be maintained by the National Archives and shall be exempt from the requirements of this section except subsections (e)(4)(A) through (G) and (e)(9) of this section.

(m) Government Contractors. When an agency provides by a contract for the operation by or on behalf of the agency of a system of records to accomplish an agency function, the agency shall, consistent with its authority, cause the requirements of this section to be applied to such system. For purposes of subsection (i) of this section any such contractor and any employee of such contractor, if such contract is agreed to on or after the effective date of this section, shall be considered to be an employee of an agency.

(n) Mailing Lists. An individual's name and address may not be sold or rented by an agency unless such action is specifically authorized by law. This provision shall not be construed to require the withholding of names and addresses otherwise permitted to be made public.

(o) Report on New Systems. Each agency shall provide adequate advance notice to Congress and the Office of Management and Budget of any proposal to establish or alter any system of records in order to permit an evaluation of the probable or potential effect of such proposal on the privacy and other personal or property rights of individuals or the disclosure of information relating to such individuals, and its effect on the preservation of the constitutional principles of federalism and separation of powers.

(p) Annual Report. The President shall submit to the Speaker of the House and the President of the Senate, by June 30 of each calendar year, a consolidated report, separately listing for each Federal agency the number of records contained in any system of records which were exempted from the application of this section under the provisions of subsections (j) and (k) of this section during the preceding calendar year, and the reasons for the exemptions, and such other information as indicates efforts to administer fully this section.

(q) Effect of Other Laws. No agency shall rely on any exemption contained in section 552 of this title to withhold from an individual any record which is otherwise accessible to such individual under the provisions of this section.

Added Pub.L. 93–579, § 3, Dec. 31, 1974, 88 Stat. 1897, and amended Pub.L. 94–183, § 2(2), Dec. 31, 1975, 89 Stat. 1057.

An Overview*

As every man goes through life he fills in a number of forms for the record, each containing a number of questions. . . . There are thus hundreds of little threads radiating from every man, millions of threads in all. If these threads were suddenly to become visible, the whole sky would look like a spider's web, and if they materialized as rubber bands, buses, trams, and even people would lose the ability to move. . . . They are not visible, they are not material, but every man is constantly aware of their existence. . . . Each man, permanently aware of his own invisible threads, naturally develops a respect for the people who manipulate the threads.

Alexander Solzhenitsyn,
Cancer Ward [1]

* "The Privacy Act of 1974: An Overview and Critique," 1976 *Washington University Law Quarterly* 667-718. Copyright 1977 by Washington University (St. Louis, MO); reprinted with permission.

This overview examines the following topics within the purview of the Privacy Act:

Computers and Privacy   page 41

The Privacy Act — A General Assessment (Legislative History, Recognition of Individual Interests, Restrictions on Federal Agencies, and Civil Remedies)   page 44

The Privacy Act and the Social Need for Information (Law Enforcement Exemptions and Privacy and the Public's Right to Know)   page 54

Introduction

Most of us have an intuitive sense of the meaning and value of privacy. As a legal matter, however, the term "privacy" has proved remarkably elusive,[2] and the dispute over what it means, what rights it encompasses, and the degree of legal protection it deserves, rages unabated. The few Supreme Court efforts to find a constitutional footing for privacy have been cautious, tentative, and confined to an examination of the individual's right to engage in activities intensely affecting his person.[3] The Court has yet to consider the constitutional status of informational privacy—the individual's interest in controlling the flow of personal information about him.[4]

Neither the paucity of case law nor the inability to define its contours precisely can diminish the importance of informational privacy to modern American society. Today, information is power; the development of the computer has enabled a person or institution acquiring information about an individual to increase its control over that individual in proportion to the data collected.[5] The decrease in individual freedom that necessarily accompanies this increase in external control is repugnant to the goals of a democratic society.[6] Underlying the debate over privacy is a consensus that the loss of informational privacy presents an unprecedented threat to the integrity of the individual—and, that the government has an affirmative duty to protect each citizen from unwarranted external control as part of its general duty to promote individual freedom. The best evidence of this consensus is the congressional decision to enact the Privacy Act of 1974 (Privacy Act).[7]

This Note is about the Privacy Act. Part II will discuss how the computer created a massive threat to individual privacy, rendered existing legal protection wholly inadequate, and left no alternative to the enactment of federal privacy legislation.[8] Part III will analyze the means by which the Privacy Act attempts to recognize and ensure the vitality of the individual's right to informational privacy.[9] Finally, Part IV will examine the manner in which the Privacy Act strives to accommodate privacy with two of the many societal interests with which it conflicts: effective law enforcement and the public's right to know.[10]

The conclusions of this Note are not optimistic. The Privacy Act is conceptually sound, but practically unenforceable. Additionally, the attempts to resolve the conflicts between privacy and interests with which it competes are wholly unsatisfactory. Nevertheless, the recognition that the Privacy Act is merely a first step dictates the conclusion that it is a monumental step.

Computers and Privacy

Unfortunately, the massive threat to privacy that gave rise to the Privacy Act emerged in large part from the government itself. Although governments have kept records for thousands of years,[11] only recently has the threat become epidemic. In the United States, the quantity of information gathered about individuals increased steadily throughout the twentieth century as it became apparent that large quantities of information were necessary for intelligent public decisions.[12] Privacy was not seriously threatened, however, because individuals were mobile and information was stored in manual files that could not easily be transported, consolidated, analyzed, or retrieved. Technological limitations and simple inefficiency preserved a reasonable balance between the individual seeking various benefits without sacrificing privacy, and the government, which needed, and could compel the surrender of, vast amounts of personal data.[13]

Recent technological advances enabled government employees to shatter that balance. With the advent of the computer, the government's ability to compile, retrieve, manipulate, analyze, and disseminate information has increased exponentially. A 1974 study of fifty-four federal agencies disclosed 858 computerized data banks containing 1.25 billion records on individual citizens.[14] The FBI's National Crime Information Center alone contained over 1.7 million files and 195 million sets of fingerprints.[15] Twenty-nine data banks, used exclusively to maintain "black lists," contained damaging information about thousands of law-abiding citizens.[16] One commentator estimates that the average American citizen is the subject of at least twenty records.[17]

For several reasons, the exponential increase in governmental recordkeeping ability poses a unique threat to personal privacy. The most obvious danger is the computer's ability to combine scattered bits of data into a comprehensive personal dossier.[18] This capacity permits government agents to make far more effective, and consequently more intrusive, use of information already in government files.[19]

Second, the increased capacity to handle information creates strong pressures to acquire more of it. Using either legal compulsion or subtle coercion,[20] federal agencies quickly seized the opportunity to acquire huge quantities of personal information,[21] much of it irrelevant to any legitimate government duty.[22] Moreover, unqualified investigators often solicited data from third parties and compiled dossiers replete with information that was inaccurate, biased, or simply fabricated by the investigator.[23] Few persons know the importance of, or even the existence of, such personal records. Until 1974, individuals aware of these records could not inspect them, challenge their accuracy, or restrict their use.[24]

Finally, the computer's own fallibility poses a significant threat to personal privacy. Contrary to popular belief, computers do err.[25] The advent of remote terminals and universal computer language makes possible inter-data bank transfers, both authorized and unauthorized. The latter constitute simple theft, to which computer records are more vulnerable than manual records.[26] Authorized information transfers raise the prospect of contextual inaccuracy.[27] Information supplied to one agency for one purpose is often transmitted to other agencies for wholly unrelated purposes.[28] Deprived of its contextual background, the data may be misinterpreted, often to the disadvantage of the person whom it concerns.

These technological forces have had a devastating impact on personal privacy. Increasingly, almost all that we do, and particularly the mistakes we make, are recorded in government files. Neither the passage of time nor departure to a new community can erase these blemishes on our records,[29] records that are consulted with increasing frequency whenever we apply for employment, credit, insurance, or other important benefits. We live in what one commentator calls a "record prison."[30] Almost all of us have committed some act at some time that would seriously jeopardize our chances in life if recorded, retained indefinitely, and disclosed on a regular basis.[31] The technological breakthroughs in information handling may deprive people of the opportunity for a fresh start in life, a disastrous result because

> [i]f we want man to be self-realized . . . [w]e have got to give him opportunities to fall on his face, to blunder occasionally, to make mistakes. We are human, and possess frailties . . . [i]f we put another wall or barrier up, or some kind of fear in front of people, they can become very reluctant to experiment and life will be very disappointing and confining for many.[32]

Moreover, data derived from a computer carries an impact disproportionate to its actual value. Too often, those who consult computerized records assume the accuracy of the data presented and rarely consider that personalized information in such files may be irrelevant to their needs, factually or contextually inaccurate, dated, or incomplete.[33] The innocent subject of the unreliable record, however, is usually either ignorant of its existence or incapable of correcting it.[34]

Finally, the mere capacity to acquire such records may seriously injure the human interests that the concept of privacy protects. The mere collection and retention of sensitive or personal information creates a state of severe psychological insecurity.[35] As people begin to feel they are under constant surveillance, they will begin to evaluate themselves and regulate their conduct with reference to what is, or may be, contained in their computerized records.[36]

None of these threats to individual freedom and dignity was planned or even foreseen. Each has arisen as the inadvertent by-product of information techniques essential to the solution of pressing social needs. Striking a balance between the individual interest in privacy and the government interest in social progress is an extraordinarily difficult task. What makes that task urgent is the speed and completeness with which the computer has destroyed the balance that previously existed.[37]

Prior to the Privacy Act of 1974, the law afforded little protection from the dangers of extensive recordkeeping systems.[38] In both constitutional and common law interpretation, courts have awkwardly followed in the footsteps of technology while attempting to construct a legal framework to protect the right of privacy.[39] Although the Supreme Court has enunciated a constitutional right of privacy which emanates from penumbras of the Bill of Rights and is necessary to ensure the vitality of specific guarantees,[40] the Court has yet to directly address informational privacy as a constitutional right.[41] The common law provides little more protection.[42]

The common law of informational privacy was designed primarily to compensate a victim for injuries inflicted by the mass media.[43] To recover on a cause of action for invasion of privacy, an individual must ordinarily prove *public disclosure* of *intimate facts*.[44] Most injuries arising from misuse of records involve neither. The law of privacy is intertwined with the law of defamation, so that communications subject to a qualified privilege under defamation law are not actionable in a suit for invasion of privacy.[45] In the majority of cases, disclosures made for employment or credit determinations are qualifiedly privileged. Traditionally, consent was a defense in a privacy suit, and courts applied it liberally when information voluntarily surrendered for a specific reason is used for totally unrelated purposes.[46] Law suits are costly and time consuming; damages are difficult to determine and frequently inadequate.[47] Finally, and perhaps most importantly, the victim is often unaware that a computerized record containing damaging information is the cause of his injury.

On a more fundamental level, it is wholly unreasonable to expect courts alone to protect personal privacy because there is no adequate definition of the concept.[48] Several leading commentators have urged that privacy is the "right to determine when, how, and to what extent information is . . . communicated to others."[49] A control-oriented definition of privacy will permit elimination of some of the grosser abuses by records custodians. This definition alone can never guide the courts to a reasonable approach to privacy, however, because it does not facilitate a quantitative assessment of the right to privacy.[50] Yet such quantification is essential because the amorphous nature of information, its many uses, and the degree to which privacy conflicts with such other critical social interests as freedom of expression and law enforcement dictate that the right to privacy can never be absolute.[51]

Commentators recognized the judicial inability to resolve the problems created by the computer and directed their attention to Congress,[52] which responded by passing the Privacy Act of 1974.[53] The remainder of this Note will assess the degree to which the Act permits effective control of government abuses of personal records and adequate resolution of the conflict between individual privacy and social responsibility.

The Privacy Act: A General Assessment

The Privacy Act of 1974 has three broad goals—to recognize individuals' interests in government records concerning them, to regulate the information practices of federal agencies, and to strike an appropriate balance between the need of the "individual American for a maximum degree of privacy over personal information he furnishes his government, and . . . that of the government for information about the individual which it finds necessary to carry out its legitimate functions."[54] The first two goals of the Act are essentially similar: increasing the individual's control over his records necessarily restricts agency control. This section will discuss the mechanisms by which the Act seeks to achieve these two generally compatible goals.

The section will begin with a brief review of the Privacy Act's chaotic legislative history, a prerequisite to understanding its many inconsistencies. Next, it will discuss the individual interests recognized by the Act, analyzing them in terms of the Act's three conceptual focal points—collection of new information, maintenance of files, and disclosure of agency records to other persons or institutions. The third part of this section will employ the same analytic framework to assess the Act's restrictions on agency information practices. Finally, this section will discuss the civil remedies available to a citizen whose rights under the Act are ignored by a federal agency.

The conclusions reached are generally pessimistic. Although the Act is conceptually sound, the mechanisms used to implement these concepts are likely to prove ineffective. To enforce its substantive provisions, the Act relies primarily on individual initiative, yet provides citizens with neither the means to discover agency violations nor the incentive to rectify them. In short, the Act is conceptually sound but pragmatically unenforceable.

Legislative History

The legislative history of the Privacy Act is both extraordinary and significant. The final enactment of the statute ended an outstanding demonstration of legislative chaos. The House of Representatives and the Senate originally passed separate, materially different privacy bills.[55] The Senate sent its bill to the House, which retained the Senate's enacting clause and substituted the House bill in its entirety thereafter.[56] Facing strong pressure to enact some type of privacy legislation before the end of the session, and lacking adequate time for a conference committee, House and Senate committee leaders held a series of informal meetings. These meetings ultimately produced a compromise bill derived in part from the original Senate bill, in part from the original House bill, and in part from entirely new amendments.[57]

The consequence of this hasty and haphazard legislative process is an internally inconsistent statute with no reliable indication of congressional intent. The original committee reports are of limited value in interpreting the final statute. The only reliable legislative history consists of a rather skimpy staff analysis of the compromise amendments appearing in the Congressional Record.[58] Consequently, courts are likely to have great difficulty interpreting the Act and vigorous enforcement may be impossible.

Recognition of Individual Interests

The Privacy Act explicitly assumes that informational privacy "is a personal and fundamental right protected by the Constitution,"[59] respect for which is essential to our government.[60] By various means, the Act attempts to enable individuals to limit the collection, maintenance, and dissemination of personal information about them.

Collection

Subsection (e)[61] of the Privacy Act establishes specific collection regulations for each federal agency that maintains a system of records. Several of these restrictions implicitly recognize the individual's interest in limiting government acquisition of personal data about him. For example, subsection (e)(3)[62] attempts to ensure that an individual's decision to surrender information about himself to the government is intelligent and voluntary. Accordingly, agencies must disclose to persons from whom they seek information:

> (A) the authority (whether granted by statute, or by executive order of the President) which authorizes the solicitation of the information and whether disclosure of such information is mandatory or voluntary;
> (B) the principal purpose or purposes for which the information is intended to be used;
> (C) the routine uses which may be made of the information, as published pursuant to paragraph (4)(D) of this subsection; and
> (D) the effects on him, if any, of not providing all or any part of the requested information. . . .[63]

In theory this section permits individuals to resist disclosures that are not explicitly authorized by statute or executive order. In practice, however, the free choice granted by this section may be illusory if, as in the past, individuals must waive their right to withhold personal information when applying for a government job or benefit.[64]

Subsection (e)(7)[65] recognizes another important individual interest—that some personal information is ordinarily beyond the scope of any legitimate government inquiry.[66] This subsection prohibits agencies from collecting or maintaining any "record describing how any individual exercises rights guaranteed by the First Amendment unless expressly authorized by statute or by the individual about whom the record is maintained or *unless pertinent to and within the scope of an authorized law enforcement activity*."[67] The concept that some information belongs only to the individual is extremely important.[68] As one commentator has noted, however, Congress' decision to define this category of "untouchable information" in terms of the first amendment was unfortunate.[69] Moreover, the exemption for law enforcement activity opens a loophole that threatens to swallow the rule,[70] a problem that Section III will consider in detail.

Maintenance of Files

Subsection (d)[71] explicitly recognizes the individual's interest in gaining access to and correcting errors in personal records. Subsection (d)(1) provides:

"Each agency that maintains a system of records shall—(1) upon request by any individual to gain access to his record or to any information pertaining to him . . . permit him . . . to review the record. . . ."[72] Subsections (d)(2)-(4)[73] enable the individual to object to the contents of a personal record, institute proceedings to correct it, and request that notice of the objection be sent to those who have previously received the record.[74] These provisions are the heart of the Privacy Act and constitute a major conceptual advance.[75] This subsection recognizes that an individual has a continuing interest in information about him collected by the government.[76] For the first time, an individual can examine his records and ensure their accuracy.

The access provisions in subsection (d) are also the key to enforcing the other provisions of the Privacy Act. The Act relies almost exclusively on individual initiative for enforcement.[77] Consequently, unless the individual has access to his files, he will lack both the knowledge and the incentive to challenge agency lapses. If an agency fails to maintain the list of disclosures required by subsection (c),[78] or retains stale and unreliable information in violation of subsections (e)(1) and (e)(5),[79] the individual can take corrective action only if he learns of the violation via the access provision of subsection (d).[80] The enforcement of the entire Act, therefore, depends on the efficacy of subsection (d) in granting individuals access to their files.

On this critical point, the Privacy Act's sound concepts are as a practical matter deficient. The original Senate bill required agencies to take affirmative action to notify every subject of the existence of a government file about him.[81] The abandonment of this provision threatens to render the Act entirely unenforceable. An individual will not know that he is the subject of a record unless he initiates a request under subsection (d). He can exercise his rights under this provision only after combing the Federal Register to discover which agencies maintain records and contacting each agency that could conceivably have a record about him.[82] Relatively few individuals have sufficient time, money, knowledge, and initiative to attempt to discover the existence of files about them, much less begin proceedings to challenge the contents of a file. Accordingly, subsection (d) is commendable for recognizing the individual's continued interest in personal information held by the government. As a mechanism to enforce the Privacy Act, however, it is virtually worthless.

Disclosure of Records

The Privacy Act recognizes another crucial aspect of the individual's continuing interest in government held data concerning him—limiting its disclosure.[83] Subsection (b) addresses this goal, providing that unless one of eleven exemptions applies, "[n]o agency shall disclose any record which is contained in a system of records by any means of communication to any person, or to another agency, except pursuant to a written request by, or with the *prior written consent* of the individual to whom the record pertains. . . ."[84] Subsection (c) enables an individual to assure agency compliance with subsection (b) by requiring agencies to keep an accounting of the date, nature, purpose, and recipient of each disclosure.[85]

Once again these provisions are conceptually sound. In the past, interagency transfers of personal information were routine,[86] and raised substantial problems of contextual inaccuracy.[87] More serious is the inequity of disclosing the individual's personal information for uses he has never contemplated and of which he would not approve.[88] An enforceable consent requirement would not only obviate these problems, but would, in addition, partially compensate for the Act's failure to require notification to individual subjects of records.[89] The request for permission to disclose personal records will notify the subject of their existence, permitting him to exercise his rights under subsection (d).[90]

For two reasons, however, subsection (b) may fail to fulfill these additional and necessary roles. First, the provision in subsection (b) permitting disclosure without notice to, or specific consent by, subjects who have given prior written consent[91] opens a major loophole. Agencies may attempt to evade the consent requirement by simply inserting routine waiver provisions in the original request for information. Accordingly, courts should construe this provision narrowly and reject an agency's claim of prior consent absent a clause in the original request specifically stipulating not only the anticipated uses, but the potential recipients of the data as well.[92] Second, the exemptions to the consent requirement are far too broad and threaten to destroy the individual's ability to control the flow of personal information. Subsection (b)(3), for instance, is perhaps the largest loophole in the Privacy Act. This subsection allows an agency to disclose personal records to other agencies without the subject's consent if the disclosure is for a "routine use."[93] The Act defines a routine use as one whose "purpose . . . is compatible with the purpose for which [the record] was collected."[94] The original Senate bill contained no such exemption and would have placed tight restrictions on interagency transfers of information.[95] Under the enacted statute, however, an agency need only publish anticipated routine uses in the Federal Register.[96] Few Americans are aware of the existence of the Federal Register; still fewer read it on a regular basis.[97] Consequently, most individuals will never learn that an agency has declared a routine use and will be unable to challenge effectively wrongful agency declarations.

As a practical matter, subsection (b) does not significantly restrict interagency transfers; it merely requires agencies to consider in advance how information will be used.[98]

Restrictions on Federal Agencies

To complement and solidify the individual interests recognized in the Privacy Act, Congress imposed specific limitations on federal agencies that gather and use personal information. The substantive restrictions contained in subsections (b) and (e) parallel the individual interests they are designed to promote.[99] These substantive rules govern collection of new data, maintenance of new and existing files, and disclosure of agency records.

The Act also establishes various procedural requirements, of which subsection (e)(4)[100] is the most critical. This subsection requires each agency that maintains a system of records to publish an annual notice in the Federal Register of the existence, character, name, and location of each system.[101] The annual notice must also specify the categories of individuals about whom information is maintained,[102] the kind of information maintained,[103] all routine uses of such data,[104] procedures by which an individual may discover if an agency's system contains a record about him,[105] and how he may gain access to the record.[106]

These procedural restrictions serve several functions. Public disclosure of the existence of record systems gives meaning to the Act's premise that there must be no secret information systems,[107] and helps preclude a government institution like the Army from ever again maintaining secret files on millions of law-abiding American citizens.[108] The procedural rules also enable individuals to exercise their right to inspect and challenge the contents of personal files, and thereby assist in the enforcement of the Act.[109]

The procedural rules will implement effectively the goals of the Privacy Act only to the extent that the substantive restrictions on the agencies are workable. To a disturbing degree, however, the substantive rules exhibit the same flaws as those sections of the Act that recognize individual interests. While conceptually sound, the substantive agency restrictions will often prove pragmatically worthless.

Collection of New Data

Subsection (e) of the Privacy Act contains explicit restrictions on the federal agencies' ability to gather new information. Subsection (e)(2)[110] recognizes the principle that the best source of accurate data about a person is the individual himself. Thus, agencies must "collect information to the greatest extent practicable directly from the subject individual when the information may result in adverse determinations about an individual's rights, benefits, and privileges under Federal programs. . . ."[111]

As usual, this provision is soundly conceived. Congress properly recognized that information provided by third parties is often erroneous or biased.[112] Moreover, a requirement that agencies collect information from the subject of a record furthers the individual's interest in knowing of the existence of files about him and limiting the government's collection of personal data.[113] The major flaw in subsection (e)(2) is not conceptual but mechanical: the Act provides no criteria by which agencies or courts can determine when it is "impractical" to collect information directly from the subject. Apparently, the agencies have effective discretion to decide the question themselves,[114] and the laudable purpose of subsection (e)(2) is largely unenforceable.

Subsection (e)(1),[115] which limits the kind of information that agencies may collect, is perhaps the most workable provision of the Act. Subsection (e)(1) requires an agency to "maintain in its records only such information about an individual as is *relevant and necessary* to accomplish a purpose of the agency required to be accomplished by statute or by executive order of the President."[116] Underlying this requirement are the congressional judgments that agencies should never acquire personal information unless necessary to the performance of a legitimate function, and that data neither collected nor maintained cannot be misused.[117] This provision should preclude agencies from asking such questions as those appearing on many civil service applications during the 1960's:

> I believe there is a God.
> I believe in the second coming of Christ.
> I go to church almost every week.
> I am very strongly attracted by members of my own sex.
> I loved my father.
> My sex life is satisfactory.[118]

Even if such inquiries were relevant to job performance, the agency would be hard-pressed to defend their necessity in accordance with (e)(1).[119] Moreover, although the enforcement provisions of the Act are generally weak, it may be difficult for agencies to ignore the subsection (e)(1) relevance and necessity requirement because agency collection practices are highly visible to the public.[120]

Maintenance of Files

The Privacy Act imposes several restrictions on agencies to complement the recognition of the individual's interest in accurate and timely personal records. If the Act's collection restraints are effective, records compiled after 1974 should be substantially correct when initially compiled. A major problem confronting Congress in drafting privacy legislation, however, was how

to ensure the correction of inaccurate, dated, or incomplete records compiled before the passage of the statute and the continued updating of all records.[121] Congress sought to achieve these goals in two ways. First, agencies must grant individuals access to their records and correct information contained therein that is erroneous or otherwise fails to comply with the Act. The deficiencies of these provisions have been noted previously.[122] The Act also imposes a general duty on agencies to maintain only relevant and necessary information and a specific duty to ensure its accuracy and timeliness before using it to make a determination about a subject.

Subsection (e)(1), discussed previously, applies to the maintenance of new and existing agency files as well as to the collection of new data. Agencies should review their record systems on a periodic basis to ensure compliance with the "relevant and necessary" requirement of subsection (e)(1).[123] Although the rationale for this requirement applies as strongly to existing records as it does to the acquisition of new data, compliance in the former instance may be harder to achieve. Because the inner workings of the agencies are hidden from public view, pressure to update old records will be far less than pressure to force compliance with collection regulations. Thus, the absence of an adequate mechanism to enforce the Act will probably result in noncompliance.

The Privacy Act also imposes a specific duty on agencies to ensure the accuracy and timeliness of information used in making determinations about a subject. Subsection (c)(5) requires agencies to "maintain all records which are used by the agency in making any determination about any individual with such accuracy, relevance, timeliness, and completeness as is reasonably necessary to assure fairness to the individual in the determination. . . ."[124] Although the desirability of accurate information in personal files should be self-evident, this section is a substantially watered down version of the measure originally proposed in the Senate. The Senate bill imposed a heavy burden on the agencies, requiring them to ensure that information contained in a record was accurate, relevant, timely, and complete whenever the record was disclosed, used to make determinations about the subject, or altered.[125] The compromise that emerged[126] as subsection (e)(5) of the Privacy Act accepts the House provision and requires an agency to assure the quality of only those records "which are used by the agency *in making any determination* about an individual."[127] Unfortunately, even if an agency does delete information in making a determination about an individual, it will undoubtedly consider such data when making the determination.[128] Consequently, the stated purpose of subsection (e)(5), fair determinations, will probably be the exception. Moreover, subsection (e)(5) will probably fail to fulfill the broader goal of accomplishing the destruction or correction of the vast quantity of existing information that violates the Privacy Act.

Disclosure and Dissemination

The recognition of an individual's continuing interest in government-held data that concerns him required the imposition of restrictions on the dissemination practices of federal agencies. The Privacy Act attempts to provide such restrictions in two ways.

First, subsection (b)[129] requires an agency to obtain the subject's consent before disclosing personal records. The problems of enforcing this subsection and the exemptions that largely defeat it have been noted.[130] The second restriction on agency dissemination is subsection (c)(6),[131] which requires that an agency "prior to disseminating any record about an individual to any person *other than an agency,* unless the dissemination is made pursuant to subsection (b)(2) of this section, make reasonable efforts to assure that such records are accurate, complete, timely, and relevant for agency purposes. . . ."[132] Once again, this subsection is conceptually sound and practically unenforceable. Its purpose is to assure that agencies transmit only reliable information to persons outside the federal government. Because the restrictions in the Privacy Act apply only to federal agencies, the subject of a record can not gain access to, or correct errors in, records disclosed to persons outside the federal government. Data disseminated to such persons should, therefore, be of the highest possible quality.[133] In practice, this subsection is likely to prove unenforceable. The individual can challenge an agency's decision to ignore this provision only by exercising his right of access under subsection (d). As noted above, the failure to provide individuals with effective notice of the existence of their records renders subsection (d) a useless enforcement device.[134] Moreover, subsection (e)(6) is inapplicable to material disclosed under the Freedom of Information Act—probably the largest category of disclosures made to persons "other than an agency."[135]

The substantive restrictions on agency practices, therefore, parallel almost exactly the individual interests recognized under the Privacy Act. In each case, the inability to enforce them obviates the value of conceptually sound approaches to protecting informational privacy. These deficiencies, and the manifold exemptions, render the Privacy Act little more than a legislative statement of unenforceable rights.

Civil Remedies

Subsection (g)[136] of the Privacy Act establishes civil remedies enabling individuals to seek equitable relief or damages from agencies that violate the Act. Other than criminal penalties of very limited scope,[137] these provisions

are the only means to enforce the agency restrictions and implement the individual interests recognized in the Privacy Act. The original Senate bill provided for an independent Privacy Commission with power to investigate, hold hearings upon, and recommend prosecution of agency violations.[138] The legislative compromise replaced this body with a purely advisory commission,[139] leaving sole responsibility for enforcing the Act to individual citizens. Unfortunately, subsection (g) provides neither the tools nor the incentives necessary to make individual enforcement a reality.

Subsection (g) permits equitable relief in two situations. If the agency disregards the access provisions of subsection (d),[140] the individual may seek injunctive relief to force the agency to let him inspect his records.[141] If the agency refuses to amend a record upon request, or fails to review the individual's request for amendment as provided in subsection (d)(3),[142] the victim may also seek a court order compelling the agency to amend the record.[143] In both cases, the courts must determine the matter de novo and are empowered to award costs and attorney's fees to a substantially successful plaintiff.[144]

In addition, an individual may seek damages from an agency that

fails to maintain any record concerning any individual with such accuracy, relevance, timeliness, and completeness as is necessary to assure fairness in any determination relating to the qualifications, character, rights, or opportunities of, or benefits to the individual that may be made on the basis of such record, and consequently a determination is made which is adverse to the individual;[145] or fails to comply with any other provision of this section, or any rule promulgated thereunder, in such a way as do [sic] have an adverse effect on an individual.[146]

Damages are only recoverable, however, if the agency acted "in a manner which was intentional or willful,"[147] in which case the individual is entitled to an award of actual damages or $1000, whichever is greater,[148] plus his costs and reasonable attorney's fees.[149] Punitive damages are not recoverable. To obtain any relief, plaintiff must normally file suit within two years after the violation occurs.[150]

It is unrealistic to expect these remedial provisions to provide adequate incentives for individuals to seek redress under the Act. First, the Act imposes an unreasonably heavy burden on the plaintiff. He must allege and prove that he has suffered an adverse determination in consequence of the agency's violation of the Act, and that the agency acted willfully or intentionally. Most plaintiffs will fail to meet these burdens. The most prevalent threats to privacy stem not from intentional action but from "inadvertent, careless, and unthinking collection, distribution, and storage of records."[151] Requiring proof of willful misbehavior assures that most abuses will go uncorrected. The requirement that the plaintiff must have suffered an adverse determination in order to recover is also unfortunate. Many agency violations will not result in determinations or cause measurable injury, further isolating agency abuse from corrective action.

Second, the Act provides insufficient recovery to stimulate private suits. Even if the plaintiff can prove actual injury, the damage award may be small. The Act's failure to provide for punitive damages virtually guarantees that the financial risks of the litigation will often exceed the rewards of the suit. The $1000 guarantee is a meager incentive to risk the expense of suing the federal government.[152] The Act thus fails to provide the adequate level of damages essential to effective citizen enforcement.

Finally, the two-year statute of limitations is unreasonable. Because agencies need not notify individuals when making adverse determinations based on personal records,[153] many individuals aggrieved by agency violations will not learn the cause of their injury until after the statute of limitations has run.

The enforcement scheme in the original Senate bill was far superior to that in the Act as passed. A strong Privacy Commission was expected to share responsibility for enforcing the Act.[154] The original Senate bill imposed liability for negligent as well as willful violations,[155] and authorized recovery of punitive damages where appropriate.[156] Substitution of the House provisions in the final Act has once again reduced the Privacy Act to a legislative statement of unenforceable rights.

The Privacy Act and the Social Need for Reform

The first two goals of the Privacy Act—recognizing the continuing individual interest in government-held data, and restricting the information practices of federal agencies—are essentially compatible. As the original Senate bill demonstrates, drafting a statute that accomplishes these goals would have been a relatively easy task. The Act's third goal—striking an appropriate balance between the individual privacy interest and the legitimate social needs for information—is far more difficult to achieve. Resolving the conflict between these essentially incompatible interests requires a thorough understanding of each, and a well defined sense of their relative importance. The most formidable task facing Congress in drafting the Privacy Act, therefore, was the accommodation of individual privacy with such interests as administrative efficiency, effective law enforcement, and the public's right to know.

Unfortunately, those sections of the Privacy Act that consider other social interests are among the most ill-conceived sections of the Act. In virtually every instance when privacy conflicted with other legitimate objectives, Congress merely chose to sacrifice privacy. In protecting the two most important social interests—effective law enforcement and the public's right to know—the complete sacrifice of privacy significantly frustrates the operation of the Act. Moreover, in each instance, it is apparent that privacy need not have been wholly subordinated to the other interest: Congress could have struck a better balance. Examination of the interaction between the Freedom of Information Act (FOIA)[157] and the Privacy Act, and of the law enforcement exemptions to the latter, illustrates this thesis.

The Law Enforcement Exemptions

The social interest in enforcing the criminal law is clear. Equally obvious is the occasional sacrifice of individual liberties that effective law enforcement requires. During the last decade, however, agencies such as the FBI and the CIA perpetrated some of the most insidious invasions of privacy in the name of "law and order." Curbing abusive practices by law enforcement agencies without seriously impairing their legitimate functions is a difficult task for any statute. One of the most disturbing aspects of the Privacy Act is its failure to evidence even an attempt to accomplish this goal.

Subsections (j)[158] and (k)[159] permit an agency to exempt certain types of record systems from many crucial provisions of the Act. Although no record system is automatically exempt, the head of an agency can easily obtain an exemption by determining that a system qualifies for exemption under subsection (j) or (k) and filing an appropriate notice in the Federal Register.[160]

Subsection (j) grants a blanket exemption to all record systems maintained by the CIA.[161] Other agencies or sub-agencies whose principal function pertains to the enforcement of criminal laws may exempt a system of records if it consists of one of three specific kinds of data.[162] Although subsection (j) enumerates ten sections to which the exemption is supposedly inapplicable, in practice the subsection grants immunity from almost every significant restriction in the Act.[163] For example, subsection (j) does not allow an exemption from the notice and consent provisions of subsection (b).[164] Under subsection (b)(7), however, any law enforcement agency of any governmental unit can acquire personal records without either notice to, or consent by, the subject, if the agency head requests the records in writing and certifies that they will be used for law enforcement purposes.[165] Similarly, although law enforcement agencies are not exempt from subsections (c)(1) and (c)(2), requiring an accounting of all disclosures,[166] subsection (c)(4) relieves agencies of the duty to make accountings of (b)(7) disclosures available to the subject on request.[167] Finally, although these agencies cannot, under subsection (j), escape the ban on collecting information about the exercise of first amendment rights,[168] subsection (e)(7) explicitly permits collection of such data if "pertinent to and within the scope of an authorized law enforcement activity."[169]

The only substantive restrictions from which law enforcement agencies can never gain immunity require them to exercise reasonable efforts to assure the reliability of, and obtain the individual's consent before disclosing, personal files to persons other than law enforcement agencies.[170] Neither provision is meaningful. The exceptions to the consent requirement of subsection (b) virtually nullify the rule.[171] The reliability restriction of subsection (e)(6) is wholly unenforceable against law enforcement agencies because subsection (j) permits exemption from the civil remedies provisions, and violation of this requirement would not constitute grounds for criminal prosecution.[172]

Subsection (k) enables an agency to exempt seven different types of records from various provisions of the Act.[173] These exemptions are not limited to record systems maintained by law enforcement agencies,[174] but they are not as extensive as those allowed under subsection (j). Subsection (k)(2), available to law enforcement records not covered by subsection (j), permits an agency to exempt

> investigatory material compiled for law enforcement purposes, other than material within the scope of Subsection (j)(2). . . . Provided, however, That if any individual is denied any right, privilege, or benefit that he would otherwise be entitled by Federal law, or for which he would otherwise be eligible, as a result of the maintenance of such material, such material shall be provided to such individual, except to the extent that the disclosure of such material would reveal the identity of a source who furnished information to the Government under an express promise [of confidentiality], or, prior to the effective date of this [Act], under an implied promise [of confidentiality].[175]

Virtually every law enforcement record qualifies for an exemption under either subsection (j) or (k)(2).[176] Although the statutory language suggests otherwise, there are but two significant distinctions between the exemptions available under these two subsections.[177] First, while an agency relying on subsection (k)(2) must ordinarily provide damaging information to an individual adversely affected by its use,[178] subsection (j) contains no such requirement. The second important distinction is that only subsection (j) exempts agencies from the civil remedies provisions of subsection (g).[179]

From the broad immunity conferred upon law enforcement agencies flows the unfortunate conclusion that Congress apparently believed legitimate law enforcement needs should always take priority over any individual privacy interest. The only legitimate grounds for exempting law enforcement records, however, are the need to protect the secrecy of a pending investigation, the safety of undercover agents, and the secrecy of certain investigative techniques.[180] None of these reasons justifies providing agencies wholesale im-munity from the individual access and challenge provisions or from civil liability.[181] Subsection (j) should include the caveat contained in subsection (k)(2),[182] modified only as necessary to protect the legitimate government interests outlined above. Finally, it is astonishing to note that an individual is more likely to acquire his personal record from a law enforcement agency by means of an FOIA suit than by one brought under the Privacy Act.[183] A rational statutory scheme would surely recognize that the subject of a person-al record has a greater interest in it than does the general public; the Privacy Act does not. Although an agency cannot withhold information from an individual based on a Privacy Act exemption when the FOIA requires disclo-sure,[184] the approach taken in the Privacy Act is extremely disturbing. It strongly suggests that Congress intended to protect privacy only when it conflicted with no other legitimate social interests. Because privacy conflicts with other interests more often than not, such an approach guarantees little protection to individual privacy.

The conclusion is inescapable that Congress refused to analyze in depth the conflict between privacy and law enforcement. Instead, whenever it perceived a conflict, Congress sacrificed the privacy interest without consid-ering whether the marginal benefit to law enforcement exceeded the marginal cost to privacy. Consequently, the Privacy Act needlessly excludes a principal enemy of individual privacy, law enforcement agencies, from its substantive restrictions.

Privacy and the Public's Right to Know

The public's right to know is, almost by definition, the antithesis of the individual's right to privacy.[185] The individual's interest in restricting disclo-sure of personal facts is almost directly opposed to the public interest in expanding public knowledge to ensure informed, democratic decision-mak-ing. Although the right to know may have constitutional foundations,[186] since 1966 its most significant legal base has been the Freedom of Information Act (FOIA).[187]

Material disclosed to the public under the FOIA is largely exempt from the Privacy Act. Subsection (b), requiring agencies to notify and obtain the con-sent of the subject of a personal record before releasing it,[188] is expressly inapplicable to material whose disclosure is required by the FOIA.[189] Under subsection (c)(1) agencies need not keep an accounting of the release of such materials.[190] Finally, subsection (e)(6), requiring agencies to make reasonable efforts to ensure the reliability of records released to persons other than an agency, does not apply when the FOIA requires disclosure.[191]

Congress obviously chose to subordinate the Privacy Act to the FOIA whenever it perceived a potential conflict between the interests protected by each Act. Because several provisions of the FOIA purport to safeguard privacy, Congress may have assumed that the FOIA had struck an appropriate balance between personal privacy and the right to know. Closer inspection of the FOIA, however, reveals that for two reasons, the Act as presently interpreted cannot protect individual privacy. First, courts interpreting the FOIA exemptions have almost completely ignored privacy interests. More fundamentally, because only the agency can invoke an exemption, the FOIA places the responsibility of protecting individual privacy in the wrong hands—with the agency rather than the individual.

The FOIA Exemptions

A brief explanation of the operation of the FOIA is necessary to understand its inability to protect individual privacy. The FOIA directs federal agencies to release identifiable records to "any person" on request.[192] If the agency fails to comply, the individual may seek injunctive relief from the federal courts.[193] The agency bears the burden of justifying its action; unless one of nine specifically defined exemptions applies, the citizen must prevail.[194] The FOIA was intended to achieve maximum public access to government records[195] in order to develop an informed electorate capable of wisely selecting and monitoring the government.[196] In recognition of this basic purpose, courts have narrowly interpreted the exemptions.[197]

Three exemptions to the FOIA are relevant to personal privacy interests. Exemption 4 permits agencies to withhold "trade secrets and commercial or financial information obtained from a person and privileged or confidential."[198] Although the statutory language and the legislative history support the application of this exemption to all types of confidential information,[199] courts now agree that Exemption 4 protects only privileged or confidential information which is commercial in nature.[200] Information is confidential for purposes of Exemption 4 only if its disclosure would injure either the government's ability to obtain information in the future or the competitive position of the party supplying the information.[201]

The rationale for this interpretation is instructive. Courts have restricted the coverage of Exemption 4 in order to further the perceived goal of the FOIA: maximum disclosure of public records. They have failed to recognize that maximum disclosure was merely a means to accomplish the FOIA's ultimate goal—governmental accountability.[202] While the two will often be synonymous, courts have failed to recognize that disclosing confidential noncommercial information could seriously injure privacy interests without contributing significantly to the public interest in government accountability.

In short, they have failed to distinguish between different types of government-held information.[203] If there is to be an intelligent compromise between the interests of personal privacy and public knowledge, however, such distinctions are critical. In light of the Privacy Act, one can plausibly argue for reinterpretation of this exemption on the ground that its disclosure impedes the policies underlying the Privacy Act without furthering those of the FOIA.[204]

Exemption 6 permits the withholding of "personnel and medical files and similar files the disclosure of which would constitute a *clearly unwarranted invasion of personal privacy.*"[205] The most significant question to arise under this exemption concerns the standard by which a court should determine when disclosure would produce a "clearly unwarranted invasion of personal privacy." Several courts have held that subsection (a)(3), requiring agencies to release information to "any person,"[206] precludes any balancing of the consequences of disclosure.[207] Several other courts, while agreeing that the Act ordinarily prohibits balancing, insist that the sixth exemption requires an exemption.[208] These courts hold that the words "clearly unwarranted invasion of privacy" leave no alternative to weighing the public benefit of disclosure against the private injury from invasion of privacy.

Both of these positions have problems. The requirement that agencies release information to "any person" was an unfortunate product of congressional frustration with agencies who abused the original disclosure section of the Administrative Procedure Act by withholding information under the pretext that the requesting party "was not properly concerned." In many instances, however, the standing of the party seeking information *is* a relevant consideration. As the Privacy Act demonstrates, the subject of a record clearly has a greater interest in examining it than does the general public. Moreover, it is impossible to determine if a given disclosure will produce an unwarranted invasion of personal privacy without considering what the requesting party intends to do with the information—i.e., his need. Strict adherence to the "any person" requirement and failure to consider the interests of the requesting party preclude sensible resolution of problems arising under the sixth exemption. The recent Supreme Court decision in *Department of the Air Force* v. *Rose*[209] has evidently settled the basic issue. The Court held that Congress adopted the exemptions to "require a balancing of the individual's right of privacy against the preservation of the basic purpose of the Freedom of Information Act—'to open agency action to the light of public scrutiny.'"[210]

The balancing approach, however, suffers from its own deficiencies. As courts and commentators noted before *Rose,* this approach may produce perverse results. When little or no public benefit will result from disclosure, balancing mandates disclosure in the absence of a serious invasion of privacy.

Similarly, when the anticipated benefit is significant, this approach would require disclosure even if it would unwarrantably invade personal privacy.[211]

The correct approach to interpreting the sixth exemption would require courts to consider the needs of the FOIA plaintiff solely for the purpose of determining the most likely effect of disclosure on the subject. If disclosure would produce a significant invasion of privacy, the exemption should attach in all cases except those involving high public officials,[212] in which case the strong public interest in disclosure would seem to leave courts no alternative to balancing interests.

Exemption 7 was one of two exemptions amended in 1974.[213] In its original form, the seventh exemption permitted agencies to withhold "investigatory files compiled for law enforcement purposes except to the extent available by law to a party other than an agency."[214] Courts uniformly held this exemption applicable to investigatory files compiled for civil as well as criminal law enforcement purposes.[215]

The 1974 amendment was designed to overrule a series of decisions by the Court of Appeals for the District of Columbia that permitted the indefinite withholding of law enforcement files despite the absence of any legitimate purpose.[216] The seventh exemption now shields from disclosure:

investigatory records compiled for law enforcement purposes, but only to the extent that the production of such records would (A) interfere with enforcement proceedings, (B) deprive a person of a right to a fair trial or an impartial adjudication, (C) constitute an unwarranted invasion of personal privacy, (D) disclose the identity of a confidential source and, in the case of a record compiled by a criminal law enforcement authority in the course of a criminal investigation, or by an agency conducting a lawful national security investigation, confidential information furnished only by the confidential source, (E) disclose investigative techniques and procedures, or (F) endanger the life or safety of law enforcement personnel.[217]

The amendment narrows the exemption by requiring proof that disclosure would interfere with either pending or imminent law enforcement proceedings. The addition of subsection (b)(7)(c), protecting personal privacy, however, constitutes a significant expansion of the exemption.[218] Before the 1974 amendments, courts interpreting Exemption 7 generally found that the exemption was designed exclusively to protect the government's case in court and preserve the secrecy of investigative techniques.[219] The privacy of the subjects of investigations was completely ignored.[220] Yet the individual privacy interest is far from trivial. Law enforcement agencies have great freedom to decide whom to investigate; public disclosure of investigatory files about an individual may produce unwarranted public humiliation,[221] particularly when no further proceedings against him are contemplated. In these instances, disclosure would often constitute the de facto conviction of an individual who, for one reason or another, could not be prosecuted in a court of law. The earlier decisions by the District of Columbia Circuit allowing the indefinite withholding of files for purely governmental reasons inadvertently protected the individual against such disclosures.[222]

The requirement of an "unwarranted invasion of personal privacy" under amended Exemption 7 is no clearer than that of a "clearly unwarranted" invasion under Exemption 6.[223] Presumably, courts would apply similar criteria for each exemption. Whether the criteria actually employed will effectively safeguard individual privacy interests remains to be seen.[224]

Interpretation of the original Exemption 7 complemented and closely paralleled the treatment accorded Exemption 4,[225] illustrating again the judicial myopia toward personal privacy interests under the FOIA. In both instances, courts ignored substantial individual interests and failed to consider whether disclosure would further the goal of the FOIA: improving government accountability. In considering both the advantages and the disadvantages of disclosure, therefore, courts consistently undervalued the privacy interest in nondisclosure and overvalued the utility of release. Although the exemptions as currently written might effectively safeguard personal privacy, the judicial bias against privacy in FOIA suits has ominous implications for the balancing process now required by exemptions 6 and 7.

The Agencies as Guardians of Privacy

More fundamental problems with the FOIA as a guardian of privacy are inherent in the structure of the Act. The FOIA is a disclosure statute—disclosure is never prohibited.[226] In general, federal agencies rather than individuals are responsible for claiming the exemptions. Neither the FOIA nor the Privacy Act[227] requires an agency to notify the subject of a record that information about him has been requested under the FOIA. Accordingly, when an individual surrenders personal information to an agency, he effectively appoints that agency legal guardian of his right to privacy.[228] Unfortunately, the agency is an incompetent guardian.

The FOIA assumes that the agencies will vigorously assert each applicable exemption because their interest always lies in withholding information. Ordinarily, agency interests coincide with the interests protected by the exemptions, and accordingly, this assumption is perfectly sound. The Department of State, for example, will always want to protect national security information from disclosure.[229] Because the agency is the best and most logical representative of these interests, it is the proper party to assert the exemption. This critical assumption of the FOIA is incorrect, however, when applied to the privacy exemptions. Unlike national security, the agency has no inherent interest in protecting individual privacy; the incentive for a strong defense is missing.[230] Moreover, judicial interpretation of the FOIA has compounded this structural defect. To prevent frivolous claims of exemptions, courts have made it increasingly difficult for agencies to withhold information. In the leading case of *Vaughn* v. *Rosen,*[231] the Court of Appeals for the District of Columbia held that conclusory allegations would not support a claim of exemption.[232] Instead, the agency must make a "relatively detailed analysis [of the material] in manageable segments,"[233] and specify which parts should be exempt and why.[234] The *Vaughn* index is an excellent means to discourage recalcitrant agencies from indulging their usual preference for secrecy. In the context of the privacy exemptions, however, the disincentives far outweigh the minimal benefits the agency obtains from withholding personal information. Many agencies may prefer to disclose information rather than fight,[235] especially in light of the absence of any penalty for wrongful disclosure under the FOIA.

Before the Privacy Act, the majority of courts further exacerbated this problem by finding that an agency could disclose information notwithstanding the applicability of one of the nine exemptions—that is, the exemptions are merely discretionary.[236] To permit the government to waive exemptions designed to protect its own interests makes perfect sense; to allow the government to waive the individual interests underlying exemptions 4, 6, and 7, however, is ludicrous. These exemptions should be mandatory.[237] Even if an agency is compelled to assert an exemption, however, its claim is likely to be half-hearted. The FOIA thus contains an inherent procedural defect that significantly reduces its ability to protect personal privacy.

Courts have proven insensitive to the problem of the wrong party in interest. The issue has arisen in a few "reverse FOIA" suits, in which plaintiffs have attempted to prevent disclosure of trade secrets protected by the fourth exemption.[238] These suits present problems comparable to the privacy exemptions because the agency's interest in retaining future information sources is not wholly synonymous with industry's interest in keeping trade secrets. Although courts have granted the reverse FOIA plaintiff standing to sue,[239] the agency decision on the merits usually prevails.[240] Courts reason that Congress granted agencies the sole power to assert an exemption, and the agency decision is reversible only if arbitrary or capricious.[241] Those parties challenging release, and the one court that has enjoined disclosure have relied, at least in part, on statutory provisions outside the FOIA.[242] The courts have yet to realize that some exemptions protect a variety of public and private interests and that public agencies cannot be expected to assert purely private interests.

This brief review of the FOIA highlights the degree to which both Congress and the courts have misunderstood the complex interaction between individual privacy and government accountability. If Congress, in drafting the

Privacy Act, did assume that the FOIA struck an appropriate balance between these two competing interests, the assumption is plainly wrong. The subject of a personal record, not its governmental custodian, is harmed by its disclosure. Yet only the latter may invoke the FOIA exemptions.[243] In construing the privacy exemptions, the courts usually overstate the public value of releasing personal data and ignore the privacy interest in nondisclosure.[244]

On a more fundamental level, the subordination of the Privacy Act to the FOIA again exposes the congressional preference for a simplistic statute to the difficult task of balancing and reconciling competing interests. This decision is tragic, not only because it wholly sacrifices privacy but because the sacrifice is unnecessary. Identifiable personal records have little to do with the FOIA's ultimate goals of developing an informed electorate and improving government accountability. Protecting individuals from the release of such files would significantly advance personal privacy interests with minimal effect on the underlying values served by the FOIA. As it did in drafting the law enforcement exemptions,[245] however, Congress preferred to adopt a blanket solution rather than make the hard choices required to fashion an effective and comprehensive approach to resolving the conflict between personal privacy and the public's right to know. In so choosing, Congress gave new meaning to Arthur Miller's plaintive lament that "in a very back-handed way, [the FOIA] probably does more to end privacy in the United States, ostensibly in pursuit of the public's right to know, than any other enactment in the last fifty or sixty years."[246]

Interaction between the FOIA and the Privacy Act

The congressional decision to exempt FOIA information from many of the substantive requirements of the Privacy Act has some curious and probably unintended consequences. The interaction of the two statutes illustrates, as nothing else, the complete congressional failure to understand the complexity of the privacy problem. In general, the Privacy Act subordinates substantial privacy interests to insignificant FOIA interests. In some respects, however, the Privacy Act may encourage a reinterpretation of the FOIA, improving the latter Act's ability to protect individual privacy interests. Nevertheless, the FOIA's defects are so great, and the congressional intent to leave it unchanged so apparent, that amendment of the FOIA is probably the only means to strike the correct balance between the individual's right to privacy and the public's right to government information.

The consent provisions in subsection (b) of the Privacy Act best illustrate Congress' inability to comprehend the inadequacy of the FOIA's privacy exemptions. Subsection (b) prohibits disclosure of a personal record without the subject's consent.[247] Subsection (b)(2) waives this requirement for material whose disclosure is required by the FOIA.[248] The original House bill contained no such provision and was intended to "make all individually identifiable information in government files exempt from public disclosure" under the FOIA.[249] The original Senate bill exempted all records whose disclosure was either *required or permitted* by the FOIA.[250] Although the final draft of the Senate bill omitted this provision,[251] an altered version of it mysteriously reappeared in the Compromise Amendments and the Act as passed.[252]

The final version of subsection (b) is a distinctly mixed blessing. In limiting the waiver of the consent requirement to instances in which the FOIA *requires* disclosure, it improves both the original Senate proposal and the FOIA by removing agency discretion to waive the FOIA privacy exemptions.[253] Specifically, if one of these exemptions applies, the FOIA does not *require* disclosure, subsection (b) of the Privacy Act still applies, and the Privacy Act *prohibits* disclosure absent the subject's consent. A corollary of this requirement is a significant improvement in the success of reverse FOIA suits. When courts have rejected such suits on the merits, the rationale has been agency discretion to waive or assert the privacy exemptions.[254] By depriving agencies of that discretion, subsection (b) makes the privacy exemptions mandatory and grants the reverse FOIA plaintiff a legal right under the Privacy Act to prevent disclosure.

Unfortunately, the structural defects in the Privacy Act and the FOIA largely nullify the practical benefit of making the FOIA privacy exemptions mandatory. A reverse FOIA suit is possible only if the subject learns of the request for his personal records in time to object. Because neither Act requires agencies to notify the subject of such requests,[255] the agency may disclose personal information before he can assert his rights. In practice, therefore, the wrong party in interest—the agency—must still assert the exemption. The agency's probable failure to represent individual interests vigorously may result in the disclosure of personal information that should remain confidential.[256]

Technically, such half-hearted agency action may violate the Privacy Act. Indeed, one commentator has noted with alarm the agencies' exposure to FOIA suits if they invoke the exemption, and to damage suits under the Privacy Act if they fail to assert it.[257] This dilemma is wholly theoretical. The plaintiff's burden of proof in a damage suit under the Privacy Act is so great that only in rare cases can the victim expect recovery.[258] In any reasonably close case, disclosure should avoid liability under both statutes.

Several other provisions of the Privacy Act exacerbate the problem created in subsection (b). Ordinarily, subsection (c) requires an agency to keep, and make available an accounting of the date, nature, purpose, and recipient of each disclosure of a personal record.[259] Subsection (c)(1) waives this obligation for disclosures required by the FOIA.[260] This provision is difficult to justify.[261] Its only benefit is to relieve agencies of the administrative task of recording what personal information is released and to whom. The damage to individual subjects far outweighs this trivial concern. The absence of an accounting assures that many individuals will never discover that agencies have wrongfully disclosed their records under the guise of the FOIA, and thereby erects still another barrier to effective enforcement of the Privacy Act. Moreover, waiving the accounting requirement prevents the subject from tracing and correcting unreliable information disclosed by federal agencies to private parties.

The inability to restrict the use of personal information subsequent to its disclosure pursuant to the FOIA would lead one to assume that federal agencies should at least be required to assure the quality of records so released. Congress recognized that because the restrictions in the Privacy Act apply only to federal agencies, disclosure to any party other than another federal agency threatens privacy more seriously than do interagency transfers.[262] Accordingly, subsection (e)(6) requires the custodial agency to check a record for accuracy, timeliness, completeness, and relevance before releasing it to parties outside the federal government.[263] The absence of an accounting requirement for FOIA disclosures rendered this subsection the individual's only protection against disclosure of unreliable data. Nevertheless, (e)(6) is inapplicable to disclosures required by the FOIA.[264] The sole rationale for this exemption is the need for speedy processing of FOIA requests;[265] acceptance thereof demonstrates a congressional preference for speed to privacy.

The Privacy Act's various exemptions for FOIA disclosures and the FOIA's inability to safeguard individual privacy require one of two conclusions: either Congress intentionally subordinated privacy interests to public information interests in *every* case of conflict, or Congress was wholly ignorant of the complex interaction between the two statutes. There are problems with each conclusion.

The first conclusion at least produces a simple rule for courts to follow when considering the conflict between individual privacy and the public's right to know. It is hard to believe, however, that Congress really intended to sacrifice privacy at every juncture. First, the unilateral sacrifice of privacy is unnecessary: requiring an accounting of FOIA disclosures, for example, would promote privacy interests without measurably impeding the operation of the FOIA. Secondly, this interpretation attributes to Congress the perverse desire to eliminate agency regulations precisely when they are most needed.[266] Given the strong congressional desire to enact privacy legislation, and the explicit recognition of the agencies as the foremost enemy of privacy, Congress surely could not have intended to leave the protection of privacy in the hands of the agencies. It makes little sense to assume that Congress intentionally subordinated the Privacy Act to the FOIA knowing the consequence to be the pointless destruction of significant aspects of the Privacy Act. It seems apparent, therefore, that Congress simply failed to realize that the FOIA could not adequately protect privacy and that subordinating the Privacy Act to the FOIA is tantamount to sacrificing privacy interests. This conclusion would suggest that courts should consider the principles underlying both the Privacy Act and the FOIA to attempt a reconciliation of their conflicting demands.

The underlying purpose of the Privacy Act is to protect informational privacy—to ensure that each individual has control over the information that directly affects his life.[267] The purpose of the FOIA is to develop an informed public able to make intelligent electoral choices and to ensure that government remains accountable to the people.[268] Focusing on the underlying purposes would permit courts to give effect to both legislative intents. If disclosure would do little to promote government accountability, releasing the information would be inappropriate, especially if it would involve a serious invasion of individual privacy. Conversely, if release would significantly improve government accountability without seriously injuring privacy interests, disclosure would be appropriate. In any given case, the courts should balance the underlying interests served by each statute.

Fortunately, the sixth exemption to the FOIA would readily permit this type of interest balancing.[269] The Supreme Court's recent interpretation of this exemption in *Department of the Air Force* v. *Rose* [270] makes it clear that courts must balance "the individual's right to privacy against the preservation of the basic purpose of the Freedom of Information Act. . . ."[271] The Privacy Act dictates that any disclosure of personal information without consent always constitutes an invasion of privacy. Unless disclosure would substantially further the underlying goals of the FOIA, courts should liberally apply the exemption to refuse disclosure without the consent of the subject.

The problem with this approach is that it would require explicit judicial recognition of congressional ignorance. Given the explicit legislative history demonstrating congressional satisfaction with the FOIA,[272] courts are more likely to conclude that Congress intentionally, if unintelligently, chose to sacrifice privacy interests in favor of the public's right to know.

In this event, amendment of the FOIA would be the most sensible course to pursue. Specifically, agencies should be required to notify the subject of a record prior to disclosing information about him in identifiable form.[273] The agency should also supply the individual with a copy of the requested record and notice that failure to object within a specified time will constitute consent to disclosure. A less desirable amendment could require agencies to keep an accounting of disclosures and to assure the reliability of records disclosed under the FOIA.

Conclusion

We live in a society in which personal information has assumed ever-increasing importance in fulfilling our most critical social responsibilities. The development of the computer and the increasing amount of personal information in governmental hands, however, poses substantial and growing dangers for the congeries of interests encompassed by the notion of privacy. The Privacy Act of 1974 attempts to resolve this dilemma, as the courts and the common law could not, by establishing substantive and procedural restrictions on the gathering and use of information about Americans by government agencies.

Although the Privacy Act is in many respects disappointing, it is nevertheless the most important piece of federal privacy legislation since the fourth amendment.[274] The Act exhibits an understanding of the serious problems posed by computers and is conceptually sound. At the very least, it constitutes an expression of congressional policy that will prompt federal agencies to exercise greater caution in handling personal information. Perhaps most important, the Privacy Act enables ambitious individuals to control the flow of information about them, to assure agency compliance with the Act, and to recover damages for serious invasions of privacy that were not actionable at common law.

The defects in the Privacy Act are structural. The failure to provide for an independent commission to aid in the enforcement of the Act was inexcusable. The Act places responsibility for assuring agency compliance almost exclusively upon the individual, but gives him neither the tools nor the incentive to do so. The absence of required notice to subjects of records, the inadequate regulations concerning existing files containing material in violation of the Privacy Act, and the unsatisfactory remedies under the Act render it an unenforceable statement of policy.

In the final analysis, however, the Privacy Act's most serious deficiency is the failure to make even a serious attempt to accommodate privacy with such crucial conflicting interests as effective law enforcement and the public's right to know. Indeed, whether by design or inadvertence, Congress adopted a scheme in both instances that systematically sacrifices the very interests the Privacy Act purports to protect. Nothing short of amendment will remedy these defects.

Notes

1.   A. Solzhenitsyn, Cancer Ward (1968), quoted in *Department of Health, Education, and Welfare, Records Computers and the Rights of Citizens* 31 (1973) [hereinafter cited as *HEW Report*].
2.   A. Westin, *Privacy and Freedom* 7 (1967).
3.   See note 40 *infra*.
4.   For discussion of the constitutional bases of informational privacy, see Note, "Informational Privacy: Constitutional Challenges to the Collection and Dissemination of Personal Information by Government Agencies," 3 *Hastings Const. L.Q.* 229 (1976).
5.   See notes 14-22 *infra* and accompanying text.
6.   See, e.g., S. Rep. No. 93-1183, 93d Cong., 2d Sess. 7 (1974): "In the past, dictatorships have always come with hobnailed boots and tanks, and machine guns, but a dictatorship of dossiers, a dictatorship of data banks can be just as repressive, just as chilling, and just as debilitating on our constitutional protections."
7.   5 U.S.C. § 552a (Supp. V 1975).
8.   See notes 11-53 *infra* and accompanying text.
9.   See notes 54-156 *infra* and accompanying text.
10.   See notes 157-273 *infra* and accompanying text.
11.   For an outstanding discussion of the history of government record keeping from Egyptian times to the present, see "Federal Data Banks, Computers and the Bill of Rights: Hearings Before the Subcomm. on Constitutional Rights of the Senate Comm. on the Judiciary," 92d Cong., 1st Sess. 836-46 (1971) (statement of A. Westin) [hereinafter cited as "Data Bank Hearings"].
12.   See A. Westin, *supra* note 2, at 321-23. Professor Westin maintains that the marked increase in data collection stems from the rejection of the theory that rational governmental action could be based on limited facts and the acceptance of a behavioral-predictive theory of information. See also *HEW Report, supra* note 1, at 34-35; Project, "Government Information and the Rights of Citizens," 73 *Mich. L. Rev.* 971, 1222 (1975).
13.   See "Data Bank Hearings," *supra* note 11, at 69 (statement of J. Rosenberg. See also Miller, "Computers, Data Banks and Individual Privacy: An Overview," 4 colum *Human Rights L. Rev.* 1 (1972); Ruggles, Pemberton & Miller, "Symposium: Computers, Data Banks, and Individual Privacy," 53 *Minn. L. Rev.* 211, 223, 228 (1968).
14.   See *Staff of the Subcomm. on Constitutional Rights of the Senate Comm. on the Judiciary*, 93d Cong., 2d Sess., *Federal Data Banks and Constitutional Rights* IV (1974) [hereinafter cited as *Data Bank Study*]; Project, *supra* note 12, at 1223-24.
15.   See Countryman, "The Diminishing Right of Privacy: The Personal Dossier & the Computer," 49 *Tex. L. Rev.* 837, 853 (1971). See also *HEW Report, supra* note 1, at 13-15; Miller, *supra* note 13, at 5.
16.   See *Data Bank Study, supra* note 14, at xxxix (summary of findings). Most of these files were compiled and computerized by the Army, HUD, and the FCC.

Perhaps most shocking was the revelation that the Army "had been systematically keeping watch on the *lawful* political activity of a number of groups and preparing incident reports and dossiers on individuals engaged in a wide range of legal protests." Miller, *supra* note 13, at 4. See Countryman, *supra* note 15, at 857. For a collection of press articles documenting the public uproar upon discovery of the Army's activities, see "Data Bank Hearings," *supra* note 11, pt. II, at 1607-09.

17.   See Project, *supra* note 12, at 1224 (citing *Records Maintained by Government Agencies, Hearings* on H.R. 9527 and *Related Bills Before a Subcomm. of the House Comm. on Government Operations,* 92d Cong., 2d Sess. 22 (1972) (statement of Representative Patten)). See also *Data Bank Study, supra* note 14, at iv; Karst, "The Files": Legal Controls Over the Accuracy and Accessibility of Stored Personal Data," 31 *Law & Contemp. Prob.* 342, 343-44 (1966). Individuals are generally unaware of the multitude of ways in which personal information is collected. For example,

> [w]hether he knows it or not, whenever an American travels on a commercial airline, reserves a room at one of the national hotel chains, rents a car, he is likely to leave distinctive electronic tracks in the memory of a computer that can tell a great deal about his activities,—his movements, his habits and associations.

"Data Bank Hearings," *supra* note 11, at 9 (statement of A. Miller).

18.   crux of the problem is that the computer has enabled government to collect "too much data." The mere compilation of vast personal dossiers offends privacy by creating a "potential 'record-prison' for millions of Americans, as past mistakes, omissions, or misunderstood events become permanent evidence . . . ." A. Westin, *supra* note 2, at 160. See *HEW Report, supra* note 1, at 12-15; Countryman, *supra* note 15, at 168; Miller, *supra* note 13, at 1-3. Professor Countryman maintains that our continued worship of efficiency and failure to discard the misconception that whatever is efficient is desirable will result in the destruction of privacy. Countryman, *supra,* at 869. He urges that "we have not, in this country, permitted efficiency to be the determining factor when individual liberty is jeopardized." *Id.* at 870. Countryman somberly concludes that the computer cannot be controlled and that "[t]he only hope for substantial protection of privacy against the computerized dossiers . . . is that they not exist—at least . . . not exist on their present scale." *Id.* at 869.

19.   For example, standardized computer languages and remote access to computer terminals allow the instantaneous transfer of information between data banks or from a data bank to any person with access to a computer terminal. Recently there has been a movement to centralize all information about an individual in one data bank. As Alan Westin has noted:

> Compared to manual files, computers offer greater storage capacity for data; greater speed of processing; lower processing cost per item of information; greater capacity for complex logical operation; simultaneous access to multiple records; ability to link data on the same person, place, or thing from different files; remote access to central facilities for input and output; and the ability to exchange information with other computer systems.

"Data Bank Hearings," *supra* note 11, at 838. See also Countryman, *supra* note 15, at 163; Miller, "Personal Privacy in the Computer Age: The Challenge of a New Technology in an Information-Oriented Society," 67 *Mich. L. Rev.* 1089, 1093-1103

(1969); Comment, "The Computer Data Bank-Privacy Controversy Revisited: An Analysis and an Administrative Proposal," 22 *Cath. U. L. Rev.* 628, 635 (1973).

Public reaction to the computer-based privacy invasion, initially slow to develop, erupted upon disclosure of formal proposals for a National Data Center, which would have consolidated information held by all government agencies. For a discussion of the trend towards centralization and the National Data Center, see *Data Bank Study, supra* note 14, at xv-xviii; Meldman, "Centralized Information Systems and the Legal Right to Privacy," 52 *Marq. L. Rev.* 335 (1969); Miller, *supra,* at 1131-40; Note, "Privacy and Efficient Government: Proposals for a National Data Center," 82 *Harv. L. Rev.* 400, 406 (1968).

Although the proposal for a National Data Center was defeated, the "vast numbers of personal dossiers already assembled by private and official compilers have effectively treated a 'National Data Bank' now." Countryman, *supra* at 863.

20.   See Miller, *supra* note 19, at 1137.

21.   "The inevitable result of using computers is that the investigator acquires two or three times as much personal information . . . as was ever collected before because of the physical or cost limitations of acquisition." A. Westin, *supra* note 2, at 160. See Ruggles, Pemberton & Miller, *supra* note 13, at 229.

22.   "Data Bank Hearings," *supra* note 11, at 11 (statement of A. Miller); Address by Senator Ervin, Spring Joint Computer Conference (May 20, 1971), reprinted in "Data Bank Hearings," *supra* note 11, pt. II, at 1552; Ruggles, Pemberton & Miller, *supra* note 13, at 229. See also S. Rep. No. 93-1183, *supra* note 6, at 11.

23.   See Countryman, *supra* note 15, at 839-43; Miller, *supra* note 19, at 1141-42.

24.   See Countryman, *supra* note 15, at 844. Professor Countryman argues that even in those rare instances when an individual realizes that constant credit or employment rejections are attributable to a damaging record, he is unable to secure access to the record, and thus relief is impossible.

25.   See Miller, *supra* note 19, at 1109-18. Accidental disclosures, dust, and related mechanical failures can also be extremely damaging to personal privacy.

26.   See "Data Bank Hearings," *supra* note 11, at 470-73 (statement of R. Henderson) (discussing security developments); Grenier, "Computers and Privacy: A Proposal for Self-Regulation," 1970 *Duke L.J.* 495, 496; Miller, *supra* note 19 at 1109-14; Comment, "Public Access to Government-Held Computerized Information," 68 *Nw. U.L. Rev.* 433 (1973).

27.   For example, where an individual is listed as a felon on a computerized record but the offense, civil disobedience, is not recorded, the party receiving the data is likely to misinterpret it. Other frequent examples of contextual inaccuracy arise when employment ratings are transmitted to users who do not have access to the rating criterion. See, e.g., *HEW Report, supra* note 1, at 19; Miller, *supra* note 19, at 1115-17; Ruggles, Pemberton & Miller, *supra* note 13, at 230; Comment, *supra* note 19, at 636-37.

28.   The computer has made it too easy for too many people to gain access to personal files. See *HEW Report, supra* note 1, at 13; Karst, *supra* note 17, at 342-43; Miller, *supra* note 13, at 230; Comment, *supra* 26, at 433.

29.   See "Data Bank Hearings," *supra* note 11, pt. I, at 31 (remarks of S. Ervin): "[A] computer has marvelous gifts of memory far beyond any human being . . . and at the

same time it lacks virtues of human beings, such as the virtue of compassion and the willingness to forget and forgive some of our offenses."

30.   A. Westin, *supra* note 2, at 160. See note 18 *supra.*

31.   See A. Westin, *supra* note 2, at 160; "Data Bank Hearings," *supra* note 11, pt. I, at 31 (remarks of S. Ervin); Comment, *supra* note 19, at 638-39.

32.   "Data Bank Hearings," *supra* note 11, at 83 (statement of J. Rosenberg).

33.   See A. Westin, *supra* note 2, at 160; Miller, *supra* note 19, at 1116; *cf.* Warren Brandeis, "The Right to Privacy," 4 *Harv. L. Rev.* 193, 196 (1890) (discussing nineteenth century tendency to rely excessively on printed words).

34.   See "Data Bank Hearings," *supra* note 11, at 17 (statement of A. Miller); Countryman, *supra* note 15, at 844.

35.   See *Data Bank Study, supra* note 14, at xviii (statement of A. Miller): "It is not essential that dossiers, files, surveillance, actually are used to repress people. If these activities give the appearance of repression that in itself has a chilling effect on the precious rights guaranteed . . . by the Constitution . . . ."

36.   See A. Westin, *supra* note 2, at 323; "Data Bank Hearings," *supra* note 11, at 10 (statement of A. Miller); Miller, *supra* note 13, at 6 (discussing impact of computers on exercise of first amendment rights); Note, *supra* note 19, at 637-39.

37.   As Professor Miller has noted:

> The computer is a many-splendored animal. It is myopic to think of it as little more than a high speed calculator with a gland condition . . . .
>
>   . . . .
>
> We must recognize that we are dealing with a new technology, whose applications are just beginning to be perceived and whose capacity to deprive us of our privacy simply cannot be measured in terms of existing systems . . . .

Ruggles, Pemberton & Miller, *supra* note 13, at 225-27.

38.   Commentators unanimously agreed that the existing legal structure was totally incapable of coping with the threats posed by computers. See, e.g., *HEW Report, supra* note 1, at 34-35; Beaney, "The Right to Privacy and American Law," 31 *Law & Contemp. Prob.* 253, 258-59 (1966); Countryman, *supra* note 15, at 864; Kalven, "Privacy in Tort Law—Were Warren and Brandeis Wrong?," 31 *Law & Contemp. Prob.* 326, 327 (1966); Karst, *supra* note 17, at 350; Meldman, *supra* note 19, at 352; Miller, *supra* note 19, at 1207; Sills, "Automated Data Processing and the Issue of Privacy," 1 *Seton Hall L. Rev.* 7, 19 (1970). See also *Shibley* v. *Time,* 40 Ohio Misc. 51, 321 N.E.2d 791 (Ct. C.P. 1974) (holding sale of names not an actionable invasion of privacy and apologizing to plaintiff for the pitiful state of the law).

39.   For discussion of the development of the right to privacy, see *HEW Report, supra* note 1, at 34-35; Long, "The Right to Privacy: The Case Against the Government," 10 *St. Louis U.L.J.* 1 (1965); Sills, *supra* note 38, at 10-17.

40.   See *Griswold* v. *Connecticut,* 381 U.S. 479 (1965) (right to privacy in penumbras of first eight amendments protects interest of married persons in using contraceptives). See also *Roe* v. *Wade,* 410 U.S. 113 (1973) (right to privacy encompasses woman's interest in having an abortion); *Stanley* v. *Georgia,* 394 U.S. 557 (1969) (right to privacy embodied in first amendment protects individual's interest in viewing pornography at home); *Katz* v. *United States,* 389 U.S. 347 (1967) (right to privacy

found in fourth amendment protects individuals against warrantless wiretap); Beaney, *supra* note 38, at 253 (1966); Gross, "The Concept of Privacy," 42 *N.Y.U.L. Rev.* 34 (1967).

41.   For a discussion of the constitutional dimensions of informational privacy, see Note, *supra* note 4.

42.   See notes 43-47 *infra.*

43.   See Meldman, *supra* note 19, at 340-48; "Data Bank Hearings," *supra* note 11, at 17 (statement of A. Miller); Miller, *supra* note 19, at 1156-60.

44.   See note 43*supra;* Karst, *supra* note 17, at 346. Accordingly, if accurate information is disclosed, an individual cannot recover absent publication to a large number of people. False disclosures will often be subject to a qualified privilege. *Id.* See note 45 *infra.*

45.   The qualified privilege covers both communications that are made in good faith and those in which the communicator has an interest. See Karst, *supra* note 17, at 346-47; Miller, *supra* note 19, at 1158-62; Note, *supra* note 19, at 631-32.

46.   See Project, *supra* note 12, at 1241-42 (discussing recent developments). Consent may be express or implied. Courts have upheld the defense notwithstanding the use of coercion to obtain the information. See Meldman, *supra* note 19, at 349; Miller, *supra* note 19, at 1170-73 (noting inappropriate applications of the defense as well as countervailing tendency of courts to scrutinize carefully claims that consent was given).

47.   See Meldman, *supra* note 19, at 352; Comment, *supra* note 19, at 631-32. See also Karst, *supra* note 17, at 351. "Restitution in any literal sense is simply impossible in the context of disclosures of sensitive data; once made, a disclosure can never be erased." *Id.*

48.   See A. Westin, *supra* note 2, at 7: "Few values so fundamental to society as privacy have been left so undefined in social theory or have been the subject of such vague and confusing writing by social scientists." See also Sills, *supra* note 38, at 11.

Commentators have argued intensely over whether there is in fact an independent right to privacy. Dean Prosser maintained that the right to privacy was merely an expedient legal device employed by courts to protect several independent interests "which are tied together by a common name but otherwise have almost nothing in common." W. Prosser, *Handbook of the Law of Torts* § 117, at 804 (4th ed. 1971). See also Sills, *supra* note 38, at 11; Note, *supra* note 19, at 406.

Professor Bloustein, Prosser's leading critic, urged that privacy is a truly independent interest that protects individual dignity and integrity. See Bloustein, "Privacy as an Aspect of Human Dignity: An Answer to Dean Prosser," 39 *N.Y.U.L. Rev.* 962, 971 (1964). For criticism of both Prosser and Bloustein, see Gross, *supra* note 40; *cf.* Kalven, *supra* note 38, at 327 (tort law should not protect privacy at all). The debate is significant, since only Bloustein's thesis is broad enough to allow the erection of new principles capable of averting the computer-based threat to privacy. See Bloustein, *supra,* at 1006; Project, *supra* note 12, at 1232-39. Specifically, Dean Prosser's theory of privacy is merely a method derived from existing case law, designed to provide sensible resolutions to problems caused by mass-media disclosure of extremely personal information. It cannot be adapted to cope with the computer-based privacy invasion.

Professor Bloustein's theory, under which privacy is defined broadly as the interest in protecting individual dignity, is more readily adaptable. The advantage of the Bloustein thesis is that it can accomodate the regulation of any kind of threat to individual dignity and assures that "new techniques could not outflank the law." The problem with the Bloustein thesis is that it provides absolutely no guide to aid in determining what constitutes an actionable invasion of privacy. If privacy is defined in such broad terms it will ultimately be necessary to delineate the scope of legal protection against the misuse of computers with rules comparable to those developed by Dean Prosser. Thus, it does not matter if privacy is defined narrowly with reference to a specific threat, such as the computer, or broadly, with accompanying legal rules to cope with that threat. The crucial point is that the legal system must recognize the need for flexibility so that the law can adapt to new technological threats. We can no more expect to transfer rules adopted today to cope with the problems of tomorrow than we can "attempt a literal transfer of rules that were framed for a vanished environment." "Data Bank Hearings," *supra* note 11, at 835 (statement of A. Westin). Thus, the legal framework must be agreed upon before the law can proceed to struggle with the problems posed by computers.

49.   A. Westin, *supra* note 2, at 7. Professor Westin maintains that protection of privacy is crucial to a free society because: (1) it fosters self-reliant citizens; (2) it allows experimentation and innovation by private parties; and, (3) it stifles government tendencies toward totalitarianism. See "Data Bank Hearings," *supra* note 11, at 835 (statement of A. Westin). Arthur Miller asserts that although privacy is impossible to define, it has begun to be seen as an "individual's ability to control the flow of information concerning or describing him." Miller, *supra* note 19, at 1107. Miller and Westin had a strong influence on the Senate subcommittee investigating computerized data banks. The committee combined the Miller and Westin conceptions and defined privacy as "the capacity . . . to determine what information about the individual will be collected and disseminated to others. Privacy also involves a subjective sense of self-determination and control over personal information." *Data Bank Study, supra* note 14, at ix. For additional proposed definitions of privacy, see Beaney, *supra* note 38, at 254; Gross, *supra* note at 34; Jourard, "Some Psychological Aspects of Privacy," 31 *Law & Contemp. Prob.* 307 (1966); Project, *supra* note 12, at 224-26; Comment, *supra* note 19, at 630-31. See *Warden* v. *Hayden,* 387 U.S. 294, 323 (1967) (Douglas, J., dissenting).

Several commentators have urged that individuals should have a property right in all information pertaining to them "with all the restraints on interference by public or private authorities and due process guarantees that our law of property has been so skillful at devising." Miller, *supra* 19, at 1223-28.

50.   See note 48 *supra.*

51.   See *HEW Report, supra* note 1, at 38-40; A. Westin, *supra* note 2, at 7; Beaney, *supra* note 38, at 256; Miller, *supra* note 19, at 1162-70, 1193-1200; Comment, *supra* note 19, at 629; notes 157-273 *infra* and accompanying text. Additionally, total protection for privacy is neither possible nor desirable. See Meldman, *supra* note 19, at 352.

52.   See, e.g., *HEW Report, supra* note 1, at 34-35; Beaney, *supra* note 38, at 264; Meldman, *supra* note 19, at 352; Comment, *supra* note 19, at 635.

53.   5 U.S.C. § 552a (Supp. V 1975).

54.   H.R. Rep. No. 93-1416, 93d Cong., 2d Sess. 4 (1974). For a discussion of the Privacy Act, see Project, *supra* note 12, at 1303-40.

55.   H.R. 16373, 93d Cong., 2d Sess. (1974); S. 3418, 93d Cong., 2d Sess. (1974).

56.   See 120 *Cong. Rec.* H11,661 (daily ed. Dec. 11, 1974).

57.   See 120 *Cong. Rec.* S21,811 (daily ed. Dec. 17, 1974).

58.   "Analysis of House and Senate Compromise Amendments to the Federal Privacy Act," printed in 120 *Cong. Rec.* S21,817 (daily ed. Dec. 17, 1974) and in 120 *Cong. Rec.* H12,243 (daily ed. Dec. 18, 1974).

59.   Privacy Act of 1974, Pub. L. No. 93-579, § 2(a)(4), 88 Stat. 1897. See H.R. Rep. No. 93-1416, *supra* note 54, at 9.

60.   See S. Rep. No. 93-1183, *supra* note 6, at 14 ("[t]he premise underlying this legislation is that good government and efficient management require that basic principles of privacy, confidentiality and due process must apply to all personal information programs . . .").

61.   5 U.S.C. § 552a(e) (Supp. V 1975).

62.   5 U.S.C. § 552a(e)(3) (Supp. V 1975).

63.   *Id.*

64.   See note 20 *supra.*

65.   5 U.S.C. § 552a(e)(7) (Supp. V 1975).

66.   This provision, like subsection e(1), see notes 115-20 *infra,* is "aimed particularly at preventing collection of protected information not immediately needed, about law-abiding Americans, on the off-chance that Government . . . might possibly have to deal with them in the future." S. Rep. No. 93-1183, *supra* note 6, at 57. For discussion of the compromise amendment, see 120 *Cong. Rec.* S21,816 (daily ed. Dec. 17, 1974).

67.   5 U.S.C. § 552a(e)(7) (Supp. V 1975) (emphasis added).

68.   See note 49 *supra.*

69.   See Project, *supra* note 12, at 1308-09 (criticizing subsection (e)(7) for failing to prohibit collection about other activities unprotected by the first amendment). See also Office of Management and Budget, Privacy Act Implementation Guidelines and Responsibilities, 40 Fed. Reg. 28,949 (1975) [hereinafter cited as OMB Guidelines]. The OMB Guidelines direct agencies to "apply the broadest reasonable interpretation" in determining whether or not a particular activity is protected by the first amendment. *Id.* at 28,965. Although the Guidelines strictly limit the use of the subsection (e)(7) exception to acquisition expressly authorized by statute, they fail to provide adequate guidance for agencies attempting to determine if the collection of information concerning a suspect's first amendment rights would be "pertinent to and within the scope of an authorized law enforcement activity." *Id.*

70.   The primary problem with this section is that the exception is overly broad. Although there are many instances in which law enforcement agencies require information pertaining to the exercise of a subject's first amendment rights, there is no way to assure that agencies will refrain from collecting such information "unless pertinent to and within the scope of an authorized law enforcement activity." The exemption may well perpetuate precisely those "fishing expeditions" that subsection (e)(7) is designed to preclude. See 120 *Cong. Rec.* H10,892 (daily ed. Nov. 20, 1974) (pur-

pose of the exemption is to assure that "political and religious activities are not used as a cover for illegal or subversive activities").

71.   5 U.S.C. § 552a(d) (Supp. V 1975).

72.   5 U.S.C. § 552a(d)(1) (Supp. V 1975).

73.   5 U.S.C. § 552a(d)(2)-(4) (Supp. V 1975).

74.   For a discussion of these provisions, see OMB Guidelines, *supra* note 69, at 28,958-60.

75.   See note 24 *supra.*

76.   See S. Rep. No. 93-1183, *supra* note 6, at 20. An agency may not refuse the subject access to a record because of lack of proper interest. See OMB Guidelines, *supra* note 69, at 28,957.

77.   See notes 136-57 *infra.*

78.   5 U.S.C. § 552a(c) (Supp. V 1975); see note 85 *infra.*

79.   See notes 115 & 124 *infra.*

80.   The individual may learn of the existence of a record if an agency requests his consent prior to disclosing a record about him pursuant to subsection (b) (conditions of disclosure). Unfortunately the broad exemptions and the general "prior consent" provision to subsection (b) will frequently prevent an individual from discovering the existence of personal records about him. See note 91 *infra* and accompanying text.

81.   See S. Rep. No. 93-1183, *supra* note 6, at 59; note 89 *infra.*

82.   See notes 96-98 *infra* and accompanying text.

83.   See S. Rep. No. 93-1183, *supra* note 6, at 68.

84.   5 U.S.C. § 552a(b) (Supp. V 1975) (emphasis added). Neither this, nor any other provision of the Privacy Act authorizes disclosure to a person other than the subject of a record. See OMB Guidelines, *supra* note 69, at 28,953.

85.   5 U.S.C. § 552a(c) (Supp. V 1975). The accounting is intended: 1) to enable individuals to discover those to whom their records have been disclosed; 2) to facilitate the correction of erroneous records; and 3) to allow individuals to force agency compliance with the disclosure provisions of subsection (b).

Subsection (c)(2) requires agencies to retain all accountings "for at least five years or the life of the record, whichever is longer, after the disclosure for which the accounting is made." 5 U.S.C. § 552a(c)(2) (Supp. V 1975). This provision was the result of a compromise between the House and Senate Committees. See 120 *Cong. Rec.* S21,817 (daily ed. Dec. 17, 1974). Subsection (c)(3) requires agencies to allow the subject of a record to examine any accounting but those required for law enforcement purposes pursuant to subsection (b)(7). See note 167 *infra.* No accounting is necessary for disclosures required by the FOIA. See notes 259-61 *infra* and accompanying text).

86.   See note 28 *supra.*

87.   See notes 27-28 *supra.*

88.   See note 28 *supra.*

89.   The original draft of the Senate bill required any agency to notify all individuals about whom the agency maintained personal imformation. This requirement was abandoned due to the allegedly prohibitive cost of notification. Instead, the Act relies totally on the initiative of concerned citizens to seek out information pertaining to them. See S. Rep. No. 93-1183, *supra* note 6, at 59.

The Senate bill also provided for a Privacy Commission responsible in part for publishing a Directory of Information Systems designed to enable individuals to discover easily if an agency maintained a personal record about them. The Act as passed contains no such provision, and individuals who wish to learn if any personal records about them exist must study the Federal Register religiously. See notes 100-06 *infra* and accompanying text.

90.   See notes 72-74 *supra*.

91.   See text accompanying note 84 *supra*.

92.   See OMB Guidelines, *supra* note 69, at 28,954. Informing an individual of the purpose for which information will be used does not constitute prior consent to disclosure of such information. *Id*.

93.   5 U.S.C. § 552a(b)(3) (Supp. V 1975).

94.   5 U.S.C. § 552a(a)(7) (Supp. V 1975). This exemption is intended to "recognize the practical limitations of restricting use of information to explicit and express purposes for which it was collected." OMB Guidelines, *supra* note 69, at 16-17. One harmless example of a routine use given in the OMB Guidelines is the transfer of information from an agency to the Treasury Department for processing of payroll checks. *Id*.

95.   See S. Rep. No. 93-1183, *supra* note 6, at 72-73. This provision constitutes a major concession to the House. See 120 *Cong. Rec.* S21,815 (daily ed. Dec. 17, 1974).

96.   5 U.S.C. § 552a(e)(4)(D) (Supp. V 1975).

97.   But see Project, *supra* note 12, at 1316.

98.   See 120 *Cong. Rec.* S21,816 (daily ed. Dec. 17, 1974); OMB Guidelines, *supra* note 69, at 28,953.

99.   See notes 62-98 *supra* and 100-33 *infra* and accompanying text.

100.   5 U.S.C. § 552a(e)(4) (Supp. V. 1975).

101.   5 U.S.C. § 552a(e)(4)(A) (Supp. V 1975). A "system of records" is defined as a group of any records under the control of any agency from which information is *retrieved by the name* of the individual or by some identifying number, symbol, or other identifying particular assigned to the individual. 5 U.S.C. § 552a(a)(5) (Supp. V 1975) (emphasis added). The Act defines the term record as

> any item, collection, or grouping of information about an individual that is maintained by an agency, including but not limited to, his education, financial transactions, medical history, and criminal or employment history and that contains his name, or . . . other identifying particular assigned to the individual . . . . 5 U.S.C. § 552a(a)(4) (Supp. V 1975).

Although the broad definition of the term "record" will preclude agencies from refusing to comply with the Act on the pretext that an element of personal information does not constitute a record, the term "system of records" is potentially a major loophole in the Act. Virtually all provisions of the Privacy Act only apply to an agency if it *maintains a system of records*. This is a legitimate limitation with respect to subsections (e)(4)(publishing requirements) and (d) (access requirements). There is no justification, however, for applying this limitation to subsections (b) (conditions of disclosure) and (c) (accounting of disclosures). The effects of failing to apply these subsections to an agency that does not maintain a system of records are disastrous.

First, these agencies can disclose personal information to anyone for any purpose. Second, the individual has no control over the use of information. Finally, agencies can avoid the Act entirely by claiming that personal records under their control do not compromise a "system." The Act itself provides no specific guidelines to aid in the determination of whether a group of records constitutes a system and those provided in the OMB Guidelines are insufficient. See OMB Guidelines *supra* note 69, at 28,963. The Guidelines merely admonish agencies: "systems . . . should not be subdivided or reorganized so that information which would otherwise have been subject to the Act is no longer subject to the Act."

102.   5 U.S.C. § 552a(e)(4)(B) (Supp. V 1975).

103.   5 U.S.C. § 552a(e)(4)(C) (Supp. V 1975).

104.   5 U.S.C. § 552a(e)(4)(D) (Supp. V 1975).

105.   5 U.S.C. § 552a(e)(4)(E)-(H) (Supp. V 1975).

106.   5 U.S.C. § 552a(e)(4)(H) (Supp. V 1975).

107.   See S. Rep. No. 93-1183, *supra* note 6, at 2; H.R. Rep. No. 93-1416, *supra* note 54, at 4; OMB Guidelines, *supra* note 69, at 28,962.

108.   See note 16 *supra.*

109.   See OMB Guidelines, *supra* note 69, at 28,962.

110.   5 U.S.C. § 552a(e)(2) (Supp. V 1975).

111.   *Id.*

112.   See OMB Guidelines,*supra* note 69, at 28,961.

113.   See 120 Cong. Rec. S21,817 (daily ed. Dec. 17, 1974) ("[A]n individual should to the greatest extent possible be in control of information about him which is given to the government.").

114.   See OMB Guidelines, *supra* note 69, at 28,961 (providing relevant considerations); Project, *supra* note 12, at 1311-15 (criticizing subsection (e)(2)).

115.   5 U.S.C. § 552a(e)(1) (Supp. V 1975).

116.   *Id.* (emphasis added).

117.   See S. Rep. No. 93-1183, *supra* note 6, at 45; OMB Guidelines, *supra* note 69, at 28,960.

118.   Ervin, "The First Amendment: A Living Thought in the Computer Age, reprinted in Data Bank Hearings" (pt. II), *supra* note 11, at 1550, 1552; see S. Rep. No. 93-1183, *supra* note 6, at 11.

119.   The OMB Guidelines recognize necessity as a requirement and declare the following kinds of questions as guidelines for determining whether information is relevant and necessary:

1) How does the information relate to the purpose (in law) for which the system is maintained?; 2) What are the adverse consequences, if any, of not collecting the information?; 3) Does the information have to be in individually identifiable form?; 4) How long must the information be retained?; 5) What is the financial cost of maintaining the record compared to the risks/adverse consequences of not maintaining it? OMB Guidelines, *supra* note 69, at 28,960.

120.   But see Project, *supra* note 12, at 1305-08.

121.   For discussion of problems with records compiled before the Privacy Act, see notes 18-36 *supra* and accompanying text.

122.   See notes 81-82 *supra* and accompanying text.

123.   See OMB Guidelines, *supra* note 69, at 28,961 (agencies should insure that record systems comply with subsection (e)(1): (1) in preparing public notices, (2) in developing new information systems, (3) upon changing a system, (4) at least annually).

124.   5 U.S.C. § 552a(e)(5) (Supp. V 1975).

125.   See S. Rep. No. 93-1183, *supra* note 6, at 50.

126.   See 120 Cong. Rec. S21,816 (daily ed. Dec. 17, 1974).

127.   5 U.S.C. § 552a(e)(5) (Supp. V 1975) (emphasis supplied).

128.   Since all records except those compiled for statistical purposes, see subsection (a)(6), *may* be used to make determinations, this section could be interpreted to require agencies to insure the quality of all records but those subject to subsection (a)(6). *Cf.* OMB Guidelines, *supra* note 69, at 28,961 (similar argument made in discussion of subsection (e)(2)). Nevertheless, the legislative history conflicts with this interpretation and its adoption is unlikely.

129.   5 U.S.C. § 552a(b) (Supp. V 1975).

130.   See notes 84-98 *supra* and accompanying text.

131.   5 U.S.C. § 552a(e)(6) (Supp. V 1975).

132.   *Id.* (emphasis added).

133.   See 120 *Cong. Rec.* S21,816 (daily ed. Dec. 17, 1974).

134.   See notes 81-82 *supra* and accompanying text.

135.   See notes 263-66 *infra* and accompanying text.

136.   5 U.S.C. § 552a(g) (Supp. V 1975).

137.   5 U.S.C. § 552a(i) (Supp. V 1975).

138.   See S. Rep. No. 93-1183, *supra* note 6, at 23-24. The Senate Committee concluded an independent commission was essential to enforcement of the Act.

139.   Privacy Act of 1974, Publ L. No. 93-579, § 5, 88 Stat. 1896.

140.   5 U.S.C. § 552a(g)(1)(B) (Supp. V 1975).

141.   5 U.S.C. § 552a(g)(3)(A) (Supp. V 1975).

142.   5 U.S.C. § 552a(g)(1)(A) (Supp. V 1975).

143.   5 U.S.C. §§552a(g)(2)(A), (g)(3)(A) (Supp. V 1975). The only apparent difference between suits brought under these subsections is that under (g)(2)(A) the individual has the burden of proving that the agency wrongfully refused to amend a record while under (g)(3)(A) the agency must justify its refusal to grant access to the subject of a record. See OMB Guidelines, *supra* note 69, at 28,969.

144.   5 U.S.C. § 552a(g)(2)(B) (Supp. V 1975).

145.   5 U.S.C. § 552a(g)(1)(C) (Supp. V 1975) (emphasis added). The Guidelines define an adverse determination as "one resulting in the denial of a right, benefit, entitlement, or employment by an agency which the individual could reasonably have expected to have been given if the record had not been deficient." OMB Guidelines, *supra* note 69, at 28,969.

146.   5 U.S.C. § 552a(g)(1)(D) (Supp. V 1975).

147.   5 U.S.C. § 552a(g)(4) (Supp. V 1975). "On a continuum between negligence and the very high standard of willful, arbitrary, or capricious conduct, this standard is viewed as only somewhat greater than gross negligence." 120 *Cong. Rec.* S21,817 (daily ed. Dec. 17, 1974).

148.   5 U.S.C. § 552a(g)(4)(A) (Supp. V 1975).

149.   5 U.S.C. § 552a(g)(4)(B) (Supp. V 1975). Unlike (g)(2) and (g)(3), which make the award of court costs and attorneys' fees discretionary, under (g)(4) costs and attorneys' fees are mandatory when an agency is adjudged liable. See OMB Guidelines, *supra* note 69, at 76.

150.   5 U.S.C. § 552a(g)(5) (Supp. V 1975). The Act contains an exception to this requirement when

> an agency has *materially and willfully misrepresented* any information required . . . to be disclosed to an individual and the *information so misrepresented is material to establishment of the liability* of the agency to the individual . . . the action may be brought at any time within two years after *discovery* by the individual of the misrepresentation. (emphasis added).

151.   S. Rep. No. 93-1183, *supra* note 6, at 24.

152.   See Project, *supra* note 12, at 1330: "The floor on recovery . . . presumably represents a compromise between the House proposal, which only allowed recovery of actual damages, and the Senate proposal, which allowed recovery of punitive damages where appropriate." (footnotes omitted).

153.   See note 150 *supra* and accompanying text.

154.   The Senate bill provided for an independent privacy commission responsible for: 1) monitoring and inspecting new information systems, 2) compiling a directory of information systems to enable individuals to take advantage of rights granted under the Act, and 3) investigating and holding hearings upon violations of the Act. See S. Rep. No. 93-1183, *supra* note 60, at 23-24.

155.   See S. 3418, § 303(c), 93d Cong., 2d Sess. (1974). ("Any person who violates the provisions of this Act . . . shall be liable to any person aggrieved thereby in an amount equal to the sum of—(1) any actual damages . . . (2) punitive damages where appropriate . . ."). See also 120 *Cong. Rec.* S21,817 (daily ed. Dec. 17, 1974). Additionally, the Senate bill obligated the Attorney General to "challenge in court any violation of the Act which might affect the public at large, but which does not yet affect any particular citizen sufficiently . . . to induce a private person to endure the practical difficulties of litigation." S. Rep. No. 93-1183, *supra* note 6, at 83. The omission of this crucial provision was inexcusable, particularly in light of the failure to allow punitive damages.

156.   See text accompanying notes 135-36 *supra.*

157.   5 U.S.C. § 552 (1970).

158.   5 U.S.C. § 552a(j) (Supp. V 1975).

159.   5 U.S.C. § 552a(k) (Supp. V 1975).

160.   See OMB Guidelines, *supra* note 69, at 28,971-72.

161.   5 U.S.C. § 552a(j)(1) (Supp. V 1975).

162.   5 U.S.C. § 552a(j)(2) (Supp. V 1975). Specifically, to qualify for exemption under subsection (j)(2), a record system must consist of information: a) compiled for the purpose of identifying suspects and offenders and which consists only of identifying data, e.g., rap sheets; b) information compiled as part of a criminal investigation; or c) identifiable records compiled at any stage of the law enforcement process.

163.   Subsection (j) does not exempt records from the requirements of subsections (b), (c)(1) and (2), (e)(4)(A)-(F), (e)(6), (7), (9), (10) and (11) and (i). 5 U.S.C. § 552a(j) (Supp. V 1975).

164.   See note 84 *supra* and accompanying text.
165.   5 U.S.C. § 552a(b)(7) (Supp. V 1975).
166.   See note 85 *supra* and accompanying text.
167.   5 U.S.C. § 552a(c)(3) (Supp. V 1975).
168.   See note 167 *supra* and accompanying text.
169.   5 U.S.C. § 552a(e)(7) (Supp. V 1975).
170.   5 U.S.C. § 552a(e)(6) & (b) (Supp. V 1975).
171.   See note 169 *supra.*
172.   See 5 U.S.C. § 552a(i) (Supp. V 1975) (restricting criminal penalties to violations of disclosure or notice provisions).
173.   See 5 U.S.C. § 552a(k) (Supp. V 1975); OMB Guidelines, *supra* note 69, at 28,972-74,
174.   See 5 U.S.C. § 552a(k)(1)-(7) (Supp. V 1975).
175.   5 U.S.C. § 552a(k)(2) (Supp. V 1975).
176.   See Project, *supra* note 12, at 1332-36.
177.   The remaining differences between subsections (j) and (k) are either unnecessary or unwarranted, and pragmatically insignificant. Subsection (j) allows an exemption from subsection (e)(2) (requiring agencies to collect information directly from subject to the "greatest extent practicable," see notes 110-11 *supra* and accompanying text), while subsection (k)(2) does not. This difference is meaningless because in criminal investigations it will obviously be impracticable to obtain most information from a suspect. Subsection (k)(2), unlike subsection (j), does not permit exemption from the requirements of subsection (e)(3), requiring agencies to inform the subject of the purpose and authority for requests for information. See notes 62-63 *supra.* This difference is also meaningless because most law enforcement agencies acquire information about a suspect from third parties, and subsection (e)(3) does not apply to requests made of third parties. See Project, *supra* note 12, at 1310.

    The final distinction between subsections (j) and (k)(2) is that only the former permits an agency to ignore the requirements of subsection (e)(5) requiring agencies to insure the quality of records used in making determinations. See note 124 *supra* and accompanying text. This exemption is not only unwarranted, it is unnecessary given the discretion allowed law enforcement agencies elsewhere in the Act regarding the kinds of information they may acquire.
178.   The legislative history emphasizes that courts should construe narrowly the exception that permits withholding information to protect the confidentiality of sources. Additionally, the Guidelines direct agencies to make express promises of confidentiality sparingly and to inform other sources that their identities may be disclosed. See 120 *Cong. Rec.* S21,816 (daily ed. Dec. 17, 1974); OMB Guidelines, *supra* note 69, at 28,973.
179.   See notes 135-44 *supra* and accompanying text.
180.   See note 217 *infra* and accompanying text (discussing FOIA exemption).
181.   See H.R. Rep. No. 93-1416, *supra* note 54, at 37-39 (additional views of Reps. Abzug, Moss, Stanton, Gude, Burton, Fasell, Culver, Collins, Rosenthal, Conyers, Jr.):

    By narrowing the exemption categories and defining them in specific terms related to the use of records rather than to the agency maintaining them,

Congress could provide agency heads with standards to meet in exercising their . . . authority to grant exemptions. Only in this way can we be assured that the Constitutional rights of individuals will be protected and will not be sacrificed to administrative discretion, expendiency or whim.

See also 120 *Cong. Rec.* H12,248 (daily ed. Dec. 18, 1974) (remarks of Representative Koch). The failure to limit the exemptions for law enforcement agencies to active criminal investigations is unfortunate, particularly in light of experience under the seventh exemption to the FOIA prior to the 1974 amendments. See notes 219-22 *infra* and accompanying text.

182.   See text accompanying note 175 *supra.*

183.   The exemptions to the Privacy Act would often permit an agency to withhold a record from the subject where the FOIA would require disclosure. In these situations, "the Privacy Act should not be used to deny access to information about an individual which would otherwise have been *required* to be disclosed to that individual under the Freedom of Information Act." Office of Management and Budget, Implementation of the Privacy Act of 1974 (Supplementary Guidance), 40 Fed. Reg. 56,741, 56,742-43 (1975).

184.   *Id.*

185.   See Emerson, "Legal Foundations of the Right to Know," 1976 *Wash. U.L.Q.* 1, 20.

186.   For discussion of the constitutional dimensions of the right to know, see Emerson, *supra* note 185.

187.   5 U.S.C. § 552 (1970).

188.   See note 84 *supra* and accompanying text.

189.   5 U.S.C. § 552a(b)(2) (Supp. V 1975).

190.   5 U.S.C. § 552a(c)(1) (Supp. V 1975).

191.   5 U.S.C. § 552a(e)(6) (Supp. V 1975).

192.   5 U.S.C. § 552(a)(3) (1970).

193.   5 U.S.C. § 552(a)(4)(B)(Supp. IV 1974).

194.   5 U.S.C. § 552(c) (1970).

195.   See e.g., *Department of the Air Force* v. *Rose,* 425 U.S. 352, 360-61 (1976); *EPA* v. *Mink,* 410 U.S. 73, 80 (1973); *Bristol-Meyers Co.* v. *FTC,* 424 F.2d 935, 938 (D.C. Cir.), *cert denied,* 400 U.S. 824 (1970). For a general review of the FOIA, see Note, "The Freedom of Information Act: A Seven Year Assessment," 74 *Colum. L. Rev.* 895 (1974). See also *EPA* v. *Mink, supra; Department of the Air Force* v. *Rose, supra;* Note, "The Freedom of Information Act and Equitable Discretion," 51 *Den. L.J.* 263 (1974); Note, "The Investigatory Files Exemption to the FOIA: The D.C. Circuit Abandons Bristol-Meyers," 42 *Geo. Wash. L. Rev.* 869 (1974); 40 *Geo. Wash. L. Rev.* 527, 527-29 (1970).

196.   See, e.g., *Soucie* v. *David,* 448 F.2d 1067, 1080 (D.C. Cir. 1971); H. R. Rep. No. 89-1497, 89th Cong., 2d Sess. 12 (1966) ("A democratic society requires an informed, intelligent electorate, and the intelligence of the electorate varies as the quantity and quality of its information varies.").

197.   See e.g., *Ditlow* v. *Shultz,* 517 F.2d 166 (D.C. Cir. 1975); *Rose* v. *Department of the Air Force,* 495 F.2d 261, 263 (2d Cir. 1974), *aff'd,* 425 U.S. 352 (1976); *Vaughn* v. *Rosen,* 484 F.2d 820, 823 (D.C. Cir. 1973), *cert. denied,* 415 U.S. 997 (1974);

Soucie v. *David,* 448 F.2d 1067 (D.C. Cir. 1971); *Wellford* v. *Hardin,* 444 F.2d 21, 24 (4th Cir. 1971); *Bristol-Meyers Co.* v. *FTC.* 424 F.2d 935, 938 (D.C. Cir.), *cert. denied,* 400 U.S. 824 (1970); *M.A. Schapiro & Co.* v. *SEC,* 339 F. Supp. 467 (D.D.C. 1972); Note, "Access to Broadcasters' Financial Statements Filed with the FCC, The Freedom of Information Act Alternative," 42 *Geo. Wash. L. Rev.* 145, 155-56 (1973); Note, "The Plain Meaning of the Freedom of Information Act: *NLRB* v. *Getman,*" 47 *Ind. L.J.* 530, 543 (1972); Note, "Public Disclosure of Internal Revenue Service Private Letter Rulings, "40 *U. Chi. L. Rev.* 832, 844-55; 45 *Ind. L.J.* 421.

Courts and commentators agree that the FOIA is a poorly drafted statute. See, e.g., *Epstein* v. *Resor,* 421 F.2d 930, 932 (9th Cir.), *cert. denied,* 398 U.S. 965 (1970); Davis, "The Information Act: A Preliminary Analysis," 34 *U. Chi. L. Rev.* 761 (1967). See Davis, *supra,* at 762-63; Note, "The Investigatory Files Exemption to the FOIA: The D.C. Circuit Abandons Bristol-Meyers," 42 *Geo. Wash. L. Rev.* 869, 872-75 (1974); Note, "The Freedom of Information Act: A Critical Review," 38 *Geo. Wash. L. Rev.* 150, 150-58 (1969); Note, "Public Disclosure of Internal Revenue Service Private Letter Rulings," 40 *U. Chi. L. Rev.* 832, 839-42 (1973). The House Report and the Attorney General's Memorandum, which generally follows it, see *United States Department of Justice, Attorney General's Memorandum on the Public Information Section of the Administrative Procedure Act III* (1967) [hereinafter cited as *Attorney General's Memorandum*] frequently give priority to the interests of privacy and confidentiality at the expense of disclosure. They conflict with the Senate Report, which emphasizes the Act's goal of providing for broad disclosure. In an attempt to further what they view as the purpose of the FOIA, courts interpreting the Act have ignored the House Report and the Attorney General's Memorandum.

198.   5 U.S.C. § 552(b)(4) (1970).

199.   The House and Senate Reports explicitly state that the fourth exemption protects confidential information that is neither commercial nor financial. See S. Rep. No. 89-813, 89th Cong., 2d Sess. 9 (1965); H.R. Rep. No. 89-1497, *supra* note 196, at 10. Courts have disregarded the legislative history because it was drawn from an earlier version of the bill that explicitly protected noncommercial information. See *Brockway v. Department of the Air Force,* 518 F.2d 1184 (8th Cir. 1975). Professor Davis sadly concludes that the legislative history is inadequate support for the proposition that confidential noncommercial information may be exempt. He insists that courts should go outside the Act to protect confidential information. See Davis, *supra* note 197, at 788-92.

200.   See *National Parks & Conservation Ass'n v. Morton,* 498 F.2d 765, 770 (D.C. Cir. 1974) (leading case). See also *Continental Oil Co.* v. *FPC,* 519 F.2d 31, 33, (5th Cir. 1975); *Getman* v. *NLRB,* 450 F.2d 670, 673 (D.C. Cir. 1971); 88 *Harv. L. Rev.* 470 (1974). For discussion of various possible interpretations of the fourth exemption, see *Attorney General's Memorandum, supra* note 197, at 32; Davis, *supra* note 197, at 787 (criticizing Attorney General).

201.   See *National Parks & Conservation Ass'n v. Morton,* 498 F.2d 765, 770 (D.C. Cir. 1974).

202.   See *HEW Report, supra* note 1, at 64-65. The FOIA amended the original Public Information Section of the Administrative Procedure Act, Act of June 11, 1946, ch. 324, § 3, 60 Stat. 238, under which an agency could withhold records if the

information were "required for good cause to be held confidential," or if the requesting individual were not "properly and directly concerned."*Id.*

By simply labeling information exempt, agencies converted this section from a disclosure provision into a withholding act. See, e.g., *EPA* v. *Mink,* 410 U.S. 73, 79 (1973); H.R. Rep. No. 89-1497, *supra* note 196, at 4; S. Rep. No. 89-813, *supra* note 199, at 3.

In order to eliminate such agency abuse and insure government accountability, the FOIA established a presumption in favor of disclosure to "any person."

203.   See Comment, "The Freedom of Information Act's Privacy Exemptions and the Privacy Act of 1974," 11 *Harv. C.R.-C.L. L. Rev.* 596 (1976).

204.   For discussion of the possible impact of the Privacy Act upon interpretation of the FOIA, see notes 253-54 *infra* and accompanying text.

205.   5 U.S.C. § 552(b)(6) (1970) (emphasis added).

206.   5 U.S.C. § 552(a)(3) (1970).

207.   See *Robles* v. *EPA,* 484 F.2d 843, 847 (4th Cir. 1973). See also Project, *supra* note 12, at 1080-85; 40 *Geo. Wash. L. Rev.* 527, 535-36 (1972).

208.   See *Wine Hobby USA, Inc.* v. *IRS,* 502 F.2d 133 (3d Cir. 1974); *Rural Housing Alliance* v. *United States Dep't. of Agriculture,* 498 F.2d 73, 78 (D.C. Cir. 1974); *Rabbitt* v. *Department of the Air Force,* 383 F. Supp. 1065, 1070 (S.D.N.Y.). See also Note, "The Plain Meaning of the Freedom of Information Act: *NLRB* v. *Getman,*" *supra* note 197, at 530. See Davis, *supra* note 197, at 806:

> This policy choice reflects pressure from the press that the public as a whole has a right to know and does not reflect a thoughtful rejection of the balancing approach that has been a part of all judge made law. When the time comes for further legislation, I think this policy choice might well be re-examined.

See also note 202 *supra.*

209.   425 U.S. 352 (1976).

210.   *Id.* at 372.

211.   See sources cited note 207 *supra.*

212.   For another feasible solution, see Comment, *supra* note 203, at 619-24.

213.   The other exemption amended in 1974 was subsection (b)(1), pertaining to national security.

214.   5 U.S.C. § 552(b)(7) (1970) (amended 1974).

215.   See, e.g., *Center for Nat'l Policy Review on Race & Urban Issues* v. *Weinberger,* 502 F.2d 370, 373 (D.C. Cir. 1974); *Aspin* v. *Department of Defense,* 491 F.2d 24 (D.C. Cir. 1973); *Cooney* v. *Sun Shipbuilding & Drydock Co.,* 288 F. Supp. 708 (E.D. Pa. 1968); *Clement Bros. Co.* v. *NLRB,* 282 F. Supp. 540 (N.D. Ga. 1968).

216.   Prior to the 1974 amendments, courts split sharply over whether an agency attempting to invoke exemption seven was required to demonstrate that proceedings based upon requested investigatory files were either pending or reasonably likely in the near future. Courts deciding most of the early cases under the seventh exemption demanded such a showing. See e.g., *Wellford* v. *Hardin,* 444 F.2d 21 (4th Cir. 1971); *Bristol-Meyers Co.* v. *FTC,* 424 F.2d 935, 938 (D.C. Cir.), *cert. denied,* 400 U.S. 824 (1970) (government may not label all files investigatory on the possibility that proceedings may be launched in future—possibility must be concrete); *M.A. Schapiro & Co.*

v. *SEC,* 339 F. Supp. 467 (D.D.C. 1972); *Frankel* v. *SEC,* 336 F. Supp. 675 (S.D.N.Y. 1971), *rev'd on other grounds,* 460 F.2d 813 (2d Cir.), *cert. denied,* 409 U.S. 889 (1972). See also Note, "The Investigatory Files Exemption," *supra* note 86; 1974 *Wash U.L.Q.* 463. The 1973 decisions by the Court of Appeals for the District of Columbia, however, held that once the court determined that an investigatory file had been compiled for law enforcement purposes its task was completed. The exemption attached indefinitely, and the unlikelihood or impossibility of future proceedings was immaterial. *Center for Nat'l Policy Review on Race & Urban Issues* v. *Weinberger,* 502 F.2d 370 (D.C. Cir. 1974); *Rural Housing Alliance* v. *Department of Agriculture,* 498 F.2d 73 (D.C. Cir. 1974); *Ditlow* v. *Brinegar,* 494 F.2d 1073 (D.C. Cir. 1974); *Aspin* v. *Department of Defense,* 491 F.2d (D.C. Cir. 1973); *Weisberg* v. *Department of Justice,* 489 F.2d 1195 (D.C. Cir. 1973) (en banc), *cert. denied,* 416 U.S. 993 (1974). See also *Evans* v. *Department of Transp.,* 446 F.2d 821 (5th Cir. 1971), *cert denied,* 405 U.S. 918 (1972); *Koch* v. *Department of Justice,* 376 F. Supp. 313, 315 (D.D.C. 1974); *Cowles Communications, Inc.* v. *Department of Justice,* 325 F. Supp. 726 (N.D. Cal. 1971).

These decisions permitted the indefinite withholding of governmental information when no legitimate purpose was served. For discussion of the District of Columbia Circuit opinions, see Clark, "Holding Government Accountable: The Amended Freedom of Information Act," 84 *Yale L.J.* 741, 761-63 (1975); Note, "The Investigatory Files Exemption to the FOIA: The D.C. Circuit Abandons Bristol-Meyers," *supra* note 195. The legislative history clearly reveals a congressional intent to overrule these decisions. See 120 Cong. Rec. S9336 (daily ed. May 30, 1974):

> (Mr. Kennedy) Does the amendment in effect override the court decisions in the court of appeals on Weisberg against the United States; Aspin Against Department of Defense; Ditlow against Brinegar; and National Center against Weisberger?
>
> (Mr. Hart) . . . That is its purpose.

217.   5 U.S.C. § 552(b)(7) (Supp. V 1975) (emphasis added).

218.   See Clark, *supra* note 216, at 762-63.

219.   Courts generally held that the seventh exemption was designed exclusively to protect governmental interests. See *Sears, Roebuck & Co.* v. *GSA,* 384 F. Supp. 996, 1004 (D.D.C. 1974) ("exemption (b)(7) is clearly designed to protect interests of the government only."). See also *Moore-McCormack Lines, Inc.* v. *L.T.O. Corp.,* 508 F.2d 945 (4th Cir. 1974); *Weisberg* v. *Department of Justice,* 489 F.2d 1195, 1199 (D.C. Cir. 1973); *Getman* v. *NLRB,* 450 F.2d 670, 673 (D.C. Cir. 1971); *Wellford* v. *Hardin,* 444 F.2d 21, 23-24 (4th Cir. 1971); *Legal Aid Soc'y* v. *Shultz,* 349 F. Supp. 771, 777 (N.D. Cal. 1972); Katz, "The Games Bureaucrats Play: Hide and Seek Under the Freedom of Information Act," *Tex. L. Rev.* 1261, 1277 (1970).

220.   For example, several courts held exemption seven inapplicable if an individual were aware of the contents of a file since no harm to the government would result from disclosure. See *Wellford* v. *Hardin,* 444 F.2d 21, 24 (4th Cir. 1971); *Sears, Roebuck & Co.,* v. *GSA,* 384 F. Supp. 996, 1004 (D.D.C. 1974); *Ditlow* v. *Volpe,* 362 F. Supp. 1321, 1325 (D.D.C. 1973), *rev'd on other grounds,* 494 F.2d 1073 (D.C. Cir.), *cert. denied,* 419 U.S. 974 (1974); *Legal Aid Soc'y* v. *Shultz,* 349 F. Supp. 771, 776 (N.D. Cal. 1972). But see *Center for Nat'l Policy Review on Race & Urban Issues*

v. *Weinberger,* 502 F.2d 370, 373-74 (D.C. Cir. 1974) (recognizing the need to protect the privacy of the subjects of past investigations); *Cowles Communications, Inc.* v. *Department of Justice,* 325 F. Supp. 726 (N.D. Cal. 1971) ("[I]n this day of increasing concern over the conflict between the citizen's right of privacy and the need of the Government to investigate, it is unthinkable that rights of privacy should be jeopardized further by making investigatory files available to private persons").

221.   See *Center for Nat'l Policy Review on Race & Urban Issues* v. *Weinberger,* 502 F.2d 370, 374 (D.C. Cir. 1974); *Cowles Communications, Inc.* v. *Department of Justice,* 325 F. Supp. 726, 729 (N.D. Cal. 1973).

222.   The District of Columbia Circuit cases effectively protected a subject's privacy because the exemption attached indefinitely once a court concluded that an investigatory file had been compiled for law enforcement purposes. See note 216 *supra.*

223.   See notes 198-204 *supra.*

224.   For further discussion of the seventh exemption, see Project, *supra* note 12, at 1085-1101.

225.   See notes 205-12 *supra* and accompanying text.

226.   See Davis, *supra* note 197, at 806. See also A. Miller, *The Assault on Privacy: Computers, Data Banks, and Dossiers* 154 (1971).

227.   See notes 81-82 *supra* and accompanying text.

228.   For a good discussion of this problem, see O'Reilly, "Governemnt Disclosure of Private Secrets Under the Freedom of Information Act," 30 *Bus. L. Rev.* 1125 (1975).

229.   See Note, "Executive Privilege and the Freedom of Information Act: The Constitutional Foundation of the Amended National Security Exemption," 1976 *Wash. U.L.Q.* 609.

230.   *HEW Report, supra* note 1, at 65. The *HEW Report* correctly recognizes that the FOIA "is an instrument for disclosing information rather than for balancing the conflicting interests that surround the public disclosure and use of personal records." *Id.* at 35. The *Report* urged: "that the [FOIA] be amended to require an agency to obtain the consent of an individual before disclosing in personally identifiable form exempted-category data about him, unless the disclosure is within the purposes of the system as specifically required by statute." *Id.* at 65-66. The *Report* correctly notes that although adopting such an amendment might result in less disclosure, it would not detract from the effectiveness of the FOIA.

231.   484 F.2d 820 (D.C. Cir. 1973), *cert. denied,* 415 U.S. 977 (1974).

232.   *Id.* at 825.

233.   *Id.* at 826.

234.   *Id.* at 827.

235.   *Vaughn* properly held that an agency wishing to reap the benefits of an exemption must show that withholding is justified. The problem is that an agency frequently derives no benefit from an exemption that protects individuals' interests. Thus, in those instances the *Vaughn* requirements are inappropriate. The FOIA should be amended to prohibit disclosure of personal information unless the subject of the data is given notice and an opportunity to be heard. See *HEW Report, supra* note 1, at 35-36; O'Reilly, *supra* note 228. For a discussion of *Vaughn,* see 87 *Harv. L. Rev.* 854 (1974).

236.   See *Charles River Park "A", Inc.* v. *Department of HUD,* 519 F.2d 935 (D.C. Cir. 1975); *Moore-McCormack Lines, Inc.* v. *I.T.O. Corp.,* 508 F.2d 945, 950 (4th Cir. 1974); Davis, *supra* note 197, at 76 ("[t]he exemptions protect against required disclosure, not against disclosure"). Although the question has been sparsely litigated, the legislative history supports the view that agencies have discretion to release exempt information. See S. Rep. No. 93-854, 93d Cong., 2d Sess. (1974) 6: "Congress did not intend the exemptions . . . to be used either to prohibit disclosure of information or to justify automatic withholding of information. Rather, they are only permissive." See also Project, *supra* note 12, at 158-60; Note, "Access to Broadcasters' Financial Statements Filed with the FCC: The Freedom of Information Act Alternative," *supra* note 197, at 157; Note, "Freedom of Information: The Statute and the Regulations," 56 *Geo.* L.J. 18, 28 (1967). But see note 237 *infra.*

237.   See *Continental Oil Co.* v. *FPC,* 519 F.2d 31, 35-36 (5th Cir. 1975) (agency cannot always disclose even if subject to exemption); *Westinghouse Elec. Corp.* v. *Schlesinger,* 392 F. Supp. 1246, 1250 (E.D. Va. 1974); *McCoy* v. *Weinberger,* 386 F. Supp. 504, 506 (W.D. Ky. 1974).

238.   See *Charles River Park "A" Inc.* v. *HUD,* 519 F.2d 935 (D.C. Cir. 1975); *Babcock & Wilcox Co.* v. *Rumsfeld,* 70 F.R.D. 595 (N.D. Ohio 1976); *Westinghouse Elec. Corp.* v. *Schlesinger,* 392 F. Supp. 1246 (E.D. Va. 1974); *Neal-Cooper Grain Co.* v. *Kissinger,* 385 F. Supp. 769 (D.D.C. 1974); *Sears Roebuck & Co.* v. *GSA,* 384 F. Supp. 996 (D.D.C.), *stay dissolved,* 509 F.2d 527 (D.C. Cir. 1974); *Hughes Aircraft Co.* v. *Schlesinger,* 384 F. Supp. 292 (C.D. Cal. 1974). For discussion of reverse FOIA suits in general, see Project, *supra* note 12, at 1157-62; Comment, "Reverse-Freedom of Information Act Suits: Confidential Information in Search of Protection," 70 *Nw. U.L. Rev.* 995 (1976).

239.   See Comment, *supra* note 238, at 1000 (no court has denied standing, but no court has considered the problem either).

240.   *Charles River Park "A" Inc.* v. *HUD,* 519 F.2d 935 (D.C. Cir. 1975); *Neal-Cooper Grain Co.* v. *Kissinger,* 385 F. Supp. 769 (D.D.C. 1974) (denial of preliminary injunction); *Sears Roebuck & Co.* v. *GSA,* 384 F. Supp. 996 (D.D.C.), *stay dissolved, 509 F.2d 527 (D.C. Cir. 1974); Hughes Aircraft Co.* v. *Schlesinger,* 384 F. Supp. 292 (C.D. Cal. 1974); *cf. Moore-McCormack Lines, Inc.* v. *I.T.O. Corp.,* 508 F.2d 945, 950 (4th Cir. 1974) (dictum that agencies have complete discretion to release exempt information).

241.   *Charles River Park "A" Inc.* v. *HUD,* 512 F.2d 935, 941-43 (D.C. Cir. 1975); *Babcock & Wilcox Co.* v. *Rumsfeld,* 70 F.R.D. 595, 601 (N.D. Ohio 1976); Comment, *supra* note 238, at 1011-13.

242.   See *Westinghouse Elec. Corp.* v. *Schlesinger,* 392 F. Supp. 1246, 1250 (E.D. Va. 1974) (relying in part on 18 U.S.C. § 1905 (1970) in granting relief in reverse FOIA suit); *Sears Roebuck & Co.* v. *GSA,* 384 F. Supp. 996, 1001-02, *stay dissolved,* 509 F.2d 527 (D.C. Cir. 1974) (rejecting several statutory grounds on which reverse FOIA plaintiff had relied).

243.   In addition to the exemptions, two provisions of the Act authorize agencies to delete identifying details from materials the disclosure of which would otherwise produce an unwarranted invasion of privacy. See 5 U.S.C. § 552(a)(2) & (b) (Supp. V. 1975). The addition to section (b) requires that "[a]ny reasonably segregable

portion of a record shall be provided to any person requesting such record after deletion of the portions which are exempt . . . ." While subsection (b) may permit broader disclosure, it does not alter the exemptions or give agencies a greater incentive to invoke them. For discussion of this provision, see Project, *supra* note 12, at 1046.

244.   Courts have blindly pursued a policy of demanding broad disclosure and have forgotten that "broad disclosure" was merely the means adopted under the FOIA to enable the public to know about *how the Federal Government conducts its activities.* See *HEW Report, supra* note 1, at 64. When that policy mandates the disclosure of personal information which not only fails to further the primary goal of the Act, but also threatens the equally important societal goal of protecting personal privacy, then it is time to re-evaluate that policy. Perhaps, as Judge MacKinnon admonished in his concurring opinion to *Getman* v. *NLRB,* 450 F.2d 670, 681 (D.C. Cir. 1971), amendment of the FOIA is the only alternative:

> [This] is not the sort of disclosure that Congress basically had in mind in enacting the [FOIA]. But in my opinion the Act as it presently exists practically requires the disclosure of [names and addresses] on demand. One need not elaborate on the various abuses that could result if lists of people as classified by the Government for particular purposes became available practically on demand in wholesale lots. If this situation is to be corrected, it will require an amendment to the Act.

For additional arguments in favor of amending the FOIA, see A. Miller, *supra* note 226, at 154-61; A. Westin, *supra* note 2, at 387, "Data Bank Hearings," *supra* note 11, at 826 (statement of A. Westin); Davis, *supra* note 197, at 291.

245.   See note 196 *supra* and accompanying text.

246.   "Data Bank Hearings," *supra* note 11, at 25 (statement of A. Miller).

247.   5 U.S.C. § 552a(b) (Supp. V 1975). See note 84 *supra* and accompanying text.

248.   5 U.S.C. § 552a(b)(2) (Supp. V 1975).

249.   H.R. Rep. No. 93-1416, *supra* note 54, at 3.

250.   S. Rep. No. 93-1183, *supra* note 6, at 71.

> This provision was included to meet the objections of press and media representatives that the statutory right of access to public records and the right to disclosure of government information might be defeated if such restrictions were placed on the public and press. The Committee believed it would be unreasonable and contrary to the spirit of the Freedom of Information Act to attempt keep, [*sic*] an accounting of the nature and purpose of access and disclosures involving the press and public or to impose guarantees of security and confidentiality on the data they acquire.

251.   See 120 *Cong. Rec.* S19,831 (daily ed. Nov. 21, 1974). The provision appeared to have been abandoned; no explanation was given.

252.   See 120 *Cong. Rec.* S21,816 (daily ed. Dec. 17, 1974).

253.   See notes 236-37 *supra* and accompanying text.

254.   See notes 238-42 *supra* and accompanying text.

255.   See note 257 *infra* and accompanying text.

256.   See notes 226-35 *supra* and accompanying text.

257.   See Comment, *supra* note 203, at 627-31.

258.   See notes 147-56 *supra* and accompanying text.

259.   5 U.S.C. § 552a(c) (Supp. V 1975). See note 85 *supra* and accompanying text.

260.   5 U.S.C. § 552a(c)(1) (Supp. V 1975).

261.   The reason given for releasing agencies from the duty to keep an accounting is that it would be contrary to the spirit of the FOIA (see note 250 *supra*); this constitutes no justification at all. Since the public's right to know is the antithesis of the individual's right to privacy, attempts to protect one interest will frequently intrude on the other. The question then should not be "is this provision of the Privacy Act contrary to the FOIA?", but rather "how can we protect privacy without seriously impairing the public's right to know?" When the problem is addressed in this light, the congressional solution embodied in subsections (b)(2) and (c)(1) of the Privacy Act is clearly unsatisfactory.

262.   See notes 133-35 *supra* and accompanying text.

263.   5 U.S.C. § 552a(e)(6) (Supp. V 1975).

264.   *Id.*

265.   See OMB Guidelines, *supra* note 69, at 60.

266.   Most disclosures to which subsection (e)(6) applies, for example, will be required by the FOIA. Nevertheless, subsection (e)(6) is by its terms inapplicable in these instances.

267.   See note 54 *supra* and accompanying text.

268.   See note 196 *supra* and accompanying text.

269.   5 U.S.C. § 552(b)(6) (1970). See notes 205-12 *supra* and accompanying text.

270.   425 U.S. 352 (1976).

271.   *Id.* at 372.

272.   The legislative history states clearly that the Privacy Act was designed to "preserve the *status quo* as interpreted by the courts regarding the disclosure of personal information under [the FOIA]." 120 *Cong. Rec.* S21,816 (daily ed. Dec. 17, 1974). See Project, *supra* note 12, at 1336-40.

273.   See note 235 *supra*.

274.   See 120 *Cong. Rec.* H12,243 (daily ed. Dec. 18, 1974) (remarks of Rep. Moorehead) (discussing significance of Privacy Act).

CHAPTER 3

Government Data Requests

How to Use FOIA and the Privacy Act

On November 2, 1977, the Committee on Government Operations approved and adopted a report entitled "A Citizen's Guide on How To Use the Freedom of Information Act and the Privacy Act in Requesting Government Documents."

Recommendation

The committee recommends the use of this guide by citizens to facilitate the exercise of their rights under the Freedom of Information and Privacy Acts. The committee also recommends that this guide be used by Federal agencies in their training programs for government employees charged with the responsibility of administering these two laws.

Introduction

"[A] people who mean to be their own governors, must arm themselves with the power knowledge gives." James Madison wrote. "A popular government without popular information or the means of acquiring it, is but a prologue to a farce or a tragedy or perhaps both."

The Freedom of Information Act (FOIA) is based upon the presumption that the government and the information of government belong to the people. Consistent with this view is the notion that the proper function of the state in respect to government information is that of custodian in service to society. Yet such a presumption did not always prevail. Prior to the enactment of the Freedom of Information Act in 1966, the burden was on the individual citizen to prove his right to look at government records. Moreover, there were no clearly delineated statutory guidelines to assist the individual seeking information and no judicial remedies for those wrongfully denied access. With the passage of the FOIA, however, the burden of proof was shifted from the individual to the government: the "need to know" standard was replaced by the "right to know" doctrine and the onus was upon the government to justify secrecy rather than the individual to obtain access. In addition, the legislation provided workable standards for what records should be open to public inspection and established judicial remedies for the aggrieved citizen. Above all, the statute made it clear that Federal agencies were hereinafter to provide the fullest possible disclosure of information to the public. In 1974, Congress enacted a series of refining amendments to the act which, among other things, encouraged even more disclosure than the original statute.

In that same year, the Privacy Act was enacted into law. This was the first time in history that Congress gave comprehensive statutory recognition to privacy. The Privacy Act extends the principle underlying the Freedom of Information Act: that government, in its role as custodian of information, is accountable to those it serves. Both acts provide for access to government records. But whereas the FOIA is designed to be used by individuals seeking many kinds of information, the Privacy Act is intended to assist individuals in obtaining information about themselves.

More specifically, the Privacy Act allows an individual to review almost all Federal files pertaining to himself. It requires that these files be accurate, complete, relevant, and up-to-date, and allows the subjects of the files to challenge the accuracy of the information contained in them. It prescribes that information gathered for one purpose not be used for another, and that whenever possible, the information be obtained directly from the individual. And perhaps most important of all, it gives the individual significant control over how information concerning him is used. With certain exceptions, it specifies that records containing personal information about individuals be disclosed to others only with the consent of the individual to whom the record pertains. As with the FOIA, civil remedies are available if an agency refuses access or declines to amend or correct a file.

While the Privacy Act places restrictions on the disclosure of personally identifiable information, it also prescribes that there be no secret record systems on individuals. As with the FOIA, the Privacy Act compels the government to reveal its information resources. Indeed, both these laws derive from the premise that secrecy in government as Chief Justice Warren observed, is "the incubator for corruption." The essential difference between them is that the Privacy Act requires the disclosure of records containing personal information to the individual who is the subject of the record but restricts the disclosure of these records to others, whereas the FOIA requires that all types of information be released to anyone making a request provided that, among other things, it does not violate the privacy of any individual.

This guide explains how to use these two important Federal laws. It is only by exercising our rights that we preserve them. The more we know about these statutes, the more effectively they will serve us. The Freedom of Information Act provides each of us with the opportunity to become better informed about the processes and practices of our government. The Privacy Act allows us to participate in those processes that use personal information in reaching decisions that can affect our lives. These acts were designed to be used by all of us. The committee hopes that this guide will further that end.

Which Act to Use

If you are interested in obtaining documents concerning the general activities of government, you should make your request under the Freedom of Information Act. If, on the other hand, you are seeking access to government records pertaining solely to you, you should make your request under the Privacy Act.

Congress intended that the two acts be considered together in the processing of requests for information. And indeed, many government agencies handle requests under both acts out of the same office. Nevertheless, it is still a good idea to make your request in a way that guarantees you the fullest possible disclosure. Therefore, if after reading this guide on how to use the two acts and noting the exemptions from disclosure which both contain, you are uncertain as to which of the acts will afford you the best results, you would be wise to make your request under both the FOIA and the Privacy Act.

The Freedom of Information Act

Legislative Background

In 1958 Congress enacted a law, introduced in the House by Congressman John Moss and in the Senate by Senator Thomas Hennings, to correct the abuse of the Government's 180-year-old "housekeeping" statute. The Moss-Hennings bill stated that the provisions of the 1789 statute, which permitted department heads to regulate the storage and use of government records, did not authorize withholding information or records from the public. This law produced some improvement with respect to the accessibility of Federal records, but the results were far from dramatic. Most agencies continued to operate in accordance with provisions of section 3 of the Administrative Procedure Act of 1946. This act was considered by many to encourage withholding rather than disclosure. Among other things, it authorized agencies to keep information secret "for good cause found," or where secrecy was in "the public interest," or where the information had a bearing on "any matter relating solely to the internal management of an agency." In addition, an agency was required to furnish information only to "persons properly and directly concerned."

It was not until 1966 that Congress enacted comprehensive legislation to deal with the problem of government secrecy. The Freedom of Information Act of 1966 was milestone legislation that reversed long-standing government information practices. Enacted as an amendment to section 3 of the Administrative Procedure Act, it replaced the vague and general language of that law, and made it clear that it was Congress' intent that "any person" should have access to identifiable records without having to demonstrate a need or even a reason. The burden of proof for withholding information, moreover, was placed on the government. The act also broadened the scope of information available to the public and provided judicial remedies for those wrongfully denied information.

Despite the substantial shift in emphasis brought about by the 1966 Act, some government agencies responded slowly and reluctantly to requests made under the law. In 1972 the House Foreign Operations and Government Information Subcommittee held fourteen days of oversight hearings relating to the administration of the FOIA by Federal agencies and concluded that the "efficient operation of the Freedom of Information Act has been hindered by five years of foot-dragging by the Federal bureaucracy." As a result of its findings, the subcommittee proposed a number of procedural and substantive changes in the law. Two years later, Congress adopted amendments to the 1966 Act over the veto of President Ford. They became law in February 1975.

The 1974 amendments were designed to speed and ease the process of obtaining access to government files. Among other things, they required agencies to publish comprehensive indexes for the administrative processing of requests for information, required that agency fees for locating and copying records be uniform and moderate, and shortened the Government's time for answering complaints brought into court. They also prohibited agencies from withholding entire documents, only parts of which were exempt, by requiring the release of nonexempt portions. In addition, they directed the courts to expedite consideration of FOIA cases, authorized judges to examine withheld documents and make an independent determination as to whether they should be released, and provided for the recovery of attorney fees by requesters who prevailed in litigation.

How to Request Government Documents

Information Available under the Freedom of Information Act

The Freedom of Information Act applies only to documents held by the administrative agencies of the executive branch of the Federal Government. It does not apply to information maintained by the legislative and judicial branches. The executive branch includes executive departments and offices, military departments, government corporations, government controlled corporations, and independent regulatory agencies. All records in possession of these entities must be released to you upon request unless the information falls within one of the nine specific and narrowly drawn categories.[1]

Among other things, the act grants public access to final opinions and orders of agencies, policy statements and interpretations not published in the Federal Register,[2] administrative staff manuals, and government records that affect the public. Presidential papers have not been considered government records and have therefore not been required to be disclosed under the act.

There are many government documents which may be of interest to you. For example:

(1) Reports compiled by the Department of Health, Education, and Welfare concerning conditions in federally supported nursing homes.

(2) Data collected by the Agriculture Department regarding the purity and quality of meat and poultry products and the harmful effects of pesticides.

(3) Records of regulatory agencies concerning such matters as air-pollution control programs, the adverse effects of television violence, and the safety records of airlines.

(4) Test results maintained by departments and agencies concerning the nutritional content of processed foods, the efficacy of drugs, and the safety and efficiency of all makes of automobiles.

(5) Consumer complaints registered with the Federal Trade Commission regarding interstate moving companies, corporate marketing practices, and faulty products.

All this and more is available to you under the Freedom of Information Act. The FOIA does not obligate Federal agencies to do research for you. For example, you cannot expect the agency to analyze documents or to collect information it does not have. However, if the information is on record—a document, a tape recording, a computer printout—the act can help you get it.

The only information that may be withheld under the act is that which falls within nine designated categories. These exemptions from disclosure are discussed under the section entitled "Reasons Why Access May be Denied."

Locating Records

To obtain the information you desire, you should first determine which agency is most likely to have it. The United States Government Manual lists all federal agencies and describes their functions. In addition, it usually lists their local and regional office addresses and telephone numbers. The Manual can be found in most libraries and can be purchased for $6.50 by writing to the Superintendent of Documents, U.S. Government Printing Office, Washington, D.C. 20402. The Congressional Directory can also be of use since, like the Manual, it lists the administrators of the various agencies. This too is available in most public libraries and can be purchased from the Government Printing Office for $6.50.

If you are unable to obtain a copy of the Manual and are unsure of the location of the record or records you want, you should write to the agency you think is most likely to have them. In most cases, if the agency doesn't have the record, it will forward your letter to the appropriate source or tell you whom to write.

If you have reason to believe that a local or field office of a federal agency has the information you are seeking, it may also be helpful to contact that office with regard to your request. Most states have local Federal offices, which are listed in the telephone books of the major cities. Or you can use the regional Federal telephone books, which list the agencies operating in each area along with the names and titles of the policy-level employees. These books can usually be obtained at cost from the regional offices.

Making a Request

When you have accumulated as much information about the record you want as is conveniently available, write a letter. It should be directed to the head of the agency whose address can be found in the Government Manual, the Congressional Directory, or in the list provided in this handbook. Or, you can write to the FOIA Officer of the agency. However, if your telephone calls have uncovered the official directly responsible for the record you want, write to that official. In any event, it is always a good idea to write "Freedom of Information Request" on the bottom left-hand corner of the envelope.

Identify the records you want as accurately as possible. Although you are not required under the FOIA to specify a document by name or title, your request must "reasonably describe" the information sought.[3] The more specific and limited the request, the greater the likelihood that it will be processed expeditiously. This could also result in savings in the cost of searching fees. (See section on fees.)

One of the principal differences between the FOIA and previous laws is that the individual seeking information is not required to demonstrate a need or even a reason for wanting it. But in some instances the probability of getting the information you desire may be enhanced by explaining your reasons for requesting it. Agency officials have the discretionary power to release files even where the law does not require it, and they may be more inclined to disclose information which could be withheld if they understand the uses to which it is to be put.

Fees

The House-Senate conference report on the 1974 amendments to the FOIA made it clear that Congress intended that "fees should not be used for the purpose of discouraging requests for information or as obstacles to disclosure of requested information."

Pursuant to the act, each agency is required to publish a uniform schedule of fees covering all the divisions of the agency. These fees may not exceed the actual costs of searching for and copying the requested documents. Moreover, agencies cannot charge for reviewing documents to determine whether all or portions of them should be withheld. Searching fees run around $5 per hour. The average charge for copying is 10¢ a page for standard size copies of 8 x 11 inches and 8 x 14 inches. Many agencies do not charge anything where the aggregate cost is less than $3 or $4.

If you want a waiver or reduction of the fees, you might benefit by stating your reasons for requesting the information since the act provides that agencies can waive or reduce fees when "furnishing the information can be considered as primarily benefiting the general public." They also have the option to disregard charges for indigent requesters. Another way to save money on reproduction expenses is to ask to see the documents at the agency rather than have copies made. Most agencies will be glad to make the necessary arrangements for this.

Sample Request Letter

Agency Head or FOIA Officer
Title
Name of Agency
Address of Agency
City, State, zip

Re: Freedom of Information Act
Request.

Dear................:

Under the provisions of the Freedom of Information Act, 5 U.S.C. 552, I am requesting access to (identify the records as clearly and specifically as possible).

If there are any fees for searching for, or copying, the records I have requested, please inform me before you fill the request. (Or: . . . please supply the records without informing me if the fees do not exceed $—.)

[Optional] I am requesting this information (state the reason for your request if you think it will assist you in obtaining the information.)

[Optional] As you know, the act permits you to reduce or waive fees when the release of the information is considered as "primarily benefiting the public." I believe that this request fits that category and I therefore ask that you waive any fees.

If all or any part of this request is denied, please cite the specific exemption(s) which you think justifies your refusal to release the information, and inform me of the appeal procedures available to me under the law.

I would appreciate your handling this request as quickly as possible, and I look forward to hearing from you within 10 days, as the law stipulates.

Sincerely,

Signature
Name
Address
City, State, zip

Requirements for Agency Responses

Federal agencies are required to respond to all requests for information within ten working days (excluding Saturdays, Sundays, and holidays) after receipt of the request. If you are in a hurry to get the material, you might want to send your letter by certified mail and ask for a return receipt so you will know when the ten days have run out. If you haven't received a reply by the end of that time (be sure to allow for the return mail), you can write a followup letter or telephone the agency to inquire about the delay.

If an agency runs into difficulty in meeting the 10-day time requirement due to "unusual circumstances,"[4] it must inform you in writing that an extension—not to exceed ten more working days—will be required. Moreover, should your request be denied, the agency must tell you the reasons for the denial and advise you to whom you can appeal within the agency. It must also give you the names and addresses of those responsible for denying the request.

In most cases, agencies will do their best to respond within the designated time periods. However, they may sometimes fail to meet the 10-day guidelines due to substantial backlogs of requests. While it is your right to contest this in court, you should also realize that the Government's failure to comply with the prescribed time limits may not of itself constitute a basis for the release of the records you seek.[5]

Reasons Why Access May Be Denied

Government agencies can refuse to disclose information if it falls within one of nine specified categories. However, the legislative history of the act makes it clear that Congress did not intend for agencies to use these exempt categories to justify the automatic withholding of information. Rather, the exemptions are intended to designate those areas in which, under certain circumstances, information may be withheld. It would be a good idea to familiarize yourself with these general exemptions before making a request so you will know in advance what sort of documents may not be available. It will also help you to understand the reasons agencies give for refusing to release information. The exemptions are usually referred to as (b) (1), (b) (2), etc., in accordance with their designations in the act.

Exemption (b) (1): Classified documents concerning national defense and foreign policy
Exemption (b) (1) relates to documents that are "(A) specifically authorized under criteria established by an Executive order to be kept secret in the interest of national defense or foreign policy and (B) are in fact properly classified pursuant to such Executive order."

This refers to information which is properly classified "Confidential," "Secret," and "Top Secret" under the terms and procedures of the Presidential order establishing the classification system.

The fact that the document you request is classified does not mean, in and of itself, that it will be withheld from you. Upon receipt of your request, the agency concerned will determine whether the document should continue to be classified. If not it will be declassified prior to its release to you. If the agency decides that the classification should be continued, it will notify you accordingly.

The 1974 amendments to the act made it clear that when FOIA requests for classified documents are taken to court, the judge has a duty to determine whether such documents are properly classified. Judges are now authorized to examine the documents in question and make their own independent determination as to whether the claims of national security are justified. The mere fact that information is classified will not automatically exempt it from disclosure. The burden is on the government to convince the court that a document is correctly classified and should be withheld.

While this new procedure involves the courts as well as the executive branch in the classification process, it should be pointed out that in most instances the courts have been reluctant to second-guess the classifications imposed by the Government.

Exemption (b) (2): Internal personnel rules and practices

Exemption (b) (2) covers matters "related solely to the internal personnel rules and practices of an agency."

For the most part, this exemption has been limited by the courts to mean information such as agency rules concerning the employees' use of parking facilities or the management of cafeterias, internal policies with regard to sick leave, vacations, and the like.

The Supreme Court's ruling in *Rose* v. *Department of the Air Force*[6] illustrates how the majority of the courts have construed this provision. In that case, an individual sought access to case summaries of Air Force Academy disciplinary proceedings against cadets. The Court held that the information should be released since it did not relate "solely to the internal personnel rules and practices" of the Academy. In the Court's view, information about the treatment of cadets, whose education is publicly financed and who furnish a good portion of the country's future military leadership, had "substantial potential for public interest outside the Government."

Therefore, if documents affect interests outside the agency or deal with practices and procedures which are not confined to internal rules and practices, they must be released.

Exemption (b) (3): Information exempt under other laws

Exemption (b) (3) protects information "specifically exempted from disclosure by statute (other than section 552b of this title), provided that statute (A) requires the matters be withheld from the public in such a manner as to leave no discretion on the issue, or (B) establishes particular criteria for withholding or refers to particular types of matters to be withheld."

This exemption permits the government to withhold information where other laws clearly require that it be withheld.

The original provision which covered information "specifically exempted from disclosure by statute" was amended in 1976 by language added to the Government in the Sunshine Act (552b of the Administrative Procedure Act as noted above). The 1976 amendment was enacted due to congressional dissatisfaction with the expansive judicial interpretation given to the word "specifically" by the Supreme Court in *FAA* v. *Robertson*.[7] In that case, the Court ruled that, according to the Federal Aviation Act of 1958, the FAA Administrator was permitted to withhold certain information unless disclosure was required "in the interest of the public." The 1976 amendment narrowed this exemption by specifying that it be used only to withhold from the public information required to be withheld by a law containing specific criteria for withholding or designating particular types of information to be withheld.

Examples of the types of information that could be withheld under this exemption include patent applications, income tax returns, and records regarding nuclear testing.

Exemption (b) (4): Confidential business information

Exemption (b) (4) protects from disclosure "trade secrets and commercial or financial information obtained from a person and privileged and confidential."

This exemption pertains to information concerning trade secrets and confidential commercial or financial data. The consensus of judicial opinion is that it does not apply to general information obtained by the Government with the understanding that it will be held in confidence.

Trade secrets data pertain to such things as processes, formulas, manufacturing plans, and chemical compositions.

Commercial and financial information includes corporate sales data, salaries and bonuses of industry personnel, and bids received by corporations in the course of their acquisitions. However, commercial and financial information other than trade secrets can be withheld from disclosure only if it meets certain criteria: it must be privileged and confidential and it must be obtained from a "person" by the Government.

The courts have defined "confidential" information as that information which if disclosed would be likely (1) to impair the government's ability to obtain similar information in the future or (2) harm the competitive position of the person who supplied it.

Information obtained from a "person" includes data supplied by corporations and partnerships as well as individual citizens. It does not apply to records which are generated by the Government such as Government-prepared documents based on Government information.

There have been a number of instances in which corporations that have submitted information to the departments and agencies have later appealed to the courts to issue injunctions against its disclosure to others. These are referred to as "reverse" FOIA cases.

Exemption (b) (5): Internal communications

Exemption (b) (5) applies to "inter-agency or intra-agency memorandums or letters which would not be available by law to a party other than an agency in litigation with the agency."

This exemption was enacted to safeguard the deliberative policymaking processes of government. Congress was concerned that staff assistants and agency personnel might be reluctant to engage in a free exchange of ideas if they knew that all their communications were subject to public disclosure. However, the Supreme Court has drawn a distinction between agency communications prior to the rendering of a decision and communications concerning a decision once it has been made. Memorandums and letters which reflect predecisional attitudes regarding policy alternatives are not required to be disclosed. But communications that relate to decisions already made must be released. In the Court's view, once a policy is adopted, the public has a right to know the basis for that decision.

The Court has also distinguished between purely factual information and information relating to the policymaking process. Factual information must always be disclosed unless it is (1) inextricably intertwined with information concerning a decisionmaking process or is (2) part of a summary of material of an otherwise public record to be used in the agency's deliberative process.

Exemption (b) (6): Protection of privacy

Exemption (b) (6) covers "personnel and medical files and similar files, the disclosure of which would constitute a clearly unwarranted invasion of personal privacy."

This exemption relates to records that contain details about the private lives of individuals. It is the only exemption that allows a balancing of interests between disclosure and nondisclosure. The public's right to know must be weighed against the individual's right to privacy. Therefore, when requesting information of a personal nature, it is always a good idea to give a brief explanation of why you want it unless, of course, it pertains to you.

In attempting to determine what constitutes a "clearly unwarranted invasion of personal privacy," the courts have taken two separate approaches. In some cases, they have balanced the potential severity of the privacy invasion against the general public interest to be served. In others, they have considered the intrusion in relation to the needs and interests of the requester.

Exemption (b) (7): Investigatory files

Exemption (b) (7) exempts from disclosure "investigatory records compiled for law enforcement purposes, but only to the extent that the production of such records would (A) interfere with enforcement proceedings, (B) deprive a person of a right to a fair trial or an impartial adjudication, (C) constitute an unwarranted invasion of personal privacy, (D) disclose the identity of a confidential source and, in the case of a record compiled by a criminal law enforcement authority in the course of a criminal investigation, or by an agency conducting a lawful national security intelligence investigation, confidential information furnished only by the confidential source, (E) disclose investigative techniques and procedures, or (F) endanger the life or physical safety of law enforcement personnel."

The original provision concerning investigatory files was interpreted by the courts to include almost any file which could be labeled "investigatory" in nature. However, the 1974 amendments to the act narrowed the exemption by providing that investigatory records could be withheld only if their release would result in one or more of six specific harms (listed above). The amendments also changed the language of the provision to cover investigatory "records" rather than investigatory "files." The fact that a particular record is an investigatory file does not mean that it is automatically exempt. Each document or part of each document in the file must now be examined to determine whether its disclosure would result in one or more of the six enumerated harms. Moreover, these portions that do not fall within any of these categories must be released.

Exemption (b) (8): Information concerning financial institutions

Exemption (b) (8) exempts from the disclosure requirement matters "contained in or related to examination, operating, or condition reports prepared by, on behalf of, or for the use of, an agency responsible for the regulation or supervision of financial institutions."

This includes, for example, investigatory reports of the Federal Reserve Board concerning Federal banks, documents prepared by the Securities Exchange Commission regarding the New York Stock Exchange, and other similar information.

Exemption (b) (9): Information concerning wells

Exemption (b) (9) exempts from disclosure "geological and geophysical information and data, including maps concerning wells."

This was added as a specific exemption because at the time of the act's passage, it was unclear whether this type of information was covered by the trade-secret provision of the act.

Appeal Procedure

If your request for information is denied, you should send a letter of appeal to the person or office specified in the agency's reply. If for some reason this information is not provided, file your appeal with the head of the agency. Include a copy of the rejection letter along with a copy of your original request, and make as strong a case as possible for your right to know. It is important to clarify the request if the denial indicates some confusion on the part of the agency as to what is being sought.

Although it is not necessary, it will strengthen your appeal if you are able to cite court rulings concerning why the agency's use of a particular exemption to withhold information is inappropriate. Depending upon your need for the information, you might want to consult a lawyer to help you with this. Furthermore, since the chances of getting the information you desire are sometimes enhanced by explaining the reasons for wanting it, you should consider doing this, especially if you have not done so in your initial request. If you plan to pursue the matter in court in the event your appeal is denied, you might also want to include this information in your letter.

Most agency regulations require that appeals be made within thirty days after the individual has been notified that his request has been denied. Therefore, if you decide to file an appeal, you should do so within this time.

The agency is required to respond to an appeal within twenty working days after receiving it. However, if the initial request was answered within the 10-day time period, an extension of up to ten working days may be granted.

If the agency denies your appeal in whole or in part, it must inform you of your right to seek judicial review. If after twenty working days from the time of the agency's receipt of your appeal you have not received a reply, you may take your case to court.

Sample Appeal Letter

Name of Agency Official
Title
Name of Agency
Address of Agency
City, State, zip

Re: Freedom of Information Act Appeal.

Dear . . . . :

This is to appeal the denial of my request for information pursuant to the Freedom of Information Act, 5 U.S.C. 522.

On . . . . (date), I received a letter from . . . . (individual's name) of your agency denying my request for access to . . . . (description of the information sought). I am enclosing a copy of this denial along with a copy of my original request. I trust that upon examination of these communications you will conclude that the information I am seeking should be disclosed.

As provided for in the Act, I will expect to receive a reply within 20 working days.

[Optional] If you decide not to release the requested information, I plan to take this matter to court.

Sincerely,

Signature
Name
Address
City, State, zip

Taking Your Case to Court

If your appeal is rejected and you are willing to invest some time and money to get the information you want, take the case to court. You can file suit in the U.S. District Court in the district where you live or do business or where the agency records are kept. Or you can take the case to the U.S. District Court in the District of Columbia.

If you have a strong case, there is a good possibility that your decision to seek judicial review will itself produce results. Unless the agency withholding the information has a well-founded reason for doing so, it may decide to release it rather than go to court. Under a directive issued by the Attorney General in May of 1977, the burden is on the Federal agencies to convince the Justice Department that they will win FOIA suits before the Department will take their cases.

As a plaintiff under the FOIA, you go into court with the presumption that right is on your side: the burden of proof is on the Government to justify withholding information. Whenever there is a doubt as to which side is right the courts are supposed to rule in favor of disclosure. Moreover, pursuant to the 1974 amendments to the act, judges are authorized to examine the contents of contested documents to determine whether all or any part of them can be withheld. The law requires that "reasonably segregable portions" of the exempt records be released: this means nonexempt portions that are intelligible.

The courts are supposed to expedite FOIA cases and, whenever possible, consider them ahead of other matters. The act also specifies that court costs and attorney fees be awarded if the plaintiff has "substantially prevailed." In other words, if it is clear that the information should have been released to you in the beginning, the government may be required to pay the court costs and your attorney's fees. In addition, if the judge finds that agency officials have acted "arbitrarily and capriciously" in withholding information, the Civil Service Commission may initiate proceedings to determine whether disciplinary action is warranted.

The Privacy Act

Legislative Background

The Privacy Act of 1974 was the culmination of many years of public and congressional concern over the threat posed to individiual privacy by the Federal Government's increasing acquisition of vast quantities of personal information on American citizens. In the 1960's both houses of Congress held numerous hearings and conducted extensive investigations into all aspects of government information-gathering techniques. This included inquiries into such things as the telephone monitoring activities of Federal agencies, the use of "lie detectors" and other privacy-invading procedures for eliciting information from Federal employees, the maintenance of Federal data banks containing large quantities of personal data on individuals, the use of criminal justice information by Federal agencies, and the military surveillance of American citizens.

These investigations, along with others, provided the background for the Privacy Act. Early in 1974, both houses of Congress considered bills which formed the basis of the Act that eventually passed the Congress. Legislation was introduced in the Senate by Senator Sam J. Ervin, Jr., and in the House by Congressman William S. Moorhead. Two separate and divergent measures were passed by these bodies, but the differences were reconciled and the Privacy Act passed the Congress in November 1974. It was signed into law by President Ford on the last day of the year and became effective in September 1975.

The underlying purpose of the Privacy Act is to give citizens more control over what information is collected by the Federal Government about them and how that information is used. The act accomplishes this in five basic ways. It requires agencies to publicly report the existence of all systems of records maintained on individuals. It requires that the information contained in these record systems be accurate, complete, relevant, and up-to-date. It provides procedures whereby individuals can inspect and correct inaccuracies in almost all Federal files about themselves. It specifies that information about an individual gathered for one purpose not be used for another without the individual's consent. And, finally, it requires agencies to keep an accurate accounting of the disclosure of records and, with certain exceptions, to make these disclosures available to the subject of the record. In addition, the bill provides sanctions to enforce these provisions.

How to Request Personal Records

Information Available under the Privacy Act

The Privacy Act applies only to personal records maintained by the executive branch of the Federal Government concerning individual citizens. It does not apply to records held by State and local governments or private organizations. The Federal agencies covered by the act include executive departments and offices, military departments, government corporations, government controlled corporations, and independent regulatory agencies. Subject to specified exceptions, files that are part of a system of records held by these agencies must be made available to the individual subject of the record upon request.[8] A system of records, as defined by the Privacy Act, is a group of records from which information is retrieved by reference to a name or other personal identifier such as a social security number.

The Federal Government is a vast storehouse of information concerning individual citizens. For example:

If you have worked for a Federal agency or Government contractor or have been a member of any branch of the armed services, the Federal Government has a file on you.

If you have participated in any federally financed project, some agency probably has a record of it.

If you have been arrested by local, State, or Federal authorities and your fingerprints were taken, the FBI maintains a record of the arrest.[9]

If you have applied for a government subsidy for farming purposes, the Department of Agriculture is likely to have this information.

If you have received veteran's benefits, such as mortgage or education loans, employment opportunities, or medical services, the Veteran's Administration has a file on you.

If you have applied for or received a student loan or grant certified by the Government, the Department of Health, Education, and Welfare has recorded this information.

If you have applied for or been investigated for a security clearance for any reason, there is a good chance that the Department of Defense has a record of it.

If you have received medicare or social security benefits, the Department of Health, Education, and Welfare has a file on you.

In addition, Federal files on individuals include such items as:

Investigatory reports of the Federal Communications Commission concerning whether individuals holding citizens band and/or amateur radio licenses are violating operating rules.

Records of the Internal Revenue Service listing the names of individuals entitled to undeliverable refund checks.

Records compiled by the State Department regarding the conduct of American citizens in foreign countries.

This is just a fraction of the information held on individual citizens. In fact, if you have engaged in any activity that you think might be of interest to the Federal Government, there is a good chance that some Federal agency has a file on you.

The only information that may be withheld under the act is that which falls within seven designated categories. These exemptions from disclosure are discussed under the section entitled "Reasons Why Access May Be Denied."

Locating Records

If you think that a particular agency maintains records concerning you, you should write to the head of that agency or to the Privacy Act Officer. Agencies are required to inform you, at your request, whether they have files on you.

If you want to make a more thorough search to determine what records other Federal departments may have, you should consult the compilation of Privacy Act notices published annually by the Federal Register. This multivolume work contains descriptions of all Federal record systems: it describes the kinds of data covered by the systems and lists the categories of individuals to whom the information pertains. It also includes the procedures that different agencies follow in helping individuals who request information about their records, and it specifies the agency official to whom you should write to find out whether you are the subject of a file.

The compilation is usually available in large reference, law, and university libraries. It can be purchased from the Superintendent of Documents, Government Printing Office, Washington, D.C. 20402. The cost per volume runs around $6 to $12. If you know which agencies you are interested in, the Superintendent of Documents can help you identify the particular volume or volumes which contain the information you want. However, this word of caution: at the present time, the compilation is poorly indexed and, as a consequence, difficult to use. Therefore, you should examine the work before ordering it.

While it may be helpful to agency officials for you to specify a particular record system which you think contains information concerning you, it is not necessary to provide this information. If you have a general idea of the record you want, don't hesitate to write the agency which you think maintains it.

Making a Request

You can make a request in writing, by telephone, or in person. One advantage to writing is that it enables you to document the dates and contents of the request and the agency's replies. This could be helpful in the event of future disputes. Be sure to keep copies of all correspondence concerning the request.

Your request should be addressed to the head of the agency which maintains the records you want or to the agency official specified in the compilation of Privacy Act notices. (See section on Locating Records.) In any event, be sure to write "Privacy Act Request" on the bottom left-hand corner of the envelope. Along with your name and permanent address, you should always give as much information as possible about the record you are seeking.[10] The more specific the inquiry, the faster you can expect a response. If you want access to a record concerning your application for a Government loan, for example, you should give the date of the application, the place where the application was filed, the specific use to which the loan was put, and any relevant identifying numbers. Of course, if you have used the Federal Register's compilation of notices and identified a particular record system which you think contains information on you, you should cite the system.

Most agencies require some proof of identity before they will release records. Therefore, when making your request, it would be a good idea to provide some identifying data such as a copy of an official document containing your complete name and address. Remember, too, to sign your request since a signature provides a form of identification. You might also want to consider having your signature notarized. If you are seeking access to a record which has something to do with a Government benefit, it could be helpful to give your social security number. Some agencies may request additional information such as a document containing your signature and/or photograph depending upon the nature and sensitivity of the material to be released.

Anyone who "knowingly and willfully" requests or receives access to a record about an individual "under false pretenses" is subject to criminal penalties. This means that a person can be prosecuted for deliberately attempting to obtain someone else's record.

Fees

Under the Privacy Act, agencies are permitted to charge fees to cover the actual costs of copying records. However, they are not allowed to charge for the time spent in locating records or in preparing them for your inspection. Copying fees are about 10 cents a page for standard size copies of 8 x 11 inches and 8 x 14 inches.

As mentioned above, fees for locating files can be charged for requests processed under the Freedom of Information Act. Therefore, if you seek access to records under the Privacy Act which can be withheld under the act but are available under the FOIA, you could be charged searching fees. However, as noted elsewhere in this guide, the legislative histories of both the FOIA and the Privacy Act clearly indicate that Congress intended that access to records not be obstructed by costs. Consequently, if you feel that an agency's fees are beyond your means, you should ask for a reduction or waiver of the charges when making your request.

Sample Request Letter

Agency Head or Privacy Act Officer
Title
Agency
Address of Agency
City, State, zip

Re: Privacy Act Request.

Dear ....:

Under the provisions of the Privacy Act of 1974, 5 U.S.C. 522a, I hereby request a copy of (or: access to) .... (describe as accurately and specifically as possible the record or records you want, and provide all the relevant information you have concerning them).

If there are any fees for copying the records I am requesting, please inform me before you fill the request. (Or: .... please supply the records without informing me if the fees do not exceed $ — .)

If all or any part of this request is denied, please cite the specific exemption(s) which you think justifies your refusal to release the information. Also, please inform me of your agency's appeal procedure.

In order to expedite consideration of my request, I am enclosing a copy of . . . . (some document of identification).

Thank you for your prompt attention to this matter.

Sincerely,

Signature
Name
Address
City, State, zip

Requirements for Agency Responses

Unlike the Freedom of Information Act, which requires agencies to respond within ten working days after receipt of a request, the Privacy Act imposes no time limits for agency responses. However, the guidelines for implementing the act's provisions recommended by the executive branch state that a request for records should be acknowledged within ten working days of its receipt. Moreover, the acknowledgment should indicate whether or not access will be granted and, if so, when and where. The records themselves should be produced within thirty working days. And, if this is not possible, the agency should tell you the reason and advise you when it is anticipated that access will be granted.

Most agencies will do their best to comply with these recommendations. Therefore, it is probably advisable to bear with some reasonable delay before taking further action.

Disclosure of Records

Agencies are required to release records to you in a form that is "comprehensible." This means that all computer codes and unintelligible notes must be translated into understandable language.

You can examine your records in person or have copies of them mailed to you, whichever you prefer. If you decide that you want to see the records at the agency and for some reason the agency is unable to provide for this, then you cannot be charged copying fees if the records are later mailed to you.

If you view the records in person, you are entitled to take someone along with you. If you do this, you will probably be asked to sign a statement authorizing the agency to disclose and discuss the record in the other person's presence.

Special rules apply to the release of medical records. In most cases, when you request to see your medical record, you will be permitted to view it directly. However, if it appears that the information contained in it could have an "adverse effect" on you, the agency may give it to someone of your choice, such as your family doctor, who would be willing to review its contents and discuss them with you.

Reasons Why Access May Be Denied

Under the Privacy Act, certain systems of records can be exempted from disclosure. Agencies are required to publish annually in the Federal Register the existence and characteristics of all record systems, including those which have been exempted from access. However, records declared exempt are not necessarily beyond your reach, since agencies do not always use the exemptions they have claimed. Therefore, don't hesitate to request any record you want. The burden is on the agency to justify withholding any information from you.

You should familiarize yourself with these exemptions before making a request so you will know in advance what kind of documents may not be available. It will also help you to understand the reasons agencies give for refusing to release information.

General Exemptions

The general exemptions apply only to the Central Intelligence Agency and criminal law enforcement agencies. The records held by these agencies can be exempt from more provisions of the act than those maintained by other agencies. However, even the systems of these agencies are subject to many of the act's basic provisions: (1) the existence and characteristics of all record systems must be publicly reported; (2) subject to specified exceptions, no personal records can be disclosed to other agencies or persons without the prior consent of the individual to whom the record pertains; (3) all disclosures must be accurately accounted for; (4) records which are disclosed must be accurate, relevant, up-to-date, and complete; and (5) no records describing how an individual exercises his first amendment rights can be maintained unless such maintenance is authorized by statute or by the individual to whom it pertains or unless it is relevant to and within the scope of an authorized law enforcement activity.

General exemptions are referred to as (j) (1) and (j) (2) in accordance with their designations in the act.

Exemption (j) (1): Files maintained by the CIA. Exemption (j) (1) covers records "maintained by the Central Intelligence Agency." This exemption permits the heads of the Central Intelligence Agency to exclude certain systems of records within the agency from many of the act's requirements. The provisions from which the systems can be exempted are primarily those permitting individual access. Consequently, in most instances, you would probably not be allowed to inspect and correct records about yourself maintained by this agency. Congress permitted the exemption of these records from access because CIA files often contain highly sensitive information regarding national security. Nevertheless, you should always bear in mind that agencies are not required to invoke all the exemptions allowed them. Therefore, if you really want to see a record containing information about you that is maintained by this agency, go ahead and make your request.

Exemption (j) (2): Files maintained by Federal criminal law enforcement agencies. Exemption (j) (2) covers records "maintained by an agency or component thereof which performs as its principal function any activity pertaining to the enforcement of criminal laws, including police efforts to prevent, control, or reduce crime or to apprehend criminals, and the activities of prosecutors, courts, correctional, probation, pardon, or parole authorities, and which consist of (A) information compiled for the purpose of identifying individual criminal offenders and alleged offenders and consisting only of identifying data and notations of arrests, the nature and disposition of criminal charges, sentencing, confinement, release, and parole and probation status; (B) information compiled for the purpose of a criminal investigation, including reports of informants and investigators, and associated with an identifiable individual; or (C) reports indentifiable to an individual compiled at any stage of the process of enforcement of the criminal laws from arrest or indictment through release from supervision."

This exemption would permit the heads of criminal law enforcement agencies such as the FBI, the Drug Enforcement Administration, and the Immigration and Naturalization Service to exclude certain systems of records from many of the act's requirements. As with the CIA, the allowed exemptions are primarily those permitting individual access. However, many agencies do not always use the exemptions avilable to them. Remember, too, the act explicitly states that records available under the FOIA must also be available under the Privacy Act. And under the FOIA, the CIA and FBI and other federal agencies are required to release all nonexempt portions of their intelligence and investigatory files. Nevertheless, even though Congress intended that Privacy Act requests be coordinated with FOIA provisions, it is still a good idea to cite these acts when seeking information of an intelligence or investigatory nature.

Specific Exemptions

There are seven specific exemptions which apply to all agencies. Under specified circumstances, agency heads are permitted to exclude certain record systems from the access and challenge provisions of the act. However, even exempted systems are subject to many of the act's requirements. In addition to the provisions listed under General Exemptions (which apply to all record systems), a record system that falls under any one of the seven specific exemptions (listed below) is subject to the following requirements: (1) information that might be used to deny a person a right, benefit, or privilege must, whenever possible, be collected directly from the individual; (2) individuals asked to supply information must be informed of the authority for collecting it, the purposes to which it will be put, and whether or not the imparting of it is voluntary or mandatory; (3) individuals must be notified when records concerning them are disclosed in accordance with a compulsory legal process, such as a court subpoena; (4) agencies must notify persons or agencies who have previously received information about an individual of any corrections or disputes over the accuracy of the information; (5) and all records must be accurate, relevant, up-to-date, and complete.[11]

Record systems which fall within the seven exempt categories are also subject to the civil remedies provisions of the act. Therefore, if an agency denies you access to a record in an exempt record system or refuses to amend a record in accordance with your request, you can contest these actions in court. You can also bring suit against the agency if you are denied a right, benefit, or privilege as a result of records which have been improperly maintained. These remedies are not available under the general exemptions.

Specific exemptions are referred to as (k) (1), (k) (2), etc., in accordance with their designations in the act.

Exemption (k) (1): Classified documents concerning national defense and foreign policy. Exemption (k) (1) covers records "subject to the provisions of section 552 (b) (1) of this title."

This refers to the first exemption of the Freedom of Information Act which excepts from disclosure records "(A) specifically authorized under criteria established by an Executive order to be kept secret in the interest of national defense or foreign policy and (B) are in fact properly classified pursuant to such Executive order." (For further discussion of the provision, see Exemption 1: Classified documents concerning national defense and foreign policy under the FOIA section of this guide.)

Exemption (k) (2): Investigatory material compiled for law enforcement purposes. Exemption (k) (2) pertains to "investigatory material compiled for law enforcement purposes, other than material within the scope of subsection (j)

(2) of this section: Provided, however, that if any individual is denied any right, privilege, or benefit that he would otherwise be entitled by Federal law, or for which he would otherwise be eligible, as a result of the maintenance of such material, such material shall be provided to such individual, except to the extent that the disclosure of such material would reveal the identity of a source who furnished information to the Government under an express promise that the identity of the source would be held in confidence, or, prior to the effective date of this section, under an implied promise that the identity of the source would be held in confidence."

This applies to investigatory materials compiled for law enforcement purposes by agencies whose principal function is other than criminal law enforcement. Included are such items as files maintained by the Internal Revenue Service concerning taxpayers who are delinquent in filing Federal tax returns, records compiled by the Customs Bureau on narcotic suspects, investigatory reports of the Federal Deposit Insurance Corporation regarding banking irregularities, and files maintained by the Securities Exchange Commission on individuals who are being investigated by the agency.

Such files cannot be withheld from you, however, if they are used to deny you a benefit, right, or privilege to which you are entitled by law unless their disclosure would reveal the identity of a confidential source. You should always bear in mind that Congress intended that information available under either the FOIA or the Privacy Act be disclosed. Moreover, since the FOIA requires agencies to release all nonexempt portions of a file, some of the information exempted under this provision might be obtainable under the FOIA. In any event, as mentioned above, when seeking information of an investigatory nature, it is a good idea to request it under both acts.

Exemption (k) (3): Secret Service intelligence files. Exemption (k) (3) covers records "maintained in connection with providing protective services to the President of the United States or other individuals pursuant to section 3056 of title 18."

This exemption pertains to files held by the Secret Service that are necessary to insure the safety of the President and other individuals under Secret Service protection.

Exemption (k) (4): Files used solely for statistical purposes. Exemption (k) (4) applies to records "required by statute to be maintained and used solely as statistical records."

This includes such items as Internal Revenue Service files regarding the income of selected individuals used in computing national income averages, and records on births and deaths maintained by the Department of Health, Education, and Welfare for compiling vital statistics.

Exemption (k) (5): Investigatory material used in making decisions concerning Federal employment, military service, Federal contracts, and security clearances. Exemption (k) (5) relates to "investigatory material compiled solely for the purpose of determining suitability, eligibility, or qualifications for Federal civilian employment, military service, Federal contracts, or access to classified information, but only to the extent that the disclosure of such material would reveal the identity of a source who furnished information to the Government under an express promise that the identity of the source would be held in confidence, or, prior to the effective date of this section, under an implied promise that the identity of the source would be held in confidence."

This exemption applies only to investigatory records which would reveal the identity of a confidential source. Since it is not customary for agencies to grant pledges of confidentiality in collecting information concerning employment, Federal contracts, and security clearances, in most instances these records would be available.

Exemption (k) (6): Testing or examination material used solely for employment purposes. Exemption (k) (6) covers "testing or examination material used solely to determine individual qualifications for appointment or promotion in the Federal service the disclosure of which would compromise the objectivity or fairness of the testing or examination process."

This provision permits agencies to withhold information concerning the testing process that would give an individual an unfair competitive advantage. It applies solely to information that would reveal test questions and answers or testing procedures.

Exemption (k) (7): Evaluation material used in making decisions regarding promotions in the armed services. Exemption (k) (7) pertains to "evaluation material used to determine potential for promotion in the armed services, but only to the extent that the disclosure of such material would reveal the identity of a source who furnished information to the Government under an express promise that the identity of the source would be held in confidence, or, prior to the effective date of this section, under an implied promise that the identity of the source would be held in confidence."

This exemption is used solely by the Armed services. Moreover, due to the nature of the military promotion process where numerous individuals compete for the same job, it is often necessary to grant pledges of confidentiality in collecting information so that those questioned about potential candidates will feel free to be candid in their assessments. Therefore, efficiency reports and other materials used in making decisions about military promotions may be difficult to get. But always remember, when seeking information of an investigatory nature, it is a good idea to request it under both the Privacy Act and the FOIA.

Appeal Procedure for Denial of Access

Unlike the FOIA, the Privacy Act provides no standard procedure for appealing denials to release information. However, many agencies have their own regulations governing this. If your request is denied, the agency should advise you of its appeal procedure and tell you to whom to address your appeal. If this information is not provided, you should send your letter to the head of the agency. Include a copy of the rejection letter along with a copy of your original request and state your reason for wanting access, if you think it will help.

If an agency withholds all or any part of your record, it must tell you which Privacy Act exemption it is claiming as a justification. It should also advise you why it believes the record can be withheld under the Freedom of Information Act since Congress intended that information sought under either the Privacy Act or the FOIA be released unless it could be withheld under both acts. Therefore, in making your appeal, it would be a good idea to cite both the FOIA and the Privacy Act. Moreover, if you are able to do so, it might also help you to explain why you think the exemptions used to refuse you access are unjustified.

Sample Letter for Appealing Denial of Access

Agency Head or Appeal Officer
Title
Agency
Agency Address
City, State, zip

Re: Privacy Act Appeal.

Dear . . . . :

On . . . . (date), I received a letter from . . . . (individual's name) of your agency denying my request for access to . . . . (description of the information sought). Enclosed is a copy of this denial along with a copy of my original request. By this letter, I am appealing the denial.

Since Congress intended that information sought under the Privacy Act of 1974, 5 U.S.C. 552a, be released unless it could be withheld under both this Act and the Freedom of Information Act, FOIA 5 U.S.C. 552, I hereby request that you also refer to the FOIA in consideration of this appeal.

[Optional] I am seeking access to these records (state the reasons for your request if you think it will assist you in obtaining the information and give any arguments you might have to justify its release).

Thank you for your prompt attention to this matter.

Sincerely,

Signature
Name
Address
City, State, zip

Amending Your Records

The Privacy Act requires agencies to keep all personal records on individuals accurate, complete, up-to-date, and relevant. Therefore, if after seeking your record, you wish to correct, delete, or add information to it, you should write to the agency official who released the information to you, giving the reasons for the desired changes as well as any documentary evidence you might have to justify the changes. Some agencies may allow you to request these corrections in person or by telephone.

While you should have no trouble in determining whether or not the information contained in your file is accurate, complete, and up-to-date, it might be somewhat more difficult to ascertain whether it is "relevant" to the agency's purpose. However, if you have doubts about anything you find in your records, you should challenge the information and force the agency to justify its retention in your file. There is one thing in particular you might look for: the Privacy Act prohibits the maintenance of information concerning how an individual exercises his first amendment rights unless (1) the maintenance is authorized by statute or the individual to whom it pertains, or (2) unless it is pertinent to and within the scope of an authorized law enforcement activity. In most instances, you would be on solid ground in challenging any information in your file describing your religious and political beliefs, activities, and associations, unless you have voluntarily given this information to the agency.

The act requires agencies to acknowledge in writing all requests for amending records within ten working days of their receipt. In addition, individuals must be notified what action will be taken regarding the requested amendments. Moreover, agencies are directed to complete action on all requests within thirty working days of their receipt.

If the agency agrees to amend your record, it must notify all past and future recipients of the changes made. However, unless the agency has kept some record of disclosures prior to September 27, 1975—the date the act went into effect—it might not be possible for it to notify all prior recipients.

Sample Letter for Request to Amend Records

Agency Head or Privacy Officer
Title
Agency
Agency Address
City, State, zip

Re: Privacy Act Request to
Amend Records.

Dear . . . .

By letter dated . . . . , I request access to (use same description as in request letter).

In reviewing the information forwarded to me, I found that it was (inaccurate) (incomplete) (outdated) (not relevant to the purpose of your agency).

Therefore, pursuant to the Privacy Act of 1974, 5 U.S.C. 552a, I hereby request that you amend my record in the following manner:
(Describe errors, new information, irrelevance, etc.)

In accordance with the Act, I look forward to an acknowledgment of this request within 10 working days of its receipt.

Thank you for your assistance in this matter.

Sincerely,

Signature
Name
Address
City, State, zip

Appeal Procedure for Agency Refusal to Amend Records

If an agency refuses to amend your records, it must advise you of the reasons for the refusal as well as the appeal procedures available to you within the agency. It must also tell you to whom to address your appeal. Amendment appeals are usually handled by agency heads or a senior official appointed by the agency head.

Your appeal letter should include a copy of your original request along with a copy of the agency's denial. You should also include any additional information you might have to substantiate your claims regarding the disputed material.

A decision on your appeal must be rendered within thirty working days from the date of its receipt. In unusual circumstances, such as the need to obtain information from retired records or another agency, an additional thirty days may be granted.

If the agency denies your appeal and still refuses to make the changes you request, you have the right to file a brief statement giving your reasons for disputing the record. This statement of disagreement then becomes part of the record and must be forwarded to all past and future recipients of your file. However, as previously noted, unless the agency has kept some record of disclosures prior to September 27, 1975, it might not be possible to notify all past recipients. The agency is also permitted to place in your file a short explanation of its refusal to change the record. This, too, becomes a part of your permanent file and is forwarded along with your statement of disagreement.

If your appeal is denied or if the agency fails to act upon it within the specified time, you can take your case to court.

Sample Letter for Appealing Agency's Refusal to Amend Records

Agency Head or Designated Official
Title
Agency
Agency Address
City, State, zip

Re: Privacy Act Appeal.

Dear ....:

By letter dated .... to Mr. .... (official) to whom you addressed your amendment request), I requested that information held by your agency concerning me be amended. This request was denied, and I am hereby appealing that denial. For your information, I am enclosing a copy of my request letter along with a copy of Mr. ....'s reply. (If you have any additional relevant information, send it too.)

I trust that upon consideration of my reasons for seeking the desired changes, you will grant my request to amend the disputed material. However, in the event you refuse this request, please advise me of the agency procedures for filing a statement of disagreement.

[Optional] I plan to initiate legal action if my appeal is denied.

Thank you for your prompt attention to this matter.

Sincerely,

Signature
Name
Address
City, State, zip

Taking Your Case to Court

Under the Privacy Act, you can sue an agency for refusing to release your records, for denial of your appeal to amend a record, and for failure to act upon your appeal within the designated time. You can also sue if you are adversely affected by the agency's failure to comply with any of the provisions of the act. For example, if you are denied a job promotion due to inaccurate, incomplete, outdated, or irrelevant information in your file, you can contest this action in court.

While the Freedom of Information Act requires individuals to use agency appeal procedures before seeking judicial review, the Privacy Act permits individuals to appeal denials of access directly to the courts (although most agencies have their own appeal procedures and you should use them when available). On the other hand, you are required by the act to use administrative appeal procedures in contesting agency refusals to amend your records.

Judicial rulings favorable to you could result in the release or amendment of the records in question. In addition, you can obtain money damages if it is proven that you have been adversely affected as a result of the agency's intentional and willful disregard of the act's provisions. You might also be awarded court costs and attorney fees.

The act provides criminal penalties for the knowing and willful disclosure of personal records to those not entitled to receive them, for the knowing and willful failures to publish the existence and characteristics of all record systems, and for the knowing and willful attempt to gain access to an individual's records under false pretenses.

If and when you do decide to go to court, you can file suit in the federal district court where you reside or do business or where the agency records are situated. Or you can take the case to the U.S. District Court in the District of Columbia. Under the Privacy Act, you are required to bring suit within two years from the date of the violation you are challenging. However, in cases where the agency has materially or willfully misrepresented information, the statute of limitations runs two years from the date you discover the misrepresentation. As with lawsuits brought under the FOIA, the burden is on the agency to justify its refusal to release or amend records.

The same advice applies here as with suits filed under the FOIA: if you go to court, you should consult a lawyer. If you cannot afford private counsel, contact your local legal aid society.

Other Rights Provided under the Privacy Act

One of the most important provisions of the Privacy Act is the one that requires agencies to obtain an individual's written permission prior to disclosing to other persons or agencies information concerning him, unless such disclosures are specifically authorized under the act. Information can be disclosed without an individual's consent under the following circumstances: to employees and officers of the agency maintaining the records who have a need for the information in order to perform their duties; if the information is required to be disclosed under the FOIA; for "routine uses," i.e., uses which are compatible with the purpose for which the information was collected;[12] to the Census Bureau; to the National Archives; to a law enforcement agency upon the written request of the agency head; to individuals acting in behalf of the health or safety of the subject of the record; to Congress; to the General Accounting Office; or pursuant to court order. In all other circumstances, however, the individual who is the subject of the record must give his written consent before an agency can divulge information concerning him to others.

Under the act, you are also entitled to know to whom information about you has been sent. Agencies must keep an accurate accounting of all disclosures made to other agencies or persons except those required under the FOIA. Moreover, this information must be maintained for at least five years or until the record disclosed is destroyed, whichever is longer. With the exception of disclosures requested by law enforcement agencies, a list of all recipients of information concerning you must be made available upon request. Therefore, if you are interested in knowing who has received records about you, you should write to the Privacy Act officer or the head of the agency that maintains the records and request that an accounting of disclosures be sent to you.

Finally, the Privacy Act places a moratorium upon any new uses of your social security number by Federal, State, and local government agencies after January 1, 1975.[13] No agency may deny you a right, benefit, or privilege to which you are entitled by law because of your refusal to disclose your number unless the disclosure is specifically authorized by statute or regulation adopted before January 1, 1975, or by a later act of Congress. Moreover, in requesting your social security number, agencies are required to tell you whether the disclosure is mandatory or voluntary, under what law or regulation the request is authorized, and what uses will be made of the number.

You should bear in mind, however, that this provision applies only to government agencies. It does not apply to the private sector: requests for your social security number by private organizations are not prohibited by law.

Notes

1.   The FOIA can be used by any member of the general public including noncitizens.
2.   The Federal Register is a government document, issued daily, in which government agencies publish their regulations implementing acts of Congress along with other notices of public interest. It also lists Executive orders and Presidential proclamations.
3.   The report of the House Government Operations Committee defines "reasonably describes" by stating that a description "would be sufficient if it enabled a professional employee of the agency who was familiar with the subject area of the request to locate the record with a reasonable amount of effort." (H.R. No. 93–876, 1974, p. 6).
4.   Under the provisions of the act, "unusual circumstances" involve such things as collecting records from field offices or other establishments, reviewing a voluminous amount of material, and consulting with another agency in order to fill the request.
5.   In July 1976, the U.S. Court of Appeals for the District of Columbia ruled that the time requirements of the FOIA are "not mandatory but directory" when certain conditions are met. If an agency can show that it is "deluged" with requests "vastly in excess" of what Congress anticipated, that the resources are "inadequate" to deal with this volume, and that "due diligence" is being exercised in processing the request, time extensions will be permitted. *Open America* v. *Watergate Special Prosecution Force*, 547 F.2d 605 (D.C. Cir. 1976).
6.   96 S.Ct. 1592, 425 U.S. 352, 48 L.Ed.2d 11 (1976).
7.   422 U.S. 255 (1975).
8.   Unlike the FOIA—which applies to anyone making a request including foreigners as well as American citizens—the Privacy Act applies only to American citizens and aliens lawfully admitted for permanent residence.
9.   If an individual is arrested more than once, he builds up a criminal history called a rap sheet. Rap sheets chronologically list all fingerprint submissions by local, State, and Federal agencies. They also contain the charges lodged against the individual and what disposition is made of the case if the arresting agency supplies this information. You can get a copy of your rap sheet by forwarding to the Identification Division of the FBI in Washington, D.C., a set of rolled-inked fingerprint impressions along with $5 in the form of a certified check or money order made out to the Treasury of the United States.

10.   If you were using a different name at the time the record was compiled, be sure to provide this information.

11.   This provision differs from the one pertaining to all record systems which requires that records which are disclosed be accurate, relevant, up-to-date, and complete. Record systems which are subject to the seven specific exemptions must at all times be accurate, relevant, up-to-date, and complete.

12.   All Federal agencies must publish annually in the Federal Register the "routine uses" of the information they maintain.

13.   This is the only provision in the Privacy Act which applies to State and local as well as Federal agencies.

CHAPTER 4

Business Data Requests

How to Use FOIA and Reverse-FOIA Action

This report, approved and adopted by the Committee on Government Operations July 19, 1978, presents an in-depth examination of the following information regarding FOIA requests for business data and reverse-FOIA action available when disclosure has been denied:

A Brief History of the Fourth Exemption of the FOIA   *page 137*

Agency Procedures for Processing Requests for Business Information
  page 145

Reverse-Freedom of Information Cases   *page 173*

Summary of Findings and Recommendations

A portrayal of every private enterprise of any consequence lies in Government files, frequently unassembled like pieces of a picture puzzle. Collection and maintenance of such information is a universal characteristic of Government operations that regulate private industry, license commercial activities, purchase and sell goods and services, and deal in numerous other ways with the Nation's businesses.

The Freedom of Information Act allows public access to much of the information accumulated by the Federal Government. This access enables interest groups, news media, business, and others to evaluate the Government's performance. The information may also reflect on the operations of private businesses.

Understandably, firms that submit confidential documents to Federal agencies have expressed concern about their release. While competitively harmful business information may be withheld under the Freedom of Information Act, other data may legitimately be sought and publicly released.

Business's concern is not merely theoretical—numerous disputes and court cases have arisen over the release of such information.

The committee concludes that the major problem in handling the disclosure of business information concerns the procedure by which agencies decide what data to release or withhold. This report is thus primarily concerned with the process of identifying and separating confidential information. Disclosure of business data has caused some administrative difficulty, but the committee has found no major abuses.

Substantial competitive harm test. Exemption 4 of the Freedom of Information Act—which permits Federal agencies to withhold trade secrets and confidential business information—is the broadest FOIA exemption applicable to records acquired from business enterprises. What constitutes withholdable confidential business information hinges on the interpretation of Exemption 4.

A number of tests for confidentiality were adopted and then abandoned by the courts. The test now used by courts and agencies is generally referred to as the "substantial competitive harm test." Under this test, commercial or financial information may be withheld under Exemption 4 if disclosure is likely to: (1) impair the Government's ability to obtain necessary information in the future; or (2) cause substantial harm to the competitive position of the person from whom the information was obtained. While this test has been criticized by some, it appears to be the best formulation to date.

Processing FOIA requests. Many difficulties with Exemption 4 have been procedural rather than substantive. Agency procedures for deciding requests for business data have not always been suited to the fourth exemption and have not always adequately recognized the interests of the data submitter or the data requester. There are a number of procedural alternatives including the five described below. The committee recommends the adoption of some in whole and some in part.

Notice to the submitter. It is consistent with basic notions of fairness that a corporate submitter be given some form of notice about the pending release of information it supplied the Government. Notice permits a submitter to explain the need for confidential treatment of data, and allows an opportunity to challenge the release in court. The committee recommends that each agency select and formally adopt a method of predisclosure notification to submitters most suitable to the agency's own circumstances, records, and FOIA caseload. Notice does not necessarily have to be provided each time a request is received for business records; ways to minimize the administrative burden are detailed in the report.

Identification of confidential information by the submitter. A requirement that confidential records be marked by the submitter at the time they are filed with the Government may help agencies narrow the amount of data whose confidentiality is later called into dispute. A submitter's confidentiality marking would not be binding on an agency but would clearly identify those portions that are not confidential and that could be publicly released without further review. The committee recommends that each agency evaluate the possible benefits of requiring the marking of confidential information by the submitter. The committee recognizes that this procedure may not be advantageous for all agencies or for all types of records.

Determination of confidentiality by agencies at the time of submission. Some agencies have adopted a limited practice of ruling on the confidentiality of a business's records at the time of submission. The committee does not recommend the use of this procedure because information loses its confidential nature over time, and it is rarely possible to adequately determine confidentiality in advance of the receipt of an actual Freedom of Information Act request. Advance determinations may also waste agency resources and bypass the FOIA's requirements that disclosable portions of records be segregated from nondisclosable parts. Agencies using advance determination procedures should only apply them to information that is voluntarily submitted or that would normally be placed in a public file. In addition, submitters should always be informed that these advance determinations of confidentiality are not final and are subject to change at any time.

Substantive disclosure rules. The committee recommends that agencies review their experience with FOIA requests for business documents in order to identify classes of documents that do not contain confidential information. Agencies should formally adopt substantive rules providing for the disclosure of such documents. Disclosure rules can simplify the FOIA decision process by identifying nonconfidential material that can be released on request. Submitters can challenge the validity of the disclosure categories when rules are published and avoid separate suits each time disclosure is requested. Because of the difficulty of deciding in advance whether it is appropriate to grant confidential treatment, however, no rules should be issued providing that specified categories of business documents are automatically exempt from disclosure.

The committee also recommends that the Office of Federal Procurement Policy consider whether detailed uniform disclosure provisions could be included in procurement regulations.

Agency proceedings. The committee recommends that agencies institute an informal proceeding consisting of written pleadings and affidavits for FOIA requests involving records that may be confidential under Exemption 4. Such a proceeding will permit the compilation of a record of the agency decision that can be used if the submitter later sues to block a disclosure determination. A proceeding will also allow the submitter a more complete opportunity to justify the need for confidentiality. Again, the number of FOIA releases disputed is limited, and the administrative burden of such proceeding should not be excessive.

Reverse FOIA cases. A "reverse Freedom of Information Act" lawsuit arises when submitters sue to prevent agencies from releasing documents under FOIA. Nothing in the FOIA specifically authorizes these lawsuits. They have developed in response to a need to allow submitters to argue for the protection of information they have provided the Government. As a result of the lack of statutory guidance, however, the courts have differed on a number of significant procedural matters.

The courts have found jurisdiction for reverse-FOIA lawsuits under several different laws, but the general Federal jurisdiction statute, 28 U.S.C. 1361, appears adequate.

A cause of action for a reverse-FOIA lawsuit clearly arises under the Administrative Procedure Act. However, some submitters have successfully argued that a cause of action arises under the FOIA, the Trade Secrets Act (18 U.S.C. § 1905), or other laws. In the event that the decision of the Supreme Court in *Chrysler* v. *Schlesinger* does not resolve this issue with sufficient clarity, the committee recommends that a specific cause of action for reverse-FOIA lawsuits be established by Congress.[1a]

The scope of judicial review of an agency's decision to disclose records has been a major procedural issue in reverse-FOIA cases. The FOIA provides for de novo examination of the disclosure issue when a requester sues to obtain documents that have been denied. This requires the court to make its own independent decision rather than to simply review the agency's decision. The act is silent on the scope of the court's review in reverse-FOIA cases. The committee believes that existing law requires a court in a reverse-FOIA case to review the agency record and determine only whether the agency as acted arbitrarily or capriciously under the standard of the Administrative Procedure Act. Some courts have nevertheless held that a more detailed, or de novo, review was appropriate. More recent cases suggest a review of the agency record is sufficient. In the event that the decision of the Supreme Court in *Chrysler* v. *Schlesinger* does not resolve this issue with sufficient clarity, the committee recommends that FOIA be amended to specify the scope of review for reverse-FOIA cases.[1b]

Courts that have prohibited the public disclosure of records in reverse-

FOIA lawsuits have not specifically recognized that the confidentiality of information diminishes over time, and that injunctions against release should be limited in duration. Courts have also not aknowledged that Federal agencies often have legal authority other than the Freedom of Information Act to disclose or share information with the public or with other Government bodies. The committee recommends that the Department of Justice and other Federal agencies take reasonable steps to ensure that nondisclosure orders issued in reverse-FOIA lawsuits be as narrow in scope, purpose, and time of effectiveness as possible.

Paperwork. The maintenance of information by Government agencies results in costs both to those submitting the information and to the agencies holding it. One of those costs is the expense of processing FOIA requests. The committee recommends that the paperwork reduction review currently being conducted by the Office of Management and Budget recognize the expense of processing FOIA requests as one of many information collection costs. Federal agencies should only collect from businesses information necessary to a legitimate agency function.

Introduction: What's At Stake

Today, the [Freedom of Information Act] is being utilized by an extremely diverse group as a means of obtaining . . . private data. The act has been employed by competitors, analysts, investors, disgruntled employees, potential and existing adverse litigants, self-styled "public interest" groups, foreign businesses and governments and a wide variety of others to obtain information concerning private businesses which, but for the FOIA, would not be available to them. Yet now, for the price of a postage stamp, such persons can generally obtain such data from Federal agencies. The use of the FOIA for such surveillance of private affairs was not intended by Congress and needs to be remedied.[1]

This statement at recent committee hearings on the Freedom of Information Act expresses a sentiment common to businessmen. The FOIA, which requires the disclosure of many documents held by federal agencies, is being employed more and more by corporations, corporate representatives, and those interested in corporate affairs to obtain information about business operations and agency regulatory activities. The burden of the increasing numbers of requests for business information has fallen on agencies processing the requests, and on those companies whose information is sought. This burden prompted the committee's examination of the FOIA's fourth exemption which covers confidential business information.

The Freedom of Information Act establishes the policy that any person can have access to identifiable agency records without stating a reason for seeking the information. Nine categories of records may be withheld from disclosure. While each exempted category has its own unique features and problems, each must be read and interpreted consistently with the underlying principles of FOIA.

In the decade since enactment of FOIA there has been considerable evolution in the approach to the law taken by the courts, the agencies, those who request documents under the act, and those who submit information to the Government. Nowhere has this been more evident than with the business records exemption. Although unchanged by the Freedom of Information Act Amendments of 1974, there have been several significant new developments with Exemption 4 in the last few years.

First, a consensus in the courts and agencies on its scope has begun to emerge. The "substantial competitive harm" test, first applied in a 1975 court decision as a measure of the scope of Exemption 4, has become the universal standard adopted by agencies and by courts. Despite its widespread use, the test has attracted a significant amount of criticism. The history of judicial interpretation of the fourth exemption is outlined in part III.

Second, a completely new concept in freedom of information law has been created: the reverse Freedom of Information Act lawsuit. A normal FOIA lawsuit is brought by a requester seeking the release of Government documents. A reverse FOIA lawsuit is brought by a person who has submitted information to the Government and who seeks to prevent its release. Almost all reverse lawsuits to date have been filed to prevent the release of business information. Because there is no provision in the law for reverse suits, courts have been left to work out procedures without any congressional guidance. Many unresolved procedural issues remain. These issues are considered in part V.

Third, while less visible and less dramatic, Federal agencies have made significant advances in their FOIA regulations. Several techniques for handling confidential business information and for processing requests for such information have been found to be useful. These procedures are analyzed in part IV.

Nature of fourth exemption information. Information that may be subject to the fourth exemption is generally acquired by the Government from a business enterprise. The relationships between the Federal Government and businesses are extensive, complex, and varied. In its interaction with business, the Government will be at different times a customer for goods or services, a licensor of commercial activity, a regulator of numerous phases of business operations, a taxer, an investigator for civil or criminal purposes, an auditor, a subsidizer, a seller of goods or services, a lender, a landlord, a tenant, an inspector, an insurer, et cetera. Each of these relationships characteristically involves the transfer of information from the business to the Government.

By virtue of its many roles and immense size, the Federal Government acquires vast quantities of information from the private sector. Businesses have a strong and identifiable interest in maintaining the confidentiality of this information and have expressed great concern about the public release by the Government of information considered by the submitter to be confidential. The large number of reverse-FOIA lawsuits filed to block disclosure of business information exemplifies this concern.

Reverse-FOIA lawsuits represent a last resort for businesses attempting to maintain the confidentiality of information under FOIA. Other measures, less drastic and less expensive, are undertaken more frequently, and a small industry has grown up to monitor the flow of business information out of Government files. One company publishes weekly logs of all FOIA requests made at the Food and Drug Administration, the Environmental Protection Agency, the Federal Trade Commission, and the Consumer Product Safety Commission. A subscription to the FDA log costs $280 per year, and the others cost $90 apiece. For $220 per year, the company will alert a subscriber by telephone that a request has been made at FDA for information supplied by that subscriber. Also, this company will for a fee make a request for information at any Federal agency without revealing the name of the actual party in interest.[2]

It is common practice for those who submit information to the Government to use FOIA to obtain a copy of each FOIA request made by competitors and others for that information, as well as a copy of the material supplied in response to the request. Where the requester is a competitor, the company may then seek information which the competitor has filed with the agency. This may, in turn, prompt more FOIA activity. A significant portion of the corporate FOIA use appears to result from this type of monitoring.[3]

Heavy corporate use of FOIA is not surprising.[4] Businesses tend to have larger and more direct interests in agency regulatory activities than do individuals, the press, or public interest groups. Businesses also have the resources to use the FOIA to carefully watch agency disclosure practices and to wage legal challenges in court over disputed releases. None of this activity is necessarily unhealthy. It is possible that some corporations might be able to use FOIA to obtain information that will enable them to become more adept at avoiding regulation. On the other hand, those who are being regulated are in the best position to know when agencies are improperly exercising their authority.[5]

Corporate concerns. Why have businesses been so active in recent years in seeking to protect information? The motivation of a company trying to maintain the confidentiality of an unpatented, secret process is obvious enough, yet only a small portion of the activity has involved trade secrets. A partial explanation of what it is that commercial enterprises consider at stake in Exemption 4 cases can be found by looking at court cases where submitters attempted to prevent disclosure of business information. The following arguments made in those cases reflect the concerns of submitters, but not necessarily the final opinion of the court:

Confidential treatment is frequently sought by Government contractors or by those who bid on Government contracts to prevent use of information by competitors. For example, in a case involving an FOIA request for component-by-component pricing schedules contained in Government contracts for computer facilities and services, the successful bidder argued for confidentiality contending that the information would permit competitors to scrutinize pricing strategy, discount policy, cost and profit margins, technical methodology, innovative approaches, combination of devices and software, and choice of equipment. The bidder thought that the information would apprise competitors of the innovative approaches reflected in the combination of devices, software, and equipment used in the bid, and that there could be competitive disadvantage in future procurements.[6] In another case, a manufacturer of nuclear ship propulsion systems objected on grounds of competition to the release of contract information that would allegedly reveal actual and negotiated cost, profit, and prices; negotiated general and administrative expenses; policies for design responsibility and for determining responsibility for delivery delays; cash flow; and other matters.[7]

Businesses have contended that the release of information relating to equal employment opportunity programs and affirmative action plans will allow knowledgeable competitors to deduce labor costs, sales volume, plans for expansion, profit margin, vulnerability to price changes, and new products.[8]

Companies that participate in Government programs are frequently required to submit detailed financial information. In one case, a landlord argued that release of gross income figures for a housing project insured by the Department of Housing and Urban Development would harm the business vis-a-vis its competitors.[9] In another case involving a nursing home receiving medicare funds, the same argument was made to prevent the release of cost reports containing income statements, balance sheets, profit and loss statements, occupancy statistics, and itemizations of departmental expenses.[10] A Government concessionaire at a national park contended that release of financial information would facilitate competitors' plans for selective pricing, market concentration, expansion plans, and takeover bids. It was also argued that suppliers, contractors, labor unions, and creditors could use the information to bargain for higher prices, wages, or interest rates.[11]

This brief sketch of arguments made in support of the withholding of information must be kept in perspective. First, the complete range of business information in Government files is by no means covered by these examples.

They only represent some suits that have been decided, and suits over other types of information that are certainly possible. Second, not all of the allegations of harm made by businesses were accepted by the courts. Some were not proved, not relevant, not true, or not of general applicability. Nevertheless, the nature of the harm that can result from disclosure of some business information is suggested.

Finally, while information provided to the Government by a business may reveal details of business operations, it reflects the functions, operations, and activities of Government as well. Information supplied to Government agencies by regulated industries can reveal what the regulators are doing and how well they are doing it. Information received from contractors or builders shows what the government is purchasing, what it costs, and how the procurement process functions. Equal employment opportunity data submitted under Federal requirements provides a way to measure the effectiveness of the Government's EEO programs. While this and other information about the interrelationships between business and Government is revealing about business activities, it is also revealing about Government activities and therefore of legitimate public interest.

Why business data is requested. The FOIA establishes the policy that all Government information should be available to the public unless there is a reason to withhold it. Business information is obtained by the Government in the course of Government activities and is therefore subject to this policy. As with all other information in Government files, no one seeking it is required or expected to justify or explain how it will be used or why it is wanted. Given the underlying principles of FOIA—and it is not the purpose of this report to reopen debate on the principles—questions about the propriety of disclosures should not be directed at the reasons behind the requests.[12]

The proper issue is whether important public or private interests in confidentiality are adequately protected. Although not directly material to this issue, an examination of how business information obtained under FOIA is used by requesters will help to maintain a balanced view of the operation of the act. Since requesters need not explain their purposes, however, it is now known in many cases how the information is used. The following list, based on hearings and staff investigations, is not presented as representative in any scientific way. While not all of these uses of FOIA are necessarily desirable, many reflect a legitimate interest in Government files.

> A company engaged in the business of interpreting the Federal procurement system for agencies and prospective vendors wrote to the committee about the importance of openness as a means of eliminating the ability to conceal fraud, corruption, or error in the procurement

process. Four specific examples of improper contracting were described in the letter and are quoted here:

1. GSA awarded a contract for ADP equipment to a company as a result of an error in evaluation of the firm's bid whereby the cost was incorrectly computed and, thereby, the winner was thought to be the low offeror but in fact was second low.

2. The Army at Aberdeen, Md., in a contract for ADP maintenance, forgot to subtract the prompt payment discount from a vendor and incorrectly awarded to the apparent low offeror as a result of the error.

3. The Navy, in a remote computing services proposal, made mathematical errors in computation of life cycle cost in [a request for proposal] issued by the Naval Regional Procurement Office in Washington, D.C.

4. GSA, in another action, lost a vendors proposal, never opened the proposal, and incorrectly awarded to another vendor.[13]

The availability of information under FOIA was viewed as a way of policing the awarding of Government contracts.

The FOIA has been used by corporations, corporate attorneys, public interest groups, and others as a means of discovery in connection with lawsuits, especially at the National Labor Relations Board and the Federal Trade Commission. One commentator has written about "the current controversy over the question of whether the FOIA is a more appropriate discovery device than historically limited agency discovery procedures and rules available to those in litigation with the agency."[14] Another witness indicated that FOIA fills a gap in discovery for appellate litigation.[15]

The FOIA is also used as an information tool by those concerned about Government policies for ensuring private compliance with civil rights laws.[16] One witness testified that "access to equal employment opportunity information . . . is essential in evaluating how companies are conforming to the important national policies which are inherent in the whole civil rights compliance program."[17] Another requester of corporate EEO information wanted it "in order to determine whether the companies . . . had discriminatory employment practices, and if so, to seek a remedy for the discrimination. That purpose would help implement an important national goal to create fair employment opportunities for all citizens. The Federal Government itself has recognized that making employment statistics regarding women and minorities available to outside groups will help further that goal."[18] The Assistant Secretary of Labor for Employment Standards Administration confirmed the value of these disclosures. He testified: "Disclosure of information as to the manner and extent of compliance by contractors assists the Department in meeting its goals and informs the public on a matter which is of interest to all citizens."[19]

Trade publications also use FOIA to acquire information about agency actions of interest to subscribers. Stuart Pape, an attorney with the Food and Drug Administration, described the operations of one company:

> They get from us a form we call form 483 which is a list of observations that our inspectors make after completing an inspection of a pharmaceutical firm, for example. They put them together listing the observations and they will ask for these forms and delete the company's name and put together a 24-a-year newsletter which pharmaceutical executives can purchase and keep abreast of the kind of observations that inspectors are making at these facilities.[20]

A more specific example of the use of these FDA documents is provided by the director of quality control of a joint purchasing corporation for a group of more than forty hospitals. FDA reports on manufacturers of medical devices and drugs are used as a basis for recommending use of a particular drug or purchasing from a specific manufacturer. The reports permit a determination of the degree of compliance with FDA requirements.

There have been many allegations that FOIA is being used for industrial espionage purposes. One witness put it this way: "[T]he Act has increasingly become a vehicle for surveillance, at public expense, of the private affairs of commercial enterprises by their adversaries."[21] Specific instances are hard to document because these requests are frequently made using strawmen or unaffiliated third party requesters and because it is difficult to ascribe motives to a request. However, it is apparent that businesses do make many FOIA requests.[22]

> It was also suggested that FOIA could be used by companies to avoid restrictions on the exchange of information imposed by antitrust laws. By making FOIA requests for information on pricing, market shares, or other types of data, it is theoretically possible for companies to indirectly transfer information that could not be transferred directly because of antitrust restrictions.[23] The committee has no evidence that the act is being used in this way.

Purpose of this report. As a result of the committee's continuing oversight of the operations of the Freedom of Information Act, it became apparent that requests for disclosure of business information are one of the most troublesome aspects of FOIA. Complaints have been received from agencies, requesters, and especially those who have submitted information to the Government. The committee has also been monitoring the flood of reverse-FOIA lawsuits. The complex procedural issues that typically arise in this litigation have been resolved in different ways by different courts, increasing confusion about the fourth exemption.

Based on preliminary staff study, the committee limited its review primarily to the procedures used by agencies and by courts in deciding cases involving business information under Exemption 4. Although there have been suggestions that the scope of the exemption be expanded in order to protect more business information, it is not clear that most of the problems derive from the coverage of the exemption. Questionable disclosure decisions (too much or too little) have many causes, including: (1) clerical errors, (2) failure to consider all relevant confidentiality arguments, (3) misinterpretation or misunderstanding of the applicable law, (4) abuse of discretion, and (5) shortcomings in the scope of the exemption.

Changing the coverage of the exemption may only affect the last type of questionable disclosure decision. Yet there is strong evidence that many Exemption 4 problems result from the first two categories. For example, when the submitter of information is not notified that disclosure is being considered or when notice is given only one or two days before disclosure or even after disclosure has been made, inappropriate releases of data may very well occur.[24]

Focusing on procedures rather than the scope of the exemption in this report should be more productive for several reasons. First, there is a clear need for procedural reform. FOIA procedures vary considerably from agency to agency and from request to request: this lack of regularity underlies many of the complaints. Second, changes in procedure are the simplest and least disruptive way to deal with the problems. The procedural and substantive problems are intertwined and overlapping; to the extent that deficiencies in release practices result from an agency's lack of proficiency in evaluating the consequences of disclosure, it is likely that any improvement in the manner in which business information is treated will diminish or eliminate many of the substantive difficulties.

Third, most of the suggestions for altering the scope of Exemption 4 are inconsistent with the underlying philosophy of FOIA. For example, it has been recommended that the act be amended to require the requester of business information to state the purpose for which the information is being sought.[25] However, this would place a burden on the requester and would revive the need-to-know test specifically rejected by FOIA. No FOIA requester should be obliged to explain the reasons for the request. A decision to withhold information should be based on the nature of the information and the need for confidentiality rather than the identity of the requester.[26] As a practical matter it would be impossible to police any kind of interest test because of the use of middlemen to make requests.

Finally, changes in the scope of Exemption 4 may not be the most effective way to eliminate potentially objectionable disclosures of business information. Specific disclosure problems might best be solved by specific legislation rather than amendments to statutes of general applicability. If the need for special protection of narrowly defined categories of information can be convincingly demonstrated, it may be appropriate for Congress to pass separate statutes specifically defining the nature, extent, and timing of disclosure.[27] The committee is willing to consider the merits of such legislation on a case-by-case basis.

A number of procedural devices used by some agencies and some courts were identified in the hearings. This report describes those procedures, discusses their compatibility with the purposes of FOIA, and, where appropriate, recommends their continued or expanded use. Many of the procedures can be implemented by the agencies under existing law, although some may require specific legislative authorization. To the extent that the courts do not on their own adopt satisfactory methods of resolving reverse-FOIA lawsuits, legislation will be necessary.

None of the procedural remedies contained in this report has been fully tested, and some doubt about their usefulness, effectiveness, and general applicability remains. As a result, the committee is not reporting any legislation at this time. However, agencies are strongly urged to consider the procedures discussed in this report and to adopt those that are appropriate. The committee intends to closely monitor agency actions in order to evaluate what changes have been made and whether there have been any improvements. If agencies fail to act or are prevented from acting by restrictions in existing law, legislation may be expected. The need for legislation governing reverse-FOIA lawsuits will have to be reevaluated after the decision of the Supreme Court in *Chrylser v. Schlesinger.*[28] That decision is expected late in 1978 or 1979.[28a]

Business data requirements of Government. This report concerns the fourth exemption of the Freedom of Information Act. More generally, it is about disclosure requirements under FOIA. In the broadest terms, the report is about Government information policy. This context is important. Only in recent years has information policy been properly acknowledged as a substantive issue that should be approached on a Government-wide basis. Several laws, such as FOIA, the Privacy Act of 1974, and the Federal Records Act, deal with aspects of information practices, but an integrated framework has yet to be developed.

The Commission on Federal Paperwork recognized the need for a broad approach when it recommended the enactment of a Fair Information Practices Act to regulate the collection, management, and utilization of all information maintained by Federal agencies.[29] While more work is necessary before information policy can be treated in such a comprehensive fashion, narrow problems must be considered with an eye toward the larger issues.

In testimony before the Subcommittee on Government Information and Individual Rights about the privacy and confidentiality report of the Commission on Federal Paperwork, Representative Frank Horton, the Chairman of the Commission, discussed the larger information management issues:

> One of the Commission's central findings was that Government does not require its officials to look upon data and information requirements as manageable resources, which are in need of, and deserve, the same kind of disciplined treatment Government affords its other resources—personnel, money, space, equipment and supplies, and other assets. Information costs are hidden and buried in all of Government's "object class accounts"—salaries, rents, utilities, contractual services, and so on. Nowhere is there a full and accurate accounting of how much Government spends in acquiring, handling, storing and disseminating its vast data, document and literature holdings.
>
> Just as Government has a responsibility to manage its own costs and resources efficiently and effectively, it also has an obligation to the private sector to minimize the burdens imposed by the Government. To fulfill this obligation, we must consider the full cost of information requests, reporting and recordkeeping, not merely the cost to the Government. Whenever we legislate, regulate, or otherwise require the public to bear information costs, we must know what they are so that decisions can be made which will equitably distribute the costs and benefits between the public and private sectors. Full accounting is necessary to manage these costs.[30]

One of the general recommendations of the Paperwork Commission was that the collection of information from the private sector be periodically reviewed and either justified or stopped.[31] The committee strongly endorses this concept. The FOIA does not require the collection of any information by Government agencies. Once information is acquired, however, the possibility that requests will be received for that information may result in other costs. Thus, one of the many factors to be considered when deciding to obtain information is the expense and difficulty for both Government and submitters of reacting to FOIA requests. Any reduction in the collection and retention of unnecessary information will minimize costs for everyone and will reduce FOIA problems.

Recommendation. The committee recommends that the paperwork reduction review currently being conducted by the Office of Management and Budget recognize the expenses of processing FOIA requests as one of many information collection costs. The committee further recommends that OMB and all other Federal agencies make every effort to collect from businesses only information that is necessary to a legitimate agency function.

Brief History of the Fourth Exemption of the Freedom of Information Act

Understanding the Fourth Exemption

The fourth exemption to the Freedom of Information Act embraces: "trade secrets and commercial or financial information obtained from a person and privileged or confidential."[32]

Initial commentators on the FOIA were greatly troubled by the sentence structure of the exemption. It contains no punctuation, but the strategic addition of commas or semicolons could have a considerable effect on its interpretation. For example, the Attorney General's 1967 Memorandum on the Public Information Section of the Administrative Procedure Act suggests at least three possible readings.[33]

This difficult grammatical issue has been resolved by the courts, and it is now recognized that Exemption 4 includes two separate categories of information. The first category of exempt information covers trade secrets. The second category covers (a) commercial or financial information (b) obtained from a person and (c) privileged or confidential. In order to fall within the second category, information must meet all three tests.[34]

This second category—commercial or financial information obtained from a person and privileged or confidential—will be referred to generically in this report as "confidential business information." The fourth exemption as a whole, including both trade secrets and confidential business information, will be referred to as the "business records exemption."

Trade Secrets

The FOIA does not define "trade secret," yet there has been little controversy over its meaning.[35] Most of the attention in fourth exemption cases has been directed at the second category of the exemption covering confidential business information.

The Restatement of Torts has a very broad definition of "trade secret":

A trade secret may consist of any formula, pattern, device or compilation of information which is used in one's business, and which gives him an opportunity to obtain an advantage over competitors who do not know or use it.[36]

If a trade secret can be any information used in a business which gives competitive advantage, then there is little or no information left that could qualify as commercial or financial information under the second category of the exemption without also qualifying as a trade secret. This definition is therefore inconsistent with the language of the act, as well as with the general approach taken by the courts to the concept of confidential business information.

A narrower defintion, and one more suitable for FOIA, has been used in at least one FOIA case:

> An unpatented, secret, commercially valuable plan, appliance, formula, or process, which is used for the making, preparing, compounding, treating or processing of articles or materials which are trade commodities.[37]

This definition keeps the two categories of the fourth exemption distinct. It will not result in the release of any additional information, however, because commercial information that is not a "plan, appliance, formula, or process" may still qualify for exemption under the second category.

Early Approaches to Confidential Business Information

The history of the fourth exemption of the FOIA has been primarily a struggle over the concept of confidential business information. The words of the exemption—"commercial or financial information obtained from a person and privileged or confidential" do not have a clear purpose, meaning, or application. Court decisions under Exemption 4 reflect a distinct evolution in interpretation. Essentially, the trend has been away from subjective tests of confidentiality adopted in early decisions and toward an objective standard by which the confidentiality of business documents can be measured. While the progression of judicial decisions has not been quite as orderly as the following discussion suggests, there is a fairly distinct pattern to the cases.

In early Exemption 4 cases, the courts applied the so-called promise of confidentiality test. An example is *General Services Administration* v. *Benson,* where the Ninth Circuit Court of Appeals concluded:

> . . . that this exemption clearly condones withholding information only when it is obtained from a person outside the agency, and that person wishes the information to be kept confidential.
>
>   . . .
>
> [T]he exemption is meant to protect information that a private individual wishes to keep confidential for his own purposes, but reveals to the government under the express or implied promise by the government that the information will be kept confidential.[38]

This approach to business record confidentiality was derived from the 1966 House Report on FOIA, which included this language:

> The exemption would include business sales statistics inventories, customer lists, scientific or manufacturing processes or developments, and negotiation positions or requirements in the case of labor-management mediation. . . . It would also include information which is given to an agency in confidence, since a citizen must be able to confide in his Government. Moreover, where the Government has obligated itself in good faith not to disclose documents or information which it receives, it should be able to honor such obligations.[39]

The promise of confidentiality test was soon abandoned by the courts. The test establishes no standards for deciding when a promise should be made, and agencies would appear to have complete discretion. Yet, as experience with the predecessors of FOIA demonstrated, agencies have no inherent interest in making documents public.[40] Thus, it is likely that promises of confidentiality would have been bestowed freely upon all who asked, especially when sought by those who regularly did business with the agency. As a result, the promise of confidentiality test could have led to the withholding of almost all documents submitted to an agency. In addition, the test provides no guidance in cases where the confidentiality issue was not initially contemplated by either party. The courts were justified in looking for another approach to business record confidentiality.[41]

The promise of confidentiality test was generally superseded by an expectation of confidentiality test derived primarily from the 1965 Senate Report on FOIA:

> This exception is necessary to protect the confidentiality of information which is obtained by the Government through questionnaires or other inquiries, but which would customarily not be released to the public by the person from whom it was obtained. This would include business sales statistics, inventories, customer lists, and manufacturing processes.[42]

By focusing on an information policy question, the expectation of confidentiality test represented a step in the proper direction. Its use reflected an awareness that confidential business information must be appraised by an objective standard:

> Regardless of whether the information was submitted on the express or implied condition that it be kept confidential, a court should determine, on an objective basis, that this is not the type of information one would reveal to its public.[43]

While an improvement over the "promise" test, the "expectation" test still involved a subjective determination: would the person who submitted the document to the Government release the information to the public? A test based solely on the intent of the submitter is frequently irrelevant and ultimately unworkable.[44] The Government's disclosure policy cannot be contingent on the subjective intent of those who submit information. For example, it clearly would be inappropriate to withhold all information, no matter how innocuous, submitted by a corporation with a blanket policy of refusing all public requests for information. Also, the expectation test would lead to inconsistent results. Documents submitted by companies with liberal information policies would be released by the Government while identical documents acquired from companies without such policies would be withheld.

The expectation of confidentiality test is inadequate even if made more general by asking whether a reasonable business enterprise would customarily release the information. Any test based on actual business policies for the release of information will prove to be inadequate because of the widespread practice of withholding information whether or not there is a legitimate reason for the withholding. As the experience of the Government with the release of its own documents under FOIA certainly indicates, estimates of the harmful consequences that result from the public disclosure of information are often exaggerated. Agency documents routinely withheld prior to the passage of FOIA are now routinely released without damage. Similarly, federal agency meetings held in secret prior to the Government in the Sunshine Act[45] are now held in public without detriment.

The proper inquiry under the fourth exemption is not whether information is customarily withheld, but why the information should be withheld. The exemptions in FOIA were provided to protect legitimate needs for confidentiality. Decisions about the release of business information in Government files must be based on the need for protection of the information and not on incidental matters such as promises of confidentiality or patterns of release. Documents may be withheld only when there is a reasonable justification for doing so.[46]

The early Exemption 4 cases relied heavily on the legislative history of FOIA. Both the "promise" and the "expectation" tests of confidentiality were derived from the committee reports. However, several commentators have stated that such a use of the reports for explication of the fourth exemption is inappropriate. Professor Kenneth Culp Davis has written about the difficulties of the legislative history:

> The most important fact about the legislative history is that no explanation appears for the addition to the fourth exemption of the words "commercial or financial." The 1964 version of the bill (S. 1666) provided for exemption of "trade secrets and other information obtained from the public and customarily privileged or confidential." That version was passed by the Senate, but the House did not act, and when the bill (S. 1160) was introduced in the 89th

Congress, two changes had been made: The word "customarily" was deleted, and the words "commercial or financial" were added.

Not only was no explanation ever made for the addition of the words "commercial or financial," but both the Senate committee and the House committee in their reports seem to read the words "commercial or financial" as if they were not there. Both reports, for instance, say the exemption would cover "information customarily subject to the doctor-patient, lawyer-client, lender-borrower, and other such privileges." Since information within the doctor-patient privilege is normally noncommercial and nonfinancial, the committees seem to be strangely ignoring the statutory words "commercial or financial." Furthermore, the Senate committee says the exemption includes "any commerical, technical, and financial data," and the House committee says that it includes "technical or financial data." The committees do not attempt to explain how the words "commercial or financial" can be stretched to include "technical." The reports on their face appear to involve a flagrant attempt to defeat the plain meaning of the words "commercial or financial."

But the discrepancy between the statutory language and the reports turns out to be a mere inadvertence. The Senate committee simply failed to alter its earlier report, based on the earlier bill without the words "commercial or financial," to reflect the addition of the words "commercial or financial." And the House committee seven months later copied most of the Senate committee report.

Committee reports explaining the earlier version of the bill that did not include the words "commercial or financial" do not seem to me to be a satisfactory basis for finding the meaning of the enacted version that did include those words.[47]

In light of this analysis, use of the legislative history of FOIA for guidance in the interpretation of the fourth exemption must be done prudently; reliance on specific language from the committee reports is clearly not advisable.

Competitive Harm Test

National Parks and Conservation Association v. *Morton* [48] was the first case to delve deeply into the purpose of the confidential business information exemption. In its decision, the District of Columbia Court of Appeals started from an earlier determination[49] that the test for confidentiality must be an objective one, but went well beyond the limited objectivity embodied in the "expectation" text:

Whether particular information would customarily be disclosed to the public by the person from whom it was obtained is not the only relevant inquiry in determining whether that information is "confidential" for purposes of section 552(b) (4). A court must also be satisfied that non-disclosure is justified by the legislative purpose which underlies the exemption. Our first task, therefore, is to ascertain the ends which Congress sought to attain in enacting the exemption for "commercial or financial" information.[50]

In its comprehensive analysis of the legislative history, the court considered the hearings, the committee reports, the general purposes of FOIA, and the factors that led to the inclusion of the business record exemption. The court found that Exemption 4 has a dual purpose: to protect the interests of the Government and to protect the interests of the person from whom information is obtained. Based on this conclusion, a twofold test for confidentiality was set forth. Commercial or financial information is confidential under Exemption 4 if disclosure is likely to have either of the following effects:

(1) to impair the Government's ability to obtain necessary information in the future; or

(2) to cause substantial harm to the competitive position of the person from whom the information was obtained.[51]

National Parks has been a very influential case. While no exhaustive survey has been made, the twofold test for confidentiality appears to have been adopted universally.

The first test does not apply when an agency requires the submission of information. Since agencies are able to subpena or otherwise exact much information, there have been few cases and the test has not been as important or as controversial as the second test.[52]

Although there are a growing number of cases applying the substantial competitive harm test, it is nevertheless difficult to generalize about it. As is true with trade secrets, each case seems to be heavily dependent on independent factual circumstances. The rapid general acceptance of the substantial competitive harm test—the first confidentiality test based solely on objective and not subjective criteria—is strong evidence that the court in National Parks made a significant stride in dealing with the problems of confidential business information.

Ever since its first use, the substantial competitive harm test has been severely criticized by many businesses and corporate attorneys who would return to the "promise" or "expectation" test of confidentiality. Their arguments are not convincing. As discussed above, these tests have a very insubstantial basis in the legislative history, and are generally inconsistent with the language of the fourth exemption as well as the policy underlying FOIA.

However, all critics of the competitive harm test cannot be dismissed so easily. While the court in National Parks may have asked the right questions in analyzing Exemption 4, it is not yet clear that it reached the only right answer. Competitive harm is an objective test for confidentiality, but it may not be the only objective test available.[53] Many contend that it is too narrow to protect all business records that should be accorded confidential treatment. One critic wrote:

> Not only does the *National Park I* "harm to competitive position" test seem fashioned out of the court's own ideology, rather than Congress' intention, but it is too restrictive even to accomplish the purpose which the court states it should serve: protecting persons who submit business data to the Government from the competitive disadvantages of disclosure. It is quite possible that business information might be useful to a competitor and yet its disclosure would not be likely to harm the proprietor's competitive position. It seems clear, however, that Congress did not intend the FOIA to enable persons to rummage through their competitors' files in search of useful information.[54]

Another aspect of competitive harm that has attracted criticism is its failure to apply to noncommercial scientific research documents. In *Washington Research Project* v. *Department of Health, Education and Welfare,*[55] the District of Columbia Court of Appeals held that Exemption 4 could not apply to such documents because noncommercial scientists are not engaged in trade or commerce. The court stated that while there may be a legitimate need for secrecy of such documents, the exemption is limited to "commercial or financial" matters and must be narrowly construed. Whether this restriction on the applicability of the fourth exemption follows directly from the language of the fourth exemption, or indirectly as a result of the adoption of the substantial competitive harm test is not entirely clear. The court's decision has been attacked for both legal and policy reasons.[56]

Beyond the Competitive Harm Test

Notwithstanding these problems, it is too early to make final judgments about the substantial competitive harm test. The boundaries of the test are still being drawn on a case-by-case basis by the courts, and it is possible that subsequent decisions may affect the availability of the exemption. When the *National Parks* case was reviewed for the second time at the appellate level,[57] the burden of proving that business documents are entitled to confidential treatment was simplified. The submitter does not have to demonstrate an actual adverse effect on competition. In determining the likelihood of substantial competitive harm, the court may exercise its judgment in view of the nature of the material sought and the competitive circumstances, and may rely on relevant and credible opinion testimony.[58]

The committee's October 1977 hearings did not delve deeply into the scope of Exemption 4. As a result, the committee is not prepared at this time to consider the merits of the substantial competitive harm test. Competitive harm can only be properly evaluated when compared with other possible tests. Unfortunately, much of the discussion about Exemption 4 has been directed at the older, now unacceptable tests for confidentiality, and not at reasonable alternatives. If there are other governmental or private interests that Exemption 4 should be protecting, they must be identified and the need for protection must be demonstrated. Some problems raised by a general confidentiality test for business documents may best be solved by legislation establishing disclosure rules for specific categories of information.[59] One area clearly in need of further study is the type and extent of protection, if any, that should be available for noncommercial scientific research proposals.

General criteria for evaluating confidentiality tests for business records can be set forth. First, a test must be objective; it should select documents for protection based on substantive reasons for confidentiality established by statute. Business records cannot be exempted from disclosure simply because they are business records, because an agency has made a promise without specific statutory foundation, or because a business would prefer its records to be confidential. In this regard, the Attorney General's May 5, 1977 letter to the heads of Federal departments and agencies is instructive because it establishes substantive criteria for withholding of documents. The Attorney General announced that the Department of Justice would not defend FOIA lawsuits simply because documents technically fall within the exemptions of the act. In order to justify defense of an FOIA lawsuit, there must be a "sufficient prospect of actual harm to legitimate public or private interests if access to the requested records were to be granted."[60] Similarly, any test for determining the confidentiality of business records must evaluate both the legitimate need for confidentiality and the consequences of disclosure.[61]

Second, a test for confidentiality cannot distinguish between requesters or consider the purpose for which the documents are requested. FOIA allows any person to make a request without stating a purpose, and this principle must be maintained.[62] Inquiries into the purpose of the requester are costly, time-consuming, subjective, and irrelevant. It is likely that a request for any business document in the possession of the Government could be framed to satisfy any purpose test. Thus, it would still be necessary to use other criteria in determining whether confidential treatment was appropriate for the document in question. Also, distinguishing between requesters would require controlling the use of the information by a successful requester in order to prevent its use by an unsuccessful requester. Such regulation by the Government of information in the hands of private citizens would be a complete reversal of the principles of freedom of information.

Finally, a confidentiality test should be as easy to apply as possible. The

competitive harm test sometimes requires courts and agencies to make difficult factual determinations about how information might be used and how
its use might affect the competitive position of the submitter of the documents. It would be ideal if decisions on disclosure depended on standards that
could always be applied quickly, simply, and cheaply. While this may be an
impossible goal, it is one that should be met to the greatest extent possible
without conflicting with the first two more important criteria.[63]

Agency Procedures for Processing Requests for Business Information

Introduction

With most FOIA requests that do not involve business information, there are
normally only two parties with an interest in the result: the Government and
the requester. Exemptions 1 (classified matters), 2 (personnel rules), and 5
(intra-agency or inter-agency memoranda), relate mostly to documents created by Federal agencies.[64] Since both the Government and the requester are
necessarily involved in FOIA requests, the interests of both are always represented.

Exemption 4 applies only to information supplied by persons outside the
Government.[65] A consequence of this is that there are likely to be three
parties with an interest in each FOIA request for business documents that may
fall under Exemption 4: the Government, the requester, and the business that
submitted the documents.[66] Three parties may also be interested in the release of information that may be covered by Exemptions 6 (personal information), 8 (reports about financial institutions), 9 (geological information), and
occasionally other exemptions, most notably Exemption 7 (investigatory
records). Because of its relationship with the Privacy Act of 1974, Exemption
6 presents some unique features not directly relevant here.[67] But Exemptions
8 and 9 both cover information obtained from commercial enterprises, and
the procedures applicable to Exemption 4 material should be applicable to
them as well.

When disputes arise with most exemptions, the two parties to the request
generally each represent a different side of the disclosure question. However,
with Exemption 4 material, the Government's role may not always be clearly
defined. When agency operations are unaffected by disclosure of documents,
some Government agencies have indicated that they have no real interest.[68]
However, the court in *National Parks* found that the fourth exemption was

intended for the benefit of persons who supply information as well as the agencies which gather it.[69] In recognition of the Government's interest in the acquisition of information, the first test fashioned by the court permits the withholding of information if disclosure is likely to impair the Government's ability to obtain necessary information in the future.[70]

The act prescribes no role for the submitter in the decision to release documents, but experience has clearly shown that the submitter can be an important party. In many cases, an agency may have little more on which to base a decision than the FOIA's general presumption in favor of release and possibly an unexplained stamp of "confidential" placed on the document by the submitter. Under the substantial competitive harm test, release depends on whether disclosure will cause substantial harm to the competitive position of the person from whom the information was obtained.[71] It may not be apparent from the face of a document how the information contained therein can be used or how use of the information can affect the competitive position of the business. Agencies do not always have sufficient resources, knowledge, or expertise to judge these issues, nor are they accustomed to making such decisions. Without participation in some form by the submitter of the information, relevant arguments against the release of documents may not be presented.[72]

A number of methods of dealing with these special Exemption 4 problems have been developed or suggested. Some of these procedures have been informally adopted by agencies or submitters, others are already included in regulations, and others are found in FOIA literature. The nature and merits of these ideas are discussed in this part of the report. The last section of this part considers the possible need to restructure or extend the time limits for decisions on FOIA requests and appeals in order to allow agencies to incorporate procedural changes.

An undercurrent in many complaints about FOIA—especially those made by submitters—is that agency review procedures are uncertain. Two statements submitted for the October hearing record reflect this. The first complained of a lack of consistency in the handling of FOIA matters:

> Uniformity in handling of FOIA requests might well ease the burden of the various agencies who have been scurrying to provide regulations to deal with these issues, as well as ease the aura of uncertainty currently surrounding the submission of data to the Government which the source believes should be mandatorily exempt from disclosure to the public.[73]

The second statement indicated that there is need for more predictable behavior by agencies when they decide FOIA cases:

> Predictability in the procedures might assuage some fears, among persons asked to submit

information to the Government, that their data will be secretly but lawfully leaked to their competition.[74]

Each of the procedures described here has some potential for improving, simplifying, or formalizing an aspect of the agency FOIA process. For example, the separation of confidential from nonconfidential information may be accomplished in part by requiring submitters to identify confidential business information at the time of submission. Another device employed by some agencies is a determination of confidentiality at the time that information is submitted rather than when an FOIA request is subsequently received. A more categorical approach to the problem may be the preparation of substantive rules governing the disclosure of specific classes of information.

Once an actual FOIA request for business information is received by an agency, other procedures may be beneficial. A requirement that the submitter receive some type of notice of the request and be permitted to argue the need for confidentiality could result in a fairer and better decision by the agency. Other changes in agency procedures, including participation by the requester and the preparation of a record of agency action may also improve the quality of the agency decision.

In general, none of these procedures is mutually exclusive. Depending on the type of information maintained and the number of FOIA requests received, an agency may be able to use all of the recommended procedures at the same time. Alternatively, some less complete combination may be more efficient and more effective. Each agency should formally adopt those procedures most suited to its own FOIA operations.

Notice to the Submitter

Whenever confidential information is shared, the originator loses some control over it, and the chances of disclosure are increased. Benjamin Franklin put it this way: three men may keep a secret if two of them are dead. In the FOIA context, a measure of control over information submitted to the government can be restored if the submitter is told that disclosure of the information is being considered.

Submitters have consistently told the committee of the importance of receiving notice, and at recent committee hearings, both submitters and requesters testified in favor of notice. It appears that notice is a useful procedure that can improve the Government's handling of business documents.

There is nothing in FOIA requiring that the submitter of information be notified by an agency that disclosure of the submitter's documents is being considered. Nor has any court held that notice is required by due process.

In discussing a submitter's due process argument, a district court found that notice requirements are:

> relative and circumstantial rather than absolute. They are determined by weighing the private rights at stake, the government's interests, the type of proceeding, the manner of notification, the likelihood of eliciting a response, and the practical difficulties of time and cost.[75]

Using this standard, the court rejected the argument that notice to submitters in FOIA matters was either constitutionally or statutorily mandated.[76]

Nevertheless, notice can serve an important and useful purpose. It allows submitters an opportunity to object to the unwarranted disclosure of information by agencies and to take action to prevent the disclosure. Without notice, the submitter may only learn of the release of a document when it is too late. In a recent article, a commentator recommended the use of notice:

> The most fundamental procedural protection for submitters is agency notification that submitter-generated information has been requested under the FOIA. Without notification submitters have no opportunity to present their nondisclosure arguments at the agency level before the final decision to disclose.[77]

Notice to submitters also has advantages for the agency that must decide on the release of documents. FOIA requests for business documents raise complex issues that may be outside the normal range of agency expertise. In a statement submitted for the record, Coopers and Lybrand described how the submitter can assist the agency:

> The need for private parties to have an opportunity to present arguments for nondisclosure is obvious. In many cases Government personnel may have no expertise enabling them to predict the possible harm that could result from disclosure. Moreover, without prompting by the affected interests, agency personnel may have no incentive to maintain the confidentiality of the private business information obtained by them under governmental authority. Unless adequately apprised of the dangers of disclosure, there may be a natural tendency for agency personnel to adopt the path of least resistance and release information on request.[78]

Allowing the submitter to explain the consequences of disclosure may lessen the chances of an unwarranted release of information. Concomitantly, arguments in favor of release made by the requester may prevent an improper decision to withhold. Both sides can participate effectively.

Notice may also result in a reduction in complaints of agency bias in favor of the release of documents. This statement in a recent article on the fourth exemption made by two attorneys who have litigated FOIA cases is typical:

Since the agency usually has no real stake in the outcome, may lack knowledge and expertise on the relevant issues, and is institutionally biased in favor of disclosure, it would seem obvious that the real party in interest, the submitter, should be a full party to any agency proceeding regarding disclosure of its business records.[79]

Those who regularly seek information from the Government under FOIA would likely contest the view that agencies are biased in favor of release. Nevertheless, giving the submitter notice and an opportunity to object to disclosure may partially reduce charges of bias. Bare claims of confidentiality can easily and thoughtlessly be made by marking documents, but submitters who are asked to justify those claims may discover upon examination that no harmful consequences will follow the release of the information. A thorough working knowledge of the standards of confidentiality may also make submitters less suspicious of the motives of Government agencies faced with the application of those standards.

Agency regulations. Some agencies have already discovered the advantages of providing notice to submitters. In a letter included in the hearing record, John Harmon, Assistant Attorney General, Department of Justice, stated the view that it is a nearly universal practice among agencies to give notice to submitters of business information, although the notice may be informal and provided only a few days in advance of the scheduled release of documents. [80] However, a review of agency regulations reveals that few agencies have formally bound themselves to notify submitters. When notice is discretionary, submitters cannot be certain that they will be told in advance of disclosure of documents. It is apparent from the testimony received that submitters are unhappy with the lack of predictability of current agency notice practices.

The problem is accommodating a submitter's interest in receiving notice without overwhelming agency FOIA operations. A requirement that notice be given for each FOIA request involving business documents might put an impossible administrative burden on some agencies. Several solutions are suggested by agencies that have found ways to limit notice without limiting its value.

Food and Drug Administration Commissioner Donald Kennedy indicated that FDA received approximately 25,000 FOIA requests in 1977, that most of these requests were for business documents, and the FDA's entire FOIA operation would have been "seriously threatened" if they were required to give notice for ever contemplated disclosure. Commissioner Donald Kennedy went on to say:

Nor do we feel that providing notice in advance of every disclosure would provide benefits justifying the time and expense involved. If the public is to have prompt access to Agency records, the disclosure process cannot be encumbered with elaborate procedures that give private persons, with an interest in confidentiality, an opportunity to negotiate each disclosure decision.[81]

FDA has not totally rejected the use of notice. When the confidentiality of records is "uncertain," the submitter is asked to provide additional information to permit the disclosure decision to be made.[82] However, the submitter is not invited to argue or to persuade FDA of the need for confidentiality.[83]

While the standard used by FDA to determine when notice will be given lacks predictability, the notice policy must be evaluated in the context of the agency's overall approach to FOIA. Commissioner Kennedy testified that FDA has rules setting disclosure guidelines for the majority of its agency records.[84] (The rules are discussed in greater detail below.) By consulting these rules, companies submitting information to FDA may be able to determine in advance whether that information is subject to release.[85]

This use of substantive disclosure rules along with notice suggests one way that notice can be effective without being required before all FOIA requests. Notice will usually be superfluous if submitters have already been informed of the release practices of agencies through published regulations. Regulations, which are contestable when issued, constitute effective and timely notice of the agency's intention to disclose. Notice can then be limited to those cases involving records not covered by regulations, cases where disclosure is to be made notwithstanding the regulations, and other special circumstances.

The Environmental Protection Agency also makes limited but effective use of a notice procedure. Under its regulations, those requested to supply information are told that claims of confidentiality must be asserted at the time the information is submitted, and that information not claimed as confidential may be released subsequently without notice.[86] This limits the need for notice to those cases where a claim of confidentiality has already been asserted, thus reducing the number of pointless notices.[87]

Types of notice. Notice may be of two distinct but related types. When given prior to the agency's decision in the FOIA request, notice invites the submitter to explain whether disclosure will result in competitive harm and how. Used in this way, notice is a preliminary part of the agency decision making process for the release of business information. Fairness requires that the FOIA requester be informed that the submitter's views have been solicited and be permitted an equal degree of involvement. Both submitter and requester should have a strictly limited period of time to respond. The nature of agency FOIA proceedings is discussed in detail below.

A second type of notice is given after the agency has decided that the documents requested are to be released. The purpose of this final notice is to allow the submitter to pursue any remedies that may prevent release.

Both types of notice may be suitable for some or most cases, with a preliminary notice given when the request is received and a final notice when a decision to release is made. A final notice should be given with enough time to permit the submitter to pursue whatever legal remedies are available. In cases where the submitter had received advance warning of the possibility of release through a preliminary notice, five days should be sufficient. When no preliminary notice was given, a final notice might allow the submitter ten days before the documents are to be disclosed.[88]

Other ways of lessening the administrative burden of notifying the submitter without necessarily sacrificing his interests are also possible. For example, if a class of information collected by an agency loses its confidential character on a predictable schedule, the agency could provide by rule that no preliminary notice will be given. For some older information, even the final notice might be skipped. Notice might also be unnecessary if an earlier decision on release of the requested documents were made within six months of the current request or the information has already become public.[89]

Recommendation. The committee believes that it is consistent with basic notions of fairness that a submitter be given some form of notice about the release of information. Notice can be accomplished by issuing regulations, by contacting submitters when requests are received, or by other means. Because there are different methods of providing notice, and because one method may not be suitable for all agencies or for all types of information, the committee does not recommend the adoption of any specific notice procedure.[90]

The committee recommends that each agency select and formally adopt a method of notifying submitters that is most suitable to its own circumstances, records, and FOIA caseload. Some may be able to use procedures similar to those of FDA or EPA, while others may find it easier and cheaper to provide notice to submitters for each request. Under existing authority, agencies have the ability to implement some type of effective notice arrangement, even if it is limited to a final notice after the agency has made the release decision.

Identification of Confidential Information by the Submitter

The most difficult problem with Exemption 4 is the identification of confidential business information. Part III of this report contains a discussion of the categories of information that have been considered as confidential within the meaning of the business record exemption. However, there is another aspect beyond the legal issue of definition. Even if a definition were agreed upon, the tremendous volume of information acquired by Government agencies from business enterprises makes the mere identification of those portions that are or may be confidential a complex legal and records management problem.

One way to begin the process of determining what information is confidential is to ask the submitter. Submitters could be required to identify confidential business information at the time of submission. Depending on the type of documents collected, their use and storage by the agency, and other recordkeeping policies, submitters could be told to segregate confidential material and file it separately or just to mark those documents or portions of documents for which confidentiality is claimed. Identification of confidential information by the submitter would only be advisory, and would be subject to agency review when and if an FOIA request were made. Information not marked as confidential would be made available to the public upon request.

Pros and cons. Mandatory identification of confidential information by the submitter at the time of submission has several advantages. First, it helps the agency to define what is at issue when an FOIA request is made. Information not marked as confidential by the submitter can be released without the need for any substantive determination by the agency and without further contact with the submitter. Both the agency and the submitter can focus their attention specifically on information that has a claim of confidentiality attached. Second, identification is cheap and simple for submitters. While proving the need for confidentiality can be difficult, simple identification of confidential information does not require extensive consideration in order to decide whether release might be harmful.[91] When in doubt, a submitter would always be free to mark information as confidential and postpone the actual determination and proof until a request is actually made. Third, for some types of documents submitted to the Government, it is already common practice for businesses to identify confidential or proprietary data. A requirement of identification could standardize the markings and their significance.

Several who provided statements for the hearing record favored a requirement that confidential information be marked by the submitter. John H. Harmon, Assistant Attorney General, Office of Legal Counsel, Department of Justice, stated that marking would be useful as long as the designations were not conclusive.[92] Texas Instruments suggested that a uniform system be established under FOIA for the designation of confidential material by the submitter.[93] Coopers & Lybrand recommended that the FOIA be amended to allow submitters to identify confidential information upon submission.[94]

There are also a number of arguments against an identification requirement. First, it imposes a burden on companies to review and mark all documents submitted to the Government. Given the large volume of submissions made, the total cost might be large. Burt A. Braverman, a corporate attorney, questioned the desirability of channeling significant amounts of business resources into marking documents in advance when few will ever be requested under FOIA.[95] Second, since not all documents submitted by businesses are requested under FOIA, much of the effort that went into marking documents will be wasted. While no information is available that would allow an accurate estimate to be made, it seems reasonable to assume that a fairly large number of business documents are never requested. Third, since the need for confidential treatment of information frequently diminishes rapidly over time, the value of the markings is limited. Finally, acting on the theory that it is better to be safe than sorry, businesses might make extensive use of a confidentiality stamp in order to protect any possible interest in confidentiality that might exist. If everything is marked confidential, then nothing will be gained.

Agency experience. Environmental Protection Agency regulations require that when a written request is made to a business for information that could be regarded by the business as entitled to confidential treatment, the business should be told that a claim of confidentiality must be asserted at the time of submission. If no claim is made, then the information will be publicly released upon request. If confidentiality is asserted, then the business will receive notice before any request is filled.[96]

EPA Deputy General Counsel Michael A. James described the benefits of this procedure:

> By doing this, the initial burden of identifying confidential business information is placed on the affected business. The advantage of this approach is that much information that might otherwise be Exemption 4 information is eliminated from consideration because the businesses do not claim it as confidential. There would be disadvantages to the Agency if businesses asserted very broad claims, but our experience has been that once businesses are made aware of the procedure EPA follows and the fact that they may later have to substantiate their claims, they tend to make claims that are limited in scope to information that is most likely to be entitled to confidential treatment.[97]

Initially, EPA found that confidentiality claims were asserted very broadly. But as businesses became more familiar with the regulation, EPA indicated that claims were more limited in scope.[98] This trend is important, since the value of simple marking depends on the cooperation of those submitting information. Businesses must resist the temptation to claim confidentiality on all documents as a matter of course. When marking is tied to notice,[99] as EPA has done, there is an incentive to mark only those items that are in fact confidential. A business that marks all submitted documents may find that it is asked to justify its claims with great frequency. Not only will this require extra effort, and expense, but unless able to make a good argument in favor of the need of confidentiality, the submitter may find the credibility of its confidentiality stamp severely diminished.[100]

The Bureau of Mines is developing a plan that should make it easier for submitters to identify confidential business information. The agency is considering revising its forms to insert a yes/no block beside each data element so that submitters can specifically identify what is confidential. Where information that may be confidential is collected on standard forms, this approach may help to avoid blanket claims.[101]

Recommendation. On balance the committee finds potential benefits in a requirement that confidential information submitted to the Government be identified at the time of submission, especially when used as a basis for providing submitters notice prior to release of marked information. A major barrier to the adoption of a simple marking requirement is the view that submitters will automatically mark everything "confidential." However, EPA's experience suggests that this concern may be overstated. While more evidence is needed before a definitive judgment can be made, there are grounds for the belief that marking will aid agencies in the administration of FOIA requests without placing an unacceptable workload on submitters of documents.

The committee recommends that all agencies evaluate the benefits of identification of confidential information by the submitter as part of a comprehensive approach to the problems of the fourth exemption. The committee recognizes that identification by the submitter may not be advantageous for all agencies or for all records received by a single agency. The Food and Drug Administration indicated that it would have little direct impact on current agency practices.[102] In light of FDA's extensive substantive disclosure regulations, an identification requirement may indeed be superfluous. However, no other agency has yet developed such comprehensive regulations. When more experience with this procedure has been achieved, the committee can consider the need for an amendment to FOIA making an identification requirement mandatory.

Determination of Confidentiality by Agencies at the Time of Submission

Identification of confidential information by the submitter discussed in the previous section is designed to help agencies rule on FOIA requests. Since a submitter's marking would not be binding on the agency, those submitting documents to the Government may not be able to tell whether their documents will be accorded confidential treatment. As a result, a business may choose not to make information available to the Government rather than take the risk that its documents will be disclosed. Even if an agency has authority to compel a business to supply information, fears about disclosure could induce a business to make it difficult for the agency to acquire the needed data. To deal with such situations, several agencies have provided for determinations of confidentiality either just before or just after the submission of documents.

Under a presubmission review procedure, the agency examines the documents marked confidential by the submitter and decides whether it will protect them should an FOIA request be received. The submitter may then have the option of withdrawing the documents if dissatisfied with the agency decision. A post-submission review is similar, although the submitter may not have the option of withdrawing the documents in the event of an adverse confidentiality determination. Both types of document review will be referred to as advance determinations of confidentiality because a decision is made in advance of the receipt of an FOIA request.

An advance determination is not the same as a promise of confidentiality. The promise of confidentiality test discussed in part III was a standard (now discarded) for determining whether information was exempt.[103] An advance determination of confidentiality is a procedure for applying the relevant standard to specific data submitted to an agency. An advance determination is not necessarily a binding decision by an agency.

Practical difficulties. There are several problems with the general use of advance determinations of confidentiality. First, if many requests for advance determination are received, an agency could quickly become overloaded, burdening regular FOIA processing. Second, since not all of the documents submitted for advance determination will be requested under FOIA, some of the effort that went into the decisionmaking will be wasted. A company that has had experience with advance determinations submitted these comments:

A fundamental problem encountered by Coopers & Lybrand in its efforts to protect against disclosure of confidential documents to the Federal Trade Commission has been the burden of complying with procedures that require it to persuade the Commission of the need for confidentiality at the time it submitted the material, before any FOIA request for disclosure has ever been made. These procedures mean that Coopers & Lybrand has had to engage in a costly and time-consuming process of submitting arguments for the confidential treatment of documents which may in fact never be the subject of an FOIA request. Additionally, information that was confidential when submitted to the Government may, because of changed circumstances no longer need to be kept confidential at the time a request is actually made.[104]

Third, and more important, an agency cannot always determine in advance whether confidentiality is appropriate or how long a document should be withheld. For some narrowly defined categories of information, a long-term promise to withhold may be possible. For example, there are probably no circumstances that would justify an agency's public release of a trade secret.[105] However, commercial or financial information loses its confidential character over time, and a determination of confidentiality made at an earlier time can become meaningless.

Also, a determination of confidentiality made without the participation of an FOIA requester may overlook relevant issues. Evidence that supported the petition for confidentiality might be impeached by evidence supplied by a requester. Without the pressure of a request for information, agencies may not view submitters' claims of confidentiality with a sufficiently critical eye. It is also possible that, because of changed circumstances, the public interest may require the release of information for which an earlier determination of confidentiality was made.[106]

Finally, it is likely that advance determinations will be unable to accommodate the act's requirement that reasonably segregable portions of a record be provided to a requester after deletion of exempt portions.[107]

Agency regulation. Agencies have adopted or proposed a variety of practices for making advance determinations of confidentiality. The Office of Federal Contract Compliance (OFCC) at the Department of Labor requires that a ruling on all confidentiality claims be made at the time that equal employment opportunity information is submitted to any agency. The contract compliance officer of each compliance agency must determine within ten days whether the material is exempt from disclosure. An appeal of an adverse decision to the Director of OFCC is permitted.[108] In practice, agencies do not make the required advance determinations,[109] apparently because it is too burdensome to make decisions in the absence of an actual request for disclosure.[110] None of the court cases dealing with the release of OFCC information indicates that an advance determination of confidentiality was ever made as part of normal agency procedure.[111]

At the Environmental Protection Agency, advance confidentiality determinations are made only for information that has been "voluntarily" submitted. This category includes information that EPA could require to be submitted under statutory or contractual authority, and information that was not required to be submitted by statute or regulation as a condition of obtaining a benefit under a regulatory program.[112]

Like EPA, the Food and Drug Administration's presubmission review of documents is also only available for information submitted on a voluntary basis.[113] Since most of the information received by FDA and by EPA is required to be submitted, advance determinations are available for only a portion of the information acquired, and the burden of making determinations is small. A brief investigation at FDA found that presubmission review was rarely used.[114]

The Securities and Exchange Commission acquires information under a completely different set of rules. The SEC's policy makes all submitted documents available to the public at the time of filing. A submitter seeking confidential treatment must segregate any confidential information and file it separately so that a determination of its status can be made. A decision that a document is entitled to confidential treatment does not preclude reconsideration when an FOIA request is made or when there is some other reason to make the information public. The SEC will attempt to give a submitter advance notice of the revocation of any grant of confidential treatment.[115]

The Nuclear Regulatory Commission has an openness policy similar to the SEC's for materials filed in connection with licensing proceedings and will make advance determinations of confidentiality when requested by the submitter. The NRC regulations[116] provide that an affidavit must be filed identifying the information sought to be withheld and stating the specific reasons under the fourth exemption that justify withholding. If a request for confidential treatment is denied, the submitter is given thirty days to withdraw the document before it becomes public.

The Federal Trade Commission has proposed comprehensive rules for advance determinations, going well beyond the limitations imposed by the other agencies.[117] The FTC proposal appears to cover most information received by the agency and is not limited to information submitted voluntarily or in a public file. Requests for protection would be required to identify the information, the period of time for which confidentiality is necessary, and the nature of the harm that would result from disclosure.[118] If the request establishes a prima facie showing that the information is exempt under FOIA, confidential treatment can be granted for a period of up to three years. An extension is possible.

Should disclosure be sought under FOIA for information accorded confidential treatment by the FTC, the submitter will be asked whether confidentiality is still required and, if so, the request will be denied. On appeal of that denial, the submitter will be notified, and the appeal will be decided based on "all facts bearing on the issue of the exempt status of the requested records." Prior to the release of the information, the submitter will be given ten days notice.[119]

If the FTC finally adopts this rule, it may be the best test to date of the value of advance determinations of confidentiality. The committee takes no position at this time. The major question is whether the costs incurred by the agency and the submitter in making the initial determination will result in benefits at a later stage in the FOIA process or will otherwise simplify the acquisition of information by the agency. Another issue will be how well the agency is able to determine the confidentiality of information in advance of actual requests.[120]

What if an FOIA request is made for documents undergoing presubmission review? Both FDA and EPA stated that they would automatically deny any FOIA request for documents in the presubmission review pipeline about which a determination of confidentiality had not yet been made. Documents already found to be confidential could, of course, be denied to the requester on that basis. FDA and EPA will allow documents not qualifying for confidential treatment to be withdrawn by the submitter irrespective of the FOIA request. EPA will keep a copy of any document returned under this procedure if an FOIA request was received while the document was in EPA's possession, but will not disclose it except upon court order.[121] FDA regulations do not permit a copy or summary of any withdrawn records to be kept.[122]

These two agencies have different theories justifying their denial of FOIA requests for material undergoing advance determinations of confidentiality. The FDA does not consider documents acquired for presubmission review to become a part of agency files until a determination of confidentiality has been made. Therefore, a request would be denied because the information is not in agency files.[123] EPA on the other hand, would deny requests for this information on the grounds that the document was exempt under the alternate test in *National Parks.*[124] Under that test, a record can be withheld because disclosure would impair the Government's ability to obtain necessary information in the future.[125]

The committee believes that both of these positions are questionable. Nothing in FOIA indicates that an agency can maintain a document in its possession for one purpose but deny that it has it for another purpose. The FDA's use of this theory as a basis for withholding would likely be rejected by the court. Allowing business documents to make "special appearances" in agency files can easily be abused and should not be permitted.[126]

There is a firmer legal basis for EPA's use of the alternate test of *National*

Parks to deny documents, although it is still far from certain that the test would properly apply. Can information received for an advance determination of confidentiality be considered as "necessary" within the meaning of the test? If the information is found to be confidential under the competitive harm standard,[127] then there is no problem denying it to the requester. But where information is not confidential and is to be reclaimed by the submitter, an agency will be hard pressed to explain how that information was "necessary."

Recommendation. The committee recommends that advance determinations of confidentiality not be used. However, if an agency wishes to experiment with this procedure, these limitations are suggested: First, advance determinations should be made only for documents submitted voluntarily to an agency or for documents that would automatically become public upon filing.[128] Second, it should be used only if there is a positive reason for believing that the procedure will be advantageous. Some, and possibly most, agencies may find that it is not necessary because few confidential business documents are voluntarily submitted. Third, at the time that a determination is made, the submitter should be told that a determination of confidentiality is not final, that it will automatically expire on a fixed date, and that the issue may be reopened at any time during this period. Agencies should establish a set cut-off date of short duration for the confidential treatment of a document. A confidentiality determination can become outdated because of the passage of time, because a certain event has occurred, because the information has been made public elsewhere, or because the determination was incorrect when made. Fourth, when a request is denied based on a prima facie or pro forma determination of confidentiality, the requester should be specifically informed of the basis of the decision, the availability of an appeal, and any differing standard used on appeal.[129] Finally, if an agency has initially accorded confidential treatment to a document, the submitter should be notified in advance of the actual release.

All of the procedures discussed above are palliatives that can only be used on a case by case basis. Documents are marked as confidential or not marked depending on the contents of individual documents. Notice is provided to the submitter when individual documents are requested. Advance determinations of confidentiality are made when individual documents are submitted to Government agencies. While these procedures help in the identification of confidential information, none provides a method for making general categorical judgments about the confidentiality of documents. There is, therefore, a need to narrow, simplify, speed the identification of, or possibly even eliminate the document-by-document decisions that current practices entail.

This can be accomplished through the issuance of substantive disclosure rules. Much of the business information regularly received by agencies is submitted on standard forms or in standardized formats. With some, but by no means all, of these documents, the factors that relate to the need for confidentiality are identifiable, predictable, and recurrent. Agencies may find it useful to make decisions about the disclosure of some classes of documents by issuing rules describing these factors and stating how they affect both confidentiality and the decision to release or withhold documents.

Both submitters and requesters can have a voice in the preparation of disclosure rules. Under the rulemaking section of the Administrative Procedure Act[130] all interested parties receive notice of any proposed rules through the Federal Register, and are entitled to submit written comments. Final agency rules may be challenged under the judicial review provisions of the Administrative Procedure Act.

FDA's Substantive Disclosure Rules

The Food and Drug Administration is clearly the leading agency in the promulgation of substantive disclosure rules. FDA Commissioner Donald Kennedy estimated that rules have been issued for the majority of agency records.[131] These "availability of specific categories of records" regulations "state the way in which specific categories of Food and Drug Administration records are handled upon a request for public disclosure."[132] Commissioner Kennedy explained the reasons for these rules:

> We think that the definition of trade secrets and confidential commercial or financial information in our own regulations are reasonably explicit. It would be very difficult, however, to make correct and consistent disclosure decisions involving potentially valuable business information without relating the definitions to the categories of records that are routinely found in FDA's possession.
>
> As a result, after we went through our rulemaking exercise, we did another kind of exercise. We searched our own files and tried to categorize the kinds of information that were contained therein and attempted to draw up a set of fairly explicit definitions and exclusions with regard to trade secrets and confidential commercial information so that in examining our own records in response to Freedom of Information requests, we would have a set of guidelines for our people that were consistent and that were understood by the public.
>
> This was a major undertaking, but we think it was a wise investment. Our own regulations and extensive preamble discussion that accompanies them describe for our own employees and for the public what the status of each kind of record is under FOI.
>
> For that reason, we try to make our disclosure decisions both more uniform and more prompt than they would otherwise be. That is not to say that we are quick as others would like us to be or would like to be ourselves in all cases. But we are certainly quicker than we

would be if we had to make an ad hoc decision in every case without a set of guidelines published as part of agency regulations.[133]

Substantive disclosure rules do not have to be limited to confidential business information. Some of the categories in FDA's regulations describe disclosure policies for broad classes of records such as administrative enforcement records, court enforcement records, correspondence, summaries of oral discussions, testing and research conducted by or with FDA funds, manuals, agreements with other agencies, and data and information obtained by contract. For example, the rules governing release of studies and reports list seven items that become available to the public upon acceptance by the responsible agency official. Three types of reports—internal audits, internal planning and budgeting documents, and legislative proposals prior to submission to Congress—are listed as not available to the public. Data and information obtained by contract are available when accepted except to the extent that they are exempt. Technical proposals of successful offerors are available, but those of unsuccessful offerors are categorically defined as exempt under the fourth exemption to FOIA.[134]

The remaining categories of records for which disclosure rules have been issued relate to specific petitions, permits, registrations, notices, files, and other information received under operational requirements. Twenty-eight specific categories are referenced in the FOIA regulations, and the rules for each category are included in the portion of FDA's regulations relating to the subject matter of the records. The categories include color additive petitions, drug establishment registrations and drug listings, new animal drug application files, master files for new drug applications, cosmetic product experience reports, electronic product information, et cetera.[135]

As an example of how detailed these rules are and how they operate, the color additive rules are described here. Unless extraordinary circumstances are shown, the rules provide that six types of data contained in a color additive petition become available for public disclosure after a notice of petition filing is published in the Federal Register. Safety and functionality data will be disclosed as will FDA tests results on color additives. Lists of ingredients and protocols for test or studies will be made public unless shown to fall under the business records exemption of FOIA. An assay or other analytical method will become available unless it serves no regulatory or compliance purpose and is shown to be exempt under the business records exemption. Adverse reaction reports and similar materials will be released after deletion of details identifying users, physicians, and hospitals.

Three types of information are listed in the color additive rules as not available for public disclosure unless previously disclosed or unless related to a product that has been abandoned and no longer represents Exemption 4 material. Manufacturing methods or processes and quantitative formulas will not be released. Production, sales, distribution, and similar data will not be disclosed unless aggregated.[136]

Problems with FDA's rules. While FDA's substantive disclosure rules represent a significant accomplishment in information policy, there is much room for improvement. The committee is opposed to FDA's rules declaring that documents are categorically exempt from disclosure. The criteria for withholding of business documents are not easily applied by rule.[137] The substantial competitive harm test requires factual determinations that are difficult to make for general categories of business documents. Further, in most instances it will not be possible to specify by rule which portions of an exempt document are segregable and therefore releasable.[138] For example, the rule stating that unsuccessful technical proposals are exempt from disclosure is misleading because certain information about these proposals may be releasable including the identity of the offeror, the date and general nature of the proposal, and other nonconfidential data.

An agency may find itself unduly restricted by its nondisclosure rules if the public interest or other circumstances warrant the release of material defined as exempt. Finally, nondisclosure rules may be counterproductive. If an agency denies an FOIA request based only on a rule, it may find it difficult to defend the denial on appeal to a court. Appeals by requesters are considered de novo by the courts, and decisions are based on an examination of the documents. Agency rules prohibiting disclosures would have little or no significance to a court and the agency may have no other defense for its decision to withhold. Because of these problems, it is doubtful that nondisclosure rules have any legal consequence.

Another difficulty is that the rules occasionally establish unclear criteria for release. For example, some of the color additive petition materials will be released if they serve no regulatory or compliance purpose. The meaning of this standard is not clear on its face. Notwithstanding the lack of desirability of FDA's nondisclosure rules, they could be improved by a citation to the applicable exemption of FOIA and a brief explanation of the reasons for the exemption's applicability.

It is apparent from this detailed description of FDA's disclosure rules that all FOIA decisions cannot be made in advance through the issuance of rules. While some records are listed as available or unavailable without qualification, others are releasable only under certain conditions or if no FOIA exemption applies. There is little purpose in a regulation that simply declares that records will be made public if not exempt under FOIA. By itself, this regulation tells little. But as part of a comprehensive description of disclosure policies, it is valuable to separate those records whose disclosability is certain and records whose disclosability is in doubt. If in instances where there is doubt, the factors that affect release can be specified, then so much the better. If not, then the decision will have to be postponed until a request is actually made. But it is still useful to narrow as much as possible the class of records whose release is uncertain.

Rules of other agencies. Unlike FDA, the Environmental Protection Agency does not specifically declare that information will or will not be disclosed through substantive disclosure rules. When EPA determines it has items of business information with common characteristics that will result in identical treatment of each item, EPA regulations provide for the issuance of a "class determination."[139] A class determination may state that a class of information is or is not voluntarily submitted; fails to meet applicable substantive criteria for confidentiality determinations;[140] or meets those criteria only during a certain period of time. EPA described the use of class determinations this way:

> EPA does not use class determinations to declare information confidential as a class. Rather, the class determination is a procedural tool to streamline the process of making *ad hoc* determinations concerning confidentiality. In the class determination we set forth the criteria that we will apply in making determinations in the class. We still make the individual determinations. The class determination notifies affected businesses of our general approach to the specific class of information, and in the case of information that would never be confidential because statute requires disclosure, we would define that information. The class determination is not a determination that specific information is confidential.[141]

Only a few class determinations have been issued to date, and a few more are under consideration. EPA estimated that less than one percent of information maintained by the agency is covered by any form of class determination.[142]

The regulations of the Office of Federal Contract Compliance at the Department of Labor are similar to those of FDA in that they provide for the release of specific types of information regularly received. These must be disclosed: Standard Form EEO–1, imposed EEO plans, final conciliation agreements, validation studies of tests, and dates of scheduled compliance reviews.[143] Contractor-submitted affirmative action plans are releasable except to the extent that they reveal major shifts or changes in contractor personnel requirements not already made public.[144] Withholding of this information can only be made after receiving a suitable explanation and verification from the contractor. Certain other classes of exempt information are also described in the regulations.

Donald Elisburg, Assistant Secretary for Employment Standards at the Department of Labor, indicated that rules for disclosure or withholding of other

OFCC information are under study. He noted limited rulemaking has been used under other Labor Department programs, but generally only to identify what information is disclosable. Mr. Elisburg made it clear that rulemaking is not a panacea:

> In most cases, . . . it would be difficult to establish a general rule which would cover all business data submitted because the circumstances of a given situation may determine whether the information, as to the particular company involved, is confidential. While we do not preclude the possibility of rulemaking in this area, our experience to date has not indicated any particular need to do so since we have been able to handle this problem through informal contacts with the organization which supplied the data.[145]

The Department of the Interior has recently issued specific disclosure rules for coal leasing information acquired under the Mineral Leasing Act. The information falls in one of five categories, and the rules indicate what events trigger the release of each category.[146]

The substantive disclosure rules of each of these agencies differ slightly. Some rules simply announce that documents will be released; others set guidelines for disclosure; and others define when documents will be made available. There is no single way to write disclosure rules, and with the exception of nondisclosure rules, all of these approaches have some validity.

Nonagency witnesses told the committee that they favored disclosure rules, and, like the agencies, each had a slightly different conception of the form the rules should take. Charles I. Derr of the Machinery and Allied Products Institute saw disclosure rules as a way to avoid use of the competitive harm test and to make Exemption 4 mandatory. Since these were desirable consequences in his view, he supported the use of disclosure rules, and stated that an approach such as that employed by EPA using guidelines established in advance "deserves further study."[147] Louis J. Schiffer of the Women's Rights Project of the Center for Law and Social Policy suggested that agencies be encouraged to promulgate regulations making determinations about the disclosability of regularly collected forms.[148]

Diane B. Cohn of the Freedom of Information Clearinghouse suggested that agencies compile lists of the categories of business documents for which FOIA requests have been made and that Congress consider enacting "reverse (b) (3) statutes" for some categories of information. The reference is to the third exemption of the FOIA. An Exemption 3 statute requires the withholding of documents; a reverse Exemption 3 statute would mandate the release of documents. In addition to these witnesses, one commentator supported the use of disclosure rules to identify categories of documents that would automatically be releasable.[149]

Burt Braverman testified that use of disclosure rules has great factual appeal, but that the consequences of disclosure of information might vary from industry to industry and even from company to company. As a remedy, he suggested including a "fair and realistic waiver provision" that allows submitters to demonstrate the need for the confidentiality of a document despite a general determination of disclosability.[150]

One possible side effect of the issuance of substantive disclosure rules may be to help agencies to process requests since requesters who are told what information is available will be able to make specific, easy to fulfill, requests.[151]

Limitations on substantive disclosure rules. As with other procedures, substantive disclosure rules can play only a limited role in the FOIA process, and some of the limitations are readily identifiable. First, disclosure rules are not suitable for all business documents. They appear to work best with information received in standardized formats. Nevertheless, such rules may also find a place with documents relating to regular agency functions—such as procurement—even though the documents differ significantly from one instance to another. For some documents, rules setting time limits on confidentiality claims might be useful.

Second, even if a rule governing disclosability can be drafted, an agency may determine that it is not worth the effort. If few requests for business documents are normally received, then it may be easier and cheaper to handle them on an *ad hoc* basis. However, an agency that chooses to handle FOIA requests on a case-by-case basis rather than issuing rules must ensure that all requesters and submitters receive fair and uniform treatment.

In addition to rules defining documents as confidential and therefore exempt from disclosure, some agencies have issued regulations restricting the use of the agency's discretionary authority to release exempt documents. One such regulation provides that the agency will not make any discretionary release of exempt business documents.[152] Flat prohibitions against discretionary releases may result in serious difficulties for an agency in cases where the public interest requires the release of confidential information. An example might be where the public health or safety is threatened. The public interest may also require the disclosure of information (not otherwise exempt) about activities that are illegal or in violation of public policy.[153]

It is likely that a court would invalidate as an abuse of discretion any regulation that prevents the release of information vital to the public interest. Regulation on discretionary release authority should only be procedural or establish guidelines for the use of the release authority.[154] An appropriate procedural restriction might be a requirement that the submitter be notified in advance of any discretionary release. Another possibility is to limit the number of people with the authority to make discretionary releases.

Finally, agencies should consider procedures for special cases where a general rule providing for disclosure may result in undue hardship or unfairness for an individual company. One method of accomplishing this is to permit submitters to specially mark information that should be withheld despite disclosure rules and to provide at the time of submission a complete justification for withholding. When the document is requested, the agency should consider the confidentiality claim without further participation by or argument from the submitter. If the document is to be released notwithstanding the special claim of confidentiality, the submitter should receive adequate advance notice. Any such remedy must be viewed as extraordinary. If used frequently by submitters, this type of special procedure would be counterproductive. The primary method of challenging a rule should be through the judicial review procedure of the Administrative Procedure Act.

Recommendations. The committee recommends that agencies review their experience with FOIA requests for business documents in order to identify categories of documents that may be suitable for treatment by disclosure rules. When new reporting requirements are imposed on business or when old ones are revised, the possibility of establishing disclosure rules for the information reported should be seriously considered.

The committee recommends that the Office of Federal Procurement Policy consider whether detailed, uniform disclosure provisions could be included in procurement regulations.[155] OFPP should also examine ways to structure government procurement documents so that nonexempt information is easily segregated from information that is or may be exempt.

Finally, the committee recommends that agencies formally adopt substantive disclosure rules when appropriate. If disclosure rules are not feasible, rules setting time limits on confidentiality claims should be considered. However, no rules should be issued providing that business documents are absolutely not releasable. Agencies such as FDA that have issued nondisclosure rules should review the utility and legality of the rules.

Agency Proceedings

With most FOIA requests, the method an agency uses to reach a decision never becomes an issue. The Freedom of Information Act has few procedural particulars, requiring only that initial determinations be made within ten days, appeals within twenty days, and that all denials be accompanied with a notification of appeal rights.[156] Agencies are not required to hold hearings or conduct adjudications, although some FOIA officers will informally consult with a requester by telephone. If a requester sues in federal district court to obtain documents that the agency has denied, the FOIA requires the court to consider the matter de novo and, as a result, courts do not normally review any part of the agency proceeding.[157]

However, when a submitter files a reverse-FOIA lawsuit—one seeking to prevent an agency from releasing documents—the agency's procedure as well as the basis for the decision to release can be crucial. Early reverse-FOIA cases were heard de novo by the courts. However, several courts have recently decided that trial de novo is not appropriate in reverse-FOIA cases and that the court should decide the case by reviewing the adequacy of the agency decision based on the record compiled by the agency.[158] Agency procedure is important not only because it may become an issue in reverse-FOIA lawsuits, but because improvements in procedure may result in fairer and less costly FOIA decisions.[159]

Agency decision procedures. The Office of Federal Contract Compliance at the Department of Labor has the most completely developed procedure for deciding on the release of business documents. In accordance with Executive Order 11246,[160] OFCC designated other Federal agencies as compliance agencies with responsibility to enforce adherence to equal employment opportunity laws by Federal contractors. Much of the information submitted by contractors to demonstrate compliance with EEO requirements is received by those agencies. OFCC regulations require submitters to identify confidential information at the time of submission and agencies to rule on those claims with ten days. However, these regulations are apparently not strictly followed by compliance agencies and confidentiality determinations are made only when a request is received.[161]

Under the criteria established in OFCC regulations, the initial determination of confidentiality is made by the individual compliance agency. If that agency decides to release the requested documents, the submitter may appeal the decision to the Labor Department's Director of OFCC.[162] The key concept of the appeal is a decision on the informal record compiled by the compliance agency. This is certainly not a new feature of administrative law, but it is relatively novel in FOIA matters. Contractors are generally given five days to submit in writing their objections to release. Requesters have also been allowed to present their views, but the agency indicated that it is rare for a requester to ask to participate. Depending on the complexity of the case, experts—typically employees of the Department of Labor—may be consulted and their views included as part of the record.[163]

By requiring a written justification of the submitter's claim of confidentiality, OFCC is able to compile all of the evidence that formed the basis for the agency's decision for possible use by a reviewing court. While not all courts have been willing to review the record compiled by the agency, OFCC is in a position that enables it to argue for such a review. In any event, the submitter is assured that its views are available to the agency decision maker.

In practice, compliance agencies have had mixed results compiling adequate records of FOIA decisions. Both cases where courts have accepted the principle of review on the record involved EEO information, and both were remanded to agencies to supplement and clarify the reasons for the decision. In *Chrysler,* the Court of Appeals found the record compiled by the Defense Supply Agency to be inadequate.[164] In *General Dynamics,* however, the administrative records were much more complete, and the remand was limited to narrow issues.[165] As agencies acquire more experience with the requirements of review on the record in FOIA cases, the need for remands should disappear entirely.

The Environmental Protection Agency also has a structured decision process for Exemption 4 cases, although it is not as strongly oriented to the preparation of a record of the agency's action. When an FOIA request is made for information marked as confidential by the submitting business, an initial pro forma denial is issued to the requester by the program office handling the request, unless the information is clearly not entitled to confidential treatment. At the same time, a letter is sent to the submitter asking for substantiation of the claim of confidentiality. The submitter is asked whether the information is available to the public elsewhere, how the information is protected, and whether release would result in substantial harm to its competitive position.[166]

A final determination of confidentiality is then made by EPA's legal office based on the submitter's substantiation.[167] The final determination is considered to be an appeal of the initial denial and is made automatically, without the need for further action by the requester. The requester has no opportunity to argue that the information should not be accorded confidential treatment. Deputy General Counsel Michael A. James said that because the requester cannot see the documents in question even for a special limited use, the requester's ability to comment knowledgeably is extremely limited.[168] He also indicated that participation by the requester would only prolong the proceeding.

Legal problems with existing procedures. While EPA's approach to FOIA requests for business information brings the submitter into the process at a timely point, the use of a pro forma denial in all cases involving colorable claims of confidentiality is of questionable legality. FOIA requires that the agency make an initial determination within ten days, and it is by no means clear that a pro forma denial qualifies as a determination within the meaning of the act. When a pro forma denial is issued, the initial determination is actually made at the appellate level, and the requester is obliged to file suit in order to have that determination reviewed. EPA cites four reasons for its approach:

First, because of the difficult legal issues that arise in these cases and the threat of reverse Freedom of Information Act cases, the Agency decided that the decision making should be centered in the legal office.

Second, because the Freedom of Information Act requires an initial response within ten days, the Agency decided that there was not time to evaluate the issues involved in a particular situation except in those cases where information is clearly not entitled to confidential treatment.

Therefore, whenever there is any doubt, the program office must issue an initial denial.

Third, because the initial denial is based on a determination that the affected business has asserted a confidentiality claim and because the denial is issued unless the information clearly is not entitled to confidential treatment, the Agency decided that a final determination should be made automatically by the EPA legal office, whether or not the requester appealed the initial denial. The Agency decided that this would give the requester a decision based on the facts of the specific situation, rather than the pro forma denial standing alone.

Fourth, because the Agency does not usually have enough information to evaluate whether specific information is entitled to confidential treatment, the Agency decided to ask the affected business to submit substantiating information.[169]

EPA makes a strong case in favor of its procedures, but fails to overcome the legal requirement that determinations and not just responses be made within ten days of the receipt of an FOIA request.[170]

The FOIA process at OFCC presents a different type of legal question. The authority for requiring an appeal of a compliance agency's decision to the Director of OFCC is uncertain. The FOIA covers the release of records in the possession of an agency, and provides only for "consultation" with another agency having a substantial interest in the determination concerning the release of those records.[171] Nothing in the Act appears to specifically authorize an appeal of one agency's FOIA decision to another agency, or an appeal by a submitter of a decision to release documents.[172] The Department of Labor, defending its practice as necessary to assure uniformity, claims legal authority for it:

The basis for the procedure is the authority of the Secretary of Labor under E.O. 11246, which designates the Secretary as the Government official responsible for the administration and enforcement of the order. He has delegated this responsibility, except the responsibility to issue rules and regulations of general applicability, to the Director of the Office of Federal Contract Compliance Programs. The order also makes contracting agencies (compliance agencies) primarily responsible for conducting compliance reviews of Federal contractors and subcontractors. The compliance agencies obtain possession of affirmative action programs in the course of compliance reviews. They hold possession of these documents as agents of the Secretary of Labor who ultimately has responsibility for the determination of contractor compliance and has control over the disposition of these documents. Therefore the Secretary has the authority to direct the FOIA release policies of compliance agencies with respect to these documents. OFCCP regulations only provide for review by the Director of agency decisions to disclose, not withhold, documents. Although as a practical matter OFCCP has not found it necessary to review agency decisions to withhold information, we believe that OFCCP could require agencies to disclose information if the Director determined it was in the public interest and furthered the purposes of the Executive order to do so.[173]

As did EPA, OFCC makes a strong policy argument justifying its FOIA procedure. However, OFCC did not explain how the procedure is authorized by or consistent with FOIA. At least some compliance agencies have been unwilling to delay the release of documents pending appeal to OFCC.[174]

Other comments. Several witnesses testified in favor of some form of agency proceeding. Charles I. Derr of the Machinery and Allied Products Institute stated that a requirement for formal agency proceedings "would substantially redress the present inequity."[175] Burt A. Braverman recommended a comprehensive scheme including the requirement that agencies notify submitters, that submitters be given adequate time to prepare and submit views, that a full hearing be held including the presentation of evidence and argument before an administrative law judge if the submitter has shown at least a reasonable possibility that the documents contain confidential information, that a written decision be issued, and that the submitter be given time to appeal that decision to the courts before the release of the documents.[176] James T. O'Reilly suggested that agencies be authorized to certify complex technical or legal issues to an administrative law judge for a recommendation.[177]

John Harmon of the Office of Legal Counsel at the Department of Justice also suggested that it would be desirable to authorize but not require routinely or automatically an administrative proceeding. The decision to conduct such a proceeding would be left with the agency, but might be requested by any of the parties, the Justice Department, or the court. An administrative law judge or outside panel might preside, with *in camera* inspection of documents and arguments permitted in order to protect the confidentiality of the information in question.[178]

All of the witnesses recognized that the present time limits are virtually an impenetrable barrier to any realistic form of agency proceeding except where the requester is willing to allow an extension. Commissioner Donald Kennedy of the Food and Drug Administration opposed any type of hearing, even an informal one, in order to preserve the benefits of prompt decisionmaking.[179]

In an important article on reverse-FOIA lawsuits, Daniel Gorham Clement discussed how the rationale for time limits in the act should be used to shape the form of any agency proceeding:

> The emphasis of the FOIA upon full and prompt disclosure will greatly shape the nature and duration of agency proceedings held to resolve FOIA requests for submitter-generated information. Time would not permit a formal agency hearing in every case in which a submitter objects to proposed disclosure, especially if existing time limits for initial agency determinations are extended to permit notification to and preparation of arguments by submitters. The presentation of witnesses, introduction of evidence, cross-examination of witnesses, and all the other elements of a formal evidentiary hearing would not only tremendously delay the processing of FOIA requests but also seriously burden agency time and budgets and place requesters—whose financial and legal resources are usually dwarfed by those of submitters—at a distinct disadvantage. Furthermore, although Congress clearly preferred the right of submitters to disclosure over the right of submitters to confidentiality, it did not provide for agency evidentiary hearings for FOIA requesters. Therefore, to provide agency hearings for submitters would seem anomalous. Moreover, ample precedent indicates that formal agency hearings are not necessary to protect fully the rights of submitters. Submitters may satisfactorily vindicate their rights at informal agency proceedings based upon written pleadings and affidavits. It is not a major sacrifice for submitters to rely upon written affidavits instead of expert testimony, especially since the alternative—providing administrative hearings for submitters—would thwart the congressional goal of expediting FOIA requests. Forgoing the live testimony of witnesses and arguments of counsel would not significantly undermine submitters' rights, particularly if submitters receive the other procedural safeguards suggested here.[180]

The best way to balance the conflicting interests of requesters, submitters, agencies, and courts may be a fast, informal, and optional written proceeding held at the discretion of the agency. Any proceeding that permits the submitter to argue for confidentiality must allow participation by the requester, and must make that participation as meaningful as possible.[181] In addition, it may be appropriate to amend the act to give submitters the right to appeal a decision to release documents within the agency. This might help to accomplish a major goal of agency proceedings: reducing the number of reverse-FOIA cases filed in Federal district court. However, it is also possible that an administrative appeal by submitters might lead to additional delays.[182]

Recommendation. The committee recommends agencies institute an informal proceeding consisting of written pleadings and affidavits for FOIA requests involving information that may be confidential under the fourth exemption. The committee is aware that the time limits of the act may not permit agencies to fully implement this recommendation.[183] Under existing law, both OFCC and EPA are able to compile a record of agency action that could be used by a court in a reverse FOIA lawsuit. While the committee has some doubts about the legality of aspects of these procedures, the compilation of a record is a good idea in Exemption 4 cases since de novo consideration by the courts has not always been required.[184] All agencies should make certain that requesters are offered a full opportunity to participate in the compilation of a record of the agency decision.

The committee takes no position at present on whether agencies should compile a record at the agency appellate level or when the initial determination is made. On the one hand, it may be appropriate to compile the record at the time the initial decision is made so that the record is available for review on appeal to the agency head. On the other hand, the preparation of a record for all requests may be too much of an administrative burden for agencies and may not be justified by the amount of litigation. Agencies should exercise discretion on a case-by-case basis depending on the nature of the information requested, the difficulty of the determination, and the likelihood of litigation.

A Note on Time Limits

The 1974 amendments to FOIA imposed strict time limits for decisions on FOIA requests and appeals. Agencies must determine whether to comply with a request within ten days after its receipt, and appeals must be decided within twenty days. These time limits can be extended for up to ten days if (1) the records requested are not at the office processing the request, or (2) a voluminous amount of records are demanded, or (3) there is a need for consultation with another agency that has a substantial interest in the documents requested. The extension can be invoked only once, during either the initial decision process or the appeal but not both.[185] Under the existing statutory framework, the maximum total time allowed from the receipt of a request until a final agency determination is forty days.

Prior to the 1974 amendments, many agencies took months rather than days to respond to FOIA requests. While the addition of time limits to the law has resulted in a major improvement in the response time for requests, not all agencies are yet in compliance with the 10-day requirement. This is a continuing problem. The committee continues to believe that timely access to records is a critical feature of the Freedom of Information Act.

Agency use of the procedures discussed in this report for FOIA requests involving business information would have a mixed effect on compliance with the time limits. Some of the procedures, such as identification of confidential information by submitters and substantive disclosure rules, are likely to make it easier for agencies to respond quickly. On the other hand, recommendations calling for notice to submitters and for informal agency proceedings will probably slow down response times. The net result should be that agencies will still be able to handle many requests for business information within ten days, but that more time may be needed to decide on requests that require an agency proceeding.

There are several ways to provide the additional time. The first makes use of the additional ten days that can be invoked under certain circumstances. When there is cause to use this extension, agencies may also be able to use the extra time to complete a proceeding. In many cases, an extra ten days will be sufficient. Alternately, should an agency choose to conduct its informal proceeding on appeal, twenty days will always be available.

Second, when agencies have in good faith attempted to comply with requests, many requesters have been willing to allow more time to complete processing. It is probable that most requesters would also agree to a short and definite extension in order to permit the completion of an informal proceeding.

Third, if in practice neither of these methods is sufficient, the committee will consider the need to extend or restructure the time limits. However, any such changes will be limited to cases involving business information and will be contingent upon the adoption and use by agencies of the procedures recommended in this report. For example, more time might be allowed within or in addition to the 40-day statutory framework when the submitter is notified of a request and given an opportunity to object to disclosure in writing. No changes in the time limits will be considered until agencies have acquired sufficient experience to determine that these procedures are practical and fair.

Reverse-Freedom of Information Cases

Introduction

A requester who has been denied documents by a Government agency may, when administrative remedies have been exhausted, sue to force disclosure. This is the typical FOIA lawsuit. But the FOIA has also been used to prevent agencies from releasing documents. This type of lawsuit has come to be known as a reverse-FOIA action because the submitter sues to prohibit the disclosure of information it had provided to the Government. The FOIA specifically authorizes suits by requesters, but contains no similar provision for suits by submitters.

Reverse-FOIA lawsuits are a relatively recent development.[186] While the law became effective in 1967, the first decision in a reverse-FOIA action was not handed down until 1973. A significant number of reverse-FOIA cases have been filed in recent years. The Department of Justice reports that approximately 76 cases were filed in 1976, 63 in 1977, and 7 in 1978 through May. There are 104 pending cases, including 34 involving EEO information, 33 involving commercial information, and 20 cases about medicare cost reports.[187] The overwhelming majority of reverse cases involves business documents.[188]

Any survey of reverse lawsuits will reveal that the cases tend to be very complex and to take a long time to resolve. Lois J. Schiffer of the Center for Law and Social Policy described how the filing of a reverse-FOIA suit affected a request for documents made by her client. In August 1975, the District of Columbia Chapter of the National Organization of Women made a FOIA request at the Social Security Administration for equal employment opportunity documents that had been filed by four insurance companies. The administrative process for this request lasted until July 1976, at which time it was decided that NOW was entitled to most of the documents it was seeking. After the final administrative determination, the companies involved went to district court and successfully obtained a stay of disclosure. In December 1976, the court ordered some of the documents released, and all parties appealed the ruling. The companies appealed directly to the Supreme Court, but that appeal was denied. The companies then sought and obtained a stay of disclosure from the Court of Appeals. As of March 1978, the case was awaiting argument before the Court of Appeals. Over 2 1/2 years have elapsed since the information was originally requested by D.C. NOW, and an end to the litigation is not yet in sight.[189] Delays of this length are not unusual in reverse FOIA lawsuits, especially in cases involving EEO information where the administrative process is more extensive than normal.[190]

Congress has never specifically authorized the courts to entertain reverse FOIA lawsuits. Indeed, the possibility that FOIA would be used to prevent the disclosure of information was not foreseen by Congress, and there is no reference to such litigation in the act or its legislative history. It is the courts that have recognized a cause of action permitting submitters to challenge the release by Federal agencies of business information that may be confidential.

Based on the pattern of reverse-FOIA suits filed to date, it is apparent that this litigation has caused substantial interference with the flow of information under FOIA. The length of time necessary to resolve reverse-FOIA cases represents a serious threat to the usefulness of FOIA as an expeditious means of making documents available. Reverse-FOIA actions filed while requests are pending disrupt agency proceedings by prematurely involving the courts and place significant new burdens on the judicial system. Finally, these suits may unduly restrict agency discretion to release information in the public interest.

On the other hand, the lawsuits provide submitters with a way to protect confidential documents from unwarranted disclosures. The courts have recognized the importance of allowing submitters a remedy and have been willing to hear reverse-FOIA actions. Judicial examination of agency release practice and policy is consistent with general principles of judicial review of agency actions reflected in the Administrative Procedure Act and other laws, including FOIA itself. It may be true many of the problems with reverse-FOIA lawsuits are a result of the lack of congressional guidance in this area. Nevertheless, the conflict between the goals of disclosure of public information and of protection of private interests will always be acute.

Jurisdiction

Several different jurisdictional bases have been used in reverse-FOIA lawsuits. Until early 1977, many courts found jurisdiction under the Administrative Procedure Act (APA). While some courts relied on the APA,[191] others consistently refused to recognize it as an independent grant of jurisdiction in any context.[192] This controversy was recently resolved by the Supreme Court. In *Califano* v. *Sanders,*[193] a case that did not involve the FOIA, the Court made it clear that the Administrative Procedure Act does not afford subject matter jurisdiction permitting judicial review of agency action. Thus, the jurisdictional basis for reverse-FOIA suits must be found elsewhere.

Many courts have found jurisdiction for reverse-FOIA lawsuits under the general Federal jurisdiction statute, 28 U.S.C. § 1331, which gives district courts original jurisdiction of all civil actions arising under United States law. Several commentators[194] have concluded that Section 1331 is the best source of jurisdiction in reverse-FOIA actions. This is reinforced by a 1976 amendment to Section 1331 eliminating the $10,000 amount-in-controversy requirement in actions brought against the United States, its agencies, officers, and employees.[195]

Section 1331 appears to be an adequate basis for jurisdiction.[196]

Basis for Relief

Submitters have generally relied on one of three legal theories as a basis for reverse-FOIA lawsuits.

Administrative Procedure Act. Section 10 of the APA provides: "A person suffering legal wrong because of agency action, or adversely affected or aggrieved by agency action within the meaning of a relevant statute, is entitled to judicial review thereof."[197] Disclosure by an agency constitutes agency action within the meaning of the APA, and the adverse consequence of that action is the alleged harm to a submitter's competitive position.[198] While the APA does not afford jurisdiction for reverse-FOIA lawsuits, it clearly provides a submitter with a cause of action for enjoining an agency from disclosing confidential information furnished by that submitter.[199] The consequences of reliance on the APA in reverse-FOIA cases for the scope of judicial review are discussed in the next section.

Freedom of Information Act. A second theory for reverse-FOIA lawsuits is derived from the FOIA itself. The act explicitly provides a judicial remedy for requesters seeking disclosure, but no corresponding remedy for submitters seeking to prevent disclosure. Nevertheless, it has been contended that submitters may sue under the FOIA in order to block disclosures that the FOIA was designed to prohibit. This contention is based on the view that Congress specifically intended to protect the submitter's need for confidentiality but that the interests in nondisclosure underlying the fourth exemption are not adequately protected unless the exemptions are mandatory.[200] Under this interpretation, agencies are not merely permitted to withhold information that is exempt, but are required to do so.

A cause of action under FOIA for reverse-FOIA cases appears to be contingent upon a determination that the exemptions are mandatory, and in several early reverse-FOIA cases, courts so held.[201] However, in later cases, courts (including, most recently, the third, seventh, and eighth circuits) have adopted the view that the exemptions are permissive.[202] Nothing in the language of FOIA directly supports the argument that the exemptions are mandatory, and the legislative history of the original law and the 1974 amendments clearly reflects the intention of the Congress that the exemptions are permissive.[203] Nearly all commentators on FOIA agree that the exemptions are permissive.[204] The Department of Justice told the committee that Exemption 4 material can be released on a discretionary basis "where such a release would not be an abuse of discretion or a violation of some other statute."[205]

The committee finds that there is no legitimate basis for holding that the exemptions are mandatory and, as a result, it is extremely doubtful that a cause of action for reverse-FOIA suits properly arises under FOIA.[206]

Trade Secrets Act. A third theory underlying reverse-FOIA lawsuits is based on the Trade Secrets Act (18 U.S.C. § 1905),[207] a criminal statute that on its face prohibits the disclosure of very broad categories of business information "except as provided by law." Submitters have inferred from this statute a private cause of action to prevent the disclosure of information that is exempt under FOIA.[208] Since the Trade Secrets Act only prohibits the disclosure of business information not authorized by law, no cause of action arises with regard to information that is not exempt because the FOIA requires that non-exempt information be released. However, it has been argued that the permissive disclosure of exempt documents is not authorized by FOIA or other statutes, that disclosure is therefore prohibited by section 1905, and that submitters can sue to prevent these disclosures.

The courts have been willing to imply a private cause of action under Federal criminal statutes only under limited circumstances. One of the necessary prerequisites is the unavailability of alternative avenues of redress.[209] Since adequate relief is available under the Administrative Procedure Act,[210] there is no reason to imply a cause of action under Section 1905.[211]

There may be additional reasons why the Trade Secrets Act may not be available to the reverse-FOIA plaintiff. The first relates to the scope of the Trade Secrets Act. While most courts that considered section 1905 and Exemption 4 concluded that both have the same scope, a recent analysis of the legislative history of section 1905 by attorney Daniel Gorham Clement demonstrates convincingly that this interpretation of section 1905 is overly broad. According to Clement's research, the current Trade Secrets Act was derived from three narrow predecessor statutes limiting disclosure of tax information, trade secrets or processes arising out of Tariff Commission investigations, and confidential statistical information acquired by the Commerce Department. The current language of section 1905 dates back to a 1940 codification intended only to consolidate these three laws.[212]

Based on this analysis, it appears that although the language of the section implies that broad categories of disclosures are prohibited, only a few are actually covered. Since section 1905 is a criminal statute, it should be strictly construed, and the narrower interpretation should be preferred. Under this view, the scope of section 1905 is extremely limited, and the section has no relevance to most reverse-FOIA cases.

The second reason against use of section 1905 is that it does not absolutely bar the release of business information within its scope. The prohibition only applies to disclosures that are not authorized by law. If agencies may release exempt information under FOIA or other statutes, then section 1905 is not applicable. In other words, if an agency has legal authority to reveal information, the disclosure is not criminal activity as defined in section 1905. The third circuit and the eighth circuit both recently held that such disclosure authority does exist. Regulations authorizing disclosure may be issued under FOIA; under 5 U.S.C. 301, the "housekeeping" statute that authorizes the issuance of regulations for the custody, use, or preservation of records; and under other specific statutes that define agency responsibilities.[213]

Recommendation. Despite the general confusion in the court cases, the committee finds that there is sufficient authority under the Administrative Procedure Act to support a reverse-FOIA cause of action. In the event that the decision of the Supreme Court in *Chrysler* v. *Schlesinger* does not resolve this issue with sufficient clarity, the committee recommends that a specific cause of action for reverse-FOIA lawsuits be established by Congress.[213a]

Scope of Review

Another issue that arises in reverse-FOIA cases is the proper scope of judicial review of the agency decision to disclose. Scope of review is the degree of scrutiny that a court gives to a decision of an administrative agency. It is especially important in reverse-FOIA cases because a more extensive review by the courts takes more time, is more expensive, and can substantially delay the FOIA process and the availability of information.

When a requester sues to require production of records improperly withheld by an agency, FOIA requires the court to determine the matter de novo. This requires the court to make its own independent decision rather than to simply review the agency's decision. The court is specifically given the authority to examine the disputed records *in camera,* and the burden of proof is on the agency to sustain its action.[214] However, nothing in the act refers to reverse-FOIA litigation and there is, therefore, no specific legislative determination of the proper scope of judicial review of an agency decision to disclose documents.

Until recently, the courts have uniformly made de novo determinations in reverse-FOIA cases.[215] However, in *Chrysler Corp.* v. *Schlesinger,*[216] the Third Circuit decided for the first time anywhere that the proper scope of judicial review of a reverse-FOIA case arising under the Administrative Procedure Act is a review of the agency record and not a de novo determination.

Arguments for de novo review. Those who favor de novo review in reverse-FOIA cases make a number of arguments for its necessity. First, since a suit seeking disclosure of records is heard de novo, a suit to prevent disclosure should be entitled to the same type of review. When deciding that trial de novo was required, the Court of Appeals for the fourth circuit said:

> Should not the person who is threatened with harm through a disclosure, which the Congress has indicated clearly is against the public policy as expressed in the FOIA itself, be the proper one to assert that right to protection from disclosure assured him under Exemption 4, in an equity action in which he can have a de novo trial? The envious competitor or the curious busybody demanding access to that private information has the right to such a de novo trial.

The Act gives it to him. But is not the same right to be implied, when the supplier, with a right that Congress gave him "not only as a matter of fairness but as a matter of right," seeks what may be regarded as correlative relief?[217]

Second, it is argued that de novo review is necessary because agencies are not qualified to make decisions about the consequences of disclosure for the submitting business. One witness stated:

> While the agency employees who pass upon disclosure requests are skilled at performing their primary functions, they are not properly qualified to assess the serious impact which disclosure of assertedly confidential commercial information will have on the submitter. Thus, most government employees who pass upon FOIA requests and claims of exemption are primarily trained to perform wholly distinct job responsibilities; they are not, however, either expert economists or judges, and have no adequate training or experience either to independently analyze the impact of threatened disclosure or to assess competing claims and expert testimony as to what effect disclosure will have. Indeed, some government agencies have admitted as much, stating before this subcommittee that they do not have the capability to independently evaluate the competitive nature and value of much of the private, commercial data which is furnished to government agencies.[218]

Third, it has been charged that "many agencies are now characterized by an institutional bias in favor of disclosure which may render these agencies insensitive to business' claims of confidentiality and may well impair the agency's ability to develop a fair and adequate record of the administrative action."[219] The appropriate remedy for this problem, it is contended, is trial de novo.

Finally, it is argued that current agency proceedings in FOIA matters do not permit the compilation of an adequate record of the agency's decision, so that de novo review by the court is necessary because a court cannot review the record for a decision when no record exists.

Arguments against de novo review. The arguments favoring de novo review in reverse-FOIA cases do not take into account the general legal requirements for review of agency actions. Normally, when any agency action is appealed to the courts, the scope of judicial review is governed by section 706 of the Administrative Procedure Act.[220] But for the FOIA's express provision of de novo review in cases brought by requesters, section 706 would require review of the agency record and a setting aside of the agency action if found to be "arbitrary, capricious, an abuse of discretion, or otherwise not in accordance with the law." Since there is no statute prescribing a different scope of review in reverse-FOIA cases, it follows that section 706 should be applicable. Some of the confusion in existing reverse FOIA cases about scope of review may derive from the reliance on statutes other than the APA as a basis for the lawsuits.[221] In cases where the courts held that the actions arose under the APA, they also held that trial de novo was inappropriate.

In FOIA appeals by requesters, Congress decided that de novo review was necessary because of the extreme reluctance of agencies to make information public,[222] and to assure that "the ultimate decision as to the propriety of the agency's action is made by the court and [to] prevent it from becoming meaningless judicial sanctioning of agency discretion."[223]

The reason that led Congress to provide de novo review in the normal FOIA lawsuit—agency reluctance to disclose—does not support de novo review for those seeking to prevent the disclosure of documents. Agency disclosure policies were well documented at the time Congress decided that de novo review was appropriate in normal FOIA lawsuits. However, evidence to substantiate allegations of the agency bias in favor of disclosure of business information has not been presented.

The charge that agencies are not well qualified to assess the consequences of disclosure is, at least in part, true. The same could be said of judges who are not specifically trained to decide complex business information issues. However, if agencies have a lack of experience or ability in the evaluation of evidence of competitive harm, it does not mean that the remedy is trial de novo in the courts. Agency errors in evaluation of evidence can be corrected through a review of the record more easily and more cheaply than through trial de novo.

It is also true that there are inadequacies in agency procedures for deciding on the release of business information. Again, however, the solution is not necessarily de novo review. Nancy Duff Campbell, visiting Associate Professor of Law at Georgetown University Law Center, summarized the practical problems with de novo review:

> De novo review dictates that courts consider the questions before them as if they were the agency faced with deciding the case in the first instance. This increases the amount of court time beyond that which is necessary simply to determine from the agency's own record whether there has been an abuse of discretion. The granting of relief to either party in the case is also thus delayed, as is the decision of other perhaps equally if not more important cases on the court's docket. While these consequences may be justified in FOIA cases where Congress has, for substantial reasons, provided for de novo review, to engender such consequences in reverse-FOIA cases seems both unwarranted and unwise.[224]

An obvious remedy for deficient agency procedures is a change in those procedures. The adoption of the improvements recommended in part IV should result in better, fairer, and more efficient decision making in reverse-FOIA matters.

Further, even when agency procedures are imperfect, remand to the agency is an alternative to de novo review by the courts. In *Chrysler,* the administrative record was found to be insufficient, and the case was returned to the agency for further proceedings. The Court of Appeals in *Chrysler* viewed the remand decision as the last step in reviewing an agency decision to disclose documents:

> It seems to us that in reverse FOIA cases under the APA a reviewing court should make the following analysis. First it should inquire whether any non-disclosure statute or non-disclosure regulation is applicable. If so, the court must conclude that the agency has acted outside the scope of its statutory authority, and should enjoin disclosure. If no nondisclosure statute or regulation applies, the court must then determine under what authority the agency intends to disclose the contested information. If the agency has concluded that the contested information does not fall within any FOIA exemption, thus mandating disclosure, the court must examine whether the agency applied the proper legal standards for the applicability of the FOIA exemptions. If, however, the agency has concluded (a) that the contested information does fall within an FOIA exemption but (b) public disclosure is, nevertheless, both desirable and permissible under the agency's own disclosure regulations, the court must undertake a two-step analysis. It must first examine whether the agency applied the proper legal standards for the applicability of the FOIA exemptions and, if so, then examine whether the agency considered the proper factors in determining that disclosure was permitted under its own disclosure regulations. . . . And, as the FOIA exemptions make clear, disclosure of certain types of information will not, in the opinion of Congress, always be in the public interest. Finally, if the agency record does not establish, or insufficiently explains, the basis for the agency's decision, so as not to permit the reviewing court to effectively perform the above analysis, the remedy is not a trial de novo, but a remand to the agency for an additional record or explanation for its decision. Interim relief, of course, can be ordered on the authority of 5 U.S.C. § 705.[225]

The step-by-step approach outlined by the court in *Chrysler* seems quite appropriate for reverse-FOIA cases. When it is necessary to remand a case to an agency, the court should allow a limited time for agency action in order to prevent excessive delays in the FOIA process.

Recommendation. The committee agrees with recent court cases holding that existing law requires judicial review of the agency record in reverse-FOIA cases under the "arbitrary and capricious" standard of the Administrative Procedure Act. Unfortunately, this interpretation has not been universally adopted. In the event that the decision of the Supreme Court in *Chrysler* v. *Schlesinger* does not resolve this issue with sufficient clarity, the committee recommends that FOIA be amended to specify the scope of review in reverse-FOIA cases.[225a]

Other Procedural Matters

Exhaustion of administrative remedies. Under FOIA, a requester may not sue for disclosure of documents until all administrative remedies, including appeal to the head of the agency, have been exhausted. Since the act provides no administrative remedies for submitters seeking to block disclosure, the courts have not recognized any prerequisites to the filing of a reverse-FOIA lawsuit. When a reverse-FOIA suit is brought by a submitter before agency action is completed, the administrative process can be shortcircuited. The filing of a suit may not only interrupt the agency decision making process, but may allow the submitter to choose the most favorable forum for the lawsuit. Many agencies agree either formally or informally to give submitters advance notice of a final decision to release documents. This helps to preserve the significance of the agency decision. Nevertheless, submitters remain free to file suit to prevent release of documents at any time before the agency has made a final decision.

Nancy Duff Campbell, Visiting Associate Professor of Law at Georgetown University Law Center, suggested that both requester and submitter should be required to exhaust administrative remedies. Under her proposal, both parties would initially submit arguments to the agency which would make a determination. Either party could appeal an adverse decision to the head of the agency, and appeals by both parties would be consolidated. Only after a final agency decision would either party be permitted to appeal to the courts.[226]

This suggestion is consistent with the emphasis placed on the administrative process in this report. By forcing submitters to state their objections at the agency level, agencies will have more information on which to base a decision, and a better record will be available for judicial review. However, a dual exhaustion requirement would increase the time needed to complete agency action on requests; the use by a submitter of the agency appeal process might significantly slow the release of information. No agency has had any experience with such a procedure.

The committee is concerned that under this proposal, submitters would be able to delay the release of information simply by appealing the initial decision to the head of the agency. How this would affect the overall flow of information under FOIA must still be evaluated.[227] Also, if obliged to exhaust administrative remedies, a submitter would have to receive some type of notice that a request for information was made in order to pursue administrative remedies. Such a notice requirement would have to be integrated with the notice options discussed in part IV of this report. The committee has no recommendation at this time.

Venue. The FOIA allows the requester to file suit in several places: the district in which the complainant resides or has his principal place of business, the district in which the agency records are located, or the District of Columbia.[228] Since the submitter can file suit any time after the request has been made, but the requester cannot go to court until the administrative process has been completed, the submitter has an initial opportunity to choose the forum. In one case involving the Consumer Product Safety Commission, Consumers Union, and thirteen television manufacturers, more than a dozen separate lawsuits were filed over a single FOIA request. Consumers Union had requested certain television related accident data submitted to the Commission by the manufacturers. When the Commission eventually agreed to release the information, the manufacturers filed reverse-FOIA lawsuits to prevent release. Seven suits were filed in Delaware and five were filed in New York or Pennsylvania. Shortly after these reverse-FOIA suits were filed, the requester sued in the District of Columbia.[229] The actions brought by the manufacturers were consolidated in Delaware,[230] but the requester's lawsuit was not consolidated or coordinated with the reverse-FOIA actions.[231] Each court initially proceeded with the case before it without specifically considering the effect of the other lawsuit.

Bringing all of the parties interested in the release of business information together in one FOIA suit is not a simple matter. Suits can be initiated at different times and in different places by the submitter or by the requester. In one instance, a submitter filed a reverse-FOIA lawsuit after a request was made, and obtained an injunction prohibiting release of documents. The requester, who was not a party to the submitter's action and who did not intervene, then filed a suit of his own. The requester's court did not find itself bound by the action of the submitter's court, and reached a different decision.[232] In this case, the courts and the Government did twice as much work as was necessary.

Another problem is that the procedural devices of the Federal Rules of Civil Procedure are not always sufficient to manage all types of reverse-FOIA lawsuits. In some cases, there may be jurisdictional limitations which prevent the requester or the submitter from joining the other party in a lawsuit. Also, since it has not been established by any court that the submitter is an indispensable party to a lawsuit filed by the requester or vice versa, the courts have not insisted that both parties participate in the same action. If a requester is required to intervene or otherwise join in a lawsuit filed by a submitter, it is possible that some requesters may be prevented from using FOIA because of the expense of the litigation. Some submitters may also be unable to protect documents if confronted by a similar requirement. It is unclear whether all of these problems can be corrected by the courts without changes in current rules of procedure.[233]

Only two witnesses specifically addressed the problems of venue in reverse-FOIA cases. Diane B. Cohn of the Freedom of Information Clearinghouse suggested that requesters be joined in reverse-FOIA suits and that requesters be given the right to transfer the action to any other district court where the requester could have filed suit under FOIA.[234] Nancy Duff Campbell, who had suggested that both requester and submitter be required to exhaust administrative remedies before filing suit, wanted the winner at the administrative level limited to a right of intervention in the loser's suit, with a preference for the requester's choice of forum. If the agency decision is adverse to both parties, the requester would have the first opportunity to appeal and to choose a forum. If the requester did not act within a fixed period, the submitter would be entitled to appeal in a forum of his choice.[235]

Recommendation. The committee recommends that FOIA be amended to provide rules governing the venue of reverse-FOIA lawsuits. The purpose of an amendment should be to limit the amount of litigation arising out of an FOIA request by allowing the submitter, requester, and government to participate in the same lawsuit. Participation in the litigation should not be a requirement of maintaining a request for documents or a claim of confidentiality. The existing preference for the rights of requesters should be maintained.

Restrictions on the Scope of Relief in Reverse-FOIA Cases

The purpose of a reverse-FOIA lawsuit is to prevent a Federal agency from releasing confidential information to the public under FOIA, and a plaintiff who is successful will obtain an injunction to that effect. While this has been the type of relief granted in the typical reverse-FOIA action, possible expansion of the scope of available relief is a cause of concern. For example, an injunction might be so broadly worded that it prohibits disclosure after the information has lost its confidential character; restricts other authorized uses of the information by an agency; or prevents persons not connected with the Government from using or disclosing the information. These possibilities are for the most part theoretical. Nevertheless, great care must be taken in reverse-FOIA cases in order to prevent the unwitting expansion of the cause of action and the creation of new and unwarranted restrictions on the availability and use of business data.

Time. Decisions in reverse-FOIA cases favorable to plaintiffs have generally not recognized the time value of confidential business information. Injunctions against release are usually permanent and contain no expiration date. Findings made by the court in reverse-FOIA cases are typically limited to a determination of the confidential character of the information at the time the request was made. Yet it is apparent that the need for confidential treatment of most business data diminishes rapidly as time passes. The competitive value of stale information is small or nonexistent.

In many cases, a court that has determined that an agency should not release business information should be able to place a specific time limit on its nondisclosure order. This could be done in one of two ways. If the court is able to decide that protection is necessary for a fixed period only, it can order the information withheld for that time and then released when the need for confidentiality has passed. Alternatively, if the court is unable to decide upon a specific termination date for confidential treatment, it can still place a time limit on the effectiveness of its decision without requiring release at the end of the period. Upon expiration of the withholding order, the issue of the availability of the documents could be raised again and the need for confidentiality reassessed. Unqualified orders to withhold information are generally inappropriate, and the courts should recognize that changed circumstances may require the reversal of an earlier conclusion that a document is confidential or that disclosure would be an abuse of discretion.

Other disclosure statutes. A second area where reverse-FOIA litigation could lead to overly broad court orders involves restrictions on disclosures made by agencies under the authority of statutes other than FOIA. While FOIA is the only law authorizing the general release of Federal records to the public, many agencies are subject to other laws requiring or permitting specific releases of information to the public, to other Federal, State, or local agencies, or to the Congress.

A good example of a law that sanctions the sharing of information among agencies is the Federal Coal Leasing Amendments Act of 1975.[236] Section 7 of that act amends the Mineral Lands Leasing Act by adding a subsection that authorizes and directs all Federal departments to provide the Secretary of the Interior with information necessary in implementing an exploratory program for coal.

Exchanges of information pursuant to this or similar laws do not constitute disclosures under the Freedom of Information Act, and no limitation imposed in a reverse-FOIA lawsuit can or should affect this authority to share data. No exchange of records between Federal agencies can be made pursuant to the legal authority of FOIA because requests under that act can only be made by a "person." As defined by the Administrative Procedure Act, "person" specifically excludes Federal agencies.[237]

Restrictions imposed in reverse-FOIA lawsuits should not directly interfere with other types of public disclosure statutes. For example, the Federal Energy Administration Act of 1974 authorizes the release of information to keep the public fully and currently informed as to the nature, extent, duration, and impact of shortages of energy supplies.[238] How this authority interacts with statutory restrictions found elsewhere is not entirely clear. However, an order in a reverse-FOIA lawsuit limiting release of information by an agency should apply only to disclosures made pursuant to the Freedom of Information Act.

A court should not flatly forbid any disclosure of business documents unless all agency disclosure authority has been considered and found lacking. The scope of agency authority to publish information under a law other than FOIA may of course be subject to court review independently of reverse-FOIA actions.

Release of business data by third parties. Since FOIA only authorizes disclosures of information by Federal agencies, restrictions imposed as a result of reverse-FOIA actions should only apply to Federal agencies. It is possible that a submitter may have other legal remedies to prevent third parties from using or disclosing information acquired from the Government. But a reverse-FOIA cause of action does not attach to the information itself. Information that has been disclosed already by an agency, regardless of the circumstances, is beyond the reach of a reverse-FOIA lawsuit. The most extreme example would be an attempt to use a reverse-FOIA suit to prevent a newspaper or its reporter from printing confidential business records obtained from a Government agency. A reverse-FOIA lawsuit may not be used as a tool of prior restraint.

Recommendation. The committee recommends that the Department of Justice and other Federal agencies take reasonable steps to ensure that nondisclosure orders issued in reverse-FOIA lawsuits be as narrow in scope, purpose, and time of effectiveness as possible.

Notes

[1a].   On April 18, 1979 the Supreme Court rendered a unanimous opinion in *Chrysler* v. *Brown,* 60 L Ed 2d 208. The court held that FOIA itself "does not afford [the submitting party] any right to enjoin agency disclosure" (at p. 220). However, the Court held that the Trade Secrets Act (18 USC 1905) is applicable to the threatened disclosure (at pp. 220-235). The court did not decide whether an agency's

discretionary decision to release a submitter's records is subject to judicial review under the Administrative Procedure Act.

[1b].   The Court in *Chrysler* v. *Brown*, 60 L Edd 2d 208, refused to decide which standard of review should apply.

1.   Business Record Exemption of the Freedom of Information Act: Hearings Before a Subcommittee of the House Committee on Government Operations, 95th Cong., 1st Sess. p. 111. (Oct. 3 and 4, 1977), (testimony of Burt A. Braverman) [hereinafter cited as Hearings].

2.   The company is FOI Services, Incorporated, Rockville, Maryland. Other companies offer similar services.

3.   See, e.g., Testimony of Donald Kennedy, Commissioner, Food and Drug Administration, in Hearings, p. 77.

4.   Statistics on the number and source of FOIA requests are frequently unreliable. At some agencies, requests for information are counted only when FOIA is specifically cited by the requester. Identical requests that do not mention the act may not be counted. At the Food and Drug Administration, for example, correspondence that is handled by the Consumer Inquiries Office is not counted as part of the FOIA workload. Although not all consumer inquiries necessarily contained requests for information, over 80,000 letters were received by that office in 1977. This compares with an FDA estimate of 25,000 FOIA requests for the same period, mostly from corporations or their representatives. Also, at FDA many requests made for information that is not yet available are required to be resubmitted at a later date. Since both the initial and the resubmitted requests are counted separately, the total number of FOIA requests is inflated. On the other hand, one service company advertises that it is able to fill 40 percent of FOIA requests for FDA documents out of its own files. Although these requests may have been generated by FOIA, they are not included in agency totals.

The number of requests and the mix of requesters vary considerably from agency to agency. At the Federal Bureau of Investigation, for example, most requests are from individuals. The FBI does not keep separate statistics on FOIA and Privacy Act requests, and a recent GAO report indicated that approximately 70 percent of all requests were from individuals. See General Accounting Office, "Timeliness and Completeness of FBI Responses to Requests under Freedom of Information and Privacy Act Have Improved" 6 (GGD-78–51, Apr. 10, 1978).

5.   In discussing the effect of FOIA on industry compliance with FDA rules, Commissioner Donald Kennedy testified that FOIA would probably leave the pharmaceutical and the food industries "at a standoff." While it might lead to a certain homogenization of practice, Kennedy doubted that it would affect industry's overall compliance rate with regulations. Hearings, p. 78.

6.   *Honeywell Information Systems, Inc.* v. *National Aeronautics and Space Administration,* Nos. 76–353, 76–377 (D.D.C. July 28, 1976).

7.   *Babcock & Wilcox Company* v. *Rumsfeld,* 70 F.R.D. 595 (N.D. Ohio 1976).

8.   See, e.g., *Sears, Roebuck and Co.* v. *General Services Administration* (II), 553 F. 2d 1378 (D.C. Cir. 1977); *Westinghouse Electric Corp.* v. *Schlesinger,* 392 F. Supp. 1246 (E.D. Va. 1974).

9.   *Charles River Park "A", Inc.* v. *Department of Housing and Urban Development,* 519 F. 2d 935 (D.C. Cir. 1973).

10.   *McCoy* v. *Weinberger,* 386 F. Supp. 504 (W.D. Ky. 1974).

11.   *National Parks and Conservation Association* v. *Kleppe* (II), 547 F. 2d 673 (D.C. Cir. 1976).

12.   See note 62 and accompanying text.

13.   Letter from Terry D. Miller, president, Government Sales Consultants, Inc., in Hearings, app. 13.

14.   W. Connolly and J. Fox, "Employer Rights and Access to Documents Under the Freedom of Information Act," 46 *Fordham Law Review* 203, 204 (1977). The committee is aware of the growing use of FOIA to augment both civil and criminal discovery proceedings. The first sentence of the opinion of the Court of Appeals in *Rabbins Tire and Rubber Co.* v. *National Labor Relations Board,* 563 F.2d 724 (5th Cir. 1977), rev'd, — U.S. — (June 6, 1978) (No. 77–911), reflects this use: "This is a Freedom of Information Act (FOIA) case, although it takes on the troubling coloration of a dispute about the discovery rights of respondents in National Labor Relations Board proceedings." 563 F.2d at 726 (footnote omitted).

In lawsuits where the Government is a party, FOIA has been used to obtain information (1) of a type not available under discovery rules, (2) at a different time than discovery rules permit, or (3) already received under discovery but requested under FOIA as a test of accuracy or completeness. When the Government is not involved in litigation, FOIA may be used to obtain information about the opposing party or about Government policies and activities related to the subject of the lawsuit. It has also been alleged that FOIA has been used to harass or interfere with ongoing investigations or prosecutions. This is done by requesting information that agency personnel intimately involved with the probe must spend time processing.

A review of the relationship between FOIA and rules of discovery involves matters beyond the scope of this report and would have taken more time than was available. However, more work on this subject, including a review of agency and judicial discovery rules and their coordination with Government information policy is needed.

15.   Testimony of Michael A. James, Deputy General Counsel, Environmental Protection Agency, in Hearings, p. 23.

16.   W. Connolly and J. Fox, *supra* note 14 at 206.

17.   Testimony of Diane B. Cohn, Freedom of Information Clearinghouse, in Hearings, p. 152.

18.   Letter from Lois J. Schiffer, Center for Law and Social Policy, in Hearings, app. 8.

19.   Hearings, p. 25.

20.   Hearings, p. 77.

21.   Testimony of Burt A. Braverman in Hearings, p. 108.

22.   See generally D. Montgomery, A. Peters and C. Weinberg, "The Freedom of Information Act: Strategic Opportunities and Threats," *Sloan Management Review* 1 (Winter, 1978).

23.   *Id.,* pp. 105-06.

24.   *Id.,* p. 100: Letter from James H. Hanes, vice president and general counsel, Dow Chemical Co., in Hearings, app. 11.

25.   See testimony of Burt A. Braverman in Hearings, p. 124–25; Letter from James H. Hanes, vice president and general counsel, Dow Chemical Co., in Hearings, app. 11.

26.   See text accompanying notes 60–62.

27.   See 5 U.S.C. § 552(b)(3) (1976).

28.   565 F. 2d 1172 (3d Cir. 1977), *cert. granted sub nom. Chrysler* v. *Brown,* 6 U.S.L.W. 3555 (Mar. 7, 1978).

[28a].   *Chrysler* v. *Brown* was handed down on April 18, 1979. See the opinion in Appendix A.

29.   Commission on Federal Paperwork, Confidentiality and Privacy 100 (1977).

30.   Hearings on the Privacy and Confidentiality Report and Final Recommendations of the Commission on Federal Paperwork before a subcommittee of the House Committee on Government Operations, 95th Cong., 1st sess., (Oct. 17, 1977).

31.   See also General Accounting Office, "Data Collected From Non-Federal Sources—Statistical and Paperwork Implications," ch. 4 (GGD–78–54, May 17, 1978).

32.   5 U.S.C. § 552(b)(4) (1976).

33.   The Attorney General had concluded that Exemption 4 covered any information, whether or not commercial or financial, given to the Government in confidence. U.S. Department of Justice, 1967 Attorney General's Memorandum of the Public Information Section of the Administrative Procedure Act 32–34 (1967). For comments on the shortcomings of the Attorney General's memorandum, see Subcommittee on Administrative Practice and Procedure of the Senate Committee on the Judiciary, 93d Cong., 2d sess., Freedom of Information Act Source Book: Legislative Materials, Cases, Articles 9 (Committee Print 1974) [hereinafter cited as Sourcebook].

34.   See, for example, *National Parks and Conservation Association* v. *Morton* (I), 498 F. 2d 765 (D.C. Cir. 1974). The Interpretation of the scope of Exemption 4 contained in the 1967 Attorney General's Memorandum is clearly incorrect. See K. Davis, *Administrative Law Treatise* § 3A.19 (Supp. 1970): K. Davis, *Administrative Law of the Seventies* § 3A.19 (1976).

35.   See note, "Would Macy's Tell Gimbel's: Government-Controlled Business Information and the Freedom of Information Act, Forwards and Backwards," 6 *Loyola University Law Journal* 594, 598 (1975). See also "A Short Guide to the Freedom of Information Act" in Department of Justice, Freedom of Information Case List 10 (Feb. 1978) [hereinafter cited as Department of Justice Short Guide].

36.   *Restatement of Torts* § 757, comment b at 5 (1939).

37.   *Consumers Union of United States* v. *Veterans' Administration,* 301 F. Supp. 796, 801 (.S.D.N.Y. 1969), appeal dismissed as moot, 436 F. 2d 1363 (2d Cir. 1971), quoting *United States ex rel. Norwegian Nitrogen Products Co.* v. *United States Tariff Commission,* 6 F. 2d 491, 495 (D.C. Cir. 1925), rev'd on other grounds, 274 U.S. 106 [47 S.Ct. 499, 71 L.Ed. 949] (1927).

38.   415 F. 2d 878, 881 (9th Cir. 1969).

39.   H.R. Rep. No. 1497, 89th Cong., 2d sess. 10 (1966).

40.   Administrative Procedure Act, Act of June 11, 1946, ch. 324, § 3, 60 Stat. 238: Act of Aug. 12, 1958, Public Law No. 85–619, 72 Stat. 547. See H.R. Rep. No. 92–1419, 92d Cong., 2d sess. 1–3 (1972).

41.   It is now generally recognized that agencies are without authority to make promises of confidentiality that are inconsistent with the disclosure standards of FOIA. "It will obviously not be enough for the agency to assert simply that it received the file under a pledge of confidentiality to the one who supplied it. Undertakings of that nature cannot, in and of themselves, override the Act." *Ackerly* v. *Levy,* 420 F. 2d 1336, 1339–40 n. 3 (D.C. Cir. 1969); *Petkas* v. *Staats,* 501 F. 2d 887, 889 (D.C. Cir. 1974).

42.   S Rep. No. 813, 89th Cong., 1st sess. 9 (1965).

43.   *M. A. Schapiro & Co.* v. *Securities and Exchange Commission,* 339 F. Supp. 467, 471 (D.D.C. 1972).

44.   In *National Parks Conservation Association* v. *Morton,* 498 F.2d 765 (D.C. Cir. 1974), the District of Columbia Court of Appeals established a new test for business record confidentiality, but did not entirely discard the expectation of confidentiality test. The court indicated that the expectation test may be relevant in determining whether information falls within the fourth exemption, but that a finding that information would not generally be made public by the submitter was not, by itself, enough to support application of the fourth exemption. How the expectation test meshes with the substantial competitive harm test is not clear. See text accompanying notes 48–56.

45.   Act of Sept. 13, 1976, Public Law No. 94–409, 90 stat. 1241, 5 U.S.C. § 552b (1976).

46.   "The touchstone of any proceedings under the act must be the clear legislative intent to assure public access to all governmental records whose disclosure would not significantly harm specific governmental interests. The policy of the act requires that the disclosure requirement be construed broadly, the exemptions narrowly." *Soucie* v. *David,* 448 F. 2d 1067 (D.C. Cir. 1971). See *Department of Air Force* v. *Rose,* 425 U.S. 352, [96 S.Ct. 1592, 48 L.Ed.2d 11] 61 (1976).

47.   K. Davis, Administrative Law Treatise § 3A.10 (1970 Supp.). See Note, 6 *Loyola University Law Journal, supra* note 35 at 600–602; 88 *Harvard Law Review* 470 (1974). See generally, Sourcebook 9; *Getman* v. *National Labor Relations Board,* 450 F.2d 620 (D.C. Cir. 1971); *Consumers Union* v. *Veterans' Administration,* 301 F. Supp. 796 (S.D.N.Y. 1969). appeal dismissed as moot. 436 F.2d 1363 (2d Cir. 1971).

48.   498 F.2d 765 (D.C. Cir. 1974).

49.   *Bristol-Myers Co.* v. *Federal Trade Commission,* 424 F.2d 935, 938 (D.C. Cir.), *cert. denied* 400 U.S. 824 (1970).

50.   498 F.2d at 767.

51.   *Id.* at 770.

52.   The court stated that where information was submitted as a mandatory condition of a concessionaire's right to operate in national parks, the first test was inapplicable regardless of whether the information was supplied "pursuant to statute, regulation or some less formal mandate." 498 F. 2d at 770. However, it is not clear when this test should be used. The Commission on Federal Paperwork wrote:

> The need for agencies to guarantee confidentiality is particularly signifi-
> cant in the field of statistical or research activities, where the Government
> must generally rely on the cooperation of the private sector to obtain com-

prehensive and reliable data. Where mandatory collection authority exists or where business entities submit information voluntarily in order to qualify for some Government benefit, such as a license, grant, or contract, it is obviously not as significant a factor.

Commission on Federal Paperwork, *Confidentiality and Privacy* 100 (1977) (footnote omitted). The Commission's last point is very well taken.

53.   The court recognized that its own analysis might be limited. "We express no opinion as to whether other governmental interests are embodied in this exemption." 498 F.2d at Cir. (1976).

54.   T. Patten and K. Weinstein, "Disclosure of Business Secrets Under the Freedom of Information Act: Suggested Limitations," 29 *Administrative Law Review* 193, 198 (1977).

55.   504 F.2d 238 (D.C. Cir. 1974). *cert. denied* 421 U.S. 693 (1975).

56.   See Department of Justice Short Guide 11. See generally letter from Neils J. Reimers, Office of Technology Licensing. Stanford University; letter from Howard W. Bremer, Wisconsin Alumni Research Foundation; letter from Reagan Scurlock, National Association of College and University Business Officers; and letter from John F. Sherman, Association of American Medical Colleges in Hearings, apps. 12, 14, 15, and 17, respectively.

57.   *National Parks and Conservation Association* v. *Kleppe* (II), 547 F.2d 673 (D.C. Cir. 1976).

58.   *Id.* at 683. See T. Patten & K. Weinstein, *supra,* note 54 at 200–01.

59.   See text accompanying note 27.

60.   This standard is frequently referred to as the "demonstrable harm" test, a somewhat misleading description. The Attorney General's letter is reproduced in 123 Congressional Record 87763 (daily ed. May 17, 1977) (remarks of Sen. Kennedy); and in Access Reports, May 17, 1977, at 2–3.

61.   The Attorney General has not explained how the requirement of a sufficient prospect of actual harm relates to the substantial competitive harm test, and at least one witness expressed concern about the creation of a new and narrower standard for the protection of business records. See testimony of Charles I. Derr, senior vice president, Machinery and Allied Products Institute, in Hearings, p. 163. See also letter from Vico E. Henriques, president, Computer and Business Equipment Manufacturers Association in Hearings, app. 8. The committee is unable to divine any difference between sufficient prospect of actual harm and substantial competitive harm, and is not aware that the May 5 letter has resulted in any changes in the treatment of cases involving the fourth exemption.

The General Accounting Office found that less than 1 percent of all pending FOIA cases were settled as a result of the policy announced in the May 5 letter. See General Accounting Office, "Timeliness and Completeness of FBI Responses to Requests Under Freedom of Information and Privacy Act Have Improved" 75 (GGD–78–51, April 10, 1978). The Attorney General's new policy was apparently directed primarily at limiting use of the fifth exemption dealing with inter-agency and intra-agency memoranda. See Department of Justice, "Freedom of Information Act Annual Report to Congress, 1977" at 18.

62.   The nature of a requester's interest in disclosure has been found to be relevant by some courts in FOIA cases involving determinations of clearly unwarranted invasions of personal privacy under the sixth exemption. See, e.g., *Getman* v. *National Labor Relations Board,* 450 F. 2d 670 (D.C. Cir. 1971). But see *Ditlow* v. *Shultz,* 517 F. 2d 166 (D.C. cir. 1975); *Robles* v. *Environmental Protection Agency,* 484 F. 2d 843 (4th Cir. 1973). In *Rose* v. *Department of Air Force,* 425 U.S. 352 (1976), the Supreme Court held that the sixth exemption requires a balancing of public interest in disclosure against the individual's right to privacy, but did not indicate whether the interest of a specific requester could be considered in the balance. In *Environmental Protection Agency* v. *Mink,* 410 U.S. 73, 79 [93 S.Ct. 827, 35 L.Ed.2d 119] (1973), the Supreme Court noted that the original public disclosure section of the Administrative Procedure Act made information available only to "persons properly and directly concerned" with the information. The FOIA eliminated this test of access and made information available to any person.

Since FOIA does not give agencies authority to restrict a requester's use of information, it is not appropriate to base a decision to disclose on the requester's stated purpose. Even if a requester agreed to limit its use of the information, the agreement could not be enforced. In balancing under the sixth exemption, only the general public interest in disclosure should be considered. If this general balancing test requires the withholding of information that an agency would otherwise prefer to disclose, it may still be possible to provide for its disclosure. For some records, the Privacy Act of 1974 permits agencies to establish a routine use authorizing disclosure if the disclosure is compatible with the purpose for which the records were collected. See 5 U.S.C. § 552a(b)(3)(1976). But see generally Commission on Federal Paperwork, *Confidentiality and Privacy* 102(1977) for a different view on this point.

63.   The discussion in this part relates to disclosures of business information required by FOIA. As discussed in part V, agencies have authority to make discretionary disclosures of information that is exempt under FOIA. See text accompanying notes 201–206. In making a decision to disclose information on a discretionary basis, an agency must carefully weigh the public interest in disclosure against the private interest in non-disclosure. See letter from John M. Harmon, Assistant Attorney General, Department of Justice, in Hearings, app. 6, especially pp. 234–235.

64.   All FOIA exemptions are included in subsection (b) of 5 U.S.C. § 552 (1976).

65.   *Grumman Aircraft Engineering Corp.* v. *Renegotiation Board,* 425 F. 2d 578, 582 (D.C. Cir. 1970); *Consumers Union* v. *Veterans' Administration,* 301 F. Supp. 796, 803 (S.D.N.Y. 1969), appeal dismissed as moot, 436 F. 2d 1363 (2d Cir. 1971). But see *Brockway* v. *Department of Air Force,* 518 F. 2d 1184 (8th Cir. 1975).

66.   It is possible that there could be a fourth party with an interest in the result of a FOIA request. When a business has submitted information containing personal data about its employees, both the business and the employees might object to its release. The business could seek confidentiality under Exemption 4 and the employees under Exemption 6. There have been some cases where businesses have argued Exemption 4 on their own behalf and Exemption 6 on behalf of their employees. See, for example, *Sears, Roebuck and Co.* v. *General Services Administration* (II), 553 F. 2d 1378 (D.C. Cir. 1977).

67.   Although there has been widespread confusion about the interaction of the

Privacy Act of 1974 and FOIA, the two Acts actually "mesh well." See the explanation in the report of the Privacy Protection Study Commission, Personal Privacy in an Information Society 520–21 (1977).

It has been suggested on occasion that some procedural protection governing the disclosure of personal information might be needed, especially notice. But in enacting the Privacy Act, Congress decided that notifying individuals prior to each disclosure made by agencies would be too unwieldy and too expensive. Consent of the person who is the subject of a record is required before some disclosures, but for most routine transfers of personal information, the Privacy Act relies on the publication of notices in the Federal Register. This does not preclude an agency from providing notice in selected cases when the disclosure of sensitive personal information is being considered.

68.   See, for example, testimony of Gerald P. Norton, Deputy General Counsel, Federal Trade Commission, before the Subcommittee on Administrative Practice and Procedure of the Senate Committee on the Judiciary, 95th Cong., 1st sess., 14 (1977). See also, T. Patten & K. Weinstein, *supra* note 54 at 202. The Food and Drug Administration has even issued a regulation requiring a submitter to defend any lawsuit arising out of a denial of an FOIA request on grounds of the fourth exemption. If the submitter fails to intervene, then FDA will disclose the information, 21 C.F.R. 20.53 (1977). While an agency may make a discretionary disclosure of exempt information, a decision to release data based solely on the failure of the submitter to intervene in a lawsuit is an improper exercise of that discretionary authority. The need for specific legislative authority for such a regulation is illustrated by the Internal Revenue Code provision for public inspection of written determinations. When the Secretary of the Treasury is sued for disclosure of a written determination, the Secretary must notify persons to whom the determination pertains. If they fail to intervene in the suit, section 6110 of the Code provides that the Secretary is not required to defend the suit.

69.   498 F. 2d at 770.

70.   See text accompanying notes 50–52.

71.   See text accompanying notes 48–58.

72.   See testimony of Michael A. James, Deputy General Counsel, Environmental Protection Agency, in Hearings, p. 5.

73.   Letter from William J. Roche, vice president, secretary, and general counsel, Texas Instruments, Inc., in Hearings, app. 10.

74.   Letter from James T. O'Reilly in Hearings, app. 9.

75.   *Pharmaceutical Manufacturers Association* v. *Weinberger,* 401 F. Supp. 444 (D.D.C. 1976) (preliminary injunction denied); 411 F. Supp. 576 (D.D.C. 1976) (permanent injunction denied).

76.   See also e.g., *Chrysler* v. *Schlesinger* 565 F. 2d 1172 (3d Cir. 1977), *cert. granted sub nom. Chrysler Corp.* v. *Brown,* 46 U.S.L.W. 3555 (Mar. 7, 1978).

77.   D. Clement, "The Rights of Submitters to Prevent Agency Disclosure of Confidential Business Information: The Reverse Freedom of Information Act Lawsuit," 55 *Texas Law Review* 587, 634 (1977) (footnotes omitted).

78.   Hearings, app. 16. See also *Westinghouse Electric Corp.* v. *Schlesinger,* 542 F. 2d 1190, 1213 (4th Cir. 1976), *cert. denied,* 431 U.S. 924 (1977).

79.   T. Patten and K. Weinstein, *supra,* note 54 at 202–03. Requesters also contend

that agencies do not adequately represent the interests of requesters. This may be especially true, in reverse-FOIA cases, where the requester is not joined as a party to the suit.

80.   Letter from John Harmon, Assistant Attorney General, Department of Justice, in Hearings, app. 6.

81.   Hearings, pp. 94–95.

82.   FDA Public Information Regulations, 21 C.F.R. § 20.45 (1977).

83.   Testimony of Donald Kennedy, Commissioner of Food and Drug Administration, in Hearings, p. 69.

84.   *Id.* pp. 68–69.

85.   A study dated Mar. 8, 1978, conducted by the staff of the Government Information and Individual Rights Subcommittee reached these conclusions about the operation of FDA's notice procedure:

"Regulated industry is dissatisfied with FDA's procedures to notify submitters prior to disclosure of submitted information.

"FDA's position on notifying submitters prior to disclosing information which they submitted to FDA is that the regulations constitute such notice and state what information is disclosable. FDA officials stated that it is not feasible to categorize circumstances under which notice should be given or types of data for notice. Only in 'close question' situations are submitters directly notified that information which they submitted to FDA may be disclosed. FDA's FOI officer stated that he had given notice to submitters only six times in the past year.

"The submitter is given notice via phone and mail. When the submitter is contacted via telephone, information is obtained in order to aid the FOI officer in deciding whether the data should be considered confidential or not. For example, use of the information in the company, whether the information provides competitive advantage, and whether such information is widely known throughout the industry are questioned. The FOI officer does not ask whether or not the data is a trade secret. He makes his determination independent of the firm's viewpoint. A letter is then sent notifying the submitter that he has five days during which to file an injunction to stop FDA from releasing the data.

"Although FDA officials and regulated industry agree that it is unrealistic to give notice every time a request is to be answered, regulated industry disagrees with FDA that its regulations constitute notice to submitters. Submitters are of the legal opinion that they should be notified in every case that their information is to be disclosed. All but one of the firms interviewed stated that they had never received notices."

86.   40 C.F.R. § 2.203(c)(1977).

87.   The Office of Federal Procurement Policy recently requested agencies to provide notice to submitters when FOIA requests for contractor information are received. See OFPP Policy Letter No. 78–3 (Mar. 30, 1978). See also "Proposed Regulations on Confidential Business Information of National Highway Traffic Safety Administration," 43 *Federal Register* 22414 (May 25, 1978).

88.   For a discussion of the problems with time limits in existing law, see text accompanying note 185.

89.   See, e.g., EPA Public Information Regulations, 40 C.F.R. §§ 2.204(d) (1)(i), (2) (1977).

90.   There are several laws requiring that submitters be notified prior to disclosure of specific categories of information. See for example, the Federal Insecticide, Fungicide, and Rodenticide Act, 7 U.S.C. § 136h (1976); the Toxic Substances Control Act, Public Law 94–469, 14, 15 U.S.C. § 2613 (1976), The Tax Reform Act of 1976. Public Law 94–455 added section 6110 to the Internal Revenue Code providing for public inspection of IRS written determinations. Included in subsection (f) is a requirement that prior to disclosure of a determination, the Secretary of the Treasury must notify persons to whom the determination pertains. Adoption of a general notice requirement would make these specific laws unnecessary.

The new information provision of the Tax Code contains two new features of relevance to Exemption 4. First, the Code now provides that in the event of a suit for additional disclosure of determinations, the Secretary must notify the person to whom the determination pertains, but that after sending the notice, the Secretary is no longer required to defend the lawsuit. Another provision of section 6110 makes the Government liable for actual damages in the event of an improper disclosure. The Privacy Act of 1974 contains a similar provision, 5 U.S.C. § 552a(g) (1976), but it only covers wrongful disclosures of personal information. Section 6110 now allows damages for improper disclosure of confidential business information. The general desirability or effectiveness of either of these new features remains to be demonstrated.

91.   One witness who favored identification of confidential information at the time of submission suggested that a brief statement of the basis for the claim of confidentiality be required, along with an indication of whether the necessity for confidentiality will be altered by time or future events. Under this proposal, the agency would not rule on the claim until a request for the information is received, at which time the submitter would be permitted to provide a more complete basis for the claim. While it is likely that any requirement that makes it more difficult for a business to claim confidentiality would tend to discourage marginal claims, it is far from certain that the benefits of any reduction in claims would offset the additional expense to business of detailing the reasons for nondisclosure upon submission. See testimony of Diane B. Cohn, Freedom of Information Clearinghouse, in Hearings, p. 153.

92.   Hearings, app. 6.

93.   Letter from William J. Roche, vice president, secretary, and general counsel, Texas Instruments, Inc., in Hearings, app. 10.

94.   Hearings, app. 16.

95.   Hearings, pp. 101–02, 137–138.

96.   40 C.F.R. §§ 2.203,–.204 (1977).

97.   Hearings, pp. 7–8.

98.   Testimony of Michael A. James, Deputy General Counsel, Environmental Protection Agency, in Hearings, pp. 9–10.

99.   The Toxic Substances Control Act, 15 U.S.C. § 2613(c) (1976), provides that submitters must receive notice prior to release of information marked as confidential.

100.   The Commission on Federal Paperwork notes that overuse of the confidentiality classification by agencies collecting information may also serve to perpetuate duplicate reporting and the paperwork burden for agencies and industry by limiting sharing of information between agencies. See Commission on Federal Paperwork, Energy 44 (1977).

101.   *Id.*

102.   Letter from Donald Kennedy, Commissioner of Food and Drug Administration in Hearings, app. 4.

103.   See text accompanying notes 38–41.

104.   Statement of Coopers & Lybrand in Hearings, app. 6.

105.   "Trade secrets" is used here in its narrow sense. See text accompanying notes 35–37. The Department of Justice suggests that the disclosure of this type of trade secret (a technical process, formula or design) might constitute an unconstitutional taking of property within the meaning of the fifth amendment. See letter from John M. Harmon, Assistant Attorney General, in Hearings, app. 6.

106.   Some corporate lawyers advise their clients not to comply with Government requests for information in order to force the issue into court where a protective order can be sought. See, for example, the comments of Herbert M. Wachtell reported in 64 *ABA Journal* 533, 34 (1978). This type of proceeding is similar to an advance determination of confidentiality made by an agency and suffers from all of the same shortcomings. While requiring an agency to notify the submitter before public disclosure may be appropriate, no court should issue an order inconsistent either procedurally or substantively with FOIA. Courts must not allow a protective order to become a device that allows submitters to avoid FOIA to the prejudice of future requesters.

107.   5 U.S.C. § 552(b) (1976).

108.   41 C.F.R. § 60–60.4d (1977). See text accompanying notes 160–164.

109.   See W. Connolly and J. Fox, *supra* note 14 at 211.

110.   See the testimony of Burt A. Braverman in Hearings, p. 138.

111.   The Department of Labor indicated that it is agency practice to provide notice of an FOIA request to the submitter whether or not the information was marked as confidential. See letter from Donald Elisburg, Assistant Secretary for Employment Standards, Department of Labor, in Hearings, app. 3.

112.   40 C.F.R. §§ 2.201(i). .206 (1977).

113.   21 C.F.R. § 20.44 (1977).

114.   A study dated Mar. 8, 1978, conducted by the staff of the Government Information and Individual Rights Subcommittee reached these conclusions about FDA's presubmission review procedure:

"Presubmission review was seldom used. FDA Bureau officials interviewed had participated in only one case of presubmission review. All except one firm interviewed had voluntarily offered information to FDA under presubmission review. The major reason that presubmission review was seldom used was that the regulations covered most of FDA's records and, therefore, informed submitters what information would be considered confidential or not. A representative from one firm stated that he would seldom use presubmission review because he considered it unwise to volunteer information to FDA which it may consider to be "unconfidential."

"The one firm which had used presubmission review volunteered information to FDA on three different occasions. It believed that presubmission review was a useful process and that it could rely on FDA not to release the information if it received an FOIA request for the information. The firm felt that presubmission review was advantageous to industry because decisions are rendered quickly and save the company time in planning its work. FDA had informed the firm of its decision on the confidentiality of the volunteered information within a month of receipt of the information. FDA officials stated that presubmission review decisions are made much more quickly than FOIA decisions because there are few presubmission review cases and they need not go through the entire formal FOIA process. FDA does not promote the presubmission review process. Industry is informed of it through FDA regulations."

115.   See § 24 of the Securities Exchange Act of 1934, 15 U.S.C. § 78x (1976); 17 CFR §240.24b-2 (1977). A denial of a request for confidential treatment can be appealed to the courts giving submitters an alternative to a reverse-FOIA lawsuit. At least one such case has been decided. See *Continental Stock Transfer and Trust Company* v. *Securities and Exchange Commission,* No. 77–4034 (2d Cir. Mar. 21, 1977), in Federal Securities Law Reports. CCH, para. 96, 172.

116.   10 C.F.R. § 2.790 (1977).

117.   43 *Federal Register* 3571 (Jan. 26, 1978).

118.   The National Highway Traffic Safety Administration recently proposed regulations providing for advance determinations. NHTSA would require submitters to support requests for confidential treatment with an affidavit stating that a diligent inquiry has been made to determine that the information has not been disclosed, or otherwise appeared publicly. See 43 *Federal Register* 22412 (May 25, 1978).

119.   The proposed FTC advance determination procedure has some similarities with EPA's method of treating information marked as confidential. EPA does not make any determination when information is submitted, although it does rely on the marking to issue a pro forma denial of a request. However, EPA automatically institutes an appeal and the entire issue of confidentiality is considered at that time. The legality of aspects of the advance determination procedure at both EPA and FTC is in doubt. See text accompanying notes 166–170.

120.   See also Proposed Regulations on Confidential Business Information of National Highway Traffic Safety Administration, 43 *Federal Register* 22412 (May 25, 1978).

121.   40 C.F.R. § 2.206(d) (1977).

122.   21 C.F.R. § 20.44(d) (1977).

123.   Letter from Donald Kennedy, Commissioner of Food and Drug Administration, in Hearings, app. 4.

124.   Letter from Michael A. James, Deputy General Counsel, Environmental Protection Agency, in Hearings, app. 1.

125.   See text accompanying notes 51–52.

126.   A related issue recently arose in *Goland* v. *Central Intelligence Agency,* Civil No. 76–0166 (D.C. Cir. May 23, 1978). There, an FOIA request was made at the CIA for a transcript of a congressional hearing that had been held in executive session. A copy of the transcript had been provided to the CIA. The transcript was marked "Secret" and the court found this to be evidence of a congressional intent to maintain congressional control over the document's confidentiality. Based on this intent, and the facts surrounding the transfer of the document to the CIA, the court held that the transcript was not an agency record within the meaning of FOIA but was a congressional document to which the act does not apply.

In dissenting from this decision, Judge Bazelon stated his view of FOIA "as an unequivocal declaration by Congress that documents which have become part of the administrative process are subject to full disclosure unless specifically exempted." Slip Op. at 9 n. 11. This reading of the law is consistent with the committee's understanding. In any event, the majority opinion in *Goland* must be construed narrowly, applying only to official congressional documents for when there is a formally stated intention to preserve confidentiality. The court's ruling can have no applicability to business documents.

127.   See text accompanying notes 48–63.

128.   See Department of Justice Short Guide 34.

129.   For a discussion of the legality of prima facie determination, see text accompanying notes 169–170.

130.   5 U.S.C. § 553 (1976).

131.   Hearings, p. 92.

132.   21 C.F.R. § 20.100(a) (1977).

133.   Hearings, pp. 68–9.

134.   21 C.F.R. § 20.100 *et seq.* (1977). Blanket rules covering the disclosure of technical proposals of both successful and unsuccessful offerors are of questionable wisdom because such proposals are likely to contain a mixture of confidential and non-confidential data. *Cf. Honeywell Information Systems, Inc.* v. *National Aeronautic and Space Administration,* Nos 76–353, 76–377 (D.D.C. July 23, 1976). See also text accompanying note 155.

135.   21 C.F.R. § 20.100(c) (1977).

136.   21 C.F.R. § 71.15 (1977).

137.   See note 105 and accompanying text.

138.   FDA does have a regulation on segregability, 21 C.F.R. § 2023 (1977), but it is not specifically cross referenced in the substantive disclosure rules.

139.   40 C.F.R. § 2.207(a) (1977). The National Highway Traffic Safety Administration has proposed class determination regulations very similar to those of EPA. See 43 *Fed. Register* 22412. 18 (May 25, 1978).

140.   *Id.* at § 2.208.

141.   Letter from Michael A. James, Deputy General Counsel, Environmental Protection Agency, in Hearings, app. 1.

142.   Class determinations have been issued governing: (1) Confidentiality of Business Information Contained in Bi-monthly Summary Report on Fuel Gas Desulfurization Systems; (2) Confidentiality of Business Information Submitted in Applications for Light Duty Motor Vehicle Certifications Through Model Year 1978; (3) Confidentiality of Business Information Submitted in Applications for Light Duty Motor Vehicle Certifications Model Year 1979. See Letter from Michael A. James, Deputy General Counsel, Environmental Protection Agency, in Hearings, app. 1.

143.   41 C.F.R. § 60–40.2 (1977).

144.   41 C.F.R. § 60–40.3 (1977).

145.   Hearings, app. 3.

146.   43 *Federal Register* 15155 (1978) (to be codified in 43 C.F.R. § 220).

147.   Hearings, p. 171.

148.   Hearings, app. 8.

149.   D. Clement, *supra* note 77 at 638.

150.   Hearings, p. 139.

151.   The Securities and Exchange Commission FOIA rules contain a list of documentary materials available to the public. 17 C.F.R. § 200.80a (1977). Some nondisclosure materials are listed in 17 C.F.R. § 200.80(b)(4) (1977).

152.   Food and Drug Administration Public Information Regulations, 21 C.F.R. § 20.61(c) (1977).

153.   See Memorandum from Peter F. Flaherty, Deputy Attorney General to Quinlan J. Shea, Director, Office of Information and Privacy Appeals, dated June 2, 1977, reproduced in 1 Access Reports—Reference File 12.2071. The memorandum establishes a Department of Justice policy that Exemption 7A (investigatory records compiled for law enforcement purposes) should not be used to conceal unlawful activities.

154.   A regulation to the effect that trade secrets (narrow definition) should not be disclosed may be acceptable. See note 105 and text accompanying notes 35–37.

155.   The Office of Federal Procurement Policy recently issued a policy letter dealing with requests for disclosure of contractor-supplied information obtained in the course of a procurement. While the letter is welcome as a first attempt to coordinate and direct procurement information policies, it fails to contain any detailed guidelines for disclosure of specific categories of data generated during the contracting process. Also, the thrust of the letter is excessively weighed in favor of the withholding rather than the release of information. OFPP Policy Letter No. 78–3 (Mar. 30, 1978).

156.   5 U.S.C. § 552(a)(6) (1976).

157.   5 U.S.C. § 552(a)(4)(B) (1976).

158.   *Chrysler Corp.* v. *Schlesinger,* 565 F. 2d 1172 (3d Cir. 1977), *cert. granted sub nom. Chrysler Corp.* v. *Brown,* 46 U.S.L.W. 3555 (Mar. 7, 1978); *General Dynamics Corp.* v. *Marshall,* No. 77–1192 (8th Cir. Feb. 14, 1978).

159.   Judicial procedures for reverse-FOIA lawsuits and the problems that have developed are discussed in part V of this report. Scope of judicial review is considered in the text accompanying notes 214–225.

160.   42 U.S.C. § 2000e note (1970).

161.   See text accompanying notes 108–111.

162.   41 C.F.R. § 60–60.4(d) (1977).

163.   Testimony of James Henry, Associate Solicitor for Labor Relations in Hearings, p. 38.

164.   *Chrysler Corp.* v. *Schlesinger,* 565 F. 2d 1172 (3d Cir. 1977), *certiorari granted sub nom. Chrysler Corp.* v. *Brown,* 46 U.S.L.W. 3555 (Mar. 7, 1978).

165.   *General Dynamics Corp.* v. *Marshall.* No. 77–1192 (8th Cir. Feb. 14, 1978).

166.   40 C.F.R. § 2.204 (1977).

167.   *Id.* at § 2.205.

168.   Hearings, p. 11. But see generally *Vaughn* v. *Rosen,* 484 F. 2d 820 (D.C. Cir. 1973), *certiorari denied* 415 U.S. 977 (1974), which outlines an indexing procedure that gives the requester an idea of what type of documents are being denied. A *Vaughn* index is only prepared at the court level.

169.   Testimony of Michael A. James, Deputy General Counsel, Environmental Protection Agency, in Hearings, pp. 4–5.

170.   See Confidentiality of Coal Information Regulation issued by the Department of Interior, 43 *Federal Register* 15155 (Apr. 11, 1978). Interior decided to delete a

proposed procedure similar to EPA's pro forma denial procedure on grounds that it might infringe on procedural rights under FOIA.

171.   5 U.S.C. § 552(a)(6)(B)(iii) (1976).

172.   See generally *Church of Scientology of California* v. *U.S. Department of Air Force,* Civ. No. 76–1008 (D.D.C. Apr. 12, 1978), in which a district court held that an agency must consider a request for records that originated with another agency.

173.   Letter from Donald Elisburg, Assistant Secretary for Employment Standards, Department of Labor in Hearings, app. 3. The problems with appeals from one agency to another may disappear when the proposed reorganization of the equal employment opportunity program becomes effective. Current plans are to have OFCC do the contract compliance work now done by the compliance agencies. See Reorganization Plan No. 1 of 1978 (proposed Feb. 24, 1978).

174.   See, e.g., *Chrysler Corp.* v. *Schlesinger,* 565 F. 2d 1172 (3d Cir. 1977), *certificate granted sub nom. Chrysler Corp.* v. *Brown,* 46 U.S.L.W. 3555 (Mar. 7, 1978).

175.   Hearings, p. 71.

176.   Hearings, pp. 134–36.

177.   Hearings, app. 9.

178.   Hearings, app. 6.

179.   Hearings, p. 96.

180.   D. Clement, *supra* note 77 at 636–37 (footnotes omitted).

181.   See note 168 and accompanying text.

182.   See text accompanying note 227.

183.   See text accompanying note 185.

184.   See text accompanying notes 214–225.

185.   5 U.S.C. § 552(a)(6) (1976).

186.   Other openness in government laws are not enlightening on this topic. The Government in the Sunshine Act, Public Law 94–409, which provides that some Government agencies must open some of their meetings to public observation, may eventually give rise to parallel litigation. A "reverse-sunshine" lawsuit to prevent the disclosure of information in an open agency meeting seems possible. See Statutory Comment, "Government in the Sunshine Act: A Danger of Overexposure," 14 *Harvard Journal on Legislation,* 620, 643–48 (1977). However, since reverse-sunshine litigation would likely require considerable judicial intervention in agency proceedings the courts might choose to take a less active role. See also R. Berg and S. Klitzman, An Interpretive Guide to the Government in the Sunshine Act, 89–90 (1978).

The Privacy Act of 1974 permits individuals to object to agency plans for disclosure of information in a system of records, but there have been few cases to date. See 5 U.S.C. 552a(3)(3)(11), (g) (1976).

187.   Letter from Barbara Allen Babcock, Assistant Attorney General, Department of Justice, to Richardson Preyer (May 19, 1978). See Department of Justice, Freedom of Information Case List 68–71 (Feb. 1978); D. Clement, *supra* note 77 at 589–90 n. 7 (collecting cases).

188.   A few reverse-FOIA suits have been filed to prevent the release of personal information that is protected by Exemption 6 of the act, that protects information the

disclosure of which would constitute a clearly unwarranted invasion of personal privacy.

189.   Hearings, app. 8.

190.   See text accompanying notes 160–165.

191.   See, for example, *Charles River Park "A", Inc.* v. *Department of Housing and Urban Development,* 519 F.2d 935 (D.C. Cir. 1975); *McCoy* v. *Weinberger,* 386 F. Supp. 504 (W.D. Ky. 1974).

192.   See Note, "Protection from Government Disclosure—The Reverse-FOIA Lawsuit," 1976 *Duke Law Journal* 330, 349 n. 95.

193.   430 U.S. 99 (1977).

194.   D. Clement, *supra* note 77 at 628; Note, 1976 *Duke Law Journal, supra* note 192 at 351; Note, "Reverse-Freedom of Information Act Suits: Confidential Information in Search of Protection," 70 *Northwestern University Law Review* 995, 1007 (1976). See *Planning Research Corp.* v. *Federal Power Commission,* 555 F.2d 970 (D.C. Cir. 1977).

195.   Act of Oct. 21, 1976, Public Law 94–574, 90 Stat. 2721.

196.   Other theories of jurisdiction have been used on occasion. For example, statutes that prohibit the disclosure of particular information may provide a jurisdictional basis for a reverse-FOIA lawsuit. Most frequently discussed in these terms is 18 U.S.C. § 1905 (1976). See *GTE Sylvania Inc.* v. *Consumer Products Safety Commission,* 404 F. Supp. 352 (D. Del. 1975) (18 U.S.C. § 1337); See generally Note, 1976 *Duke Law Journal, supra* note 192 at 349–351. The need for these alternate theories of jurisdiction is highly questionable given the availability of Section 1331. See text accompanying notes 207–211.

197.   5 U.S.C. § 702 (1976).

198.   Harm to competitive position is the interpretation of the fourth exemption now generally accepted. See text accompanying notes 48–53.

199.   See D. Clement, *supra* note 77 at 626; Note, 70 *Northwestern University Law Review, supra* note 194 at 1012.

200.   See, e.g., *Pennzoil Co.* v. *Federal Power Commission,* 534 F.2d 627 (5th Cir. 1976); *Hughes Aircraft Co.* v. *Schlesinger,* 384 F. Supp. 292 (C.D. Cal. 1974). See generally D. Clement, *supra* note 77 at 950–602; Note 70, *Northwestern University Law Review, supra* note 194 at 1009–11.

201.   See, for example, *Westinghouse Electric Corp.* v. *Schlesinger,* 542 F.2d 1190 (4th Cir. 1976), *certiorari denied sub nom. Brown* v. *Westinghouse Electric Corp.,* 431 U.S. 924 (1977).

202.   *Chrysler Corp.* v. *Schlesinger,* 565 F.2d 1172 (3d Cir. 1977), *certiorari granted sub nom. Chrysler Corp.* v. *Brown,* 46 U.S.L.W. 3555 (Mar. 7, 1978); *General Dynamics Corp.* v. *Marshall,* No. 77–1192 (8th Cir. Feb. 14, 1978); *Sears, Roebuck and Co.* v. *Eckerd,* (No. 77–1417) (7th Cir. Apr. 25, 1978). See also D. Clement, *supra* note 77 at 600 n. 46 (collecting cases).

203.   The Senate report on the 1974 amendments states: "Congress did not intend the exemptions in the FOIA to be used either to prohibit disclosure of information or to justify automatic withholding of information. Rather, they are only permissive. They merely mark the outer limits of information that may be withheld where the agency makes a specific affirmative determination that the public interest and the specific

circumstances presented dictate—as well as that the intent of the exemption allows—that the information should be withheld." S. Rep. No. 93–854, 93d Cong. 2d Sess. 6 (1974). See also H.R. Rep. No. 93–876, 93d Cong., 2d Sess. (1974); H.R. Rep. No. 92–1419, 92d Cong., 2d Sess. (1972); H.R. Rep. No. 1497, *supra* note 39; S. Rep. No. 813, *supra* note 42.

204.   Davis, "The Information Act: A Preliminary Analysis," 34 *University of Chicago Law Review* 761, 766 (1967); Note, 6 *Loyola University Law Review, supra* note 35 at 597; Note, 70 *Northwestern University Law Review, supra* note 194 at 1009; Note, "A Review of the Fourth Exemption of the Freedom of Information Act," 9 *Akron Law Review* 673, 690 (1976); Note, 1976 *Duke Law Journal, supra* note 192 at 333–39; D. Drachsler, "The Freedom of Information Act and the 'Right' of Non-disclosure," 28 *Administrative Law Review* 1, 2 (1976); D. Clement, *supra* note 77 at 591–602.

205.   Letter from John M. Harmon, Assistant Attorney General, Department of Justice, in Hearings, app. 6. See also text accompanying notes 60–61.

206.   Many submitters and their representatives have argued strongly that the exemptions are or should be mandatory. However, the committee has received little or no specific evidence that agencies are habitually releasing exempt documents arbitrarily or without cause. Arguments that a document is being released on a discretionary basis are usually made by an agency only as an alternative to a primary argument that the document is not exempt. The committee's experience acquired during formal and informal oversight of FOIA is that agency release policies under the fourth exemption are generally conservative. Some agencies have by regulation eliminated their authority to make discretionary releases of confidential business information. For a discussion of the wisdom of such regulations, see text accompanying notes 152–154.

207.   18 U.S.C. § 1905 (1976) provides:

"Whoever, being an officer or employee of the United States or of any department or agency thereof, publishes, divulges, discloses, or makes known in any manner or to any extent not authorized by law any information coming to him in the course of his employment or official duties or by reason of any examination or investigation made by, or return, report or record made to or filed with, such department or agency or officer or employee thereof, which information concerns or relates to the trade secrets, processes, operations, style of work, or apparatus, or to the identity, confidential statistical data, amount or source of any income, profits, losses, or expenditures of any person, firm, partnership, corporation, or association; or permits any income return or copy thereof or any book containing any abstract or particulars thereof to be seen or examined by any person except as provided by law; shall be fined not more than $1,000 or imprisoned not more than one year, or both; and shall be removed from office or employment."

208.   Other nondisclosure statutes have been used in this way in reverse-FOIA suits, but 18 U.S.C. § 1905 (1976) has been used most often. *Cf. Charles River Park "A" v. Department of Housing and Urban Development,* 519 F.2d 935, 941 n. 6 (D.C. Cir. 1975) (no need to reply on 18 U.S.C. 1905 in this case). See *Associated Dry Goods Corp.* v. *Equal Employment Opportunity Commission,* 419 F. Supp. 814 (E.D. Va. 1976) (18 U.S.C. § 1337 and 42 U.S.C. § 200e); *Chrysler Corp.* v. *Schlesinger,*

565 F. 2d 1172 (3d Cir. 1977) (44 U.S.C. § 3508 found not applicable to this case), *cert. granted sub nom. Chryser Corp.* v. *Brown,* 46 U.S.L.W. 3555 (Mar. 7, 1978).
209.   *Holloway* v. *Bristol-Myers Corp.,* 485 F.2d 986 (D.C. Cir. 1973). See *Cort* v. *Ash,* 422 U.S. 66 [95 S.Ct. 2080, 45 L.Ed.2d 26] (1975); *Securities Investor Protection Corp.* v. *Barbour,* 421 U.S. 412 [95 S.Ct. 1733, 44 L.Ed.2d 263] (1975); *Chrysler Corp.* v. *Schlesinger,* 565 F.2d 1172 (3d Cir. 1977), *certiorari granted sub nom. Chrysler Corp.* v. *Brown,* 46 U.S.L.W. 3555 (Mar. 7, 1978); *General Dynamics Corp.* v. *Marshall,* No. 77–1192 (8th Cir. Feb. 14, 1978); *Sears, Roebuck and Co.* v. *Eckerd,* No. 77–1477 (7th Cir. Apr. 25, 1978); *Charles River Park "A", Inc.* v. *Department of Housing and Urban Development,* 519 F.2d 935, 941 n. 6 (D.C. Cir. 1975); Note, 1976 *Duke Law Journal, supra* note 192 at 349–51; D. Clement, *supra* note 77 at 624–26.
210.   See text accompanying notes 197–199.
211.   Submitters have also used the Trade Secrets Act in reverse-FOIA cases other than as the basis for a cause of action. They have argued that it qualifies as a nondisclosure statute under the third exemption of FOIA which refers to matters that are "specifically exempted from disclosure by statute . . . provided that such statute (A) requires that the matters be withheld from the public in such a manner as to leave no discretion on the issue, or (B) establishes particular criteria for withholding or refers to particular types of matters to be withheld." 5 U.S.C. 552(b)(3) (1976). The Government in the Sunshine Act, Act of Sept. 13, 1976, Public Law 94–409, 90 Stat. 1241, amended Exemption 3 by adding a proviso setting criteria for qualifying statutes. Prior to this amendment some courts incorrectly held that section 1905 was an Exemption 3 statute. See *Westinghouse Electric Corp.* v. *Schlesinger* (542 F. 2d 1190) (4th Cir., 1976), *cert. denied.* 431 U.S. 924 (1977)). The better view is that Section 1905 was never an Exemption 3 statute. See *National Parks & Conservation Association* v. *Kleppe* (547 F. 2d 673 (D.C. Cir. 1976)). The committee has never considered that section 1905 qualified under Exemption 3, and since the Sunshine Act only narrowed the scope of the exemption, it is not possible for section 1905 to qualify under the amended exemption. The reaction of the D.C. Circuit to the Sunshine Act amendments is especially curious. The court ordered the district court to reconsider its earlier holding that section 1905 was not an Exemption 3 statute. See *Sears, Roebuck and Co.* v. *General Services Administration* (II), 553 F. 2d 1378 (D.C. Cir. 1977).
212.   D. Clement, *supra* note 77 at 607–17; *Sears, Roebuck and Co.* v. *Eckerd,* No. 77–1417 (7th Cir. Apr. 25, 1978). Clement's article was also cited favorably on this issue by the third circuit in *Chrysler Corp.* v. *Schlesinger,* but the question of the scope of section 1905 was not reached in that case.
213.   *Chrysler Corp.* v. *Schlesinger,* 565 F. 2d 1172 (3d Cir. 1977, *cert. granted sub nom. Chrysler* v. *Brown,* 46 U.S.L.W. 3555 (Mar. 7, 1978); *General Dynamics Corp.* v. *Marshall,* No 77–1192 (8th Cir. Feb 14, 1978). *Accord, Sears, Roebuck and Co* v. *Eckerd* No. 77–1417 (7th Cir. Apr. 25, 1978). See Note, 1976 *Duke Law Journal, supra* note 192 at 343–44; D. Clement, *supra* note 677 at 617–24. The Attorney General's May 5, 1977, letter directly supports the proposition that agencies may release exempt documents. See text accompanying note 60. But see *Westinghouse Electric Corp.* v. *Schlesinger* 542 F. 2d 1190 (4th Cir. 1976), *cert. denied,* 431 U.S. 924 (1976).

[213a].   On April 18, 1979 the Supreme Court rendered a unanimous opinion in *Chrysler* v. *Brown,* 60 L Ed 2d 208. The court held that FOIA "does not afford [the submitting party] any right to enjoin agency disclosure" (at p. 220). However, the Court held that the Trade Secrets Act (18 usc 1905) is applicable to the threatened disclosure (at pp. 220–235). The court did not decide whether an agency's discretionary decision to release a submitter's records is subject to judicial review under the Administrative Procedure Act.

214.   5 U.S.C. § 552(a)(4)(B) (1976).

215.   See D. Clement, *supra* note 77 at 631 n. 205 (collecting cases).

216.   565 F. 2d 1172 (3d Cir. 1977), *cert. granted sub nom. Chrysler* v. *Brown* 46 *U.S.L.W.* 3555 (Mar. 7, 1978).

217.   *Westinghouse Electric Corp.* v. *Schlesinger* 542 F. 2d 1190, 1213 (4th Cir. 1976), *cert. denied,* 431 U.S. 924 (1977).

218.   Testimony of Burt A. Braverman in Hearings, pp. 143–44 (footnote omitted).

219.   *Id.* p. 145.

220.   5 U.S.C. § 706 (1976).

221.   See text accompanying notes 196 and 208.

222.   See Testimony of Nancy Duff Campbell, Visiting Associate Professor of Law, Georgetown University Law Center, in Hearings, p. 53.

223.   S. Rep. No. 813, 89th Cong., 1st Sess. 8 (1965).

224.   Hearings, pp. 53–4.

225.   565 F. 2d 1172, 1192, *Accord, General Dynamics Corp.* v. *Marshall,* No. 77–1192 (8th Cir. Feb. 14, 1978).

[225a].   The court in *Chrylser* v. *Brown,* 60 L Ed 2d 208, refused to decide which standard of review should apply.

226.   Hearings, pp. 60–63.

227.   See text accompanying note 182.

228.   5 U.S.C. § 552(a)(4)(B) (1976).

229.   *Consumers Union of the United States* v. *Consumer Products Safety Commission,* 400 F. Supp. 848 (D.D.C. 1975), rev'd and remanded, 561 F. 2d 349 (D.C. Cir.), rehearing denied, 565 F. 2d 721 (D.C. Cir. 1977), vacated and remanded for further consideration in light of permanent injunction entered by United States District Court for Delaware *sub nom. GTE Sylvania Inc.* v. *Consumers Union* 46 *U.S.L.W.* 3452 (Jan. 17, 1978) (No. 77–508).

230.   *GTE Sylvania Inc.* v. *Consumer Products Safety Commission,* 404 F. Supp. 352 (D. Del. 1975). A permanent injunction barring disclosure was granted on December 8, 1977, Civil Action No. 75–104 (D. Del. 1977).

231.   See Testimony of Nancy Duff Campbell, Visiting Associate Professor of Law, Georgetown University Law Center, in Hearings, pp. 60–61.

232.   *Robertson* v. *Department of Defense,* 402 F. Supp. 1342 (D.D.C. 1975).

233.   The Federal Rules of Civil Procedure provide for joinder of parties (rule 19), for intervention by one party in the lawsuit of another (rule 24), and for the consolidation of lawsuits involving common questions of law or fact (rule 42). It seems likely that these rules are sufficient to bring together in one place the relevant parties in most reverse-FOIA lawsuits. However, there has been little exploration of procedural alter-

natives in cases decided to date so that shortcomings in existing rules are not readily apparent.

234.   Hearings, p. 155.
235.   Hearings, pp. 60–63.
236.   Act of August 4, 1976. Public Law 94–377, 90 Stat. 1083.
237.   5 U.S.C. § 551(2) (1976).

Bibliography

Selected Law Review Articles and Notes

Access to information? Exemptions from disclosure under the Freedom of Information Act and the Privacy Act of 1974. *Willamette L J* 13: 135–71, Win '76.

Administrative Law: abuse of discretion. Any disclosure of FOIA-exempt information without weighing benefit to the agency, harm to the public, and the possibility of compromise is an abuse of discretion. *St. Mary's L J* 8: 543–50, '76.

Administrative Law: attorney fees under the Freedom of Information Act. Commercial interest and in propia persona appearances. *Wayne L Rev* 24: 1045–60, Mr '78.

Administrative disclosure of private business records under the Freedom of Information Act: an analysis of alternative methods of review. *Syracuse L Rev* 28: 923–80, Fall '77.

Backdooring the NLRB: use and abuse of the amended FOIA for administrative discovery. *Loyola U L J* (Chicago) 8: 145–85, Fall '76.

Belair, R.R. Agency implementation of the Privacy Act and the Freedom of Information Act: impact on the government's collection, maintenance, and dissemination of personally identifiable information. *John Marshall J of Practice and Procedure* 10: 465–512, Spr '77.

————. Less government secrecy and more personal privacy? Experience with the Freedom of Information and Privacy Acts. *Civil Liberties Rev* 4: 10–18, My/Je '77.

Campbell, N.D. Reverse Freedom of Information Act litigation: the need for congressional action. *Georgetown L J* 67: 103–205, Oct '78.

Clement, D.G. Rights of submitters to prevent agency disclosure of confidential business information: the reverse Freedom of Information Act lawsuit. *Tex L Rev* 55: 587–644.

Clifford, D.K. Scientists and freedom of information. *Victoria U of Wellington L Rev* 9: 451–64, Oct '78.

Connolly, W.B. and Fox, J.C. Employer rights and access to documents under the Freedom of Information Act. *Fordham L Rev* 46: 203–40, Nov '77.

Corporate dilemma in "reverse-FOIA" lawsuits: Chyrsler v. Schlesinger (565 F 2d 1172). *U Pitt L Rev* 40: 93–119, Fall '78.

Cox, M.P. Walk through section 552 of the Administrative Procedure Act: the Freedom of Information Act, the Privacy Act, and the government in the Sunshine Act. *U Cin L Rev* 46: 969–87, '78.

DeDeo, C. and Irving, J.S. Right to Privacy and Freedom of Information: the NLRB and issues under the Privacy and Freedom of Information Acts. *NYU Conference on Labor* 29: 49–90, '76.

Disclosure of union authorization cards under the Freedom of Information Act: interpreting the personal privacy exemptions. *Minn L Rev* 62: 949–86, Je '78.

Effect of the 1976 amendment to exemption three of the Freedom of Information Act. *Columbia L Rev* 76: 1029–47, Oct '76.

Executive privilege and the Freedom of Information Act: the constitutional foundation of the amended national security exemption. *Wash U L Q* 1976: 609–66, Fall '76.

Findler, W.E. and Jones, R.H. Freedom of Information Act in military aircrash cases. *J of Air Law and Commerce* 43: 535–53, '77.

FOIA and Privacy Act interface: toward a resolution of statutory conflict. *Loyola U L J* (Chicago) 8: 570–93, Spr '77.

Freedom of Information Act: 1974 amended time provisions interpreted. *U Miami L Rev* 32: 212–27, Dec '77.

Freedom of Information Act: a potential alternative to conventional criminal discovery. *Am Crim L Rev* 14: 73–161, Sum '76.

Freedom of Information Act: a survey of litigation under the exemptions. *Miss L J* 48: 784–817, Spr '77.

Freedom of Information Act: labor law. An employer charged with an unfair labor practice is not entitled under the FOIA to NLRB files compiled pursuant to investigation of the charge when the enforcement proceeding is pending. *Geo Wash L Rev* 45: 114–26, Nov '76.

Fuselier, L.A. and Moeller, A.J. Jr. NLRB investigatory records: disclosure under the Freedom of Information Act. *U Richmond L Rev* 10: 541–55, Spr '76.

Hanus, J.J. and Relyea, H.C. Policy assessment of the Privacy Act of 1974. *Am U L Rev* 23: 555–93, Spr '76.

Hunter, H.O. Statutory and judicial responses to the problem of access to government information. *Det Coll L Rev* 1979: 51–87, Spr '79.

In camera inspection of national security files under the Freedom of Information Act. *Kan L Rev* 26: 617–24, Sum '78.

Impact of the FOIA on NLRB discovery procedures. *U Mich J of Law Reform* 10: 476–96, Spr '77.

Kovach, K.A. Retrospective look at the Privacy and Freedom of Information Acts. *Labor L J* 27:548–64, Sept '76.

Linderman, T.G. Freedom of Information: animal drug regulations. *Food Drug Cosmetic L J* 33: 274–80, Je '78.

Miller , A. and Sobol, M.J. Example of the Third Circuit's expansion of exemption six of the Freedom of Information Act to include union authorization cards. *Villanova L Rev* 23: 751–62, My '78.

New York Freedom of Information Law: how to obtain copies of official regulations, decisions, etc. *Columbia Human Rights L Rev* 9–10: 43–53, Fall-Win '77-'78 & Spr-Sum '78.

Patten, T.L. and Weinstein, K.W. Disclosure of business secrets under the Freedom of Information Act: suggested limitations. *Adm Law Rev* 29: 193–208, Spr. '77.

Privacy Act of 1974: an overview and critique. *Wash U L Q* 1976: 667–718, Fall '76.

Review of the fourth exemption of the Freedom of Information Act. *Akron L Rev* 9: 673–94, Spr '76.

Rosenbloom, H.D. More IRS information may become public due to amended Freedom of Information Act. *J Taxation* 45: 258–63, Nov '76.

Snyder, J.L. Developments on Freedom of Information Act reveal trend toward greater disclosure. *J Taxation* 50: 48–52, Jan '79.

Steinberg, M.I. 1974 amendments to the Freedom of Information Act: the safety valve provision § 552(a)(6)(C) excusing agency compliance with statutory time limits, a proposed interpretation. *Notre Dame Law* 52: 235–60, Dec '76.

Ward, P.C. Public's access to government: Freedom of Information, Privacy, and Sunshine Acts, an address. *Law Library J* 70: 509–17, Nov '77.

What is record? Two approaches to the Freedom of Information Act's threshold requirement. *Brigham Young U L Rev* 1978: 408–35, '78.

Wildes, L. Nonpriority program of the immigration and naturalization service goes public: the litigative use of the Freedom of Information Act. *San Diego L Rev* 14: 42–75, Dec '76.

Addresses of Selected Government Agencies

ACTION:
   ACTION
   806 Connecticut Avenue, N.W.
   Washington, D.C. 20525
Administrative Conference of the United States:
   Administrative Conference of the United States
   Suite 500
   2120 L Street, N.W.
   Washington, D.C. 20037
Agriculture, Department of:
   Department of Agriculture
   Washington, D.C. 20250
Air Force, Department of the:
   Department of the Air Force
   The Pentagon
   Washington, D.C. 20330
Alcohol, Drug Abuse, and Mental Health Administration:
   Alcohol, Drug Abuse, and Mental Health Administration
   5600 Fishers Lane
   Rockville, Maryland 20857
Alcohol, Tobacco and Firearms, Bureau of:
   Bureau of Alcohol, Tobacco, and Firearms
   1200 Pennsylvania Avenue, N.W.
   Washington, D.C. 20226
American Battle Monuments Commission:
   American Battle Monuments Commission
   40014 Forrestal Bldg.
   Washington, D.C. 20314
Appalachian Regional Commission
   Appalachian Regional Commission
   1666 Connecticut Avenue, N.W.
   Washington, D.C. 20235
Arms Control and Disarmament Agency:
   U.S. Arms Control and Disarmament Agency
   320 21st Street
   Washington, D.C. 20451
Army, Department of the:

Department of the Army
The Pentagon
Washington, D.C. 20314
Census, Bureau of the:
    Bureau of the Census
    Federal Building 3
    Washington, D.C. 20233
Central Intelligence Agency:
    Central Intelligence Agency
    Washington, D.C. 20505
Civil Aeronautics Board:
    Civil Aeronautics Board
    1825 Connecticut Avenue, N.W.
    Washington, D.C. 20428
Civil Rights Commission:
    Civil Rights Commission
    1121 Vermont Avenue, N.W.
    Washington, D.C. 20425
Civil Service Commission:
    Civil Service Commission
    1900 E Street, N.W.
    Washington, D.C. 20415
Coastal Plains Regional Commission:
    Coastal Plains Regional Commission
    1725 K Street, N.W.
    Washington, D.C. 20006
Commerce, Department of:
    Department of Commerce
    Washington, D.C. 20230
Commodity Futures Trading Commission:
    Commodity Futures Trading Commission
    2033 K Street, N.W.
    Washington, D.C. 20581
Community Services Administration:
    Community Services Administration
    1200 19th Street, N.W.
    Washington, D.C. 20506
Comptroller of the Currency, Office of:
    Office of Comptroller of the Currency
    490 L'Enfant Plaza E., S.W.
    Washington, D.C. 20219
Consumer Product Safety Commission:

1111 18th Street, N.W.
Consumer Product Safety Commission
Washington, D.C. 20207
Copyright Office:
Copyright Office
Library of Congress
Washington, D.C. 20559
Customs Service, United States:
U.S. Customs Service
1301 Constitution Avenue, N.W.
Washington, D.C. 20229
Defense, Department of:
Department of Defense
The Pentagon
Washington, D.C. 20301
Defense Contracts Audits Agency:
Defense Contracts Audits Agency
Cameron Station
Alexandria, Virginia 22314
Defense Intelligence Agency:
Defense Intelligence Agency
RDS–3A
Washington, D.C. 20301
Defense Investigative Service:
Defense Investigative Service
D0020
Washington, D.C. 20304
Defense Logistics Agency:
Defense Logistics Agency
Cameron Station
Alexandria, Virginia 22314
Defense Mapping Agency:
Defense Mapping Agency
Naval Observatory
Washington, D.C. 20305
Disease Control, Center for:
Center for Disease Control
Atlanta, Georgia 30333
Economic Development Administration:
Department of Commerce
14th & Constitution Avenue, N.W.
Washington, D.C. 20230

Education, Office of:
    Office of Education
    400 Maryland Avenue, S.W.
    Washington, D.C. 20202
Energy, Department of:
    Department of Energy
    U.S. Department of Energy
    Washington, D.C. 20461
Environmental Protection Agency:
    Environmental Protection Agency
    401 M Street, S.W.
    Washington, D.C. 20460
Environmental Quality, Council on:
    Council on Environmental Quality
    722 Jackson Place, N.W.
    Washington, D.C. 20006
Equal Employment Opportunity Commission:
    Equal Employment Opportunity Commission
    2401 E Street, N.W.
    Washington, D.C. 20506
Export-Import Bank of the U.S.:
    Export-Import Bank of the U.S.
    811 Vermont Avenue, N.W.
    Washington, D.C. 20571
Farm Credit Administration:
    Farm Credit Administration
    490 L'Enfant Plaza, S.W.
    Washington, D.C. 20578
Federal Aviation Administration:
    Federal Aviation Administration (FAA)
    800 Independence Avenue, S.W.
    Washington, D.C. 20591
Federal Bureau of Investigation:
    Federal Bureau of Investigation
    9th and Pennsylvania Avenue, N.W.
    Washington, D.C. 20535
Federal Communications Commission:
    Federal Communications Commission
    1919 M Street, N.W.
    Washington, D.C. 20554
Federal Deposit Insurance Corporation:
    Federal Deposit Insurance Corporation

550 17th Street, N.W.
Washington, D.C. 20429
Federal Election Commission:
    Federal Election Commission
    1325 K Street, N.W.
    Washington, D.C. 20463
Federal Highway Administration:
    Federal Highway Administration
    400 7th Street, S.W.
    Washington, D.C. 20590
Federal Home Loan Bank Board:
    Federal Home Loan Bank Board
    320 First Street, N.W.
    Washington, D.C. 20552
Federal Maritime Commission
    1100 L Street, N.W.
    Washington, D.C. 20573
Federal Mediation and Conciliation Service:
    Federal Mediation and Conciliation Service
    2100 K Street, N.W.
    Washington, D.C. 20427
Federal Power Commission:
    Federal Power Commission
    825 North Capitol Street
    Washington, D.C. 20426
Federal Trade Commission:
    Federal Trade Commission
    6th and Pennsylvania Avenue, N.W.
    Washington, D.C. 20580
Food and Drug Administration:
    Food and Drug, Administration
    5600 Fishers Lane
    Rockville, Maryland 20857
Foreign Claims Settlement Commission:
    Foreign Claims Settlement Commission
    1111 20th Street, N.W.
    Washington, D.C. 20579
General Accounting Office:
    General Accounting Office
    441 G. Street, N.W.
    Washington, D.C. 20548
General Services Administration

General Services Administration
18th and F Streets, N.W.
Washington, D.C. 20405
Health Care Financing Administration:
Health Care Financing Administration
330 C Street, S.W.
Washington, D.C. 20201
Health, Education, and Welfare, Department of:
U.S. Department of Health, Education, and Welfare
200 Independence Avenue, S.W.
Washington, D.C. 20201
Health Resources Administration:
Health Resources Administration
3700 East West Highway
Hyattsville, Maryland 20782
Health Service Administration:
Health Services Administration
5600 Fishers Lane
Rockville, Maryland 20857
Housing and Urban Development, Department of:
Department of Housing and Urban Development
Washington, D.C. 20410
Immigration and Naturalization Service:
Immigration and Naturalization Service
425 I Street, N.W.
Washington, D.C. 20536
Indian Claims Commission:
Indian Claims Commission
1730 K Street, N.W.
Washington, D.C. 20006
Information Agency, U.S. (USIA):
U.S. Information Agency
1750 Pennsylvania Avenue, N.W.
Washington, D.C. 20547
Interior, Department of:
Department of the Interior
18th and C Street, N.W.
Washington, D.C. 20240
Internal Revenue Service:
Internal Revenue Service
1111 Constitution Avenue, N.W.
Washington, D.C. 20224

International Development, Agency for (AID):
    Agency for International Development
    21st and Virginia Avenue, N.W.
    Washington, D.C. 20532
International Trade Commission, U.S.:
    U.S. International Trade Commission
    701 E Street, N.W.
    Washington, D.C. 20436
Interstate Commerce Commission:
    Interstate Commerce Commission
    12th and Constitution Avenue, N.W.
    Washington, D.C. 20423
Justice, Department of:
    Department of Justice
    Washington, D.C. 20530
Labor, Department of:
    Department of Labor
    Washington, D.C. 20210
Law Enforcement Assistance Administration:
    Law Enforcement Assistance Administration
    633 Indiana Avenue, N.W.
    Washington, D.C. 20531
Maritime Administration:
    Maritime Administration
    Washington, D.C. 20230
National Aeronautics and Space Administration:
    National Aeronautics and Space Administration
    400 Maryland Avenue, S.W.
    Washington, D.C. 20546
National Archives and Records Service:
    National Archives and Records Service
    Washington, D.C. 20408
National Credit Union Administration:
    National Credit Union Administration
    2025 M Street, N.W.
    Washington, D.C. 20456
National Endowment for the Arts:
    National Endowment for the Arts
    806 15th Street, N.W.
    Washington, D.C. 20506
National Endowment for the Humanities:
    National Endowment for the Humanities

Washington, D.C. 20506
National Highway Traffic Safety Administration:
National Highway Traffic Administration
400 7th Street, S.W.
Washington, D.C. 20590
National Institute of Education:
National Institute of Education
1200–19th Street, N.W.
Washington, D.C. 20208
National Institutes of Health:
National Institutes of Health
9000 Rockville Pike
Rockville, Maryland 20014
National Labor Relations Board
National Labor Relations Board
1717 Pennsylvania Avenue, N.W.
Washington, D.C. 20570
National Oceanic and Atmospheric Administration:
National Oceanic and Atmospheric Administration
6010 Executive Blvd.
Rockville, Maryland 20852
National Railroad Passenger Corporation:
National Railroad Passenger Corporation (AMTRAK):
955 North L'Enfant Plaza, S.W.
Washington, D.C. 20024
National Science Foundation:
National Science Foundation
1800 G Street, N.W.
Washington, D.C. 20550
National Security Agency:
National Security Agency
Fort George Meade, Maryland 20755
National Security Council:
National Security Council
Old Executive Office Building
Washington, D.C. 20506
National Transportation Safety Board:
National Transportation Safety Board
800 Independence Avenue, S.W.
Washington, D.C. 20594
Navy, Department of the:
Department of the Navy

The Pentagon
Washington, D.C. 20350
Nuclear Regulatory Commission:
Nuclear Regulatory Commission
Washington, D.C. 20555
Occupational Safety and Health Review Commission:
Occupational Safety and Health Review Commission
1825 K Street, N.W.
Washington, D.C. 20006
Office of Management and Budget:
Office of Management and Budget
Old Executive Office Building
Washington, D.C. 20503
Overseas Private Investment Corporation:
Overseas Private Investment Corporation
1129 20th Street, N.W.
Washington, D.C. 20527
Postal Service, U.S.:
U.S. Postal Service
475 L'Enfant Plaza, S.W.
Washington, D.C. 20260
Prisons, Bureau of:
Bureau of Prisons
320 First Street, N.W.
Washington, D.C. 20534
Public Health Service:
Public Health Service
200 Independence Avenue, S.W.
Washington, D.C. 20201
Railroad Retirement Board:
Railroad Retirement Board
844 N. Rush Street
Chicago, Illinois 60611
Renegotiation Board:
Renegotiation Board
2000 M Street, N.W.
Washington, D.C. 20446
Secret Service:
U.S. Secret Service
1800 G Street, N.W.
Washington, D.C. 20223
Securities and Exchange Commission:

Securities and Exchange Commission
500 North Capitol Street
Washington, D.C. 20549
Selective Service System:
600 E Street, N.W.
Washington, D.C. 20435
Small Business Administration:
Small Business Administration
1441 L Street, N.W.
Washington, D.C. 20416
Social Security Administration:
Social Security Administration
6401 Security Blvd.
Baltimore, Maryland 21235
State, Department of:
Department of State
Washington, D.C. 20520
Tennessee Valley Authority (TVA):
Tennessee Valley Authority
400 Commerce Avenue
Knoxville, Tennessee 37902
Transportation, Department of:
Department of Transportation
400 7th Street, S.W.
Washington, D.C. 20590
Treasury, Department of:
Department of the Treasury
1500 Pennsylvania Avenue, N.W.
Washington, D.C. 20220
Urban Mass Transit Administration:
Urban Mass Transit Administration
400 7th Street, S.W.
Washington, D.C. 20590
Veterans Administration:
Veterans Administration
Vermont Avenue, N.W.
Washington, D.C. 20420

Appendices

A. Chrysler v. Brown, 441 U.S. 281 (1979)
[1] Opinion of the Court   223
[2] Analysis   248

B. Two Government Memoranda to All Agencies and Legal Departments re: Chrysler v. Brown
[1] Memorandum from Ass't Attorney General Barbara Babcock to All Agency General Counsels on "Reverse" Freedom of Information Act Cases. Issued June 21, 1979
   251
[2] Memorandum from Robert L. Saloschin, Director, Office of Information Law and Policy, To All Federal Departments and Agencies on Chrysler v. Brown. Issued June 19, 1979
   258

C. State-by-State Freedom of Information Statutes
265

APPENDIX **A**

Chrysler v. Brown

441 U.S. 281
(Argued November 28, 1978 and decided April 18, 1979)

[1] Opinion of the Court

Mr. Justice **Rehnquist** delivered the opinion of the Court.

The expanding range of federal regulatory activity and growth in the Government sector of the economy have increased federal agencies' demand for information about the activities of private individuals and corporations. These developments have paralleled a related concern about secrecy in Government and abuse of power. The Freedom of Information Act (hereinafter "FOIA") was a response to this concern, but it has also had a largely unforeseen tendency to exacerbate the uneasiness of those who comply with governmental demands for information. For under the FOIA third parties have been able to obtain Government files containing information submitted by corporations and individuals who thought the information would be held in confidence.

This case belongs to a class that has been popularly denominated "reverse-FOIA" suits. The Chrysler Corporation (hereinafter "Chrysler") seeks to enjoin agency disclosure on the grounds that it is inconsistent with the FOIA and 18 USC § 1905 [18 USCS § 1905], a criminal statute with origins in the 19th century that proscribes disclosure of certain classes of business and personal information. We agree with the Court of Appeals for the Third Circuit that the FOIA is purely a disclosure statute and affords Chrysler no private right of action to enjoin agency disclosure. But we cannot agree with that court's conclusion that this disclosure is "authorized by law" within the meaning of § 1905. Therefore, we vacate the Court of Appeals' judgment and remand so that it can consider whether the documents at issue in this case fall within the terms of § 1905.

I

As a party to numerous Government contracts, Chrysler is required to comply with Executive Orders 11246 and 11375, which charge the Secretary of Labor with ensuring that corporations who benefit from Government contracts provide equal employment opportunity regardless of race or sex.[1] The U.S. Department of Labor's Office of Federal Contract Compliance Programs (OFCCP) has promulgated regulations which require Government contractors to furnish reports and other information about their affirmative action programs and the general composition of their work forces.[2]

The Defense Logistics Agency (DLA) (formerly the Defense Supply Agency) of the Department of Defense is the designated compliance agency responsible for monitoring Chrysler's employment practices.[3] OFCCP regulations require that Chrysler make available to this agency written affirmative action programs (AAPs) and annually submit Employer Information Reports, known as EEO-1 Reports. The agency may also conduct "compliance reviews" and "complaint investigations," which culminate in Compliance Review Reports (CRRs) and Complaint Investigation Reports (CIRs), respectively.[4]

Regulations promulgated by the Secretary of Labor provide for public disclosure of information from records of the OFCCP and its compliance agencies. Those regulations state that notwithstanding exemption from mandatory disclosure under the Freedom of Information Act, 5 USC § 552 [5 USCS § 552],

> "records obtained or generated pursuant to Executive Order 11246 (as amended) . . . shall be made available for inspection and copying . . . if it is determined that the requested inspection or copying furthers the public interest and does not impede any of the functions of the OFCC[P] or the Compliance Agencies except in the case of records disclosure of which is prohibited by law."[5]

---

1.   Executive Order 11246, 3 CFR 339 (1964–1965 Comp), probihits discrimination on the basis of "race, creed, color, or national origin" in federal employment or by Government contractors. Under § 202 of this Executive order, most Government contracts must contain a provision whereby the contractor agrees not to discriminate in such a fashion and to take affirmative action to ensure equal employment opportunity. With promulgation of Executive Order 11375, 3 CFR 684 (1966–1970 Comp), in 1967, President Johnson extended the requirements of the 1965 order to prohibit discrimination on the basis of sex.

2.   41 CFR §§ 60-1.3, 60-1.7 (1977).

3.   For convenience all references will be to DLA.

4.   *Id.,* §§ 60-1.20, 60-1.24. The term "alphabet soup" gained currency in the early days of the New Deal as a description of the proliferation of new agencies such as WPA and PWA. The terminology required to describe the present controversy suggests that the "alphabet soup" of the New Deal era was, by comparison, a clear broth.

5.   *Id.,* § 60-40.2(a) (1977). The regulations also state that EEO-1 reports "shall be disclosed," id., § 60-40.4, and that AAPs "must be disclosed" if not within limited exceptions. Id., §§ 60-40.2(b)(1), 60-40.3.

It is the voluntary disclosure contemplated by this regulation, over and above that mandated by the FOIA, which is the gravamen of Chrysler's complaint in this case.

This controversy began in May of 1975 when the DLA informed Chrysler that third parties had made a FOIA request for disclosure of the 1974 AAP for Chrysler's Newark, Del. assembly plant and an October 1974 CIR for the same facility. Nine days later Chrysler objected to release of the requested information, relying on OFCCP's disclosure regulations and on exemptions to the FOIA. Chrysler also requested a copy of the CIR, since it had never seen it. DLA responded the following week that it had determined that the requested material was subject to disclosure under the FOIA and the OFCCP disclosure rules, and that both documents would be released five days later.

On that day Chrysler filed a complaint in the United States District Court for Delaware seeking to enjoin release of the Newark documents. The District Court granted a temporary restraining order barring disclosure of the Newark documents and requiring that DLA give five days' notice to Chrysler before releasing any similar documents. Pursuant to this order, Chrysler was informed on July 1, 1975, that DLA had received a similar request for information about Chrysler's Hamtramck, Mich. plant. Chrysler amended its complaint and obtained a restraining order with regard to the Hamtramck disclosure as well.

Chrysler made three arguments in support of its prayer for an injunction: that disclosure was barred by the FOIA; that it was inconsistent with 18 USC § 1905 [18 USCS § 1905], 42 USC § 2000e-8(e) [42 USCS § 2000e-(8)], and 44 USC § 3508 [44 USCS § 3508], which for ease of reference will be referred to as the "confidentiality statutes"; and finally that disclosure was an abuse of agency discretion insofar as it conflicted with OFCCP rules. The District Court held that it had jurisdiction under 28 USC § 1331 [28 USCS § 1331] to subject the disclosure decision to review under the Administrative Procedure Act. 5 USC §§ 701–706 [5 USCS §§ 701–706]. It conducted a trial de novo on all of Chrysler's claims; both sides presented extensive expert testimony during August 1975.

On April 20, 1976, the District Court issued its opinion. It held that certain of the requested information, the "manning" tables, fell within Exemption 4 of the FOIA.[6] The District Court reasoned from this holding that the tables may or must be withheld, depending on applicable agency regulations, and that here a governing regulation required that the information be withheld. Pursuant to 5 USC § 301 [5 USCS § 301], the enabling statute which gives federal department heads control over department records, the Secretary of

---

6.   Manning tables are lists of job titles and of the number of people who perform each job.

Labor has promulgated a regulation, 29 CFR § 70.21(a) (1977), stating that no officer or employee of the Department is to violate 18 USC § 1905 [18 USCS § 1905]. That section imposes criminal sanctions on Government employees who make unauthorized disclosure of certain classes of information submitted to a Government agency, including trade secrets and confidential statistical data. In essence the District Court read § 1905 as not merely a prohibition of unauthorized disclosure of sensitive information by Government employees, but as a restriction on official agency actions taken pursuant to promulgated regulations.

Both sides appealed, and the Court of Appeals for the Third Circuit vacated the District Court's judgment. It agreed with the District Court that the FOIA does not compel withholding of information that falls within its nine exemptions. It also, like the District Court, rejected Chrysler's reliance on the confidentiality statues, either because there was no implied private right of action to proceed under the statute, or because the statute, by its terms, was not applicable to the information at issue in this case. It agreed with the District Court that analysis must proceed under the APA. But it disagreed with that court's interpretation of 29 CFR § 70.21(a). By the terms of that regulation, the specified disclosures are only proscribed if "not authorized by law," the standard of 18 USC § 1905 [18 USCS § 1905]. In the Court of Appeals' view, disclosures made pursuant to OFCCP disclosure regulations are "authorized by law" by virtue of those regulations. Therefore it held that 29 CFR § 70.21(a) was inapplicable.

The Court of Appeals also disagreed with the District Court's view of the scope of review under the APA. It held that the District Court erred in conducting a de novo review; review should have been limited to the agency record. However, the Court of Appeals found that record inadequate in this case and directed that the District Court remand to the agency for supplementation. Because of a conflict in the circuits[7] and the general importance of these "reverse-FOIA" cases, we granted certiorari and now vacate the judgment of the Third Circuit and remand for further proceedings.

II

We have decided a number of FOIA cases in the last few years.[8] Although

---

7.   Compare *Westinghouse Electric Corp.* v. *Schlesinger,* 542 F2d 1190 (CA4 1976), *cert denied,* 431 US 924, 53 L Ed 2d 239, 97 S Ct 2199 (1977), with *Sears, Roebuck & Co.* v. *Eckerd,* 575 F2d 1197 (CA7 1978); *General Dynamics Corp.* v. *Marshall,* 572 F2d 1211 (CA8 1978); *Pennzoil Co.* v. *FPC,* 534 F2d 627 (CA5 1976); *Charles River Park "A," Inc.* v. *Department of HUD,* 171 US App DC 286, 519 F2d 935 (1975).

8.   *NLRB* v. *Robbins Tire and Rubber Co.,* 437 US 214, 57 L Ed 2d 159, 98 S Ct 2311 (1978); *Department of Air Force* v. *Rose,* 425 US 352, 48 L Ed 2d 11, 96 S Ct 1592 (1976); *FAA* v. *Robertson,* 422 US 255, 45 L Ed 2d 164, 95 S Ct 2140 (1975);

we have not had to face squarely the question whether the FOIA ex proprio vigore forbids governmental agencies from disclosing certain classes of information to the public, we have in the course of at least one opinion intimated an answer.[9] We have, moreover, consistently recognized that the basic objective of the Act is disclosure.[10]

In contending that the FOIA bars disclosure of the requested equal employment opportunity information, Chrysler relies on the Act's nine exemptions and argues that they require an agency to withhold exempted material. In this case it relies specifically on Exemption 4:

"(b) [FOIA] does not apply to matters that are—

. . . . .

"(4) trade secrets and commercial or financial information obtained from a person and privileged or confidential . . . ." 5 USC § 552(b)(4) [5 USCS § 552(b)(4)].

Chrysler contends that the nine exemptions in general, and Exemption 4 in particular, reflect a sensitivity to the privacy interests of private individuals and nongovernmental entities. That contention may be conceded without inexorably requiring the conclusion that the exemptions impose affirmative

---

NLRB v. *Sears, Roebuck & Co.,* 421 US 132, 44 L Ed 2d 29, 95 S Ct 1504 (1975); *Renegotiation Bd.* v. *Grumman Aircraft Engineering Corp.,* 421 US 168, 44 L Ed 2d 57, 95 S Ct 1491 (1975); *Renegotiation Bd.* v. *Bannercraft Clothing Co.,* 415 US 1, 39 L Ed 2d 123, 94 S Ct 1028 (1974); *EPA* v. *Mink,* 410 US 73, 35 L Ed 2d 119, 93 S Ct 827 (1973).

9.   "Subsection (b) of the Act creates nine exemptions from compelled disclosures. These exemptions are explicitly made exclusive, 5 USC § 552(c) [5 USCS § 552(c)], and are plainly intended to set up concrete, workable standards for determining whether particular material *may* be withheld or *must* be disclosed." *EPA* v. *Mink,* 410 US 73, 79, 35 L Ed 2d 119, 93 S Ct 827 (1973) (emphasis added).

10.   We observed in *Department of the Air Force* v. *Rose,* 425 US 352, 361, 48 L Ed 2d 11, 96 S Ct 1592 (1976), that "disclosure, not secrecy, is the dominant objective of the Act." The legislative history is replete with references to Congress' desire to loosen the agency's grip on the data underlying governmental decision making.

"A democratic society requires an informed, intelligent electorate, and the intelligence of the electorate varies as the quality and quantity of its information varies . . . . [The FOIA] provides the necessary machinery to assure the availability of Government information necessary to an informed electorate." HR Rep No. 1497, 89th Cong, 2d Sess, 12 (1966).

Although the theory of an informed electorate is vital to the proper operation of a democracy, there is nowhere in our present law a statute which affirmatively provides for that information." S Rep No. 813, 89th Cong, 1st Sess, 3 (1965).

duties on an agency to withhold information sought.[11] In fact, that conclusion is not supported by the language, logic or history of the Act.

The organization of the Act is straightforward. Subsection (a), 5 USC § 552(a) [5 USCS § 552(a)], places a general obligation on the agency to make information available to the public and sets out specific modes of disclosure for certain classes of information. Subsection (b), 5 USC § 552(b) [5 USCS § 552(b)], which lists the exemptions, simply states that the specified material is not subject to the disclosure obligations set out in subsection (a). By its terms, subsection (b) demarcates the limits of the agency's obligation to disclose; it does not foreclose disclosure.

That the FOIA is exclusively a disclosure statute is, perhaps, demonstrated most convincingly by examining its provision for judicial relief. Subsection (a)(4)(B) gives federal district courts "jurisdiction to enjoin the agency from withholding agency records and to order the production of any agency records improperly withheld from the complainant." 5 USC § 552(a)(4)(B) [5 USCS § 552(a)(4)(B)]. That provision does not give the authority to bar disclosure, and thus fortifies our belief that Chrysler, and courts which have shared its view, have incorrectly interpreted the exemption provisions to the FOIA. The Act is an attempt to meet the demand for open government while preserving workable confidentiality in governmental decisionmaking.[12] Congress appreciated that with the expanding sphere of governmental regulation and enterprise, much of the information within Government files has been submitted by private entities seeking Government contracts or responding to unconditional reporting obligations imposed by law. There was sentiment that Government agencies should have the latitude, in certain circumstances, to

---

11.   See, e.g., HR Rep No. 1497, 89th Cong, 2d Sess, 10 (1966) (emphasis added): "[Exemption 4] would assure the confidentiality of information obtained by the Government through questionnaires or through material submitted and disclosures made in procedures such as the mediation of labor-management controversies. It exempts such material if it would not customarily be made public by the person from whom it was obtained by the Government . . . . It would . . . include information which is given to an agency in confidence, since a citizen must be able to confide in his Government. Moreover, *where the Government has obligated itself in good faith not to disclose documents or information which it receives, it should be able to honor such obligations."*

The italicized passage is obviously consistent with Exemption 4's being an exception to the disclosure mandate of the FOIA and not a limitation on agency discretion.

12.   See S Rep No. 813, 89th Cong, 1st Sess, 3 (1965):

"It is not an easy task to balance the opposing interests, but it is not an impossible one either. It is not necessary to conclude that to protect one of the interests, the other must, of necessity, either be abrogated or substantially subordinated. Success lies in providing a workable formula which encompasses, balances, and protects all interests, yet places emphasis on the fullest responsible disclosure."

afford the confidentiality desired by these submitters.[13] But the congressional concern was with the *agency's* need or preference for confidentiality; the FOIA by itself protects the submitters' interest in confidentiality only to the extent that this interest is endorsed by the agency collecting the information.

Enlarged access to governmental information undoubtedly cuts against the privacy concerns of nongovernmental entities, and as a matter of policy some balancing and accommodation may well be desirable. We simply hold here that Congress did not design the FOIA exemptions to be mandatory bars to disclosure.[14]

This conclusion is further supported by the legislative history. The FOIA was enacted out of dissatisfaction with § 3 of the Administrative Procedure Act, which had not resulted in as much disclosure by the agencies as Congress later thought desirable.[15] Statements in both the Senate and House Reports on the effect of the exemptions support the interpretation that the exemptions were only meant to permit the agency to withhold certain information, and were not meant to mandate nondisclosure. For example, the House Report states:

> "[The FOIA] sets up workable standards for the categories of records which *may* be exempt from disclosure. . . .
>
> ". . . There may be legitimate reasons for nondisclosure and [the FOIA] is designed to *permit* nondisclosure in such cases.
>
> "[The FOIA] lists in a later subsection the specific categories of information which *may*

---

13.   *Id.,* at 9; n 11, *supra.*

14.   It is informative in this regard to compare the FOIA with the Privacy Act of 1974, 5 USC § 552a [5 USCS § 552a]. In the latter Act Congress explicitly requires agencies to withhold records about an individual from most third parties unless the subject gives his permission. Even more telling is 49 USC § 1357 [49 USCS § 1357], a section which authorizes the Administrator of the FAA to take antihijacking measures, including research and development into protection devices.

"Notwithstanding [FOIA], the Administrator shall prescribe such regulations as he may deem necessary to prohibit disclosure of any information obtained or developed in the conduct of research and development activities under this subsection if, in the opinion of the Administrator, the disclosure of such information—

.   .   .

"(B) would reveal trade secrets or privileged or confidential commercial or financial information obtained from any person . . . . *Id.,* § 1357(d)(2)(B).

15.   Section 3 of the original Administrative Procedure Act provided that an agency should generally publish or make available organizational data, general statements of policy, rules and final orders. Exception was made for matters "requiring secrecy in the public interest" or "relating solely to the internal management of an agency." This original version of § 3 was repealed with passage of the FOIA. See *EPA* v. *Mink,* 410 US 73, 35 L Ed 2d 119, 93 S Ct 827 (1973).

be exempted from disclosure."[16]

We therefore conclude that Congress did not limit an agency's discretion to disclose information when it enacted the FOIA. It necessarily follows that the Act does not afford Chrysler any right to enjoin agency disclosure.

III

Chrysler contends, however, that even if its suit for injunctive relief cannot be based on the FOIA, such an action can be premised on the Trade Secrets Act, 18 USC § 1905 [18 USCS § 1905]. The Act provides:

> "Whoever, being an officer or employee of the United States or of any department or agency thereof, publishes, divulges, discloses, or makes known in any manner or to any extent not authorized by law any information coming to him in the course of his employment or official duties or by reason of any examination or investigation made by, or return, report or record made to or filed with, such department or agency or officer or employee thereof, which information concerns or relates to the trade secrets, processes, operations, style of work, or apparatus, or to the identity, confidential statistical data, amount or source of any income, profits, losses, or expenditures of any person, firm, partnership, corporation, or association; or permits any income return or copy thereof or any book containing any abstract or particulars thereof to be seen or examined by any person except as provided by law; shall be fined not more than $1,000 or imprisoned not more than one year, or both; and shall be removed from office or employment."

There are necessarily two parts to Chrysler's argument: that § 1905 is applicable to the type of disclosure threatened in this case, and that it affords Chrysler a private right of action to obtain injunctive relief.

A

The Court of Appeals held that § 1905 was not applicable to the agency disclosure at issue here because such disclosure was "authorized by law" within the meaning of the Act. The court found the source of that authorization to be the OFCCP regulations that DLA relied on in deciding to disclose information on the Hamtramck and Newark plants.[17] Chrysler contends here that these agency regulations are not "law" within the meaning of § 1905.

It has been established in a variety of contexts that properly promulgated, substantive agency regulations have the "force and effect of law."[18] This

---

16.   HR Rep No. 1497, 89th Cong, 2d Sess, 2, 5–7 (1966) (emphasis added). See also S Rep No. 813, 89th Cong, 1st Sess, 10 (1965). Congressman Moss, the House sponsor of the FOIA, described the exemptions on the House floor as indicating what documents "may be withheld." 112 Cong Rec 13641 (1966).
17.   41 CFR §§ 60.40-1 to 60.40-4.
18.   E. G., *Batterton* v. *Francis,* 432 US 416, 425 n 9, 53 L Ed 2d 448, 97 S Ct 2399 (1977); *Foti* v. *Immigration & Naturalization Serv.,* 375 US 217, 223, 11 L Ed 2d 281,

doctrine is so well established that agency regulations implementing federal statutes have been held to pre-empt state law under the Supremacy Clause.[19] It would therefore take a clear showing of contrary legislative intent before the phrase "authorized by law" in § 1905 could be held to have a narrower ambit than the traditional understanding.

The origins of the Trade Secrets Act can be traced to Rev Stat 3167, an Act which barred unauthorized disclosure of specified business information by Government revenue officers.[20] There is very little legislative history concerning the original bill, which was passed in 1864. It was reenacted numerous times, with some modification, and remained part of the revenue laws until 1948.[21] Congressional statements made at the time of these re-enactments indicate that Congress was primarily concerned with unauthorized disclosure of business information by feckless or corrupt revenue agents,[22] for in the early days of the Bureau of Internal Revenue, it was the field agents

---

84 S Ct 306 (1963); *United States* v. *Mersky,* 361 US 431, 437–438, 4 L Ed 2d 423, 80 S Ct 459 (1960); *Atchison, T. & S. F. R. Co.* v. *Scarlett,* 300 US 471, 474, 81 L Ed 748, 57 S Ct 541 (1937).

19.   *Paul* v. *United States,* 371 US 245, 9 L Ed 2d 292, 83 S Ct 426 (1963); *Free* v. *Bland,* 369 US 663, 8 L Ed 2d 180, 82 S Ct 1089 (1962); *Public Utilities Commission* v. *United States,* 355 US 534, 2 L Ed 2d 470, 78 S Ct 446 (1958).

20.   Revenue Act of 1864, ch 173, § 38, 13 Stat 228.

21.   The last version was codified as 18 USC § 216 (1940) [18 USCS § 216]:

"It shall be unlawful for any collector, deputy collector, agent, clerk, or other officer or employee of the United States to divulge or to make known in any manner whatever not provided by law to any person the operations, style or work or apparatus of any manufacturer or producer visited by him in the discharge of his official duties, or the amount, source of income, profits, losses, expenditures, or any particular thereof, set forth or disclosed in any income return, or to permit any income return or copy thereof or any book containing any abstract or particulars thereof to be seen or examined by any person except as provided by law; and it shall be unlawful for any person to print or publish in any manner whatever not provided by law any income, profits, losses, or expenditures appearing in any income return; and any offense against the foregoing provision shall be a misdemeanor and be punished by a fine not exceeding $1,000 or by imprisonment not exceeding one year, or both, at the discretion of the court; and if the offender be an officer or employee of the United States he shall be dismissed from office or discharged from employment."

22.   See, e. g., 26 Cong Rec 6893 (1894) (Sen. Aldrich) (expressing concern that taxpayer's confidential information is "to be turned over to the tender mercies of poorly paid revenue agents"); *id.,* 6924 (Sen. Teller) (exposing records to the "idle curiosity of a revenue officer"). See also Cong Globe, 38th Cong, 1st Sess, 2997 (1864) (Rep. Brown) (expressing concern that 1864 revenue provisions would allow "every little petty officer" to investigate the affairs of private citizens).

who had substantial contact with confidential financial information.[23]

In 1948, Rev Stat 3167 was consolidated with two other statutes—involving the Tariff Commission and the Department of Commerce—to form the Trade Secrets Act.[24] The statute governing the Tariff Commission was very similar to Rev Stat 3167, and it explicitly bound members of the Commission as well as Commission employees.[25] The Commerce Department statute embodied some differences in form. It was a mandate addressed to the Bureau of Foreign and Domestic Commerce and to its Director, but there was no reference to Bureau employees and it contained no criminal sanctions.[26] Unlike the other statutes it also had no exception for disclosures "authorized

---

23.   There was virtually no Washington bureaucracy created by the Act of July 1, 1862, 12 Stat 432, the statute to which the present Internal Revenue Service can be traced. Researchers report that during the Civil War 85% of the operations of the Bureau of Internal Revenue were carried out in the field—"including the assessing and collection of taxes, the handling of appeals, and punishment for frauds"—and this balance of responsibility was not generally upset until the 20th Century. L. Schmeckebier & F. Eble, The Bureau of Internal Revenue 8, 40–43 (1923). Agents had the power to enter any home or business establishment to look for taxable property and examine books of accounts. Information was collected and processed in the field. It is therefore not surprising to find that congressional comments during this period focused on potential abuses by agents in the field and not on breaches of confidentiality by a Washington-based bureaucracy.

24.   See HR Rep No. 304, 80th Cong, 1st Sess, A127–128 (1947).

25.   The Tariff Commission statute, last codified as 19 USC § 1335 (1940), [19 USCS § 1335], provided:

"It shall be unlawful for any member of the commission, or for any employee, agent, or clerk of the commission, or any other officer or employee of the United States, to divulge, or to make known in any manner whatever not provided for by law, to any person, the trade secrets or processes of any person, firm, copartnership, corporation, or association embraced in any examination or investigation conducted by the commission, or by order of the commission, or by order of any member thereof. Any offense against the provisions of this section shall be a misdemeanor and be punished by a fine not exceeding $1,000, or by imprisonment not exceeding one year, or both, in the discretion of the court, and such offender shall also be dismissed from office or discharged from employment."

26.   Title 15 USC § 176b (1940) [15 USCS § 176b]:

"Any statistical information furnished in confidence to the Bureau of Foreign and Domestic Commerce by individuals, corporations, and firms shall be held to be confidential, and shall be used only for the statistical purposes for which it is supplied. The Director of the Bureau of Foreign and Domestic Commerce shall not permit anyone other than the sworn employees of the Bureau to examine such individual reports, nor shall he permit any statistics of domestic commerce to be published in such manner as to reveal the identity of the individual, corporation, or firm furnishing such data."

by law." In its effort to "consolidate[ ]" the three statutes, Congress enacted § 1905 and essentially borrowed the form of Rev Stat 3167 and the Tariff Commission statute.[27] We find nothing in the legislative history of § 1905 and its predecessors which lends support to Chrysler's contention that Congress intended the phrase "authorized by law," as used in § 1905, to have a special, limited meaning.

Nor do we find anything in the legislative history to support the Government's suggestion that § 1905 does not address formal agency action—i.e., that it is essentially an "anti-leak" statute that does not bind the heads of governmental departments or agencies. That would require an expansive and unprecedented holding that any agency action directed or approved by an agency head is "authorized by law," regardless of the statutory authority for that action. As Attorney General Brownell recognized not long after § 1905 was enacted, such a reading is difficult to reconcile with Congress' intent to consolidate the Tariff Commission and Commerce Department statutes, both of which explicitly addressed ranking officials, with Rev Stat 3167.[28] It is also inconsistent with a settled understanding—previously shared by the Department of Justice—that has been continually articulated and relied upon in Congress during the legislative efforts in the last three decades to increase public access to Government information.[29] Although the existence of this

(*Text continued on page 235*)

---

27.   HR Rep No. 304, supra n 24, at A127.

28.   In a December 1, 1953 opinion, the Attorney General advised the Secretary of the Treasury that he should regard himself as bound by § 1905. The Attorney General noted: "The reviser of the Criminal Code describes the provision as a consolidation of three other sections formerly appearing in the United States Code. Of the three, two expressly operated as prohibitions on the heads of agencies." 41 Op Atty Gen 166, 167 (footnote omitted). See also *id.,* at 221 (Atty. Gen. Brownell advising FCC Chairman to regard himself as bound).

29.   If we accepted the Government's position, 18 USC § 1905 [18 USCS § 1905] would simply be irrelevant to the issue of public access to agency information. The FOIA and other such "access" legislation are concerned with formal agency action— to what extent can an agency or department or, put differently, the head of an agency or department withhold information contained within the governmental unit's files. It is all but inconceivable that a government employee would *withhold* information which his superiors had directed him to release; and these Acts are simply not addressed to *disclosure* by a government employee that is not sanctioned by the employing agency. This is not to say that the actions of individual employees might not be inconsistent with the access legislation. But such actions are only inconsistent insofar as they are imputed to the agencies themselves. Therefore, if § 1905 is not addressed to formal agency action—i. e., action approved by the agency or department head—there should have been no concern in Congress regarding the interrelationship of § 1905 and the access legislation, for they would then address totally different types of disclosure.

In fact, the legislative history of all the significant access legislation of the last 20 years evinces a concern with this relationship and a concomitant universal assumption that § 1905 embraces formal agency action. Congress was assured that the 1958 amendment to 5 USC § 301 [5 USCS § 301], the housekeeping statute that affords department heads custodial responsibility for department records, would not circumscribe the confidentiality mandated by § 1905. The 1958 amendment simply clarified that § 301 itself was not substantive authority to withhold information. See pp ———, 60 L Ed 2d 230–231, infra. Also in 1958 the Subcommittee on Constitutional Rights of the Senate Committee on the Judiciary conducted hearings on the power of the President to withhold information from Congress. As part of the investigative effort, a list was compiled of all statutes restricting disclosure of Government information. Section 1905 was listed among them. Hearings on S 921 before the Subcommittee on Constitutional Rights of the Senate Committee on the Judiciary, 85th Cong, 2d Sess, pt 2, at 986 (1958). Two years later the House Committee on Government Operations conducted a study on statutory authorities restricting or requiring the release of information under the control of executive departments or independent agencies, and again prominent among the statutes "affecting the availability of information to the public" was 18 USC § 1905 [18 USCS § 1905]. House Committee on Government Operations, Federal Statutes on the Availability of Information 262 (Comm Print March 1960) (§ 1905 denominated as statute prohibiting the disclosure of certain information).

In *FAA* v. *Robertson,* 422 US 255, 264–265, 45 L Ed 2d 164, 95 S Ct 2140 (1975), we recognized the importance of these lists in Congress' later deliberations concerning the FOIA, particularly in the consideration of the original Exemption 3. That exemption excepted from the operation of the FOIA matters "specifically exempted from disclosure by statute." As we noted in Robertson:

"When the House Committee on Government Operations focused on Exemption 3, it took note that there are 'nearly 100 statutes or parts of statutes which restrict public access to specific Government records. *These would not be modified* by the public records provisions of [the FOIA].' HR Rep No. 1497, 89th Cong, 2d Sess, 10 (1966). (Emphasis added.)" *Id.,* at 265, 45 L Ed 2d 164, 95 S Ct 2140.

In determining that the statute at issue in *Robertson,* 49 USC § 1504 [49 USCS § 1504], was within Exemption 3, we observed that the statute was on these prior lists and that the CAB had brought the statute to the attention of both the House and Senate Committees as an exempting statute during the hearings on the FOIA. *Id.,* at 264, and n 11, 45 L Ed 2d 164, 95 S Ct 2140. In fact, during those hearings 18 USC § 1905 [18 USCS § 1905] was the most frequently cited restriction on agency or department disclosure of information. Hearings on HR 5012 et al before the Subcommittee of the House Committee on Government Operations, 89th Cong, 1st Sess, 283 (1965) (cited by 28 agencies as authority for withholding information). Among those citing the statute was the Department of Justice. *Id.,* at 386 ("commercial information received or assembled in connection with departmental functions must be withheld pursuant to these requirements"). See also *id.,* at 20 (colloquy between Rep. Moss and Asst. Atty. Gen. Schlei); Attorney General's Memorandum on the Public Information Section of the Administrative Procedure Act 31–32 (June 1967) (18 USC § 1905 [18 USCS understanding is not by any means dispositive, it does shed some light on the intent of the enacting Congress. See *Red Lion Broadcasting Co.* v. *FCC,* 395 US 367, 380–381, 23 L Ed 2d 371, 89 S Ct 1794 (1969); *Federal Housing Administration* v. *The Darlington, Inc.,* 358 US 84, 90, 3 L Ed 2d 132, 79 S Ct 141 (1958). In sum, we conclude that § 1905 does address formal agency action and that the appropriate inquiry is whether OFCCP's regulations provide the "authoriz[ation] by law" required by the statute.

In order for a regulation to have the "force and effect of law," it must have certain substantive characteristics and be the product of certain procedural requisites. The central distinction among agency regulations found in the Administrative Procedure Act (APA) is that between "substantive rules" on the one hand and "interpretive rules, general statements of policy, or rules of agency organization, procedure, or practice" on the other.[30] A "substantive rule" is not defined in the APA, and other authoritative sources essentially offer definitions by negative inference.[31] But in *Morton* v. *Ruiz,* 415 US 199,

---

§ 1905] among the "nearly 100 statutes" mentioned in the House Report).

Most recently, in its report on the Government in the Sunshine Act, the House Committee on Government Operations observed:

"[T]he Trade Secrets Act, 18 USC § 1905 [18 USCS § 1905], which relates only to the disclosure of information where disclosure is 'not authorized by law," would not permit the withholding of information otherwise required to be disclosed by the Freedom of Information Act, since the disclosure is there authorized by law. Thus, for example, if material did not come within the broad trade secrets exemption contained in the Freedom of Information Act, section 1905 would not justify withholding; on the other hand, if material is within the trade secrets exemption of the Freedom of Information Act and therefore subject to disclosure if the agency determines that disclosure is in the public interest, section 1905 must be considered to ascertain whether the agency is forbidden from disclosing the information." HR Rep No, 880, 94th Cong, 2d Sess, at 23 (1976).

30.   5 USC § 553(b), (d) (1976) [5 USCS § 553(b), (d)].

31.   Neither the House nor Senate report attempted to expound on the distinction. In prior cases we have given some weight to the Attorney General's Manual on the Administrative Procedure Act (1947), since the Justice Department was heavily involved in the legislative process that resulted in the Act's enactment in 1946. See *Vermont Yankee Nuclear Power Corp.* v. *NRDC,* 435 US 519, 546, 55 L Ed 2d 460, 98 S Ct 1197 (1978); *Power Reactor Co.* v. *Electricians,* 367 US 396, 408, 6 L Ed 2d 924, 81 S Ct 1529 (1961); *United States* v. *Zucca,* 315 US 91, 96, 100 L Ed 964, 76 S Ct 671 (1956).

The Manual refers to substantive rules as rules that "implement" the statute. "Such rules have the force and effect of law." Manual, at 30 n 3. In contrast it suggests that "interpretive rules" and "general statements of policy" do not have the force and effect of law. Interpretive rules are "issued by an agency to advise the public of the agency's construction of the statutes and rules which it administers." *Ibid.* General statements of policy are "statements issued by an agency to advise the public prospec-

39 L Ed 2d 270, 94 S Ct 1055 (1974), we noted a characteristic inherent in the concept of a "substantive rule." We described a substantive rule—or a "legislative-type rule," id., at 236, 39 L Ed 2d 270, 94 S Ct 1055—as one "affecting individual rights and obligations." Id., at 232, 39 L Ed 2d 270, 94 S Ct 1055. This characteristic is an important touchstone for distinguishing those rules that may be "binding" or have the "force of law." Id., at 235, 236, 39 L Ed 2d 270, 94 S Ct 1055.

That an agency regulation is "substantive," however, does not by itself give it the "force and effect of law." The legislative power of the United States is vested in the Congress, and the exercise of quasi-legislative authority by governmental departments and agencies must be rooted in a grant of such power by the Congress and subject to limitations which that body imposes. As this Court noted in *Batterton* v. *Francis,* 432 US 416, 425 n 9, 53 L Ed 2d 448, 97 S Ct 2399 (1977):

> "Legislative, or substantive, regulations are 'issued by an agency pursuant to statutory authority and . . . implement the statute, as, for example, the proxy rules issued by the Securities and Exchange Commission . . . . Such rules have the force and effect of law.' "[32]

Likewise the promulgation of these regulations must conform with any procedural requirements imposed by Congress. *Morton* v. *Ruiz,* supra, at 232, 39 L Ed 2d 270, 94 S Ct 1055. For agency discretion is not only limited by substantive, statutory grants of authority, but also by the procedural requirements which "assure fairness and mature consideration of rules of general application." *NLRB* v. *Wyman-Gordon Co.,* 394 US 759, 764, 22 L Ed 2d 709, 89 S Ct 1426 (1969). The pertinent procedural limitations in this case are those found in the APA.

The regulations relied on by the Government in this case as providing "authoriz[ation] by law" within the meaning of § 1905 certainly affect individual rights and obligations; they govern the public's right to information in records obtained under Executive Order 11246 and the confidentiality rights of those who submit information to OFCCP and its compliance agencies. It is a much closer question, however, whether they are the product of a congressional grant of legislative authority.

In his published memorandum setting forth the disclosure regulations at issue in this case, the Secretary of Labor states that the authority upon which he relies in promulgating the regulations are § 201 of Executive Order 11246,

---

tively of the manner in which the agency proposes to exercise a discretionary power." *Ibid.* See also Final Report of Attorney General's Committee on Administrative Procedure 27 (1941).

32.   Quoting US Department of Justice, Attorney General's Manual on the Administrative Procedure Act 30 n 3 (1947).

as amended, and 29 CFR § 70.71, which permits units in the Department of Labor to promulgate supplemental disclosure regulations consistent with 29 CFR pt 70 and the FOIA. 38 Fed Reg 3192–3194 (1973). Since materials that are exempt from disclosure under the FOIA are by virtue of Part II of this opinion outside the ambit of that Act, the Government cannot rely on the FOIA as congressional authorization for disclosure regulations that permit the release of information within the Act's nine exemptions.

Section 201 of Executive Order 11246 directs the Secretary of Labor to "adopt such rules and regulations and issue such orders as he deems necessary and appropriate to achieve the purposes thereof." But in order for such regulations to have the "force and effect of law," it is necessary to establish a nexus between the regulations and some delegation of the requisite legislative authority by Congress. The origins of the congressional authority for Executive Order 11246 are somewhat obscure and have been roundly debated by commentators and courts.[33] The order itself as amended establishes a program to eliminate employment discrimination by the Federal Government and by those who benefit from Government contracts. For purposes of this case, it is not necessary to decide whether Executive Order 11246 as amended is authorized by the Federal Property and Administration Services Act of 1949,[34] Titles VI and VII of the Civil Rights Act of 1964,[35] the Equal Employ-

---

33.   See, e.g., *Contractors Assn. of Eastern Pennsylvania* v. *Secretary of Labor,* 442 F2d 159 (CA3), *cert denied,* 404 US 854, 30 L Ed 2d 95, 92 S Ct 98 (1971); Hearings on the Philadelphia Plan and S 931 before the Subcomm on Separations of Powers of the Senate Comm on the Judiciary, 91st Cong, 1st Sess (1969); Jones, "The Bugaboo of Employment Quotas, 1970 *Wis L Rev* 341; "Leiken, Preferential Treatment in the Skilled Building Trades: An Analysis of the Philadelphia Plan," 56 *Cornell L Rev* 84 (1970); Note, "The Philadelphia Plan: A Study in the Dynamics of Executive Power," 39 *Chi L Rev* 723 (1972); Note, "Executive Order 11246: Anti-Discrimination Obligations in Government Contracts," 44 *NYUL Rev* 590 (1969).

The Executive Order itself merely states that it is promulgated "[u]nder and by virtue of the authority vested in [the President] of the United States by the Constitution and statutes of the United States." 3 CFR 339 (1964–1965 Comp).

34.   Pub L No. 81-152, 63 Stat 377, as amended, 40 USC §§ 471–514 [40 USCS §§ 471–514]. The Act as amended is prefaced with the following declaration of policy:

"It is the intent of the Congress in enacting this legislation to provide for the Government an economical and efficient system for (a) the procurement and supply of personal property and nonpersonal services, including related functions such as contracting, inspection, storage, issue, specifications, property identification and classification, transportation and traffic management, establishment of pools or systems for transportation of Government personnel and property by motor vehicle within specific areas, management of public utility services, repairing and converting, establishment of inventory levels, establishment of forms and procedures, and representation

ment Opportunity Enforcement Act of 1972,[36] or some more general notion that the Executive can impose reasonable contractual requirements in the exercise of its procurement authority.[37] The pertinent inquiry is whether

---

before Federal and State regulatory bodies; (b) the utilization of available property; (c) the disposal of surplus property; and (d) records management." 40 USC § 471 [40 USCS § 471]. The Act explicitly authorizes Executive orders "necessary to effectuate [its] provisions." *Id.,* § 486(a). However, nowhere in the Act is there a specific reference to employment discrimination.

Lower courts have suggested that § 486(a) was the authority for predecessors of Executive Order 11246. *Farmer* v. *Philadelphia Electric Co.,* 329 F2d 3 (CA3 1964); *Farkas* v. *Texas Instrument, Inc.,* 375 F2d 629 (CA5), *cert denied,* 389 US 977, 19 L Ed 2d 471, 88 S Ct 480 (1967). But as the Third Circuit noted in *Contractors Assn. of Eastern Pennsylvania* v. *Secretary of Labor,* 442 F2d 159, 167 (CA3 1971), these suggestions were dicta and made without any analysis of the nexus between the Federal Property and Administrative Services Act and the Executive orders. It went on to hold, however, that § 486(a) was authority for at least some aspects of Executive Order 11246 on the ground that "it is in the interest of the United States in all procurement to see that its suppliers are not over the long run increasing its costs and delaying its programs by excluding from the labor pool available minority workmen." 442 F2d, at 170.

35.   42 USC §§ 2000d to 2000d-4; 2000e to 2000e-17 [42 USCS §§ 2000d-4; 2000e to 2000e-17]. Significantly, the question has usually been put in terms of whether Executive Order 11246 is inconsistent with these titles of the Civil Rights Act of 1964. See, e. g., *Contractors Assn. of Eastern Pennsylvania* v. *Secretary of Labor,* 442 F2d 159, 171–174 (1971).

Title VI grants federal agencies that are "empowered to extend Federal financial assistance to any program or activity, by way of grant, loan, or contract" the authority to promulgate rules "which shall be consistent with achievement of the objectives of the statute authorizing the financial assistance in connection with which the action is taken." Such rules must be approved by the President, and their enforcement is subject to congressional review. "In the case of any action terminating, or refusing to grant or continue, assistance because of failure to comply with a requirement imposed pursuant to this section, the head of the Federal department or agency shall file with the committees of the House and Senate having legislative jurisdiction over the program or activity involved a full written report of the circumstances and the grounds for such action." Section 602 of the Civil Rights Act of 1964, 42 USC § 2000d-1 [42 USCS § 2000d-1]. Executive Order 11246 contains no provision for congressional review, and therefore is not promulgated pursuant to § 602. Cf. Executive Order 11247, 3 CFR 348 (1964–1965 Comp). Titles VI and VII contain no other express substantive delegation to the President.

36.   This is an argument that Congress ratified Executive Order 11246 as amended, when it rejected a series of amendments to the Equal Employment Opportunity Enforcement Act that were designed to cut back on affirmative action efforts under the Executive order.

37.   See *Farkas* v. *Texas Instrument, Inc.,* 375 F2d 629 (CA5), *cert denied,* 389 US

under any of the arguable *statutory* grants of authority, the OFCCP disclosure regulations relied on by the Government are reasonably within the contemplation of that grant of authority. We think that it is clear that when it enacted these statutes, Congress was not concerned with public disclosure of trade secrets or confidential business information, and, unless we were to hold that any federal statute that implies some authority to collect information must grant *legislative* authority to disclose that information to the public, it is simply not possible to find in these statutes a delegation of the disclosure authority asserted by the Government here.[38]

The relationship between any grant of legislative authority and the disclosure regulations becomes more remote when one examines § 201 of the Executive order. It speaks in terms of rules and regulations "necessary and appropriate" to achieve the purposes of the Executive order. Those purposes are an end to discrimination in employment by the Federal Government and those who deal with the Federal Government. One cannot readily pull from the logic and purposes of the Executive order any concern with the public's access to information in Government files or the importance of protecting trade secrets or confidential business statistics.

The "purpose and scope" section of the disclosure regulations indicates two underlying rationales: OFCCP's general policy "to disclose information to the public," and its policy "to cooperate with other public agencies as well as private parties seeking to eliminate discrimination in employment." 41 CFR § 60-40.1 (1977). The Government argues that "[t]he purpose of the Executive Order is to combat discrimination in employment, and a disclosure policy

---

977, 19 L Ed 2d 471, 88 S Ct 480 (1967); *Farmer v. Philadelphia Electric Co.* 329 F2d 3 (CA3 1964); *cf. Perkins* v. *Lukens Steel,* 310 US 113, 84 L Ed 1108, 60 S Ct 869 (1940); *Youngstown Sheet and Tube Co.* v. *Sawyer,* 343 US 579, 637, 96 L Ed 1153, 72 S Ct 863, 47 Ohio Ops 430, 62 Ohio L Abs 417, 26 ALR2d 1378 (1952) (Jackson, J., concurring).

38.   The Government cites *Jones* v. *Rath* Packing Co., 430 US 519, 536, 51 L Ed 2d 604, 97 S Ct 1305 (1977), for the proposition that "it has long been acknowledged that administrative regulations consistent with the agencies' substantive statutes have the force of law." Government Brief, at 38 n 24. The legislative delegation in that case, however, was quite explicit. The issue was whether state regulation of the labeling of meats and flour was pre-empted by the Federal Meat Inspection Act (FMIA), the Federal Food, Drug, and Cosmetic Act (FDCA) and the Fair Packaging and Labeling Act. The FMIA provides that meat or a meat product is misbranded

"(5) if in a package or other container unless it bears a label showing . . . (B) an accurate statement of the quantity of the contents in terms of weight, measure, or numerical count: *Provided,* That . . . reasonable variations may be permitted, and exemptions as to small packages may be established, by regulations prescribed by the Secretary." Section 1(n)(5) of the FMIA, 21 USC § 601(n)(5) [21 USCS § 601(n)(5)]. There is a similar provision in the FDCA.

designed to further this purpose is consistent with the Executive Order and an appropriate subject for regulation under its aegis." Government Brief, at 48. Were a grant of legislative authority as a basis for Executive Order 11246 more clearly identifiable, we might agree with the Government that this "compatibility" gives the disclosure regulations the necessary legislative force. But the thread between these regulations and any grant of authority by the Congress is so strained that it would do violence to established principles of separations of powers to denominate these particular regulations "legislative" and credit them with the "binding effect of law."

This is not to say that any grant of legislative authority to a federal agency by Congress must be specific before regulations promulgated pursuant to them can be binding on courts in a manner akin to statutes. What is important is that the reviewing court reasonably be able to conclude that the grant of authority contemplates the regulations issued. Possibly the best illustration remains Justice Frankfurter's opinion for the Court in *National Broadcasting Co.* v. *United States,* 319 US 190, 87 L Ed 1344, 63 S Ct 997 (1943). There the Court rejected the argument that the Communications Act of 1934 did not give the Federal Communications Commission authority to issue regulations governing chain broadcasting beyond the specification of technical, engineering requirements. Before reaching that conclusion, however, the Court probed the language and logic of the Communications Act and its legislative history. Only after this careful parsing of authority did the Court find that the regulations had the force of law and were binding on the courts unless they were arbitrary or not promulgated pursuant to prescribed procedures.

"Our duty is at an end when we find that the action of the Commission was based upon findings supported by evidence, and was made pursuant to authority granted by Congress. It is not for us to say that the 'public interest' will be furthered or retarded by the Chain Broadcasting Regulations. The responsibility belongs to the Congress for the grant of valid legislative authority and to the Commission for its exercise." Id., at 224, 87 L Ed 1344, 63 S Ct 997.

The Government argues, however, that even if these regulations do not have the force of law by virtue of Executive Order 11246, an explicit grant of legislative authority for such regulations can be found in 5 USC § 301 [5 USCS § 301], commonly referred to as the "housekeeping statute."[39] It provides:

---

39.   See HR Rep No. 1461, 85th Cong, 2d Sess, 1 (1958):

"The law has been called an office 'housekeeping' statute, enacted to help General Washington get his administration underway by spelling out the authority for executive officials to set up offices and file Government documents. The documents involved are papers pertaining to the day-to-day business of Government which are not

"The head of an Executive department or military department may prescribe regulations for the government of his department, the conduct of its employees, the distribution and performance of its business, and the custody, use, and preservation of its records, papers, and property. This section does not authorize withholding information from the public or limiting the availability of records to the public."

The antecedents of § 301 go back to the beginning of the Republic, when statutes were enacted to give heads of early Government departments authority to govern internal departmental affairs. Those laws were consolidated into one statute in 1874 and the current version of the statute was enacted in 1958.

Given this long and relatively uncontroversial history, and the terms of the statute itself, it seems to be simply a grant of authority to the agency to regulate its own affairs. What is clear from the legislative history of the 1958 amendment to § 301 is that this section was not intended to provide authority for limiting the scope of § 1905.[40]

The 1958 amendment to § 301 was the product of congressional concern that agencies were invoking § 301 as a source of authority to withhold information from the public. Congressman Moss sponsored an amendment that added the last sentence to § 301, which specifically states that this section "does not authorize withholding information from the public." The Senate Report accompanying the amendment stated:

"Nothing in the legislative history of [§ 301] shows that Congress intended this statute to be a grant of authority to the heads of the executive departments to withhold information from the public or to limit the availability of records to the public." S Rep No. 1621, 85th Cong, 2d Sess, 2 (1958).

The logical corollary to this observation is that there is nothing in the legislative history of § 301 to indicate it is a substantive grant of legislative power to promulgate rules authorizing the *release* of trade secrets or confidential business information. It is indeed a "housekeeping statute," authorizing what

---

restricted under other specific laws nor classified as military information or secrets of state."

The Secretary of Labor did not cite this statute as authority for the OFCCP disclosure regulations. 38 Fed Reg 3192–3193 (1973).

40.   This does not mean, of course, that disclosure regulations promulgated on the basis of § 301 are "in excess of statutory jurisdiction, authority, or limitations" for purposes of § 10(e)(B)(3) of the Administrative Procedure Act, 5 USC § 706(2)(C) [5 USCS § 706(2)(C)]. It simply means that disclosure pursuant to them is not "authorized by law" within the meaning of § 1905.

the APA terms "rules of agency organization, procedure or practice" as opposed to "substantive rules."[41]

This would suggest that regulations pursuant to § 301 could not provide the "authoriz[ation] by law" required by § 1905. But there is more specific support for this position. During the debates on the 1958 amendment Congressman Moss assured the House that the amendment would "not affect the confidential status of information given to the Government and carefully detailed in title 18, United States Code, section 1905." 104 Cong Rec 6550 (1958).

The Government argues that this last statement is of little significance, because it is only made with reference to the amendment. But that robs Congressman Moss's statement of any substantive import. If Congressman Moss thought that records within the terms of § 1905 could be released on the authority of a § 301 regulation, why was he (and presumably the House) concerned with whether the amendment affected § 1905? Under the Government's interpretation, records released pursuant to § 301 are outside § 1905 by virtue of the first sentence of § 301.

The remarks of a single legislator, even the sponsor, are not controlling in analyzing legislative history. Congressman Moss's statement must be considered with the Reports of both Houses and the statements of other congressmen, all of which refute the Government's interpretation of the relationship between § 301 and § 1905.[42] Of greatest significance, however, is the

---

41.   The House Committee on Government Operations cited approvingly an observation by legal experts that

"[§ 301] merely gives department heads authority to regulate within their departments the way in which requests for information are to be dealt with—for example, by centralizing the authority to deal with such requests in the department head." HR Rep No. 1461, 85th Cong, 2d Sess, 7 (1958).

It noted that the members of its Special Subcommittee on Government Information "unanimously agreed that [§ 301] originally was adopted in 1789 to provide for the day-to-day office housekeeping in the Government departments, but through misuse it has become twisted into a claim of authority to withhold information." *Id.,* at 12. There are numerous remarks to similar effect in the Senate report and the floor debates. See, e.g., S Rep No. 1621, 85th Cong, 2d Sess, 2 (1958); 104 Cong Rec 6549 (Rep. Moss), 6560 (Rep. Fascell), 15690–15696 (colloquy between Sens. Hruska and Johnston).

42.   Throughout the floor debates references are made to 78 statutes that require the withholding of information, and assurances are consistently given that these statutes are not in any way affected by § 301. E.g., 104 Cong Rec 6548 (1958) (Rep. Brown), 6549–6550 (Rep. Moss). It is clear from Congressman Moss's comments that § 1905 is one of those statutes. 104 Cong Rec 6549–6550 (1958). There is also frequent reference to trade secrets as not being disclosable and the confidentiality of that information as not being affected by § 301. HR Rep No. 1461. 85th Cong, 2d

"housekeeping" nature of § 301 itself. On the basis of this evidence of legislative intent, we agree with the Court of Appeals for the District of Columbia Circuit that "[s]ection 301 does not authorize regulations limiting the scope of section 1905." *Charles River Park "A," Inc.* v. *HUD,* 519 F2d 935, 942–943 (1975).

There is also a procedural defect in the OFCCP disclosure regulations which precludes courts from affording them the force and effect of law. That defect is a lack of strict compliance with the APA. Recently we have had occasion to examine the requirements of the APA in the context of "legislative" or "substantive" rulemaking. In *Vermont Yankee Nuclear Power Corp.* v. *Natural Resources Defense Council, Inc.,* 435 US 519, 55 L Ed 2d 460, 98 S Ct 1197 (1978), we held that courts could only in "extraordinary circumstances" impose procedural requirements on an agency beyond those specified in the APA. It is within an agency's discretion to afford parties more procedure, but it is not the province of the courts to do so. In *Vermont Yankee* we recognized that the APA is " 'a formula upon which opposing social interests and political forces have come to rest.' " Id., at 547, 55 L Ed 2d 460, 98 S Ct 1197 (quoting *Wong Yang Sung* v. *McGrath,* 339 US 33, 40, 94 L Ed 616, 70 S Ct 445 (1950)). Courts upset that balance when they override informed choice of procedures and impose obligations not required by the

---

Sess, 2 (1958); 104 Cong Rec 6558 (1958) (Rep. Fascell), 6564 (Rep. Wright). The following exchange between Congressmen Meador and Moss is also instructive.

"Mr. MEADER. Mr. Chairman, I should like the attention of the gentleman from California [Mr. Moss], the sponsor of the measure. I would like to read three paragraphs from the additional views I submitted to the report which appear upon page 62 of the report. I said:

"I believe there is unanimous sentiment in the Government Operations Committee on the following points:

"1. That departments and agencies of the Government have construed [§ 301] to authorize them to withhold information from the public and to limit the availability of records to the public.

"2. That this interpretation is a strained and erroneous interpretation of the intent of Congress in [§ 301] which merely authorized department heads to make regulations governing day-to-day operation of the department—a so-called housekeeping function; and that [§ 301] was not intended to deal with the authority to *release* or withhold information or records.

.   .   .   .

"I now yield to the gentleman from California to state whether or not those three points as I have set them forth in my additional views in the report on this measure accurately state what he understands to be the consensus of the judgment of the members of the Government Operations Committee in reporting out this legislation?

"Mr. MOSS. That is correct as I interpret it." 104 Cong Rec 6562 (1958) (emphasis added).

APA. By the same token courts are charged with maintaining the balance: ensuring that agencies comply with the "outline of minimum essential rights and procedures" set out in the APA. HR Rep No. 1980, 79th Cong, 2d Sess, 16 (1946); see *Vermont Yankee Nuclear Power Corp.*, supra, at 549 n 21, 55 L Ed 2d 460, 98 S Ct 1197. Certainly regulations subject to the APA cannot be afforded the "force and effect of law" if not promulgated pursuant to the statutory procedural minimum found in that Act.[43]

Section 4 of the APA, 5 USC § 553 [5 USCS § 553], specifies that an agency shall afford interested persons general notice of proposed rulemaking and an opportunity to comment before a substantive rule is promulgated.[44] "Interpretive rules, general statements of policy or rules of agency organiza-

---

43.   See, e.g., *Morton* v. *Ruiz,* 415 US 199, 39 L Ed 2d 270, 94 S Ct 1055 (1974); *United States* v. *Allegheny-Ludlum Steel Corp.,* 406 US 742, 758, 32 L Ed 2d 453, 92 S Ct 1941 (1972).

44.   5 USC § 553 (1976) [5 USCS § 553]:

"(a) This section applies, according to the provisions thereof, except to the extent that there is involved—

"(1) a military or foreign affairs function of the United States; or

"(2) a matter relating to agency management or personnel or to public property, loans, grants, benefits, or contracts.

"(b) General notice of proposed rule making shall be published in the Federal Register, unless persons subject thereto are named and either personally served or otherwise have actual notice thereof in accordance with law. The notice shall include—

"(1) a statement of the time, place, and nature of public rule making proceedings;

"(2) reference to the legal authority under which the rule is proposed; and

"(3) either the terms or substance of the proposed rule or a description of the subjects and issues involved.

Except when notice or hearing is required by statute, this subsection does not apply—

"(A) to interpretative rules, general statements of policy, or rules of agency organization, procedure, or practice; or

"(B) when the agency for good cause finds (and incorporates the finding and a brief statement of reasons therefor in the rules issued) that notice and public procedure thereon are impracticable, unnecessary, or contrary to the public interest.

"(c) After notice required by this section, the agency shall give interested persons an opportunity to participate in the rule making through submission of written data, views, or arguments with or without opportunity for oral presentation. After consideration of the relevant matter presented, the agency shall incorporate in the rules adopted a concise general statement of their basis and purpose. When rules are required by statute to be made on the record after opportunity for an agency hearing, sections 556 and 557 of this title apply instead of this subsection.

"(d) The required publication or service of a substantive rule shall be made not less than 30 days before its effective date, except—

"(1) a substantive rule which grants or recognizes an exemption or relieves a restriction;

tion, procedure or practice" are exempt from these requirements. When the Secretary of Labor published the regulations pertinent in this case, he stated:

> "As the changes made by this document relate solely to interpretive rules, general statements of policy, and to rules of agency procedure and practice, neither notice of proposed rule making nor public participation therein is required by 5 USC 553 [5 USCS § 553]. Since the changes made by this document either relieve restrictions or are interpretative rules, no delay in effective date is required by 5 USC 553(d) [5 USCS § 553(d)]. These rules shall therefore be effective immediately.
>
> "In accordance with the spirit of the public policy set forth in 5 USC 553 [5 USCS § 553], interested persons may submit written comments, suggestions, data, or arguments to the Director, Office of Federal Contract Compliance. . . ." 38 Fed Reg 3192, 3193 (1973).

Thus the regulations were essentially treated as interpretative rules and interested parties were not afforded the notice of proposed rulemaking required for substantive rules under 5 USC § 553(b) [5 USCS § 553(b)]. As we observed in *Batterton* v. *Francis,* 432 US 416, 425 n 9, 55 L Ed 2d 448, 97 S Ct 2399 (1977), "a court is not required to give effect to an interpretative regulation. Varying degrees of deference are accorded to administrative interpretations, based on such factors as the timing and consistency of the agency's position, and the nature of its expertise." We need not decide whether these regulations are properly characterized "interpretative rules." It is enough that such regulations are not properly promulgated as substantive rules, and therefore not the product of procedures which Congress prescribed as necessary prerequisites to giving a regulation the binding effect of law.[45] An interpretative regulation or general statement of agency policy cannot be the "authoriz[ation] by law" required by § 1905.

"(2) interpretative rules and statements of policy; or

"(3) as otherwise provided by the agency for good cause found and published with the rule.

"(e) Each agency shall give an interested person the right to petition for the issuance, amendment, or repeal of a rule."

45.   The regulations at issue in Jones v Rath Packing Co., see n 38, *supra,* were the product of notice of proposed rulemaking and comment. 32 Fed Reg 10729 (1967); 35 Fed Reg 1552 (1970).

We also note that the Government's reliance on *FCC* v. *Schreiber,* 381 US 279, 14 L Ed 2d 383, 85 S Ct 1459 (1965), is misplaced. In that case the Court held that a FCC rule—that investigatory proceedings would be public unless a hearing examiner found that "the public interest, the proper dispatch of the business . . . or the ends of justice" would be served by closed sessions—was consistent with the pertinent congressional grant of authority and not arbitrary or unreasonable. This Court held that the District Court impermissibly invaded the province of the agency when it imposed its own notions of proper procedures. *Cf. Vermont Yankee Nuclear Power Corp.* v *Natural Resources Defense Council, Inc.,* 435 US 519, 55 L Ed 2d 460, 98 S Ct 1197

This disposition best comports with both the purposes underlying the APA and sound administrative practice. Here important interests are in conflict: the public's access to information in the Government's files and concerns about personal privacy and business confidentiality. The OFCCP's regulations attempt to strike a balance. In enacting the APA, Congress made a judgment that notions of fairness and informed administrative decisionmaking require that agency decisions be made only after affording interested persons notice and an opportunity to comment. With the consideration that is the necessary and intended consequence of such procedures, OFCCP might have decided that a different accommodation was more appropriate.

B

We reject, however, Chrysler's contention that the Trade Secrets Act affords a private right of action to enjoin disclosure in violation of the statute. In *Cort* v. *Ash,* 422 US 66, 45 L Ed 2d 26, 95 S Ct 2080 (1975), we noted that this Court has rarely implied a private right of action under a criminal statute and where it has done so "there was at least a statutory basis for inferring that a civil cause of action of some sort lay in favor of someone."[46] Nothing in § 1905 prompts such an inference. Nor are other pertinent circumstances outlined in *Cort* present here. As our review of the legislative history of § 1905—or lack of same—might suggest, there is no indication of legislative intent to create a private right of action. Most importantly, a private right of action under § 1905 is not "necessary to make effective the congressional purpose," *J. I. Case Co.* v. *Borak,* 377 US 426, 433, 12 L Ed 2d 423, 84 S Ct 1555 (1964), for we find that review of DLA's decision to disclose Chrysler's employment data is available under the APA.[47]

(1978). There was no question in the case regarding the applicability of § 1905. Moreover, the respondents had made a broad request that *"all* testimony and documents to be elicited from them . . . should be received in camera." 381 US, at 295, 14 L Ed 2d 383, 85 S Ct 1459 (emphasis in original). The Court held that when specific information was requested that might actually injure Schreiber's firm competitively, "there would be ample opportunity to request that it be received in confidence, and to seek judicial protection if the request were denied." *Id.,* at 296, 14 L Ed 2d 383, 85 S Ct 1459.

46.   *Cort* v. *Ash,* 422 US 66, 79, 45 L Ed 2d 26, 95 S Ct 2080 (1975), citing *Wyandotte Transportation Co.* v. *United States,* 389 US 191, 19 L Ed 2d 407, 88 S Ct 379 (1967); *J. I. Case Co.* v. *Borak,* 377 US 426, 12 L Ed 2d 423, 84 S Ct 1555 (1964); *Texas & Pacific R. Co.* v. *Rigsby,* 241 US 33, 60 L Ed 874, 36 S Ct 482 (1916).

47.   Jurisdiction to review agency action under the APA is found in 28 USC § 1331 [28 USCS § 1331]. See *Califano* v. *Sanders,* 430 US 99, 51 L Ed 2d 192, 97 S Ct 980 (1977).

Chrysler does not argue in this Court, as it did below, that private rights of action are available under 42 USC § 2000e-8(e) [42 USCS § 2000e-8(e)] and 44 USC § 3508 [44 USCS § 3508].

IV

While Chrysler may not avail itself of any violations of the provisions of § 1905 in a separate cause of action, any such violations may have a dispositive effect on the outcome of judicial review of agency action pursuant to § 10 of the APA. Section 10(a) of the APA provides that "[a] person suffering legal wrong because of agency action, or adversely affected or aggrieved by agency action . . . , is entitled to judicial review thereof." 5 USC § 702 (1976) [5 USCS § 702]. Two exceptions to this general rule of reviewability are set out in § 10. Review is not available where "statutes preclude judicial review" or where "agency action is committed to agency discretion by law." 5 USC § 701(a)(1), (2) (1976) [5 USCS § 701(a)(1), (2)]. In *Citizens to Preserve Overton Park, Inc.* v. *Volpe,* 401 US 402, 410, 28 L Ed 2d 136, 91 S Ct 814 (1971), the Court held that the latter exception applies "where 'statutes are drawn in such broad terms that in a given case there is no law to apply.' " Quoting S Rep No. 752, 79th Cong, 1st Sess, 26 (1945). Were we simply confronted with the authorization in 5 USC § 301 [5 USCS § 301] to prescribe regulations regarding "the custody, use, and preservation of [agency] records, papers and property," it would be difficult to derive any standards limiting agency conduct which might constitute "law to apply." But our discussion in Part III demonstrates that § 1905 and any "authoriz[ation] by law" contemplated by that section place substantive limits on agency action.[48] Therefore we conclude that DLA's decision to disclose the Chrysler reports is reviewable agency action and Chrysler is a person "adversely affected or aggrieved" within the meaning of § 10(a).

Both Chrysler and the Government agree that there is APA review of DLA's decision. They disagree on the proper scope of review. Chrysler argues that there should be de novo review, while the Government contends that such review is only available in extraordinary cases and this is not such a case.

The pertinent provisions of § 10(e) of the APA, 5 USC § 706 (1976) [5 USCS § 706], provide that a reviewing court shall

"(2) hold unlawful and set aside agency action, findings, and conclusions found to be—
"(A) arbitrary, capricious, an abuse of discretion, or otherwise not in accordance with law;

. . .

"(F) unwarranted by the facts to the extent that the facts are subject to trial de novo by the reviewing court."

For the reasons previously stated, we believe any disclosure that violates §

---

48.   By regulation the Secretary of Labor also has imposed the standards of § 1905 on OFCCP and its compliance agencies. 29 CFR § 70.21 (1977).

1905 is "not in accordance with law" within the meaning of 5 USC § 706(2)(A) [5 USCS § 706(2)(A)]. De novo review by the District Court is ordinarily not necessary to decide whether a contemplated disclosure runs afoul of § 1905. The District Court in this case concluded that disclosure of some of Chrysler's documents was barred by § 1905, but the Court of Appeals did not reach the issue. We shall therefore vacate the Court of Appeals' judgment and remand for further proceedings consistent with this opinion in order that the Court of Appeals may consider whether the contemplated disclosures would violate the prohibition of § 1905.[49] Since the decision regarding this substantive issue—the scope of § 1905—will necessarily have some effect on the proper form of judicial review pursuant to § 706(2), we think it unnecessary, and therefore unwise, at the present stage of this case for us to express any additional views on that issue.

Vacated and remanded.

[2] Analysis of Chrysler v. Brown

On April 18, 1979, The Supreme Court handed down a unanimous decision in *Chrysler* v. *Brown,* 441 US 281, 60 L Ed 2d 208, — S Ct — (1979), which will heavily effect the attempts by corporations to preclude disclosure to third persons under the Freedom of Information Act (FOIA) of confidential information submitted by them to the government. These attempts to enjoin agency disclosure, known as "reverse-FOIA" actions, were addressed by the Supreme Court for the first time in this decision.

The FOIA places a general obligation on an agency to make information available to the public on request and then specifies nine categories of materials that are "exempt" from disclosure. The U.S. Courts of Appeals had divided on whether, assuming the particular material was demonstrated to be exempt, a government agency was nevertheless free *voluntarily* to release the

---

49.   Since the Court of Appeals assumed for purposes of argument that the material in question was within an exemption to the FOIA, that court found it unnecessary expressly to decide that issue and it is open on remand. We, of course, do not here attempt to determine the relative ambits of Exemption 4 and § 1905, or to determine whether § 1905 is an exempting statute within the terms of the amended Exemption 3, 5 USC § 552(b)(3) (1976) [5 USCS § 552(b)(3)]. Although there is a theoretical possibility that material might be outside Exemption 4 yet within the substantive provisions of § 1905, and that therefore the FOIA might provide the necessary "authoriz[ation] by law" for purposes of § 1905, that possibility is at most of limited practical significance in view of the similarity of language between Exemption 4 and the substantive provisions of § 1905.

information to the requesting party, regardless of an objection by the party who had originally submitted the information.

The view of most courts was that the nine exemptions were "discretionary," that although an agency could not be compelled to release exempt records, it had the discretion to do so if it deemed disclosure desirable.[1] Several other courts viewed the exemptions as being "mandatory," that the agencies were prohibited from disclosing exempt materials.[2]

In *Chrysler,* the Supreme Court opted for the "discretionary" point of view. The Court determined that "the congressional concern was with the *agency's* need or preference for confidentiality; the FOIA by itself protects the submitter's interest in confidentiality only to the extent that this interest is endorsed by the agency collecting the information.

> "We simply hold here that Congress did not design the FOIA exemptions to be mandatory bars to disclosure . . .
> "We therefore conclude that Congress did not limit an agency's discretion to disclose information when it enacted FOIA. It necessarily follows that the Act does not afford [the submitting party] any right to enjoin agency disclosure."[3]

Whether the above language implies that an agency has unreviewable discretion to direct the release of "exempt" documents and thus the submitting party is powerless to maintain any action to enjoin, or more narrowly, whether it simply rejects the "mandatory" approach in favor of the "discretionary" approach is far from clear.[4]

The Courts of Appeals which had adopted the "discretionary" approach had never considered an agency's "discretion" as unreviewable. Rather they reviewed the agency decision to disclose under the "abuse of discretion" standard of § 706(2)(A) of the Administrative Procedure Act.

The above ambiguity however is rendered largely moot by the Court's view of 18 USC 1905 (the Trades Secrets Act). In general, § 1905 prohibits any government agency, unless "authorized by law," from disclosing or divulging any information which "concerns or relates to the trade secrets,

---

1.   See, e.g., *Chrysler* v. *Schlesinger,* 565 F.2d 1172 (3rd Cir. 1977); *Superior Oil Co.* v. *FERC,* 563 F2d 191(5th Cir. 1977); *Sears, Roebuck and Co.* v. *Eckerd,* 575 F2d 1197 (7th Cir. 1978); *General Dynamics Corp.* v. *Marshall,* 572 F2d 1211 (8th Cir. 1978).

2.   See, e.g., *Westinghouse Elec. Corp.* v. *Schlesinger,* 542 F 2d 1190 (4th Cir. 1976).

3.   *Chrysler* v. *Brown,* 60 L Ed 2d 220 (1979). (9-10)

4.   There is language in the Supreme Court's opinion which would directly support a narrow holding, e.g., "We simply hold here that Congress did not design the FOIA exemptions to be mandatory bars to disclosure." Id. at 219 (9).

processes, operations, style of work, or apparatus, or to the identity, confidential statistical data, amount or source of any income, profits, losses, or expenditures of any person, firm, partnership, corporation, or association."

The Supreme Court held that § 1905 is applicable to a threatened disclosure by interpreting the "authorized by law" provision in a narrow manner. An agency regulation authorizing discretionary disclosure of FOIA "exempt" documents does not constitute "law" under § 1905 unless the regulation is "substantive" in nature, originally adopted in full conformity with the Administrative Procedure Act, and "reasonable within the contemplation" of the basic grant of statutory authority to the agency.[5]

In *Chrysler* the Department of Labor agency regulations involved did not meet this test. First, the Court ruled that neither a statute nor a previous executive order adopted for the purpose of eliminating discrimination by government contractors (the area of duty of the agency involved) envisioned regulations authorizing disclosure of information to the public.[6] Neither FOIA nor 5 USC § 301 (the "housekeeping statute") authorized the agency's disclosure regulations.[7]

Second, the regulations in question had not been adopted in conformity with the procedural requirements of the APA.

Hence, the agency regulations did not constitute "law" under § 1905 and release by the government of documents falling within the purview of § 1905 were prohibited.

It should be noted that if materials are found to be within the protection of § 1905 and not within the exception, the prohibition against disclosure is in effect "mandatory" since "any disclosure that violates § 1905 is 'not in accordance with law'."[8] There is no "discretion" in an agency to release such materials to a FOIA requesting party.

A number of questions were left unresolved by the opinion. Whether in a case *not* within the purview of § 1905 an agency's decision to release a submitter's material is reviewable under the APA was left unanswered. The Court explicitly declined to decide the scope of § 1905, though it hinted strongly that it is at least as broad as Exemption 4.[9] The Court also did not decide whether the standard of review in reverse-discrimination cases is either the "arbitrary, capricious, and abuse of discretion," or de novo standards of review.

---

5.   Id., 441 US at 294-316, 60 LEd2d at 220-234 (*supra,* 230-246).
6.   Id., 441 US at 295-308, 60 LEd2d at 220-228 (*supra,* 230-240).
7.   Id., 441 US at 290-294, 312; 60 LEd2d at 218-220, 231 (*supra,* 226-230, 243).
8.   Id., 441 US at 318, 60 LEd2d at 235 (*supra,* 247-248).
9.   Id., 441 US at 319, 60 LEd2d at 235 (*supra,* 248).

Two Government Memoranda to All Agencies and Legal Departments re: Chrysler v. Brown

[1] Memorandum from Ass't Attorney General Barbara Babcock to All Agency General Counsels on "Reverse" Freedom of Information Act Cases. Issued June 21, 1979.

TO: All Agency General Counsels
FROM: Barbara Allen Babcock
           Assistant Attorney General
           Civil Division
SUBJECT: Current and Future Litigation Under
           Chrysler v. *Brown*

The purpose of this letter is to direct your attention to a recent Supreme Court decision, *Chrysler Corp.* v. *Brown,* 47 U.S.L.W. 4434 (April 18, 1979), which will have a significant impact upon the Government's litigation of so-called "reverse" Freedom of Information Act cases—lawsuits for injunctive relief brought against the Government by private parties who, having submitted information to federal agencies, seek to prevent agency disclosure of this information pursuant to FOIA requests. Inasmuch as your agency may at this time or in the future be a party defendant to at least one such pending case, you should become fully apprised of the import of the *Chrysler* decision and of the approach which the Department of Justice now intends to pursue in such cases in light of *Chrysler.* I apologize for the length and complexity of what follows, but urge you to address it carefully because we are very close to a just resolution of this difficult problem.

I would first like to emphasize that the Supreme Court's ruling in *Chrysler* decisively resolved a number of important issues in the Government's favor,

251

such that our ability to defend Government disclosure in "reverse" cases is now greatly enhanced. The Court unequivocally determined, for example, that an agency's invocation of the Freedom of Information Act's exemptions is permissive, not mandatory, and that a private party which submits data to the Government has an enforceable interest under the FOIA in the confidentiality of such data "only to the extent that this interest is endorsed by the agency collecting the information." 47 U.S.L.W. at 4437. The *Chrysler* decision similarly put to rest any notion that a private cause of action to enjoin Government disclosure of submitted data may be implied either from the Freedom of Information Act, 5 U.S.C. §552, or from the Trade Secrets Act, 18 U.S.C. §1905; such a cause of action, the Court ruled, may arise only under the general judicial review provisions of the Administrative Procedure Act, 5 U.S.C. §§701, *et seq. See id.* at 4444. Significantly, the Court further held that such judicial review should "ordinarily" be limited to review of the administrative record and should not be undertaken *de novo* by district courts. *See id.* Thus, the Supreme Court in *Chrysler* upheld the significant procedural victories won by the Government in the Third Circuit below and in the other circuits which followed the Third Circuit's lead. *See Chrysler Corp.* v. *Schlesinger,* 565 F.2d 1172 (3rd Cir. 1977); *see also Sears, Roebuck & Co.* v. *Eckerd* 575 F.2d 1197 (7th Cir. 1978); *General Dynamics Corp.* v. *Marshall,* 572 F.2d 1211 (8th Cir. 1978).

However, the Court did rule adversely to the Government regarding the impediment to disclosure posed by 18 U.S.C. § 1905 and the ability of federal agencies to overcome that impediment through the promulgation of disclosure regulations in satisfaction of § 1905's exception for disclosures which are "authorized by law." By holding that there must exist some identifiable "nexus" between such a disclosure regulation and the delegation of legislative authority for its promulgation, the Court adopted a standard more demanding than that advocated by the Government for the satisfaction of § 1905's "authorized by law" exception. *See id.* at 4438-44. Although the Court thus dealt with § 1905's "authorized by law" exception, it expressly decline to define the substantive scope of § 1905, and remanded that vital issue to the Third Circuit. *See id.* at 4444 & n.49.

Chrysler's interpretation of § 1905's "authorized by law" exception has created the necessity in almost all pending "reverse" FOIA cases for agencies to determine for the first time whether the disputed data falls within the substantive scope of § 1905. Because of this necessity for further agency review, and in light of the fact that most "reverse" FOIA cases have been in litigation for many months or years, the Department of Justice has determined that it is in the Government's best interest to seek their immediate remand to the agencies for the creation of new administrative records. Although such an undertaking will of course involve a substantial expenditure of administrative resources in the new future, I am firmly convinced that it is absolutely essential to the Government's defense of the pending litigation and that it will ultimately minimize both the administrative and litigative burden of defending the Government's disclosure determinations in all such cases. Only through the careful re-creation of the administrative process for these pending cases can we maximize our future ability to defend all such "reverse" cases successfully in the wake of *Chrysler.*

In order to facilitate this administrative process on remand, I have outlined the following procedures and standards as appropriate guidelines for your agency's creation of new administrative records.

(1) First, you should undertake to contact the original data requester in order to ensure that there continues to exist an actual case or controversy surrounding the data at issue. It could well be that with the passage of time the requester has lost interest in the request, has obtained the data (or like data) elsewhere, or possibly even now considers the data to be uselessly out of date. It would not be at all unreasonable to require an updated expression of interest from at least one bona fide Freedom of Information Act requester before considering the matter to be still "live." Indeed, you should invite the requester's active participation in the administrative process through the submission of any evidence known to the requester that would support disclosure.

(2) Second, you should take all steps necessary to ensure that the administrative record generated on remand will be fully adequate for judicial review under the Administrative Procedure Act. You should be cognizant of the factors which some courts have deemed relevant in examining administrative records under the APA in "reverse" FOIA cases. *See, e.g., Chrysler Corp. v. Schlesinger,* 565 F.2d 1172, 1192 (3rd Cir. 1977), *vacated on other grounds,* 47 U.S.L.W. 4434 (April 18, 1979); *GTE Sylvania, Inc.* v. *Consumer Product Safety Commission,* 404 F.Supp. 352, 366-67 (D.Del. 1975), *aff'd,* No. 78-1328 (3rd Cir., April 30, 1979). You should solicit from the submitter detailed written objections to disclosure, and your administrative decision should include a full explanation and documentation of all reasons supporting your acceptance or rejection of the submitter's various objections. Furthermore, to the extent that your decision is based upon evidence submitted by the requester, you should explain the relevance of such evidence to your decision.

(3) The following primary legal arguments are routinely raised by submitters in "reverse" FOIA cases: (a) that the submitted data falls within a non-disclosure statute that triggers the FOIA's Exemption 3; (b) that the data falls within the scope of Exemption 4; (c) that the data falls within the scope of Exemption 6; and (d) that disclosure of the data is

prohibited by §1905. The appropriate approach for addressing upon remand each of these primary legal arguments is discussed below. If your agency encounters additional arguments not discussed herein, or in the event that your agency has a problem in any particular case with respect to the proper application of the following legal standards, please contact the Department of Justice attorney assigned to the case. In addition, you should refer substantial prelitigation questions regarding general FOIA law or policy to the Department's Office of Information Law and Policy.

(a) Where a submitter claims that the data falls within the scope of a non-disclosure statute which the submitter asserts to be an Exempting 3 statute, you should employ the following approach:

(i) You should determine whether the non-disclosure statute identified by the submitter qualifies as an Exemption 3 statute by virtue of satisfying either of the alternative clauses of 5 U.S.C. §552(b)(3), as interpreted by applicable case law. *See, e.g., Lee Pharmaceuticals v. Kreps,* 577 F.2d 610 (9th Cir. 1978); *Seymour v. Barabba,* 559 F.2d 806 (D.C. Cir. 1977). In this regard you should follow the Government's policy, as stated in the attached memorandum from the Department of Justice's Office of Information Law and Policy, that §1905 is not an Exemption 3 statute.

(ii) If it is determined that the statute identified by the submitter is an Exemption 3 statute, you should then determine whether the data falls within the scope of that statute. Any data falling within the scope of an Exemption 3 statute should not be disclosed, *unless* the Exemption 3 statute is one which vests discretion in the agency to determine whether or not to withhold data, *and* the agency decides in the exercise of such discretion not to withhold such data.

(iii) Even if the submitter fails to raise an Exemption 3 objection, you should nevertheless determine whether any Exemption 3 statute applies to the data.

(b) Where Exemption 4 or § 1905 or both are raised by the submitter, you would employ the following approach:

(i) You should first determine whether the data falls within Exemption 4. *See, e.g., National Parks and Conservation Ass'n v. Morton,* 498 F.2d 765 (D.C. Cir. 1974).

(ii) If it is determined that the data falls within Exemption 4, you should next determine whether the data should nevertheless be disclosed as a matter of administrative discretion. Such a determination should be clearly set forth, together with an indication of the matters considered in reaching that determination.

(iii) If it is determined that the data does not fall within Exemption 4, then you should further determine whether the data would nevertheless be appropriate for discretionary disclosure even if arguably protected by that exemption. Such a finding should be similarly stated with full justification, even though rendered only in the hypothetical.

(iv) With respect to all data within Exemption 4 which the agency desires to disclose as a matter of discretion, you should make § 1905 findings as requested in paragraph (d), below, and you should also determine whether such discretionary disclosure would be prohibited by any statute other than § 1905 or by any agency regulation.

(c) Where Exemption 6 is raised by the submitter, you should determine whether the data falls within that exemption, as interpreted by the Supreme Court in *Department of the Air Force* v. *Rose,* 425 U.S. 352 (1976).

(d) Where 18 U.S.C. § 1905 is either raised by the submitter or possibly applicable, you should make the determinations requested in paragraph (b), above, and in addition make the following determinations:

(i) You should first determine whether disclosure of the data by your agency is contemplated by a statute which would meet *Chrysler's* "nexus" test, thus satisfying § 1905's "authorized by law" exception. An example of such a statute may be found at 42 U.S.C. § 1306, which has recently been held to authorize HEW disclosure regulations in satisfaction of § 1905 under the *Chrysler* test. *See Cedars Nursing and Convalescent Center, Inc.* v. *Aetna Life & Casualty Insurance Co.,* — F. Supp. —, Civil No. 79-1416 (E.D. Pa., May 7, 1979). This determination should be made in careful consultation with the Department of Justice.

(ii) Regardless of the outcome of the inquiry described in paragraph (i), above, you should next determine the substantive applicability of § 1905 to the data at issue. For this purpose, you should view the statute as being not broader in scope than the combined scopes of the three predecessor statutes of which it is a consolidation—the Revenue Act of 1864, last codified at 18 U.S.C. § 216 (1940); a Tariff Commission statute, last codified at 19 U.S.C. § 1335 (1940); and a Commerce Department statute, last codified at 15 U.S.C. § 176b (1940)—

and accordingly determine whether the contested data falls within the substantive reach of § 1905 as so defined. *See Muniz* v. *Hoffman,* 422 U.S. 454 (1975); *United States* v. *Cook,* 384 U.S. 257 (1966). A copy of the text of § 1905's predecessor statutes is attached hereto.

(4) Finally, you should make all ultimate administrative disclosure determinations upon remand as follows:

(a) *All* data determined *not* to fall within any FOIA exemption ("nonexempt data") must be disclosed, regardless of the applicability of §1905, as follows:

(i) If the nonexempt data does not fall within § 1905, as defined above, it must be disclosed pursuant to the statutory mandate imposed upon your agency by the FOIA.

(ii) If the nonexempt data does fall within § 1905, as defined above, it must nonetheless be disclosed for the reason that the FOIA itself would "authorize" the disclosure, thus rendering § 1905 inapplicable.

(b) With respect to all data determined to fall within an FOIA exemption, your disclosure decisions should be made as follows:

(i) All data which the agency has determined to be prohibited from disclosure by any statute (other than § 1905, which is discussed separately below) or by any agency regulation must be withheld.

(ii) All data found not to be prohibited from disclosure under subparagraph (i), immediately above, and also found to fall *outside* the substantive scope of § 1905, may be disclosed.

(iii) All data found not to be prohibited from disclosure under subparagraph (i), above, and also found to fall *inside* the substantive scope of § 1905 must be withheld, *unless* the agency can identify either a "nexus" statute or an agency regulation based upon a "nexus" statute to "authorize" disclosure, in which case the data may be disclosed.

(iv) Any discretionary determination to disclose FOIA exempt data should be based upon a consideration in the administrative record of both (1) the harm likely to result from such disclosure; and (2) other factors, such as furthering the public interest or advancing the mission of the agency, which counterbalance such harm. In this regard, please consult Part V of [Robert Saloschin's] memorandum from the Department's Office of Information Law and Policy.

(5) After completing a new administrative record upon remand by making the ultimate disclosure determinations as requested in paragraph (4), above,

and prior to disclosing any disputed data, please promptly contact the Department of Justice attorney assigned to the case who will both inform you regarding the status of any pending injunction prohibiting disclosure, and will also request your assistance in filing the new record before the district court.

I realize that the above approach may at first appear difficult to follow, but I am confident that upon careful analysis and implementation you will agree that adherence to such an approach on remand will provide the optimum basis for favorable judicial review of your agency's disclosure determinations. Daniel J. Metcalfe, 633-3183, and Vincent Garvey, 633-3442, of my staff will be available to answer any questions and to provide any assistance required with respect to this process. We look forward to a mutually cooperative relationship which will maximize our ability to defend all Government disclosure determinations in the wake of *Chrysler.*

Attachments

ATTACHMENT

15 U.S.C. § 176a(1940)

"Any statistical information furnished in confidence to the Bureau of Foreign and Domestic Commerce by individuals, corporations and firms shall be held to be confidential, and shall be used only for the statistical purposes for which it is supplied. The Director of the Bureau of Foreign and Domestic Commerce shall not permit anyone other than the sworn employees of the Bureau to examine such individual reports, nor shall he permit any statistics of domestic commerce to be published in such manner as to reveal the identity of the individual, corporation, or firm furnishing such data."

18 U.S.C. § 216(1940)

"It shall be unlawful for any collector, deputy collector, agent, clerk, or other officer or employee of the United States to divulge or to make known in any manner whatever not provided by law to any person the operations, style of work, or apparatus of any manufacturer or producer visited by him in the discharge of his official duties, or the amount or source of income, profits, losses, expenditures, or any particular thereof, set forth or disclosed in any income return, or to permit any income return or copy thereof or any book containing any abstract or particulars thereof to be seen or examined by any person except as provided by law; and it shall be unlawful for any person to print or publish in any manner whatever not provided by law any income return, or any part thereof or source of income, profits, losses, or expenditures appearing in any income return; and any offense against the foregoing provision shall be a misdeameanor and be punished by a fine not exceeding $1,000 or by imprisonment not exceeding one year, or both, at the discretion of the court; and if the offender be an officer or employee of the United States he shall be dismissed from office or discharged from employment."

19 U.S.C. § 1335(1940)

"It shall be unlawful for any member of the commission, or for any employee, agent, or clerk of the commission, or any other officer or employee of the United States, to divulge, or to make known in any manner whatever not provided for by law, to any person, the trade secrets or processes of any person, firm, co-partnership, corporation, or association embraced in any examination or investigation conducted by the commission, or by order of the commission, or by order of any member thereof. Any offense against the provisions of this section shall be a misdemeanor and be punished by a fine not exceeding $1,000, or by imprisonment not exceeding one year, or both, in the discretion of the court, and such offender shall also be dismissed from office or discharged from employment."

[2] Memorandum from Robert L. Saloschin, Director, Office of Information Law and Policy, To All Federal Departments and Agencies on *Chrysler* v. *Brown.* Issued June 19, 1979.

TO: All Federal Department and Agencies
           Attention: Principal Legal and Administrative
                      Contacts on FOIA Matters
FROM: Robert L. Saloschin, Director Office of
           Information Law and Policy
SUBJECT: Statement Concerning The Supreme Court's
           Decision in *Chrysler* v. *Brown*

The following statement pertains to important matters involved in the administration of the Freedom of Information Act (FOIA) by most federal agencies, particularly agencies which receive requests for access to information submitted by and pertaining to business firms. The statement has been adopted by this Office, after full discussion within the Department's Freedom of Information Committee.

This statement sets forth the position of the Department of Justice on some of the questions left undecided by the recent Supreme Court decision in *Chrysler Corp.* v. *Brown,* 47 U.S.L.W. 4434 (April 18, 1979), and is being issued as guidance to agencies in this field.

I. *Narrative Summary of the Chrysler case to present time.*

Chrysler Corporation, as a party to numerous Government contracts, was required to comply with Executive Orders 11246 and 11375, which charge the Secretary of Labor with ensuring that corporations that benefit from Government contracts provide equal employment opportunity regardless of race or sex. Regulations promulgated by the Department of Labor's Office of Federal Contract Compliance Programs (OFCCP) require Government contractors to furnish reports about their affirmative action programs and the composition of their work forces, and provide that notwithstanding exemption from mandatory disclosure under the Freedom of Information Act (FOIA), such records shall be made available for inspection if determined to be in the public interest, except in the case of records whose disclosure is prohibited by law. After the Department of Defense's Defense Logistics Agency (DLA), the designated compliance agency responsible for monitoring the corporation's employment practices, informed Chrysler that third parties had made a FOIA request for disclosure of certain materials that had been furnished to the DLA by Chrysler, Chrysler objected to their release. The DLA determined that the materials were subject to disclosure under the FOIA and OFCCP disclosure rules, and Chrysler then sued to enjoin release of the documents.

The United States District Court for the District of Delaware found in 1976 that release of lists of internally used job titles and the number of people who perform each job, known as "manning tables," could cause the company substantial competitive harm within the test of *National Parks and Conservation Association* v. *Morton,* 498 F.2d 765, 770 (D.C. Cir. 1974). The Court further found that an employee disclosing the manning tables would face criminal liability under 18 U.S.C. § 1905; that such disclosure was forbidden by 29 C.F.R. § 70.21(a), regulations promulgated by the Secretary of Labor pursuant to 5 U.S.C. § 301, the general housekeeping statutes; and entered a permanent injunction against the disclosure of the manning tables. The Court held that its jurisdiction over the matter arose from 28 U.S.C. § 1331 and in part under the Fifth Amendment. The Court rejected Chrysler's claim that additional commercial data in the AAP's which it found to be far less detailed than that found in EEO-1's also met the *National Park* test for invocation by the Government of the fourth exemption of the Freedom of Information Act. *Chrysler Corp.* v. *Schlesinger,* 412 F.Supp. 171 (D. Del. 1976).

Both Chrysler and the Government appealed the lower court decision. The Court of Appeals for the Third Circuit held that (1) neither the Freedom of Information Act nor 18 U.S.C. § 1905 created a cause of action to enjoin disclosure, but the Administrative Procedure Act does; (2) the disclosure of these records was authorized by law within the meaning of 18 U.S.C. § 1905 because the Office of Federal Contract Compliance regulations for disclosure of information which it received from government contractors concerning hiring of minorities and women, are authorized by the statute providing that the head of executive departments may prescribe regulations for preservation of records, 5 U.S.C. § 301, referred to above as the general housekeeping statute; and (3) the record was insufficient to permit determination of the basis for the decision to disclose the information. The Court of Appeals vacated the judgment of the district court and remanded the case for further agency proceedings. *Chrysler* v. *Schlesinger,* 565 F.2d 1174 (3rd Cir. 1977).

Chrysler Corporation sought review of the Court of Appeals decision in the Supreme Court. The Supreme Court opinion issued on April 18, 1979, noted a number of significant issues but only resolved some of them. The present posture of the case is that the Supreme Court vacated the Court of Appeal's judgment and remanded the case back to the Court of Appeals for consideration of whether the contemplated disclosures would violate the prohibition of 18 U.S.C. § 1905. Chrysler's brief will be filed shortly and the Government's approximately two weeks later.

II. *Questions Decided and Left Undecided by the Supreme Court*

The issues that the Supreme Court resolved are:

1. The Freedom of Information Act is exclusively a disclosure statute. Therefore, submitters have no private right of action under it to enjoin agency disclosure. The Court explicitly found that Congressional concern in enacting the statute was with the *agency's* need or preference for confidentiality. Thus, the FOIA by itself protects the interest in confidentiality of private entities submitting information only to the extent that this interest is endorsed by the agency collecting the information.

2. The exemptions in FOIA are not mandatory but discretionary.

3. 18 U.S.C. § 1905 does not create a private cause of action, but it is an independent prohibition against certain releases of business information by agencies.

4. A private right of action under 18 U.S.C. § 1905 is not necessary to make effective its congressional purpose, since an agency's decision to make a disclosure contrary to 18 U.S.C. § 1905 is reviewable under the Administrative Procedure Act.

5. *De novo* review by the courts is ordinarily not necessary to decide whether a contemplated disclosure would violate 18 U.S.C. § 1905.

The three significant issues which were not disposed of by the Supreme Court are: the substantive *scope* of 18 U.S.C. § 1905 the substantive *scope* of the fourth exemption to the FOIA; and whether 18 U.S.C. § 1905 is an exemption three statute. The Court did, however, deal with the question whether agency regulations could provide legal authorization for releases of business information that would otherwise be prohibited as falling within the substantive scope of 18 U.S.C. § 1905, and apparently held that agency regulations can accomplish this only if they were adopted with proper rule-making procedures and have a "nexus" with some statute dealing with disclosure of business information. The Court further held that 5 U.S.C. §301, the general housekeeping statute, is not such a statute, nor is the Freedom of Information Act as to material which is exempt under its terms.

III. *Question of Criminal Prosecution under 18 U.S.C. § 1905.*

Since the *Chrysler* decision, the Assistant Attorney General of the Criminal Division has issued an instruction on prosecution policy concerning 18 U.S.C. § 1905, to all United States Attorneys. After noting that there "are no reported annotations dealing with prosecution under this statute," the instruction declares that the policy of the Criminal Division is not to prosecute government employees for a violation of 18 U.S.C. § 1905 if the release of information in question was made in "a good faith effort to comply with the Freedom of Information Act and the appropriate applicable regulations." Furthermore, United States Attorneys are directed to consult with the Public Integrity Section of the Criminal Division prior to initiating any action involving a potential violation of the statute. This instruction has been issued as an insert to the United States Attorneys' Manual, where it appears as a new Section, 9-2.025.

IV. *18 U.S.C. § 1905 vis-a-vis FOIA.*

18 U.S.C. § 1905 is an independent prohibition against release, in response to a FOIA request or otherwise, of information within its scope if such release is not "authorized by law." A release of records that are not exempt under FOIA in response to a FOIA request is *required* by law, and therefore is "authorized by law" within the meaning of 18 U.S.C. § 1905 even if disclosure of such records would otherwise be prohibited by the latter statute.

The Justice Department does not consider 18 U.S.C. § 1905 a third exemption statute. This position represents the overwhelming weight of authority including two Congressional reports, H.R. Rep. No. 95-1382, 95th Cong., 2d Sess., 23 (1976); as well as numerous court decisions. Although the Fourth Circuit in *Westinghouse Electric Corp.* v. *Schlesinger,* 542 F.2d 1190 (1976), *cert. denied,* 431 U.S. 924 (1977), upheld the lower court holding that 18 U.S.C. § 1905 is a (b) (3) statute weeks after the Sunshine Act amendment of that exemption, the Court made no reference to this amendment. Courts in several other cases have reached the opposite conclusion, including *Nationwide Mutual Insurance Co.* v. *Friedman,* 451 F.Supp. 736 (D. Md. 1978), *Westinghouse Electric Corporation* v. *Brown,* 443 F.Supp. 1225 (E.D. Va. 1977), and *Crown Central Petroleum Corp.* v. *Kleppe,* 424 F.Supp. 744 (D.

Md. 1976), all in the Fourth Circuit. The court in *Nationwide* distinguished the Fourth Circuit's opinion in *Westinghouse* by saying, "This decision was prior to the change in provision (b) (3) and relied heavily on the reasoning in *Robertson.*" In *Crown Central,* the court quoted the House Government Operations Committee Report for the proposition that Section 1905 was not intended to fall under the new (b) (3). *See also General Dynamics Corp.* v. *Marshall,* 572 F.2d 1211 (8th Cir. 1978), vacated, — U.S. —(1979); *United Technologies Corp.* v. *Marshall,* 464 F.Supp. 845 (D.Conn. 1979); *Westchester General Hospital, Inc.* v. *Department of Health, Education and Welfare,* 464 F. Supp. 236 (M.D. Fla. 1979); and *St. Mary's Hospital, Inc.* v. *Califano,* 462 F. Supp 315 (S.D. Fla. 1978).

Accordingly, unless the requested records contain information that is exempt under FOIA (Exemption 4 is the most likely exemption for information from business firms claimed to be confidential), there is no need to consider whether the information is within the scope of 18 U.S.C. § 1905. However, if the records do contain exempt business information, 18 U.S.C. § 1905 may prohibit its release and therefore must be considered, in two respects.

First, as to the scope of 18 U.S.C. § 1905, the legislative history of § 1905 shows that the scope of that section is not as broad as its literal language. Section 1905 is a product of the 1948 codification to Title 13. It was intended to consolidate three predecessor statutes. The Supreme Court has twice analyzed the same 1948 codification and held that Congress did not, in the predecessor statutes, intend to make substantive changes in the predecessor statutes, including those consolidated. Therefore, seeming substantive changes inadvertently resulting from the codification would not be given full force and effect. *Muniz* v. *Hoffman,* 422 U.S. 454 (1975); *United States* v. *Cook,* 384 U.S. 257 (1966). Construing the statute literally would seem to produce unreasonable results; *e.g.,* making it a crime for a federal employee to disclose that the telephone company is in the telephone business unless the employee was "authorized to law" to do so. Moreover, even if the 1948 codification is read to have effected substantive changes, the meaning of § 1905 must still be determined in light of the predecessor statutes.

Second, the applicability of 18 U.S.C. § 1905 to particular information may be conditioned by other legislation. Therefore, we recommend that agencies examine the statutes under which they operate before receipt of a FOIA request to determine if they provide a sufficient "nexus" for regulations providing for the discretionary release of exempt, privately-submitted commercial or financial information. (This Office would welcome information from your agency on the results of such an examination.) It is preferable to make these determinations in advance rather than in the often pressurized context of responding to a specific request. In this regard agencies will wish to consult a post-*Chrysler* decision, *Cedars Nursing & Convalescent Center*

v. *Aetna Life and Casualty*, C.A. No. 70-1416 (E.D. Pa. May 7, 1979), in which the Court found that 42 U.S.C. §1306 provided a sufficient "nexus" for the promulgation of a discretionary disclosure regulation which satisfied the "authorized by law" requirement of §1905.

V. *Position Concerning Exempt Business Information to which 18 U.S.C. § 1906 is not, or may not be, applicable.*

Although the Justice Department has consistently maintained what the Supreme Court confirmed in *Chrysler*, namely, that FOIA exemptions give agencies discretion to withhold and do not prohibit release, this does not mean that agencies have unlimited discretion to make releases regardless of the circumstances and the effects upon legitimate private interests. Where Exemption 4 clearly applies because of the likelihood of substantial competitive injury to the firm which submitted the information, its release by the agency without justification would be an abuse of discretion and, as such, contrary to law. Normally, justification, if it exists, will be based upon the public health, safety, or some other recognized aspect of the public interest, including the advancement of the agency's mission. The prospect of private benefit to the submitter's competitors would not in itself constitute such justification.

VI. *Administration action where submitter may object to release.*

Where a FOIA requester seeks access to business information over the objections of the submitter, the agency should be prepared to support a decision either to release or to withhold. Agencies planning to deny a FOIA request have always been faced with the possible need to sustain the burden of justifying a denial in court. Agencies planning to grant access over a submitter's objections must also face the possible need to defend such a proposed release in a "reverse" suit. In preparing to do this, the most pressing concern facing agencies is the necessity of developing adequate administrative records to explain a possible decision to disclose. This must be done to fulfill the Government's responsibility to make an informed, well-reasoned administrative determination. The legitimate concerns of the private commercial sector must be adequately protected by the Government. The Justice Department is committed to the policy that federal agencies should always give private submitters of commercial and financial information an opportunity to express their views on whether such information can, should, or must be withheld. Either upon receipt of a FOIA request for these types of records or as soon as any question arises of granting access the agency should notify the submitter.

Each agency should attempt to establish equitable and expeditious procedures for insuring that adequate consideration will be given to submitters' objections to release, together with any supporting information, and to requesters' arguments in favor of release, and that an administrative record is made of the basis for a possible agency decision to disclose. In designing such procedures, agencies may wish to consider the thoughtful discussion in House Report 95-1382 of July 20, 1978, entitled "Freedom of Information Act Requests For Business Data and Reverse FOIA Lawsuits."

If the agency determines that the records are exempt but wishes to release them as a matter of discretion over the submitters' objections, it must consider whether such a discretionary release would be an abuse of discretion or contrary to law within the meaning of the Administrative Procedure Act. The first step in this analysis is to determine whether the records are within the scope of § 1905. If they are not, release would be appropriate in any instance where release is not otherwise prohibited and a counterbalancing public interest would be served by such action. If they are, however, the agency must ascertain whether there is an applicable statute which either authorizes release itself or provides a sufficient "nexus" within the meaning of *Chrysler* to support the promulgation of a disclosure regulation, and whether such a regulation has been validly promulgated. If either of these criteria is met, release is "authorized by law" within the meaning of § 1905. In either situation, the agency should develop an administrative record which sets forth the basis for its decision to make a discretionary release in sufficient detail. If the agency determines that the records are not exempt and must be released despite the submitters' objection, an administrative record should also be made of how that determination was reached. . . .

State-by-State Freedom of Information Statutes

Alabama Code
Title 41

§ 145. (2695) Every citizen entitled to inspect and copy public records. Every citizen has a right to inspect and take a copy of any public writing of this state, except as otherwise expressly provided by statute.

§ 146. (5030) (7439) (5133) (3949) (4158) (772) (652) Refusal of public officer to permit examination of records. Any public officer, having charge of any book or record, who shall refuse to allow any person to examine such record free of charge, must, on conviction, be fined not less than fifty dollars.

§ 147. (2696) Public officers bound to give copies. Every public officer having the custody of a public writing, which a citizen has a right to inspect, is bound to give him, on demand, a certified copy of it, on payment of the legal fees therefor, and such copy is admissible as evidence in like cases and with like effect as the original writing.

Alaska Statutes
Title 9

Sec. 09.25.100. Disposition of tax information. Information in the possession of the department of revenue which discloses the particulars of the business or affairs of a taxpayer or other person is not a matter of public record, except for purposes of investigation and law enforcement. The information shall be kept confidential except when its production is required in an official investigation or court proceeding. These restrictions do not prohibit the publication of statistics presented in a manner that prevents the identification of particular reports and items, or prohibit the publication of tax lists showing the names of taxpayers who are delinquent and relevant information which may assist in the collection of delinquent taxes. (§ 3.21 ch 101 SLA 1962)

Sec. 09.25.110. Inspection and copies of public records. Unless specifically provided otherwise the books, records, papers, files, accounts, writings, and transactions of all agencies and departments are pulic records and are open to inspection by the public under reasonable rules during regular office hours. The public officer having the custody of public records shall give on request and payment of costs a certified copy of the public record. (§ 3.22 ch 101 SLA 1962)

Sec. 09.25.120. Inspection and copying of public records. Every person has a right to inspect a public writing or record in the state, including public writings and records in recorders' offices except (1) records of vital statistics and adoption proceedings which shall be treated in the manner required by AS 18.50.010—18.50.380; (2) records pertaining to juveniles; (3) medical and related public health records; (4) records required to be kept confidential by a federal law or regulation or by state law. Every public officer having the custody of records not included in the exceptions shall permit the inspection, and give on demand and on payment of the legal fees therefor a certified copy of the writing or record, and the copy shall in all cases be evidence of the original. Recorders shall permit memoranda, transcripts, and copies of the public writings and records in their offices to be made by photography or otherwise for the purpose of examining titles to real estate described in the public writings and records, making abstracts of title or guaranteeing or insuring the titles of the real estate, or building and maintaining title and abstract plants; and shall furnish proper and reasonable facilities to persons having lawful occasion for access to the public writings and records for those purposes, subject to reasonable rules and regulations, in conformity to the direction of the court, as are necessary for the protection of the writings and records and to prevent interference with the regular discharge of the duties of the recorders and their employees. (§ 3.23 ch 101 SLA 1962)

Arizona Revised Statutes
Volume 12, Title 39

§ 39–121.01. Copies; printouts or photographs of public records. In this article, unless the context otherwise requires:

1. "Officer" means any person elected or appointed to hold any elective or appointive office of any public body and any chief administrative officer, head, director, superintendent or chairman of any public body.

2. "Public body" means the state, any county, city, town, school district, political subdivision or tax-supported district in the state, any branch, department, board, bureau, commission, council or committee of the foregoing, and any public organization or agency, supported in whole or in part by funds from the state or any political subdivision thereof, or expending funds provided by the state or any political subdivision thereof.

3. All officers and public bodies shall maintain all records reasonably necessary or appropriate to maintain an accurate knowledge of their official activities and of any of their activities which are supported by funds from the state or any political subdivision thereof.

4. Each public body shall be responsible for the preservation, maintenance and care of that body's public records and each officer shall be responsible for the preservation, maintenance and care of that officer's public records. It shall be the duty of each such body to carefully secure, protect and preserve public records from deterioration, mutilation, loss or destruction, unless disposed of pursuant to §§ 41–1344, 41–1347 and 41–1351.

5. Any person may request to examine or be furnished copies, printouts or photographs of any public record during regular office hours. The custodian of such records shall furnish such copies, printouts or photographs and may charge a reasonable fee if the facilities are available, subject to the provisions of § 39–122. The fee shall not exceed the commercial rate for like service except as otherwise provided by statute.

6. If the custodian of a public record does not have facilities for making copies, printouts or photographs of a public record which a person has a right to inspect, such person shall be granted access to the public record for the purpose of making copies, printouts or photographs. The copies, printouts or photographs shall be made while the public record is in the possession, custody and control of the custodian thereof and shall be subject to the supervision of such custodian. Added Laws 1975, Ch. 147, § 1. As amended Laws 1976, Ch. 104, § 17.

§ 39–121.02. Action upon denial of access; expenses and attorney fees; damages.

A. Any person who has requested to examine or copy public records pursuant to the provisions of this article, and who has been denied access to or the right to copy such records, may appeal the denial through a special action in the superior court, pursuant to the rules of procedure for special actions against the officer or public body.

B. If the court determines that a person was wrongfully denied access to or the right to copy a public record and if the court finds that the custodian of such public record acted in bad faith, or in an arbitrary or capricious manner, the superior court may award to the petitioner legal costs, including reasonable attorney fees, as determined by the court.

C. Any person who is wrongfully denied access to public records pursuant to the provisions of this article shall have a cause of action against the officer or public body for any damages resulting therefrom. Added Laws 1975, Ch. 147, § 1.

Arkansas Statutes, 1947-1968 Replacement
1977 Cumulative Pocket Supplement
Volume 2A, Title 12

12-2801. Title of Act. This Act [§§ 12-2801—12-2807] shall be known and cited as the "Freedom of Information Act" of 1967. [Acts 1967, No. 93, § 1, p. 208.]

12-2802. Declaration of public policy. It is vital in a democratic society that public business be performed in an open and public manner so that the electors shall be advised of the performance of public officials and of the decisions that are reached in public activity and in making public policy. Toward this end, this act [§§ 12-2801—12-2807] is adopted, making it possible for them, or their representatives, to learn and to report fully the activities of their public officials. [Acts 1967, No. 93, § 2, p. 208.]

12-2803. Definitions. "Public records" are writings, recorded sounds, films, tapes, or data compilations in any form (a) required by law to be kept, or (b) otherwise kept and which constitute a record of the performance or lack of performance of official functions which are or should be carried out by a public official or employee, a governmental agency, or any other agency wholly or partially supported by public funds or expending public funds.

All records maintained in public offices or by public employees within the scope of their employment shall be presumed to be public records. Provided, that compilations, lists, or other aggregations of "personal information," determined to be confidential by the State Information Practices Board pursuant to its duties set forth in sub-section [sub-subsection] 2 of subsection (k) of Section 4 of Act 730 of 1975, being Arkansas Stat. Ann. 16-801, et seq., shall not be considered to be "public records" within the terms of this Act [§§ 12-2801—12-2807] and shall not be supplied to private individuals or organizations.

"Public meetings" are the meetings of any bureau, commission or agency of the State, or any political subdivision of the State, including municipalities and counties, boards of education, and all other boards, bureaus, commissions or organizations in the State of Arkansas, except grand juries, supported wholly or in part by public funds, or expending public funds. [Acts 1967, No. 93, § 3, p. 208; 1977, No. 652, § 1, p. —]

12-2804. Examination and copying of public records. Except as otherwise specifically provided herein, by laws now in effect, or laws hereinafter specifically enacted to provide otherwise, all public records shall be open to inspection and copying by any citizen of the State of Arkansas during the regular business hours of the custodian of the records. It is the specific intent of this Section that State income tax returns; medical, scholastic, and adoption records; the site files and records maintained by the Arkansas Historic Preservation Program and the Arkansas Archeological Survey; grand jury minutes; unpublished drafts of judicial or quasi-judicial opinions and decisions; undisclosed investigations by law enforcement agencies of suspected criminal activity; unpublished memoranda, working papers, and correspondence of the Governor, Legislators, Supreme Court Justices, and the Attorney General; documents which are protected from disclosure by order or rule of court; files which, if disclosed, would give advantage to competitors or bidders; and other similar records which by law are required to be closed to the public shall not be deemed to be made open to the public under the provisions of this Act [§§ 12-2801—12-2807].

Reasonable access to public records and reasonable comforts and facilities for the full exercise of the right to inspect and copy such records shall not be denied to any citizen.

If a public record is in active use or in storage and, therefore, not available, at the time a citizen asks to examine it, the custodian shall certify this fact in writing to the applicant and set a date and hour within three (3) days, at which time the record will be available for the exercise of the right given by this Act. [Acts 1967, No. 93, § 4, p. 208; 1977, No. 652, § 2, p.—.]

12-2806. Enforcement. Any citizen denied the rights granted to him by this Act [§§ 12-2801—12-2807] may appeal immediately from such denial to the Pulaski Circuit Court, or to the Circuit Court of the residence of the aggrieved party, if an agency of the State is involved, or to any of the Circuit Courts of the appropriate judicial districts when an agency of a county, municipality, township or school district, or a private organization supported by or expending public funds is involved. Upon written application of the person denied the rights provided for in this Act, or any interested party, it shall be mandatory upon the Circuit Court having jurisdiction, to fix and assess a day the petition is to be heard within seven [7] days of the date of the application of the petitioner, and to hear and determine the case. Those who refuse to comply with the orders of the court shall be found guilty of contempt of court. [Acts 1967, No. 93, § 6, p. 208.]

12-2807. Penalty. Any person who wilfully and knowingly violates any of the provisions of this Act [§§ 12-1801—12-2807] shall be guilty of a misdemeanor and shall be punished by a fine of not more than $200, or 30 days in jail, or both. [Acts 1967, No. 93, § 7, p. 208.]

California Codes, West's Annotated
1978 Cumulative Supplement

§ 6250. Legislative findings and declarations.

In enacting this chapter, the Legislature, mindful of the right of individuals to privacy, finds and declares that access to information concerning the conduct of the people's business is a fundamental and necessary right of every * * * *person in* this state.

(Added by Stats.1968, c. 1473, p. 2946, § 39. Amended by Stats.1970, c. 575, p. 1150, § 1.)

§ 6251. Short title.

This chapter shall be known and may be cited as the California Public Records Act.

(Added by Stats.1968, c. 1473, p. 2946, § 39.)

§ 6252. Definitions.

As used in this chapter:

(a) "State agency" means every state office, officer, department, division, bureau, board, and commission or other state agency, except those agencies provided for in Article IV (except Section 20 thereof) or Article VI of the California Constitution.

(b) "Local agency" includes a county; city, whether general law or chartered; city and county; school district; municipal corporation; district; political subdivision; or any board, commission or agency thereof; or other local public agency.

(c) "Person" includes any natural person, corporation, partnership, firm, or association.

(d) "Public records" includes any writing containing information relating to the conduct of the public's business prepared, owned, used, or retained by any state or local agency regardless of physical form or characteristics. *"Public records" in the custody of or maintained by the Governor's office means any writing prepared on or after January 6, 1975.*

(e) "Writing" means handwriting, typewriting, printing, photostating, photographing, and every other means of recording upon any form of communication or representation, including letters, words, pictures, sounds, or symbols, or combination thereof, and all papers, maps, magnetic or paper tapes, photographic films and prints, magnetic or punched cards, discs, drums, and other documents.

(Added by Stats.1968, c. 1473, p. 2946, § 39. Amended by Stats.1970, c. 575, p. 1151, § 2; Stats.1975, c. 1246, p. ——. § 2.)

§ 6253. Public records open to Inspection; time; guidelines and regulations governing procedure.

(a) Public records are open to inspection at all times during the office hours of the state or local agency and every citizen has a right to inspect any public record, except as hereafter provided. Every agency may adopt regulations stating the procedures to be followed when making its records available in accordance with this section.

The following state and local bodies shall establish written guidelines for accessibility of records. A copy of these guidelines shall be posted in a conspicuous public place at the offices of such bodies, and a copy of such guidelines shall be available upon request free of charge to any person requesting that body's records:

Department of Motor Vehicles
Department of Consumer Affairs
Department of Transportation
Department of Real Estate
Department of Corrections
Department of the Youth Authority
Department of Justice
Department of Insurance
Department of Corporations
Secretary of State
State Air Resources Board
Department of Water Resources
Department of Parks and Recreation
San Francisco Bay Conservation and Development Commission
State Department of Health *Services*
Employment Development Department
* * * *State Department of Social Services*
State Department of Mental Health
State Department of Developmental Services
State Department of Alcohol and Drug Abuse
State Office of Statewide Health Planning and Development
Public Employees' Retirement System
Teachers' Retirement Board
Department of Industrial Relations
Department of General Services
Department of Veterans Affairs
Public Utilities Commission
California Coastal Zone Conservation Commission
All regional coastal zone conservation commissions
State Water Quality Control Board

San Francisco Bay Area Rapid Transit District
All regional water quality control boards
Los Angeles County Air Pollution Control District
Bay Area Air Pollution Control District
Golden Gate Bridge, Highway and Transportation District.

(b) Guidelines and regulations adopted pursuant to this section shall be consistent with all other sections of this chapter and shall reflect the intention of the Legislature to make such records accessible to the public.
(Added by Stats.1968, c. 1473, p. 2946, § 39. Amended by Stats.1973, c. 664, p. 1215, § 1; Stats.1974, c. 544, p. 1249, § 7; Stats.1975, c. 957, p. 2140, § 6; Stats.1977, c. 1252, p.—, § 96, operative July 1, 1978.)
§ 6253.5 Initiative, referendum and recall petitions deemed not public records.

Notwithstanding the provisions of Section 6252 and 6253, statewide, county, city, and district initiative, referendum, and recall petitions and all memoranda prepared by the county clerks in the examination of such petitions indicating which registered voters have signed particular petitions shall not be deemed to be public records and shall not be open to inspection except by the public officer or public employees who have the duty of receiving, examining or preserving such petitions or who are responsible for the preparation of such memoranda; *provided, however, that the Attorney General, the Secretary of State, the Fair Political Practices Commission, a district attorney, and a city attorney shall be permitted to examine such material upon approval of the appropriate superior court.*
(Added by Stats.1974, c. 1410, p. 3106, § 10; Stats.1974, c. 1445, p. 3155, § 9. Amended by Stats.1975, c. 678, p. 1483, § 26; Stats.1977, c. 556, p.—, § 4.)
§ 6254. Exemption of particular records.

Except as provided in Section 6254.7, nothing in this chapter shall be construed to require disclosure of records that are:

(a) Preliminary drafts, notes, or interagency or intra-agency memoranda which are not retained by the public agency in the ordinary course of business, provided that the public interest in withholding such records clearly outweighs the public interest in disclosure;

(b) Records pertaining to pending litigation to which the public agency is a party, or to claims made pursuant to Division 3.6 (commencing with Section 810) of Title 1 of the Government Code, until such litigation or claim has been finally adjudicated or otherwise settled;

(c) Personnel, medical, or similar files, the disclosure of which would constitute an unwarranted invasion of personal privacy;

(d) Contained in or related to:

(1) Applications filed with any state agency responsible for the regulation or supervision of the issuance of securities or of financial institutions, including, but not limited to, banks, savings and loan associations, industrial loan companies, credit unions, and insurance companies;

(2) Examination, operating, or condition reports prepared by, on behalf of, or for the use of any state agency referred to in subdivision (1);

(3) Preliminary drafts, notes, or interagency or intra-agency communications prepared by, on behalf of, or for the use of any state agency referred to in subdivision (1); or

(4) Information received in confidence by any state agency referred to in subdivision (1).

(e) Geological and geophysical data, plant production data and similar information relating to utility systems development, or market or crop reports, which are obtained in confidence from any person;

(f) Records of complaints to or investigations conducted by, or records of intelligence information or security procedures of, the office of the Attorney General and the Department of Justice, and any state or local police agency, or any such investigatory or security files compiled by any other state or local police agency, or any such investigatory or security files compiled by any other state or local agency for correctional, law enforcement or licensing purposes, except that local police agencies shall disclose the names and addresses of persons involved in, or witnesses other than confidential informants to, the incident, the description of any property involved, the date, time, and location of the incident, all diagrams, statements of the parties involved in the incident, the statements of all witnesses, other than confidential informants, to the persons involved in an incident, or an authorized representative thereof, an insurance carrier against which a claim has been or might be made, and any person suffering bodily injury or property damage as the result of the incident caused by arson, burglary, fire, explosion, robbery, vandalism, or a crime of violence as defined by subdivision (b) of Section 13960, unless the disclosure would endanger the safety of a witness or other person involved in the investigation, disclosure would endanger the successful completion of the investigation or a related investigation;

(g) Test questions, scoring keys, and other examination data used to administer a licensing examination, examination for employment, or academic examination, except as provided for in Chapter 3 (commencing with Section 99150) of Part 65 of the Education Code;

(h) The contents of real estate appraisals, engineering or feasibility estimates and evaluations made for or by the state or local agency relative to the acquisition of property, or to prospective public supply and construction contracts, until such time as all of the property has been acquired or all of the contract agreement obtained, provided, however, the law of eminent domain shall not be affected by this provision;

(i) Information required from any taxpayer in connection with the collection of local taxes which is received in confidence and the disclosure of the information to other persons would result in unfair competitive disadvantage to the person supplying such information;

(j) Library and museum materials made or acquired and presented solely for reference or exhibition purposes;

(k) Records the disclosure of which is exempted or prohibited pursuant to provisions of federal or state law, including, but not limited to, provisions of the Evidence Code relating to privilege;

(l) Correspondence of and to the Governor or employees of the Governor's office or in the custody of or maintained by the Governor's legal affairs secretary, provided public records shall not be transferred to the custody of the Governor's legal affairs secretary to evade the disclosure provisions of this chapter;

(m) In the custody or maintained by the Legislative Counsel;

(n) Statements of personal worth or personal financial data required by a licensing agency and filed by an applicant with such licensing agency to establish his personal qualification for the license, certificate, or permit applied for; and

(o) Financial data contained in applications for financing under Division 27 (commencing with Section 44500) of the Health and Safety Code, where an authorized officer of the California Pollution Control Financing Authority determines that disclosure of such financial data would be competitively injurious to the applicant and such data is required in order to obtain guarantees from the United States Small Business Administration. The California Pollution Control Financing Authority shall adopt rules for review of individual requests for confidentiality under this section and for making available to the public those portions of an application which are subject to disclosure under this chapter.

(p) Records of the University of California, Hastings College of the Law, and the California State University and Colleges prepared for or during collective bargaining sessions, or minutes of such sessions.

Nothing in this section is to be construed as preventing any agency from opening its records concerning the administration of the agency to public inspection, unless disclosure is otherwise prohibited by law.

(Added by Stats.1968, c. 1473, p. 2946, § 39. Amended by Stats.1970, c. 1231, p. 2157, § 11.5; Stats.1970, c. 1295, p. 2396, § 1.5; Stats.1975, c. 1231, p. 3123, § 1; Stats.1975, c. 1246, p. 3209, § 3; Stats.1976, c. 314, p. 629, § 1; Stats.1977, c. 579, p. —, § 60; Stats.1977, c. 650, p. —, § 1, urgency, eff. Sept. 8, 1977; Stats.1978, c. 1217, § 3; Stats.1978, c. 744, p.

—, § 4, operative July 1, 1979; Stats.1978, c. 1217, § 4, operative July 1, 1979.)

§ 6254.7 Air pollution data; public records; notices and orders to building owners; trade secrets.

(a) All information, analyses, plans, or specifications that disclose the nature, extent, quantity, or degree of air contaminants or other pollution which any article, machine, equipment, or other contrivance will produce, which any air pollution control district or any other state or local agency or district requires any applicant to provide before such applicant builds, erects, alters, replaces, operates, sells, rents, or uses such article, machine, equipment, or other contrivance, are public records.

(b) All air or other pollution monitoring data, including data compiled from stationary sources, are public records.

(c) All records of notices and orders directed to the owner of any building of violations of housing or building codes, ordinances, statutes, or regulations which constitute violations of standards provided in Section 1941.1 of the Civil Code, and records of subsequent action with respect to such notices and orders, are public records.

(d) *Except as otherwise provided in subdivision (e),* trade secrets are not public records under this section. "Trade secrets," as used in this section, may include, but are not limited to, any formula, plan, pattern, process, tool, mechanism, compound, procedure, production data, or compilation of information which is not patented, which is known only to certain individuals within a commercial concern who are using it to fabricate, produce, or compound an article of trade or a service having commercial value and which gives its user an opportunity to obtain a business advantage over competitors who do not know or use it.

(e) Notwithstanding any other provision of law, all air pollution emission data, including those emission data which constitute trade secrets as defined in subdivision (d), are public records. Data used to calculate emission data are not emission data for the purposes of this subdivision and data which constitute trade secrets and which are used to calculate emission data are not public records.

(Added by Stats.1970, c. 1295, p. 2397, § 2. Amended by Stats.1971, c. 1601, p. 3448, § 1; Stats.1972, c. 400, p. 722, § 1; Stats.1973, c. 186, p. 488, § 1, urgency, eff. July 9, 1973.)

§ 6254.8 Employment contracts between state or local agency and public official or employee; public record.

Every employment contract between a state or local agency and any public official or public employee is a public record which is not subject to the provisions of Sections 6254 and 6255.

(Added by Stats.1974, c. 1198, p. 2588, § 1.)

Library references

    Records   14.

    C.J.S. Records § 35 et seq.

§ 6255. Justification for withholding of records.

    The agency shall justify withholding any record by demonstrating that the record in question is exempt under express provisions of this chapter or that on the facts of the particular case the public interest served by not making the record public clearly outweighs the public interest served by disclosure of the record.

(Added by Stats.1968, c. 1473, p. 2947, § 39.)

§ 6256. Copies of records.

    Any person may receive a copy of any identifiable public record or * * * copy * * * thereof. *Upon request, an exact copy shall be provided unless impracticable to do so.* Computer data shall be provided in a form determined by the agency.

(Added by Stats.1968, c. 1473, p. 2947, § 39. Amended by Stats.1970, c. 575, p. 1151, § 3.)

§ 6257. Request for copy; fee.

    A request for a copy of an identifiable public record or information produced therefrom, or a certified copy of such record, shall be accompanied by payment of a * * * fee or deposit * * * *to* the state or local agency, provided such fee shall not exceed * * * *the actual cost of providing the copy,* or the prescribed statutory fee, * * * *if any, whichever is less.*

(Added by Stats.1968, c. 1473, p. 2947, § 39. Amended by Stats.1975, c. 1246, p. 1246, § 8; Stats.1976, c. 822, p. 2024, § 1.)

§ 6258. Proceedings to enforce right to Inspect or to receive copy of record.

    Any person may institute proceedings *for injunctive or declarative relief* in any court of competent jurisdiction to enforce his right to inspect or to receive a copy of any public record *or class of public records* under this chapter. The times for responsive pleadings and for hearings in such proceedings shall be set by the judge of the court with the object of securing a decision as to such matters at the earliest possible time.

(Added by Stats.1968, c. 1473, p. 2948, § 39. Amended by Stats.1970, c. 575, p. 1151, § 4.)

§ 6259. Order of court; contempt; court costs and attorney fees.

    Whenever it is made to appear by verified petition to the superior court of the county where the records or some part thereof are situated that certain public records are being improperly withheld from a member of the public, the court shall order the officer or person charged with withholding the records to disclose the public record or show cause why he should not do so. The court shall decide the case after examining the record in camera, if permitted by subdivision (b) of Section 915 of the Evidence Code, papers filed by the parties and such oral argument and additional evidence as the court may allow.

If the court finds that the public official's decision to refuse disclosure is not justified under the provisions of Section 6254 or 6255, he shall order the public official to make the record public. If the judge determines that the public official was justified in refusing to make the record public, he shall return the item to the public official without disclosing its content with an order supporting the decision refusing disclosure. Any person who fails to obey the order of the court shall be cited to show cause why he is not in contempt of court. *The court shall award court costs and reasonable attorney fees to the plaintiff should the plaintiff prevail in litigation filed pursuant to this section. Such costs and fees shall be paid by the public agency of which the public official is a member of employee and shall not become a personal liability of the public official. If the court finds that the plaintiff's case is clearly frivolous, it shall award court costs and reasonable attorney fees to the public agency.*

(Added by Stats.1968, c. 1473, p. 2948, § 39. Amended by Stats.1975, c. 1246, p. —, § 9.)

§ 6260. Effect of chapter on prior rights and proceedings.

The provisions of this chapter shall not be deemed in any manner to affect the status of judicial records as it existed immediately prior to the effective date of this section, nor to affect the rights of litigants, including parties to administrative proceedings, under the laws of discovery of this state, *nor to limit or impair any rights of discovery in a criminal case.*

(Added by Stats.1968, c. 1473, p. 2948, § 39. Amended by Stats.1976, c. 314, p. 629, § 2.)

§ 6261. Itemized statement of total expenditures and disbursement of any agency.

Notwithstanding Section 6252, an itemized statement of the total expenditures and disbursement of any agency provided for in Article VI of the California Constitution shall be open for inspection.

(Added by Stats.1975, c. 1246, p. —, § 3.5.)

Colorado Revised Statutes
Volumes 10, 12

Part 2

24-72-201. Legislative declaration. It is declared to be the public policy of this state that all public records shall be open for inspection by any person at reasonable times, except as provided in this part 2 or as otherwise specifically provided by law.

Source: L. 68, p. 201, § 1; C.R.S. 1963, § 113-2-1.

24-72-202. Definitions. As used in this part 2, unless the context otherwise requires:

(1) "Custodian" means and includes the official custodian or any authorized person having personal custody and control of the public records in question.

(2) "Official custodian" means and includes any officer or employee of the state or any agency, institution, or political subdivision thereof who is responsible for the maintenance, care, and keeping of public records, regardless of whether such records are in his actual personal custody and control.

(3) "Person" means and includes any natural person, corporation, partnership, firm, or association.

(4) "Person in interest" means and includes the person who is the subject of a record or any representative designated by said person; except that if the subject of the record is under legal disability, "person in interest" means and includes his parent or duly appointed legal representative.

(5) "Political subdivision" means and includes every county, city and county, city, town, school district, and special district within this state.

(6) "Public records" means and includes all writings made, maintained, or kept by the state or any agency, institution, or political subdivision thereof for use in the exercise of functions required or authorized by law or administrative rule or involving the receipt or expenditure of public funds. It does not include criminal justice records which are subject to the provisions of part 3 of this article.

(7) "Writings" means and includes all books, papers, maps, photographs, cards, tapes, recordings, or other documentary materials, regardless of physical form or characteristics.

Source: L. 68, p. 201, § 2; C.R.S. 1963, § 113-2-2; Amended, L. 77, p. 50, § 2.

24-72-203. Public records open to inspection. (1) All public records shall be open for inspection by any person at reasonable times, except as provided in this part 2 or as otherwise provided by law, but the official custodian of any public records may make such rules and regulations with reference to the inspection of such records as are reasonably necessary for the protection of such records and the prevention of unnecessary interference with the regular discharge of the duties of the custodian or his office.

(2) If the public records requested are not in the custody or control of the person to whom application is made, such person shall forthwith notify the applicant of this fact, in writing if requested by the applicant. In such notification he shall state in detail to the best of his knowledge and belief the reason

for the absence of the records from his custody or control, their location, and what person then has custody or control of the records.

(3) If the public records requested are in the custody and control of the person to whom application is made but are in active use or in storage and therefore not available at the time an applicant asks to examine them, the custodian shall forthwith notify the applicant of this fact, in writing if requested by the applicant. If requested by the applicant, the custodian shall set a date and hour within three working days at which time the records will be available for inspection.

Source: L. 68, p. 202, § 3; C.R.S. 1963, § 113-2-3.

24-72-204. Allowance or denial of inspection-grounds-procedure-appeal.

(1) The custodian of any public records shall allow any person the right of inspection of such records or any portion thereof except on one or more of the following grounds or as provided in subsection (2) or (3) of this section:

(a) Such inspection would be contrary to any state statute.

(b) Such inspection would be contrary to any federal statute or regulation issued thereunder having the force and effect of law.

(c) Such inspection is prohibited by rules promulgated by the supreme court or by the order of any court.

(2) (a) The custodian may deny the right of inspection of the following records, unless otherwise provided by law, on the ground that disclosure to the applicant would be contrary to the public interest:

(I) Repealed, L. 77, p. 1250, § 4.

(II) Test questions, scoring keys, and other examination data pertaining to administration of a licensing examination, examination for employment, or academic examination; except that written promotional examinations and the scores or results thereof conducted pursuant to the state personnel system or any similar system shall be available for inspection, but not copying or reproduction, by the person in interest after the conducting and grading of any such examination;

(III) The specific details of bona fide research projects being conducted by a state institution; and

(IV) The contents of real estate appraisals made for the state or a political subdivision thereof relative to the acquisition of property or any interest in property for public use, until such time as title to the property or property interest has passed to the state or political subdivision; except that the contents of such appraisal shall be available to the owner of the property at any time, and except as provided by the Colorado rules of civil procedure. If condemnation proceedings are instituted to acquire any such property, any owner thereof who has received the contents of any appraisal pursuant to this section shall, upon receipt thereof, make available to said state or political subdivision a copy of the contents of any appraisal which he has obtained relative to the proposed acquisition of the property.

(b) If the right of inspection of any record falling within any of the classifications listed in this subsection (2) is allowed to any officer or employee of any newspaper, radio station, television station, or other person or agency in the business of public dissemination of news or current events, it shall be allowed to all such news media.

(3) (a) The custodian shall deny the right of inspection of the following records, unless otherwise provided by law; except that any of the following records, other than letters of reference concerning employment, licensing, or issuance of permits, shall be available to the person in interest under this subsection (3):

(I) Medical, psychological, sociological, and scholastic achievement data on individual persons, exclusive of coroners' autopsy reports; but either the custodian or the person in interest may request a professionally qualified person, who shall be furnished by the said custodian, to be present to interpret the records;

(II) Personnel files, except applications and performance ratings; but such files shall be available to the person in interest and to the duly elected and appointed public officials who supervise his work;

(III) Letters of reference;

(IV) Trade secrets, privileged information, and confidential commercial, financial, geological, or geophysical data furnished by or obtained from any person;

(V) Library and museum material contributed by private persons, to the extent of any limitations placed thereon as conditions of such contributions; and

(VI) Addresses and telephone numbers of students in any public elementary or secondary school.

(b) Nothing in this subsection (3) shall prohibit the custodian of records from transmitting data concerning the scholastic achievement of any student to any prospective employer of such student, nor shall anything in this subsection (3) prohibit the custodian of records from making available for inspection, from making copies, print-outs, or photographs of, or from transmitting data concerning the scholastic achievement or medical, psychological, or sociological information of any student to any law enforcement agency of this state, of any other state, or of the United States where such student is under investigation by such agency and the agency shows that such data is necessary for the investigation.

(c) Nothing in this subsection (3) shall prohibit the custodian of the records of a school, including any institution of higher education, or a school district from transmitting data concerning standardized tests, scholastic achievement, or medical, psychological, or sociological information of any student to the custodian of such records in any other such school or school district to which such student moves, transfers, or makes application for transfer, and the written permission of such student or his parent or guardian shall not be required therefor. No state educational institution shall be prohibited from transmitting data concerning standardized tests or scholastic achievement of any student to the custodian of such records in the school, including any state educational institution, or school district in which such student was previously enrolled, and the written permission of such student or his parent or guardian shall not be required therefor.

(4) If the custodian denies access to any public record, the applicant may request a written statement of the grounds for the denial, which statement shall cite the law or regulation under which access is denied and shall be furnished forthwith to the applicant.

(5) Any person denied the right to inspect any record covered by this part 2 may apply to the district court of the district wherein the record is found for an order directing the custodian of such record to show cause why he should not permit the inspection of such record. Hearing on such application shall be held at the earliest practical time. Unless the court finds that the denial of the right of inspection was proper, it shall order the custodian to permit such inspection and, upon a finding that the denial was arbitrary or capricious, it may order the custodian personally to pay the applicant's court costs and attorney fees in an amount to be determined by the court.

(6) If, in the opinion of the official custodian of any public record, disclosure of the contents of said record would do substantial injury to the public interest, notwithstanding the fact that said record might otherwise be available to public inspection, he may apply to the district court of the district in which such record is located for an order permitting him to restrict such disclosure. Hearing on such application shall be held at the earliest practical time. After hearing, the court may issue such an order upon a finding that disclosure would cause substantial injury to the public interest. In such action the burden of proof shall be upon the custodian. The person seeking permission to examine the record shall have notice of said hearing served upon him in the manner provided for service of process by the Colorado rules of civil procedure and shall have the right to appear and be heard.
Source: L. 68, p. 202, § 4; L. 69, pp. 925, 926, §§ 1, 1; C.R.S. 1963, § 113-2-4.
24-72-205. Copies, printouts, or photographs of public records. (2) If the custodian does not have facilities for making copies, printouts, or photographs of records which the applicant has the right to inspect, the applicant shall be granted access to the records for the purpose of making copies, printouts, or photographs. The copies, printouts, or photographs shall be

made while the records are in the possession, custody, and control of the custodian thereof and shall be subject to the supervision of such custodian. When practical, they shall be made in the place where the records are kept, but, if it is impractical to do so, the custodian may allow arrangements to be made for this purpose. If other facilities are necessary, the cost of providing them shall be paid by the person desiring a copy, printout, or photograph of the records. The official custodian may establish a reasonable schedule of times for making copies, printouts, or photographs and may charge the same fee for the services rendered by him or his deputy in supervising the copying, printing out, or photographing as he may charge for furnishing copies under subsection (1) of this section.

Source: L. 68, p. 204, § 5; C.R.S. 1963, § 113-2-5.

24-72-206. Violation - penalty. Any person who willfully and knowingly violates the provisions of this part 2 is guilty of a misdemeanor and, upon conviction thereof, shall be punished by a fine of not more than one hundred dollars, or by imprisonment in the county jail for not more than ninety days, or by both such fine and imprisonment.

Source: L. 68, p. 204, § 6; C.R.S. 1963, § 113-2-6.

Part 3
Criminal Justice Records

24-72-301. Legislative declaration. (1) The general assembly hereby finds and declares that the maintenance, access and dissemination, completeness, accuracy, and sealing of criminal justice records are matters of statewide concern and that, in defining and regulating those areas, only statewide standards in a state statute are workable.

(2) It is further declared to be the public policy of this state that criminal justice agencies shall maintain records of official actions, as defined in this part 3, and that such records shall be open to inspection by any person and to challenge by any person in interest, as provided in this part 3, and that all other records of criminal justice agencies in this state may be open for inspection as provided in this part 3 or as otherwise specifically provided by law.

Source: Added, L. 77, p. 1244, § 1.

24-72-302. Definitions. As used in this part 3, unless the context otherwise requires:

(1) "Arrest and criminal records information" means information reporting the arrest, indictment, or other formal filing of criminal charges against a person; the identity of the criminal justice agency taking such official action relative to an accused person; the date and place that such official action was taken relative to an accused person; the name, birth date, last known address,

and sex of an accused person; the nature of the charges brought or the offenses alleged against an accused person; and one or more dispositions relating to the charges brought against an accused person.

(2) "Basic identification information" means the name, birth date, last known address, physical description, sex, and fingerprints of any person.

(3) "Criminal justice agency" means any court with criminal jurisdiction and any agency of the state or of any county, city and county, home rule city and county, home rule city or county, city, town, territorial charter city, governing boards of institutions of higher education, school district, special district, judicial district, or law enforcement authority which performs any activity directly relating to the detection or investigation of crime; the apprehension, pretrial release, posttrial release, prosecution, defense, correctional supervision, rehabilitation, evaluation, or treatment of accused persons or criminal offenders; or criminal identification activities or the collection, storage, or dissemination of criminal justice information.

(4) "Criminal justice records" means all books, papers, cards, photographs, tapes, recordings, or other documentary materials, regardless of form or characteristics, which are made, maintained, or kept by any criminal justice agency in the state for use in the exercise of functions required or authorized by law or administrative rule.

(5) "Custodian" means the official custodian or any authorized person having personal custody and control of the criminal justice records in question.

(6) "Disposition" means a decision not to file criminal charges after arrest; the conclusion of criminal proceedings, including conviction, acquittal, or acquittal by reason of insanity; the dismissal, abandonment, or indefinite postponement of criminal proceedings; formal diversion from prosecution; sentencing, correctional supervision, and release from correctional supervision, including terms and conditions thereof; outcome of appellate review of criminal proceedings; or executive clemency.

(7) "Official action" means an arrest; indictment; charging by information; disposition; pretrial or posttrial release from custody; judicial determination of mental or physical condition; decision to grant, order, or terminate probation, parole, or participation in correctional or rehabilitative programs; and any decision to formally discipline, reclassify, or relocate any person under criminal sentence.

(8) "Official custodian" means any officer or employee of the state or any agency, institution, or political subdivision thereof who is responsible for the maintenance, care, and keeping of criminal justice records, regardless of whether such records are in his actual personal custody and control.

(9) "Person" means any natural person, corporation, partnership, firm, or association.

(10) "Person in interest" means the person who is the primary subject of a criminal justice record or any representative designated by said person by power of attorney or notarized authorization; except that, if the subject of the record is under legal disability, "person in interest" means and includes his parents or duly appointed legal representative.

Source: Added, L. 77, p. 1244, § 1.

24-72-303. Records of official actions required - open to inspection.

(1) Each official action as defined in this part 3 shall be recorded by the particular criminal justice agency taking the official action. Such records of official actions shall be maintained by the particular criminal justice agency which took the action and shall be open for inspection by any person at reasonable times, except as provided in this part 3 or as otherwise provided by law. The official custodian of any records of official actions may make such rules and regulations with reference to the inspection of such records as are reasonably necessary for the protection of such records and the prevention of unnecessary interference with the regular discharge of the duties of the custodian or his office.

(2) If the requested record of official action of a criminal justice agency is not in the custody or control of the person to whom application is made, such person shall forthwith notify the applicant of this fact in writing, if requested by the applicant. In such notification, he shall state, in detail to the best of his knowledge and belief, the agency which has custody or control of the record in question.

(3) If the requested record of official action of a criminal justice agency is in the custody and control of the person to whom application is made, but is in active use or in storage and therefore not available at the time an applicant asks to examine it, the custodian shall forthwith notify the applicant of this fact in writing, if requested by the applicant. If requested by the applicant, the custodian shall set a date and hour within three working days at which time the record will be available for inspection.

Source: Added, L. 77, p. 1246, § 1.

24-72-304. Inspection of criminal justice records. (1) Except for records of official actions which must be maintained and released pursuant to this part 3, all criminal justice records, at the discretion of the official custodian, may be open for inspection by any person at reasonable times, except as otherwise provided by law, and the official custodian of any such records may make such rules and regulations with reference to the inspection of such records as are reasonably necessary for the protection of such records and the prevention of unnecessary interference with the regular discharge of the duties of the custodian or his office.

(2) If the requested criminal justice records are not in the custody or control of the person to whom application is made, such person shall forth-

with notify the applicant of this fact in writing, if requested by the applicant. In such notification, he shall state, in detail to the best of his knowledge and belief, the reason for the absence of the records from his custody or control, their location, and what person then has custody or control of the records.

(3) If the requested records are not in the custody and control of the criminal justice agency to which the request is directed, but are in the custody and control of a central repository for criminal justice records pursuant to law, the criminal justice agency to which the request is directed shall forward the request to the central repository. If such a request is to be forwarded to the central repository, the criminal justice agency receiving the request shall do so forthwith and shall so advise the applicant forthwith. The central repository shall forthwith reply directly to the applicant.

Source: Added, L. 77, p. 1246, § 1.

24-72-305. Allowance or denial of inspection - grounds - procedure - appeal.

(1) The custodian of criminal justice records may allow any person to inspect such records or any portion thereof except on the basis of any one of the following grounds or as provided in subsection (5) of this section:

(a) Such inspection would be contrary to any state statute;

(b) Such inspection is prohibited by rules promulgated by the supreme court or by the order of any court.

(2) to (4) Repealed, L. 78, p. 407, § 4, effective May 5, 1978.

(5) On the ground that disclosure would be contrary to the public interest, and unless otherwise provided by law, the custodian may deny access to records of investigations conducted by or of intelligence information or security procedures of any sheriff, district attorney, or police department or any criminal justice investigatory files compiled for any other law enforcement purpose.

(6) If the custodian denies access to any criminal justice record, the applicant may request a written statement of the grounds for the denial, which statement shall be provided to the applicant within seventy-two hours, shall cite the law or regulation under which access is denied or the general nature of the public interest to be protected by the denial, and shall be furnished forthwith to the applicant.

(7) Any person denied access to inspect any criminal justice record covered by this part 3 may apply to the district court of the district wherein the record is found for an order directing the custodian of such record to show cause why said custodian should not permit the inspection of such record. A hearing on such application shall be held at the earliest practical time. Unless the court finds that the denial of inspection was proper, it shall order

the custodian to permit such inspection and, upon a finding that the denial was arbitrary or capricious, it may order the custodian to pay the applicant's court costs and attorney fees in an amount to be determined by the court. Upon a finding that the denial of inspection of a record of an official action was arbitrary or capricious, the court may also order the custodian personally to pay to the applicant a penalty in an amount not to exceed twenty-five dollars for each day that access was improperly denied.

Source: Added, L. 77, p. 1246, § 1; IP (1) amended and (2), (3), and (4) repealed, L. 78, pp. 403, 407, §§ 1, 4.

24-72-306. Copies, printouts, or photographs of criminal justice records - fees authorized. (1) Criminal justice agencies may assess reasonable fees, not to exceed actual costs, including but not limited to personnel and equipment, for the search, retrieval, and copying of criminal justice records and may waive fees at their discretion. Where fees for certified copies or other copies, printouts, or photographs of such records are specifically prescribed by law, such specific fees shall apply. Where the criminal justice agency is an agency or department of any county or municipality, the amount of such fees shall be established by the governing body of the county or municipality.

(2) If the custodian does not have facilities for making copies, printouts, or photographs of records which the applicant has the right to inspect, the applicant shall be granted access to the records for the purpose of making copies, printouts, or photographs. The copies, printouts, or photographs shall be made while the records are in the possession, custody, and control of the custodian thereof and shall be subject to the supervision of such custodian. When practical, they shall be made in the place where the records are kept, but, if it is impractical to do so, the custodian may allow other arrangements to be made for this purpose. If other facilities are necessary, the cost of providing them shall be paid by the person desiring a copy, printout, or photograph of the records. The official custodian may establish a reasonable schedule of times for making copies, printouts, or photographs and may charge the same fee for the services rendered by him or his deputy in supervising the copying, printing out, or photographing as he may charge for furnishing copies under subsection (1) of this section.

Source: Added, L. 77, p. 1248, § 1.

24-72-307. Challenge to accuracy and completeness - appeals. (1) Any person in interest who is provided access to any criminal justice records pursuant to this part 3 shall have the right to challenge the accuracy and completeness of records to which he has been given access, insofar as they pertain to him, and to request that said records be corrected.

(2) If the custodian refuses to make the requested correction, the person in interest may request a written statement of the grounds for the refusal, which statement shall be furnished forthwith.

(3) In the event that the custodian requires additional time to evaluate the merit of the request for correction, he shall so notify the applicant in writing forthwith. The custodian shall then have thirty days from the date of his receipt of the request for correction to evaluate the request and to make a determination of whether to grant or refuse the request, in whole or in part, which determination shall be forthwith communicated to the applicant in writing.

(4) Any person in interest whose request for correction of records is refused may apply to the district court of the district wherein the record is found for an order directing the custodian of such record to show cause why he should not permit the correction of such record. A hearing on such application shall be held at the earliest practical time. Unless the court finds that the refusal of correction was proper, it shall order the custodian to make such correction, and, upon a finding that the refusal was arbitrary or capricious, it may order the criminal justice agency for which the custodian was acting to pay the applicant's court costs and attorney fees in an amount to be determined by the court.

Source: Added, L. 77, p. 1248, § 1.

24-72-308. Sealing or limiting release of records. (1) (a) Any person in interest may petition the district court of his residence or of the district in which the arrest and criminal records information pertaining to him is located for the sealing of all or any part of said record, except basic identification information.

(b) Any person in interest may petition the county in which the arrest and criminal records information pertaining to him is located for the limiting of release of all or any part of said record, except basic identification information. If a criminal action has previously been filed in a court, the petition provided for in this paragraph (b) shall be made a part of such action, and no additional docket fee shall be required. Such a petition shall be filed pursuant to and shall be governed by the provisions of subsection (1.1) of this section.

(1.1) (a) An order limiting the release of all or any part of said record may be obtained if:

(I) The record is a record of an official action involving conviction for a misdemeanor or a petty offense after which the individual has not been formally charged with another crime, other than a petty offense or a class 3 or class 4 misdemeanor traffic offense, for a period of five years following completion of sentence or satisfaction of conditions imposed in lieu of sentence; or

(II) The record is a record of an official action involving conviction for a felony after which the individual has not been formally charged with a crime, other than a petty offense or a class 3 or class 4 misdemeanor traffic offense, for a period of seven years following completion of sentence or satisfaction of conditions imposed in lieu of sentence.

(b) The state court administrator shall prepare and distribute to the clerks of the courts a standardized form to be used for all petitions for the limiting of release of said records. The clerks shall make the form available at their offices and upon request shall mail the form to any person requesting the same.

(c) Within five days of the receipt of such a form which has been completed and notarized, the clerk of the court shall send copies thereof to the district attorney and the Colorado bureau of investigation.

(d) If the district attorney or the Colorado bureau of investigation does not file a response objecting to the petition for the limiting of release of said records within thirty days after receipt of the petition by the clerk of the court, the court shall grant the petition and order that the record shall only be released to the person in interest or to a criminal justice agency of this state or to a similar agency of the United States government or any of the states of the United States of America. This order shall be made and entered without further action by the petitioner and without his appearance.

(e) (I) If the district attorney or the Colorado bureau of investigation files a response objecting to the petition for the limiting of release of said records within thirty days after receipt of the petition by the clerk of the court, stating that it can show unto the court that the provisions of paragraph (a) of this subsection (1.1) do not apply to the petitioner, the court shall deny the petition unless the petitioner files a written request for a hearing thereon within sixty days after the original date of receipt of the petition by the clerk of the court.

(II) At the time of filing the response objecting to the petition, the district attorney or the Colorado bureau of investigation shall serve upon the petitioner a copy of the response and a notice indicating to the petitioner that his petition will be denied unless he files a written request for a hearing within sixty days after the original date of receipt of the petition by the clerk of the court.

(f) If a request for a hearing is received within the sixty-day period, the court shall set a date for a hearing, which hearing may be closed at the court's discretion, and notify the petitioner and the district attorney or the Colorado bureau of investigation of the date of said hearing. At the hearing, the court shall grant the petition unless the district attorney or the Colorado bureau of investigation shows that none of the provisions of paragraph (a) of this subsection (1.1) apply to the petitioner. Upon granting the petition, the court shall order that the record shall only be released to the person in interest or to a criminal justice agency of this state or to a similar agency of the United States government or any of the states of the United States of America. The hearing shall be held and the petition granted or denied whether or not the petitioner appears.

(g) The response and notice required by paragraph (e) of this subsection (1.1) and the notification required by paragraph (f) of this subsection (1.1) shall be served upon the petitioner by depositing the same in the United States mail, postage prepaid, certified, and return receipt requested, addressed to the petitioner at the address provided in the petition.

(h) Any order entered pursuant to this subsection (1.1) shall be directed to every custodian who may have custody of any part of arrest and criminal records information which is the subject of the order. Whenever a court enters an order pursuant to this subsection (1.1), it shall provide the Colorado bureau of investigation with a copy thereof. The Colorado bureau of investigation shall forward copies of such an order to every custodian which has furnished information to it pursuant to section 24-32-412 (3) concerning the subject of the order.

(i) Every custodian of the arrest and criminal records information subject to the order, within thirty days after entry of the order unless it is stayed pending an appeal, shall advise the court and the petitioner in writing of compliance with the order.

(j) Court orders sealing or limiting the release of records of official actions entered pursuant to this section shall not limit the operation of rules of discovery promulgated by the supreme court of Colorado.

(k) All arrest and criminal records information, whether existing prior to or after May 5, 1978, except basic identification information, is subject to an order limiting the release thereof in accordance with this subsection (1.1).

(1.2) (a) A court shall enter an order limiting access to arrest and criminal records information when the record is a record of an official action in which the individual is acquitted or in which the charges are dismissed. The order shall be entered as a matter of course, upon the court's own motion, thirty days after the dismissal or acquittal unless the defendant requests in writing or in open court that the record remain open. The defendant may subsequently withdraw the request that the record remain open by submitting a written authorization to the court to enter the order. Upon receipt of such an authorization, the court shall enter the order. The provisions of paragraphs (h) and (j) of subsection (1.1) of this section shall apply to any order entered pursuant to this paragraph (a).

(b) An order limiting access to arrest and criminal records information entered pursuant to this subsection (1.2) shall state that the record shall only be released to the person in interest or to a criminal justice agency of this state or to a similar agency of the United States government or any of the states of the United States of America.

(1.3) (a) The custodian of any record of an arrest shall not allow inspection of the record of that arrest if the records in his custody and control do not show that the arrest was followed by the commencement of a trial thereon within two years after the arrest or was followed by a disposition prior to a trial within two years after the arrest; except that, subject to the provisions of subsections (1.1) and (1.2) of this section, the custodian shall allow the inspection of such a record if the person seeking the inspection provides information to the custodian which shows that the arrest has been followed by the commencement of a trial within two years after the arrest or has been followed by a disposition prior to a trial within two years after the arrest.

(b) For the purposes of this subsection (1.3), "disposition" includes deferred prosecution and deferred sentencing.

(c) This subsection (1.3) shall not restrict the right of the person in interest to inspect his own records, nor shall it deny access thereto by a criminal justice agency of this state or by a similar agency of the United States government or any of the states of the United States of America.

(2) Upon the filing of a petition or the entering of a court order relating to the sealing of records, the court shall set a date for a hearing, which hearing may be closed at the court's discretion, and shall notify the district attorney, the arresting agency, and any other person or agency who the court has reason to believe may have relevant information related to the sealing of such record.

(3) (a) Upon a finding that the harm to privacy of the person in interest or dangers of unwarranted adverse consequences outweigh the public interest in retaining the records, the court may order such records, or any part thereof except basic identification information, to be sealed. If the court finds that neither sealing of the records nor maintaining of the records unsealed by the agency would serve the ends of justice, the court may enter an appropriate order limiting access to such records.

(b) Any order entered pursuant to this subsection (3) shall be directed to every custodian who may have custody of any part of arrest and criminal records information which is the subject of the order. Whenever a court enters an order pursuant to this subsection (3), it shall provide the Colorado bureau of investigation with a copy thereof. The Colorado bureau of investigation shall forward copies of such an order to every custodian which has furnished information to it pursuant to section 24-32-412 (3) concerning the subject of the order.

(c) Every custodian of the arrest and criminal records information subject to the order, within thirty days after entry of the order unless it is stayed pending an appeal, shall advise the court and the petitioner in writing of compliance with the order.

(4) Upon the entry of an order to seal the records, or any part thereof, the subject official actions shall be deemed never to have occurred, and the

person in interest and all criminal justice agencies may properly reply, upon any inquiry in the matter, that no such action ever occurred and that no such record exists with respect to such person.

(5) Inspection of the records included in the order may thereafter be permitted by the court only upon petition by the person in interest who is the subject of such records or by the district attorney and only to those persons and for such purposes named in such petition.

(6) Employers, educational institutions, state and local government agencies, officials, and employees shall not, in any application or interview or otherwise, require an applicant to disclose any information contained in sealed records. An applicant need not, in answer to any question concerning arrest and criminal records information that has been sealed, include a reference to or information concerning such sealed information and may state that no such action has ever occurred. Such an application may not be denied solely because of the applicant's refusal to disclose arrest and criminal records information that has been sealed.

(7) All arrest and criminal records information existing prior to December 31, 1977, except basic identification information, is also subject to sealing in accordance with this part 3.

(8) Nothing in this section shall be construed to authorize the physical destruction of any criminal justice records; except that, upon the petition of a person in interest who has received a pardon after a conviction, the court shall order the physical destruction of the arrest and criminal records information relating to that pardon.

(9) (a) Whenever a defendant has charges against him dismissed, is acquitted, or is sentenced following a conviction, he shall be advised by the judge of his rights concerning the sealing or limiting the release of his criminal justice records if he complies with the applicable provisions of subsections (1) to (3) of this section.

(b) Whenever a defendant completes his sentence or satisfies conditions imposed in lieu of sentence, the person having immediate supervision of the defendant when he is released or the prison facility releasing the defendant shall again advise the defendant of his right to petition for an order of court sealing or limiting the release of his criminal justice records if he complies with the applicable provisions of subsections (1) to (3) of this section.

Source: Added, L. 77, p. 1249, § 1; (1) and (2) amended, (3) (b) R&RE, and (1.1) to (1.3) and (9) added, L. 78, pp. 403, 406, §§ 2, 3.

24-72-309. Violation-penalty. Any person who willfully and knowingly violates the provisions of this part 3 is guilty of a misdemeanor and, upon conviction thereof, shall be punished by a fine of not more than one hundred dollars, or by imprisonment in the county jail for not more than ninety days, or by both such fine and imprisonment.

Source: Added, L. 77, p. 1250, § 1.

30-10-101. Offices - inspection of records - failure to comply - penalty. (1) Every sheriff, county clerk and recorder, county treasurer, and clerk of the district and county courts shall keep his respective office at the county seat of the county and in the office provided by the county, if any such has been provided, or, if there is none provided, then at such place as the board of county commissioners shall direct. Subject to the provisions of part 2 of article 72 of title 24, C.R.S. 1973, and any judicially recognized right of privacy, all books and papers required to be in such offices shall be open to the examination of any person, but no person, except parties in interest, or their attorneys, shall have the right to examine pleadings or other papers filed in any cause pending in such court.

(2) Any person or corporation and their employees engaged in making abstracts or abstract books shall have the right, during usual business hours and subject to such rules and regulations as the officer having the custody of such records may prescribe, to inspect and make memoranda, copies, or photographs of the contents of all such books and papers for the purpose of their business; but any such officer may make reasonable and general regulations concerning the inspection of such books and papers by the public. If, for the purpose of making such photographs, it becomes necessary to remove such records from the room where they are usually kept to some other room in the courthouse where such photographic apparatus may be installed for such purpose, the county clerk, in his discretion, may charge to the person or corporation making such photographic reproductions, a fee of one dollar per hour for the service of the deputy who has charge of such records while they are being so photographed; but such fees shall not be charged to one person or corporation unless the same fee is likewise charged to every person or corporation photographing such records.

(3) If any person or officer refuses or neglects to comply with the provisions of this section, he shall forfeit for each day he so refuses or neglects the sum of five dollars, to be collected by civil action, in the name of the people of the state of Colorado, and pay it into the school fund; but this shall not interfere with or take away any right of action for damages by any person injured by such neglect or refusal.

Source: G. L. § 554; L. 1885, p. 157, § 1; R. S. 08, § 1352; L. 13, p. 227, § 1; L. 19, p. 368, § 1; C. L. § 8829; CSA, C. 45, § 176; CRS 53, § 35-1-1; C.R.S. 1963, § 35-1-1; L. 77, p. 1435, § 1.

Connecticut General Statutes, Annotated
1977 Cumulative Annual Pocket Parts
Volume 2

[§ 1–18a. (P.A. 75–342, § 1) Definitions].

As used in this act and in chapter 3, the following words and phrases shall have the following meanings, except where such terms are used in a context which clearly indicates the contrary:

(a) "Public agency" or "agency" means any executive, administrative or legislative office of the state or any political subdivision of the state and any state or town agency, any department, institution, bureau, board, commission or official of the state or of any city, town, borough, municipal corporation, school district, regional district or other district or other political subdivision of the state, and also includes any judicial office, official or body of the court of common pleas, probate court and juvenile court but only in respect to its or their administrative functions.

(b) "Meeting" means any hearing or other proceeding of a public agency and any convening or assembly of a quorum of a multi-member public agency, whether in person or by means of electronic equipment, to discuss or act upon a matter over which the public agency has supervision, control, jurisdiction or advisory power, but shall not include any chance meeting, or a social meeting neither planned nor intended for the purpose of discussing matters relating to official business. "Meeting" shall not include strategy or negotiations with respect to collective bargaining nor a caucus of members of a single political party notwithstanding that such members also constitute a quorum of a public agency. "Caucus" means a convening or assembly of the enrolled members of a single political party who are members of a public agency within the state or a political subdivision.

(c) "Person" means natural person, partnership, corporation, association or society.

(d) "Public records of files" means any recorded data or information relating to the conduct of the public's business prepared, owned, used, received or retained by a public agency, whether such data or information be handwritten, typed, tape-recorded, printed, photostated, photographed or recorded by any other method.

(e) "Executive sessions" means a meeting of a public agency at which the public is excluded for one or more of the following purposes:

(1) Discussion concerning the appointment, employment, performance, evaluation, health or dismissal of a public officer or employee, provided that such individual may require that discussion be held at an open meeting;

(2) strategy and negotiations with respect to pending claims and litigation;

(3) matters concerning security strategy or the deployment of security personnel, or devices affecting public security;

(4) discussion of the selection of a site or the lease, sale or purchase of real estate by a political subdivision of the state when publicity regarding such construction would cause a likelihood of increased price until such time as all of the property has been acquired or all proceedings or transactions concerning same have been terminated or abandoned; and

(5) discussion of any matter which would result in the disclosure of public records or the information contained therein described in subsection (b) of section 1-19.

(1975, P.A. 75-342, § 1.)

§ 1-19. Access to public records.

(a) Except as otherwise provided by any federal law or state statute, all records maintained or kept on file by any public agency, whether or not such records are required by any law or by any rule or regulation, shall be public records and every person shall have the right to inspect or copy such records at such reasonable time as may be determined by the custodian thereof. Each such agency shall keep and maintain all public records in its custody at its regular office or place of business in an accessible place and, if there is no such office or place of business, the public records pertaining to such agency shall be kept in the office of the clerk of any political subdivision or the secretary of the state, as the case may be. Any certified record hereunder attested as a true copy by the clerk, chief or deputy or such other person designated or empowered by law to so act, of such agency shall be competent evidence in any court of this state of the facts contained therein. Each such agency shall make, keep and maintain a record of the proceedings of its meetings.

(b) Nothing in sections 1-15, 1-18a, 1-19 to 1-19b, inclusive, and 1-21 to 1-21k, inclusive, shall be construed to require disclosure of (1) preliminary drafts or notes provided the public agency has determined that the public interest in withholding such documents clearly outweighs the public interest in disclosure; personnel or medical files and similar files the disclosure of which would constitute an invasion of personal privacy; (2) records of law enforcement agencies not otherwise available to the public which records were compiled in connection with the detection or investigation of crime, if the disclosure of said records would not be in the public interest because it would result in the disclosure of (A) the identity of informants not otherwise known, (B) information to be used in a prospective law enforcement action if prejudicial to such action, (C) investigatory techniques not otherwise known to the general public, or (D) arrest records of a juvenile, which shall also include any investigatory files, concerning the arrest of such juvenile, compiled for law enforcement purposes; (3) records pertaining to pending claims and litigation to which the public agency is a party until such litigation or claim has been finally adjudicated or otherwise settled; (4) trade secrets, which for purposes of sections 1–15, 1–18a, 1–19 to 1–19b, inclusive, and 1–21 to 1–21k, inclusive, are defined as unpatented, secret, commercially valuable plans, appliances, formulas, or processes, which are used for the making, preparing, compounding, treating or processing of articles or materials which are trade commodities obtained from a person and which are recognized by law as confidential, and commercial or financial information given in confidence, not required by law and obtained from the public; (5) test questions, scoring keys and other examination data used to administer a licensing examination, examination for employment or academic examinations; (6) the contents of real estate appraisals, engineering or feasibility estimates and evaluations made for or by an agency relative to the acquisition of property or to prospective public supply and construction contracts, until such time as all of the property has been acquired or all proceedings or transactions have been terminated or abandoned, provided the law of eminent domain shall not be affected by this provision; (7) statements of personal worth or personal financial data required by a licensing agency and filed by an applicant with such licensing agency to establish his personal qualification for the license, certificate or permit applied for; (8) records, reports and statements of strategy or negotiations with respect to collective bargaining; (9) records, tax returns, reports and statements exempted by federal law or state statutes or communications privileged by the attorney-client relationship.

(c) The records referred to in subsection (b) shall not be deemed public records for the purposes of sections 1–15, 1–18a, 1–19 to 1–19b, inclusive, and 1–21 to 1–21k, inclusive, provided disclosure pursuant to the provisions of said sections shall be required of all records of investigation conducted with respect to any tenement house, lodging house or boarding house as defined in chapter 352, or any nursing home, home for the aged or rest home, as defined in chapter 333, by any municipal building department or housing code inspection department, any local or district health department, or any other department charged with the enforcement of ordinances or laws regulating the erection, construction, alteration, maintenance, sanitation, ventilation or occupancy of such buildings.

(1971, P.A. 193; 1975, P.A. 75–342, § 2, eff. Oct. 1, 1975; 1976, P.A. 76–294.)

[§ 1–19a. (P.A. 75–342, § 4) Computer storage system; printouts].

Any public agency which maintains its records in a computer storage system shall provide a printout of any data properly identified.

(1975, P.A. 75–342, § 4.)

[§ 1–19b. (P.A. 75–342, § 3) Construction of act].

Nothing in this act shall be: (1) Construed as preventing any public agency

from opening its records concerning the administration of such agency to public inspection, or (2) construed as authorizing the withholding of information in personnel files, birth records or of confidential tax data from the individual who is the subject of such records, or (3) be deemed in any manner to affect the status of judicial records as they existed prior to Oct. 1, 1975, nor to affect the rights of litigants, including parties to administrative proceedings, under the laws of discovery of this state.
(1975, P.A. 75–342, § 3.)
§ 1–20a. Public employment contracts as public record.

Any contract of employment to which the state or a political subdivision of the state is a party shall be deemed to be a public record for the purposes of sections 1–19 and 1–20.
(1973, P.A. 73–271.)

Delaware Code, Annotated
1979 Cumulative Supplement
Article 29

§ 6411. Organization regulations; rules of procedure.
For the benefit of the public, each agency shall adopt the following regulations:

(1) A general description of its organization, its methods of operations and the manner, including addresses and telephone numbers, whereby the public may obtain information and otherwise deal with the agency; and

(2) A statement of the nature and requirements of all rules of practice and procedure used by the agency to exercise its statutory authority in compliance with this chapter. (60 Del. Laws, c. 585, § 1.)
§ 6412. Public information.

(a) Each agency shall make available promptly to the public upon request, for inspection, originals or legible copies of the following:

(1) Its regulations, orders, decisions, opinions and licenses;

(2) Any documents, papers and other materials considered by the agency in taking agency action; or

(3) Any records of the agency reasonably specified by the requesting person.

(b) When making its documents and other materials available to the public the agency may:

(1) Take reasonable precautions to preserve the integrity and security of such documents or materials;

(2) Make available only at reasonable, specified intervals documents and materials being actively used by the agency;

(3) Limit the availability of information to its regular business hours and place of business;

(4) Decline to make available documents and other materials which:

a. Relate solely to the agency's internal procedural and personnel practices;

b. Pertain to ongoing enforcement investigations which have not yet resulted in agency action;

c. Are specifically exempted from disclosure by law; or

d. Are confidential or privileged for the same or similar reasons as the Court would hold its records confidential or privileged;

(5) Make a reasonable charge for the cost of reproducing or copying such documents or materials.

(c) The Court shall have jurisdiction of all actions to compel an agency to produce or disclose any documents, materials or information and the agency shall have the burden of sustaining its refusal to produce or disclose as requested. (60 Del. Laws, c. 585, § 1.)

§ 10001. Declaration of policy.

It is vital in a democratic society that public business be performed in an open and public manner so that the citizens shall be advised of the performance of public officials and of the decisions that are made by such officials in formulating and executing public policy. Toward this end, this chapter is adopted, and shall be construed. (60 Del. Laws, c. 641, § 1.)

§ 10002. Definitions.

(a) "Public body" means any regulatory, administrative, advisory, executive or legislative body of the State or any political subdivision of the State including, but not limited to, any board, bureau, commission, department, agency, committee, counsel, legislative committee, association or any other entity established by an act of the General Assembly of the State, which (1) is supported in whole or in part by public funds; (2) expends or disburses public funds; or (3) is specifically charged by any other public body to advise or make recommendations.

(b) "Public business" means any matter over which the public body has supervision, control, jurisdiction or advisory power.

(c) "Public funds" are those funds derived from the State or any political subdivision of the State, but not including grants-in-aid.

(d) "Public record" is written or recorded information made or received by a public body relating to public business. For purposes of this chapter, the following records shall not be deemed public.

(1) Any personnel, medical or pupil file, the disclosure of which would

constitute an invasion of personal privacy, under this legislation or under any State or federal law as it relates to personal privacy;

(2) Trade secrets and commercial or financial information obtained from a person which is of a privileged or confidential nature;

(3) Investigatory files compiled for civil or criminal law-enforcement purposes including pending investigative files, pretrial and presentence investigations and child custody and adoption files where there is no criminal complaint at issue;

(4) Criminal files and criminal records, the disclosure of which would constitute an invasion of personal privacy. Any person may, upon proof of identity, obtain a copy of his personal criminal record. All other criminal records and files are closed to public scrutiny. Agencies holding such criminal records may delete any information, before release, which would disclose the names of witnesses, intelligence personnel and aids or any other information of a privileged and confidential nature;

(5) Intelligence files compiled for law-enforcement purposes, the disclosure of which could constitute an endangerment to the local, state or national welfare and security;

(6) Any records specifically exempted from public disclosure by statute or common law;

(7) Any records which disclose the identity of the contributor of a bona fide and lawful charitable contribution to the public body whenever public anonymity has been requested of the public body with respect to said contribution by the contributor;

(8) Any records involving labor negotiations or collective bargaining;

(9) Any records pertaining to pending or potential litigation which are not records of any court;

(10) Any record of discussions allowed by § 10004(b) of this title to be held in executive session; or

(11) Any records which disclose the identity or address of any person holding a permit to carry a concealed deadly weapon; provided, however, all records relating to such permits shall be available to all bona fide law-enforcement officers.

(e) "Meeting" means the formal or informal gathering of a quorum of the members of any public body for the purpose of discussing or taking action on public business.

(f) "Agenda" shall include but is not limited to a general statement of the major issues expected to be discussed at a public meeting.

(g) "Public body," "public record" and "meeting" shall not include activities of the Farmers Bank of the State of Delaware or the University of Delaware, except that the Board of Trustees of the University shall be a "public body," and University documents relating to the expenditure of public funds

shall be "public records," and each meeting of the full Board of Trustees shall be a "meeting." (60 Del. Laws, c. 641, § 1; 61 Del. Laws, c. 55, § 1.)
Effect of amendment.—61 Del. Laws, c. 55, effective May 23, 1977, added paragraph (11) in subsection (d).

§ 10003. Examination and copying of public records.

(a) All public records shall be open to inspection and copying by any citizen of the State during regular business hours by the custodian of the records for the appropriate public body. Reasonable access to and reasonable facilities for copying of these records shall not be denied to any citizen. If the record is in active use or in storage and, therefore, not available at the time a citizen requests access, the custodian shall so inform the citizen and make an appointment for said citizen to examine such records as expediently as they may be made available. Any reasonable expense involved in the copying of such records shall be levied as a charge on the citizen requesting such copy.

(b) It shall be the responsibility of the public body to establish rules and regulations regarding access to public records as well as fees charged for copying of such records. (60 Del. Laws, c. 641, § 1.)

§ 10004. Open meetings.

(a) Every meeting of all public bodies shall be open to the public except those closed pursuant to subsections (b), (c), (d) and (g) of this section.

(b) A public body at any meeting may call for an executive session closed to the public pursuant to subsection (c) of this section for any of the following purposes:

(1) Discussion of individual citizen's qualifications to hold a job or pursue training unless the citizen requests that such a meeting be open;

(2) Preliminary discussions on site acquisitions for any publicly funded capital improvements;

(3) Activities of any law-enforcement agency in its efforts to collect information leading to criminal apprehension;

(4) Strategy sessions with respect to collective bargaining, pending or potential litigation, when an open meeting would have effect on the bargaining or litigation position of the public body;

(5) Discussions which would disclose the identity of the contributor of a bona fide and lawful charitable contribution to the public body whenever public anonymity has been requested of the public body with respect to said contribution by the contributor;

(6) Discussion of the content of documents, excluded from the definition of "public record" in § 10002 of this title where such discussion may disclose the contents of such documents;

(7) The hearing of student disciplinary cases unless the student requests a public hearing;

(8) The hearing of employee disciplinary or dismissal cases unless the employee requests a public hearing;

(9) Personnel matters in which the names, competency and abilities of individual employees or students are discussed;

(10) Training and orientation sessions conducted to assist members of the public body in the fulfillment of their responsibilities;

(11) Discussion of potential or actual emergencies related to preservation of the public peace, health, and safety;

(12) Where the public body has requested an attorney-at-law to render his legal advice or opinion concerning an issue or matter under discussion by the public body and where it has not yet taken a public stand or reached a conclusion in the matter; or

(13) Preliminary discussions resulting from tentative information relating to the management of the public schools in the following areas: School attendance zones; personnel needs; and fiscal requirements.

(c) A public body may hold an executive session closed to the public upon affirmative vote of a majority of members present at a meeting of the public body. The purpose for such executive session shall be announced ahead of time and shall be limited to the purposes listed in subsection (b) of this section. Executive sessions may be held only for the discussion of public business, and all voting on public business must be made at a public meeting and the results of the vote made public, unless disclosure of the existence or results of the vote would disclose information properly the subject of an executive session pursuant to subsection (b) of this section.

(d) This section shall not prohibit the removal of any person from a public meeting who is willfully and seriously disruptive of the conduct of such meeting.

(e) (1) This subsection concerning notice of meetings shall not apply to any emergency meeting which is necessary for the immediate preservation of the public peace, health or safety, or to the General Assembly.

(2) All public bodies shall give public notice of their regular meetings at least 7 days in advance thereof. The notice shall include the agenda, if such has been determined at the time, and the dates, times and places of such meetings; however, the agenda shall be subject to change to include additional items or the deletion of items at the time of the public body's meeting.

(3) All public bodies shall give public notice of the type set forth in paragraph (2) of this subsection of any special or rescheduled meeting no later than 24 hours before such meeting.

(4) Public notice required by this subsection shall include, but not be limited to, conspicuous posting of said notice at the principal office of the public holding the meeting, or if no such office exists at the place where

meetings of the public body are regularly held, and making a reasonable number of such notices available.

(5) When the agenda is not available as of the time of the initial posting of the public notice it shall be added to the notice at least 6 hours in advance of said meeting.

(f) Each public body shall make available for public inspection and copying as a public record minutes of all regular, special and emergency meetings. Such minutes shall include a record of those members present and a record, by individual members, of each vote taken and action agreed upon. Such minutes or portions thereof, and any public records pertaining to executive sessions conducted pursuant to this section, may be withheld from public disclosure so long as public disclosure would defeat the lawful purpose for the executive session, but no longer.

(g) This section shall not apply to the proceedings of:

(1) Grand juries;

(2) Petit juries;

(3) Special juries;

(4) The deliberations of any court;

(5) The board of Pardons and Parole; and

(6) Public bodies having only 1 member. (60 Del. Laws, c. 641, § 1.)

§ 10005. Enforcement.

Any action taken at a meeting in violation of this chapter may be voidable by the Court of Chancery. Any citizen may challenge the validity under this chapter of any action of a public body by filing suit within 30 days of the citizen's learning of such action but in no event later than 6 months after the date of the action. Any citizen denied access to public records as provided in this chapter may bring suit within 10 days of such denial. Venue in such cases where access to public records is denied shall be placed in a court of competent jurisdiction for the county or city in which the public body ordinarily meets or in which the plaintiff resides. Remedies permitted by this section include a declaratory judgment, writ of mandamus and other appropriate relief. (60 Del. Laws, c. 641, § 1.)

District of Columbia Code Encyclopedia
1978-1979 Cumulative Annual Pocket Part
Title I

An Act (1-178)
In the Council of the District of Columbia

November 19, 1976

To create a Freedom of Information Act; to create rights;

and for other purposes.

Be it enacted by the Council of the District of Columbia,
That this act may be cited as the "Freedom of Information Act of 1976."
Sec. 2. The District of Columbia Administrative Procedure Act (D.C. Code,
sec. 1-1501 et seq.) as amended, is further amended by adding to the end
thereof the following:
Title II Freedom of Information
"Public Policy"
Sec. 201. Generally the public policy of the District of Columbia is that all
persons are entitled to full and complete information regarding the affairs of
government and the official acts of those who represent them as public
officials and employees. To that end, provisions of this act shall be construed
with the view toward expansion of public access and the minimization of
costs and time delays to persons requesting information.
Right of Access to Public Records: Allowable Costs
"Time Limits"
Sec. 202. (a) Any person has a right to inspect, and at his or her discretion,
to copy any public record of the Mayor or an agency, except as otherwise
expressly provided by section 204 of this title, in accordance with reasonable
rules that shall be issued by the Mayor or an agency after notice and comment, concerning the time and place of access.
(b) The Mayor or an agency may establish and collect fees not to exceed the
actual cost of searching for or making copies of records, but in no instance
shall the total fee for searching exceed 10 dollars for each request. For
purposes of this subsection "request" means a single demand for any number
of documents made at one time to an individual agency. Documents may be
furnished without charge or at a reduced charge where the Mayor or agency
determines that waiver or reduction of the fee is in the public interest because
furnishing the information can be considered as primarily benefiting the general public. Notwithstanding the foregoing, fees shall not be charged for
examination and review by the Mayor or an agency to determine if such
documents are subject to disclosure.
(c) The Mayor or an agency, upon request reasonably describing any public
record, shall within 10 days (except Saturdays, Sundays, and legal public
holidays) of the receipt of any such request either make the requested public
record accessible or notify the person making such request of its determina-

tion not to make the requested public record or any part thereof accessible and the reasons therefor.

(d) In unusual circumstances, the time limit prescribed in subsection (c) of this section may be extended by written notice to the person making such request setting forth the reasons for extension and expected date for determination. Such extension shall not exceed 10 days (except Saturdays, Sundays and legal public holidays). For purposes of this subsection, and only to the extent necessary for processing of the particular request, 'unusual circumstances' are limited to:

(1) the need to search for, collect, and appropriately examine a voluminous amount of separate and distinct records which are demanded in a single request; or

(2) the need for consultation, which shall be conducted with all practicable speed, with another agency having a substantial interest in the determination of the request or among two or more components of the agency having substantial subject-matter interest therein.

(e) Any failure on the part of the Mayor or an agency to comply with a request under subsection (a) of this section within the time provisions of subsections (c) and (d) of this section shall be deemed a denial of the request, and the person making such request shall be deemed to have exhausted his administrative remedies with respect to such request, unless such person chooses to petition the Mayor pursuant to section 207 of this title to review the deemed denial of the request.

"Letters of Denial"

Sec. 203. (a) Denial by the Mayor or an agency of a request for any public record shall contain at least the following:

(1) the specific reasons for the denial, including citations to the particular exemption(s) under section 204 of this title relied on as authority for the denial;

(2) the name(s) of the public official(s) or employee(s) responsible for the decision to deny the request; and

(3) notification to the requester of any administrative or judicial right to appeal under section 207 of this title.

(b) The Mayor and each agency of the District of Columbia shall maintain a file of all letters of denial of requests for public records. This file shall be made available to any person on request for purposes of inspection and/or copying.

"Exemptions"

Sec. 204. (a) The following matters may be exempt from disclosure under the provisions of this title:

(1) Trade secrets and commercial or financial information obtained from outside the government, to the extent that disclosure would result in substan-

tial harm to the competitive position of the person from whom the information was obtained;

(2) Information of a personal nature where the public disclosure thereof would constitute a clearly unwarranted invasion of personal privacy;

(3) Investigatory records compiled for law enforcement purposes, but only to the extent that the production of such records would-

(A) interfere with enforcement proceedings,

(B) deprive a person of a right to a fair trial or an impartial adjudication,

(C) constitute an unwarranted invasion of personal privacy,

(D) disclose the identity of a confidential source and, in the case of a record compiled by a law enforcement authority in the course of a criminal investigation, or by an agency conducting a lawful national security intelligence investigation, confidential information furnished only by the confidential source,

(E) disclose investigative techniques and procedures not generally known outside the government,

(F) endanger the life or physical safety of law enforcement personnel;

(4) Inter-agency or intra-agency memorandums or letters which would not be available by law to a party other than an agency in litigation with the agency;

(5) Test questions and answers to be used in future license, employment, or academic examinations, but not previously administered examinations or answers to questions thereon;

(6) Information specifically exempted from disclosure by statute (other than this section), provided that such statute-

(A) requires that the matters be withheld from the public in such a manner as to leave no discretion on the issue, or

(B) establishes particular criteria for withholding or refers to particular types of matters to be withheld; and

(7) Information specifically authorized by Federal law under criteria established by a Presidential Executive order to be kept secret in the interest of national defense or foreign policy which is in fact properly classified pursuant to such Executive order.

(b) Any reasonably segregable portion of a public record shall be provided to any person requesting such record after deletion of those portions which may be withheld from disclosure under subsection (a) of this section.

(c) This section does not authorize withholding of information or limit the availability of records to the public, except as specifically stated in this section. This section is not authority to withhold information from the Council of the District of Columbia. This section shall not operate to permit nondisclosure of information of which disclosure is authorized or mandated by other law.

"Recording of Final Votes"

Sec. 205. Each agency having more than one member shall maintain and make available for public inspection a record of the final votes of each member in each proceeding of that agency.

"Information Which Must be Made Public"

Sec. 206. Without limiting the meaning of other sections of this title, the following categories of information are specifically made public information:

(a) the names, salaries, title, and dates of employment of all employees and officers of the Mayor and an agency;

(b) administrative staff manuals and instructions to staff that affect a member of the public;

(c) final opinions, including concurring and dissenting opinions, as well as orders, made in the adjudication of cases;

(d) those statements of policy and interpretations of policy, acts, and rules which have been adopted by the Mayor or an agency;

(e) correspondence and materials referred to therein, by and with the Mayor or an agency relating to any regulatory, supervisory, or enforcement responsibilities of the agency, whereby the agency determines, or states an opinion upon, or is asked to determine or state an opinion upon, the rights of the District, the public, or any private party;

(f) information in or taken from any account, voucher, or contract dealing with the receipt or expenditure of public or other funds by public bodies; and

(g) the minutes of all proceedings of all agencies.

"Administrative Appeals and Enforcement"

Sec. 207. (a) Any person denied the right to inspect a public record of a public body may petition the Mayor to review the public record to determine whether it may be withheld from public inspection. Such determination shall be made in writing with a statement of reasons therefor in writing within 10 days (excluding Saturdays, Sundays, and legal holidays) of the submission of the petition.

(1) If the Mayor denies the petition or does not make a determination within the time limits provided in this subsection, or if a person is deemed to have exhausted his or her administrative remedies pursuant to subsection (e) of section 202, the person seeking disclosure may institute proceedings for injunctive or delcaratory relief in the Superior Court for the District of Columbia.

(2) If the Mayor decides that the public record may not be withheld, he shall order the public body to disclose the record immediately. If the public body continues to withhold the record, the person seeking disclosure may bring suit in the Superior Court for the District of Columbia to enjoin the public body from withholding the record and to compel the production of the requested record. "(b) In any suit filed under subsection (a) of this section,

the Superior Court for the District of Columbia may enjoin the public body from withholding records and order the production of any records improperly withheld from the person seeking disclosure. The burden is on the Mayor or the agency to sustain its action. In such cases the court shall determine the matter *de novo,* and may examine the contents of such records *in camera* to determine whether such records or any part thereof shall be withheld under any of the exemptions set forth in section 204 of this title.

(c) If a person seeking the right to inspect or to receive a copy of a public record prevails in whole or in part in such suit, he or she may be awarded reasonable attorney fees and other costs of litigation.

"Oversight"

Sec. 208. On or before the 30th day of June of each calendar year, the Mayor shall compile and submit to the Council of the District of Columbia a report covering the public-record-disclosure activities of each agency and of Executive Branch as a whole during the preceeding calendar year. The report shall include:

(1) The number of determinations made by each agency not to comply with requests for records made to such agency under this title and the reasons for each such determination;

(2) The number of appeals made by persons under Section 207(a) of this title, the result of such appeals, and the reason for the action upon each appeal that results in a denial of information;

(3) The names and titles or positions of each person responsible for the denial of records requested under this title, and the number of instances of participation for each such person;

(4) A copy of the fee schedule and the total amount of fees collected by each agency for making records available under this title;

(5) such other information as indicates efforts to administer fully this title; and

(6) for the prior calendar year, a listing of the total number of cases arising under this title, the total number of cases in which a request was denied in whole or in part, the total number of times in which each exemption provided under Section 204 of this title was cited as a reason for denial of a request, and the total amount of fees collected under section 202(b) of this act. Such report shall also include a description of the efforts undertaken by the Mayor to encourage agency compliance with this title.

"Definition"

Sec. 209. For purposes of this title, the terms "Mayor," "Council," "District," "agency," "rule," "rulemaking," "person," "party," "order," "relief," "proceeding," "public record," and "adjudication" shall have the meaning as provided in section 102 of Title I of this Act."

Florida Statutes, Annotated
1977 Cumulative Annual Pocket Part
Volume A

119.01 General state policy on public records.

It is the policy of this state that all state, county, and municipal records shall at all times be open for a personal inspection by any person.

Amended by Laws 1973, c. 73–98, § 1, eff. Oct. 1, 1973; Laws 1975, c. 75–225, § 2, eff. July 1, 1975.

119.011 Definitions.

For the purpose of this chapter:

(1) "Public records" means all documents, papers, letters, maps, books, tapes, photographs, films, sound recordings or other material, regardless of physical form or characteristics, made or received pursuant to law or ordinance or in connection with the transaction of official business by any agency.

(2) "Agency" shall mean any state, county, district, authority, or municipal officer, department, division, board, bureau, commission or other separate unit of government created or established by law and any other public or private agency, person, partnership, corporation, or business entity acting on behalf of any public agency.

Amended by Laws 1973, c. 73–98, § 2, eff. Oct. 1, 1973; Laws 1975, c. 75–225, § 3, eff. July 1, 1975.

119.012 Records made public by public fund use.

If public funds are expended by an agency defined in subsection 119.011(2) in payment of dues or membership contributions to any person, corporation, foundation, trust, association, group, or other organization, then all the financial, business and membership records pertaining to the public agency from which or on whose behalf the payments are made, of the person, corporation, foundation, trust, association, group, or organization to whom such payments are made shall be public records and subject to the provisions of s. 119.07. Laws 1975, c. 75–225, § 3, eff. July 1, 1975.

119.02 Penalty.

Any public official who shall violate the provisions of subsection 119.07(1) shall be subject to suspension and removal or impeachment and, in addition, shall be guilty of a misdemeanor of the second degree, punishable as provided in s. 775.082 or s. 775.083.

Amended by Laws 1975, c. 75–225, § 6, eff. July 1, 1975.

119.07 Inspection and examination of records; exemptions.

(1) Every person who has custody of public records shall permit the records to be inspected and examined by any person desiring to do so, at

reasonable times, under reasonable conditions, and under supervision by the custodian of the records or his designee. The custodians shall furnish copies or certified copies of the records upon payment of fees as prescribed by law or, if fees are not prescribed by law, upon payment of the actual cost of duplication of the copies. Unless otherwise provided by law, the fees to be charged for duplication of public records shall be collected, deposited, and accounted for in the manner prescribed for other operating funds of the agency.

(2)(a) All public records which presently are provided by law to be confidential or which are prohibited from being inspected by the public, whether by general or special law, shall be exempt from the provisions of subsection (1).

(b) All public records referred to in ss. 794.03, 198.09, 199.222, 658.10(1), 624.319(3), (4), 624.311(2), and 63.181, are exempt from the provisions of subsection (1).

(c) Examination questions and answer sheets of examinations administered by a governmental agency for the purpose of licensure, certification, or employment shall be exempt from the provisions of subsection (1). However, an examinee shall have the right to review his own completed examination. Amended by Laws 1975, c. 75–225, § 4, eff. July 1, 1975.

119.08 Photographing public records.

(1) In all cases where the public or any person interested has a right to inspect or take extracts or make copies from any public record, instruments or documents, any person shall hereafter have the right of access to said records, documents or instruments for the purpose of making photographs of the same while in the possession, custody and control of the lawful custodian thereof, or his authorized deputy.

(2) Such work shall be done under the supervision of the lawful custodian of the said records, who shall have the right to adopt and enforce reasonable rules governing the said work. Said work shall, where possible, be done in the room where the said records, documents or instruments are by law kept, but if the same in the judgment of the lawful custodian of the said records, documents or instruments be impossible or impracticable, then the said work shall be done in such other room or place as nearly adjacent to the room where the said records, documents and instruments are kept as determined by the lawful custodian thereof.

(3) Where the providing of another room or place is necessary, the expense of providing the same shall be paid by the person desiring to photograph the said records, instruments or documents. While the said work hereinbefore mentioned is in progress, the lawful custodian of said records may charge the person desiring to make the said photographs for the services of a deputy of the lawful custodian of said records, documents or instruments

to supervise the same, or for the services of the said lawful custodian of the same in so doing at a rate of compensation to be agreed upon by the person desiring to make the said photographs and the custodian of the said records, documents or instruments, or in case the same fail to agree as to the said charge, then by the lawful custodian thereof.

119.09 Assistance of the division of archives, history and records management of the department of state.

The division of archives, history and records management of the department of state shall have the right to examine into the condition of public records and shall give advice and assistance to public officials in the solution of their problems of preserving, creating, filing and making available the public records in their custody. When requested by the division, public officials shall assist the division in the preparation of an inclusive inventory of public records in their custody to which shall be attached a schedule, approved by the head of the governmental unit or agency having custody of the records and the division, establishing a time period for the retention or disposal of each series of records. Upon the completion of the inventory and schedule, the division shall (subject to the availability of necessary space, staff and other facilities for such purposes) make available space in its records center for the filing of semicurrent records so scheduled and in its archives for noncurrent records of permanent value and shall render such other assistance as needed, including the microfilming of records so scheduled.

119.10 Violation of chapter a misdemeanor.

Any person willfully and knowingly violating any of the provisions of this chapter shall be guilty of a misdemeanor of the first degree, punishable as provided in § 775.082 or § 775.083.

119.11 Accelerated hearing; Immediate compliances

(1) Whenever an action is filed to enforce the provisions of this chapter, the court shall set an immediate hearing, giving the case priority over other pending cases.

(2) Whenever a court orders an agency to open its records for inspection in accordance with this chapter, the agency shall comply with such order within 48 hours, unless otherwise provided by the court issuing such order, or unless the appellate court issues a stay order within such 48-hour period. The filing of a notice of appeal shall not operate as an automatic stay.

(3) A stay order shall not be issued unless the court determines that there is substantial probability that opening the records for inspection will result in significant damage.

Added by Laws 1975, c. 75–225, § 5, eff. July 1, 1975.

119.12 Attorney's fees.

(1) Whenever an action has been filed against an agency to enforce the provisions of this chapter and the court determines that such agency unrea-

sonably refused to permit public records to be inspected, the court shall assess a reasonable attorney's fee against such agency.

(2) Whenever an agency appeals a court order requiring it to permit inspection of records pursuant to this chapter and such order is affirmed, the court shall assess a reasonable attorney's fees for the appeal against such agency.

Added by Laws 1975, c. 75–225, § 5, eff. July 1, 1975.

Georgia Code, Annotated
1978 Cumulative Pocket Part
Title 40

40-801c Short title.

This Chapter shall be known and may be cited as the "Georgia Records Act." (Acts 1972, pp. 1267, 1268.)

40-802c Definitions.

For the purpose of this Chapter:

(a) "Department" means the Department of Archives and History.

(b) "Records" means all documents, papers, letters, maps, books (except books in formally organized libraries), microfilm, magnetic tape, or other material regardless of physical form or characteristics made or received pursuant to law or ordinance or in performance of functions by any agency.

(c) "Agency" means any State office, department, division, board, bureau, commission, authority or other separate unit of State government created or established by law.

(d) "Georgia State Archives" means an establishment maintained by the department for the preservation of those records and other papers that have been determined by the department to have sufficient historical and other value to warrant their continued preservation by the State and have been accepted by the department for deposit in its custody.

(e) "Records center" means an establishment maintained by the department primarily for the storage, processing, servicing, and security of public records that must be retained for varying periods of time but need not be retained in an agency's office equipment or space.

(f) "Vital records" means any record vital to the resumption or continuation of operations, or both, to the re-creation of the legal and financial status of government in the State, or to the protection and fulfillment of obligations to citizens of the State.

(g) "Retention schedule" means a set of disposition instructions prescribing how long, where, and in what form a record series shall be kept;

(h) "Record series" means documents or records that are filed in a unified arrangement, having similar physical characteristics or relating to a similar function or activity;

(i) "Records management" means the application of management techniques to the creation, utilization, maintenance, retention, preservation and disposal of records undertaken to reduce costs and improve efficiency of record keeping. Records management includes management of filing and microfilming equipment and supplies; filing and information retrieval systems; files, correspondence, reports and forms management; historical documentation; micrographics; retention programming and vital records protection.

(j) "Court record" means all documents, papers, letters, maps, books (except books formally organized in libraries), microfilm, magnetic tape, or other material regardless of physical form or characteristics made or received pursuant to law or ordinance or in the necessary performance of any judicial function created or received by an official of the Supreme Court, Court of Appeals, and any superior, state, juvenile, probate, county or justice of the peace court, and includes records or the offices of the judge, clerk, prosecuting attorney, public defender, court reporter, or any employee of the court.

(Acts 1972, pp. 1267, 1268; 1973, pp. 691, 692; 1975, pp. 675, 676; 978, H.B. No. 1638, Act No 1207.)

40-803c State Records Committee; creation; Membership; duties

(a) There is hereby created the State Records Committee, to be composed of the Governor, the Secretary of State, the Attorney General and the State Auditor, or their designated representatives. It shall be the duty of the committee to review, approve, disapprove, amend or modify retention schedules submitted by agency heads, school boards, county governments and municipal governments through the department for the disposition of records based on administrative, legal, fiscal or historical values. Such retention schedules, once approved, shall be authoritative, directive and have the force and effect of law. A retention schedule may be determined by three members of the committee. Retention schedules may be amended by the committee on change of program mission or legislative changes affecting the records. The Secretary of State shall serve as chairman of the committee and shall schedule meetings of the committee as required. Three members shall constitute a quorum. Each agency head has the right of appeal to the committee for actions taken under this Section.

(b) The Supreme Court may, by rule of the court, provide for retention schedules for court records. The State Records Committee may recommend retention schedules for court records to the Supreme Court. The destruction of court records by retention schedule shall not be construed as affecting the status of that court as a court of record.

(Acts 1978, H. B. No. 1638, Act No. 1207, eff. April 3, 1978.)

40-804c Duties of department.

It shall be the duty of the department to:

(a) Establish and administer, under the direction of a State records management officer (who shall be employed under the rules and regulations of the State Merit System), a records management program;

(b) Develop and issue procedures, rules, and regulations establishing standards for efficient and economical management methods relating to the creation, maintenance, utilization, retention, preservation, and disposition of records, filing equipment, supplies, microfilming of records, and vital records program;

(c) Assist State agencies in implementing records programs by providing consultative services in records management, conducting surveys in order to recommend more efficient records management practices, and providing training for records management personnel;

(d) Operate a records center or centers which shall accept all records transferred to it through the operation of approved retention schedules, provide secure storage and reference service for the same and submit written notice to the applicable agency of intended destruction of records in accordance with approved retention schedules.

Acts 1972, pp. 1267, 1269; 1975, pp. 675, 677.)

40-805c Duty of agencies.

It shall be the duty of each agency to:

(a) Cause to be made and preserved records containing adequate and proper documentation of the organization, functions, policies, decisions, procedures, and essential transactions of the agency and designed to furnish the information necessary to protect the legal and financial rights of the Government and of persons directly affected by the agency's activities;

(b) Cooperate fully with the department in complying with the provisions of this Chapter;

(c) Establish and maintain an active and continuing program for the economical and efficient management of records and assist the department in the conduct of records management surveys;

(d) Implement records management procedures and regulations issued by the department;

(e) Submit to the department, in accordance with the rules and regulations of the department, a recommended retention schedule for every record series in its custody, except that schedules for common-type files may be established by the department. No records will be scheduled for permanent retention in an office. No records will be scheduled for retention any longer than is absolutely necessary in the performance required functions. Records requiring retention for several years will transferred to the records center for low-cost storage at the earliest possible date following creation.

(f) Establish necessary safeguards against the removal or loss of records and such further safeguards as may be required by regulations of the department. Such safeguards shall include notification to all officials and employees of the agency that no records in the custody of the agency are to be alienated or destroyed except in accordance with the provisions of this Chapter.

(g) Designate an agency records management officer who shall establish and operate a records management program.

(Acts 1972, pp. 1267, 1269; 1975, pp. 675, 677, 678.)

40-806c Construction of Chapter; confidential records.

(a)Nothing in this Chapter shall be construed to divest agency heads of the authority to determine the nature and form of records required in the administration of their several departments. Notwithstanding this Section agency heads shall carry out provisions of section 40-805c.

(b) Any records designated confidential by law shall be so treated by the department in the maintenance, storage and disposition of such confidential records. These records shall be destroyed in such a manner that they cannot be read, interpreted, or reconstructed.

(Acts 1972, pp. 1267, 1270; 1975, pp. 675, 678; Acts 1978, H. B. No. 1638, No. 1207.)

40-807c Disposal of records.

(a) All records created or received in the performance of duty and paid for by public funds are deemed to be public property and shall constitute a record of public acts;

(b) The destruction of records shall occur only through the operation of an approved retention schedule. Such records shall not be placed in the custody of private individuals or institutions or semi-private organizations unless authorized by retention schedules;

(c) The alienation, alteration, theft or destruction of records by any person or persons in a manner not authorized by an applicable retention schedule is punishable as a misdemeanor;

(d) No person acting in compliance with the provisions of this Chapter shall be held personally liable.

(Acts 1972, pp. 1267, 1270; 1975, pp. 675, 679.)

40-808c Photostatic copies of records as primary evidence.

Photostatic copies of records, produced from microfilm and printout copies of computer records shall be received in any court of this State as primary evidence of the recitals contained therein.

(Acts 1972, pp. 1267, 1270.)

40-809c Certified copies.

The department may make certified copies under seal of any records or any preservation duplicates transferred or deposited in the Georgia State Archives, or the records center, or may make reproductions of such records.

Such certified copies or reproductions, when signed by the director of the department, shall have the same force and effect as if made by the agency from which the records were received. The department may establish and charge reasonable fees for such services.

(Acts 1972, pp. 1267, 1271.)

40-810c Title to records.

(a) Title to any record transferred to the Georgia State Archives as authorized by this Chapter shall be vested in the department. The department shall not destroy any record transferred to it by an agency without consulting with the proper official of the transferring agency prior to submitting a retention schedule requesting such destruction to the State Records Committee. Access to records of Constitutional Officers shall be at the discretion of the Constitutional Officer who created, received, or maintained the records, but no limitation on access to such records shall extend more than 25 years after creation of the records.

(b) Title to any record transferred to the records center shall remain in the agency transferring such records to the records center.

(Acts 1972, pp. 1267, 1271; 1973, pp. 691, 692; 1975, pp. 675, 679.)

40-811c Establishment of records management program county and municipal governments and school boards.

(a) County and municipal governments and school boards may:

(1) adopt and utilize State rules and regulations as a basis of establishing a records management program; or

(2) submit to the State Records Committee proposed retention schedules for their approval. Once approved these schedules have the same force and effect as if they were approved for an agency of State government.

(Acts 1978, H. B. No. 1638, Act No. 1207, eff. April 3, 1978.)

40-812c Confidential, classified or restricted records; restrictions on access; lifting of restrictions.

(a) This section applies only to those records (1) that are confidential, classified or restricted by Acts of the General Assembly, or may be declared to be confidential, classified or restricted by future Acts of the General Assembly, unless said future Acts specifically exempt these records from the provisions of this section; and (2) that have been, or are in the future, deposited in the Georgia State Archives or in other State-operated archival institutions because of their value for historical research;

(b) All restrictions on access to records covered by this section are hereby lifted and removed 75 years after the creation of the record;

(c) Restrictions on access to records covered by this section may be lifted and removed as early as 20 years after the creation of the record on unanimous approval in writing of the State Records Committee;

(d) Applications requesting that the State Records Committee review and consider lifting such restrictions may be made either by the director of the department or by the head of the agency that transferred the record to the Archives.

(Acts 1975, pp. 675, 680.)

40-813c Same; use for research purposes.

(a) Records that are by law confidential, classified or restricted may be used for research purposes by private researchers providing that (1) the researcher is qualified to perform such research; (2) the research topic is designed to produce a study that would be of potential benefit to the State or its citizens; and (3) the researcher will agree in writing to protect the confidentiality of the information contained in the records. When the purpose of the confidentiality is to protect the rights of privacy of any person or persons who are named in the records the researcher must agree, in either his notes or in his finished study or in any manner, not to refer to said person in such a way that they can be identified. When the purpose of the confidentiality is to protect other information the researcher must agree not to divulge that information;

(b) The head of the agency that created the records (or his designee) shall determine whether or not the researcher and his research topic meets the qualifications set forth in subsection (a) above prior to accepting the signed agreement from the researcher and granting permission to use the confidential records;

(c) The use of such confidential records for research shall be considered a privilege and the agreement signed by the researcher shall be binding on him. Researchers who violate the confidentiality of these records shall be punishable in the same manner as would government employees or officials found guilty of this offense.

(Acts 1975, pp. 675, 680.)

40-814c Construction of certain laws and rules and regulations.

(a) All laws or parts of laws prescribing how long or in what form records shall be kept are hereby repealed;

(b) Whenever laws or rules and regulations prescribed where a record series must be kept, the custodian of such records shall be considered in compliance with said laws, rules and regulations if he transfers said records to a local holding area, a records center, or the Georgia State Archives when he does so in accordance with an approved retention schedule.

(Acts 1975, pp. 675, 681.)

40-2701 Right of public to inspect records.

All State, county and municipal records, except those, which by order of a court of this State or by law, are prohibited from being open to inspection by the general public, shall be open for a personal inspection of any citizen of Georgia at a reasonable time and place, and those in charge of such records shall not refuse this privilege to any citizen.

(Acts 1959, p. 88.)

40-2702 Supervision of persons photographic records; charge for services of deputy.

In all cases where a member of the public interested has a right to inspect or take extracts or make copies from any public records, instruments or documents, any such person shall hereafter have the right of access to said records, documents or instruments for the purpose of making photographs of the same while in the possession, custody and control of the lawful custodian thereof, or his authorized deputy. Such work shall be done under the supervision of the lawful custodian of the said records, who shall have the right to adopt and enforce reasonable rules governing the said work. Said work shall be done in the room where the said records, documents or instruments are by law kept. While the said work hereinbefore mentioned is in progress, the lawful custodian of said records may charge the person desiring to make the said photographs for the services of a deputy of the lawful custodian of said records, documents or instruments to supervise the same, or for the services of the said lawful custodian of the same in so doing at a rate of compensation to be agreed upon by the person desiring to make the said photographs and the custodian of the said records, documents or instruments.

(Acts 1959, pp. 88, 89.)

40-2703 Exception of certain records.

The provisions of this Chapter shall not be applicable to records that are specifically required by the Federal Government to be kept confidential or to medical records and similar files, the disclosure of which would be an invasion of personal privacy. All records of hospital Authorities other than the foregoing shall be subject to to the provisions of this Chapter. All State officers and employees shall have a privilege to refuse to disclose the identity of any person who has furnished medical or other similar information which has or will become incorporated into any medical or public health investigation, study or report of the Department of Human Resources. The identity of such informant shall not be admissible in evidence in any court of the State unless the said court finds that the identity of the informant already has been otherwise disclosed.

(Acts 1967, p. 455; 1970, p. 163.)

Hawaii Revised Statutes
Volume 2, Chapter 92

§92–50 Definitions. As used in this part, "public record" means any written or printed report, book or paper, map or plan of the State or of a county and their respective subdivisions and boards, which is the property thereof, and in or on which an entry has been made or is required to be made by law, or which any public officer or employee has received or is required to receive for filing, but shall not include records which invade the right of privacy of an individual. [L 1975, c 166, pt of §2]

§92–51 Public records; available for inspection; cost of copies. All public records shall be available for inspection by any person during established office hours unless public inspection of such records is in violation of any other state or federal law, provided that except where such records are open under any rule of court, the attorney general and the responsible attorneys of the various counties may determine which records in their offices may be withheld from public inspection when such records pertain to the preparation of the prosecution or defense of any action or proceeding, prior to its commencement, to which the State or county is or may be a party, or when such records do not relate to a matter in violation of law and are deemed necessary for the protection of a character or reputation of any person.

Certified copies of extracts from public records shall be given by the officer having the same in custody to any person demanding the same and paying or tendering twenty cents per folio of one hundred words for such copies or extracts. [L 1975, c 166, pt of §2]

§92–52 Denial of inspection; application to circuit courts. Any person aggrieved by the denial by the officer having the custody of any public record of the right to inspect the record or to obtain copies of extracts thereof may apply to the circuit court of the circuit wherein the public record is found for an order directing the officer to permit the inspection of or to furnish copies of extracts of the public records. The court shall grant the order after hearing upon a finding that the denial was not for just and proper cause. [L 1975, c 166, pt of §2]

Idaho General Laws, Annotated
1976 Cumulative Pocket Supplement
Volumes 2, 10

9-302. Furnishing of certified copy—Duty of officer having custody—Copy as evidence—Fees.—Every public officer having the custody of a public writing, which a citizen has a right to inspect, is bound to give him, on demand, a certified copy of it, on payment of the legal fees therefor, and such copy is admissible as evidence in like cases and with like effect as the original writing. When the amount of the legal fees for such certified copies is not otherwise specified, the officer furnishing the copies shall demand and receive therefor twenty cents for each folio of one hundred words: provided, however, that when the copies are furnished said public officer, and that proofreading and correction alone is necessary, said officer shall, whether the amount of legal fees for certified copies is specified herein or elsewhere, charge five cents per folio, which shall be in lieu of all other charges, including certificate. [C. C. P. 1881, § 903; R. S., R. C., & C. L., § 5966; C. S., § 7941; am. 1923, ch. 64, § 1, p. 71; am. 1925, ch. 124, § 1, p. 170; I. C. A., § 16-302.]

9-301. Public writings—Right to inspect and take copy. Every citizen has a right to inspect and take a copy of any public writing of this state, except as otherwise expressly provided by statute. [C.C.P. 1881, § 902; R.S., R.C., & C.L., § 5965; C.S., § 7940; I.C.A., § 16-301.]

Volume 10

59-1009. Official records open to inspection. The public records and other matters in the office of any officer are, at all times during office hours, open to the inspection of any citizen of this state. [R.S., § 454; am. R.C., § 341; reen. C.L., § 341; C.S., § 479; I.C.A., § 57-1009.]

59-1011. Funishing account books—Examination by citizens. It shall be the duty of the state and county officers respectively charged with furnishing books and stationery for public use, to furnish suitable books for the purpose to such officers; and such books shall be subject to examination by any citizen at any reasonable time, and such citizen shall be entitled to take memoranda from the same without charges being imposed: provided, if any person or persons desire certified copies of any such account, the officer or person in charge of said books shall be entitled to demand and receive fees for the same, as for copies of other public records in his control. [1901, p. 208, § 2; reen. R.C. & C.L., § 343; C.S., § 481; I.C.A., § 57-1011.]

Illinois, Smith-Hurd Annotated Statutes
1979 Cumulative Annual Pocket Part
Chapters 13, 116

§ 9. Custody of records—Public inspection.

The county clerk shall have the care and custody of all the records, books and papers appertaining to and filed or deposited in their respective offices, and the same, except as otherwise provided in the "Vital Statistics Act," enacted by the Seventy-Second General Assembly, shall be open to the inspection of all persons without reward. As amended 1961, Aug. 8, Laws 1961, p. 2917, § 1.

Chapter 116

§ 43.5 Definitions.

For the purposes of this Act:

"Secretary" means Secretary of State.

"Record" or "records" means all books, papers, maps, photographs, or other official documentary materials, regardless of physical form or characteristics, made, produced, executed or received by any agency in the State in pursuance of state law or in connection with the transaction of public business and preserved or appropriate for preservation by that agency or its successor as evidence of the organization, function, policies, decisions, procedures, operations, or other activities of the State or of the State Government, or because of the informational data contained therein. Library and museum material made or acquired and preserved solely for reference or exhibition purposes, extra copies of documents preserved only for convenience of reference, and stocks of publications and of processed documents are not included within the definition of records as used in this Act.

"Agency" means all parts, boards, and commissions of the executive branch of the State government including but not limited to all departments established by the "Civil Administrative Code of Illinois," as heretofore or hereafter amended.

"Public Officer" or "public officers" means all officers of the executive branch of the State government, all officers created by the "Civil Administrative Code of Illinois," as heretofore or hereafter amended, and all other officers and heads, presidents, or chairmen of boards, commissions, and agencies of the State government.

"Commission" means the State Records Commission.

"Archivist" means the Secretary of State. 1957, July 6, Laws 1957, p. 1687, § 2.

§ 43.6 Reports and records of obligation, receipt and use of public funds as public records.

Reports and records of the obligation, receipt and use of public funds of the State are public records available for inspection by the public. These records shall be kept at the official place of business of the State or at a designated place of business of the State. These records shall be available for public inspection during regular office hours except when in immediate use by persons exercising official duties which require the use of those records. The person in charge of such records may require a notice in writing to be submitted 24 hours prior to inspection and may require that such notice specify which records are to be inspected. Nothing in this section shall require the State to invade or assist in the invasion of any person's right to privacy. Nothing in this Section shall be construed to limit any right given by statute or rule of law with respect to the inspection of other types of records.

Warrants and vouchers in the keeping of the State Comptroller may be destroyed by him as authorized in "An Act in relation to the reproduction and destruction of records kept by the Comptroller," approved August 1, 1949, as now or hereafter amended.

1957, July 6, Laws 1957, p. 1687, § 3. Amended by P.A. 77–1870, § 1, eff. Oct. 1, 972; P.A. 79–139, § 2, eff. Oct. 1, 1975.

§ 43.7 Right of access by public—Reproductions—Fees.

Any person shall have the right of access to any public records of the expenditure or receipt of public funds as defined in Section 3[1] for the purpose of obtaining copies of the same or of making photographs of the same while in the possession, custody and control of the lawful custodian thereof, or his authorized deputy. The photographing shall be done under the supervision of the lawful custodian of said records, who has the right to adopt and enforce reasonable rules governing such work. The work of photographing shall, when possible, be done in the room where the records, documents or instruments are kept. However, if in the judgment of the lawful custodian of the records, documents or instruments, it would be impossible or impracticable to perform the work in the room in which the records, documents or instruments are kept, the work shall be done in some other room or place as nearly adjacent as possible to the room where kept. Where the providing of a separate room or place is necessary, the expense of providing for the same shall be borne by the person or persons desiring to photograph the records, documents or instruments. The lawful custodian of the records, documents or instruments may charge the same fee for the services rendered by him or his assistant in supervising the photographing as may be charged for furnishing a certified copy or copies of the said record, document or instrument. In the event that the lawful custodian of said records shall deem it advisable in his judgment to furnish photographs of such public records, instruments or documents in lieu of allowing the same to be photographed, then in such event he may furnish photographs of such records and charge a fee of 35¢ per page when the page to be photographed does not exceed legal size and $1.00 per page when the page to be photographed exceeds legal size and where the fees and charges therefor are not otherwise fixed by law. 1957, July 6, Laws 1957, p. 1687, § 4.

Indiana Statutes, Annotated
1977 Cumulative Pocket Supplement
Title 5

Public Proceedings

5-14-1-1 [57-601]. Construction of act. Pursuant to the fundamental philosophy of the American constitutional form of representative government which holds to the principal [principle] that government is the servant of the people, and not the master of them, it is hereby declared to be the public policy of the state of Indiana that all of the citizens of this state are, unless otherwise expressly provided by law, at all times entitled to full and complete information regarding the affairs of government and the official acts of those whom the people select to represent them as public officials and employees.

To that end, the provisions of this act [5-14-1-1—5-14-1-6] shall be liberally construed with the view of carrying out the above declaration of policy. [Acts 1953, ch. 115, § 1, p. 427.]

5-14-1-2 [57-602]. Definitions. As used in this chapter [5-14-1-1—5-14-1-6]:

The term "public records" shall mean any writing in any form necessary, under or required, or directed to be made by any statute or by any rule or regulation of any administrative body or agency of the state or any of its political subdivisions. [Acts 1953, ch. 115, § 2, p. 427; 1977, P.L. 57, § 2, p. —.]

(2) The term "public proceedings" shall mean the transaction of governmental functions affecting any or all of the citizens of the state by any administrative body or agency of the state, or any of its political subdivisions when such administrative body or agency is convened for the purpose of transacting the governmental function with which it is charged under any statute or under any rule or regulation of such administrative body or agency. [Acts 1953, ch. 115, § 2, p. 427.]

5-14-1-3 [57-603]. Right of inspection of public records. Except as may now or hereafter be otherwise specifically provided by law, every citizen of this state shall, during the regular business hours of all administrative bodies or agencies of the state, or any political subdivision thereof, have the right to inspect the public records of such administrative bodies or agencies, and to make memoranda abstracts from the records so inspected. [Acts 1953, ch. 115, § 3, p. 427.]

5-14-1-5 [57-605]. Exceptions to chapter—Confidential records. Nothing in this chapter [5-14-1-1—5-14-1-6] contained shall be construed to modify or repeal any existing law with regard to public records which, by law, are declared to be confidential. [Acts 1953, ch. 115, § 5, p. 427; 1977, P.L. 57, § 3, p. —.]

5-14-1-6 [57-606]. Violation of act by official—Separability. (a) Any public official of the state, or of any political subdivision thereof, who denies to any citizen the rights guaranteed to such citizen under the provisions of section 3 [5-14-1-3] of this chapter is guilty of an infraction.

(b) Any citizen who has been denied the rights guaranteed under section 3 of this chapter, may bring a complaint to compel inspection. The citizen need not allege or prove any special damage different from that suffered by the public at large.

(c) Each section, subsection, sentence, clause and phrase of this chapter [5-14-1-1—5-14-1-6] is declared to be an independent section, subsection, sentence, clause or phrase, and the finding or holding of any section, subsection, sentence, clause or phrase to be unconstitutional, void or ineffective for any cause shall not affect any other section, subsection, sentence or part thereof. [Acts 1953, ch. 115, § 6, p. 427; 1971, P.L. 51, § 1, p. 264; 1977, P.L. 57, § 4, p. —.]

Iowa Code, Annotated
1978-1979 Cumulative Annual Pocket Part
Volume 4A

68A.1 Public records defined.

Wherever used in this chapter, "public records" includes all records and documents of or belonging to this state or any county, city, town, township, school corporation, political subdivision, or tax-supported district in this state, or any branch, department, board, bureau, commission, council, or committee of any of the foregoing.

Acts 1967 (62 G.A.) ch. 106, § 1, eff. Aug. 9, 1967.

68A.2 Citizen's right to examine.

Every citizen of Iowa shall have the right to examine all public records and to copy such records, and the news media may publish such records, unless some other provision of the Code expressly limits such right or requires such records to be kept secret or confidential. The right to copy records shall include the right to make photographs or photographic copies while the records are in the possession of the lawful custodian of the records. All rights under this section are in addition to the right to obtain certified copies of records under section 622.46.

Acts 1967 (62 G.A.) ch. 106, § 2, eff. Aug. 9, 1967.

68A.3 Supervision.

Such examination and copying shall be done under the supervision of the lawful custodian of the records or his authorized deputy. The lawful custodian may adopt and enforce reasonable rules regarding such work and the protection of the records against damage or disorganization. The lawful custodian shall provide a suitable place for such work, but if it is impracticable to do such work in the office of the lawful custodian, the person desiring to examine or copy shall pay any necessary expenses of providing a place for such work. All expenses of such work shall be paid by the person desiring to examine or copy. The lawful custodian may charge a reasonable fee for the services of the lawful custodian or his authorized deputy in supervising the records during such work. If copy equipment is available at the office of the lawful custodian of any public records, the lawful custodian shall provide any person a reasonable number of copies of any public record in the custody of the office upon the payment of a fee. The fee for the copying service as determined by the lawful custodian shall not exceed the cost of providing the service.

Amended by Acts 1976 (66 G.A.) ch. 1079, § 1.

68A.4 Hours when available.

The rights of citizens under this chapter may be exercised at any time during the customary office hours of the lawful custodian of the records. However, if the lawful custodian does not have customary office hours of at least thirty hours per week, such right may be exercised at any time from nine o'clock a.m. to noon and from one o'clock p.m. to four o'clock p.m. Monday through Friday, excluding legal holidays, unless the citizen exercising such right and the lawful custodian agree on a different time.

Acts 1967 (62 G.A.) ch. 106, § 4, eff. Aug. 9, 1967.

68A.5 Enforcement of rights.

The provisions of this chapter and all rights of citizens under this chapter may be enforced by mandamus or injunction, whether or not any other remedy is also available. In the alternative, rights under this chapter also may be enforced by an action for judicial review according to the provisions of the Iowa administrative procedure Act, if the records involved are records of an "agency" as defined in that Act.

Amended by Acts 1974 (65 G.A.) ch. 1090, § 210, eff. July 1, 1975.

1974 Amendment: Re-wrote the section.

68A.6 Penalty.

It shall be unlawful for any person to deny or refuse any citizen of Iowa any right under this chapter, or to cause any such right to be denied or refused. Any person knowingly violating or attempting to violate any provision of this chapter where no other penalty is provided shall be guilty of a simple misdemeanor.

Amended by Acts 1976 (66 G.A.) ch. 1245 (ch. 4), § 28, eff. Jan. 1, 1978.

1976 Amendment. Added "simple" misdemeanor and deleted a specified penalty.

68A.7 Confidential records.

The following public records shall be kept confidential, unless otherwise ordered by a court, by the lawful custodian of the records, or by another person duly authorized to release information:

1. Personal information in records regarding a student, prospective student, or former student of the school corporation or educational institution maintaining such records.

2. Hospital records and medical records of the condition, diagnosis, care, or treatment of a patient or former patient, including outpatient.

3. Trade secrets which are recognized and protected as such by law.

4. Records which represent and constitute the work product of an attorney, which are related to litigation or claim made by or against a public body.

5. Peace officers investigative reports, except where disclosure is authorized elsewhere in this Code.

6. Reports to governmental agencies which, if released, would give advantage to competitors and serve no public purpose.

7. Appraisals or appraisal information concerning the purchase of real or personal property for public purposes, prior to public announcement of a project.

8. Iowa development commission information on an industrial prospect with which the commission is currently negotiating.

9. Criminal identification files of law enforcement agencies. However, records of current and prior arrests shall be public records.

10. Personal information in confidential personnel records of the military department of the state.

11. Personal information in confidential personnel records of public bodies including but not limited to cities, towns, boards of supervisors and school districts.

Acts 1967 (62 G.A.) ch. 106, § 7, eff. Aug. 9, 1967.

68A.8 Injunction to restrain examination.

In accordance with the rules of civil procedure the district court may grant an injunction restraining the examination (including copying) of a specific public record, if the petition supported by affidavit shows and if the court finds that such examination would clearly not be in the public interest and would substantially and irreparably injure any person or persons. The district court shall take into account the policy of this chapter that free and open examination of public records is generally in the public interest, even though such examination may cause inconvenience or embarrassment to public officials or others. Such injunction shall be subject to the rules of civil procedure except that the court in its discretion may waive bond. Reasonable delay by any person in permitting the examination of a record in order to seek an injunction under this section is not a violation of this chapter, if such person believes in good faith that he is entitled to an injunction restraining the examination of such record.

Acts 1967 (62 G.A.) ch. 106, § 8, eff. Aug. 9, 1967.

68A.9 Denial of federal funds.

If it is determined that any provision of this chapter would cause the denial of funds, services or essential information from the United States government which would otherwise definitely be available to an agency of this state, such provision shall be suspended as to such agency, but only to the extent necessary to prevent denial of such funds, services, or essential information. Acts 1967 (62 G.A.) ch. 106, § 11, eff. Aug. 9, 1967.

Kansas Statutes, Annotated
1977 Cumulative Pocket Part Supplement
Volumes 3A, 6A

45-201. Official public records open to inspection; exceptions; "official public records" defined. (a) All official public records of the state, counties, municipalities, townships, school districts, commissions, agencies and legislative bodies, which records by law are required to be kept and maintained, except those of the district court concerning proceedings pursuant to the juvenile code which shall be open unless specifically closed by the judge or by law, adoption records, records of the birth of illegitimate children, and records specifically closed by law or by directive authorized by law, shall at all times be open for a personal inspection by any citizen, and those in charge of such records shall not refuse this privilege to any citizen.

(b) For the purposes of this act and the act of which this act is amendatory, the term "official public records" shall not be deemed to apply to personally identifiable records, files, and data which are described in K.S.A. 1976 Supp.

72-6214 and the accessibility and availability of which is limited by the terms of said section.

History: K.S.A. 45-201; L. 1976, ch. 228, § 2; L. 1976, ch. 151, § 6; Jan. 10, 1977.

45-202. Same; photographing records, when; rules. In all cases where the public or any person interested has a right to inspect or take extracts or make copies from any such public records, instruments or documents, any such person shall have the right of access to said records, documents or instruments for the purpose of making photographs of the same while in the possession, custody and control of the lawful custodian thereof, or his authorized deputy. Such work shall be done under the supervision of the lawful custodian of the said records who shall have the right to adopt and enforce reasonable rules governing the said work. Said work shall, where possible, be done in the room where the said records, documents or instruments are by law kept, but if the same in the judgment of the lawful custodian of the said records, documents or instruments be impossible or impracticable, then the said work shall be done in such other room or place as nearly adjacent as may be available. [L. 1957, ch. 455, § 2; June 29.]

45-203. Same; penalties for violations. Any official who shall violate the provisions of this act shall be subject to removal from office and in addition shall be deemed guilty of a misdemeanor. [L. 1957, ch. 455, § 3; June 29.]

Volume 6A

(Relating to motor fuel tax investigations; references are to Director of Taxation)

79-3420. Examination of books, records, property and equipment; secrecy required; exceptions. The director, or any deputy or agent appointed in writing by him, is hereby authorized to examine the books, papers, records, storage tanks, tank wagons, trucks, and any other equipment of any distributor, dealer, carrier, or any other person, pertaining to the use, storage, transportation, or sale and delivery of liquid fuels or motor fuels, to verify the accuracy of any report, statement, or payment made under the provisions of this act, or to ascertain whether or not all reports and tax payments required by this act have been made; but any information gained by the director, his deputies or agents, as the result of the reports, investigations, and verifications herein required to be made, shall be confidential, and shall not be divulged by any person except as herein provided. Every distributor, dealer, transporter, and consumer, and every person handling or possessing any liquid fuels or motor-vehicle fuels shall give said director, or his deputy or agent appointed in writing, full and free access during reasonable business hours to all the papers, records, and property hereinbefore mentioned, with full opportunity to examine the same: *Provided, however,* That the director may publish the gallons received by each licensed motor-vehicle fuel distributor and the deductions claimed by such distributor and may make available or furnish information to the taxing officials of any other state or of the federal government, or the director of property valuation, in the manner as provided in K.S.A. 74-2424 and acts amendatory thereof. [K.S.A. 79-3420; L. 1971, ch. 317, § 1; July 1.]

(Relating to LP-gas taxes)

79-3499. Records, invoices, bills of lading; preservation; examination of records and equipment; secrecy required. Each LP-gas user or LP-gas dealer shall maintain and keep for a period of three (3) years, such record or records of LP-gas purchased, sold or placed into the fuel supply tank or tanks of motor vehicles within this state by such LP-gas user or LP-gas dealer, together with invoices, bills of lading and other pertinent records and papers as may be required by the director for the reasonable administration of the act.

Every person who sells LP-gas to any person must, at the time of such sale and delivery, make and deliver to the purchaser, consignee or an agent thereof, an invoice covering each such delivery showing the date, the name and address of the seller, the number of gallons of LP-gas, the place of delivery, the name and address of the buyer, and such other information as the director may require. Each such invoice must be identified by consecutive numbers printed thereon, and each seller or consignor must be able to account for each numbered delivery invoice and each copy thereof.

Every person who purchases, accepts or receives any LP-gas must, at the time of delivery or acceptance of such LP-gas demand and receive an invoice as required by this section covering such LP-gas. All invoices required by this section must be furnished by the respective sellers and persons distributing such fuel.

The director and/or secretary of revenue, or any deputy or agent appointed in writing by either of them, is hereby authorized to examine the books, papers, records, storage tanks, and any other equipment of any LP-gas user or LP-gas dealer, or any other person, pertaining to the use, storage, transportation, or sale and delivery of LP-gas, to verify the accuracy of any report, statement, or payment made under the provisions of this act, or to ascertain whether or not all reports and tax payments required by this act have been made; but any information gained by the director, the secretary of revenue, their deputies or agents, as the result of the reports, investigation, and verifications herein required to be made, shall be confidential, and shall not be divulged by any person, except as shall be necessary in the administration and enforcement of this act or any rules and regulations promulgated by the director, pursuant thereto, or as provided in this act. Every LP-gas user or LP-gas dealer, and every person handling or possessing any such LP-gas shall give said director, the secretary of revenue, or their deputies or agents appointed in writing, full and free access during reasonable business hours to all the papers, records, and property hereinbefore mentioned, with full opportunity to examine the same. [K.S.A. 79-3499; L. 1973, ch. 402, § 16; July 1.]

Kentucky Revised Statutes
1978 Cumulative Supplement
Volume 3

Open Records

61.870. Definitions. As used in KRS 61.872 to 61.884:

(1) "Public agency" means every state or local officer, state department, division, bureau, board, commission and authority; every legislative board, commission, committee and officer; every county and city governing body, council, school district board, special district board, municipal corporation, court or judicial agency, and any board, department, commission, committee, subcommittee, ad hoc committee, council or agency thereof; and any other body which is created by state or local authority in any branch of government or which derives at least twenty-five per cent (25%) of its funds from state or local authority.

(2) "Public records" means all books, papers, maps, photographs, cards, tapes, discs, recordings or other documentary materials regardless of physical form or characteristics, which are prepared, owned, used, in the possession of or retained by a public agency. "Public record" shall not include any records owned by a private person or corporation that are not related to functions, activities, programs or operations funded by state or local authority.

(3) "Official custodian" means the chief administrative officer or any other officer or employe of a public agency who is responsible for the maintenance, care and keeping of public records, regardless of whether such records are in his actual personal custody and control.

(4) "Custodian" means the official custodian or any authorized person having personal custody and control of public records. (Enact. Acts 1976, ch. 273, § 1.)

61.872. Right to inspection—Limitation. (1) All public records shall be open for inspection by any person, except as otherwise provided by KRS 61.870 to 61.884 and suitable facilities shall be made available by each public agency for the exercise of this right. No person shall remove original copies of public records from the offices of any public agency without the written permission of the official custodian of the record.

(2) Any person shall have the right to inspect public records during the regular office hours of the public agency. The official custodian may require written application describing the records to be inspected.

(3) If the person to whom the application is directed does not have custody or control of the public record requested, such person shall so notify the applicant and shall furnish the name and location of the custodian of the public record, if such facts are known to him.

(4) If the public record is in active use, in storage or not otherwise available, the official custodian shall immediately so notify the applicant and shall designate a place, time and date, for inspection of the public records, not to exceed three (3) days from receipt of the application, unless a detailed explanation of the cause is given for further delay and the place, time and earliest date on which the public record will be available for inspection.

(5) If the application places an unreasonable burden in producing voluminous public records or if the custodian has reason to believe that repeated requests are intended to disrupt other essential functions of the public agency, the official custodian may refuse to permit inspection of the public records. However, refusal under this section must be sustained by clear and convincing evidence. (Enact. Acts 1976, ch. 273, § 2.)

61.874. Abstracts, memoranda, copies—Agency may prescribe fee.

(1) Upon inspection, the applicant shall have the right to make abstracts of the public records and memoranda thereof, and to obtain copies of all written public records. When copies are requested, the custodian may require a written request and advance payment of the prescribed fee. If the applicant desires copies of public records other than written records, the custodian of such records shall permit the applicant to duplicate such records, however, the custodian may insure that such duplication will not damage or alter the records.

(2) The public agency may prescribe a reasonable fee for making copies of public records which shall not exceed the actual cost thereof not including the cost of staff required. (Enact. Acts 1976, ch. 273, § 3.)

61.876. Agency to adopt rules and regulations. (1) Each public agency shall adopt rules and regulations in conformity with the provisions of KRS 61.870 to 61.884 to provide full access to public records, to protect public records from damage and disorganization, to prevent excessive disruption of its essential functions, to provide assistance and information upon request and to insure efficient and timely action in response to application for inspection, and such rules and regulations shall include, but shall not be limited to:

(a) The principal office of the public agency and its regular office hours;

(b) The title and address of the official custodian of the public agency's records;

(c) The fees, to the extent authorized by KRS 61.874 or other statute, charged for copies;

(d) The procedures to be followed in requesting public records.

(2) Each public agency shall display a copy of its rules and regulations pertaining to public records in a prominent location accessible to the public.

(3) The executive department for finance and administration may promulgate uniform rules and regulations for all state administrative agencies. (Enact. Acts 1976, ch. 273, § 4.)

61.878. Right of inspection only on order of court. (1) The following public records are excluded from the application of KRS 61.870 to 61.884 and shall be subject to inspection only upon order of a court of competent jurisdiction:

(a) Public records containing information of a personal nature where the public disclosure thereof would constitute a clearly unwarranted invasion of personal privacy.

(b) Records confidentially disclosed to an agency and compiled and maintained for scientific research, in conjunction with an application for a loan, the regulation of commercial enterprise, including mineral exploration records, unpatented, secret commercially valuable plans, appliances, formulae, or processes, which are used for the making, preparing, compounding, treating, or processing of articles or materials which are trade commodities obtained from a person and which are generally recognized as confidential, or for the grant or review of a license to do business and if openly disclosed would permit an unfair advantage to competitors of the subject enterprise. This exemption shall not, however apply to records the disclosure or publication of which is directed by other statute.

(c) Public records pertaining to a prospective location of a business or industry where no previous public disclosure has been made of the business' or industry's interest in locating in, relocating within or expanding within the commonwealth. Provided, however, That this exemption shall not include those records pertaining to application to agencies for permits or licenses necessary to do business or to expand business operations within the state, except as provided in paragraph (b) above.

(d) The contents of real estate appraisals, engineering or feasibility estimates and evaluations made by or for a public agency relative to acquisition of property, until such time as all of the property has been acquired; Provided, however, the law of eminent domain shall not be affected by this provision.

(e) Test questions, scoring keys and other examination data used to administer a licensing examination, examination for employment or academic examination before the exam is given or if it is to be given again.

(f) Records of law enforcement agencies or agencies involved in administrative adjudication that were compiled in the process of detecting and investigating statutory or regulatory violations if the disclosure of the information would harm the agency by revealing the identity of informants not otherwise known or by premature release of information to be used in a prospective law enforcement action or administrative adjudication. Unless exempted by other provisions of KRS 61.870 to 61.884, public records exempted under this provision shall be open after enforcement action is completed or a decision is made to take no action. Provided, however that the exemptions provided by this subsection shall not be used by the custodian of the records to delay or impede the exercise of rights granted by KRS 61.870 to 61.884.

(g) Preliminary drafts, notes, correspondence with private individuals, other than correspondence which is intended to give notice of final action of a public agency;

(h) Preliminary recommendations, and preliminary memoranda in which opinions are expressed or policies formulated or recommended;

(i) All public records or information the disclosure of which is prohibited by federal law or regulation;

(j) Public records or information the disclosure of which is prohibited or restricted or otherwise made confidential by enactment of the general assembly.

(2) No exemption in this section shall be construed to prohibit disclosure of statistical information not descriptive of any readily identifiable person.

(3) If any public record contains material which is not excepted under this section, the public agency shall separate the excepted and make the nonexcepted material available for examination.

(4) The provisions of this section shall in no way prohibit or limit the exchange of public records or the sharing of information between public agencies when the exchange is serving a legitimate governmental need or is necessary in the performance of a legitimate government function. (Enact. Acts 1976, ch. 273, § 5.)

61.880. Denial of inspection—Role of attorney general. (1) Each public agency, upon any request for records made under KRS 61.870 to 61.884, shall determine within three (3) days (excepting Saturdays, Sundays, and legal holidays) after the receipt of any such request whether to comply with the request and shall notify in writing the person making the request, within the three (3) day period, of its decision. An agency response denying, in whole or in part, inspection of any record shall include a statement of the specific exception authorizing the withholding of the record and a brief explanation of how the exception applies to the record withheld. The response shall be issued by the official custodian or under his authority, and it shall constitute final agency action.

(2) A copy of the written response denying inspection of a public record shall be forwarded immediately by the agency to the attorney general of the commonwealth of Kentucky. If requested by the person seeking inspection, the attorney general shall review the denial and issue within ten (10) days (excepting Saturdays, Sundays and legal holidays) a written opinion to the agency concerned, stating whether the agency acted consistent with provisions of KRS 61.870 to 61.884. A copy of the opinion shall also be sent by the attorney general to the person who requested the record in question. The burden of proof in sustaining the action shall rest with the agency and the attorney general may request additional documentation from the agency for substantiation. The attorney general may also request a copy of the records involved but they shall not be disclosed.

(3) Each agency shall notify the attorney general of any actions filed against that agency in circuit court regarding the enforcement of KRS 61.870 to 61.884.

(4) In the event a person feels the intent of KRS 61.870 to 61.884 is being subverted by an agency short of denial of inspection, including but not limited to the imposition of excessive fees or the misdirection of the applicant, the person may complain in writing to the attorney general and the complaint shall be subject to the same adjudicatory process as if the record had been denied.

(5) If the attorney general upholds, in whole or in part, the request for inspection, the public agency involved may institute proceedings within thirty (30) days for injunctive or declaratory relief in the circuit court of the district where the public record is maintained. If the attorney general disallows the request or if the public agency continues to withhold the record notwithstanding the opinion of the attorney general, the person seeking disclosure may institute such proceedings. (Enact. Acts 1976, ch. 273, § 6.)

61.882. Jurisdiction of circuit court in action seeking right of inspection— Burden of proof—Costs—Attorney fees. (1) The circuit courts of this state shall have jurisdiction to enforce the purposes of KRS 61.870 to 61.884, by injunction or other appropriate order on application of any citizen of this state.

(2) In order for the circuit courts of this state to exercise their jurisdiction to enforce the purposes of KRS 61.870 to 61.884, it shall not be necessary to have forwarded any request for the documents to the attorney general pursuant to KRS 61.880, or for the attorney general to have acted in any manner upon a request for his opinion.

(3) In any such action, the court shall determine the matter de novo and the burden of proof shall be on the public agency to sustain its action. The

court on its own motion, or on motion of either of the parties, may view the records in controversy in camera before reaching a decision. Any noncompliance with the order of the court may be punished as contempt of court.

(4) Courts shall take into consideration the basic policy of KRS 61.570 to 61.884 that free and open examination of public records is in the public interest and the exceptions provided for by KRS 61.870 to 61.884 or otherwise provided for by law shall be strictly construed, even though such examination may cause inconvenience or embarrassment to public officials or others. Except as otherwise provided by law or rule of court, proceedings arising under this section take precedent on the docket over all other causes and shall be assigned for hearing and trial at the earliest practicable date.

(5) Any person who prevails against an agency in any action in the courts seeking the right to inspect and copy any public record may, upon a finding that the records were wilfully withheld in violation of KRS 61.870 to 61.884, be awarded all costs, including reasonable attorney fees, incurred in connection with such legal action. If such person prevails in part, the court may in its discretion award him costs or an appropriate portion thereof. In addition, it shall be within the discretion of the court to award such person an amount not to exceed twenty-five dollars ($25.00) for each day that he was denied the right to inspect or copy said public record. The costs or award shall be paid by such person or agency as the court shall determine is responsible for the violation. (Enact. Acts 1976, ch. 273, § 7.)

61.884. Person's access to record relating to him. Any person shall have access to any public record relating to him or in which he is mentioned by name, upon presentation of appropriate identification, subject to the provisions of KRS 61.878. (Enact. Acts 1976, ch. 273, § 8.)

Louisiana Statutes, West's Annotated
1976 Cumulative Annual Pocket Part
Volume 24

§ 1. General definitions.

A. All records, writings, accounts, letters and letter books, maps, drawings, memoranda and papers, and all copies or duplicates thereof, and all photographs or other similar reproductions of the same, having been used, being in use, or prepared for use in the conduct, transaction or performance of any business, transaction, work, duty or function which was conducted, transacted or performed by or under the authority of the Constitution or the laws of this state, or the ordinances or mandates or orders of any municipal or parish government or officer or any board or commission or office established or set up by the Constitution or the laws of this state, or concerning or relating to the receipt or payment of any money received or paid by or under the authority of the Constitution or the laws of this state are public records, subject to the provisions of this Chapter except as hereinafter provided.

B. All electric logs produced from wells drilled in search of oil and gas which are filed with the Commissioner of Conservation shall remain confidential upon the request of the owner so filing for periods as follows:

For wells shallower than fifteen thousand feet a period of one year, plus one additional year when evidence is submitted to the Commissioner of Conservation that the owner of the log has a leasehold interest in the general area in which the well was drilled and the log produced; for wells fifteen thousand deep or deeper, a period of two years, plus two additional years when evidence is submitted to the Commissioner of Conservation that the owner of the log has such an interest in the general area in which the well was drilled and the log produced; provided however that no release will be required of logs produced from wells drilled in the off-shore area.

At the expiration of time in which any log or logs shall be held as confidential by the Commissioner of Conservation as provided for above said log or logs shall be placed in the open files of the Department of Conservation and any party or firm shall have the right to examine and/or reproduce, at their own expense, copies of said log or logs by photography or other means not injurious to said records.

Amended by Acts 1973, No. 135, § 1; Acts 1973, Ex.Sess., No. 4, § 1.

§ 2. Records involved in legislative investigations.

Subject to the proviso set forth in Sub-section B of R.S. 44:3, the provisions of this Chapter shall not apply to any records, writings, accounts, letters, letter books, photographs or copies thereof, in the custody or control of any attorney or counsel whose duties or functions are performed by or under the authority of the legislature and which concern or hold relation to any case, cause, charge or investigation being conducted by or through the legislature, until after the case, cause, charge or investigation has been finally disposed of.

After final disposition, the records, writings, accounts, letters, letter books, photographs or copies thereof, are public records and subject to the provisions of this Chapter.

§ 3. Records of prosecutive, investigative, and law enforcement agencies.

A. Nothing in this Chapter shall be construed to require disclosure of records, or the information contained therein, held by the offices of the attorney general, district attorneys, sheriffs, police departments, marshals, investigators, correctional agencies, investigative agencies, or intelligence agencies of the state, which records are:

(1) Records pertaining to pending criminal litigation or any criminal litiga-

tion which can be reasonably anticipated, until such litigation has been finally adjudicated or otherwise settled; or

(2) Records containing the identity of a confidential source of information or records which would tend to reveal the identity of a confidential source of information; or

(3) Records containing security procedures, investigative training information or aids, investigative techniques, investigative technical equipment or instructions on the use thereof, or internal security information.

B. All records, files, documents, and communications, and information contained therein, pertaining to or tending to impart the identity of any confidential source of information of any of the state officers, agencies, or departments mentioned in Paragraph A above, shall be privileged, and no court shall order the disclosure of same except on grounds of due process or constitutional law. No officer or employee of any of the officers, agencies, or departments mentioned in Paragraph A above shall disclose said privileged information or produce said privileged records, files, documents, or communications, except as a court order as provided above or with the written consent of the chief officer of the agency or department where he is employed or in which he holds office, and to this end said officer or employee shall be immune from contempt of court and from any and all other criminal penalties for compliance with this paragraph.

C. Whenever the same is necessary, judicial determination pertaining to compliance with this section or with constitutional law shall be made after a contradictory hearing as provided by law. An appeal by the state or an officer, agency, or department thereof shall be suspensive.

D. Nothing in this section shall be construed to prevent any and all prosecutive, investigative, and law enforcement agencies from having among themselves a free flow of information for the purpose of achieving coordinated and effective criminal justice.
Amended by Acts 1972, No. 448, § 1.

§ 4. Tax returns; records relating to old age assistance; dependent children; liquidation proceedings; banks; insurance ratings.

This Chapter shall not apply:

(1) To any tax returns.

(2) To the name of any person or any other information from the records, papers or files of the state or its political subdivisions or agencies, concerning persons applying for or receiving old age assistance, aid to the blind, or aid to dependent children.

(3) To any records, writings, accounts, letters, letter books, photographs or copies thereof, in the custody or control of any officer, employee, agent or agency of the state whose duties and functions are to investigate, examine, manage in whole or in part, or liquidate the business of any private person,

firm or corporation in this state, when the records, writings, accounts, letters, letter books, photographs or copies thereof, pertain to the business of the private person, firm or corporation, and are in their nature confidential.

(4) To any records, writings, accounts, letters, letter books, photographs or copies thereof in the custody or control of the state bank commissioner or agent, insofar as the records relate to solvent banks engaged in the banking business at the time of application for inspection.

(5) To any daily reports or endorsements filed by insurance companies doing business in this state with the Louisiana Casualty and Surety Rating Commission in accordance with the laws of this state.

(6) To any records, writings, accounts, letters, letter books, photographs or copies or memoranda thereof in the custody or control of the Supervisor of Public Funds, unless otherwise provided by law.

(7) To any records, writings, accounts, letters, letter books, photographs or copies or memoranda thereof, and any report or reports concerning the fitness of any person to receive, or continue to hold, a license to practice medicine or midwifery, in the custody or control of the Louisiana State Board of Medical Examiners. As amended Acts 1950, No. 155, § 1.

§ 5. Records in custody of governor.

This Chapter shall not apply to any of the books, records, writings, accounts, letters, letter books, photographs or copies thereof, ordinarily kept in the custody or control of the governor in the usual course of the duties and business of his office.

The provisions of this Section shall not prevent any person otherwise herein authorized so to do from examining and copying any books, records, papers, accounts or other documents pertaining to any money or moneys or any financial transactions in the control of or handled by or through the governor.

§ 8. Louisiana office building corporation, special provisions.

A. The private, nonprofit corporation known as the Louisiana Office Building Corporation, incorporated in the parish of East Baton Rouge on June 30, 1965, is hereby declared to be a quasi-public corporation. All papers, documents, contracts, legal agreements, correspondence, minutes of meetings and any other record whatsoever of said corporation are hereby declared to be matters of public record, and shall be open to inspection by state officials and employees, members of the Legislature and legislative staff personnel and the general public. The officers, members of the board of directors, agents and employees of said corporation are hereby authorized and directed to grant access to any record of said corporation upon request. The procedure for access to records under the authority of this Section shall be in keeping with the general provisions for access to public records contained in Chapter 1 of this Title.

B. All officers, directors and employees of the Louisiana Office Building Corporation who are also elected officials of the State of Louisiana shall be subject to the provisions of the code of ethics for state elected officials contained in R.S. 42:1141–1148 with reference to actions taken in their capacities as such officers, directors or employees of the said corporation. All other officers, directors and employees of the corporation shall be subject to the provisions of the code of ethics for state employees contained in R.S. 42.1111–1123 to the same extent as any state employees.

C. All books and records of the Louisiana Office Building Corporation shall be subject to audit and review by the Legislative Auditor to the same extent as all other state departments or agencies. Added Acts 1966, No. 429, §§ 1–3.

§ 9. Records of violations of municipal ordinances and of state statutes classified as misdemeaners.

A. Any person who has been arrested for a violation of a municipal ordinance or for violation of a state statute which is classified as a misdemeanor, except in cases of arrests for a first or second violation of any ordinance and/or statute making criminal the driving of a motor vehicle while under the influence of alcoholic beverages or narcotic drugs, as denounced by R.S. 14:98, and such proceedings having been disposed of by nolle prosequi, acquittal, or dismissal, may make a written motion to the clerk of court of the court of record to have the record of arrest destroyed, whether the arrest record is on file in the records of the clerk of court or on file with a police department, sheriff's office, or any other such official agency empowered to arrest.

B. Any criminal court of record in which there was a nolle prosequi, an acquittal, or dismissal of a crime set forth above shall at the time of discharge of a person from its control, enter an order annulling, cancelling, or rescinding the record of arrest, and disposition, and further ordering the destruction of the arrest record and order of disposition. Upon the entry of such an order the person against whom the arrest has been entered shall be restored to all civil rights lost or suspended by virtue of the arrest, unless otherwise provided in this section, and shall be treated in all respects as not having been arrested.

C. Notwithstanding any other provision of this section to the contrary, the provisions of this section shall in no case be construed to effect in any way whatsoever the practices and procedures in effect on July 29, 1970, relating to the administration of the implied consent law.

D. Whoever violates any provisions of this section shall be punished by a fine of not more than two hundred fifty dollars or by imprisonment of not more than ninety days, or both, if the conviction is for a first violation; second and subsequent violations shall be punished by a fine of not more than five hundred dollars or imprisonment of six months, or both.

Added by Acts 1970, No. 445, § 1. Amended by Acts 1972, No. 715, §§ 2, 3; Acts 1974, No. 531, § 1.

§ 10. Confidential nature of documents and proceedings of judiciary commission.

All documents filed with, and evidence and proceedings before the judiciary commission are confidential. The record filed by the commission with the supreme court and proceedings before the supreme court are not confidential. Added by Acts 1975, No. 55, § 1.

§ 31. Right to examine records.

The right to examine, copy, photograph and take memoranda of any and all public records, except as otherwise provided in this Chapter, may be exercised by:

(1) Any elector of the state.

(2) Any taxpayer who has paid any tax collected by or under the authority of the state if payment was made within one year from the date the taxpayer applies to exercise the right.

(3) Any duly authorized agent of paragraphs (1) and (2) above.

§ 32. Duty to permit examination; prevention of alteration; payment for overtime.

All persons having custody or control of any public record shall present it to any person who is authorized by the provisions of this Chapter and who applies during the regular office hours or working hours of the person to whom the application is made. The persons in custody or control of a public record shall make no inquiry of any person authorized by this Chapter who applies for a public record, beyond the purpose of establishing his authority; and shall not review nor examine or scrutinize any copy, photograph or memoranda in the possession of any authorized person; and shall give, grant and extend to the authorized persons all reasonable comfort and facility for the full exercise of the right granted by this Chapter; provided, that nothing herein contained shall prevent the lawful custodian of a record from maintaining such vigilance as is required to prevent alteration of any such record while same is being examined by a person under the authority of this section; and provided further, that notwithstanding the requirements contained hereinabove, examinations of records under the authority of this section must be conducted during regular office or working hours. If the chief of the office or the person next in authority among those present in the office shall authorize examination of records in other than regular office or working hours, the persons designated to represent the lawful custodian of such record during such examinations shall be entitled to reasonable compensation to be paid to them by the office, agency or department having lawful custody of such record, out of funds provided in advance by the person examining such record in other than regular office or working hours.

Amended by Acts 1968, No. 473, § 1.

§ 33. Availability of records.

If the public record applied for is immediately available, because of its not being in active use at the time of the application, the public record shall be immediately presented to the authorized person applying for it. If the public record applied for is not immediately available, because of its being in active use at the time of the application, then the chief of the office, or the person next in authority among those present, shall promptly certify this in writing to the applicant, and in his certificate shall fix a day and hour within three days for the exercise of the right granted by this Chapter.

The fact that the public records are being audited shall in no case be construed as a reason or justification for a refusal to allow inspection of the records except when the public records are in active use by the auditor.

§ 34. Absence of records.

If any public record applied for by any authorized person is not in the custody or control of the person to whom the application is made, such person shall promptly certify this in writing to the applicant, and shall in the certificate state in detail to the best of his knowledge and belief, the reason for the absence of the record from his custody or control, its location, what person then has custody of the record and the manner and method in which, and the exact time at which it was taken from his custody or control. He shall include in the certificate ample and detailed answers to all inquiries of the applicant that may facilitate the exercise of the right granted by this Chapter.

§ 35. Suits to enforce provisions; preference.

Any suit brought in any court of original jurisdiction to enforce the provisions of this Chapter shall be tried by preference and in a summary manner. All appellate courts to which the suits are brought shall place them on its preferential docket and shall hear them without delay. The appellate courts shall also render a decision in these suits within ten days after hearing them.

§ 36. Preservation of records.

All persons having custody or control of any public record, other than conveyance, probate, mortgage or other permanent record required by existing law to be kept for all time, shall exercise diligence and care in preserving the public record for a period of at least six years from the date on which the public record was made. However, where copies of an original record exist, the original alone shall be kept. When only duplicate copies of a record exist, only one copy of the duplicate copies need be kept.

All existing records or records hereafter accumulated by the department of revenue may be destroyed after five years from the thirty-first day of December of the year in which the tax to which the records pertain became due; provided that these records shall not be destroyed in any case where there is a contest relative to the payment of taxes or where a claim has been made for a refund or where litigation with reference thereto is pending. As amended Acts 1954, No. 473, § 1.

§ 40. Additional copies of records by microphotographic process; purchase of equipment; funds available for payment

A. The several clerks of court and ex officio recorders and registers of conveyances and recorders of mortgages, throughout the state, are hereby authorized at their option to make additional copies, by means of the microphotographic process, of all original acts and/or records thereof, including criminal records, of every nature and kind in their custody by virtue of their various official capacities as such clerks of court and ex officio recorders and registers of conveyances and recorders of mortgages, filed or recorded in their offices prior to July 20, 1964 and subsequent thereto.

B. Such clerks of court and ex officio recorders and registers are hereby authorized to purchase the necessary microphotographic equipment and equipment used to retrieve from storage microfilm copies, to lease such equipment or to contract with competent independent contractors, or both, according to the discretion of said clerks of court and ex officio recorders and registers, to cause the records described in this section to be copied and reproduced by means of the microphotographic process.

C. Each such clerk of court and ex officio recorder and register is hereby authorized to defray the cost of copying, reproducing and retrieving the records described in this section, including the cost of microphotographic and retrieval equipment and services, out of any funds available in the clerk's salary fund.

D. In the parish of Orleans the judges of the civil district court and the criminal district court, and in the remainder of the state the respective police juries or other governing authorities of the several parishes, are authorized to provide the necessary funds, when such funds are not already available, to enable said clerk of courts and ex officio recorders and registers to carry out the provisions of this section.

E. The several clerks of court, including the clerk of the criminal district court in the parish of Orleans, shall make and retain in their custody a copy, by means of the microphotographic process, of all original criminal records of every nature and kind which have been in their custody for a period of five or more years. Said clerks of court may destroy such original criminal records which have been in their custody for a period of five or more years and which have been copied and retained by means of the microphotographic process.

Acts 1958, No. 350, §§ 1 to 4. Amended by Acts 1964, No. 415, § 1; Acts 1972, No. 498, §§ 1,2.

Maine Revised Statutes, Annotated
1976-1977 Cumulative Pocket Supplement
Volume 2, Title 1

§ 408. Public records available for public inspection.

Except as otherwise provided by statute, every person shall have the right to inspect and copy any public record during the regular business hours of the custodian or location of such record: provided that, whenever inspection cannot be accomplished without translation of mechanical or electronic data compilations into some other form, the person desiring inspection may be required to pay the State in advance the cost of translation and both translation and inspection may be scheduled to occur at such time as will not delay or inconvenience the regular activities of the agency or official having custody of the record sought and provided further that the cost of copying any public record to comply with this section shall be paid by the person requesting the copy.

§ 409. Appeals.

1. Records. If any body or agency or official, who has custody or control of any public record, shall refuse permission to so inspect or copy or abstract a public record, this denial shall be made by the body or agency or official in writing, stating the reason for the denial, within 10 days of the request for inspection by any person. Any person aggrieved by denial may appeal therefrom, within 10 days of the receipt of the written notice of denial, to any Superior Court within the State. If a court, after a trial de novo, determines such denial was not for just and proper cause, it shall enter an order for disclosure. Appeals shall be privileged in respect to their assignment for trial over all other actions except writs of habeas corpus and actions brought by the State against individuals.

2. Actions. If any body or agency approves any ordinances, orders, rules, resolutions, regulations, contracts, appointments or other official action in an executive session, this action shall be illegal and the officials responsible shall be subject to the penalties hereinafter provided. Upon learning of any such action, any person may appeal to any Superior Court in the State. If a court, after a trial de novo, determines this action was taken illegally in an executive session, it shall enter an order providing for the action to be null and void. Appeals shall be privileged in respect to their assignment for trial over all other actions except writs of habeas corpus or actions brought by the State against individuals.

3. Proceedings not exclusive. The proceedings authorized by this section shall not be exclusive of any other civil remedy provided by law.

1975, c. 758.

§ 410. Violations.

A willful violation of any requirement of this subchapter is a Class E crime. 1975, c. 758.

Maryland Code, Annotated
Volume 7A, Article 76A

Maryland
Regular Session
Chapter 1006, Laws 1978, House Bill #1326

An Act concerning
Public Information Act
For the purpose of eliminating unnecessary definitions; adding
and revising definitions; providing a policy statement; providing that State and local governments may maintain only necessary and relevant information about persons under certain conditions; providing greater access in certain circumstances to investigative, intelligence, and security records; generally revising the provisions relating to the right to inspect public records; making changes in the provisions permitting denial of public records or any portion thereof; providing an administrative review; providing for judicial enforcement; creating civil liability for violations; providing for appropriate personnel disciplinary action; providing for the removal of the subsections allowing special treatment of public records in Hartford County; providing for statutory limitation on the right to bring an action; and clarifying language.

Section 1. Be it enacted by the General Assembly of Maryland, that section(s) of the Annotated Code of Maryland be repealed, amended, or enacted to read as follows:
Article 76A – Public Information
1.(A) In this article the following words have the meanings indicated.
(B) "Public records" when not otherwise specified shall include any paper, correspondence, form, book, photograph, photostat, film, microfilm, sound recording, map, drawing, or other written document, regardless of physical form or characteristics, and including all copies thereof, that have been made by any branch of the State government, including the legislative, judicial and executive branches, by any branch of a political subdivision, and by any agency or instrumentality of the State or a political subdivision, or received by them in connection with

the transaction of public business. The term "public records" also includes the salaries of all employees of the State, of a political subdivision, and any agency or instrumentality thereof, both in the classified and non-classified service.

(C) "Applicant" means and includes any person requesting disclosure of public records.

(D) "Written Documents" means and includes all books, papers, maps, photographs, cards, tapes, records, computerized records, or other documentary materials, regardless of physical form or characteristics.

(E) "Political subdivision" means and includes every county, city and county, city, incorporated and unincorporated town, school district, and special district within the State.

(F) "Official custodian" means and includes each and every officer or employee of the State or any agency, institution, or political subdivision thereof, who is responsible for the maintenance, care, and keeping of public records, regardless of whether such records are in his actual personal custody and control.

(G) "Custodian" means and includes the official custodian or any authorized person having personal custody and control of the public records in question.

(H) "Person" means and includes any natural person, corporation, partnership, firm, association, or governmental agency.

(I) "Person in interest" means and includes the person who is the subject of a record or any representative designated by said person, except that if the subject of the record is under legal disability, the term "person in interest" shall mean and include the parent or duly appointed legal representative.

1.(a) The State, counties, municipalities, and political subdivisions, or any agencies thereof, may maintain only such information about a person as is relevant and necessary to accomplish a purpose of the governmental entity or agency which is authorized or required to be accomplished by statute, executive order of the governor or the chief executive of a local jurisdiction, judicial rule, or other legislative mandate. Moreover, all persons are entitled to information regarding the affairs of government and the official acts of those who represent them as public officials and employees. To this end, the provisions of this act shall be construed in every instance with the view toward public access, unless an unwarranted invasion of the privacy of a person in interest would result therefrom, and the minimization of costs and time delays to persons requesting information.

2.(a) All public records shall be open for inspection by any person at reasonable times, except as provided in this article or as otherwise provided by law. The official custodian of any public record shall make and publish such rules and regulations with reference to the timely inspection and production of such record as shall be reasonably necessary for the protection of such record and the prevention of unnecessary interference with the regular discharge of the duties of the custodian or his office.

(b) If the public records requested are not in the custody or control of the person to whom written application is made, such person shall, within ten working days of the receipt of the request, notify the applicant of this fact and if known, the custodian of the record and the location or possible location thereof.

(c) If the public records requested are in the custody and control of the person to whom written application is made but are not immediately available, the custodian shall, within ten working days of the receipt of the request, notify the applicant of this fact and shall set forth a date and hour within a reasonable time at which time the record will be available for the exercise of the right given by this article.

(d) In Charles County, except for records kept by officials, agencies, or departments of the State of Maryland, public information shall be regulated by § 6 of this article.

3.(a) The custodian of any public records shall allow any person the right of inspection of such records or any portion thereof except on one or more of the following grounds or as provided in subsection (b) or (c) of this section:

(i) Such inspection would be contrary to any State statute;

(ii) Such inspection would be contrary to any federal statute or regulation issued thereunder having the force and effect of law;

(iii) Such inspection is prohibited by rules promulgated by the Court of Appeals, or by the order of any court of record; or

(iv) Such public records are privileged or confidential by law.

(b) The custodian may deny the right of inspection of the following records or appropriate portions thereof, unless otherwise provided by law, if disclosure to the applicant would be contrary to the public interest:

(i) Records of investigations conducted by, or of intelligence information or security procedures of, any sheriff, county attorney, city attorney, state's attorney, the Attorney General, police department, or any investigatory files compiled for any other law-enforcement, judicial, correctional, or prosecution purposes, but the right of a person in interest to inspect the records may be denied only to the extent that the production of them would (a) interfere with valid and proper law-enforcement proceedings, (b) deprive another person of a right to a fair trial or an impartial adjudication, (c) constitute an unwarranted invasion of person privacy, (d) disclose the identity of a confidential source, (e) disclose investigative techniques and procedures, (f) prejudice any investigation, or (g) endanger the life or physical safety of any person;

(ii) Test questions, scoring keys, and other examination data pertaining to administration of licenses or employment or academic examinations; except that written promotional examinations and the scores or results thereof shall be available for inspection, but not copying or reproduction, by the person in interest after the conducting and grading of any such examination;

(iii) The specific details of bona fide research projects being conducted by an institution of the State or a political subdivision, except that the name, title, expenditures, and the time when the final project summary shall be available;

(iv) The contents of real estate appraisals made for the State or a political subdivision thereof, relative to the acquisition of property or any interest in property for public use, until such time as title of the property or property interest has passed to the state or political subdivisions, except that the contents of such appraisal shall be available to the owner of the property at any time, and except as provided by statute.

(v) Interagency or intraagency memorandums or letters which would not be available by law to a private party in litigation with the agency.

(c) The custodian shall deny the right of inspection of the following records or any portion thereof, unless otherwise provided by law:

(i) Medical, psychological, and sociological data on individual persons, exclusive of coroners' autopsy reports;

(ii) Adoption records or welfare records on individual persons;

(iii) Personnel files except that such files shall be available to the person in interest, and the duly elected and appointed officials who supervise the work of the person in interest;

(iv) Trade secrets, information privileged by law, and confidential commercial, financial, geological, or geophysical data furnished by or obtained from any person;

(v) Library, archives, and museum material contributed by private persons, to the extent of any limitations placed thereon as conditions of such contribution;

(vi) Hospital records relating to medical administration, medical staff, personnel, medical care, and other medical information, whether on individual persons or groups, or whether of a general or specific classification;

(vii) School district records containing information relating to the biography, family, physiology, religion, academic achievement, and physical or mental ability of any student except to the person in interest or to the officials duly elected and appointed to supervise him; and

(viii) Circulation records maintained by public libraries showing personal transactions by those borrowing from them.

(d) Whenever the custodian denies a written request for access to any public record or any portion thereof under this section, the custodian shall provide the applicant with a written statement of the grounds for the denial, which statement shall cite the law or regulation under which access is denied and all remedies for review of this denial available under this article. The statement shall be furnished to the applicant within ten working days of denial. In addition, any reasonably severable portion of a record shall be provided to any person requesting such record after deletion of those portions which may be withheld from disclosure.

(e) If, in the opinion of the official custodian of any public record which is otherwise required to be disclosed under this article, disclosure of the contents of said record would do substantial injury to the public interest, the official custodian may temporarily deny disclosure pending a court determination of whether disclosure would do substantial injury to the public interest provided that, within ten working days of the denial, the official custodian applies to the circuit court of the county where the record is located or where he maintains his principal office for an order permitting him to continue to deny or restrict such disclosure. The failure of the official custodian to apply for a court determination following a temporary denial of inspection will result in his becoming subject to the sanctions provided in this article for failure to disclose authorized public records required to be disclosed. After hearing, the court may issue such an order upon a finding that disclosure would cause substantial injury to the public interest. The person seeking permission to examine the record shall have notice of the application sent to the circuit court served upon him in the manner provided for service of process by the Maryland Rules of Procedure and shall have the right to appear and be heard.

4.(a) In all cases in which a person has the right to inspect any public records such person shall have the right to be furnished copies, printouts, or photographs for a reasonable fee to be set by the official custodian. Where fees for certified copies or other copies, printouts, or photographs of such record are specifically prescribed by law, such specific fees shall apply.

(b) If the custodian does not have the facilities for making copies, printouts, or photographs of records which the applicant has the right to inspect, then the applicant shall be granted access to the records for the purpose of making copies, printouts, or photographs. The copies, printouts, or photographs shall be made while the records are in the possession, custody, and control of the custodian thereof and shall be subject to the supervision of such custodian. When practical, they shall be made in the place where the records are kept, but if it is impractical to do so, the custodian may allow arrangements to be made for this purpose. If other facilities are necessary the cost of providing them shall be paid by the person desiring a copy, printout, or photograph of the records. The official custodian may establish a reasonable schedule of times for making copies, printouts, or photographs and may charge a reasonable fee for the services rendered by him or his deputy in supervising the copying, printingout, or photographing as he may charge for furnishing copies under this section.

5.(a) Except in cases of temporary denials under section 3(e) of this subtitle any applicant denied the right to inspect public records where the official custodian of the records is an agency subject to the provisions of subtitle 24 of article 41 of this code may ask for an administrative review of this decision in accordance with section 251 through 254 of article 41 of this code, however, this remedy need not be exhausted prior to filing suit in the circuit court pursuant to this article.

(b) (1) On complaint of any person denied the right to inspect any record covered by this Article, the circuit court in the jurisdiction in which the complainant resides, or has his principal place of business, or in which the records are situated, has jurisdiction to enjoin the State, any county, municipality, or political subdivision, any agency, official or employee thereof, from withholding records and to order the production of any records improperly withheld from the complainant. In such case, the court may examine the contents of the records in camera to determine whether the records or any part thereof may be withheld under any of the exemptions set forth in section 3, and the burden is on the defendant to sustain its action. In carrying this burden the defendant may submit to the court for review a memorandum justifying the withholding of the records.

(2) Notwithstanding any other provision of law, the defendant shall serve an answer or otherwise plead to any complaint made under this subsection within 30 days after service upon the defendant of the pleading in which the complaint is made, unless the court otherwise directs for good cause shown.

(3) Except as to cases the court considers of greater importance, proceedings before the court, as authorized by this section, and appeals therefrom shall take precedence on the docket over all other cases and shall be heard at the earliest practicable date and expedited in every way.

(4) In addition to any other relief which may be granted to a complainant, in any suit brought under the provisions of this section in which the court determines that the defendant has knowingly and wilfully failed to disclose or fully disclose records and information to any person who, under this Article, is entitled to receive it, and the defendant knew or should have known that the person was entitled to receive it, any defendant governmental entity or entities shall be liable to the complainant in an amount equal to the sum of the actual damages sustained by the individual as a result of the refusal or failure and such punitive damages as the court deems appropriate.

(5) In the event of noncompliance with an order of the court, the court may punish the responsible employee for contempt.

(6) The court may assess against any defendant governmental entity or entities reasonable attorney fees and other litigation costs reasonably incurred in any case under this section in which the court determines that the applicant has substantially prevailed.

(C) Whenever the court orders the production of any records improperly withheld from the applicant, and in addition, finds that the custodian acted arbitrarily or capriciously in withholding the public record, the court shall forward a certified copy of its finding to the appointing authority of the custodian, upon receipt thereof, the appointing authority shall, after appropriate investigation, take such disciplinary action as is warranted under the circumstances.

(D) Any person who wilfully and knowingly violates the provisions of this article shall be guilty of a misdemeanor and, upon conviction thereof, shall be punished by a fine not to exceed $100.

Article – Courts and Judicial Proceedings

5–110. An action to enforce any criminal or civil liability created under sections 1 through 5 of article 76A of this code may be brought within two years from the date on which the cause of action arises, except that if the defendant has materially and wilfully misrepresented any information required under those sections to be disclosed to a person and the information so misrepresented is material to the establishment of liability of the defendant to the person under those sections, the action may be brought at any time within two years after discovery by the person of the misrepresentation.

Massachusetts General Laws, Annotated
1979 Cumulative Annual Pocket Part
Volume 8A, Chapter 66

§ 3. "Record," defined; quality of paper and film; microfilm records.

The word "record" in this chapter shall mean any written or printed book or paper, or any photograph, microphotograph, map or plan. All written or printed public records shall be entered or recorded on paper made of linen rags and new cotton clippings, well sized with animal sizing and well finished, or on one hundred per cent bond paper sized with animal glue or gelatin, and preference shall be given to paper of American manufacture marked in water line with the name of the manufacturer. All photographs, microphotographs, maps and plans which are public records shall be made of materials approved by the supervisor of records. Public records may be made by handwriting, or by typewriting, or in print, or by the photographic process, or by the microphotographic process, or by any combination of the same. When the photographic or microphotographic process is used, the recording officer, in all instances where the photographic print or microphotographic film is illegible or indistinct, may make, in addition to said photographic or microphotographic record, a typewritten copy of the instrument, which copy shall be filed in a book kept for the purpose. In every such instance the recording officer shall cause cross references to be made between said photographic or microphotographic record and said typewritten record. If in the judgment of the recording officer an instrument offered for record is so illegible that a photographic or microphotographic record thereof would not be sufficiently legible, he may, in addition to the making of such record, retain the original in his custody, in which case a photographic or other attested copy thereof shall be given to the person offering the same for record, or to such person as he may designate.

Amended by St.1975, c. 282.

§ 16. Surrender of church records; jurisdiction of superior court.

If a church, parish, religious society, monthly meeting of the people called Friends or Quakers, or any similar body of persons who have associated themselves together for holding religious meetings, shall cease for the term of two years to hold such meetings, the persons having the care of any records or registries of such body, or of any officers thereof, shall deliver all such records, except records essential to the control of any property or trust funds belonging to such body, to the custodian of a depository provided by the state organization of the particular denomination or to the clerk of the city or town where such body is situated and such clerk may certify copies thereof upon the payment of the fee as provided by clause (25) of section thirty-four of chapter two hundred and sixty-two. If any such body, the records or registries of which, or of any officers of which, have been so delivered, shall resume meetings under its former name or shall be legally incorporated, either alone or with a similar body, the clerk of such city or town or the custodian of said depository shall, upon written demand by a person duly authorized, deliver such records or registries to him if he shall in writing certify that to the best of his knowledge and belief said meetings are to be continued or such incorporation has been legally completed. The superior court shall have jurisdiction in equity to enforce this section.

§ 17A. Public assistance records; public inspection; destruction.

· The records of the department of public welfare relative to all public assistance, and the records of the commission for the blind relative to aid to the blind, shall be public records; provided that they shall be open to inspection only by public officials of the commonwealth, which term shall include members of the general court, representatives of the federal government and those responsible for the preparation of annual budgets for such public assistance, the making or recommendations relative to such budgets, or the approval or authorization of payments for such assistance, or for any purposes directly connected with the administration of such public assistance including the use of said records by the department of public welfare in concert with related wage reports to ascertain or confirm any fraud, abuse or improper payments to an applicant for or recipient of public assistance; and provided, further, that information relative to the record of an applicant for public assistance or a recipient thereof may be disclosed to him or his duly authorized agent. The commonwealth shall destroy public assistance records ten years after the discontinuance of aid granted under the provisions of chapters sixty-nine, one hundred and seventeen, one hundred and eighteen, one hundred and eighteen A, one hundred and eighteen D and one hundred and nineteen, in such manner as the commissioner or director may prescribe.

§ 17C. Failure to maintain public records of meetings; orders to maintain.

Upon proof of failure of a governmental body as defined in section eleven A of chapter thirty A, section nine F of chapter thirty-four and section twenty-three A of chapter thirty-nine, or by any member or officer thereof to carry out any of the provisions prescribed by this chapter for maintaining public records, a justice of the supreme judicial or the superior court sitting within and for the county in which such governmental body acts or, in the case of a governmental body of the commonwealth, sitting within and for any county, shall issue an appropriate order requiring such governmental body or member or officer thereof to carry out the provisions of this chapter. Such order may be sought by complaint of three or more registered voters, by the attorney general, or by the district attorney for the county in which the governmental body acts. The order of notice on the complaint shall be returnable no later than ten days after the filing thereof and the complaint shall be heard and determined on the return day or on such day thereafter as the court shall fix, having regard to the speediest possible determination of the cause consistent with the rights of the parties; provided, however, that orders with respect to any of the matters referred to in this section may be issued at any time on or after the filing of the complaint without notice when such order is necessary to fulfill the purposes of this section. In the hearing of any such complaint the burden shall be on the respondent to show by a preponderance of the evidence that the actions complained of in such complaint were in accordance with and authorized by section eleven B of chapter thirty A, by section nine G of chapter thirty-four or by section twenty-three B of chapter thirty-nine. All processes may be issued from the clerk's office in the county in which the action is brought and, except as aforesaid, shall be returnable as the court orders.

Any such order may also, when appropriate, require the records of any such meeting of a governmental body to be made a public record unless it shall have been determined by such justice that the maintenance of secrecy with respect to such records is authorized by section eleven B of chapter thirty, by section nine G of chapter thirty-four or by section twenty-three B. The remedy created hereby is not exclusive, but shall be in addition to every other available remedy.

§ 10. Public inspection of records; copies; compliance with requests; remedies.

(a) Every person having custody of any public record, as defined in clause Twenty-sixth of section seven of chapter four, shall, at reasonable times and without unreasonable delay, permit it, or any segregable portion of a record which is an independent public record, to be inspected and examined by any person, under his supervision, and shall furnish one copy thereof upon payment of a reasonable fee. Every person for whom a search of public records is made shall, at the direction of the person having custody of such records, pay the actual expense of such search.

(b) A custodian of a public record shall, within ten days following receipt of a request for inspection or copy of a public record, comply with such request. Such request may be delivered in hand to the office of the custodian or mailed via first class mail. If the custodian refuses or fails to comply with such a request, the person making the request may petition the supervisor of records for a determination whether the record requested is public. Upon the determination by the supervisor of records that the record is public, he shall order the custodian of the public record to comply with the person's request. If the custodian refuses or fails to comply with any such order, the supervisor of records may notify the attorney general or the appropriate district attorney thereof who may take whatever measures he deems necessary to insure compliance with the provisions of this section. The administrative remedy provided by this section shall in no way limit the availability of the administrative remedies provided by the commissioner of administration and finance with respect to any officer or employee of any agency, executive office, department or board; nor shall the administrative remedy provided by this section in any way limit the availability of judicial remedies otherwise available to any person requesting a public record. If a custodian of a public record refuses or fails to comply with the request of any person for inspection or copy of a public record or with an administrative order under this section, the supreme judicial or superior court shall have jurisdiction to order compliance.

(c) In any court proceeding pursuant to paragraph (b) there shall be a presumption that the record sought is public, and the burden shall be upon the custodian to prove with specificity the exemption which applies.

Michigan Compiled Laws, Annotated
1979-1980 Cumulative Annual Pocket Part
Volume 39

750.492 Inspection and use of public records.

Sec. 492. * * * Any officer having the custody of any county, city or township records in this state who shall when requested fail or neglect to furnish proper and reasonable facilities for the inspection and examination of the records and files in his office and for making memoranda of transcripts therefrom during the usual business hours, which shall not be less than 4 hours per day, to any person having occasion to make examination of them for any lawful purpose shall be guilty of a misdemeanor, punishable by imprisonment in the county jail not more than 1 year, or by a fine of not more than $500.00. The custodian of said records and files may make such reasonable rules * * * with reference to the inspection and examination of them as shall be necessary for the protection of said records and files, and to prevent interference with the regular discharge of the duties of such officer. The officer shall prohibit the use of pen and ink in making copies or notes of records and files in his office. No books, records and files shall be removed from the office of the custodian thereof, * * * except by the order of the judge of any court of competent jurisdiction, or in response to a subpoena duces tecum issued therefrom, or for audit purposes conducted pursuant to Act No. 71 of the Public Acts of 1919, as amended, being sections 21.41 to 21.53 of the Compiled Laws of 1948, Act No. 52 of the Public Acts of 1929, being sections 14.141 to 14.145 of the Compiled Laws of 1948 or Act No. 2 of the Public Acts of 1968, being sections 141.421 to 141.433 of the Compiled Laws of 1948 with the permission of the official having custody of the records if the official is given a receipt listing the records being removed. Amended by P.A.1970, No. 109, § 1, Imd. Eff. July 23.

Minnesota Statutes, Annotated
1977 Cumulative Annual Pocket Part
Volume 3

15.17 Official records.

Subdivision 1. Must be kept. All officers and agencies of the state, and all officers and agencies of the counties, cities, villages, and towns, shall make and keep all records necessary to a full and accurate knowledge of their official activities. All such public records shall be made on paper of durable quality and with the use of ink, carbon papers, and typewriter ribbons of such quality as to insure permanent records. Every public officer, and every county officer with the approval of the county board, is empowered to record or copy public records by any photographic, photostatic, microphotographic, or microfilming device, approved by the Minnesota historical society, which clearly and accurately records or copies them, and such public officer or such county officer may make and order that such photographs, photostats, micro-photographs, microfilms, or other reproductions, be substituted for the originals thereof, and may direct the destruction or sale for salvage or other disposition of the originals from which the same were made. Any such photographs, photostats, microphotographs, microfilms, or other reproductions so made shall for all purposes be deemed the original recording of such papers, books, documents and records so reproduced when so ordered by any officer with the approval of the county board, and shall be admissible as evidence in all courts and proceedings of every kind. A facsimile or exemplified or certified copy of any such photograph, photostat, microphotograph, microfilm, or other reproduction, or any enlargement or reduction thereof, shall have the same effect and weight as evidence as would a certified or exemplified copy of the original.

. . .

Subd. 4. Accessible to public. Every custodian of public records shall keep them in such arrangement and condition as to make them easily accessible for convenient use. Photographic, photostatic, microphotographic, or microfilmed records shall be considered as accessible for convenient use regardless of the size of such records. Except as otherwise expressly provided by law, he shall permit all public records in his custody to be inspected,

examined, abstracted, or copied at reasonable times and under his supervision and regulation by any person; and he shall, upon the demand of any person, furnish certified copies thereof on payment in advance of fees not to exceed the fees prescribed by law. Full convenience and comprehensive accessibility shall be allowed to researchers including historians, genealogists and other scholars to carry out extensive research and complete copying of all public records except as otherwise expressly provided by law.
Amended by Laws 1973, c. 422, § 1.

Mississippi Code 1972, Annotated
Volume 19

§ 89–5–25. How instrument recorded and book indexed—records public—copies.

(1) It shall be the duty of the clerk of the chancery court to whom any written instrument is delivered to be recorded, and which is properly recordable in his county, to record the same without delay in a well bound book of good paper, to be provided by him for that purpose, together with the acknowledgments of proofs and the certificates thereof, and also the plats of surveys, schedules, and other papers thereto annexed, by entering them word for word in a fair handwriting, or typewriting, or by filling up printed forms, or by recording by photostat machine or other equally permanent photographic process, and entering at the margin or foot of the page the hour and minute, the day of the month, and the year when the instrument was delivered to him for record, and when recorded. He shall also carefully preserve all instruments of writing, which are properly acknowledged and delivered to him to be recorded, and after recording deliver them to the party entitled thereto on demand. He shall also put a complete alphabetical index, both direct and reverse, to each book, except as provided in subsection (2), herein; and every person shall have access, at proper times, to such books, and be entitled to transcripts from the same on paying the lawful fees. He shall record the deeds and other instruments in the order of time in which they are filed for record as far as practicable.

(2) In counties having a population in excess of 119,000 with an assessed valuation of all taxable property therein in excess of $63,000,000.00, and having two cities wholly located therein, each with a population in excess of 30,000 persons according to the preceding Federal Census, wherein the clerk of the chancery court has a well kept general index, both direct and reverse, for each kind or class of record books as required by section 89–5–33, the board of supervisors may, by order spread upon its minutes, authorize the

clerk of the chancery court to omit putting such index in each separate book of the records to which such general index is kept.

(3) This section shall not be construed to authorize and empower the boards of supervisors to purchase any photostat machines or other equally permanent photographic processes.

Missouri Statutes, Vernon's Annotated
1977 Cumulative Annual Pocket Part
Volume 8

109.180. Public records open to inspection—refusal to permit inspection, penalty.

Except as otherwise provided by law, all state, county and municipal records kept pursuant to statute or ordinance shall at all reasonable times be open for a personal inspection by any citizen of Missouri, and those in charge of the records shall not refuse the privilege to any citizen. Any official who violates the provisions of this section shall be subject to removal on impeachment and in addition shall be deemed guilty of a misdemeanor and upon conviction shall be punished by a fine not exceeding one hundred dollars, or by confinement in the county jail not exceeding ninety days, or by both the fine and the confinement. (L.1961 p. 548 § 1)

109.190. Right of person to photograph public records—regulations.

In all cases where the public or any person interested has a right to inspect or take extracts or make copies from any public records, instruments or documents, any person has the right of access to the records, documents or instruments for the purpose of making photographs of them while in the possession, custody and control of the lawful custodian thereof or his authorized deputy. The work shall be done under the supervision of the lawful custodian of the records who may adopt and enforce reasonable rules governing the work. The work shall, where possible, be done in the room where the records, documents or instruments are by law kept, but if that is impossible or impracticable, the work shall be done in another room or place as nearly adjacent to the place of custody as possible to be determined by the custodian of the records. While the work authorized herein is in progress, the lawful custodian of the records may charge the person desiring to make the photographs a reasonable rate for his services or for the services of a deputy to supervise the work and for the use of the room or place where the work is done. (L.1961 p. 548 § 2)

Montana Revised Codes, 1947
1975 Cumulative Pocket Supplement
Volume 7

93-1001-2. (10540) Public writings defined. Public writings are:
1. The written acts or records of the acts of the sovereign authority, of official bodies and tribunals, and of public officers, legislative, judicial, and executive, whether of this state, of the United States, of a sister state, or of a foreign country;
2. Public records, kept in this state, of private writings.
93-1001-4. (10542) Every citizen entitled to inspect and copy public writings. Every citizen has a right to inspect and take a copy of any public writings of this state, except as otherwise expressly provided by statute.
93-1001-5. (10543) Public officer bound to give copies. Every public officer having the custody of a public writing, which a citizen has a right to inspect, is bound to give him, on demand, a certified copy of it, on payment of the legal fees therefor, and such copy is admissible as evidence in like cases and with like effect as the original writing.

Nebraska Revised Statutes, 1971
1976 Cumulative Supplement
Volume 5

84-712. Public records; free examination; memorandum and abstracts. Except as otherwise expressly provided by statute, all citizens of this state, and all other persons interested in the examination of the public records, are hereby fully empowered and authorized to examine the same, and to make memoranda and abstracts therefrom, all free of charge, during the hours the respective offices may be kept open for the ordinary transaction of business.
84-712.01. Public records; right of citizens; full access. Sections 84-712 to 84-712.03 shall be liberally construed whenever any state, county or political subdivision fiscal records, audit, warrant, voucher, invoice, purchase order, requisition, payroll, check, receipt or other record of receipt, cash or expenditure involving public funds is involved in order that the citizens of this state shall have full rights to know of, and have full access to information on the public finances of the government and the public bodies and entities created to serve them.
Source: Laws 1961, c. 454, § 2, p. 1383.

84-712.02. Public records; claimants before federal veterans agencies; certified copies free of charge. When it shall be requested by any claimant before the United States Veterans' Bureau or any claimant before the United States Bureau of Pensions, his or her agent or attorney, that certified copies of any public record be furnished for the proper and effective presentation of any such claim in such bureau, the officer in charge of such public records shall furnish or cause to be furnished such claimant, his or her agent or attorney, a certified copy thereof free of charge.

84-712.03. Public records; denial of rights; remedies; violation; penalties. Any person denied any rights granted by sections 84-712 to 84-712.03 may file for speedy relief by a writ of mandamus in the district court within whose jurisdiction the state, county or political subdivision officer who has custody of said public record can be served. Any official who shall violate the provisions of sections 84-712 to 84-712.03 shall be subject to removal or impeachment and in addition shall be deemed guilty of a misdemeanor and shall, upon conviction thereof, be fined not exceeding one hundred dollars, or be imprisoned in the county jail not exceeding three months.

Nevada Revised Statutes
Volume 8

In General
239.010 Public books, records open to inspection; penalty.
1. All public books and public records of state, county, city, district, governmental subdivision and quasi-municipal corporation officers and offices of this state (and all departments thereof), the contents of which are not otherwise declared by law to be confidential, shall be open at all times during office hours to inspection by any person, and the same may be fully copied or an abstract or memorandum prepared therefrom, and any copies, abstracts or memoranda taken therefrom may be utilized to supply the general public with copies, abstracts or memoranda of the records or in any other way in which the same may be used to the advantage of the owner thereof or of the general public.
2. Any officer having the custody of any of the public books and public records described in subsection 1 who refuses any person the right to inspect such books and records as provided in subsection 1 is guilty of a misdemeanor.
[1:149:1911; RL § 3232; NCL § 5620]—(NRS A 1963, 26; 1965, 69)
239.015 Removal, transfer, storage of records authorized when necessary; copies to be provided.

1. A custodian of records may remove books of records, maps, charts, surveys and other papers for storage in an appropriate facility if he believes that the removal of such records is necessary for their protection or permanent preservation, or he may arrange for their transfer to another location for duplication or reproduction.

2. If a county recorder receives a request for a particular item which has been stored pursuant to subsection 1, he shall produce a microfilmed copy of such item or the original within 3 working days.

(Added to NRS by 1975, 748)

239.020 Certified copies of public records to be provided without charge to Veterans' Administration. Whenever a copy of any public record is required by the Veterans' Administration to be used in determining the eligibility of any person to participate in benefits made available by the Veterans' Administration, the official charged with the custody of such public record shall, without charge, provide the applicant for the benefit or any person acting on his behalf or the representative of the Veterans' Administration with a certified copy or copies of such records.

[1:30:1947; 1943 NCL § 6879.15]

239.030 Furnishing of certified copies of public records. Every officer having custody of public records, the contents of which are not declared by law to be confidential, shall furnish copies certified to be correct to any person who requests them and pays or tenders such fees as may be prescribed for the service of copying and certifying.

[1:73:1909; RL § 2045; NCL § 2976]—(NRS A 1973, 353)

New Hampshire Revised Statutes, Annotated
1977 Supplement
Volume 2

91-A:4 Minutes and Records Available for Public Inspection. Every citizen during the regular or business hours of all such bodies or agencies, and on the regular business premises of such bodies or agencies, has the right to inspect all public records, including minutes of meetings of the bodies or agencies, and to make memoranda abstracts, photographic or photostatic copies, of the records or minutes so inspected, except as otherwise prohibited by statute or section 5 of this chapter.

Source. 1967, 251:1, eff. Aug. 26, 1967.

91-A:5 Exemptions. The records of the following bodies are exempted from the provisions of this chapter:

I. Grand and petit juries.

II. Parole and pardon boards.

III. Personal school records of pupils.

IV. Records pertaining to internal personnel practices, confidential, commercial, or financial information, personnel, medical, welfare, and other files whose disclosure would constitute invasion of privacy.

Source. 1976, 251:1, eff. Aug. 26, 1967.

91-A:7 Violation. Any person aggrieved by a violation of this chapter may petition the superior court for injunctive relief. The courts shall give proceedings under this chapter priority on the court calendar. Such a petitioner may appear with or without counsel. The petition shall be deemed sufficient if it states facts constituting a violation of this chapter, and may be filed by the petitioner or his counsel with the clerk of court or any justice thereof. Thereupon the clerk of court or any justice shall order service by copy of the petition on the person or persons charged. When any justice shall find that time probably is of the essence, he may order notice by any reasonable means, and he shall have authority to issue an order ex parte when he shall reasonably deem such an order necessary to insure compliance with the provisions of this chapter.

Source. 1967, 251:1. 1977, 540:5, eff. Sept. 13, 1977.

91-A:8 [New] Remedies. Any body or agency which, in violation of the provisions of this chapter, refuses to provide a public document or refuses access to a public proceeding, to a person who reasonably requests the same, shall be liable for reasonable attorney's fees and costs incurred in making the information available or the proceeding open to the public provided the court renders final judgment in favor of such request.

Source. 1973, 113:1, eff. July 7, 1973.

New Jersey Statutes, Annotated
1979-1980 Cumulative Annual Pocket Part
Title 47

47:1A-1. Legislative findings.

The Legislature finds and declares it to be the public policy of this State that public records shall be readily accessible for examination by the citizens of this State, with certain exceptions, for the protection of the public interest. L.1963, c. 73, § 1.

47:1A-2. Public records; right of Inspection; copies; fees.

Except as otherwise provided in this act or by any other statute, resolution of either or both houses of the Legislature, executive order of the Governor, rule of court, any Federal law, regulation or order, or by any regulation promulgated under the authority of any statute or executive order of the Governor, all records which are required by law to be made, maintained or kept on file by any board, body, agency, department, commission or official of the State or of any political subdivision thereof or by any public board, body, commission or authority created pursuant to law by the State or any of its political subdivisions, or by any official acting for or on behalf thereof (each of which is hereinafter referred to as the "custodian" thereof) shall, for the purposes of this act, be deemed to be public records. Every citizen of this State, during the regular business hours maintained by the custodian of any such records, shall have the right to inspect such records. Every citizen of this State shall also have the right, during such regular business hours and under the supervision of a representative of the custodian, to copy such records by hand, and shall also have the right to purchase copies of such records. Copies of records shall be made available upon the payment of such price as shall be established by law. If a price has not been established by law for copies of any records, the custodian of such records shall make and supply copies of such records upon the payment of the following fees which shall be based upon the total number of pages or parts thereof to be purchased without regard to the number of records being copied:

First page to tenth page .... $0.50 per page
Eleventh page to twentieth page .... 0.25 per page
All pages over 20 .... 0.10 per page

If the custodian of any such records shall find that there is no risk of damage or mutilation of such records and that it would not be incompatible with the economic and efficient operation of the office and the transaction of public business therein, he may permit any citizen who is seeking to copy more than 100 pages of records to use his own photographic process, approved by the custodian, upon the payment of a reasonable fee, considering the equipment and the time involved, to be fixed by the custodian of not less than $5.00 or more than $25.00 per day. L.1963, c. 73, § 2.

47:1A–3. Records of Investigations in progress.

Notwithstanding the provisions of this act, where it shall appear that the record or records which are sought to be examined shall pertain to an investigation in progress by any such body, agency, commission, board, authority or official, the right of examination herein provided for may be denied if the inspection, copying or publication of such record or records shamm be inimical to the public interest; provided, however, that this provision shall not be construed to prohibit any such body, agency, commission, board, authority or official from opening such record or records for public examination if not otherwise prohibited by law. L.1963, c. 73, § 3.

47:1A–4. Proceedings to enforce right to inspect or copy.

Any such citizen of this State who has been or shall have been denied for any reason the right to inspect, copy or obtain a copy of any such record as provided in this act may apply to the Superior Court of New Jersey by a proceeding in lieu of prerogative writ for an order requiring the custodian of the record to afford inspection, the right to copy or to obtain a copy thereof, as provided in this act. L.1963, c. 73, § 4.

New Mexico Statutes, Annotated
1975 Pocket Supplement
Volumes 10, 5

71-5-1. Right to inspect public records—Exceptions. Every citizen of this state has a right to inspect any public records of this state except:

A. records pertaining to physical or mental examinations and medical treatment of persons confined to any institutions;

B. letters of reference concerning employment, licensing or permits;

C. letters or memorandums which are matters of opinion in personnel files or students' cumulative files; and

D. as otherwise provided by law.

71-5-2. Officers to provide opportunity and facilities for inspection. All officers having the custody of any state, county, school, city or town records in this state shall furnish proper and reasonable opportunities for the inspection and examination of all the records requested of their respective offices and reasonable facilities for making memoranda abstracts therefrom, during the usual business hours, to all persons having occasion to make examination of them for any lawful purpose.

71-5-3. Penalties for violation of act. If any officer having the custody of any state, county, school, city or town records in this state shall refuse to any citizen of this state the right to inspect any public records of this state, as provided in this act [71-5-1 to 71-5-3], such officer shall be guilty of a misdemeanor and shall, upon conviction thereof, be fined not less than two hundred and fifty dollars ($250.00) nor more than five hundred dollars ($500.00), or be sentenced to not less than sixty (60) days nor more than six (6) months in jail, or both such fine and imprisonment for each separate violation.

Volume 5

34-2-17. Disclosure of information. A. All certificates, applications, records, and reports made for the purpose of this act [34-2-1 to 34-2-25] to, and directly or indirectly identifying, a patient or former patient or an individual whose involuntary referral for mental health care has been sought under this act shall be kept confidential and shall not be disclosed by any person except in so far:

(1) as the individual identified or his legal guardian, if any, (or, if he is a minor, his parent or legal guardian) shall consent; or

(2) as disclosure may be necessary to carry out any of the provisions of this act; or

(3) as a court may direct upon its determination that disclosure is necessary for the conduct of proceedings before it and that failure to make such disclosure would be contrary to the public interest.

B. Nothing in this section shall preclude disclosure, upon proper inquiry, of information contained in such certificates, applications, records or reports, to abstractors in connection with title matters relating to title in real property in which the patient has or had some interest, or lawyers, or information as to his current medical condition to any of the family of a patient or to his relatives or friends.

C. Any person violating any provision of this section shall be guilty of a misdemeanor and subject to a fine of not more than five hundred dollars ($500) and imprisonment for not more than one [1] year.

5-6-23. Formation of public policy. A. The formation of public policy or the conduct of business by vote shall not be conducted in secret.

B. All meetings of a quorum of members of any board, commission or other policy-making body of any state agency, or any agency or authority of any county, municipality, district or any political subdivision held for the purpose of formulating public policy, discussing public business or for the purpose of taking any action within the authority of or the delegated authority of such board, commission or other policy-making body, are declared to be public meetings open to the public at all times, except as otherwise provided in the constitution or the provisions of this act [5-6-23 to 5-6-26].

C. Any such meetings at which the discussion or adoption of any proposed resolution, rule, regulation or formal action occurs, and at which a majority or quorum of the body is in attendance, shall be held only after reasonable notice to the public. The affected body shall determine at least annually in a public meeting what notice shall be reasonable when applied to such body.

D. Such minutes as may reasonably be required by the board, commission or other policy-making body shall be recorded and be open to public inspection.

E. The provisions of this section shall not apply to adjudicatory or personnel matters nor to meetings pertaining to issuance, suspension, renewal or revocation of a license, nor meetings of grand juries. Nothing in this section shall be construed to deny or permit an aggrieved person the right to demand a public hearing.

New York Consolidated Laws, McKinney's Annotated
1978-1979 Cumulative Annual Pocket Part
Book 46

Public Officers Law
Article 6 - Freedom of Information Law [New]
Sec.
84. Legislative declaration.
85. Short title.
86. Definitions.
87. Access to agency records.
88. Access to state legislative records.
89. General provisions relating to access to records; certain cases.
90. Severability.
    Former Art. 6. Renumbered 7.
§ 84. Legislative declaration.
    The legislature hereby finds that a free society is maintained when government is responsive and responsible to the public, and when the public is aware of governmental actions. The more open a government is with its citizenry, the greater the understanding and participation of the public in government.
    As state and local government services increase and public problems become more sophisticated and complex and therefore harder to solve, and with the resultant increase in revenues and expenditures, it is incumbent upon the state and its localities to extend public accountability wherever and whenever feasible.
    The people's right to know the process of governmental decision-making and to review the documents and statistics leading to determinations is basic to our society. Access to such information should not be thwarted by shrouding it with the cloak of secrecy or confidentiality.
    The legislature therefore declares that government is the public's business and that the public, individually and collectively and represented by a free press, should have access to the records of government in accordance with the provisions of this article.
Added L.1977, c. 933, § 1.
§ 85. Short title.

This article shall be known and may be cited as the "Freedom of Information Law."

Added L.1977, c. 933, § 1.

§ 86. Definitions.

As used in this article, unless the context requires otherwise:

1. "Judiciary" means the courts of the state, including any municipal or district court, whether or not of record.

2. "State legislature" means the legislature of the state of New York, including any committee, subcommittee, joint committee, select committee, or commission thereof.

3. "Agency" means any state or municipal department, board, bureau, division, commission, committee, public authority, public corporation, council, office or other governmental entity performing a governmental or proprietary function for the state or any one or more municipalities thereof, except the judiciary or the state legislature.

4. "Record" means any information kept, held, filed, produced or reproduced by, with or for an agency or the state legislature, in any physical form whatsoever including, but not limited to, reports, statements, examinations, memoranda, opinions, folders, files, books, manuals, pamphlets, forms, papers, designs, drawings, maps, photos, letters, microfilms, computer tapes or discs, rules, regulations or codes.

Added L.1977, c. 933, § 1.

§ 87. Access to agency records.

1. (a) Within sixty days after the effective date of this article, the governing body of each public corporation shall promulgate uniform rules and regulations for all agencies in such public corporation pursuant to such general rules and regulations as may be promulgated by the committee on public access to records in conformity with the provisions of this article, pertaining to the administration of this article.

(b) Each agency shall promulgate rules and regulations, in conformity with this article and applicable rules and regulations promulgated pursuant to the provisions of paragraph (a) of this subdivision, and pursuant to such general rules and regulations as may be promulgated by the committee on public access to records in conformity with the provisions of this article, pertaining to the availability of records and procedures to be followed, including, but not limited to:

i. the times and places such records are available;

ii. the persons from whom such records may be obtained, and

iii. the fees for copies of records which shall not exceed twenty-five cents per photocopy not in excess of nine inches by fourteen inches, or the actual cost of reproducing any other record, except when a different fee is otherwise prescribed by law.

2. Each agency shall, in accordance with its published rules, make available for public inspection and copying all records, except that such agency may deny access to records or portions thereof that:

(a) are specifically exempted from disclosure by state or federal statute;

(b) if disclosed would constitute an unwarranted invasion of personal privacy under the provisions of subdivision two of section eighty-nine of this article;

(c) if disclosed would impair present or imminent contract awards or collective bargaining negotiations;

(d) are trade secrets or are maintained for the regulation of commercial enterprise which if disclosed would cause substantial injury to the competitive position of the subject enterprise;

(e) are compiled for law enforcement purposes and which, if disclosed, would:

i. interfere with law enforcement investigations or judicial proceedings;

ii. deprive a person of a right to a fair trial or impartial adjudication;

iii. identify a confidential source or disclose confidential information relating to a criminal investigation; or

iv. reveal criminal investigative techniques or procedures, except routine techniques and procedures;

(f) if disclosed would endanger the life or safety of any person;

(g) are inter-agency or intra-agency materials which are not:

i. statistical or factual tabulations or data;

ii. instructions to staff that affect the public; or

iii. final agency policy or determinations; or

(h) are examination questions or answers which are requested prior to the final administration of such questions.

3. Each agency shall maintain:

(a) a record of the final vote of each member in every agency proceeding in which the member votes;

(b) a record setting forth the name, public office address, title and salary of every officer or employee of the agency; and

(c) a reasonably detailed current list by subject matter, of all records in the possession of the agency, whether or not available under this article.

Added L.1977, c. 933, § 1.

§ 88. Access to state legislative records

1. The temporary president of the senate and the speaker of the assembly shall promulgate rules and regulations for their respective houses in conformity with the provisions of this article, pertaining to the availability, location and nature of records, including, but not limited to:

(a) the times and places such records are available;

(b) the persons from whom such records may be obtained;

(c) the fees for copies of such records, which shall not exceed twenty-five cents per photocopy not in excess of nine inches by fourteen inches, or the actual cost of reproducing any other record, except when a different fee is otherwise prescribed by law.

2. The state legislature shall, in accordance with its published rules, make available for public inspection and copying:

(a) bills and amendments thereto, fiscal notes, introducers' bill memoranda, resolutions and amendments thereto, and index records;

(b) messages received from the governor or the other house of the legislature, and home rule messages;

(c) legislative notification of the proposed adoption of rules by an agency;

(d) members' code of ethics statements;

(e) transcripts or minutes, if prepared, and journal records of public sessions including meetings of committees and subcommittees and public hearings, with the records of attendance of members thereat and records of any votes taken;

(f) internal or external audits and statistical or factual tabulations of, or with respect to, material otherwise available for public inspection and copying pursuant to this section or any other applicable provision of law;

(g) administrative staff manuals and instructions to staff that affect members of the public;

(h) final reports and formal opinions submitted to the legislature;

(i) final reports or recommendations and minority or dissenting reports and opinions of members of committees, subcommittees, or commissions of the legislature;

(j) any other files, records, papers or documents required by law to be made available for public inspection and copying.

3. Each house shall maintain and make available for public inspection and copying: (a) a record of votes of each member in every session and every committee and subcommittee meeting in which the member votes;

(b) a record setting forth the name, public office address, title, and salary of every officer or employee; and

(c) a current list, reasonably detailed, by subject matter of any records required to be made available for public inspection and copying pursuant to this section.

Added L.1977, c. 933, § 1.

§ 89. General provisions relating to access to records; certain cases.

The provisions of this section apply to access to all records, except as hereinafter specified:

1. (a) The committee on public access to records is continued and shall consist of the lieutenant governor or the delegate of such officer, the secretary of state or the delegate of such officer, whose office shall act as secretariat

for the committee, the commissioner of the office of general services or the delegate of such officer, the director of the budget or the delegate of such officer, and six other persons, none of whom shall hold any other state or local public office, to be appointed as follows: four by the governor, at least two of whom are or have been representatives of the news media, one by the temporary president of the senate, and one by the speaker of the assembly. The persons appointed by the temporary president of the senate and the speaker of the assembly shall be appointed to serve, respectively, until the expiration of the terms of office of the temporary president and the speaker to which the temporary president and speaker were elected. The four persons presently serving by appointment of the governor for fixed terms shall continue to serve until the expiration of their respective terms. Thereafter, their respective successors shall be appointed for terms of four years. The committee shall hold no less than four meetings annually. The members of the committee shall be entitled to reimbursement for actual expenses incurred in the discharge of their duties.

(b) The committee shall:

i. furnish to any agency advisory guidelines, opinions or other appropriate information regarding this article;

ii. furnish to any person advisory opinions or other appropriate information regarding this article;

iii. promulgate rules and regulations with respect to the implementation of subdivision one and paragraph (c) of subdivision three of section eighty-seven of this article;

iv. request from any agency such assistance, services and information as will enable the committee to effectively carry out its powers and duties; and

v. report on its activities and findings, including recommendations for changes in the law, to the governor and the legislature annually, on or before December fifteenth.

2. (a) The committee on public access to records may promulgate guidelines regarding deletion of identifying details or withholding of records otherwise available under this article to prevent unwarranted invasions of personal privacy. In the absence of such guidelines, an agency may delete identifying details when it makes records available.

(b) An unwarranted invasion of personal privacy includes, but shall not be limited to:

i. disclosure of employment, medical or credit histories or personal references of applicants for employment;

ii. disclosure of items involving the medical or personal records of a client or patient in a medical facility;

iii. sale or release of lists of names and addresses if such lists would be used for commercial or fund-raising purposes;

iv. disclosure of information of a personal nature when disclosure would result in economic or personal hardship to the subject party and such information is not relevant to the work of the agency requesting or maintaining it; or

v. disclosure of information of a personal nature reported in confidence to an agency and not relevant to the ordinary work of such agency.

(c) Unless otherwise provided by this article, disclosure shall not be construed to constitute an unwarranted invasion of personal privacy pursuant to paragraphs (a) and (b) of this subdivision:

i. when identifying details are deleted;

ii. when the person to whom a record pertains consents in writing to disclosure;

iii. when upon presenting reasonable proof of identity, a person seeks access to records pertaining to him.

3. Each entity subject to the provisions of this article, within five business days of the receipt of a written request for a record reasonably described, shall make such record available to the person requesting it, deny such request in writing or furnish a written acknowledgement of the receipt of such request and a statement of the approximate date when such request will be granted or denied. Upon payment of, or offer to pay, the fee prescribed therefor, the entity shall provide a copy of such record and certify to the correctness of such copy if so requested, or as the case may be, shall certify that it does not have possession of such record or that such record cannot be found after diligent search. Nothing in this article shall be construed to require any entity to prepare any record not possessed or maintained by such entity except the records specified in subdivision three of section eighty-seven and subdivision three of section eighty-eight.

4. (a) Any person denied access to a record may within thirty days appeal in writing such denial to the head, chief executive or governing body of the entity, or the person therefor designated by such head, chief executive, or governing body, who shall within seven business days of the receipt of such appeal fully explain in writing to the person requesting the record the reasons for further denial, or provide access to the record sought. In addition, each agency shall immediately forward to the committee on public access to records a copy of such appeal and the determination thereon.

(b) Any person denied access to a record in an appeal determination under the provisions of paragraph (a) of this subdivision may bring a proceeding for review of such denial pursuant to article seventy-eight of the civil practice law and rules. In the event that access to any record is denied pursuant to the provisions of subdivision two of section eighty-seven of this article, the agency involved shall have the burden of proving that such record falls within the provisions of such subdivision two.

5. Nothing in this article shall be construed to limit or abridge any otherwise available right of access at law or in equity of any party to records. Added L.1977, c. 933, § 1.

§ 90. Severability

If any provision of this article or the application thereof to any person or circumstances is adjudged invalid by a court of competent jurisdiction, such judgment shall not affect or impair the validity of the other provisions of the article or the application thereof to other persons and circumstances. Added L.1977, c. 933, § 1.

North Carolina General Statutes
1977 Cumulative Supplement
Volume 3B

§ 132-1. "Public records" defined. "Public record" or "public records" shall mean all documents, papers, letters, maps, books, photographs, films, sound recordings, magnetic or other tapes, electronic data-processing records, artifacts, or other documentary material, regardless of physical form or characteristics, made or received pursuant to law or ordinance in connection with the transaction of public business by any agency of North Carolina government or its subdivisions. Agency of North Carolina government or its subdivisions shall mean and include every public office, public officer or official (State or local, elected or appointed), institution, board, commission, bureau, council, department, authority or other unit of government of the State or of any county, unit, special district or other political subdivision of government. (1935, c. 265, s. 1; 1975, c. 787, s. 1.)

§ 132-1.1. Confidential communications by legal counsel to public board or agency; not public records. Public records, as defined in G.S. 132-1, shall not include written communications (and copies thereof) to any public board, council, commission or other governmental body of the State or of any county, municipality or other political subdivision or unit of government, made within the scope of the attorney-client relationship by any attorney-at-law serving any such governmental body, concerning any claim against or on behalf of the governmental body or the governmental entity for which such body acts, or concerning the prosecution, defense, settlement or litigation of any judicial action, or any administrative or other type of proceeding to which the governmental body is a party or by which it is or may be directly affected. Such written communication and copies thereof shall not be open to public inspection, examination or copying unless specifically made public by the governmental body receiving such written communications; provided, however, that such written communications and copies thereof shall become public records as defined in G.S. 132-1 three years from the date such communication was received by such public board, council, commission or other governmental body. (1975, c. 662.)

§ 132-4. Disposition of records at end of official's term. Whoever has the custody of any public records shall, at the expiration of his term of office, deliver to his successor, or, if there be none, to the Department of Cultural Resources, all records, books, writings, letters and documents kept or received by him in the transaction of his official business; and any such person who shall refuse or neglect for the space of 10 days after request made in writing by any citizen of the State to deliver as herein required such public records to the person authorized to receive them shall be guilty of a misdemeanor and upon conviction imprisoned for a term not exceeding two years or fined not exceeding one thousand dollars ($1,000) or both. (1935, c. 265, s. 4; 1943, c. 237; 1973, c. 476, s. 48; 1975, c. 696, s. 1.)

§ 132-5. Demanding custody. Whoever is entitled to the custody of public records shall demand them from any person having illegal possession of them, who shall forthwith deliver the same to him. If the person who unlawfully possesses public records shall without just cause refuse or neglect for 10 days after a request made in writing by any citizen of the State to deliver such records to their lawful custodian, he shall be guilty of a misdemeanor and upon conviction imprisoned for a term not exceeding two years or fined not exceeding one thousand dollars ($1,000) or both. (1935, c. 265, s. 5; 1975, c. 696, s. 2.)

§ 132-5.1. Regaining custody; civil remedies. (a) The Secretary of the Department of Cultural Resources or his designated representative or any public official who is the custodian of public records which are in the possession of a person or agency not authorized by the custodian or by law to possess such public records may petition the Superior Court in the county in which the person holding such records resides or in which the materials in issue, or any part thereof, are located for the return of such public records. The court may order such public records to be delivered to the petitioner upon finding that the materials in issue are public records and that such public records are in the possession of a person not authorized by the custodian of the public records or by law to possess such public records. If the order of delivery does not receive compliance, the petitioner may request that the court enforce such order through its contempt power and procedures.

(b) At any time after the filing of the petition set out in subsection (a) or contemporaneous with such filing, the public official seeking the return of the public records may be ex parte petition request the judge or the court in which the action was filed to grant one of the following provisional remedies:

(1) An order directed at the sheriff commanding him to seize the materi-

als which are the subject of the action and deliver the same to the court under the circumstances hereinafter set forth; or

(2) A preliminary injunction preventing the sale, removal, disposal or destruction of or damage to such public records pending a final judgment by the court.

(c) The judge or court aforesaid shall issue an order of seizure or grant a preliminary injunction upon receipt of an affidavit from the petitioner which alleges that the materials at issue are public records and that unless one of said provisional remedies is granted, there is a danger that such materials shall be sold, secreted, removed out of the State or otherwise disposed of so as not to be forthcoming to answer the final judgment of the court respecting the same; or that such property may be destroyed or materially damaged or injured if not seized or if injunctive relief is not granted.

(d) The aforementioned order of seizure or preliminary injunction shall issue without notice to the respondent and without the posting of any bond or other security by the petitioner. (1975, c. 787, s. 2.)

§ 132-9. Access to records. Any person who is denied access to public records for purposes of inspection, examination or copying may apply to the appropriate division of the General Court of Justice for an order compelling disclosure, and the court shall have jurisdiction to issue such orders. (1935, c. 265, s. 9; 1975, c. 787, s. 3.)

North Dakota Century Code
Volume 9

44-04-18. Access to public records. Except as otherwise specifically provided by law, all records of public or governmental bodies, boards, bureaus, commissions or agencies of the state or any political subdivision of the state, or organizations or agencies supported in whole or in part by public funds, or expending public funds, shall be public.

Ohio Revised Code, Pages Annotated
Title 1

State Government

§ 149.43 Availability of public records.

As used in this section, "public record" means any record required to be kept by any governmental unit, including, but not limited to, state, county, city, village, township, and school district units, except records pertaining to physical or psychiatric examinations, adoption, probation, and parole proceedings, and records the release of which is prohibited by state or federal law.

All public records shall be open at all reasonable times for inspection. Upon request, a person responsible for public records shall make copies available at cost, within a reasonable period of time.

§ 149.44 Availability of records in centers and archival institutions.

Any state records center or archival institution established pursuant to sections 149.31 and 149.331 [149.33.1] of the Revised Code is an extension of the departments, offices, and institutions of the state and all state records transferred to records centers and archival institutions shall be available for use by the originating agencies and agencies or individuals so designated by the office of origin. The state records administrator and the state archivist shall establish regulations and procedures for the operation of state records centers and archival institutions respectively.

HISTORY: 131 v 631. Eff 11-1-65.

§ 149.99 Penalty.

Whoever violates section 149.43 or 149.351 [149.35.1] of the Revised Code shall forfeit not more than one hundred dollars for each offense to the state. The attorney general shall collect the same by civil action.

HISTORY: 130 v 155, § 1 (Eff 9-27-63); 131 v 177. Eff 11-1-65.

Oklahoma Statutes, Annotated
1976-1977 Cumulative Annual Pocket Part
Title 51

§ 24. Records open for public inspection.

It is hereby made the duty of every public official of the State of Oklahoma, and of its sub-divisions, who are required by law to keep public records pertaining to their said offices, to keep the same open for public inspection for proper purposes, at proper times and in proper manner, to the citizens and taxpayers of this State, and its sub-divisions, during all business hours of the day; provided, however, the provisions of this act shall not apply to Income Tax Returns filed with the Oklahoma Tax Commission, or other records required by law to be kept secret. Laws 1943, p. 126, § 1.

Oregon Revised Statutes

192.410 Definitions for ORS 192.410 to 192.500. As used in ORS 192.410 to 192.500:

(1) "Public body" includes every state officer, agency, department, division, bureau, board and commission; every county and city governing body, school district, special district, municipal corporation, and any board, department, commission, council, or agency thereof; and any other public agency of this state.

(2) "State agency" includes every state officer, agency, department, division, bureau, board and commission.

(3) "Person" includes any natural person, corporation, partnership, firm or association.

(4) "Public record" includes any writing containing information relating to the conduct of the public's business, prepared, owned, used or retained by a public body regardless of physical form or characteristics.

(5) "Writing" means handwriting, typewriting, printing, photostating, photographing and every means of recording, including letters, words, pictures, sounds, or symbols, or combination thereof, and all papers, maps, magnetic or paper tapes, photographic films and prints, magnetic or punched cards, discs, drums, or other documents.
[1973 c.794 §2]

192.420 Right to inspect public records. Every person has a right to inspect any public record of a public body in this state, except as otherwise expressly provided by ORS 192.500
[1973 c.794 §3]

192.430 Functions of custodian of public records. The custodian of any public records, unless otherwise expressly provided by statute, shall furnish proper and reasonable opportunities for inspection and examination of the records in his office and reasonable facilities for making memoranda or abstracts therefrom, during the usual business hours, to all persons having occasion to make examination of them. The custodian of the records may make reasonable rules and regulations necessary for the protection of the records and to prevent interference with the regular discharge of his duties.
[1973 c.794 §4]

192.440 Certified copies of public records; fees. (1) The custodian of any public record which a person has a right to inspect shall give him, on demand, a certified copy of it, if the record is of a nature permitting such copying, or shall furnish reasonable opportunity to inspect or copy.

(2) The public body may establish fees reasonably calculated to reimburse it for its actual cost in making such records available.

[1973 c.794 §5]

192.450 Petition to review denial of right to inspect state public record; appeal from decision of Attorney General denying inspection. (1) Subject to ORS 192.480, any person denied the right to inspect or to receive a copy of any public record of a state agency may petition the Attorney General to review the public record to determine if it may be withheld from public inspection. The burden is on the agency to sustain its action. The Attorney General shall issue his order denying or granting the petition, or denying it in part and granting it in part, within three business days from the day he receives the petition.

(2) If the Attorney General grants the petition and orders the state agency to disclose the record, or if he grants the petition in part and orders the state agency to disclose a portion of the record, the state agency may institute proceedings for injunctive or declaratory relief in the Circuit Court for Marion County. If the Attorney General denies the petition in whole or in part, or if the state agency continues to withhold the record or a part of it notwithstanding an order to disclose by the Attorney General, the person seeking disclosure may institute such proceedings.

(3) The Attorney General shall serve as counsel for the state agency in a suit filed under subsection (2) of this section if the suit arises out of a determination by him that the public record should not be disclosed, or that a part of the public record should not be disclosed if the state agency has fully complied with his order requiring disclosure of another part or parts of the public record, and in no other case. In any case in which the Attorney General is prohibited from serving as counsel for the state agency, the agency may retain special counsel.

[1973 c.794 §6]

192.460 Procedure to review denial of right to inspect other public records. ORS 192.450 is equally applicable to the case of a person denied the right to inspect or receive a copy of any public record of a public body other than a state agency, except that in such case the district attorney of the county in which the public body is located, or if it is located in more than one county the district attorney of the county in which the administrative offices of the public body are located, shall carry out the functions of the Attorney General, and any suit filed shall be filed in the circuit court for such county, and except that the district attorney shall not serve as counsel for the public body in the cases permitted under subsection (3) of ORS 192.450, unless he ordinarily serves as counsel for it.

[1973 c.794 §7]

192.470 Petition form; procedure when petition received. (1) A petition to the Attorney General or district attorney requesting him to order a public record to be made available for inspection or to be produced shall be in substantially the following form, or in a form containing the same information:

(Date)
    I (we), _____ (names) _____ , the undersigned, request the Attorney General (or District Attorney of _____ County) to order (name of govern-mental body) and its employees to (make available for inspection) (produce a copy or copies of) the following records:
    1. (Name or description of record)
    2. (Name or description of record)
I (we) asked to inspect and/or copy these records on _____ (date) _____ at _____ (address) _____ . The request was denied by the following person(s):
    1. (Name of public officer or employee; title or position, if known)
    2. (Name of public officer or employee; title or position, if known)
(Signature(s))

This form should be delivered or mailed to the Attorney General's office in Salem, or the district attorney's office in the county courthouse.

(2) Promptly upon receipt of such a petition, the Attorney General or district attorney shall notify the public body involved. The public body shall thereupon transmit the public record disclosure of which is sought, or a copy, to the Attorney General, together with a statement of its reasons for believing that the public record should not be disclosed. In an appropriate case, with the consent of the Attorney General, the public body may instead disclose the nature or substance of the public record to the Attorney General.
[1973 c.794 §10]

192.480 Procedure to review denial by elected official of right to inspect public records. In any case in which a person is denied the right to inspect or to receive a copy of a public record in the custody of an elected official, or in the custody of any other person but as to which an elected official claims the right to withhold disclosure, no petition to require disclosure may be filed with the Attorney General or district attorney, or if a petition is filed it shall not be considered by the Attorney General or district attorney after a claim of right to withhold disclosure by an elected official. In such case a person denied the right to inspect or to receive a copy of a public record may institute proceedings for injunctive or declaratory relief in the appropriate circuit court, as specified in ORS 192.450 or 192.460, and the Attorney General or district attorney may upon request serve or decline to serve, in his discretion, as counsel in such suit for an elected official for which he ordinarily serves as counsel. Nothing in this section shall preclude an elected official from requesting advice from the Attorney General or a district attorney as to whether a public record should be disclosed.

[1973 c.794 §8]

192.490 Court authority in reviewing action denying right to inspect public records; docketing; attorney fees. (1) In any suit filed under ORS 192.450 to 192.480, the court has jurisdiction to enjoin the public body from withholding records and to order the production of any records improperly withheld from the person seeking disclosure. The court shall determine the matter de novo and the burden is on the public body to sustain its action. The court, on its own motion, may view the documents in controversy in camera before reaching a decision. Any noncompliance with the order of the court may be punished as contempt of court.

(2) Except as to causes the court considers of greater importance, proceedings arising under ORS 192.450 to 192.480 take precedence on the docket over all other causes and shall be assigned for hearing and trial at the earliest practicable date and expedited in every way.

(3) If a person seeking the right to inspect or to receive a copy of a public record prevails in such suit, he shall be awarded his reasonable attorney fees. If such person prevails in part, the court may in its discretion award him his reasonable attorney fees, or an appropriate portion thereof.

[1973 c.794 §9]

192.500 Public records exempt from disclosure. (1) The following public records are exempt from disclosure under ORS 192.410 to 192.500 unless the public interest requires disclosure in the particular instance:

(a) Records of a public body pertaining to litigation to which the public body is a party if the complaint has been filed, or if the complaint has not been filed, if the public body shows that such litigation is reasonably likely to occur. This exemption does not apply to litigation which has been concluded, and nothing in this paragraph shall limit any right or opportunity granted by discovery or deposition statutes to a party to litigation or potential litigation;

(b) Trade secrets. "Trade secrets," as used in this section, may include, but are not limited to, any formula, plan, pattern, process, tool, mechanism, compound, procedure, production data, or compilation of information which is not patented, which is known only to certain individuals within a commercial concern who are using it to fabricate, produce, or compound an article of trade or a service or to locate minerals or other substances, having commercial value, and which gives its user an opportunity to obtain a business advantage over competitors who do not know or use it;

(c) Investigatory information compiled for criminal law purposes, except that the record of an arrest or the report of a crime shall not be confidential unless and only so long as there is a clear need in a particular case to delay disclosure in the course of an investigation. Nothing in this paragraph shall limit any right constitutionally guaranteed, or granted by statute, to disclosure or discovery in criminal cases;

(d) Test questions, scoring keys, and other examination data used to administer a licensing examination, examination for employment, or academic examination before the examination is given and if the examination is to be used again;

(e) Information consisting of production records, sale or purchase records or catch records, or similar business records of a private concern or enterprise, required by law to be submitted to or inspected by a governmental body to allow it to determine fees or assessments payable or to establish production quotas, and the amounts of such fees or assessments payable or paid, to the extent that such information is in a form which would permit identification of the individual concern or enterprise. Nothing in this paragraph shall limit the use which can be made of such information for regulatory purposes or its admissibility in any enforcement proceeding;

(f) Information relating to the appraisal of real estate prior to its acquisition;

(g) The names and signatures of employes who sign authorization cards or petitions for the purpose of requesting representation or decertification elections; and

(h) Investigatory information relating to any complaint filed under ORS 659.040 or 659.045, until such time as the complaint is resolved under ORS 659.050, or a final administrative determination is made under ORS 659.060.

(2) The following public records are exempt from disclosure under ORS 192.410 to 192.500:

(a) Communications within a public body or between public bodies of an advisory nature to the extent that they cover other than purely factual materials and are preliminary to any final agency determination of policy or action. This exemption shall not apply unless the public body shows that in the particular instance the public interest in encouraging frank communication between officials and employes of public bodies clearly outweighs the public interest in disclosure;

(b) Information of a personal nature such as that kept in a personal, medical or similar file, if the public disclosure thereof would constitute an unreasonable invasion of privacy, unless the public interest by clear and convincing evidence requires disclosure in the particular instance. The party seeking disclosure shall have the burden of showing that public disclosure would not constitute an unreasonable invasion of privacy;

(c) Information submitted to a public body in confidence and not otherwise required by law to be submitted, where such information should reasonably be considered confidential, the public body has obliged itself in good faith not to disclose the information, and when the public interest would suffer by the disclosure;

(d) Information or records of the Corrections Division, including the State Board of Parole and Probation, to the extent that disclosure thereof would interfere with the rehabilitation of a person in custody of the division or substantially prejudice or prevent the carrying out of the functions of the division, if the public interest in confidentiality clearly outweighs the public interest in disclosure;

(e) Records, reports and other information received or compiled by the Superintendent of Banks in his administration of ORS chapters 723, 724, 725 and 726, not otherwise required by law to be made public, to the extent that the interests of lending institutions, their officers, employes and customers in preserving the confidentiality of such information outweighs the public interest in disclosure;

(f) Reports made to or filed with the court under ORS 137.075 or 137.530;

(g) Any public records or information the disclosure of which is prohibited by federal law or regulations;

(h) Public records or information the disclosure of which is prohibited or restricted or otherwise made confidential or privileged under ORS 1.440, 7.211, 7.215, 41.675, 44.040, 57.850, 146.780, 173.230, 179.495, 181.540, 306.129, 308.290, 314.835, 314.840, 336.195, 341.290, 342.850, 344.600, 351.065, 411.320, 416.230, 418.135, 418.770, 419.567, 432.060, 432.120, 432.425, 432.430, 474.160, 476.090, 483.610, 656.702, 657.665, 706.720, 706.730, 715.040, 721.050, 731.264 or 744.017; and

(i) Public records or information described in this section, furnished by the public body originally compiling, preparing or receiving them to any other public officer or public body in connection with performance of the duties of the recipient, if the considerations originally giving rise to the confidential or exempt nature of the public records or information remain applicable.

(3) If any public record contains material which is not exempt under subsection (1), (2) or (4) of this section, as well as material which is exempt from disclosure, the public body shall separate the exempt and nonexempt material and make the nonexempt material available for examination.

(4) (a) Upon application of any public body prior to convening of the 1975 regular session of the Legislative Assembly, the Governor may exempt any class of public records, in addition to the classes specified in subsection (1) of this section, from disclosure under ORS 192.410 to 192.500 unless the public interest requires disclosure in the particular instance, if he finds that the class of public records for which exemption is sought is such that unlimited public access thereto would substantially prejudice or prevent the carrying out of any public function or purpose, so that the public interest in confidentiality of such records substantially outweighs the public interest in disclosure.

Such exemption from disclosure shall be limited or conditioned to the extent the Governor finds appropriate.

(b) Prior to the granting of any exemption under this subsection the Governor shall hold a public hearing after notice as provided by ORS 183.335, or he may designate the Attorney General to hold the required hearing.

(c) Any exemption granted under this subsection shall expire upon adjournment of the 1975 regular session of the Legislative Assembly.

Pennsylvania Statutes, Purdon's Annotated
1979-1980 Cumulative Annual Pocket Part
Title 65

§ 66.1 Definitions.

In this act the following terms shall have the following meanings:

(1) "Agency." Any department, board or commission of the executive branch of the Commonwealth, any political subdivision of the Commonwealth, the Pennsylvania Turnpike Commission, or any State or municipal authority or similar organization created by or pursuant to a statute which declares in substance that such organization performs or has for its purpose the performance of an essential governmental function.

(2) "Public Record." Any account, voucher or contract dealing with the receipt or disbursement of funds by an agency or its acquisition, use or disposal of services or of supplies, materials, equipment or other property and any minute, order or decision by an agency fixing the personal or property rights, privileges, immunities, duties or obligations of any person or group of persons: Provided, That the term "public records" shall not mean any report, communication or other paper, the publication of which would disclose the institution, progress or result of an investigation undertaken by an agency in the performance of its official duties, except those reports filed by agencies pertaining to safety and health in industrial plants; it shall not include any record, document, material, exhibit, pleading, report, memorandum or other paper, access to or the publication of which is prohibited, restricted or forbidden by statute law or order or decree of court, or which would operate to the prejudice or impairment of a person's reputation or personal security, or which would result in the loss by the Commonwealth or any of its political subdivisions or commissions or State or municipal authorities of Federal funds, excepting therefrom however the record of any conviction for any criminal act.

As amended 1971, June 17, P.L. 160, No. 9, § 1.

§ 66.2 Examination and inspection.

Every public record of an agency shall, at reasonable times, be open for examination and inspection by any citizen of the Commonwealth of Pennsylvania. 1957, June 21, P.L. 390, § 2.

§ 66.3 Extracts, copies, photographs or photostats.

Any citizen of the Commonwealth of Pennsylvania shall have the right to take extracts or make copies of public records and to make photographs or photostats of the same while such records are in the possession, custody and control of the lawful custodian thereof or his authorized deputy. The lawful custodian of such records shall have the right to adopt and enforce reasonable rules governing the making of such extracts, copies, photographs or photostats. 1957, June 21, P.L. 390, § 3.

§ 66.4 Appeal from denial of right.

Any citizen of the Commonwealth of Pennsylvania denied any right granted to him by section 2 or section 3 of this act,[1] may appeal from such denial to the Court of Common Pleas of Dauphin County if an agency of the Commonwealth is involved, or to the court of common pleas of the appropriate judicial district if a political subdivision or any agency thereof is involved. If such court determines that such denial was not for just and proper cause under the terms of this act, it may enter such order for disclosure as it may deem proper. 1957, June 21, P.L. 390, § 4.

§ 66.4 Appeal from denial of right.

Repealed in Part

Section 508(a)(90) of the "Appellate Court Jurisdiction Act of 1970," 1970, July 31, P.L. 673, No. 223, (17 P.S. § 211.508(a) (90)), provided that the jurisdiction of the court named in this section is transferred to and vested in the Commonwealth Court and that this section is repealed in so far as it relates to the Court of Common Pleas of Dauphin County.

Rhode Island General Laws, 1956
1977 Pocket Supplement
Volume 7

45-43-7. Meetings—Records. All regular council of local government meetings shall be open to the public and all records of its proceedings, resolutions and actions shall be open to public view.

South Carolina Code Laws, 1976 Annotated
1978 Cumulative Supplement
Title 30

This act shall be known and cited as the "Freedom of Information Act."
§ 30-4-20. Definitions. (a) "Public body" means any department of the State, any state board, commission, agency and authority, any public or governmental body or political subdivision of the State, including counties, municipalities, townships, school districts and special purpose districts, or any organization, corporation or agency supported in whole or in part by public funds or expending public funds and includes any quasi-governmental body of the State and its political subdivisions, including, without limitation, such bodies as the South Carolina Public Service Authority and the South Carolina State Ports Authority.

(b) "Person" includes any individual, corporation, partnership, firm, organization or association.

(c) "Public record" includes all books, papers, maps, photographs, cards, tapes, recordings or other documentary materials regardless of physical form or characteristics prepared, owned, used, in the possession of or retained by a public body. Records such as income tax returns, medical records, hospital medical staff reports, scholastic records, adoption records and other records which by law are required to be closed to the public shall not be deemed to be made open to the public under the provisions of this act nor shall the definition of public records include those records concerning which the public body, by favorable public vote of three-fourths of the membership taken within fifteen working days after receipt of written request, concludes that the public interest is best served by not disclosing them. *Provided,* however, nothing herein shall authorize or require the disclosure of records of the Board of Financial Institutions pertaining to applications and surveys for charters and branches of banks and savings and loan associations or surveys and examinations of such institutions required to be made by law.

(d) "Meeting" means the convening of a quorum of the constituent membership of a public body, whether corporal or by means of electronic equipment, to discuss or act upon a matter over which the public body has supervision, control, jurisdiction or advisory power.

(e) "Quorum" unless otherwise defined by applicable law means a simple majority of the constituent membership of a public body.

Inspection of public records. (a) Any person has a right to inspect or copy any public record of a public body, except as otherwise provided by Section 5, in accordance with reasonable rules concerning time and place of access.

(b) The public body may establish and collect fees not to exceed the actual cost of searching for or making copies of records. Such records shall be furnished at the lowest possible cost to the person requesting the records. Records shall be provided in a form that is both convenient and practical for use by the person requesting copies of the records concerned, if it is equally convenient for such public body to provide the records in such form. Documents may be furnished when appropriate without charge or at a reduced charge where the agency determines that waiver or reduction of the fee is in the public interest because furnishing the information can be considered as primarily benefiting the general public. Fees shall not be charged for examination and review to determine if such documents are subject to disclosure. Nothing in this act shall prevent the custodian of the public records from charging a reasonable hourly rate for making records available to the public nor requiring a reasonable deposit of such costs prior to searching for or making copies of the records.

(c) Each public body, upon written request for records made under this act, shall within fifteen days (excepting Saturdays, Sundays and legal public holidays) of the receipt of any such request notify the person making such request of its determination and the reasons therefor. Such a determination shall constitute the final opinion of the public body as to the public availability of the requested public record.

Matters exempt from disclosure.
SECTION 5. (a) The following matters may be exempt from disclosure under the provisions of this act:

(1) Trade secrets, which are defined as unpatented, secret, commercially valuable plans, appliances, formulas, or processes, which are used for the making, preparing, compounding, treating or processing of articles or materials which are trade commodities obtained from a person and which are generally recognized as confidential.

(2) Information of a personal nature where the public disclosure thereof would constitute unreasonable invasion of personal privacy, including, but not limited to, information as to gross receipts contained in applications for business licenses.

(3) Records of law enforcement and public safety agencies not otherwise available by law that were compiled in the process of detecting and investigating crime if the disclosure of the information would harm the agency by:

(A) Disclosing identity of informants not otherwise known;

(B) The premature release of information to be used in a prospective law enforcement action;

(C) Disclosing investigatory techniques not otherwise known outside the government;

(D) By endangering the life, health or property of any person.

(4) Matters specifically exempted from disclosure by statute or law.

(5) Documents incidental to proposed contractual arrangements and proposed sale or purchase of property.

(6) Salaries of employees below the level of department head; *provided,* however, that complete salary schedules showing compensation ranges for each employee classification, including longevity steps, where applicable shall be made available.

(7) Correspondence or work products of legal counsel for a public body and any other material that would violate attorney-client relationships.

(b) If any public record contains material which is not exempt under item (a) of this section, the public body shall separate the exempt and nonexempt material available for examination.

Certain matters public information.
SECTION 6. Without limiting the meaning of other sections of this act, the following categories of information are specifically made public information subject to the restrictions and limitations of Sections 3, 5 and 8 of this act:

(1) The names, sex, race, title and dates of employment of all employees and officers of public bodies;

(2) Administrative staff manuals and instructions to staff that affect a member of the public;

(3) Final opinions, including concurring and dissenting opinions, as well as orders, made in the adjudication of cases;

(4) Those statements of policy and interpretations of policy, statute and the Constitution which have been adopted by the public body;

(5) Written planning policies and goals and final planning decisions;

(6) Information in or taken from any account, voucher or contract dealing with the receipt or expenditure of public or other funds by public bodies;

(7) The minutes of all proceedings of all public bodies and all votes at such proceedings, with the exception of all such minutes and votes taken at meetings closed to the public pursuant to Section 8.

Meetings of public bodies to be open.
SECTION 7. Every meeting of all public bodies shall be open to the public unless closed pursuant to Section 8 of this act.
When meetings may be closed
SECTION 8. (a) A public body may hold a meeting closed to the public for one or more of the following reasons:

(1) Discussion of employment, appointment, compensation, promotion, demotion, discipline or release of an employee, or the appointment of a person to a public body; *provided,* however, that if an adversary hearing

involving the employee, other than under a grievance procedure provided in Chapter 17 of Title 8 of the 1976 Code, is held such employee shall have the right to demand that the hearing be conducted publicly.

(2) Discussion of negotiations incident to proposed contractual arrangements and proposed sale or purchase of property, the receipt of legal advice, settlement of legal claims, or the position of the public agency in other adversary situations involving the assertion against said agency of a claim.

(3) Discussion regarding the development of security personnel or devices.

(4) Investigative proceedings regarding allegations of criminal misconduct.

(5) Prior to going into executive session the public agency shall vote in public on the question and when such vote is favorable the presiding officer shall announce the purpose of the executive session. Any formal action taken in executive session shall thereafter be ratified in public session prior to such action becoming effective. As used in this item "formal action" means a recorded vote committing the body concerned to a specific course of action.

(b) Any public body may hold a closed meeting for the purpose of receiving an administrative briefing by an affirmative vote of three-fourths of its members present and voting when required by some exceptional reason so compelling as to override the general public policy in favor of public meetings; *provided,* that no budgetary matters shall be discussed in such closed session except as otherwise provided by law. Such reasons and the votes of the members shall be recorded and be matters of public record. No regular or general practice or pattern of holding closed meetings shall be permitted.

(c) No chance meeting, social meeting or electronic communication shall be used in circumvention of the spirit of requirements of this act to act upon a matter over which the public body has supervision, control, jurisdiction or advisory power.

(d) This act shall not prohibit the removal of any person who wilfully disrupts a meeting to the extent that orderly conduct of the meeting is seriously compromised.

(e) Sessions of the General Assembly may enter into executive sessions authorized by the Constitution of this State and rules adopted pursuant thereto.

Notice of meetings required.
SECTION 9. (a) All public bodies shall give written public notice of their regular meetings at the beginning of each calendar year. The notice shall include the dates, times and places of such meetings. Agendas, if any, for regularly scheduled meetings shall be posted on a bulletin board at the office or meeting place of the public body at least twenty-four hours prior to such meetings. All public bodies shall post on such bulletin board public notice for any called, special or re-scheduled meetings. Such notice shall be posted as

early as is practicable but not later than twenty-four hours before the meeting. The notice shall include the agenda, date, time and place of the meeting. This requirement shall not apply to emergency meetings of public bodies.

(b) Legislative committees shall post their meeting times during weeks of the regular session of the General Assembly and shall comply with the provisions for notice of special meetings during those weeks when the General Assembly is not in session. Subcommittees of standing legislative committees shall give reasonable notice during weeks of the legislative session only if it is practicable to do so.

(c) Written public notice shall include but need not be limited to posting a copy of the notice at the principal office of the public body holding the meeting or, if no such office exists, at the building in which the meeting is to be held.

(d) All public bodies shall make an effort to notify local news media, or such other news media as may request notification of the times, dates, places and agenda of all public meetings, whether scheduled, rescheduled or called, and the efforts made to comply with this requirement shall be noted in the minutes of the meetings.

Minutes required.

SECTION 10. (a) All public bodies shall keep written minutes of all of their public meetings. Such minutes shall include but need not be limited to:

(1) The date, time and place of the meeting.

(2) The members of the public body recorded as either present or absent.

(3) The substance of all matters proposed, discussed or decided and, at the request of any member, a record, by an individual member, of any votes taken.

(4) Any other information that any member of the public body requests be included or reflected in the minutes.

(b) The minutes shall be public records and shall be available within a reasonable time after the meeting except where such disclosures would be inconsistent with Section 8 of this act.

(c) All or any part of a meeting of a public body may be recorded by any person in attendance by means of a tape recorder or any other means of sonic reproduction, except when a meeting is closed pursuant to Section 8 of this act, provided that in so recording there is no active interference with the conduct of the meeting. *Provided,* further, that the public body shall not be required to furnish recording facilities or equipment.

Injunctive relief.

SECTION 11. (a) Any citizen of the State may apply to the circuit court for injunctive relief to enforce the provisions of this act in appropriate cases provided such application is made no later than sixty days following the date which the alleged violation occurs or sixty days after ratification of such act in public session whichever comes later. The court may order equitable relief as it deems appropriate.

(b) If a person seeking such relief prevails, he may be awarded reasonable attorney fees and other costs of litigation. If such person prevails in part, the court may in its discretion award him reasonable attorney fees or an appropriate portion thereof.

Penalties.
SECTION 12. Any person or group of persons who willfully violates the provisions of this act shall be deemed guilty of a misdemeanor and upon conviction shall be fined not more than one hundred dollars or imprisoned for not more than thirty days for the first offense, shall be fined not more than two hundred dollars or imprisoned for not more than sixty days for the second offense and shall be fined three hundred dollars or imprisoned for not more than ninety days for the third or subsequent offense.
Repeal.
SECTION 13. Act 1396 of 1972, as amended by Act 608 of 1976, is repealed.
Time effective.
SECTION 14. This act shall take effect upon approval by the Governor.

Approved, July 18, 1978

South Dakota Compiled Laws, 1974 Revision
1978 Pocket Supplement
Volume 2, Title 1

1-26-2. Agency materials available for public inspection—Derogatory materials. Each agency shall make available for public inspection all rules, final orders, decisions, opinions, intra-agency memoranda, together with all other materials, written statements of policy or interpretations formulated, adopted, or used by the agency in the discharge of its functions. An agency shall hold confidential materials derogatory to a person but such information shall be made available to the person to whom it relates.

Source: SDC 1939, § 55.1203; SL 1966, ch 159, § 2; 1972, ch 8, § 4.
1-27-1. Records open to inspection. In every case where the keeping of a record, or the preservation of a document or other instrument is required of an officer or public servant under any statute of this state, such record, document, or other instrument shall be kept available and open to inspection

by any person during the business hours of the office or place where the same is kept.

Source: SL 1935, ch 177, § 1; SDC 1939, § 48.0701, SL 1977, ch 16, § 2.

Amendments: The 1977 amendment substituted "any statute of this state" for "the laws of this state."

1-27-2. Repealed by SL 1977, ch 16, § 3.

1-27-3. Records declared confidential or secret. Section 1-27-1 shall not apply to such records as are specifically enjoined to be held confidential or secret by the laws requiring them to be so kept.

Source: SL 1935, ch 177, § 2; SDC 1939, § 48.0701; SL 1977, ch 16, § 1.

Amendments: The 1977 amendment inserted "confidential or."

Tennessee Code, Annotated
1977 Cumulative Supplement
Volume 3A

15-304. Records open to public inspection. All state, county and municipal records shall at all times, during business hours, be open for personal inspection by any citizen of Tennessee, and those in charge of such records shall not refuse such right of inspection to any such citizen, unless otherwise provided by law or regulations made pursuant thereto. [Acts 1957, ch. 285, § 1.]

15-305. Confidential records. (1) The medical records of patients in state hospitals and medical facilities, and the medical records of persons receiving medical treatment, in whole or in part, at the expense of the state, shall be treated as confidential and shall not be open for inspection by members of the public. Additionally, all investigative records of the Tennessee bureau of criminal identification shall be treated as confidential and shall not be open to inspection by members of the public. The information contained in such records shall be disclosed to the public only in compliance with a subpoena or an order of a court of record, however, such investigative records of the Tennessee bureau of criminal identification shall be open to inspection by elected members of the general assembly if such inspection is directed by a duly adopted resolution of either house or of a standing or joint committee of either house. Records shall not be available to any member of the executive branch except those directly involved in the investigation in the Tennessee bureau of investigation itself and the governor himself. The records, documents and papers in the possession of the military department which involve the security of the United States and/or the state of Tennessee, including but not restricted to national guard personnel records, staff studies and investigations, shall be treated as confidential and shall not be open for inspection by members of the public.

(2) The records of students in public educational institutions shall be treated as confidential. Information in such records relating to academic performance, financial status of a student or his parent or guardian, medical or psychological treatment or testing shall not be made available to unauthorized personnel of the institution or to the public or any agency, except those agencies authorized by the educational institution to conduct specific research or otherwise authorized by the governing board of the institution, without the consent of the student involved or the parent or guardian of a minor student attending any institution of elementary or secondary education, except as otherwise provided by law or regulation pursuant thereto and except in consequence of due legal process or in cases when the safety of persons or property is involved. The governing board of the institution, the state department of education, and the Tennessee higher education commission shall have access on a confidential basis to such records as are required to fulfill their lawful functions. Statistical information not identified with a particular student may be released to any person, agency, or the public; and information relating only to an individual student's name, age, address, dates of attendance, grade levels completed, class placement and academic degrees awarded may likewise be disclosed.

(3) Any record designated "confidential" shall be so treated by agencies in the maintenance, storage and disposition of such confidential records. These records shall be destroyed in such a manner that they cannot be read, interpreted, or reconstructed. The destruction shall be in accordance with an approved records disposition authorization from the public records commission.

(4)(a) The following books, records and other materials in the possession of the office of the attorney general and reporter which relate to any pending or contemplated legal or administrative proceeding in which the office of the attorney general and reporter may be involved shall not be open for public inspection:

(i) Books, records or other materials which are confidential or privileged by state law;

(ii) Books, records or other materials relating to investigations conducted by federal law enforcement or federal regulatory agencies, which are confidential or privileged under federal law;

(iii) The work product of the attorney general and reporter or any attorney working under his supervision and control; or

(iv) Communications made to or by the attorney general and reporter or any attorney working under his supervision and control in the context of the attorney-client relationship.

(v) Books, records and other materials in the possession of other departments and agencies which are available for public inspection and copying pursuant to §§ 15-304 and 15-307. It is the intent of this section to leave subject to public inspection and copying pursuant to §§ 15-304 and 15-307 such books, records and other materials in the possession of other departments even though copies of the same books, records and other materials which are also in the possession of the attorney general's office are not subject to inspection or copying in the office of the attorney general, provided such records, books and materials are available for copying and inspection in such other departments.

(b) Books, records and other materials made confidential by this subsection which are in the possession of the office of the attorney general and reporter shall be open to inspection by the elected members of the general assembly if such inspection is directed by a duly adopted resolution of either house or of a standing or joint committee of either house and is required for the conduct of legislative business.

(c) Except for the provisions of subsection (b) hereof, the books, records and materials made confidential or privileged by this subsection shall be disclosed to the public only in the discharge of the duties of the office of the attorney general. [Acts 1957, ch. 285, § 2; 1970 (Adj. S.), ch. 531, §§ 1, 2; 1973, ch. 99, § 1; 1975, ch. 127, § 1; 1976 (Adj. S.), ch. 552, § 1; 1976 (Adj. S.), ch. 777, § 1; 1977, ch. 152, § 3; 1978 (Adj. S.), ch. 544, § 1; 1978 (Adj. S.), ch. 890, § 2.]

15-306. Violations. (1) Any official who shall violate the provisions of §§ 15-304—15-307 shall be deemed guilty of a misdemeanor.

(2) [Deleted by 1977 amendment.] [Acts 1957, ch. 285, § 3; 1975, ch. 127, § 2; 1977, ch. 152, § 4.]

15-307. Right to make copies of public records. In all cases where any person has the right to inspect any such public records, such person shall have the right to take extracts or make copies thereof, and to make photographs or photostats of the same while such records are in the possession, custody and control of the lawful custodian thereof, or his authorized deputy; provided, however, the lawful custodian of such records shall have the right to adopt and enforce reasonable rules governing the making of such extracts, copies, photographs or photostats. [Acts 1957, ch. 285, § 4.]

15-308. Records of convictions of traffic and other violations—Availability. Any public official having charge or custody of or control over any public records of convictions of traffic violations or any other state, county or municipal public offenses shall made available to any citizen, upon request, during regular office hours, a copy or copies of any such record requested by such citizen, upon the payment of a reasonable charge or fee therefor. Such official is authorized to fix a charge or fee per copy that would reasonably defray the cost of producing and delivering such copy or copies. [Acts 1974 (Adj. S.), ch. 581, § 1.]

15-310. Disposition of records. The disposition of all state records shall occur only through the process of an approved records disposition authorization. Records authorized for destruction shall be disposed of according to the records disposition authorization and shall not be given to any unauthorized person, transferred to another agency, political subdivision, private or semi-private institution. [Acts 1978 (Adj. S.), ch. 544, § 2.]

Effective Dates. Acts 1978 (Adj. S.), ch. 544, § 5. February 22, 1978.

15-401. Definitions. 1. "Section" shall mean the records management section of the department of finance and administration.

2. "Public record" or "public records" shall mean all documents, papers, letters, maps, books, photographs, microforms, electronic data processing output, films, sound recordings, or other material regardless of physical form or characteristics made or received pursuant to law or ordinance or in connection with the transaction of official business by any governmental agency.

3. "Permanent records" shall mean those records which have permanent administrative, fiscal, historical or legal value.

4. "Temporary records" shall mean those records which cease to have value immediately after departmental use and need not be retained for any purpose.

5. "Working papers" shall mean those records created to serve as input for final reporting documents, including electronic data processed records, and/or computer output microfilm, and those records which become obsolete immediately after agency use or publication.

6. "Agency" shall mean any department, division, board, bureau, commission, or other separate unit of government created or established by the constitution, by law or pursuant to law.

7. "Disposition" shall mean preservation of the original records in whole or in part, preservation by photographic or other reproduction processes, or outright destruction of the records. [Acts 1974 (Adj. S.), ch. 739, § 1; 1975, ch. 286, § 2.]

Texas Penal Code, Vernon's Annotated
1979-1980 Cumulative Annual Pocket Part
Volume 17

Art. 6252—17a. Access by public to information in custody of governmental agencies and bodies

Declaration of policy
Section 1. Pursuant to the fundamental philosophy of the American constitutional form of representative government which holds to the principle that government is the servant of the people, and not the master of them, it is hereby declared to be the public policy of the State of Texas that all persons are, unless otherwise expressly provided by law, at all times entitled to full and complete information regarding the affairs of government and the official acts of those who represent them as public officials and employees. The people, in delegating authority, do not give their public servants the right to decide what is good for the people to know and what is not good for them to know. The people insist on remaining informed so that they may retain control over the instruments they have created. To that end, the provisions of this Act shall be liberally construed with the view of carrying out the above declaration of public policy.

Definitions
Sec. 2. In this Act:
(1) "Governmental body" means:
(A) any board, commission, department, committee, institution, agency, or office within the executive or legislative branch of the state government, or which is created by either the executive or legislative branch of the state government, and which is under the direction of one or more elected or appointed members;
(B) the commissioners court of each county and the city council or governing body of each city in the state;
(C) every deliberative body having rulemaking or quasi-judicial power and classified as a department, agency, or political subdivision of a county or city;
(D) the board of trustees of every school district, and every county board of school trustees and county board of education;
(E) the governing board of every special district;
(F) the part, section, or portion of every organization, corporation, commission, committee, institution, or agency which is supported in whole or in part by public funds, or which expends public funds. Public funds as used herein shall mean funds of the State of Texas or any governmental subdivision thereof;
(G) the Judiciary is not included within this definition.
(2) "Public records" means the portion of all documents, writings, letters, memoranda, or other written, printed, typed, copied, or developed materials which contain public information.
Public information
Sec. 3. (a) All information collected, assembled, or maintained by governmental bodies pursuant to law or ordinance or in connection with the transac-

tion of official business is public information and available to the public during normal business hours of any governmental body, with the following exceptions only:

(1) information deemed confidential by law, either Constitutional, statutory, or by judicial decision;

(2) information in personnel files, the disclosure of which would constitute a clearly unwarranted invasion of personal privacy; provided, however, that all information in personnel files of an individual employee within a governmental body is to be made available to that individual employee or his designated representative as is public information under this Act;

(3) information relating to litigation of a criminal or civil nature and settlement negotiations, to which the state or political subdivision is, or may be, a party, or to which an officer or employee of the state or political subdivision, as a consequence of his office or employment, is or may be a party, that the attorney general or the respective attorneys of the various political subdivisions has determined should be withheld from public inspection;

(4) information which, if released, would give advantage to competitors or bidders;

(5) information pertaining to the location of real or personal property for public purposes prior to public announcement of the project, and information pertaining to appraisals or purchase price of real or personal property for public purposes prior to the formal award of contracts therefor;

(6) drafts and working papers involved in the preparation of proposed legislation;

(7) matters in which the duty of the Attorney General of Texas or an attorney of a political subdivision, to his client, pursuant to the Rules and Canons of Ethics of the State Bar of Texas are prohibited from disclosure, or which by order of a court are prohibited from disclosure;

(8) records of law enforcement agencies that deal with the detection and investigation of crime and the internal records and notations of such law enforcement agencies which are maintained for internal use in matters relating to law enforcement;

(9) private correspondence and communications of an elected office holder relating to matters the disclosure of which would constitute an invasion of privacy;

(10) trade secrets and commercial or financial information obtained from a person and privileged or confidential by statute or judicial decision;

(11) inter-agency or intra-agency memorandums or letters which would not be available by law to a party other than one in litigation with the agency;

(12) information contained in or related to examination, operating, or condition reports prepared by, on behalf of, or for the use of an agency

responsible for the regulation or supervision of financial institutions, and/or securities, as that term is defined in the Texas Securities Act;

(13) geological and geophysical information and data including maps concerning wells, except information filed in connection with an application or proceeding before any agency;

(14) student records at educational institutions funded wholly, or in part, by state revenue; but such records shall be made available upon request of educational institution personnel, the student involved, or that student's parent, legal guardian, or spouse;

(15) birth and death records maintained by the Bureau of Vital Statistics in the State of Texas;

(16) the audit working papers of the State Auditor.

(b) This section does not authorize withholding of information or limit the availability of records to the public, except as specifically stated in this section. This section is not authority to withhold information from individual members or committees of the legislature to use for legislative purposes.

(c) The custodian of the records may in any instance within his discretion make public any information contained within Section 3, Subsection (a) 6, 9, 11, and 15.

(d) It is not intended that the custodian of public records may be called upon to perform general research within the reference and research archives and holdings of state libraries.

Application for public information
Sec. 4. On application for public information to the custodian of information in a governmental body by any person, the custodian shall promptly produce such information for inspection or duplication, or both, in the offices of the governmental body. If the information is in active use or in storage and, therefore, not available at the time a person asks to examine it, the custodian shall certify this fact in writing to the applicant and set a date and hour within a reasonable time when the record will be available for the exercise of the right given by this Act. Nothing in this Act shall authorize any person to remove original copies of public records from the offices of any governmental body without the written permission of the custodian of the records.

Custodian of public records described
Sec. 5. (a) The chief administrative officer of the governmental body shall be the custodian of public records, and the custodian shall be responsible for the preservation and care of the public records of the governmental body. It shall be the duty of the custodian of public records, subject to penalties provided in this Act, to see that the public records are made available for public inspection and copying; that the records are carefully protected and pre-

served from deterioration, alteration, mutilation, loss, removal, or destruction; and that public records are repaired, renovated, or rebound when necessary to preserve them properly. When records are no longer currently in use, it shall be within the discretion of the agency to determine a period of time for which said records will be preserved.

(b) Neither the custodian nor his agent who controls the use of public records shall make any inquiry of any person who applies for inspection or copying of public records beyond the purpose of establishing proper identification and the public records being requested; and the custodian or his agent shall give, grant, and extend to the person requesting public records all reasonable comfort and facility for the full exercise of the right granted by this Act.

Specific information which is public

Sec. 6. Without limiting the meaning of other sections of this Act, the following categories of information are specifically made public information:

(1) reports, audits, evaluations, and investigations made of, for, or by, governmental bodies upon completion;

(2) the names, sex, ethnicity, salaries, title, and dates of employment of all employees and officers of governmental bodies;

(3) information in any account, voucher, or contract dealing with the receipt or expenditure of public or other funds by governmental bodies, not otherwise made confidential by law;

(4) the names of every official and the final record of voting on all proceedings in governmental bodies;

(5) all working papers, research material, and information used to make estimates of the need for, or expenditure of, public funds or taxes by any governmental body, upon completion of such estimates;

(6) the name, place of business, and the name of the city to which local sales and use taxes are credited, if any, for the named person, of persons reporting or paying sales and use taxes under the Limited Sales, Excise, and Use Tax Act;

(7) descriptions of an agency's central and field organization and the established places at which, the employees (and in the case of a uniformed service, the members) from whom, and the methods whereby, the public may obtain information, make submittals or requests, or obtain decisions;

(8) statements of the general course and method by which an agency's functions are channeled and determined, including the nature and requirements of all formal and informal procedures available;

(9) rules of procedure, descriptions of forms available or the places at which forms may be obtained, and instructions as to the scope and contents of all papers, reports, or examinations;

(10) substantive rules of general applicability adopted as authorized by

law, and statements of general policy or interpretations of general applicability formulated and adopted by the agency;

(11) each amendment, revisions, or repeal of 7, 8, 9 and 10 above;

(12) final opinions, including concurring and dissenting opinions, as well as orders, made in the adjudication of cases;

(13) statements of policy and interpretations which have been adopted by the agency;

(14) administrative staff manuals and instructions to staff that affect a member of the public;

(15) information currently regarded by agency policy as open to the public.

Attorney general opinions

Sec. 7. (a) If a governmental body receives a written request for information which it considers within one of the exceptions stated in Section 3 of this Act, but there has been no previous determination that it falls within one of the exceptions, the governmental body within a reasonable time, no later than ten days, after receiving a written request must request a decision from the attorney general to determine whether the information is within that exception. If a decision is not so requested, the information shall be presumed to be public information.

(b) The attorney general shall forthwith render a decision, consistent with standards of due process, to determine whether the requested information is a public record or within one of the above stated exceptions. The specific information requested shall be supplied to the attorney general but shall not be disclosed until a final determination has been made. The attorney general shall issue a written opinion based upon the determination made on the request.

Writ of mandamus

Sec. 8. If a governmental body refuses to request an attorney general's decision as provided in this Act, or to supply public information or information which the attorney general has determined to be a public record, the person requesting the information or the attorney general may seek a writ of mandamus compelling the governmental body to make the information available for public inspection.

Cost of copies of public records

Sec. 9. (a) The cost to any person requesting noncertified photographic reproductions of public records comprised of pages up to legal size shall not be excessive. The State Board of Control shall from time to time determine the actual cost of standard size reproductions and shall periodically publish these cost figures for use by agencies in determining charges to be made pursuant to this Act.

(b) Charges made for access to public records comprised in any form other than up to standard sized pages or in computer record banks, microfilm records, or other similar record keeping systems, shall be set upon consultation between the custodian of the records and the State Board of Control, giving due consideration to the expenses involved in providing the public records making every effort to match the charges with the actual cost of providing the records.

(c) It shall be the policy of all governmental bodies to provide suitable copies of all public records within a reasonable period of time after the date copies were requested. Every governmental body is hereby instructed to make reasonably efficient use of each page of public records so as not to cause excessive costs for the reproduction of public records.

(d) The charges for copies made in the district clerk's office and the county clerk's office shall be as otherwise provided by law.

(e) No charge shall be made for one copy of any public record requested from state agencies by members of the legislature in performance of their duties.

(f) The charges for copies made by the various municipal court clerks of the various cities and towns of this state shall be as otherwise provided by ordinance.

Distribution of confidential information prohibited
Sec. 10. (a) Information deemed confidential under the terms of this Act shall not be distributed.

(b) Any person who violates Section 10(a) of this Act shall be deemed guilty of a misdemeanor and upon conviction shall be punished by confinement in the county jail not to exceed six (6) months or fined in an amount not to exceed $1,000, or by both such fine and confinement.

Bond for payment of costs for preparation of public records or cash prepayment
Sec. 11. A bond for payment of costs for the preparation of such public records, or a prepayment in cash of the anticipated costs for the preparation of such records, may be required by the head of the department or agency as a condition precedent to the preparation of such record where the record is unduly costly and its reproduction would cause undue hardship to the department or agency if the costs were not paid.

Penalties
Sec. 12. Any person who wilfully destroys, mutilates, removes without per-

mission as provided herein, or alters public records shall be guilty of a misdemeanor and upon conviction shall be fined not less than $25 nor more than $4,000, or confined in the county jail not less than three days nor more than three months, or both such fine and confinement.

Procedures for inspection of public records
Sec. 13. Each governmental body may promulgate reasonable rules of procedure by which public records may be inspected efficiently, safely, and without delay.

Interpretation of this act
Sec. 14. (a) This Act does not prohibit any governmental body from voluntarily making part or all of its records available to the public, unless expressly prohibited by law; provided that such records shall then be available to any person.

(b) This Act does not authorize the withholding of information or limit the availability of public records to the public, except as expressly so provided.

(c) This Act does not give authority to withhold information from individual members or committees of the Legislature of the State of Texas to use for legislative purposes.

(d) This Act shall be liberally construed in favor of the granting of any request for information.

(e) Nothing in this Act shall be construed to require the release of information contained in education records of any educational agency or institution except in conformity with the provisions of the Family Educational Rights and Privacy Act of 1974, as enacted by Section 513 of Public Law 93–380, codified as Title 20 U.S.C.A. Section 1232g, as amended.

Severability
Sec. 15. If any provision of this Act or the application thereof to any person or circumstances is held invalid, such invalidity shall not affect other provisions or applications of the Act which can be given effect without the invalid provision or application, and to this end the provisions of this Act are declared to be severable.
Acts 1973, 63rd Leg., p. 1112, ch. 424, eff. June 14, 1973. Sec. 14(e) added by Acts 1975, 64th Leg., p. 809, ch. 314, § 1, eff. May 27, 1975.

Utah Code, Annotated
1977 Pocket Supplement
Volumes 7, 10

63-2-66. Archives and records service—Access—Certified copies. The archivist shall keep the public archives in his custody in such arrangement and condition as to make them accessible for convenient use and shall permit them to be inspected, examined, abstracted or copied at reasonable times under his supervision by any person. He shall upon the demand of any person furnish certified copies thereof on payment in advance of reasonable fees as determined by the director of finance. Copies of public records transferred pursuant to law from the office of origin to the custody of the archivist when certified by the archivist under the seal of the Utah state archives shall have the same legal force and effect as if certified by their original custodian.

78-26-1. Classes of public writings. Public writings are divided into four classes:

(1) Laws.

(2) Judicial records.

(3) Other official documents.

(4) Public records, kept in this state, of private writings, which such records may be made by handwriting, typewriting, or as a photostatic microphotographic, photographic, or similar reproduction of such private writings.

78-26-2. Right to inspect and copy. Every citizen has a right to inspect and take a copy of any public writing of this state except as otherwise expressly provided by statute.

78-26-3. Officials to furnish certified copies. Every public officer having the custody of a public writing which a citizen has the right to inspect is bound to give him, on demand, a certified copy of it, on payment of the legal fees therefor.

78-26-4. Public and private statutes defined. Statutes are public and private. A private statute is one which concerns only certain designated individuals, and affects only their private rights. All other statutes are public, in which are included statutes creating or affecting corporations.

Vermont Statutes, Annotated
1976 Cumulative Pocket Supplement
Title 1, Chapter 5

Subchapter 3. Access to Public Records
§ 315. Statement of policy.

It is the policy of this subchapter to provide for free and open examination of records consistent with Chapter I, Article 6 of the Vermont Constitution. Officers of government are trustees and servants of the people and it is in the public interest to enable any person to review and criticize their decisions even though such examination may cause inconvenience or embarrassment. All people, however, have a right to privacy in their personal and economic pursuits, which ought to be protected unless specific information is needed to review the action of a governmental officer. Consistent with these principles, the general assembly hereby declares that certain public records shall be made available to any person as hereinafter provided. To that end, the provisions of this subchapter shall be liberally construed with the view towards carrying out the above declaration of public policy.—Added 1975, No. 231 (Adj. Sess.).

§ 316. Access to public records and documents.

(a) Any person may inspect or copy any public record or document of a public agency, on any day other than a Saturday, Sunday, or a legal holiday, between the hours of nine o'clock and twelve o'clock in the forenoon and between one o'clock and four o'clock in the afternoon; provided, however, if the public agency is not regularly open to the public during those hours, inspection or copying may be made during customary office hours.

(b) If a photocopying machine or other mechanical device maintained for use by a public agency is used by the agency to copy the public record or document requested, the person requesting the copy may be charged the actual cost of providing the copy, which cost may be collected by the public agency. Nothing in this section shall exempt any person from paying fees otherwise established by law for obtaining copies of public records or documents, but if such fee is established for the copy, no additional costs or fees shall be charged.

(c) A public agency having photocopying or other mechanical copying facilities shall utilize those facilities to produce copies. If the public agency does not have such facilities, nothing in this section shall be construed to require the public agency to provide or arrange for photocopying service, to use or permit the use of copying facilities other than its own, to permit operation of its copying facilities by other than its own personnel, to permit removal of the public record by the requesting person for purposes of copying, or to make its own personnel available for making handwritten or typed copies of the public record or document requested.

(d) A public agency may make reasonable rules to prevent disruption of operations, to preserve the security of public records or documents, and to protect them from damage. Added 1975, No. 231 (Adj. Sess.).

§ 317. Definitions; public agency; public records and documents.

(a) As used in this subchapter, "public agency" or "agency" means any agency, board, department, commission, committee, branch or authority of the state or any agency, board, committee, department, branch, commission or authority of any political subdivision of the state.

(b) As used in this subchapter, "public record" or "public document" means all papers, staff reports, individual salaries, salary schedules or any other written or recorded matters produced or acquired in the course of agency business except:

(1) records which by law are designated confidential or by a similar term;

(2) records which by law may only be disclosed to specifically designated persons;

(3) records which, if made public pursuant to this subchapter, would cause the custodian to violate duly adopted standards of ethics or conduct for any profession regulated by the state;

(4) records which, if made public pursuant to this subchapter, would cause the custodian to violate any statutory or common law privilege;

(5) records dealing with the detection and investigation of crime, including those maintained on any individual or compiled in the course of a criminal or disciplinary investigation by any police or professional licensing agency; provided, however, records relating to management and direction of a law enforcement agency and records reflecting the initial arrest of a person and the charge shall be public;

(6) a tax return and related documents, correspondence and certain types of substantiating forms which include the same type of information as in the tax return itself filed with or maintained by the Vermont department of taxes or submitted by a person to any public agency in connection with agency business;

(7) personal documents relating to an individual, including information in any files maintained to hire, evaluate, promote or discipline any employee of a public agency, information in any files relating to personal finances, medical or psychological facts concerning any individual or corporation; provided, however, that all information in personnel files of an individual employee of any public agency shall be made available to that individual employee or his designated representative;

(8) test questions, scoring keys, and other examination instruments or data used to administer a license, employment, or academic examination;

(9) trade secrets, including, but not limited to, any formulae, plan, pattern, process, tool, mechanism, compound, procedure, production data, or compilation of information which is not patented, which is known only to certain individuals within a commercial concern, and which gives its user or owner an opportunity to obtain business advantage over competitors who do not know it or use it;

(10) lists of names compiled or obtained by a public agency when disclosure would violate a person's right to privacy or produce public or private gain, provided; however, that this section does not apply to lists which are by law made available to the public;

(11) student records at educational institutions funded wholly or in part by state revenue; provided, however, that such records shall be made available upon request under the provisions of the Federal Family Educational Rights and Privacy Act of 1974 (P.L. 93–380) and as amended;

(12) records concerning formulation of policy where such would constitute a clearly unwarranted invasion of personal privacy, if disclosed;

(13) information pertaining to the location of real or personal property for public agency purposes prior to public announcement of the project and, information pertaining to appraisals or purchase price of real or personal property for public purposes prior to the formal award of contracts thereof;

(14) records which are relevant to litigation to which the public agency is a party of record, provided all such matters shall be available to the public after ruled discoverable by the court before which the litigation is pending, but in any event upon final termination of the litigation;

(15) records relating specifically to negotiation of contracts including but not limited to collective bargaining agreements with public employees;

(16) any voluntary information provided by an individual, corporation, organization, partnership, association, trustee, estate, or any other entity in the state of Vermont, which has been gathered prior to the enactment of this subchapter, shall not be considered a public document.—Added 1975, No. 231 (Adj. Sess.).

(17) records of inter-departmental and intra-departmental communications in any County, City, Town, Village, Town School District, Incorporated School District, Union School District, Consolidated Water District, Fire District, or any other political subdivision of the state to the extent that they cover other than primarily factual materials and are preliminary to any determination of policy or action or precede the presentation of the budget at a meeting held in accordance with 1 V.S.A. Section 312

§ 318. Procedure.

(a) Upon request the custodian of a public record shall promptly produce the record for inspection, except that:

(1) if the record is in active use or in storage and therefore not available

for use at the time the person asks to examine it, the custodian shall so certify this fact in writing to the applicant and set a date and hour within one calendar week of the request when the record will be available for examination;

(2) if the custodian considers the record to be exempt from inspection under the provisions of this subchapter, he shall so certify in writing stating his reasons for denial of access to the record. Such certification shall be made within two business days, unless otherwise provided in division (5) of this subsection. The custodian shall also notify the person of his right to appeal to the head of the agency any adverse determination;

(3) if appealed to the head of the agency, the head of the agency shall make a determination with respect to any appeal within five days, excepting Saturdays, Sundays, and legal public holidays, after the receipt of such appeal. If an appeal of the denial of the request for records is in whole or in part upheld, the agency shall notify the person making such request of the provisions for judicial review of that determination under section 319 of this title;

(4) if a record does not exist, the custodian shall certify in writing that the record does not exist under the name given to him by the applicant or by any other name known to the custodian;

(5) in unusual circumstances as herein specified the time limits prescribed in this subsection may be extended by written notice to the person making such request setting forth the reasons for such extension and the date on which a determination is expected to be dispatched. No such notice shall specify a date that would result in an extension for more than ten working days. As used in this division, "unusual circumstances" means to the extent reasonably necessary to the proper processing of the particular request:

(A) the need to search for and collect the requested records from field facilities or other establishments that are separate from the office processing the request;

(B) the need to search for, collect, and appropriately examine a voluminous amount of separate and distinct records which are demanded in a single request; or

(C) the need for consultation, which shall be conducted with all practicable speed, with another agency having a substantial interest in the determination of the request or among two or more components of the agency having substantial subject matter interest therein, or with the attorney general.

(b) Any person making a request to any agency for records under subsection (a) of this section shall be deemed to have exhausted his administrative remedies with respect to each request if the agency fails to comply within the applicable time limit provisions of this section. Upon any determination by an agency to comply with a request for records, the records shall be made available promptly to the person making such request. Any notification of denial of any request for records under this section shall set forth the names and titles or positions of each person responsible for the denial of such request. Added 1975, No. 231 (Adj. Sess.).

§ 319. Enforcement.

(a) Any person aggrieved by the denial of a request for public records under this subchapter may apply to the superior court in the county in which the complainant resides, or has his personal place of business, or in which the public records are situated, or in the superior court of Washington County, to enjoin the public agency from withholding agency records and to order the production of any agency records improperly withheld from the complainant. In such a case the court shall determine the matter de novo, and may examine the contents of such agency records in camera to determine whether such records or any part thereof shall be withheld under any of the exemptions set forth in section 317 of this title, and the burden is on the agency to sustain its action.

(b) Except as to cases the court considers of greater importance, proceedings before the superior court, as authorized by this section, and appeals therefrom, take precedence on the docket over all cases and shall be assigned for hearing and trial or for argument at the earliest practicable date and expedited in every way.

(c) If the public agency can show the court that exceptional circumstances exist and that the agency is exercising due diligence in responding to the request, the court may retain jurisdiction and allow the agency additional time to complete its review of the records.

(d) The court may assess against the public agency reasonable attorney fees and other litigation costs reasonably incurred in any case under this section in which the complainant has substantially prevailed. Added 1975, No. 231 (Adj. Sess.).

§ 320. Penalties.

(a) Whenever the court orders the production of any public agency records, improperly withheld from the complainant and assesses against the agency reasonable attorney fees and other litigation costs, and the court additionally issues a written finding that the circumstances surrounding the withholding raise questions whether the agency personnel acted arbitrarily or capriciously with respect to the withholding, the department of personnel if applicable to that employee, shall promptly initiate a proceeding to determine whether disciplinary action is warranted against the officer or employee who was primarily responsible for the withholding. The department, after investigation and consideration of the evidence submitted, shall submit its findings and recommendations to the administrative authority of the agency concerned and shall send copies of the findings and recommendations to the officer or employee or his representative. The administrative authority shall take the corrective action that the department recommends.

(b) In the event of noncompliance with the order of the court, the superior court may punish for contempt the responsible employee or official, and in the case of a uniformed service, the responsible member. Added 1975, No. 231 (Adj. Sess.).

Virginia Code, 1950
1976 Cumulative Supplement
Volume 1

§ 2.1-340.1. Policy of chapter. It is the purpose of the General Assembly by providing this chapter to ensure to the people of this Commonwealth ready access to records in the custody of public officials and free entry to meetings of public bodies wherein the business of the people is being conducted. This chapter recognizes that the affairs of government are not intended to be conducted in an atmosphere of secrecy since at all times the public is to be the beneficiary of any action taken at any level of government. To the end that the purposes of this chapter may be realized, it shall be liberally construed to promote an increased awareness by all persons of governmental activities and afford every opportunity to citizens to witness the operations of government. Any exception or exemption from applicability shall be narrowly construed in order that no thing which should be public may be hidden from any person. (1976, c. 467.)

§ 2.1-341. Definitions.

(b) *"Official records"* means all written or printed books, papers, letters, documents, maps and tapes, photographs, films, sound recordings, reports or other material, regardless of physical form or characteristics, made and received in pursuance of law by the public officers of the State and its counties, municipalities and subdivisions of government in the transaction of public business.

(e) *"Public body"* shall mean any of the groups, agencies or organizations enumerated in subsection (a) of this section.

(f) *"Scholastic records"* means those records, files, documents, and other materials containing information about a student and maintained by a public body which is an educational agency or institution or by a person acting for such agency or institution, but, for the purpose of access by a student, does not include (i) financial records of a parent or guardian nor (ii) records of instructional, supervisory, and administrative personnel and educational personnel ancillary thereto, which are in the sole possession of the maker thereof and which are not accessible or revealed to any other person except a substitute. c.1968, c. 479; 1970, c. 456; 1974, c. 332; 1975, c. 307.)

§ 2.1-341.1. Notice of chapter. Any person elected, reelected, appointed or reappointed to any body not excepted from this chapter shall be furnished by the public body's administrator or legal counsel with a copy of this chapter within two weeks following election, reelection, appointment or reappointment. (1976, c. 467.)

§ 2.1-342. Official records to be open to inspection; procedure for requesting records and responding to request; charges; exceptions to application of chapter. (a) Except as otherwise specifically provided by law, all official records shall be open to inspection and copying by any citizens of this State during the regular office hours of the custodian of such records. Access to such records shall not be denied to any such citizen of this State, nor to representatives of newspapers and magazines with circulation in this State, and representatives of radio and television stations broadcasting in or into this State; provided, that the custodian of such records shall take all necessary precautions for their preservation and safekeeping. Any public body covered under the provisions of this chapter shall make an initial response to citizens requesting records open to inspection within fourteen calendar days from the receipt of the request by the public body. Such citizen request shall designate the requested records with reasonable specificity. If the requested records or public body are excluded from the provisions of this chapter, the public body to which the request is directed shall within fourteen calendar days from the receipt of the request tender a written explanation as to why the records are not available to the requestor. Such explanation shall make specific reference to the applicable provisions of this chapter or other Code sections which make the requested records unavailable. In the event a determination of the availability of the requested records may not be made within the fourteen-calendar-day period, the public body to which the request is directed shall inform the requestor as such, and shall have an additional ten calendar days in which to make a determination of availability. A specific reference to this chapter by the requesting citizen in his records request shall not be necessary to invoke the time limits for response by the public body. The public body may make reasonable charges for the copying and search time expended in the supplying of such records; however, in no event shall such charges exceed the actual cost of the public body in supplying such records. Such charges for the supplying of requested records shall be estimated in advance at the request of the citizen.

(b) The following records are excluded from the provisions of this chapter:

(1) Memoranda, correspondence, evidence and complaints related to criminal investigations, reports submitted to the State and local police in confidence, and all records of persons imprisoned in a penal institution in this State provided such records relate to the said imprisonment.

(2) Confidential records of all investigations of applications for licenses and all licensees made by or submitted to the Alcoholic Beverage Control Board.

(3) State income tax returns, scholastic records and personnel records, except that such access shall not be denied to the person who is the subject thereof, and medical and mental records, except that such records can be personally reviewed by the subject person or a physician of the subject person's choice; provided, however, that the subject person's mental records may not be personally reviewed by such person when the subject person's treating physician has made a part of such person's records a written statement that in his opinion a review of such records by the subject person would be injurious to the subject person's physical or mental health or well-being. Where the person who is the subject of scholastic or medical and mental records is under the age of eighteen, his right of access may be asserted only by his parent or guardian, except in instances where the person who is the subject thereof is an emancipated minor or a student in a state-supported institution of higher education.

(4) Memoranda, working papers and correspondence held by members of the General Assembly or by the office of the Governor or Lieutenant Governor, Attorney General or the mayor or other chief executive officer of any political subdivision of the State or the president or other chief executive officer of any state-supported institutions of higher education.

(5) Memoranda, working papers and records compiled specifically for use in litigation and material furnished in confidence with respect thereto.

(6) Confidential letters and statements of recommendation placed in the records of educational agencies or institutions respecting (i) admission to any educational agency or institution, (ii) an application for employment, or (iii) receipt of an honor or honorary recognition. (1968, c. 479; 1973, c. 461; 1974, c. 332; 1975, cc. 307, 312; 1976, cc. 640, 709.)

§ 2.1-343. Meetings to be public except as otherwise provided; minutes: information as to time and place.—Except as otherwise specifically provided by law and except as provided in §§ 2.1-344 and 2.1-345, all meetings shall be public meetings. Minutes shall be recorded at all public meetings. Information as to the time and place of each meeting shall be furnished to any citizen of this State who requests such information. Requests to be notified on a continual basis shall be made at least once a year in writing and include name, address, zip code and organization if any, together with an adequate supply of stamped self-addressed envelopes. (1968, c. 479; 1973, c. 461; 1976, c. 467.)

§ 2.1-344. Executive or closed meetings.—(a) Executive or closed meetings may be held only for the following purposes:

(1) Discussion or consideration of employment, assignment, appointment,

promotion, demotion, salaries, disciplining or resignation of public officers, appointees or employees of any public body.

(2) Discussion or consideration of the condition, acquisition or use of real property for public purpose, or of the disposition of publicly held property.

(3) The protection of the privacy of individuals in personal matters not related to public business.

(4) Discussion concerning a prospective business or industry where no previous announcement has been made of the business' or industry's interest in locating in the community.

(5) The investing of public funds where competition or bargaining are involved, where if made public initially the financial interest of the governmental unit would be adversely affected.

(6) Consultation with legal counsel and briefings by staff members, consultants or attorneys, pertaining to actual or potential litigation, or other legal matters within the jurisdiction of the public body.

(b) No meeting shall become an executive or closed meeting unless there shall have been recorded in open meeting an affirmative vote to that effect by the public body holding such meeting, which motion shall state specifically the purpose or purposes hereinabove set forth in this section which are to be the subject of such meeting and a statement included in the minutes of such meeting which shall make specific reference to the applicable exemption or exemptions as provided in subsection (a) or § 2.1-345. A general reference to the provisions of this chapter or to the exemptions of subsection (a) shall not be sufficient to satisfy the requirements for an executive or closed meeting. The public body holding such an executive or closed meeting shall restrict its consideration of matters during the closed portions to only those purposes specifically exempted from the provisions of this chapter.

(c) No resolution, ordinance, rule, contract, regulation or motion adopted, passed or agreed to in an executive or closed meeting shall become effective unless such public body, following such meeting, reconvenes in open meeting and takes a vote of the membership on such resolution, ordinance, rule, contract, regulation or motion.

(d) Nothing in this section shall be construed to prevent the holding of conferences between two or more public bodies, or their representatives, but these conferences shall be subject to the same regulations for holding executive or closed sessions as are applicable to any other public body. (1968, c. 479; 1970, c. 456; 1973, c. 461; 1974, c. 332; 1976, cc. 467, 709.)

§ 2.1-345. Agencies to which chapter inapplicable—The provisions of this chapter shall not be applicable to:

(1) Deliberations of standing and other committees of the General Assembly. Provided that, unless such action contravenes the rules of a body of the General Assembly under provisions of Article IV, § 7 of the Constitution of

Virginia, when bills or other legislative matters are considered in executive or closed meetings, final votes thereon shall be taken in open meetings.

(2) Legislative interim study commissions and committees, including the Virginia Code Commission; provided, however, that final votes shall be taken in open meetings.

(3) The Virginia Advisory Legislative Council and its committees; provided, however, that final votes shall be taken in open meetings.

(4) Study committees or commissions appointed by the Governor; provided, however, that final votes shall be taken in open meetings.

(5) Boards of visitors or trustees of state-supported institutions of higher education; provided, that, except for the actions excluded by § 2.1-344, announcements of the actions of such boards are made available immediately following the meetings, with membership of such boards then available for discussion of actions taken, and that the official minutes of the board meetings are made available to the public not more than three working days after such meetings.

(6) Parole boards; petit juries; grand juries; and the Virginia State Crime Commission.

(7) Study commissions or study committees appointed by the governing bodies of counties, cities and towns; provided, however, that final votes shall be taken in open meetings and provided, further, that no such committee or commission appointed by such governing bodies, the membership of which includes more than one member of a three member governing body or includes more than two members of a governing body having four or more members, shall be deemed to be study commissions or study committees under the provisions of this section. (1968, c. 479; 1971, Ex. Sess., c. 1; 1973, c. 461; 1974, c. 332.)

§ 2.1-346. Proceedings for enforcement of chapter. Any person denied the rights and privileges conferred by this chapter may proceed to enforce such rights and privileges by petition for mandamus or injunction, supported by an affidavit showing good cause, addressed to the court of record, having jurisdiction of such matters, of the county or city in which such rights and privileges were so denied. Any such petition alleging such denial by a board bureau, commission, authority, district or agency of the State government or by a standing or other committee of the General Assembly, shall be addressed to the Circuit Court of the city of Richmond. Such petition shall be heard within seven days of the date when the same is made; provided, if such petition is made outside of the regular terms of the circuit court of a county which is included in a judicial circuit with another county or counties, the hearing on such petition shall be given precedence on the docket of such court over all cases which are not otherwise given precedence by law. Such petition shall allege with reasonable specificity the circumstances of the denial of the rights and privileges conferred by this chapter. A single instance of denial of such rights and privileges conferred by this chapter shall be sufficient to invoke the remedies granted herein. If the court finds the denial to be in violation of the provisions of this chapter, the court may award costs and reasonable attorney's fees to the petitioning citizen. Such costs and fees shall be paid by the public body in violation of this chapter. The court may award costs and reasonable attorney's fees to the public body if the court finds that the petition was based upon a clearly inadequate case. (1968, c. 479; 1976, c. 709.)

§ 2.1-346.1. Violations and penalties. In a proceeding commenced against members of governing bodies under § 2.1-346 for a violation of §§ 2.1-342, 2.1-343 or 2.1-344, the court, if it finds that a violation was willfully and knowingly made, shall impose upon such person or persons in his or her individual capacity, whether a writ of mandamus or injunctive relief is awarded or not, a civil penalty of not less than twenty-five dollars nor more than five hundred dollars, which amount shall be paid into the State Literary Fund. (1976, c. 467.)

Washington Revised Code, Annotated
1977 Pocket Part
Title 42

42.17.250 Duty to publish procedures.

(1) Each state agency shall separately state and currently publish in the Washington Administrative Code and each local agency shall prominently display and make available for inspection and copying at the central office of such local agency, for guidance of the public:

(a) descriptions of its central and field organization and the established places at which, the employees from whom, and the methods whereby, the public may obtain information, make submittals or requests, or obtain copies of agency decisions;

(b) statements of the general course and method by which its operations are channeled and determined, including the nature and requirements of all formal and informal procedures available;

(c) rules of procedure;

(d) substantive rules of general applicability adopted as authorized by law, and statements of general policy or interpretations of general applicability formulated and adopted by the agency; and

(e) each amendment or revision to, or repeal of any of the foregoing.

(2) Except to the extent that he has actual and timely notice of the terms

thereof, a person may not in any manner be required to resort to, or be adversely affected by, a matter required to be published or displayed and not so published or displayed. [Enacted Laws 1973 ch 1 § 25, effective January 1, 1973 (Initiative Measure No. 276 § 25).]

42.17.260 Documents and indexes to be made public.

(1) Each agency, in accordance with published rules, shall make available for public inspection and copying all public records. To the extent required to prevent an unreasonable invasion of personal privacy, an agency shall delete identifying details when it makes available or publishes any public record; however, in each case, the justification for the deletion shall be explained fully in writing.

(2) Each agency shall maintain and make available for public inspection and copying a current index providing identifying information as to the following records issued, adopted, or promulgated after January 1, 1973:

(a) Final opinions, including concurring and dissenting opinions, as well as orders, made in the adjudication of cases;

(b) Those statements of policy and interpretations of policy, statute, and the Constitution which have been adopted by the agency;

(c) Administrative staff manuals and instructions to staff that affect a member of the public;

(d) Planning policies and goals, and interim and final planning decisions;

(e) Factual staff reports and studies, factual consultant's reports and studies, scientific reports and studies, and any other factual information derived from tests, studies, reports, or surveys, whether conducted by public employees or others; and

(f) Correspondence, and materials referred to therein, by and with the agency relating to any regulatory, supervisory, or enforcement responsibilities of the agency, whereby the agency determines, or opines upon, or is asked to determine or opine upon, the rights of the state, the public, a subdivision of state government, or of any private party.

(3) An agency need not maintain such an index, if to do so would be unduly burdensome, but it shall in that event:

(a) Issue and publish a formal order specifying the reasons why and the extent to which compliance would unduly burden or interfere with agency operations; and

(b) Make available for public inspection and copying all indexes maintained for agency use.

(4) A public record may be relied on, used, or cited as precedent by an agency against a party other than an agency and it may be invoked by the agency for any other purpose only if—

(a) It has been indexed in an index available to the public; or

(b) Parties affected have timely notice (actual or constructive) of the terms thereof.

(5) This chapter shall not be construed as giving authority to any agency to give, sell or provide access to lists of individuals requested for commercial purposes, and agencies shall not do so unless specifically authorized or directed by law: *Provided, however,* That lists of applicants for professional licenses and of professional licensees shall be made available to those professional associations or educational organizations recognized by their professional licensing or examination board, upon payment of a reasonable charge therefor: *Provided further,* That such recognition may be refused only for a good cause pursuant to a hearing under the provisions of chapter 34.04 RCW. [Enacted Laws 1973 ch 1 § 26, effective January 1, 1973 (Initiative Measure No. 276 § 26); Amended by Laws 1st Ex Sess 1975 ch 294 § 14, effective July 2, 1975.]

42.17.270 Facilities for copying—Availability of public records.

Public records shall be available for inspection and copying, and agencies shall, upon request for identifiable public records, make them promptly available to any person. Agency facilities shall be made available to any person for the copying of public records except when and to the extent that this would unreasonably disrupt the operations of the agency. Agencies shall honor requests received by mail for identifiable public records unless exempted by provisions of this chapter. [Enacted Laws 1973 ch 1 § 27, effective January 1, 1973 (Initiative Measure No. 276 § 27); Amended by Laws 1st Ex Sess 1975 ch 294 § 15, effective July 2, 1975.]

42.17.280 Times for inspection and copying.

Public records shall be available for inspection and copying during the customary office hours of the agency: *Provided,* that if the agency does not have customary office hours of at least thirty hours per week, the public records shall be available from nine o'clock a. m. to noon and from one o'clock p. m. to four o'clock p. m. Monday through Friday, excluding legal holidays, unless the person making the request and the agency or its representative agree on a different time. [Enacted Laws 1973 ch 1 § 28, effective January 1, 1973 (Initiative Measure No. 276 § 28).]

42.17.290 Protection of public records—Public access.

Agencies shall adopt and enforce reasonable rules and regulations, consonant with the intent of this chapter to provide full public access to public records, to protect public records from damage or disorganization, and to prevent excessive interference with other essential functions of the agency. Such rules and regulations shall provide for the fullest assistance to inquirers and the most timely possible action on requests for information. Nothing in this section shall relieve agencies from honoring requests received by mail for copies of identifiable public records. [Enacted Laws 1973 ch 1 § 29, effective

January 1, 1973 (Initiative Measure No. 276 § 28); Amended by Laws 1st Ex Sess 1975 ch 294 § 16, effective July 2, 1975.]

42.17.300 Charges for copying.

No fee shall be charged for the inspection of public records. Agencies may impose a reasonable charge for providing copies of public records and for the use by any person of agency equipment to copy public records, which charges shall not exceed the amount necessary to reimburse the agency for its actual costs incident to such copying. [Enacted Laws 1973 ch 1 § 30, effective January 1, 1973 (Initiative Measure No. 276 § 30).]

42.17.310 Certain personal and other records exempt.

(1) The following shall be exempt from public inspection and copying:

(a) Personal information in any files maintained for students in public schools, patients or clients of public institutions or public health agencies, welfare recipients, prisoners, probationers, or parolees.

(b) Personal information in files maintained for employees, appointees, or elected officials of any public agency to the extent that disclosure would violate their right to privacy.

(c) Information required of any taxpayer in connection with the assessment or collection of any tax if the disclosure of the information to other persons would violate the taxpayer's right to privacy or would result in unfair competitive disadvantage to such taxpayer.

(d) Specific intelligence information and specific investigative records compiled by investigative, law enforcement, and penology agencies, and state agencies vested with the responsibility to discipline members of any profession, the nondisclosure of which is essential to effective law enforcement or for the protection of any person's right to privacy.

(e) Information revealing the identity of persons who file complaints with investigative, law enforcement, or penology agencies, other than the public disclosure commission, if disclosure would endanger any person's life, physical safety, or property: *Provided,* That if at the time the complaint is filed the complainant indicates a desire for disclosure or nondisclosure, such desire shall govern: *Provided, further,* That all complaints filed with the public disclosure commission about any elected official or candidate for public office must be made in writing and signed by the complainant under oath.

(f) Test questions, scoring keys, and other examination data used to administer a license, employment, or academic examination.

(g) Except as provided by chapter 8.26 RCW, the contents of real estate appraisals, made for or by any agency relative to the acquisition or sale of property, until the project or prospective sale is abandoned or until such time as all of the property has been acquired or the property to which the sale appraisal relates is sold, but in no event shall disclosure be denied for more than three years after the appraisal.

(h) Valuable formulae, designs, drawings, and research data obtained by any agency within five years of the request for disclosure when disclosure would produce private gain and public loss.

(i) Preliminary drafts, notes, recommendations, and intra-agency memorandums in which opinions are expressed or policies formulated or recommended except that a specific record shall not be exempt when publicly cited by an agency in connection with any agency action.

(j) Records which are relevant to a controversy to which an agency is a party but which records would not be available to another party under the rules of pretrial discovery for causes pending in the superior courts.

(2) The exemptions of this section shall be inapplicable to the extent that information, the disclosure of which would violate personal privacy or vital governmental interests, can be deleted from the specific records sought. No exemption shall be construed to permit the nondisclosure of statistical information not descriptive of any readily identifiable person or persons.

(3) Inspection or copying of any specific records, exempt under the provisions of this section, may be permitted if the superior court in the county in which the record is maintained finds, after a hearing with notice thereof to every person in interest and the agency, that the exemption of such records, is clearly unnecessary to protect any individual's right of privacy or any vital governmental function.

(4) Agency responses refusing, in whole or part, inspection of any public record shall include a statement of the specific exemption authorizing the withholding of the record (or part) and a brief explanation of how the exemption applies to the record withheld. [Enacted Laws 1973 ch 1 § 31, effective January 1, 1973 (Initiative Measure No. 276 § 31); Amended by Laws 1st Ex Sess 1975 ch 294 § 17, effective July 2, 1975.]

42.17.315 Certain records obtained by colleges, universities, libraries or archives exempt.

Notwithstanding the provisions of RCW 42.17.260 through 42.17.340, as now or hereafter amended, no state college, university, library, or archive shall be required by chapter 42.17 RCW to make available for public inspection and copying any records or documents obtained by said college, university, library, or archive through or concerning any gift, grant, conveyance, bequest, or devise, the terms of which restrict or regulate public access to such records or documents: *Provided,* That his section shall not apply to any public records as defined in RCW 40.14.010. [Added by Laws 1st Ex Sess 1975 ch 294 §22, effective July 2, 1975.]

42.17.320 Prompt responses required.

Responses to requests for public records shall be made promptly by agencies. Denials of requests must be accompanied by a written statement of the specific reasons therefor. Agencies shall establish mechanisms for the most prompt possible review of decisions denying inspection, and such review shall be deemed completed at the end of the second business day following the denial of inspection and shall constitute final agency action for the purposes of judicial review. [Enacted Laws 1973 ch 1 § 32, effective January 1, 1978 (Initiative Measure No. 276 § 32); Amended by Laws 1st Ex Sess 1975 ch 294 § 18, effective July 2, 1975.)

42.17.330 Court protection of public records.

The examination of any specific public record may be enjoined if, upon motion and affidavit, the superior court for the county in which the movant resides or in which the record is maintained, finds that such examination would clearly not be in the public interest and would substantially and irreparably damage vital governmental functions. [Enacted Laws 1973 ch 1 § 33, effective January 1, 1973 (Initiative Measure No. 276 § 33); Amended by Laws 1st Ex Sess 1975 ch 294 § 19, effective July 2, 1975.]

42.17.340 Judicial review of agency actions.

(1) Upon the motion of any person having been denied an opportunity to inspect or copy a public record by an agency, the superior court in the county in which a record is maintained may require the responsible agency to show cause why it has refused to allow inspection or copying of a specific public record or class of records. The burden of proof shall be on the agency to establish that refusal to permit public inspection and copying is required.

(2) Judicial review of all agency actions taken or challenged under RCW 42.17.250 through 42.17.320 shall be de novo. Courts shall take into account the policy of this chapter that free and open examination of public records is in the public interest, even though such examination may cause inconvenience or embarrassment to public officials or others. Courts may examine any record in camera in any proceeding brought under this section.

(3) Any person who prevails against an agency in any action in the courts seeking the right to inspect or copy any public record shall be awarded all costs, including reasonable attorney fees, incurred in connection with such legal action. In addition, it shall be within the discretion of the court to award such person an amount not to exceed twenty-five dollars for each day that he was denied the right to inspect or copy said public record. [Enacted Laws 1973 ch 1 § 34, effective January 1, 1973 (Initiative Measure No. 276 § 34); Amended by Laws 1st Ex Sess 1975 ch 294 § 20, effective July 2, 1975.]

CJS Records §§ 35 et seq.

Ops Atty Gen 1973 No. 4 (availability, for inspection and copying, of records of school district relating to district employees' salaries and payroll deductions).

Key Number Digests: Records   14.
Administration and Enforcement

42.17.350 Public disclosure commission—Established—Membership—Per diem.

There is hereby established a "Public Disclosure Commission" which shall be composed of five members who shall be appointed by the governor, with the consent of the senate. All appointees shall be persons of the highest integrity and qualifications. No more than three members shall have an identification with the same political party. The original members shall be appointed within sixty days after the effective date of this act. The term of each member shall be five years except that the original five members shall serve initial terms of one, two, three, four, and five years, respectively, as designated by the governor. No member of the commission, during his tenure, shall (1) hold or campaign for elective office; (2) be an officer of any political party or political committee; (3) permit his name to be used, or make contributions, in support of or in opposition to any candidate or proposition; (4) participate in any way in any election campaign; or (5) lobby or employ or assist a lobbyist. No member shall be eligible for appointment to more than one full term. A vacancy on the commission shall be filled within thirty days of the vacancy by the governor, with the consent of thesenate, and the appointee shall serve for the remaining term of his predecessor. A vacancy shall not impair the powers of the remaining members to exercise all of the powers of the commission. Three members of the commission shall constitute a quorum. The commission shall elect its own chairman and adopt its own rules of procedure in the manner provided in chapter 34.04 RCW. Any member of the commission may be removed by the governor, but only upon grounds of neglect of duty or misconduct in office.

Each member shall receive per diem in the amount of forty dollars in lieu of expenses for each day or portion thereof spent in performance of his duties as a member of the commission, and in addition shall be reimbursed for travel expenses actually incurred while engaged in the business of the commission as provided in chapter 43.03 RCW. The compensation provided pursuant to this section shall not be considered salary for purposes of the provisions of any retirement system created pursuant to the general laws of this state.

Nothing in this section shall prohibit the commission, or any of its members or staff on the authority of the commission, from responding to communications from the legislature or any of its members or from any state agency or from appearing and testifying at an open public meeting (as defined by RCW 42.30.030) or a hearing to adopt rules held pursuant to RCW 34.04.025 on matters directly affecting the exercise of their duties and powers under this chapter. [Enacted Laws 1973 ch 1 § 35, effective January 1, 1973 (Initiative Measure No. 276 § 35); Amended by Laws 1st Ex Sess 1975 ch 294 § 23, effective July 2, 1975.]

42.17.360 Commission—Duties.

The commission shall:

(1) Develop and provide forms for the reports and statements required to be made under this chapter;

(2) Prepare and publish a manual setting forth recommended uniform methods of bookkeeping and reporting for use by persons required to make reports and statements under this chapter;

(3) Compile and maintain a current list of all filed reports and statements;

(4) Investigate whether properly completed statements and reports have been filed within the times required by this chapter;

(5) Upon complaint or upon its own motion, investigate and report apparent violations of this chapter to the appropriate law enforcement authorities;

(6) Prepare and publish an annual report to the governor as to the effectiveness of this chapter and its enforcement by appropriate law enforcement authorities; and

(7) Enforce this chapter according to the powers granted it by law. [Enacted Laws 1973 ch 1 § 36, effective January 1, 1973 (Initiative Measure No. 276 § 36).]

42.17.370 Commission—Additional powers.

The commission is empowered to:

(1) Adopt, promulgate, amend, and rescind suitable administrative rules and regulations to carry out the policies and purposes of this chapter, which rules and regulations shall be promulgated pursuant to the provisions of chapter 34.04 RCW;

(2) Prepare and publish such reports and technical studies as in its judgment will tend to promote the purposes of this chapter, including reports and statistics concerning campaign financing, lobbying, financial interests of elected officals, and enforcement of this chapter;

(3) Make from time to time, on its own motion, audits and field investigations;

(4) Make public the time and date of any formal hearing set to determine whether a violation has occurred, the question or questions to be considered, and the results thereof;

(5) Administer oaths and affirmations, issue subpoenas, and compel attendance, take evidence and require the production of any books, papers, correspondence, memorandums, or other records which the commission deems relevant or material for the purpose of any investigation authorized under this chapter, or any other proceeding under this chapter;

(6) Adopt and promulgate a code of fair campaign practices;

(7) Relieve, by published regulation of general applicability, candidates or political committees of obligations to comply with the provisions of this chapter relating to election campaigns, if they have not received contributions

nor made expenditures in connection with any election campaign of more than one thousand dollars; and

(8) Enact regulations prescribing reasonable requirements for keeping accounts of and reporting on a quarterly basis costs incurred by state agencies, counties, cities, and other municipalities and political subdivisions in preparing, publishing, and distributing legislative information. The term "legislative information", for the purposes of this subsection, means books, pamphlets, reports, and other materials prepared, published, or distributed at substantial cost, a substantial purpose of which is to influence the passage or defeat of any legislation. The state auditor in his regular examination of each agency under chapter 43.09 RCW shall review such regulations, accounts, and reports and make appropriate findings, comments, and recommendations in his examination reports concerning those agencies.

(9) The commission, after hearing, by order approved and ratified by a majority of the membership of the commission, may suspend or modify any of the reporting requirements hereunder in a particular case if it finds that literal application of this chapter works a manifestly unreasonable hardship and if it also finds that such suspension or modification will not frustrate the purposes of the chapter. The commission shall find that a manifestly unreasonable hardship exists if reporting the name of an entity required to be reported under RCW 42.17.240(1)(g)(ii) would be likely to adversely affect the competitive position of any entity in which the person filing the report or any member of his immediate family holds any office, directorship, general partnership interest, or an ownership interest of ten percent or more. Any suspension or modification shall be only to the extent necessary to substantially relieve the hardship. The commission shall act to suspend or modify and reporting requirements only if it determines that facts exist that are clear and convincing proof of the findings required hereunder. Any citizen shall have standing to bring an action in Thurston county superior court to contest the propriety of any order entered hereunder within one year from the date of the entry of such order. [Enacted Laws 1973 ch 1 § 37 effective January 1, 1973 (Initiative Measure No. 276 § 37); Amended by Laws 1st Ex Sess 1975 ch 294 § 25, effective July 2, 1975; Laws 1st Ex Sess 1977 ch 336 § 7.]

Ops Atty Gen 1973 No. 14 (procedures for obtaining relief from reporting requirements).

42.17.380 Secretary of state, attorney general—Duties.

(1) The secretary of state, through his office, shall perform such ministerial functions as may be necessary to enable the commission to carry out its responsibilities under this chapter. The office of the secretary of state shall be designated as the place where the public may file papers or correspond with the commission and receive any form or instruction from the commission.

(2) The attorney general, through his office, shall supply such assistance

as the commission may require in order to carry out its responsibilities under this chapter. The commission may employ attorneys who are neither the attorney general nor an assistant attorney general to carry out any function of the attorney general prescribed in this chapter. [Enacted Laws 1973 ch 1 § 38, effective January 1, 1973 (Initiative Measure No. 276 § 38); Amended by Laws 1st Ex Sess 1975 ch 294 § 26, effective July 2, 1975.]

42.17.390 Civil remedies and sanctions.

(1) One or more of the following civil remedies and sanctions may be imposed by court order in addition to any other remedies provided by law:

(a) If the court finds that the violation of any provision of this chapter by any candidate or political committee probably affected the outcome of any election, the result of said election may be held void and a special election held within sixty days of such finding. Any action to void an election shall be commenced within one year of the date of the election in question. It is intended that this remedy be imposed freely in all appropriate cases to protect the right of the electorate to an informed and knowledgeable vote.

(b) If any lobbyist or sponsor of any grass roots lobbying campaign violates any of the provisions of this act, his registration may be revoked or suspended and he may be enjoined from receiving compensation or making expenditures for lobbying: *Provided,* however, that imposition of such sanction shall not excuse said lobbyist from filing statements and reports required by this chapter.

(c) Any person who violates any of the provisions of this act may be subject to a civil penalty of not more than ten thousand dollars for each such violation.

(d) Any person who fails to file a properly completed statement or report within the time required by this act may be subject to a civil penalty of ten dollars per day for each day each such delinquency continues.

(e) Any person who fails to report a contribution or expenditure may be subject to a civil penalty equivalent to the amount he failed to report.

(f) The court may enjoin any person to prevent the doing of any act herein prohibited, or to compel the performance of any act required herein. [Enacted Laws 1973 ch 1 § 39, effective January 1, 1973 (Initiative Measure No. 276 § 39).]

CJS Elections §§ 329, 356, Statutes § 6.

Key Number Digests: Elections   317. Statutes   34.

42.17.400 Enforcement.

(1) The attorney general and the prosecuting authorities of political subdivisions of this state may bring civil actions in the name of the state for any appropriate civil remedy, including but not limited to the special remedies provided in RCW 42.17.390.

(2) The attorney general and the prosecuting authorities of political subdivi-

sions of this state may investigate or cause to be investigated the activities of any person who there is reason to believe is or has been acting in violation of this chapter, and may require any such person or any other person reasonably believed to have information concerning the activities of such person to appear at a time and place designated in the county in which such person resides or is found, to give such information under oath and to produce all accounts, bills, receipts, books, papers and documents which may be relevant or material to any investigation authorized under this chapter.

(3) When the attorney general or the prosecuting authority of any political subdivision of this state requires the attendance of any person to obtain such information or the production of the accounts, bills, receipts, books, papers, and documents which may be relevant or material to any investigation authorized under this chapter, he shall issue an order setting forth the time when and the place where attendance is required and shall cause the same to be delivered to or sent by registered mail to the person at least fourteen days before the date fixed for attendance. Such order shall have the same force and effect as a subpoena, shall be effective state-wide, and, upon application of the attorney general or said prosecuting authority, obedience to the order may be enforced by any superior court judge in the county where the person receiving it resides or is found, in the same manner as though the order were a subpoena. The court, after hearing, for good cause, and upon application of any person aggrieved by the order, shall have the right to alter, amend, revise, suspend, or postpone all or any part of its provisions. In any case where the order is not enforced by the court according to its terms, the reasons for the court's actions shall be clearly stated in writing, and such action shall be subject to review by the appellate courts by certiorari or other appropriate proceeding.

(4) Any person who has notified the attorney general and the prosecuting attorney in the county in which the violation occurred in writing that there is reason to believe that some provision of this chapter is being or has been violated may himself bring in the name of the state any of the actions (hereinafter referred to as a citizen's action) authorized under this chapter. This citizen action may be brought only if the attorney general and the prosecuting attorney have failed to commence an action hereunder within forty-five days after such notice and such person has thereafter further notified the attorney general and prosecuting attorney that said person will commence a citizen's action within ten days upon their failure so to do, and the attorney general and the prosecuting attorney have in fact failed to bring such action within ten days of receipt of said second notice. If the person who brings the citizen's action prevails, the judgment awarded shall escheat to the state, but he shall be entitled to be reimbursed by the state of Washington for costs and attorney's fees he has incurred: *Provided,* That in the case of a citizen's action

which is dismissed and which the court also finds was brought without reasonable cause, the court may order the person commencing the action to pay all costs of trial and reasonable attorney's fees incurred by the defendant.

(5) In any action brought under this section, the court may award to the state all costs of investigation and trial, including a reasonable attorney's fee to be fixed by the court. If the violation is found to have been intentional, the amount of the judgment, which shall for this purpose include the costs, may be trebled as punitive damages. If damages or trebled damages are awarded in such an action brought against a lobbyist, the judgment may be awarded against the lobbyist, and the lobbyist's employer or employers joined as defendants, jointly, severally, or both. If the defendant prevails, he shall be awarded all costs of trial, and may be awarded a reasonable attorney's fee to be fixed by the court to be paid by the state of Washington. [Enacted Laws 1973 ch 1 § 40, effective January 1, 1973 (Initiative Measure No. 276 § 40); Amended by Laws 1st Ex Sess 1975 ch 294 § 27, effective July 2, 1975.]

Defendants in a citizen's action instituted under RCW 42.17.400(4) (Initiative 276, § 40(4)) are sufficiently protected from any chilling effect of frivolous and abusive lawsuits interfering with their exercise of First Amendment rights. *Frits* v. *Gorton* (1974) 83 Wn 2d 275, 517 P2d 911.

42.17.410 Limitation on actions.

Any action brought under the provisions of this chapter must be commenced within six years after the date when the violation occurred. [Enacted Laws 1973 ch 1 § 41, effective January 1, 1973 (Initiative Measure No. 276 § 41).]

42.17.420 Date of mailing deemed date of receipt.

When any application, report, statement, notice, or payment required to be made under the provisions of this chapter has been deposited post-paid in the United States mail properly addressed, it shall be deemed to have been received on the date of mailing. It shall be presumed that the date shown by the post office cancellation mark on the envelope is the date of mailing. [Enacted Laws 1973 ch 1 § 42, effective January 1, 1973 (Initiative Measure No. 276 § 42).]

42.17.430 Certification of reports.

Every report and statement required to be filed under this chapter shall identify the person preparing it, and shall be certified as complete and correct, both by the person preparing it and by the person on whose behalf it is filed. [Enacted Laws 1973 ch 1 § 43, effective January 1, 1973 (Initiative Measure No. 276 § 43).]

42.17.440 Statements and reports public records.

All statements and reports filed under this chapter shall be public records of the agency where they are filed, and shall be available for public inspection and copying during normal business hours at the expense of the person requesting copies, provided that the charge for such copies shall not exceed actual cost to the agency. [Enacted Laws 1973 ch 1 § 44, effective January 1, 1973 (Initiative Measure No. 276 § 44).]

CJS Records §§ 35 et seq.

Key Number Digests: Records   14.

42.17.450 Duty to preserve statements and reports.

Persons with whom statements or reports or copies of statements or reports are required to be filed under this chapter shall preserve them for not less than six years. The commission, however, shall preserve such statements or reports for not less than ten years. [Enacted Laws 1973 ch 1 § 45, effective January 1, 1973 (Initiative Measure No. 276 § 45).]

CJS Records §§ 34, 40.

Key Number Digests: Records   13.

42.17.900 Effective date.

The effective date of this act shall be January 1, 1973. [Enacted Laws 1973 ch 1 § 49, effective January 1, 1973 (Initiative Measure No. 276 § 49).]

42.17.910 Severability.

If any provision of this act, or its application to any person or circumstance is held invalid, the remainder of the act, or the application of the provision to other persons or circumstances is not affected. [Enacted Laws 1973 ch 1 § 46, effective January 1, 1973 (Initiative Measure No. 276 § 46).]

42.17.911 Severability—1975 1st ex.s. c 294.

If any provision of this 1975 amendatory act, or its application to any person or circumstance is held invalid, the remainder of the act, or the application of one provision to other persons or circumstances is not affected. [Enacted Laws 1st Ex Sess 1975 ch 294 § 29, effective July 2, 1975.]

CJS Statutes § 92.

Key Number Digests: Statutes   64.

42.17.920 Construction.

The provisions of this act are to be liberally construed to effectuate the policies and purposes of this act. In the event of conflict between the provisions of this act and any other act, the provisions of this act shall govern. [Enacted Laws 1973 ch 1 § 47, effective January 1, 1973 (Initiative Measure No. 276 § 47).]

42.17.930 Chapter, section headings not part of law.

Chapter and section captions or headings as used in this act do not constitute any part of the law. [Enacted Laws 1973 ch 1 § 48, effective January 1, 1973 (Initiative Measure No. 276 § 48).]

42.17.940 Repealer.

Chapter 9, Laws of 1965, as amended by section 9, chapter 150, Laws of 1965 ex. sess., and RCW 29.18.140; and chapter 131, Laws of 1967 ex. sess. and RCW 44.64; and chapter 82, Laws of 1972 (42nd Leg. 2nd Ex. Sess.) and

Referendum Bill No. 24; and chapter 98, Laws of 1972 (42nd Leg. 2nd Ex. Sess.) and Referendum Bill No. 25 are each hereby repealed. [Enacted Laws 1973 ch 1 § 50, effective January 1, 1973 (Initiative Measure No. 276 § 50).]
42.18.130 State employee.

"State employee" means any individual who is appointed by an agency head, as defined in RCW 42.18.040, or his designee, and serves under the supervision and authority of an agency as defined in RCW 42.18.030.

Notwithstanding the foregoing, the term "state employee" shall not include any of the following:

(1) Officers and employees is the legislative and judicial branches of the state of Washington; and

(2) A reserve of the Washington national guard, when he is not on active duty and is not otherwise a state employee.

An individual shall not be deemed an employee solely by reason of his being subject to recall to active service.

Every state employee shall be deemed either "intermittent" or "regular" as determined by the definitions contained in RCW 42.18.070 and 42.18.100 respectively.

The term "state employee" also includes any member of a commission, board, committee or any other multi-member governing body of an agency. [Amended by Laws 1973 ch 137 § 1.]
42.18.290 Civil action against present or former state employees.

The attorney general of the state of Washington may bring a civil action in the superior court of the county in which the violation was alleged to have occurred against any state employee, former state employee or other person who shall have violated or knowingly assisted any other person in violating any provision of this chapter and in such action may recover the following damages on behalf of the state of Washington: (1) From each such person a civil penalty of either five hundred dollars or an amount not exceeding three times the amount of the economic value of anything received or sought in violation of* this 1973 amendatory act; and (2) any damages sustained by the state, which are caused by the conduct constituting the violation. [Amended by Laws 1973 ch 137 § 2.]
42.18.300 Civil action against other violators.

The attorney general of the state of Washington may bring a civil action in the superior court of Thurston county against any person who shall violate RCW 42.18.230. In such action the attorney general shall be awarded the following damages for the state of Washington: (1) A civil penalty of either one thousand dollars or an amount not exceeding three times the economic

---

*   Reviser's Note: "this 1973 amendatory act" [1973 c 137] consists of the 1973 c 137 amendments to RCW 42.18.130, 42.18.230, and 42.18.300 and the repeal of RCW 42.18.340.

value of anything which has been given, transferred, or delivered in violation of RCW 42.18.230; and (2) any damages sustained by the state which are caused by the conduct constituting the violation. [Amended by Laws 1973 ch 137 § 3.]
42.18.340 General penalty
Repealed by Laws 1973 ch 137 § 4.

West Virginia Code, Annotated
1978 Cumulative Supplement
Volume 9, Article 1

§ 29B-1-1. Declaration of policy.
Pursuant to the fundamental philosophy of the American constitutional form of representative government which holds to the principle that government is the servant of the people, and not the master of them, it is hereby declared to be the public policy of the State of West Virginia that all persons are, unless otherwise expressly provided by law, entitled to full and complete information regarding the affairs of government and the official acts of those who represent them as public officials and employees. The people, in delegating authority, do not give their public servants the right to decide what is good for the people to know and what is not good for them to know. The people insist on remaining informed so that they may retain control over the instruments of government they have created. To that end, the provisions of this article shall be liberally construed with the view of carrying out the above declaration of public policy. (1977, c. 147.)
§ 29B-1-2. Definitions.
As used in this article:
(1) "Custodian" means the elected or appointed official charged with administering a public body.
(2) "Person" includes any natural person, corporation, partnership, firm or association.
(3) "Public body" means every state officer, agency, department, including the executive, legislative and judicial departments, division, bureau, board and commission; every county and city governing body, school district, special district, municipal corporation, and any board, department, commission, council or agency thereof; and any other body which is created by state or local authority or which is primarily funded by the state or local authority.
(4) "Public record" includes any writing containing information relating to the conduct of the public's business, prepared, owned and retained by a public body.

(5) "Writing" includes any books, papers, maps, photographs, cards, tapes, recordings or other documentary materials regardless of physical form or characteristics. (1977, c. 147.)

§ 29B-1-3. Inspection and copying.

(1) Every person has a right to inspect or copy any public record of a public body in this State, except as otherwise expressly provided by section four [§ 29B-1-4] of this article.

(2) A request to inspect or copy any public record of a public body shall be made directly to the custodian of such public record.

(3) The custodian of any public records, unless otherwise expressly provided by statute, shall furnish proper and reasonable opportunities for inspection and examination of the records in his office and reasonable facilities for making memoranda or abstracts therefrom, during the usual business hours, to all persons having occasion to make examination of them. The custodian of the records may make reasonable rules and regulations necessary for the protection of the records and to prevent interference with the regular discharge of his duties.

(4) All requests for information must state with reasonable specificity the information sought. The custodian, upon demand for records made under this statute, shall as soon as is practicable but within a maximum of five days not including Saturdays, Sundays or legal holidays:

(a) Furnish copies of the requested information;

(b) Advise the person making the request of the time and place at which he may inspect and copy the materials; or

(c) Deny the request stating in writing the reasons for such denial.

Such a denial shall indicate that the responsibility of the custodian of any public records or public body to produce the requested records or documents is at an end, and shall afford the person requesting them the opportunity to institute proceedings for injunctive or declaratory relief in the circuit court in the county where the public record is kept.

(5) The public body may establish fees reasonably calculated to reimburse it for its actual cost in making reproductions of such records. (1977, c. 147.)

§ 29B-1-4. Exemptions.

The following categories of information are specifically exempt from disclosure under the provisions of this article:

(1) Trade secrets, as used in this section, which may include, but are not limited to, any formula, plan pattern, process, tool, mechanism, compound, procedure, production data, or compilation of information which is not patented which is known only to certain individuals within a commercial concern who are using it to fabricate, produce or compound an article or trade or a service or to locate minerals or other substances, having commercial

value, and which gives its users an opportunity to obtain business advantage over competitors;

(2) Information of a personal nature such as that kept in a personal, medical or similar file, if the public disclosure thereof would constitute an unreasonable invasion of privacy, unless the public interest by clear and convincing evidence requires disclosure in the particular instance: Provided, that nothing in this article shall be construed as precluding an individual from inspecting or copying his own personal, medical or similar file;

(3) Test questions, scoring keys and other examination data used to administer a licensing examination, examination for employment or academic examination;

(4) Records of law-enforcement agencies that deal with the detection and investigation of crime and the internal records and notations of such law-enforcement agencies which are maintained for internal use in matters relating to law enforcement;

(5) Information specifically exempted from disclosure by statute;

(6) Records, archives, documents or manuscripts describing the location of undeveloped historic, prehistoric, archaeological, paleontological and battlefield sites or constituting gifts to any public body upon which the donor has attached restrictions on usage or the handling of which could irreparably damage such record, archive, document or manuscript;

(7) Information contained in or related to examination, operating or condition reports prepared by, or on behalf of, or for the use of any agency responsible for the regulation or supervision of financial institutions, except those reports which are by law required to be published in newspapers; and

(8) Internal memoranda or letters received or prepared by any public body. (1977, c. 147.)

§ 29B-1-5. Enforcement.

(1) Any person denied the right to inspect the public record of a public body may institute proceedings for injunctive or declaratory relief in the circuit court in the county where the public record is kept.

(2) In any suit filed under subsection one of this section, the court has jurisdiction to enjoin the custodian or public body from withholding records and to order the production of any records improperly withheld from the person seeking disclosure. The court shall determine the matter de novo and the burden is on the public body to sustain its action. The court, on its own motion, may view the documents in controversy in camera before reaching a decision. Any custodian of any public records of the public body found to be in noncompliance with the order of the court to produce the documents or disclose the information sought, may be punished as being in contempt of court.

(3) Except as to causes the court considers of greater importance, proceed-

ings arising under subsection one of this section shall be assigned for hearing and trial at the earliest practicable date. (1977, c. 147.)

§ 29B-1-6. Violation of article; penalties.

Any custodian of any public records who shall willfully violate the provisions of this article shall be guilty of a misdemeanor, and, upon conviction thereof, shall be fined not less than one hundred dollars nor more than five hundred dollars, or be imprisoned in the county jail for not more than ten days, or, in the discretion of the court, by both such fine and imprisonment. (1977, c. 147.)

Wisconsin Statutes, West's Annotated
1978-1979 Cumulative Annual Pocket Part
Volume 3

19.21 Custody and delivery of official property and records.

(1) Each and every officer of the state, or of any county, town, city, village, school district, or other municipality or district, is the legal custodian of and shall safely keep and preserve all property and things received from his predecessor or other persons and required by law to be filed, deposited, or kept in his office, or which are in the lawful possession or control of himself or his deputies, or to the possession or control of which he or they may be lawfully entitled, as such officers.

(2) Except as expressly provided otherwise, any person may with proper care, during office hours and subject to such orders or regulations as the custodian thereof prescribes, examine or copy any of the property or things mentioned in sub. (1). Any person may, at his own expense and under such reasonable regulations as the custodian prescribes, copy or duplicate any materials, including but not limited to blueprints, slides, photographs and drawings. Duplication of university expansion materials may be performed away from the office of the custodian if necessary.

(3) Upon the expiration of his term of office, or whenever his office becomes vacant, each such officer, or on his death his legal representative, shall on demand deliver to his successor all such property and things then in his custody, and his successor shall receipt therefor to said officer, who shall file said receipt, as the case may be, in the office of the secretary of state, county clerk, town clerk, city clerk, village clerk, school district clerk, or clerk or other secretarial officer of the municipality or district, respectively; but if a vacancy occurs before such successor is qualified, such property and things shall be delivered to and be receipted for by such secretary or clerk, respec-

tively, on behalf of the successor, to be delivered to such successor upon the latter's receipt.

(4) Any person who violates this section shall, in addition to any other liability or penalty, civil or criminal, forfeit not less than $25 nor more than $2,000; such forfeiture to be enforced by a civil action on behalf of, and the proceeds to be paid into the treasury of the state, municipality, or district, as the case may be.

(5) (a) Any city council or village board may provide by ordinance for the destruction of obsolete public records. Prior to any such destruction at least 60 days' notice in writing of such destruction shall be given the historical society which shall preserve any such records it determines to be of historical interest. The historical society may, upon application, waive such notice. No assessment roll containing forest crop acreage may be destroyed without prior approval of the secretary of revenue.

(b) The period of time any city or village public record shall be kept before destruction shall be as prescribed by ordinance unless a specific period of time is provided by statute. The period prescribed in such ordinance shall be not less than 2 years with respect to water stubs, receipts of current billings and customer's ledgers of any municipal utility, and 7 years for other records unless a shorter period has been fixed by the public records board pursuant to s. 16.61(3) (e).

(c) Any city council or village board may also provide by ordinance for the keeping and preservation of public records by the use of microfilm or other reproductive device. Any photographic reproduction shall be deemed an original record for all purposes if it meets the standards established in s. 16.61(7), so far as the same may be applicable.

(6) Counties having a population of 500,000 or more may provide by ordinance for the destruction of obsolete public records without regard to ss. 59.715 to 59.717 and may undertake a management of records service. The period of time any public record shall be kept before destruction shall be determined by ordinance except that the specific period of time expressed within s. 59.715 shall apply as to those records or documents. Prior to any destruction of records, except those specified within s. 59.715 as well as those having a confidential character as determined by the county, at least 60 days' notice of such destruction shall be given in writing, to the historical society, which may preserve any such records it determines to be of historical interest; however no notice need be given for any of the aforesaid class of records for which destruction has previously been approved by the historical society or in which it has indicated that it has no interest for historical purposes. The county board may also provide, by ordinance, a program for the keeping, preservation, retention and disposition of public records including the establishment of a committee on public records and may institute a

record management service for the county and may appropriate funds to accomplish such purposes.

19.21 Custody and delivery of official property and records.

. . .

(5)(b) The period of time any city or village public record shall be kept before destruction shall be as prescribed by ordinance unless a specific period of time is provided by statute. The period prescribed in such ordinance shall be not less than 2 years with respect to water stubs, receipts of current billings and customer's ledgers of any municipal utility, and 7 years for other records unless a shorter period has been fixed by the public records board pursuant to s. 16.61(3)(c).

(c) Any city council or village board may also provide by ordinance for the keeping and preservation of public records by the use of microfilm or other reproductive device. Any photographic reproduction shall be deemed an original record for all purposes if it meets the standards established in s. 16.61(7), so far as the same may be applicable.

. . .

(7) Any school district, except a city school district or a school district in a city of the 1st class, may provide for the destruction of obsolete school records. Prior to any such destruction, at least 60 days' notice in writing of such destruction shall be given the historical society, which shall preserve any such records it determines to be of historical interest. The historical society may, upon application, waive the notice. The period of time a school district record shall be kept before destruction shall be not less than 7 years. This section shall not apply to pupil records under s. 118.125.

59.13 Official oaths and bonds.

(1) Each county officer named in this chapter, except county supervisors, shall execute and file an official bond and take and file the official oath within 20 days after receiving official notice of . . . election or appointment, or if not officially notified, within 20 days after the commencement of the term for which . . . elected or appointed. Every county supervisor shall take and file the official oath within 20 days after receiving official notice of . . . election or appointment, or if not officially notified, within 20 days after the commencement of the term for which . . . elected or appointed. Every deputy appointed by any such officer shall take and file the official oath and if . . . the deputy neglects shall forfeit $100. Such official bonds shall be in sums and with sureties, as follows:

. . .

(1) (h) Surveyor, . . . $5,000.

. . .

(3) Each such bond shall be guaranteed by the number of personal sureties prescribed by law, or if not prescribed, by the number fixed by the county

board within the limitations, if any, prescribed by law, or by a surety company as provided by . . . 632.17(2). In the case of the county clerk, county treasurer and county abstractor the county board may by resolution require them to furnish bonds guaranteed by surety companies and direct that the premiums be paid as provided in s. 19.01(8).

. . .

59.14 Offices, where kept; when open.

(1) Every sheriff, clerk of the circuit court, register of deeds, county treasurer, register of probate . . ., county clerk and county surveyor shall keep his office at the county seat in the offices provided by the county or by special provision of law; or if there is none, then at such place as the county board directs. The county board may also require any elective or appointive county official to keep his office at the county seat. In an office to be provided by the county. All such officers shall keep such offices open during the usual business hours each day, Sundays excepted, and except that the county board of each county may permit said officers to close their offices on Saturday or on legal holidays for such time as the county board directs, and with proper care shall open to the examination of any person all books and papers required to be kept in his office and permit any person so examining to take notes and copies of such books, records, papers or minutes therefrom.

. . .

(3) Any county board may be ordinance provide that the cut-off reception time for the filing and recording of documents shall be advanced by one-half hour in any official business day during which time the register of deeds office is open to the public. In order to complete the processing, recording and indexing to conform to the day of reception but for all other purposes the office shall remain open to the public.

59.71 Records where kept; public examination; rebinding; transcribing.

(1) The books, records, papers and accounts of the county board shall be deposited with the respective county clerks and shall be open without any charge to the examination of all persons.

(2) When any book . . ., public record or the record of any town, village or city plat in any county office shall, from any cause, become unfit for use in whole or in part, the county board shall . . . order that . . . the book, record or plat be rebound or transcribed . . . . If the order . . . is to rebind such book, record or plat, . . . the rebinding must be done under the direction of the officer in charge of . . . the book, record or plat, and in his . . . office . . . . If the order . . . is to transcribe such book, record or plat, . . . the officer having charge of the same . . . shall provide a suitable book for that purpose; and thereupon such officer shall transcribe the same in the book so provided and carefully compare the transcript with the originals, and make the same a correct copy thereof, and shall attach to such transcript a certificate over

his official signature that he has carefully compared the matter therein contained with, and that the same is a correct and literal copy of the book, record or plat from which the same was transcribed, naming such book. Such copy of book, record or plat, so certified, shall have the same effect in all respects as the original, and such original book, record or plat shall be deposited with the county treasurer and carefully preserved except in counties having a population of 500,000 or more where a book containing a tract index is rewritten or transcribed, the original book may be destroyed. The order of the county board directing the transcribing of any book, record or plat duly certified by the county clerk shall, with such certificate, be recorded in each copy of book, record or plat transcribed. The fee of the officer for such service shall be fixed by the board, not exceeding . . . 10 cents per folio, or if such books or any part thereof consist of printed forms, not to exceed . . . 5 cents per folio for such books or records, to be paid by the county.

Wyoming Statutes
1975 Cumulative Supplement
Volume 4

§ 9-692.1. Classification and definitions. Definitions as used in this act [§§ 9-692.1 to 9-692.5]:

(a) The term "public records" when not otherwise specified shall include any paper, correspondence, form, book, photograph, photostat, film, microfilm, sound recording, map drawing, or other document, regardless of physical form or characteristics, and including all copies thereof, that have been made by the State of Wyoming and any counties, municipalities and political subdivisions thereof and by any agencies of the State of Wyoming, counties, municipalities, and political subdivisions thereof, or received by them in connection with the transaction of public business, except those privileged or confidential by law.

(b) Public records shall be classified as follows:

(i) The term "official public records" shall include all original vouchers, receipts and other documents necessary to isolate and prove the validity of every transaction relating to the receipt, use and disposition of all public property and public income from all sources whatsoever; all agreements and contracts to which the State of Wyoming or any agency or subdivision thereof may be a party; all fidelity, surety and performance bonds; all claims filed against the State of Wyoming or any agency or subdivision thereof; all records or documents required by law to be filed with or kept by any agency or the

State of Wyoming; and all other documents or records determined by the records committee to be official public records.

(ii) The term "office files and memoranda" shall include all records, correspondence, exhibits, books, booklets, drawings, maps, blank forms, or documents not above defined and classified as official public records; all duplicate copies of official public records filed with any agency of the State of Wyoming or subdivision thereof; all documents and reports made for the internal administration of the office to which they pertain but not required by law to be filed or kept with such agency; and all other documents or records, determined by the records committee to be office files and memoranda.

(c) The term "writings" means and includes all books, papers, maps, photographs, cards, tapes, recordings or other documentary materials, regardless of physical form or characteristics.

(d) The term "political subdivision" means and includes every county, city and county, city, incorporated and unincorporated town, school district and special district within the state.

(e) The term "official custodian" means and includes any officer or employee of the state or any agency, institution or political subdivision thereof, who is responsible for the maintenance, care and keeping of public records, regardless of whether such records are in his actual personal custody and control.

(f) The term "custodian" means and includes the official custodian or any authorized person having personal custody and control of the public records in question.

(g) The term "person" means and includes any natural person, corporation, partnership, firm or association.

(h) The term "person in interest" means and includes the person who is the subject of a record or any representative designated by said person, except that if the subject of the record is under legal disability, the term "person in interest" shall mean and include the parent or duly appointed legal representative. (Laws 1969, ch. 145, § 1.)

§ 9-692.2. Inspection—Generally. (a) All public records shall be open for inspection by any person at reasonable times, except as provided in this act [§§ 9-692.1 to 9-692.5] or as otherwise provided by law, but the official custodian of any public records may make such rules and regulations with reference to the inspection of such records as shall be reasonably necessary for the protection of such records and the prevention of unnecessary interference with the regular discharge of the duties of the custodian or his office.

(b) If the public records requested are not in the custody or control of the person to whom application is made, such person shall forthwith notify the applicant of this fact.

(c) If the public records requested are in the custody and control of the person to whom application is made but are in active use or in storage, and therefore not available at the time an applicant asks to examine them, the custodian shall forthwith notify the applicant of this fact. (Laws 1969, ch. 145, § 2.)

§ 9-692.3. Same—Grounds for denying right of inspection; statement of grounds for denial; order to show cause; order to restrict disclosure; hearing. —(a) The custodian of any public records shall allow any person the right of inspection of such records or any portion thereof except on one or more of the following grounds or as provided in subsection (b) or (d) of this section:

(i) Such inspection would be contrary to any state statute;

(ii) Such inspection would be contrary to any federal statute or regulation issued thereunder having the force and effect of law; or

(iii) Such inspection is prohibited by rules promulgated by the supreme court, or by the order of any court of record.

(b) The custodian may deny the right of inspection of the following records, unless otherwise provided by law, on the ground that disclosure to the applicant would be contrary to the public interest;

(i) Records of investigations conducted by, or of intelligence information or security procedures of, any sheriff, county attorney, city attorney, the attorney general, police department or any investigatory files compiled for any other law enforcement or prosecution purposes;

(ii) Test questions, scoring keys and other examination data pertaining to administration of a licensing examination, examination for employment or academic examination; except that written promotional examinations and the scores or results thereof shall be available for inspection, but not copying or reproduction, by the person in interest after the conducting and grading of any such examination;

(iii) The specific details of bona fide research projects being conducted by a state institution;

(iv) The contents of real estate appraisals made for the state or a political subdivision thereof, relative to the acquisition of property or any interest in property for public use, until such time as title of the property or property interest has passed to the state or political subdivision, except that the contents of such appraisal shall be available to the owner of the property at any time, and except as provided by Wyoming Statutes.

(v) Interagency or intraagency memorandums or letters which would not be available by law to a private party in litigation with the agency.

(c) If the right of inspection of any record falling within any of the classifications listed in this subsection is allowed to any officer or employee of any newspaper, radio station, television station or other person or agency in the business of public dissemination of news or current events, it may be allowed to all such news media.

(d) The custodian shall deny the right of inspection of the following records, unless otherwise provided by law:

(i) Medical, psychological, and sociological data on individual persons, exclusive of coroners' autopsy reports;

(ii) Adoption records or welfare records on individual persons;

(iii) Personnel files except that such files shall be available to the duly elected and appointed officials who supervise the work of the person in interest. Applications, performance ratings and scholastic achievement data shall be available only to the person in interest and to the duly elected and appointed officials who supervise his work;

(iv) Letters of reference;

(v) Trade secrets, privileged information and confidential commercial, financial, geological or geophysical data furnished by or obtained from any person;

(vi) Library, archives and museum material contributed by private persons, to the extent of any limitations placed thereon as conditions of such contributions; and

(vii) Hospital records relating to medical administration, medical staff, personnel, medical care, and other medical information, whether on individual persons or groups, or whether of a general or specific classification;

(viii) School district records containing information relating to the biography, family, physiology, religion, academic achievement and physical or mental ability of any student except to the person in interest or to the officials duly elected and appointed to supervise him.

(e) If the custodian denies access to any public record, the applicant may request a written statement of the grounds for the denial, which statement shall cite the law or regulation under which access is denied, and it shall be furnished forthwith to the applicant.

(f) Any person denied the right to inspect any record covered by this act [§§ 9-692.1 to 9-692.5] may apply to the district court of the district wherein the record is found for any order directing the custodian of such record to show cause why he should not permit the inspection of such record.

(g) If, in the opinion of the official custodian of any public record, disclosure of the contents of said record would do substantial injury to the public interest, notwithstanding the fact that said record might otherwise be available to public inspection, he may apply to the district court of the district in which such record is located for an order permitting him to restrict such disclosure. After hearing, the court may issue such an order upon a finding that disclosure would cause substantial injury to the public interest. The person seeking permission to examine the record shall have notice of said hearing served upon him in the manner provided for service of process by the Wyoming Rules of Civil Procedure and shall have the right to appear and be heard. (Laws 1969, ch. 145, § 3.)

§ 9-692.4. Copies, printouts or photographs; fees.—(a) In all cases in which a person has the right to inspect any public records he may request that he be furnished copies, printouts or photographs for a reasonable fee to be set by the official custodian. Where fees for certified copies or other copies, printouts or photographs of such record are specifically prescribed by law, such specific fees shall apply.

(b) If the custodian does not have the facilities for making copies, printouts or photographs of records which the applicant has the right to inspect, then the applicant shall be granted access to the records for the purpose of making copies, printouts or photographs. The copies, printouts or photographs shall be made while the records are in the possession, custody and control of the custodian thereof and shall be subject to the supervision of such custodian. When practical, they shall be made in the place where the records are kept, but if it is impractical to do so, the custodian may allow arrangements to be made for this purpose. If other facilities are necessary the cost of providing them shall be paid by the person desiring a copy, printout or photograph of the records. The official custodian may establish a reasonable schedule of times for making copies, printouts or photographs and may charge a reasonable fee for the services rendered by him or his deputy in supervising the copying, printingout or photographing as he may charge for furnishing copies under this section. (Laws 1969, ch. 145, § 4.)

§ 9-692.5. Penalty.—Any person who willfully and knowingly violates the provisions of this act [§§ 9-692.1 to 9-692.5] shall be guilty of a misdemeanor and, upon conviction thereof, shall be punished by a fine not to exceed one hundred dollars ($100.00). (Laws 1969, ch. 145, § 5.)

Index to State Statutes

Alabama   265
Alaska   265
Arizona   266
Arkansas   268
California   270
Colorado   277
Connecticut   293
Delaware   296
District of Columbia   301
Florida   307
Georgia   310
Hawaii   317
Idaho   318
Illinois   319
Indiana   321
Iowa   322
Kansas   325
Kentucky   328
Louisiana   333
Maine   341
Maryland   342
Massachusetts   349
Michigan   352
Minnesota   353
Mississippi   354
Missouri   355

Montana   356
Nebraska   356
Nevada   357
New Hampshire   358
New Jersey   359
New Mexico   361
New York   363
North Carolina   369
North Dakota   371
Ohio   371
Oklahoma   372
Oregon   373
Pennsylvania   379
Rhode Island   380
South Carolina   381
South Dakota   386
Tennessee   387
Texas   390
Utah   398
Vermont   399
Virginia   404
Washington   409
West Virginia   423
Wisconsin   426
Wyoming   430

General Index

A

Administrative Procedure Act of 1946, 92, 175-176, 235-238, 241-244, 246-250
Agency disclosures (see also **Business information; Freedom of Information Act; Government information; Privacy Act**)
    FOIA requirements for (general), 1-9, 20, 63-67, 96-97
        general exemptions, 5-6
        noncompliance, 3-5, 6-7, 21
        personnel rules, 98
        request procedures, 19-20, 94-96
        specific exemptions, 12-19
        trivia information, 12-13
    Privacy Act requirements for (general), 27-29, 44-48
        general exemptions, 36, 110-111
        noncompliance, 33-35, 52-54, 119-120
        specific exemptions, 36-37, 112-115
Appeal procedures (see **Privacy Act; Reverse-FOIA Action**)
Archival records
    Privacy Act protection of, 37-38
Armed services information
    Privacy Act protection of, 37, 114-115

B

Bank and oil well information
    FOIA protection of, 19, 101-102
Business information (see also **Freedom of Information Act**)
    Chrysler Corporation v. Brown, 22-23, (see also **Appendices A** and **B**)
    Competitive harm test, 124, 141-145
    Confidential, agency determinations of, 155-160
    Confidential, submitter identification of, 151-154
    Early approaches to record confidentiality, 138-143
    Expectation of confidentiality standard, 139-141
    FOIA effect on, 22-24

Business information—Cont.
National Parks and Conservation Association v. Morton, 141-143
Promise of confidentiality test, 138-139
Public interest in, 131-135
Reverse-FOIA action, 126-127 (see also **Reverse-FOIA action**)
Substantive disclosure rules, 160-165
Trade secrets (see **Trade secrets**)

C

CIA files
Privacy Act protection of, 36, 111
Chrysler Corporation v. Brown, 22-23
Analysis of, 248-250
Memoranda concerning, 251-264
Text of, 223-248
Chrysler Corporation v. Schlesinger, 126, 135, 178, 181
Committee on Government Operations
FOIA recommendations, 89, 123-124
Privacy Act recommendations, 89
Common law
Covering informational privacy, 43-44
Confidential business information (see **Business information**)
Competitive harm test, 124, 141-145
Computerized data banks
And personal privacy, 41-44

D

Deliberative privileges, 14
De novo review (see also **Reverse-FOIA action**)
In reverse-FOIA cases, 178-181

E

Exemptions, FOIA (see **Freedom of Information Act**)
Exemptions, Privacy Act (see **Privacy Act**)
Expectation of confidentiality standard, 139-141

F

Fair Information Practices Act of 1974, 135
Fair trial, right to
And FOIA, 18
Federal civilian employment information
Privacy Act protection of, 37, 114
Federal service employment information
Privacy Act protection of, 37, 114
Federal withholding statutes
Other than FOIA, 13, 22-24, 98-99
Food and Drug Administration
Disclosure rules promulgated by, 160-163
Freedom of Information Act (FOIA) (see also **Business information;**
     Government information)
Agency disclosure requirements, 1-9, 20, 63-67, 96-97
Agency noncompliance under, 3-5, 6-7, 21 (see also **Reverse-FOIA**
     action)
  appeal procedures, 102-104
Committee on Government Operations recommendations, 89, 123-124
Defined, 1-7, 8, 90
Effect on business information, 22-24
Exemptions
  agency trivia information, 12, 98
  bank and oil well information, 19, 101-102
  communications within executive branch, 14, 101
  confidential business information, 13-14, 58-59, 99-100, 124 (see
       also **Business information; Trade secrets**)
  invasions of personal privacy, 14-15, 18, 58-63, 100-101
  investigatory records, 15-19, 60-61, 101
  law enforcement personnel safety information, 19, 60-61
  national security information, 12, 19, 97-98
  other federal withholding statutes, 13, 22-24, 98-99
Government information available under (general), 93-94
History of, 89-90
Interrelationship with Privacy Act, 21-22, 63-66
Law enforcement procedures and, 15-19, 60-61, 101
Legislative background of, 91-93
Problems, aids to, 25-26 (see also **Bibliography,** at Selected
       Government Agencies)
State statutes concerning (see **Appendix C**)
Text on, 1-7

Freedom of Information Act (FOIA)—Cont.
Vaughn index, 16-17, 62

G

Government information (see also **Freedom of Information Act; Privacy Act**)
Agency disclosure procedures
under FOIA, 96-97
under Privacy Act, 27-29, 47-48, 109-110
Concerning government activities
and FOIA, 91-93
Concerning personal information
and Privacy Act, 91, 105-106
FOIA exemptions, 97-102 (see also **Freedom of Information** at Exemptions)
Information available
under FOIA, 93-94
under Privacy Act, 31-32, 105-106
Locating documents, 94, 106-107
Moss-Hennings bill, 91-92
Privacy Act exemptions, 36-39, 110-115
Request procedures
under FOIA, 94-96
under Privacy Act, 107-109

H

House Foreign Operations and Government Subcommittee, 92

I

Informants, law enforcement
FOIA protection of, 15-19
Internal agency information
FOIA protection of, 14, 100
Investigatory information
Law enforcement
and FOIA, 15-19, 60-61, 101
and Privacy Act, 36, 55-57, 111, 112-113

L

Law enforcement information (see **Investigatory information**)

M

Mailing lists
Privacy Act protection of, 38
Moss-Hennings bill, 91-92

N

National Crime Information Center, 41
National Parks and Conservation Association v. Morton, 141-143
National security information
FOIA protection of, 12, 19, 97-98
Privacy Act protection of, 112

P

Personal records, 116-120
Privacy Act (see also **Government information**)
Agency disclosure requirements, 27-29, 44-48
Agency noncompliance under
appeal procedures, 115-116, 117-120
civil remedies, 33-35, 52-54, 119-120
criminal penalties, 35-36
Amending personal records, 116-120
Committee on Government Operations recommendations, 89
Common law and, 43-44
Defined, 90
Exemptions
armed services information, 37, 114-115
archival records, 37-38
CIA files, 36, 111
federal civilian employment information, 37, 114
general, 36, 110-111
government documents, 110-115
law enforcement, 36, 55-57, 111, 112-113
national security information, 112

Privacy Act—Cont.
  Exemptions—Cont.
    secret service intelligence files, 113
    specific, 36-37, 112-115
    statistical records, 113
  FOIA exemptions and, 58-61, 61-63
  Goals of, 44-45
  Government information available under, 31-32, 105-106
  History of, 43-44, 89-90
  Interrelationship with FOIA, 21-22, 63-66
  Legislative background of, 45, 104-105
  Need for reform, 54-55, 67
  Pertinent terms defined, 27
  Recordkeeping systems and, 41-44, 46-47, 55-57
  Restrictions on federal agencies and, 49-52
  Text of, 27-39
  Vaughn index, 62
Privacy, personal (see also **Privacy Act**)
  And FOIA, 14-15, 18, 58-61, 100-101
  And the public's right to know, 57-58, 90
Promise of confidentiality test, 138-139

R

Recordkeeping systems
  And Privacy Act, 41-44, 46-47, 55-57
Reverse-FOIA action, 62, 100, 126-128, 171, 173-175
  De novo review, 178-181
  Exhaustion of administrative remedies and, 182
  Jurisdiction, 175
  Legal bases of, 175-178
  Restrictions on, 184-186
  Scope of relief, 178-181
  Venue, 183-184
Right to know doctrine, 90

S

Secret service intelligence files
  Privacy Act protection of, 113

Statistical records
Privacy Act protection of, 113
Statutes, state
FOIA (see **Appendix C**)

T

Trade secrets (see also **Business information**)
Defined, 137-138
FOIA protection of, 13-14, 22-24, 58-59, 62, 124
FOIA regulations governing, 13-14, 22-24, 127-130
Trade Secrets Act, 176-178, 235-238, 241-244, 246-250

V

Vaughn index, 16-17, 62